Central Debates in British Politics

Central Debates in British Politics

Edited by
**JUSTIN FISHER,
DAVID DENVER
AND JOHN BENYON**

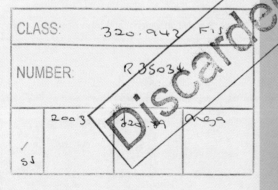
PEARSON
Longman

Harlow, England • London • New York • Boston • San Francisco • Toronto
Sydney • Tokyo • Singapore • Hong Kong • Seoul • Taipei • New Delhi
Cape Town • Madrid • Mexico City • Amsterdam • Munich • Paris • Milan

Pearson Education Limited
Edinburgh Gate
Harlow
Essex CM20 2J
England
and Associated Companies throughout the world

Visit us on the World Wide Web at:
www.pearsoned.co.uk

© Pearson Education Limited 2003

ISBN-10: 0-582-43727-X
ISBN-13: 978-0-582-43727-2

British Library Cataloguing-in-Publication Data
A catalogue record for this book is available from the British Library

Library of Congress Cataloging-in-Publication Data
Central debates in British politics / edited by Justin Fisher, David Denver, and John Benyon.
    p. cm.
  Includes bibliographical references.
  ISBN 0-582-43727-X (pbk.)
  1. Great Britain—Politics and government—1997-. I. Fisher, Justin. II. Denver, D. T. III.
Benyon, John.

JN231 .C35 2002
320.941—dc21
                                                              2002066059

10 9 8 7 6 5 4 3
07 06 05

Typeset in 9.5/12pt Giovanni Book by 35
Printed and bound in Malaysia

Contents

Preface

Textbooks dealing with British government and politics now seem to appear (or be published in revised editions) with increasing frequency. There is probably a simple explanation for this – in the last few decades there have been significant changes in the international context of UK politics, and in the system of government and the terms of political debate. At the start of the twenty-first century, change continues apace and traditional accounts of the British political system current in, say, the 1970s, are now completely out of date.

Clearly, one major change concerns the UK's relationship with the European Union, as the country has become increasingly entwined in the institutions, policies and practices of the EU. Looking beyond Europe, the forces created by the globalisation of the international economy have increasingly important effects on the ability of British governments to pursue independent economic policies and thus may be said to restrict sovereignty. In domestic terms, there has been much constitutional change since 1997, with the prospect of more to come. For example, following referendums (themselves constitutional novelties), there has been a substantial devolution of power to Scotland, Wales and Northern Ireland. Scotland now has its first parliament since 1707 and Wales its first ever national Assembly. In London (again following a referendum) there is now, for the first time ever in the UK, a directly-elected executive – the mayor. In Westminster itself, the composition of the House of Lords has been radically altered and further changes are in the pipeline. New electoral systems have been introduced for many non-Westminster elections, and there is the possibility of change for elections to the House of Commons as well. Recent years have also seen the most radical overhaul in electoral law since the extension of the franchise to all adults and the incorporation of the European Convention on Human Rights into British law.

Change has also occurred in political representation in the United Kingdom. There has been growing concern about an apparent disengagement with conventional politics. This has led to questions about the role and effectiveness of political parties, about how democratic they are internally and whether other institutions, such as pressure groups and the mass media, are now viable alternative vehicles for political representation. This has led to questions about what it means to be a citizen and about the redress of grievances. There are also questions about new forms of regulation. Both politics and society are subject to increasing regulation with the courts and judiciary, and related quasi-judicial bodies and quangos, having increasingly important roles to play.

These changes pose questions about how Britain is, and should be, governed and the contributions to this book focus on the debates around these issues. Many of the trends and developments are, of course, contentious – there is little consensus on them among politicians, academics working in the field or people in general – and such disagreement is intrinsic to political discussion. The title of the book highlights this – it is about topics on which there is much scope for debate – and we hope that the various chapters will stimulate debates among students of politics. To this end, we have assembled a group of authors who are experts in their respective fields and who explain the various arguments surrounding their particular topic. We have asked the

contributors to include four dimensions to their chapters – the background to the debate, associated theoretical concerns, summaries of the central issues and, in the light of these previous sections, an update. By structuring chapters in this way, we hope that all will stimulate lively debate about both the empirical material and the theoretical concerns. New issues will inevitably arise after publication, but we hope that the chapters will continue to provide a solid foundation on which the changing debates can be based. New issues and developing debates will, we hope, be included in subsequent editions of the book.

The book is organised into six parts. In the **introduction**, we set out the context for the book. These chapters detail the changing social, economic and political contexts of contemporary British politics, as well as broad theoretical questions which are relevant to the study of British politics, or indeed the politics of any other country. One of the aims of the book is to integrate theoretical concerns more closely with the study of British politics and we hope that the introductory chapters, as well as the theoretical sections in each chapter, provide material which will encourage students to think more generally about the issues raised.

Part II is devoted to the **changing constitutional picture** in Britain. We examine the future of the United Kingdom, debates about changing electoral systems, change in the national legislature and the impact of Britain's membership of the European Union. Part III deals with the broad concept of **representation**. It covers questions about elections, democracy within parties, representation through pressure groups and the media, and finally a discussion of the idea of citizenship.

Part IV examines **executives and governance**. It deals first with important new debates about the relationship between various arms of the executive and concludes with a discussion of how local governance has changed dramatically in recent years. The fifth section is concerned with a number of key **policy** areas, namely the economy, health, the environment and foreign policy. There is also a chapter on conscience issues – those that do not form part of official party policies. Like all of the chapters in the book, these are informed and influenced by the changing contexts of British politics. Other policy areas could have been chosen, of course, but we have selected four which we think are most pertinent for general debate and are most useful for courses in British government and politics. No doubt, new policy issues will become significant in future years – indeed, transport looks as though it may be one of these and this will be reflected in future editions.

Finally, Part V deals with **regulation** in British politics. No study of Britain can ignore the increasing role of quangos, tribunals and the courts, while any study must acknowledge the way in which the British system has endeavoured to deal with a perpetual problem that exists in all countries – the question of appropriate standards of behaviour in public life.

Overall, we think that we have covered many (but by no means all) of the central debates in British politics – but if users of the book think that there are serious omissions, we would be pleased to hear from them.

This book is a product of a collective effort. We would like to thank all the authors for producing such excellent chapters in good time. All authors stuck to their brief and, against the backdrop of the Quality Assurance Agency Subject Review in Politics for many, and the Research Assessment Exercise for all, their contributions are much appreciated. The editors should also like to thank Pearson Education and the many staff with whom we have dealt, but in particular, Ruth Haggerty and Richard Whitbread, who have ensured that the project has finally reached publication.

Justin Fisher
David Denver
John Benyon
February 2002

Contributors

John Benyon is Professor of Politics at the University of Leicester

Feargal Cochrane is Lecturer in Politics at the University of Lancaster

Philip Cowley is Lecturer in Politics at the University of Nottingham

David Denver is Professor of Politics at the University of Lancaster

Keith D. Ewing is Professor of Public Law at King's College, University of London

Keith Faulks is Reader in Citizenship at the University of Central Lancashire

Justin Fisher is Lecturer in Political Science at Brunel University

Robert Garner is Reader in Politics at the University of Leicester

Paul G. Harris is Senior Lecturer in International Relations at London Guildhall University and Associate Professor of Politics at Lingnan University, Hong Kong

Peter J. Laugharne is Senior Lecturer in Politics at London Guildhall University

Helen Margetts is Professor of Political Science at University College, London

James Mitchell is Professor of Politics at the University of Strathclyde

Michael Moran is Professor of Politics at the University of Manchester

Ralph Negrine is Director of the Centre for Mass Communication Research at the University of Leicester

Robert Pyper is Professor of Government and Public Management at Glasgow Caledonian University

Roger Scully is Lecturer in European Politics, University of Wales, Aberystwyth

Martin J. Smith is Professor of Politics at the University of Sheffield

Jim Tomlinson is Professor of Economic History at Brunel University

Paul Webb is Professor of Politics at the University of Sussex

David Wilson is Professor of Public Administration at De Montfort University

Acknowledgements

We are grateful to the following for permission to reproduce copyright material:

Tables 5.1 and 5.3, from and adapted from, respectively, *The Politicos Guide to Electoral Reform in Britain*, reproduced with permission of Politicos (Dunleavy, P., Margetts, H. and Weir, S. 1998); Table 5.2 from 'Mixed electoral systems in Britain and the Jenkins Commission on electoral reform', *British Journal of Politics and International Relations*, Vol. 1(1), pp. 12–38, reproduced by permission of Blackwell Publishers (Dunleavy, P. and Margetts, H. 1999); Table 5.3 adapted from 'Remodelling the 1997 General Election,' in Denver, D., Fisher, J., Cowley, P. and Patties, C. (eds) 'Split-ticket voting at the 1997 British general and local elections', *British Elections and Parties Review, Volume 8, The 1997 General Election,* © Frank Cass Publishers (Dunleavy, P. and Margetts, H. 1998); Table 6.2 from *CREST Welsh Referendum Study 1997* and Table 23.3 from 'Trust in the political system,' in Jowell, R., Curtice, J., Park, A., Brook, L., Thomson, K. and Bryson, C. (eds) *British Social Attitudes The 14th Report*, reproduced with permission from the National Centre for Social Research (*CREST Welsh Referendum Study*, 1997; Curtice, J. and Jowell, R. 1997); Table 7.1 from the website at http://www.parliament.uk, Table 7.4 from the website at http://www.parliament.uk/commons/selcom/ctteesys.htm and Table 7.5 from the website at http://www.publications.parliament.uk, Parliamentary copyright is reproduced with the permission of the Controller of Her Majesty's Stationery Office on behalf of

Parliament; Table 7.2 and Figures in Tables 7.3(b) and Table 12.2 from Butler, D. and Kavanagh, D., *The British General Election of 2001*, 2001, Palgrave, Figures in Table 7.3(a) from Butler, D. and Kavanagh, D., *The British General Election of 1997*, 2001, Macmillan, Table 20.1 from Garner, R., *Environmental Politics*, 2000, Macmillan, reproduced with permission of Palgrave Macmillan (Butler, D. and Kavanagh, D. 2001a,b; Garner, R. 2000); Tables 8.1 and 23.2 from the website at www.mori.co.uk, reproduced with permission of MORI; Table 10.1 from *British Election Study 2001*, reproduced with permission of Paul F. Whiteley (British Election Study, 2001); Table 11.1 from *The Politics of the New Europe: Atlantic to the Urals*, © Addison Wesley Longman Ltd, 1997 (Budge, I. K. *et al.* 1997); Table 11.2 (adapted) data reproduced with permission of the Conservatives Office; Table 11.2 (adapted) data from *Labour Party NEC Annual Reports*, courtesy of The Labour Party; Table 11.2 (adapted) data from The Liberal Democrats Information Office; Table 11.2 (adapted) with permission of the authors, from Berrington, H. and Hague, R. (1997) 'The Liberal Democrat campaign', *Parliamentary Affairs*, Vol. 50(4), pp. 555–68 and Table 12.2 (adapted) with permission of the author, from Seymour-Ure, C. (1997) 'Editorial opinion in the national press,' *Parliamentary Affairs*, Vol. 50, pp. 586–608, by permission of Oxford University Press/ Hansard Society; Table 12.1 adapted from *The Guardian* 1997, © The Guardian; Table 12.2 adapted from *Political Communications: The General Election Campaign of 1983*, Cambridge University Press (Crewe, I. and Harrop, M. 1983); Table 15.1 from the Cabinet Office website, February 2001 and Table 22.1 from Cabinet Office, *Public Bodies* (various years), Crown copyright material is reproduced with the permission of the Controller of Her Majesty's Stationery Office and the Queen's Printer for Scotland; Table 16.1 from 'Council of Europe', *Local and Regional Authorities in Europe*, No. 56, 'Only European Communities legislation as printed in the *Official Journal of the European Communities* is authentic' (European Commission, 1996); Table 16.2 adapted from *Local Elections Handbook, 1994, 1996 and 1998*, reproduced with permission of Professor Colin Rallings (Rallings, C. and Thrasher, M. 1994, 1996, 1998); Table 16.3 from *Census of Councillors* (Local Government Management Board, 1998); Table 18.1 adapted from *OECD Health Data*, copyright OECD, 1998; Table 21.1 derived and adapted from *The Public Clash of Private Values: The Politics of Morality Policy*, Chatham House (Mooney, C. Z. 2001); Table 22.2 from *The Untouchables*, reproduced with permission of the author (Hall, W. and Weir, S. 1996); Table 23.1 from *Annual Report of the Committee on Standards in Public Life 1999–2000* (Committee on Standards in Public Life).

Whilst every effort has been made to trace the owners of copyright material, in a few cases this has proved impossible and we would be grateful to hear from anyone with information which would enable us to do so.

PART ONE Introduction:
British Politics in
Context

The Contexts of British Politics

David Denver and
Justin Fisher

CHAPTER ONE

Political activity does not take place in a vacuum. Politics is only one aspect of any society – albeit an important aspect – and is set within a broader context. Indeed, we have used the plural 'contexts' in the title of this chapter to emphasise that the background to politics includes a number of different elements. We can identify distinct historical, social, economic, international and cultural contexts, each of which impinge importantly on current British politics and the debates which form the substance of this book. As is made clear in the other introductory chapter, these debates also involve enduring theoretical and practical questions about politics, but the way in which contemporary political issues are framed, interpreted and assessed is in large part a consequence of recent changes in the contexts of politics. Moreover, as we shall see, the social, economic, international and cultural contexts have been characterised by very rapid change in recent years.

The International Context

All states are part of an international system in which they interact with other states. The interaction may involve conflict, bilateral or multilateral co-operation, or co-operation mediated through international organisations such as NATO or the European Union. There are also non-state actors at the international level, such as multinational corporations or international currency speculators, which states may seek to regulate. The position of the United Kingdom in this international system has changed dramatically over the last fifty years and this clearly impinges on domestic politics. Two salient features are worth picking out – Britain's decline from world power and its increased involvement in Europe.

Decline from world power

At the end of the Second World War, Britain was one of three great powers in the world – the others being the United States and the Soviet Union. At the Potsdam conference in 1945 it was the British, American and Soviet leaders who determined the shape of the post-war world. In part, Britain's status rested on the fact that it had a huge empire but the post-war period was to see the dissolution of the Empire. India, Ceylon and Burma gained independence in the 1940s and twenty other former colonies became independent states between 1950 and 1964. In some ways decolonisation was something of a triumph since, in most cases, the transition was orderly and peaceful. Nonetheless, it left the UK in a much weaker position in the world. Economic weakness also contributed to Britain's decline. The Second World War had exhausted and impoverished the country and economic recovery was slow so that it was simply unable to afford to continue to play a world role. Overseas military bases were gradually closed as commitments were scaled down. For many people the Suez crisis in 1956 was the critical turning point, which made the country's diminished status clear to all. The Egyptian leader, Nasser, had nationalised the Suez Canal and, perceiving this as a threat to British interests, the government sent troops to Egypt. The pound came under pressure, however, and, as a condition for supporting the pound, the United States forced Britain to withdraw its troops within a few weeks. This outcome came as a shock to British public opinion, which still thought of Britain as a major power. As Reynolds comments, 'For an Egyptian ex-colonel to twist the lion's tail, and get away with it, was a palpable and lasting blow to national self-esteem and international prestige' (1991: 205).

Britain's decline from world power after 1945 was spectacular (see Sanders, 1990) and since the 1970s the country has been – at best – a middle-ranking power. With the notable exception of the Falklands conflict, activity in the field of foreign affairs has not been unilateral but undertaken in co-operation with other states under the auspices of organisations such as the United Nations or NATO. Moreover, rather than having worldwide interests to defend and promote, the focus of external concerns is now mostly upon Europe.

Involvement in Europe

The UK finally joined what was then called the European Economic Community on 1 January 1973 and this action was ratified in a referendum two years later. Ever since, the question of 'Europe' has remained controversial and this is explored in Chapter 8 by Roger Scully. Despite the clear majority which voted for membership of the EEC in the referendum, Britain entered Europe rather unwillingly – entry was seen as a cure for Britain's persistent economic weakness – and has since been aptly described as an 'awkward partner' (see George, 1994). Much of the debate over Britain's position in Europe centres on the question of sovereignty. There are two slightly different strands involved. First, there is the idea that the UK is a sovereign state, which means that its people have the right to govern themselves and to follow whatever policies they choose without 'interference' from outside. Second, in the British constitutional tradition, within the UK itself Parliament is sovereign – it has ultimate authority to decide on any matter. In both cases membership of the EU appears to involve a loss of sovereignty to European-wide institutions and this underlies much of the hostility towards 'Europe' and to further European integration. Others argue, however, that the economic and other benefits of being in Europe outweigh any diminution in sovereignty and that Britain's future outside the EU would be bleak. These issues have sharply divided the British public and also divided the major political parties over a long period and, if anything, divisions have sharpened over the whether the UK should join the European single currency, which is likely to be the subject of a referendum within the next few years. The outcome of such a referendum is far from certain, but what is clear is that it is now impossible to ignore the European dimension in British politics. In a whole series of areas – from the retiring age for women to the measures in which spirits are sold and the abolition of duty free allowances for travellers within the EU – Britain has had to fall in line with decisions emanating from the institutions of the European Union.

The Social Context

There is an intimate relation between what might be characterised as the 'social' and the 'political'. To use slightly old-fashioned terminology, the social context of politics strongly influences both the inputs and the outputs of the political system. That is to say, the kinds of demand that are made, and the issues that are raised, frequently reflect social changes and policies are produced in response to such demands. For example, in the immediate post-1945 period, the population of the UK was overwhelmingly white. From the late 1950s, however, immigration from former colonies resulted in the establishment of significant ethnic minority communities. By the 1990s members of ethnic minorities accounted for about 6% of the population, heavily concentrated in particular locations such as London, and Leicester, and the proportion was increasing. This change in the ethnic make-up of the population provoked a variety of demands – for more control of immigration, for legislation to protect the rights of ethnic minority residents, and so on. As a result, there has been a series of immigration acts, a raft of 'race'-related legislation has been passed and specialist agencies such as the Commission for Racial Equality established. In addition, the political parties have been forced to find ways of appealing to ethnic minorities (see Saggar, 2000).

Clearly there have been other changes in British society which have influenced politics in important ways and continue to do so. It is impossible to discuss these in any detail here. However, we can sketch some of the more obvious changes, but readers will be able to think of others and how they impact on both the input and output side of the political system.

The growth in the number of older people

People live longer than they used to. In 1960 those aged 65 and over constituted 11.7% of the population. By 1997 the figure was 15.7% (Office for National Statistics, 1999: 38). This simple demographic fact has major implications for politics. First, there are more pensioners whose concerns political parties must address. In this respect it is significant that in the aftermath of the 2000 local elections, although it had helped poorer pensioners in other ways, the government's bad performance was widely attributed to the fact that it had increased the basic state pension by only 75p. Perhaps more important in the long run is the cost imposed on the social security budget by an ageing population. Not only do older people have to have pensions, they also place extra demands on the National Health Service. Someone has to pay for this and it has to be through taxes paid by the shrinking population of working age. The difficulty is that the parties see increasing taxation as a sure vote loser.

Changing patterns of family life

To a large extent society is organised around what is frequently termed the 'traditional' family – two married parents with children. This is still the most common form of family arrangement but things have become more complex. Marriage itself has declined – the number of first marriages in 1996 was less than half what it had been in 1970 – and divorce has increased sharply (Office for National Statistics, 2000: 37). The proportion of births outside marriage rose from less than 10% in 1974 to almost 40% in 1997 (Office for National Statistics, 2000: 43). Between 1961 and 1998/99 the proportion of households comprising a couple (whether married or not) with children fell from 48% to 29% while single-person households rose from 11% to 29% (Office for National Statistics, 2000: 34). Some have suggested that there has been breakdown in traditional family life and that this is to blame for increased lawlessness on the part of young people and various other social ills. Whether or not this contentious suggestion has any basis, it is certainly the case that governments have to plan to provide housing for more single-person households and support for lone-parent families.

The decline of the working class

If by 'middle class' we mean people who have a non-manual occupation, then Britain became a middle-class society in 1981. The Census of that year found, for the first time ever, that among males in employment manual workers were in a minority. That minority has shrunk ever since. By the late 1990s the manual working class constituted less than one-third of the population. This had important consequences for the Labour Party in particular. For much of its life Labour had been the party of the working class. Now Labour could not win elections with the support of the working class alone. In response, although there were other factors in this, Labour in the 1990s under Tony Blair became 'New Labour', a party for all classes.

The changing position of women

For a variety of reasons the position of women in British society has changed substantially over the past twenty years. Women now form more than half of the workforce and they constituted a record 18% of MPs after both the 1997 and 2001 elections. The aspirations of women have been recognised in equal pay legislation and other policies outlawing sex discrimination. More generally, greater 'gender awareness', produced in no small part by the efforts of women themselves, is evident in many ways – in how political parties choose candidates, in 'equal opportunities' policies relating to making all sorts of appointments, in the media, and so on.

As noted above, there have been numerous other important changes in British society over the past twenty years or so which have important implications for politics and policy – the explosion in university education, the decline of religious practice (if not of belief), the emergence of satellite and cable television are three that spring to mind. We have done enough, however, to show that we live in a rapidly changing society and that this conditions the agenda of politics as well as political behaviour in all its forms.

The Economic Context

Politics and economics are intimately interconnected. Getting the economy right is one of the first aims of governments since so much else depends on economic success. It is widely believed, moreover, that governments which succeed in making the economy buoyant will be rewarded by the voters at the polls. There are numerous accounts of the management of the British economy and of economic performance (see, for example, Gamble, 1994a), but for students of politics there are three salient issues – relative economic decline, the changing structure of the economy and economic globalisation.

Relative economic decline

For most of the twentieth century, and certainly since 1945, the British economy has been in relative decline. This should not be confused with an absolute decline, of course. At the start of the twenty-first century the Gross Domestic Product (GDP) was much greater than it had been even thirty years before. British citizens enjoyed a much higher standard of living than their forebears. In absolute terms, the UK had enjoyed almost continuous economic growth. When compared to other countries, however, Britain was falling behind and steadily slipping down the economic league. As Jim Tomlinson shows in this book (Chapter 17), at various times there were severe problems relating to inflation, unemployment and the balance of payments.

As already noted, relatively poor economic performance was one of the main reasons why governments sought to join the European Union and it was also the backdrop to a steady scaling-down of defence commitments. The country could no longer afford to maintain military bases in far-flung corners of the world. Moreover, lacking steady growth on a par with that achieved by our competitors, UK governments were unable to fulfil their policy aspirations in other areas. Persistent failure led in the mid-1970s to the abandonment of Keynesian policies, which had dominated economic thinking for thirty years and which involved government management of the economy, and, especially after 1979, the espousal of monetarist policies, which involve greater reliance on market forces. As part of this new approach many formerly publicly-owned industries were privatised while other old industries (such as coal) were allowed to go to the wall. Opinion remains divided as to whether these policies produced an 'economic miracle' and also whether Labour's famously 'prudent' handling of the economy produced a lasting turnaround in economic fortunes. Nonetheless, there is no doubt that 'the economy' remains a central issue – perhaps *the* central issue – in British politics.

The structure of the economy

One aspect of the changing structure of the economy has already been touched on – the division between the private and the public sector. The list of industries that have been privatised in the last twenty years is a long one, including essential services such as telecommunications, gas, electricity, water and railways. Despite a feeling that there was nothing left worth privatising and clear public hostility to the policy, the Labour government elected in 1997 pushed on with plans to part-privatise the London Underground and the air traffic control system. The area of the economy in which government has a direct stake and ultimately responsibility has, therefore, shrunk dramatically.

Government policy has had less influence in the other major change in the structure of the economy – the balance between manufacturing and services. In 1971, 36% of employees worked in manufacturing and 53% in services. By 1992 the figures were 21% and 72% respectively (Central Statistical Office, 1993). The decline in the older and more traditional manufacturing sector – coal, steel, shipbuilding and textiles, for example – was even steeper than the overall figures suggest. A shifting balance between manufacturing and services is common to all modern societies and is partly explained by the increased efficiency of manufacturing. As more modern machinery is installed – robots in car plants, for example – fewer workers are needed to produce the same, or greater, amount of goods. Nonetheless, during the 1980s complaints about the decline of British manufacturing, arguably as a consequence of the Thatcher government's economic policies, were loud and long. Under Tony Blair, it was argued, the strength of the pound relative to the Euro was wreaking havoc among manufacturing industries. Whatever the cause, this trend has important political implications since regions which are more reliant on manufacturing suffer disproportionately in terms of unemployment, wage levels, and so on. Governments have had to manage the decline of industries on which Britain's industrial might was built in the nineteenth century.

Globalisation

From the 1980s, as world markets became increasingly deregulated, commentators began to emphasise the extent to which governments were unable to manage their national economies due to the emergence of a global economy. Multinational corporations could move their businesses around the world – as in Ford deciding to cease car production at Dagenham in the spring of 2000 and moving it to Germany – and capital moved freely around the world's stock markets. The pressures of international economic developments left governments with limited scope to pursue independent economic policies, even in relation to simple matters such as corporation taxes. This thesis is not accepted in its entirety by all (see Chapter 17, for example), but it is clear that economic globalisation poses severe challenges to British governments.

The Cultural Context

By 'cultural' we do not mean 'high culture', such as opera or art. These are more properly described as cultural forms or expressions. Rather, we are concerned with a broader meaning of culture – the values, attitudes and beliefs that are widely shared across the population. Thus Japanese culture is different from western culture in that there are different patterns of values, attitudes and beliefs and the different countries of Europe have themselves different cultures. The 'political culture' of a society concerns the values, attitudes and beliefs that relate fairly directly to politics (see Kavanagh, 1972; Miller et al., 1995).

The decline of the civic culture

In the late 1950s a pioneering and influential cross-national study of political culture was carried out by two American political scientists, Gabriel Almond and Sydney Verba (Almond and Verba, 1965). Basing their analysis on surveys of the relevant electorates, Almond and Verba argued that of the five countries studied (the USA, Mexico, Italy, Germany and the UK) it was Britain which most closely approximated what they called the 'civic culture' – the political culture which fits best with democratic political structures and which, in Brian Barry's words, involves 'a judicious mixture of respect for authority and sturdy independence' (Barry, 1970: 48). Relevant attributes of British electors included knowledge of and positive feelings towards the existing governing arrangements, trust in political leaders, a lack of extreme hostility towards political opponents and an adequate level of participation in politics. The effective functioning of British democracy was also aided by the fact that British voters exhibited attitudes of deference towards governments. That is, having elected a government, the British were happy to leave them to get on with the business of governing, broadly accepting that they had the right to do what they wanted and generally complying with government decisions and policies.

Almond and Verba's analysis was not without critics (Kavanagh, 1971), but by the mid-1970s the happy picture painted by Almond and Verba seemed seriously out of date. Governing arrangements were being seriously questioned in Scotland and Wales, while violence continued in Northern Ireland; the country was plagued by strikes, some with manifestly political motives; the country, it was claimed, was becoming ungovernable. By the end of the 1970s Dennis Kavanagh (1980) argued that the civic culture – and, in particular, social and political deference – had declined in the previous two decades. Britons were more dissatisfied with the political system, with politicians and with policies and were more likely to engage in protest behaviour than before.

Uncertainties over national identity

One of the core elements of any society's political culture is the extent to which the citizens of a state identify themselves as a community. The United Kingdom has always been a multinational state, albeit with one large nation (English) and three smaller ones. Nonetheless, for most of its existence citizens of the state had shared a common sense of Britishness. For people in Scotland and Wales this was additional to their sense of being Scots and Welsh, but in England 'English' and 'British' were virtually interchangeable terms. During the last third of the twentieth century, however, the idea of Britishness was increasingly questioned. In part this was due to stronger feelings of national identity in Scotland and Wales and continuing struggles in Northern Ireland, but the situation was also complicated by the presence of a growing number of ethnic minority citizens. By the late 1990s, and especially after the establishment of the Scottish Parliament and Welsh national Assembly, there was a wave of discussion – involving serious journalists and political commentators as well as academics – about the meaning of Britishness and, consequently, the future of the United Kingdom (see, for example, Marr, 2000).

The Historical Political Context

Nothing in politics starts from scratch. There is a history to every issue and every event. This may range from the history of particular individuals – where they come from, what their life experiences have been – to the shared history of the society as a whole. It is clear that an understanding of current debates over Northern Ireland, for example, or the UK's relationship with the European Union must involve an awareness of what has happened in the past. The same is true of every issue and for that reason most chapters in the book have a brief chronological account of the issue under discussion.

Any account of the broad historical context of British politics could go back a very long way indeed – certainly to the Bill of Rights of 1688, which established the supremacy of Parliament over the monarchy. It might also include the Act of Union of 1707, which created the British Parliament, and the Great Reform Act of 1832, which began the process of democratising politics. Although these are part of the story, however, the great majority of British citizens are unlikely to be aware of them. Contrariwise, broad changes in the character of British politics since 1945 are a part of the historical background to current issues which is more familiar and we will examine these in more depth.

The post-1945 consensus (1940s–1970s)

At the 1945 general election the electorate returned a majority Labour government for the first time and, under Prime Minister Clement Attlee, Labour set about implementing a programme that was radically different from anything that had been seen before. This included taking major industries – such as coal, steel and the railways – into public ownership, establishing the welfare state and beginning to dismantle the Empire. Despite initial misgivings, the Conservatives came to accept most of Labour's changes and, with hindsight, the whole period from the late 1940s to the mid-1970s came to be referred to as an era of political consensus (see Kavanagh and Morris, 1989). What was there consensus about?

First, the political parties generally agreed about the nature of the regime, the rules of the game and the role of the state. The 'nature of the regime' refers to such basic matters as the fact that the United Kingdom was a unitary state and a parliamentary democracy with a constitutional monarchy. Although there were occasional stirrings of Scottish and Welsh nationalism, especially from the late 1960s, it was not until the 1970s that a devolved system of government began to be seriously considered. Similarly, it was not until the 'troubles' erupted in Northern Ireland in the late 1960s that the constitutional settlement with Ireland agreed in 1922 began to be questioned. In general terms, the fundamental nature of the regime was broadly accepted by parties and voters throughout the consensus period. The same can be said of the 'rules of the game'. There was little questioning of the electoral system, for example, or of parliamentary and policy-making procedures. In addition, once Labour's reforms were in place, there was broad agreement that the state should play an active and positive role in society, especially in key areas such as welfare and the economy.

Second, the consensus extended to the substance of policy. The *defence policy* of governments of both parties was based on membership of NATO and the UK having nuclear weapons. In *foreign affairs*, the Attlee government began the process of decolonisation – India being granted independence in 1947, quickly followed by Ceylon and Burma – but it continued throughout the 1950s and early 1960s under Conservative governments. Later in the period (1973), a Conservative government took Britain into the European Community but membership was reaffirmed by a Labour government in 1975 (after a referendum on the issue). In *economic policy*, all parties gave a high priority to maintaining full employment – a concern which itself was produced by memories of the 1930s – and followed Keynesian demand management policies. From 1948 to 1970 unemployment never exceeded 3% of the workforce. The state took full responsibility for managing the economy on a day-to-day basis. The active and, in this case, benign state was also the keynote of *welfare policy*. It was accepted that the state, through a comprehensive welfare system, should look after people 'from the cradle to the grave' and the proportion of public expenditure devoted to welfare rose from 32% in 1953 to 44% in 1973.

Third, there was consensus on the style of conflict resolution. Conflict is inevitable in any society – indeed, without conflict there would be no politics – and *in extremis* it can only be resolved by civil war. In the era of consensus in British politics, however, compromise and bargaining were the order of the day. Industrial relations disputes would end with a mutually agreed deal being struck around the table, for example. An important part of this approach to conflict was the recognition that affected groups – whether trade unions, manufacturers, relevant pressure groups or whatever – had to be involved in the making of decisions which affected them. This style of conflict resolution particularly involved trade unions. All agreed that they should have an input and during the

1960s commentators described the system which emerged as *corporatism* – a system in which decisions on policy (especially economic policy) were made on the basis of consultation between government and representatives of trade unions and employers. The final aspect of conflict resolution to which all parties subscribed was to defuse issues by turning to experts. Important problems such as the persistence of poverty, the structure and functions of local government, the effectiveness of the civil service were re-defined as technical problems and hence de-politicised. Royal Commissions were appointed to investigate and come up with agreed solutions.

In broad terms, then, the period from the late 1940s to the mid-1970s can be characterised as one of consensus. Moreover, it was a consensus based on *collectivism* which, according to Samuel Beer, involves 'government intervention with the economic and social system as a whole' (1965: 80). We do not wish to give the impression that British politics in this period was a matter of 'all pals together' (for a critique, see Pimlott, 1988). There were issues that deeply divided the parties (both internally and from one another) and the wider society – the Suez crisis in 1956, for example, or the issue of nuclear disarmament. There were also important differences of emphasis between the parties. Labour generally favoured higher public spending and more central direction of the economy, while the Conservative approach was more cautious. Nonetheless, with hindsight, it seems fair to suggest that there was a broad agreement on the matters referred to above which embraced the front benches of both parties, top-level civil servants and the majority of the electorate.

The consensus questioned in the 1970s

During the 1970s the value of the consensus that had characterised politics began to be questioned – both by practising politicians and political scientists. Obvious problems included spiralling public expenditure, at best a very sluggish economy and an economic performance which compared poorly with those of competitors, and over-mighty trade unions which contributed to inflation and led to industry being plagued by strikes. Concern with these and other difficulties was reflected in four academic interpretations of the state of British politics.

'Directionless consensus'
In an article written in 1969, in which he examined the impact of parties on government policies, Richard Rose concluded that the British system could be characterised as 'government by directionless consensus' (1969: 442). Rose's argument relates mainly to the consensus on the rules of the policy-making game and the style of conflict resolution – seeking to accommodate interests affected by policy, trying to build agreement, maintaining a culture of secrecy. In policy-making, he suggests, achieving consensus among affected groups becomes an end in itself rather than the disciplined pursuit of a specific policy objective or the establishing of long-term goals. However, Rose's critique can be extended to cover substantive elements of the consensus as well, since he argues that civil servants, who are the key policy-makers, seek to defend the *status quo* and established departmental policies.

'Overload'

In 1975 Anthony King published a short but influential article in which he argued that the collectivist consensus was leading to 'overload' for British government and the result was a series of policy failures. Put simply, people expected government to do too much for them. Expectations of what governments should do for citizens were so great that government had come to be regarded 'as a sort of unlimited-liability insurance company, in the business of insuring all persons at all times against every conceivable risk' (King, 1975: 286). At the same time it was becoming more difficult for governments to deliver what was expected, partly because of the poor performance of the economy but mainly because governments were dependent upon, and unable to rely on, powerful groups (such as trade unions or currency speculators) to comply with government aims. The only solution, according to King, was to reduce popular expectations about the number of things that governments should do.

'Pluralist stagnation'

A more sustained and powerful critique of the post-war consensus was provided in the early 1980s by Samuel Beer (1982), an American political scientist who was a perceptive analyst of British politics. Subtitled 'The Political Contradictions of Collectivism', Beer's short but brilliant book argued that by the 1970s British government had come to be characterised by immobility and incoherence and that this was largely a consequence of the style of politics that had developed. Pluralist politics involves groups seeking to promote and defend their interests but the problem in Britain in the 1970s was that too many groups were now involved in a 'benefits scramble', a 'subsidy scramble' and a 'pay scramble'. In the first two cases people were looking to the government to provide benefits or subsidies of one kind or another and parties found it difficult to refuse demands from any particular group. The result was a concern simply to placate the various interests – 'stagnation' – and a loss of control over public expenditure. The government was also unable to resist apparently deserving cases for pay rises – nurses, for example – and the result was a meaningless leapfrogging of pay rates, increased public expenditure and inflation.

'Adversary politics'

The consensus on the nature of the regime and rules of the game was also attacked in 1975 by S.E. Finer (1975). Finer characterised the system that had developed as one of 'adversary politics'. The convention was that the opposition opposed government policies, almost for the sake of it. When a new government took office it would set about undoing the work of the previous government and implementing policies that had been developed in opposition with an eye to winning elections rather than being based on a serious analysis of the issue concerned. The result is destabilising discontinuities in policy. Thus, as Kavanagh (1990: 211) points out, between 1945 and 1975 government policy on prices changed, on average, every thirteen months. Crucially, Finer argues that the adversary system is underpinned by the first-past-the-post electoral system which – at least up to 1979 – tended to produce clear government majorities (enabling them to carry through their policies virtually unhindered) but also fairly regular changes in government. The start of a solution is to change the electoral system to one that is more proportional. It is worth noting that Finer's argument is rather different from that of Richard Rose mentioned above. Rose suggests that parties have little impact on policy; Finer that they have too much impact.

By the end of the 1970s, then, the post-war consensus was being criticised by academics. It was also being criticised by politicians and in the 'winter of discontent' (1978–79) the kinds of problem that had been identified came to a peak as many public sector workers went on strike. The government appeared paralysed, the country appeared ungovernable. In the general election which followed, the Conservatives under Margaret Thatcher won a large majority and proceeded to make a sharp break with the preceding consensus.

Thatcherism (1980s)

There is no doubt that Mrs Thatcher's period in office marked a sharp break with the past. As a result – and also because of her personal dominance of her governments – she became the first Prime Minister to have an 'ism' attached to her name to describe a distinctive approach to politics. There is a very large literature on 'Thatcherism' (see, for example, Kavanagh, 1990; Gamble, 1994b) but, summarising drastically, the approach that it describes has three main interlinked elements.

Style of leadership

Mrs Thatcher had no desire to achieve consensus on her policies, even within her own party. Rather, she was a 'conviction' politician, saying that she regarded believers in consensus politics as 'quislings' and 'traitors'. Consensus was achieved only 'by abandoning all beliefs, principles and values' (Young, 1989: 223–4). Indeed, she is quoted as having said:

> The Old Testament Prophets did not say, 'Brothers I want a consensus.' They said: 'This is my faith, this is what I passionately believe. If you believe it too, then come with me.'
>
> (Gamble, 1994b: v)

She was also ruthless in quashing opposition. Ministers who disagreed with her were unceremoniously sacked. She came close to viewing opposition to her policies as illegitimate, calling striking miners 'the enemy within' (Thatcher, 1993: 370) for example, and abolishing the Greater London Council and Metropolitan County Councils which were controlled by Labour and significant centres of opposition. Unlike most British Prime Ministers, Mrs Thatcher was confrontational and aggressive in her dealings with 'wet' colleagues, political opponents and the leaders of other countries in the European Community. This style of leadership was seen by Thatcher supporters as 'resolute' and her resolution was never more clearly demonstrated or admired than during the Falklands conflict of 1982. It was not for nothing that she was nicknamed the 'Iron Lady'.

General political values

Thatcherism embraced a number of general values. These included a preference for individualism over collectivism, which represented a clear break from the past. She famously suggested that 'there is no such thing as society, only individuals and their families' (but see discussion of this claim in Thatcher, 1993: 626). This preference was reflected in numerous policy areas such as welfare, where the aim was to break the 'dependency culture', and in a desire to 'roll back the state', that is reduce the role of the state (including local government) in the lives of citizens. Thus council houses were sold off and the powers of local education authorities pruned. Individualism was accompanied by support for 'Victorian values' – thrift, hard work, traditional family life, and so on – which added a moral dimension to Thatcherism. Hard work should be rewarded, families (rather than the state) should care for dependent relatives. Finally, strong nationalism – 'standing up for Britain' – was a core element of Thatcherism, exemplified not only in the Falklands but in her refusal to consider any form of devolution within the UK and her hostility to increased integration in the European Union.

Economic policy

Thatcherism involved an explicit rejection of the Keynesian consensus on economic policy. Keynesianism had, in fact, begun to fall into disrepute during the 1970s – specifically in 1976 when the Labour government was forced to apply for a loan from the International Monetary Fund and had to agree to public expenditure cuts. Nonetheless, during Mrs Thatcher's first government (1979–83) Keynesianism was abandoned and replaced by monetarism as the basis of economic policy. Full-blooded monetarism was later dropped, but economic policy continued to be dominated by a focus on inflation rather than unemployment and a preference for markets rather than the managed economy. Nationalised industries were privatised, for example, to expose them to the supposed benefits of competition.

Not surprisingly, Margaret Thatcher's term in office was, and remains, controversial. She generated strong emotions, being greatly admired by some sections of the electorate (and almost worshipped by the then Conservative-supporting press) but heartily disliked by others. Judgements differ about whether she carried through an essential modernisation of the British economy or merely succeeded in destroying the manufacturing industry, whether she expanded freedom by reducing the role of the state or created a more unequal and divided society. What is undeniable is that the Thatcher period was a highly significant period in British politics and its influence can still be felt today.

Mrs Thatcher fell from office in late 1990 and was replaced by John Major. Major was a very different personality and there is no doubt that his leadership style was different. He appeared to be more pragmatic and more concerned to carry his colleagues with him. Rightly or wrongly, he came to be seen as weak and indecisive. Partly this was a result of having a much smaller parliamentary major-ity but, nonetheless, public perceptions of Major were clearly very different from those of Mrs Thatcher. There is more debate over whether or not the policies pur-sued by Major continued to be inspired by Thatcherism (see Ludlam and Smith, 1996; Kavanagh, 1997: ch. 9). Certainly there was no 'Majorism'. Although Major introduced some new ideas, such as citizens' charters, and was less explicitly hostile to Europe, the consensus of opinion among commentators is that his term of office largely involved a continuation of Thatcherism. As both Ludlam and Smith conclude after an extensive review, 'it is the persistence of Thatcherite objectives that stands out. . . . Major's direction has been one of implementing Thatcherism rather than challenging its key precepts. In policy area after policy area, Major has maintained the Thatcherite agenda' (1996: 279).

Blair and New Labour

Tony Blair became Labour leader in 1994. He inherited a party that had lost four elections in a row and had come close (in 1983) to being relegated to third place. After 1983 the then leader, Neil Kinnock, realised that something had to be done and began to 'modernise'. Important changes were made in respect of policies, structures and organisation (Seyd, 1993). Under Tony Blair, however, the process of modernisation was accelerated and included the ditching of the old Clause 4 of the party's constitution which committed it to public ownership. By 1997, according to Patrick Seyd at least, 'the party had been changed out of all recognition' (1998: 49). Not the least of the changes was that it was now widely (if unofficially) known as 'New Labour'. The changes appeared to have the desired effect as Labour won the 1997 election in a landslide and performed a similar feat in 2001.

Did Labour's victories herald a dramatic shift away from the Thatcherite legacy? While still in opposition Blair began to develop ideas that suggested that there would be such a shift. These ideas revolved around concepts known as 'the stakeholder society' and 'the third way' (between, presumably, individualism and collectivism). The former rapidly receded and the latter remained rather vague. In its first term, however, some claimed that there was only limited evidence of a sharp break with the past, with the exception of constitutional matters. Labour pledged to stick to the previous government's spending plans, made no attempt to reverse any of the privatisations (planning, instead, to extend it to new areas such as air traffic control) or to amend significantly Thatcher's industrial relations legislation, and sought to reduce the welfare budget. By the same token, it did introduce the minimum wage as well as establishing the New Deal programme to reduce unemployment, funding this from a windfall tax on the privatised utilities. Moreover, it used the taxation system – especially various indirect taxes – to redistribute income from the better off to the less well off. In addition, Labour proclaimed a goal of full employment, a policy not promoted by governments since the 1970s. 'New Labour' may in some ways be rather different from 'Old Labour', but the claim that it is simply Thatcherism in disguise is at best a highly contentious one.

This, then, is where we are today. The style and concerns of British politics at the start of the twenty-first century did not just drop from the sky. Rather, they are products of a long series of developments building upon and reacting to previous experience. It is within this broad historical context, as well as in the changing international, social economic and cultural contexts, that the issues considered in the chapters that follow are debated.

References

Almond, G. and Verba, S. (1965) *The Civic Culture*, Boston, MA: Little, Brown and Co.

Barry, B. (1970) *Sociologists, Economists and Democracy*, London: Collier-Macmillan.

Beer, S. (1965) *Modern British Politics*, London: faber & faber.

Beer, S. (1982) *Britain against Itself: The Political Contradictions of Collectivism*, London: W.W. Norton and Co.

Central Statistical Office (1993) *Social Trends 23*, London: HMSO Stationery Office.

Finer, S.E. (1975) *Adversary Politics and Electoral Reform*, London: Wigram.

Gamble, A. (1994a) *Britain in Decline: Economic Policy, Political Strategy and the British State*, Basingstoke: Macmillan.

Gamble, A. (1994b) *The Free Economy and the Strong State: The Politics of Thatcherism* (second edition), Basingstoke: Macmillan.

George, S. (1994) *An Awkward Partner: Britain in the European Community* (second edition), Oxford: Oxford University Press.

Kavanagh, D. (1971) 'The deferential English: a comparative critique', *Government and Opposition*, Vol. VI, No. 3.

Kavanagh, D. (1972) *Political Culture*, London: Macmillan.

Kavanagh, D. (1980) 'Political culture in Great Britain: the decline of the civic culture', in G. Almond and S. Verba (eds) *The Civic Culture Revisited*, Boston, MA: Little, Brown and Co.

Kavanagh, D. (1990) *Thatcherism and British Politics* (third edition), Oxford: Oxford University Press.

Kavanagh, D. (1997) *The Reordering of British Politics: Politics after Thatcher*, Oxford: Oxford University Press.

Kavanagh, D. and Morris P. (1989) *Consensus Politics from Attlee to Thatcher*, Oxford: Blackwell.

King, A. (1975) 'Overload: problems of governing in the 1970s', *Political Studies*, Vol. XXIII, Nos 2 & 3, pp. 284–96.

Ludlam, S. and Smith, M. (1996) *Contemporary British Conservatism*, Basingstoke: Macmillan.

Marr, A. (2000) *The Day Britain Died*, London: Profile Books.

Miller, W., Timpson, A. and Lessnoff, M. (1995) *Political Culture in Contemporary Britain*, Oxford: Clarendon Press.

Office for National Statistics (1999) *Social Trends 29*, London: HMSO.

Office for National Statistics (2000) *Social Trends 30*, London: HMSO.

Pimlott, B. (1988) 'The myth of consensus', in L.M. Smith (ed.) *The Making of Britain*, London: Macmillan.

Reynolds, D. (1991) *Britannia Overruled*, London: Longman.

Rose, R. (1969) 'The variability of party government: a theoretical and empirical critique', *Political Studies*, Vol. XVI, No. 4, pp. 413–45.

Saggar, S. (2000) *Race and Representation: Electoral Politics and Ethnic Pluralism in Britain*, Manchester: Manchester University Press.

Sanders, D. (1990) *Losing an Empire, Finding a Role: British Foreign Policy since 1945*, Basingstoke: Macmillan.

Seyd, P. (1993) 'Labour: the great transformation', in A. King (ed.) *Britain at the Polls 1992*, Chatham, NJ: Chatham House, pp. 70–100.

Seyd, P. (1998) 'Tony Blair and New Labour', in A. King (ed.) *New Labour Triumphs: Britain at the Polls*, Chatham, NJ: Chatham House, pp. 49–73.

Thatcher, M. (1993) *The Downing Street Years*, London: HarperCollins.

Young, H. (1989) *One of Us*, London: Macmillan.

Enduring Questions about Politics

*Justin Fisher and
David Denver*

CHAPTER TWO

Many students of politics tend to shy away from studying political theory or philosophy. They frequently complain that it is abstract, dealing with ideas and arguments that seem remote from the realities of day-to-day political discussion and activity. In fact, however, theoretical issues underpin political debates. Whether those involved are aware of it or not, differences of opinion on contemporary political issues often reflect deeper theoretical debates on matters that have concerned students of politics for a very long time. These matters, which we refer to as 'enduring questions' about politics, include questions relating to such issues as the nature and limits of liberty, the desirability and achievability of equality, the proper role of the state, the nature of democracy and many more. These sorts of issue are the stuff of political theory, but they also frame debates and underlie arguments in politics. It should be noted that the questions raised in these areas are mainly *normative*. That is to say, they concern values; they relate to what *ought to be* the case rather than what *is* the case. It is a characteristic of normative statements that they are incapable of disproof – there is no 'right' answer – and that is why debates about them continue. Thus if someone believes that the government ought to abolish student tuition fees, then that is a value judgement and is not, in itself, either true or false. The contrast is with *positive* statements – statements of fact. Thus, if it is claimed that the government has raised x million pounds from tuition fees, then that can be easily checked and shown to be either true or false.

In this chapter we discuss some of these enduring normative questions in the context of British political debates and in the chapters that follow we have attempted to draw explicit connections between the practicalities of the topics discussed and more abstract and theoretical issues.

Liberty

Appeals to liberty or freedom feature a great deal in political debate. Almost every political doctrine – socialism, liberalism, conservatism and even (as famously argued by Jean-Jacques Rousseau) some forms of totalitarianism – proclaim liberty, in one form or another, as a desirable outcome. Liberty is almost universally thought to be 'a good thing'. The problem is, however, that there is disagreement about the meaning of liberty as well as about how much of it ordinary citizens should have.

In broad terms, liberty or freedom can be conceptualised as having two major meanings that have been identified as 'positive' and 'negative' freedom (Berlin, 1969). *Negative freedom* refers to the extent to which people have the liberty to pursue their preferences without restraint or coercion. Thus, we have liberty if we have freedom *from* constraint. Of course, any law is a form of constraint but these have to be justified by reference to other values, such as maintaining order or providing collective benefits. Proponents of this notion of liberty seek to minimise constraints and to protect individuals from abuses of power by government. They also support the individual against what John Stuart Mill referred to as 'the tyranny of the majority' (Mill, 1985: 62) – in other words, those who hold unconventional and unpopular views should not be forced to conform to majority opinion. In general, according to Mill, people should be free to do whatever they like as long as it does not harm others.

Some argue that this conception of liberty or freedom is too narrow. They suggest that liberty also involves freedom *to* pursue preferences (as well as *from* constraint). 'Real' freedom can only be achieved if the obstacles which prevent people pursuing their preferences fully are removed. Thus, before the advent of state education only those who had the ability to pay for it received an adequate education. By providing universal free education – which involved a diminution of some people's negative liberty by forcing them to pay taxes – the state removed an obstacle and gave individuals the *freedom to* pursue their educational goals and preferences and much else. This is an example of *positive freedom*.

As the example shows, the two conceptions of liberty can be in conflict with one another. In order to increase positive freedom, society – usually in the form of the state – may have to impinge upon negative freedom. This is the case with almost all public spending programmes, for example, since they frequently involve forcing some citizens to pay more taxation in order to fund improvements in the positive freedom of others. Similarly, to return to the example of education, making attendance at school compulsory – which is likely to be in the best interests of the majority of children – involves diminishing the negative freedom of parents who would like their children to be educated in a less conventional way.

There are many examples of debates concerning liberty and freedom in British politics. The Thatcher and Major administrations (1979–97), for example, placed great emphasis upon negative freedom in the economic sphere, arguing that business should be able to function with as little restraint as possible. Such restraints included trade union action and government regulations, which tend to infringe business freedom. As a consequence, government activity was referred to as *interference* rather than *intervention* or *involvement*. Of course, rhetoric does not always match outcomes. For example, although the Thatcher administration succeeded in moving utilities such as gas and electricity from public into private ownership, thus increasing negative freedom for the utilities, it also created a regulatory structure that severely restricted the negative freedom of the new businesses.

While Mrs Thatcher's government may have promoted at least rhetoric in support of negative freedom in the economic sphere, the same was not always true in other areas. Schools were required to adopt the National Curriculum, for example, which impinged upon their freedom to construct curricula as they saw fit. And, in a classic illustration of the paradox of Conservative liberalism, while supporting the expansion of economic liberty in the growth of extraterrestrial broadcasting, the government also re-affirmed its intention to maintain limits on what broadcasters, terrestrial or extraterrestrial, could transmit.

In more recent times, the question of the extent of negative liberty that should be allowed has been clearly illustrated by the debate over fox-hunting. Large majorities of the public and of MPs appear to support the banning of fox-hunting. Yet, such a ban would clearly constitute an infringement of the liberty of those who wish to hunt foxes (the 'tyranny of the majority') – on the assumption that foxes have no rights in the matter. The question of whether animals can be said to have rights is itself one which divides opinion among political theorists and more widely (see, for example, LaFollette, 1997: chs 9–13). If, for example, we argue that foxes have rights, then the denial of liberty of fox-hunters would arguably be justified. Contrariwise, if we don't suggest that foxes have intrinsic rights, then we must consider on what basis the state can legitimately infringe the negative liberty of fox-hunters. All of which illustrates that theoretical concerns are critical to our reasoning on such matters.

In terms of positive freedom, the introduction of a minimum wage provides a good example of the tensions inherent in the concept of liberty. A statutory minimum wage, prescribing minimum hourly rates of pay for most employees, was introduced soon after Labour's 1997 election victory. In terms of positive liberty, the stipulation that there is a minimum wage potentially provides recipients with the liberty to pursue their preferences to buy things that they previously could not afford, for example. By the same token, increasing positive liberty by means of the minimum wage also involves decreasing the negative liberty of employers who are no longer free to pay wages at a level which they believe to be appropriate for the job.

Clearly, then, the idea of liberty has different meanings and action or policy based on one interpretation of liberty may be seen as harmful if another interpretation is adopted. As we shall see throughout this book, questions of liberty resonate throughout British politics, but in seeking to understand them, we must be clear about which interpretation is being emphasised and about whose liberty may be compromised in the pursuit of liberty for others.

Equality

There is much greater disagreement over whether equality is a desirable or attainable goal. Most people would accept that in a democracy citizens should be treated equally by the law and have equal political rights (such as 'one person, one vote'). Most would probably also subscribe in a vague way to the view that there should be equality of opportunity in terms of education, employment, participation in social institutions, and so on. The idea of equality of outcomes is rather more controversial.

'Equal opportunities' has close theoretical links with positive freedom. The intention is to provide a framework in which barriers that prevent people progressing in their chosen sphere are removed. Thus, successive British governments have outlawed discrimination on grounds of race/ethnicity, sex and disability (but not, except in Northern Ireland, religion) and set up agencies to ensure compliance. The European Convention on Human Rights, incorporated into English law in 2000 (earlier in the case of Scotland) widened the list to include sexual orientation, which had the effect of undermining the previously-existing policy of banning homosexuals from serving in the armed forces. In addition, numerous institutions and companies in Britain have adopted 'equal opportunities practices' when making appointments or considering applicants for employment or, indeed, when choosing candidates to fight elections.

The notion and implementation of equal opportunities are not without difficulty, however. It could be argued that inequality in achievements is caused by myriad factors but that the family one is born into has a fundamental influence, conditioning much that happens in later life. The achievement of fully equal opportunities may, therefore, involve a solution advocated by Plato in his vision of the ideal state. Families need to be abolished and children brought up communally. Since that would be unacceptable it could be argued that while removing barriers by law might help, ultimately ensuring absolute equality of opportunity is a chimera – an unachievable ideal.

The practice of equal opportunities has also attracted criticism in that what it can involve is *un*equal opportunities for specially favoured groups. Creating equal opportunities can, on occasions, involve unequal treatment. Such criticism has gone furthest in the United States where 'affirmative action' – which involves positive discrimination in favour of groups which, it is argued, have been unfairly treated previously (such as women and blacks) – has been attacked in election campaigns and declared unconstitutional in some states on the grounds that it denies equal opportunity to members of non-favoured groups. In Britain, equal opportunities policies and practices have mainly focused on three specific groups – women, ethnic minorities and people with disabilities. This is largely because of concerted and well-organised political campaigns to promote their cause. But this focus potentially disadvantages other groups, some of whom have also been under-represented in public life – working-class men, for example. So how far should equal opportunities policies go? Which groups should be advantaged? Does the promotion of affirmative action for some groups lead to acceptable disadvantage for others?

The ideas and practice of equality of opportunity are, then, not beyond criticism and there is a further consideration. Inequality of opportunity is often inferred from inequality of outcomes. Thus, the fact that women and ethnic minorities are under-represented in the House of Commons or in the higher reaches of management is used to argue that they must have experienced discrimination or not had an equal opportunity to succeed. This reasoning lies behind efforts, especially in the Labour Party, to introduce procedures to increase women's representation. Prior to the 1997 general election, the party changed its selection procedures to ensure that at least half of winnable constituencies were required to choose a candidate from an all-female short-list, and the policy did contribute to a substantial increase in the number of women elected to Parliament. Paradoxically, the policy was challenged and ruled to be contrary to the Sex Discrimination Act. Undeterred, Labour adopted a new selection policy for the Scottish Parliament and Welsh Assembly elections in 1999, requiring 'twinned' constituencies to select one man and one woman and this had the desired effect on the gender balance of Labour members in the two bodies. These measures went some way to producing the desired outcome – more women representatives. The theoretical question is whether the desirable ends justified the means.

Equality of outcome may be thought of as the 'purest' form of equality and in many respects it commands little support. Few advocate complete equality of income for everyone, for example (although many favour *more* equality); few demand that university professors should reflect the social composition of the nation. Critics argue that equality of outcomes in these sorts of area, as well as being an impossible goal, would harm society as it would remove incentives to achievement and lead to a drab and stagnant society. It is sometimes argued that elected political representatives should somehow be a 'microcosm of the nation' (see, for example Pitkin, 1967; Phillips, 1995) – in others words, that the social composition of Parliament should reflect the social composition of the nation. But, there are potential difficulties in attempting to achieve this goal, even if one agrees with the basic idea. Should Parliament attempt to reflect all groups? Clearly this is impossible since there are so many permutations. But attempts could still be made to ensure composition of certain principal characteristics, such as sex and ethnicity. Yet that leads to a problem of deciding which groups are to be targeted. None of this is necessarily to argue against these ideas; merely to highlight that attempts to increase equality in areas like these can often lead to questions that must be debated. Is the unequal treatment of some groups permissible to increase the equality of others? As should be clear by now, the idea of equality is fraught with difficulties. It should also be clear that attempts to increase equality of whatever kind are bound to come into conflict with at least the negative conception of liberty. Much political debate in Britain involves disagreement over how the two should be balanced.

The Role of the State

We will not enter into discussion here about how 'the state' should be defined (see for example Dunleavy and O'Leary, 1987; Marsh and Stoker, 1995). For our purposes it refers to the institutions of government which are normally in the hands of a political party when it wins an election (although the judiciary is an obvious exception). The question is to what extent the power of the state should be used by governments to shape society.

There have been three important strands of thought on this issue in Britain – liberal, social democratic and conservative. However, as will become apparent, these are not terms consistent with the names of particular political parties. The *liberal* view of the state has links with the negative view of liberty discussed above. Having its origins in the late eighteenth century and being particularly influential during the nineteenth century, this view suggests that the role of the state ought to be as small as possible. State 'interference' in the economy or in people's lives is to be avoided – partly because it is inefficient but also because it diminishes liberty. The state should, of course, provide for the defence of the nation, ensure law and order, possibly provide a safety net for the very poorest and generally provide a framework of law. Beyond that, however, people should be left to get on with their lives as best they can without being constrained at every turn by a 'nanny' state.

In stark contrast, the *social democratic* tradition takes a much more positive view of the state. Originating at the start of the twentieth century and dominant in Britain (and in most other western societies) from 1945 to about 1980, this view connects to the positive conception of freedom and argues that the state should be used to provide collectively what individuals on their own, or the market, cannot. This includes direct provision of a wide range of welfare services – pensions, health care, education, housing – as well as regulation of a wide range of services – broadcasting, licensing, building – in the collective interest. As far as the economy is concerned, this perspective favours state involvement in planning, day-to-day management and regulation. In its heyday the social democratic vision also involved state ownership of key sectors of the economy – gas, electricity supply, water, railways, coal mines, and so on. In a useful phrase frequently used in the United States, the social democratic tradition favours 'big government'.

Lying somewhere between these two there is also a *conservative* perspective on the role of the state, again originating in the late eighteenth and early nineteenth centuries. In this case a strong state is regarded as desirable but not primarily to undertake welfare and other provisions. Rather, it is required to maintain the social order, which is hierarchical (or ought to be). Other institutions, such as the Church, also have a part to play in this, but a weak state will lead to anarchy. To avoid this, firm action by the state is required. Indeed, if maintaining the social order and the cohesion of society requires the provision of, say, decent housing for the working class, then that is properly something that the state should undertake. This was precisely the reasoning behind the introduction of an Artisan's Dwellings Act by a Conservative government under Benjamin Disraeli in 1875.

The social democratic view prevailed in British politics from 1945 to 1980, even under Conservative governments. Many key industries and services were publicly owned, expenditure on welfare increased sharply and regulation of numerous areas of activity by the state was widely accepted. After the election of Margaret Thatcher as Prime Minister in 1979, however, this situation began to be reversed. A more liberal interpretation of the role of the state was in evidence. Industries were privatised, attempts were made to cut welfare spending and deregulation became a 'buzz word'. At the same time, the conservative view remained influential as the government tried to use the 'strong state' to maintain the social order and traditional values – as in, for example, curbing the powers of local government and prescribing what should be taught in school (see, for example, Gamble, 1994). Since the coming to power of the Labour government there has been no wholesale return to the kind of social democratic state seen in the 1950s. No industry has been re-nationalised and while welfare spending has been increased in some areas, in others the government has sought to limit spending. Indeed, Tony Blair has talked of a 'third way' in politics, which seems to involve combining different elements of the three theoretical perspectives that we have outlined (Blair,

1998; Giddens, 1998). As the Blair and Thatcher examples illustrate, governments and political parties do not often pursue one particular view of the state whole-heartedly and to the exclusion of others. Rather, they are mixed up in different ways. The same probably applies to the views of individuals like you and us.

Nonetheless differing views of the role of the state still lie behind much con-temporary political debate. Should the railways be regulated, subsidised, left to run on their own or taken into public ownership? Should university education be provided freely by the state or paid for by those who benefit from it? Should the state seek to discourage smoking tobacco (or cannabis, for that matter) or leave people free to choose for themselves? Does the state really have to be involved in deciding when pubs open and close? Answers to these specific questions must clearly be informed by the more general theoretical perspectives on the role of the state, which we have outlined in this section.

Democracy

Like 'liberty' (but not 'equality'), 'democracy', once derided by elites as rule by the ignorant mass, is a word which now attracts almost universal approval. Moreover, the collapse of the former communist states (which frequently described them-selves as 'democratic republics') is said to represent the 'triumph of democracy'. Nonetheless – you will by now be unsurprised to learn – there are disagreements about what 'democracy' involves. A simple listing of some of the phrases associ-ated with democracy illustrates the difficulty: 'government by the people', 'majority rule', 'the rule of law', 'representative government', 'free speech', 'individual and minority rights', 'popular participation in politics' and, of course, 'liberty' and 'equality'. Clearly the concept comes burdened with numerous connotations and expectations.

An initial distinction needs to be made between political democracy and democracy in other arenas. The concept has been stretched to include 'industrial democracy', 'social democracy' and 'economic democracy'. Critics of democratic practice in western societies have suggested that political democracy on its own is not enough to secure 'true' democracy and that it must be extended into all aspects of life (including the family). In Britain, however, democracy has been rigidly confined to politics, for the most part, and that is what we shall concern ourselves with here.

A key problem for democracy is how to secure government by the people. In modern industrialised societies with populations running into millions, it is clearly impossible to have direct government by the people on a day-to-day basis. The solution is to have a representative democracy in which citizens elect repres-entatives to act on their behalf. For the political thinker Thomas Paine, this was the most sensible form of democracy, because most people were too busy in their everyday lives to concern themselves with intricate political debates (Paine, 1969).

This raises a number of questions in the British context, however. The first con-cerns the electoral system to be used. In recent years there has been considerable criticism of the system used to elect the House of Commons – largely on the grounds that the relationship between votes and seats is highly disproportionate – and alternatives have been mooted. Alternative, more proportional election methods have, indeed, been introduced for elections to the devolved institutions in Scotland, Wales and Northern Ireland, for the European Parliament and also for the new form of local government in London, but all have raised further questions of democratic concern, particularly in relation to the formation of coalition governments in Scotland and Wales which included the Liberal Democrats whose performance in the election, on their own, had been relatively weak. In other words, it could be argued that the more proportional electoral systems had provided the Liberal Democrats with a disproportionate amount of power as a result of their entering the coalitions.

In a few specific cases in recent years 'government by the people' has been more direct in that important policy matters – for the most part constitutional issues – have been put to the electorate in referendums. These examples of *direct* democracy have been rare, however, and only once (in 1975 on the question of membership of the European Economic Community) involved the entire national electorate. They are considered in more detail in Chapter 6.

A second problem relating to representative democracy concerns the meaning of representation. To say that someone is representative or a representative of some group can mean at least three different things:

1. He/she may be typical of the group, sharing at least some of their characteristics and/or attitudes.
2. He/she may be a delegate from the group whose task is simply to transmit its views or opinions.
3. He/she may be appointed by the group and trusted to defend and promote its interests whatever the circumstances.

It is apparent that individual MPs cannot be representatives in the first two senses since constituency electorates are socially diverse and have widely varying opinions on political issues. It might be argued, however, that the House of Commons as a whole should be representative in the first sense. Yet, the only way of ensuring that the House of Commons reflects the electorate as a whole would be to choose MPs as some sort of random sample. The case against doing so is put by Harrop and Miller:

> We may not want representation by 'people like us' so much as by 'people who will act effectively on our behalf'. Who wants representation in a court of law, or even at a press conference, by an advocate as dull-witted, shifty-eyed, inarticulate and ignorant as themselves?
>
> (Harrop and Miller, 1987: 246)

Individual MPs can be representatives in the third sense since they usually try to advance the interests of their constituencies, but in most circumstances this is secondary to their support for their party and, in the British case, it is parties that provide representative government. This involves the idea of trusteeship but it is parties rather than individuals that are entrusted to represent the voters. In all but the most exceptional cases, candidates are supported on the basis of their party label and the parties in Parliament broadly represent their supporters and hence, together, the electorate as a whole. Problems of representation remain, however. What of electors whose favoured party is defeated in their constituency? The argument would be that their views are represented by MPs of their party elected elsewhere. It is also the case that some voters remain entirely unrepresented or under-represented – there are no Green Party MPs, for example, and the Liberal Democrats' share of seats in the House of Commons after the 2001 general election (7.9%) was much smaller than the share of votes they received (18.3%). These difficulties with the adequacy of representation derive from the nature of the electoral system.

There is a clear tension in democracy between majority rule and respect for individual or group rights. This is keenly felt in the United States where the Constitution includes a Bill of Rights which enumerates the rights of citizens, including, notoriously, the right to keep and bear arms. Although there is some controversy over the interpretation of the relevant clause, this means that even if a majority wanted to outlaw the private ownership of guns, they would find it difficult, at the least, to do so. So, elective democracy aims somehow to reflect the 'will of the people' but then problems arise if the majority wish to deprive a minority of their 'democratic rights'. Until recently this has been less of a problem in Britain since there was no codification of rights until the European Convention was adopted in 2000. Indeed, there are clear examples of Parliament legislating in clear defiance of majority opinion. Capital punishment, for example, was abolished in the 1960s, despite a large majority favouring its retention, and Parliament has repeatedly voted down attempts to restore it despite consistent majority support for such a move among the public at large. This is a good example of MPs viewing their role as being to act as trustees rather than delegates. Nonetheless, the question of individual rights is bound to become more controversial in future as cases are taken to the courts under the European Convention, especially when unpopular minorities seek to have their rights upheld.

At the start of the new century British democracy faces significant challenges. The first, and most obvious, comes from Europe. This issue is taken up later but it is worth emphasising here that the European Union is not democratic in the same way as national governments. Citizens do not elect members of the Commission (the driving force of the Union) and many important decisions are made by unelected officials. There is a directly elected European Parliament but its powers are limited and its activity rarely reported in Britain. As subsequent chapters show, European law (which takes precedence over national law) and the EU generally play an increasingly large role in domestic politics. From the abolition of duty free allowances to the requirement to price and sell meat in metric units, European decisions have overridden opinion in Britain. The apparent inability of citizens – or their representatives – to influence European policy significantly or to hold key European political actors to account clearly presents significant challenges to democracy as conventionally understood.

A second challenge to democracy arises from what has been termed 'globalisation', especially economic and financial globalisation. As markets have developed and as technology has made global trade easier, so challenges to the supremacy of national governments have arguably grown, although as Jim Tomlinson argues, the extent of the challenge is debatable (see Chapter 17). A good example is the Internet. In blunt terms, national laws are virtually unenforceable on the Internet. On television, for example, news broadcasters are bound by law to be impartial in terms of political content. This applies to both terrestrial and satellite broadcasters. The consequence of this is that, by and large, viewers trust the political information they receive from television more than they do from newspapers, where impartiality is not required. On the Internet, however, any such law would be unenforceable and so website broadcasts can be as biased or impartial as they choose. Similarly, whereas broadcasting content can be regulated on television, this cannot be done on the web.

International markets challenge democracy in other ways as well. Multinational corporations, for example, can exert pressure on governments to pursue particular policies, such as joining the Euro or even to extract government grants or tax-breaks. Faced with the risk that such companies may re-locate to another country, governments can find themselves in a very difficult situation. Veiled threats of re-location have already surfaced in the context of the debate over the European single currency. Perhaps the most significant market, however, is international finance. The UK, or indeed any other country, does not have complete control over its interest rates or monetary policy. Britain's interest rates are affected, among other things, by the value of its currency, which is determined by its value on the foreign exchange markets. If the currency is valued too low, then Britain may raise its interest rates in order to improve the value of sterling and vice versa. In addition, the interest rates of other countries affect British rates. If the USA, for example, raises its rates, Britain is almost certain to follow to prevent a flight of currency from Britain. Other international markets can also affect domestic economies. In the late 1990s, for example, the economic crash in the Far East led to economic difficulties in Britain. The consequence of all this is that governments do not have complete freedom to use economic policy to promote the programmes on which they were elected. A rapid rise in interest rates, for example, could lead to a recession, which in turn would threaten Britain's ability to fund certain programmes from public spending. In short, global financial markets are interdependent, and their effect can be to challenge the ability of democratically-elected governments to fulfil their promises.

Third, it can be argued that the mass media also pose a threat to democracy. On the one hand, the media – a 'free press' – may be seen as a vital component of democracy. Indeed, the mass media are sometimes described as the 'fourth estate' – independent observers and critics of government providing citizens with information and ensuring that governments do not abuse their power. On the other hand, the concentration of media ownership in Britain – involving newspapers, commercial radio and independent television companies – has given rise to a cause for concern, with Rupert Murdoch's News International group singled out for particular criticism. Calls have been made to regulate media ownership in order to provide greater diversity and to prevent 'media moguls' having undue influence over voters and the political agenda. The campaign in the press during the summer of 2000 about naming and shaming alleged paedophiles illustrates the potential of the media to influence the agenda. It was regarded as irresponsible by the government and many commentators but was defended on the grounds that it promoted and reflected majority opinion rather than that of the liberal elite. It was, in a sense, democratic.

A final threat to consider is the increasing role of appointed, rather than elected, bodies in Britain. A feature of British politics in recent years, as David Wilson discusses (Chapter 16), has been the growth of unelected bodies in charge of many aspects of British political life. Quangos have thus challenged the authority of democratically-elected bodies at both a national and a local level. And, as Keith Ewing discusses (Chapter 24), the role of the judiciary in Britain is increasing, especially now that the European Convention on Human Rights has been incorporated into British law. In one sense, the roles of quangos and the judiciary are very different. In some cases, quangos represent the replacement of elected bodies with appointed ones, while the judiciary is charged in some sense with protecting aspects of democratic life, such as rights. However, where they are similar is that both can, and do, challenge the will of representatives elected by the public. And, as Ewing shows, this can result in the overturning of policies enacted by elected representatives on the grounds of judicial interpretation. In short, 'the will of the people', embodied in their elected representatives, can be legitimately be frustrated by unelected institutions of British political life.

Conclusion

The point of this chapter has been to emphasise that fundamental questions of political theory resonate throughout British politics. Questions of liberty, equality, democracy and the like are not ones that should be considered only within the confines of political theory courses. They are of critical importance and help frame our understanding of political debates (which of course is why most courses require students to take them). It is no use saying that one wants freedom to do something without knowing what freedom means. So throughout this book, we hope that you will consider these and other theoretical questions when examining each topic. As a consequence, a section on theoretical considerations features in each chapter to flag up questions and debates, and enrich our understanding of British politics.

References

Berlin, I. (1969) *Four Essays on Liberty*, Oxford: Oxford University Press.

Blair, T. (1998) *The Third Way*, London: Fabian Pamphlet 588.

Dunleavy, P. and O'Leary, B. (1987) *Theories of the State*, Basingstoke: Macmillan.

Gamble, A. (1994) *The Free Economy and the Strong State: The Politics of Thatcherism*, Basingstoke: Macmillan.

Giddens, A. (1998) *The Third Way: The Renewal of Social Democracy*, Cambridge: Polity Press.

Harrop, M. and Miller, W.L. (1987) *Elections and Voters*, Basingstoke: Macmillan.

LaFollette, H. (ed.) (1997) *Ethics in Practice*, Oxford: Blackwell.

Marsh, D. and Stoker, G. (eds) (1995) *Theories and Methods in Political Science*, Basingstoke: Macmillan.

Mill, J.S. (1985) *On Liberty*, Harmondsworth: Penguin.

Paine, T. (1969) *The Rights of Man*, Harmondsworth: Penguin.

Phillips, A. (1995) *The Politics of Presence*, Oxford: Clarendon Press.

Pitkin, H.F. (1967) *The Concept of Representation*, Cambridge: Cambridge University Press.

PART TWO   Constitutional
             Issues

Devolution and the Future of the Union I

James Mitchell

CHAPTER THREE

Because Britain's common political institutions are central to the British people's common identity, if you attack those institutions, you are attacking that common identity and the qualities that come with it.
(William Hague, Speech to Centre for Policy Studies, 24 January 1999)

Today it is not simply that we share a common island, and a common language, but that we also share a commitment to openness and internationalism, to public service and to justice, to creativity and inventiveness, to democracy and tolerance.
(Gordon Brown and Douglas Alexander, *New Scotland New Britain*, London: The Smith Institute, 1999: 31)

Across the political divide it is accepted that the establishment of devolved institutions marks a radical change in British constitutional politics. The Scottish Parliament and the Assemblies in Wales and Northern Ireland are important not only in the parts of the United Kingdom over which they hold jurisdiction but they also have important repercussions for the state as a whole. For Conservatives and those opposed to devolution, these constitutional changes challenge the integrity of the state itself. They challenge the authority of Parliament at Westminster, a symbol of national unity. For Labour devolutionists, contrariwise, the unreformed constitution was creating pressures threatening the integrity of the state. For them, shared values and a shared political culture bind Britain together and devolution would allow for a degree of distinctiveness within the state.

Devolutionists fondly quote John Smith, late leader of the Labour Party, who referred to devolution as the 'settled will of the Scottish people'. By way of contrast, Ron Davies, former Labour Welsh Secretary of State, has referred to devolution as a process and not an end-point. Indications since the establishment of the Parliament and Assembly suggest that Ron Davies has proved to be more correct. The nationalist parties, the Scottish National Party (SNP) and Plaid Cymru, are the second parties behind Labour in Scotland and Wales. Support for further devolution or even independence seems more likely than ever. Tensions and unresolved matters exist which may provide a dynamic for further change. Devolution, it would appear, is only the start of a constitutional journey. Its end is far from clear.

To understand where Britain may be heading it is necessary to understand the pressures which led to devolution in the first place. It is then necessary to consider whether devolution can meet these demands and also some of the repercussions of the changes. Will the new institutions serve to bind the peoples of the UK together in a common union or will they provoke demands for more change? Will a common set of values be undermined by devolution or will these common values ensure that the state remains united? Are there signs of unintended consequences of devolution which might undermine the state or will devolution be accommodated, making the UK more explicitly a pluralistic 'nation of nations'?

Background

The demand for constitutional reform has long existed in Scotland and Wales. In 1886, a Scottish Home Rule Association was set up to argue for 'home rule all round', for local Parliaments in each of the constituent nations of the UK. Welsh demands for some kind of autonomy ran in parallel with Scottish demands. Plaid Cymru was formed in 1925 and the SNP came into existence in 1934 as the result of the merger of two home rule parties. After 1945, a petition for Scottish home rule was signed by vast numbers of people in Scotland. Despite this, home rule was not a central issue in the politics of Scotland or Wales until the 1960s. Before then, popular support for change was sporadic and fairly shallow. People might have been willing to tell pollsters that they supported a Scottish Parliament or sign a petition, but when they entered the polling booths there was a reluctance to treat home rule as a priority. Labour and the Conservatives would occasionally flirt with Scottish and Welsh nationalism for electoral purposes but neither supported radical constitutional change. Each party accepted the constitutional order. So deeply embedded in British political culture was this consensus that it was hardly even recognised. There may have debates on whether there should be a Welsh Office, modelled on the Scottish Office which had been established in 1885, but the notion that Scotland or Wales should have a Parliament or Assembly was supported only on the fringes of the two main parties.

By the early 1960s, however, evidence of growing support for constitutional change or, at least, evidence of growing dissatisfaction with the *status quo* was emerging. Nationalists started to become serious challengers in a few areas. In 1966, Plaid Cymru won its first parliamentary seat in a by-election in Carmarthen and in the following year the SNP won Hamilton, previously a rock-solid Labour stronghold. Major upsets for the main parties occurred in local elections around this time too. The Conservative Party was the first to respond when Ted Heath, its leader at the time, announced to a startled Scottish Conservative conference in 1968 that a future Tory government would introduce a measure of devolution. Harold Wilson's Labour government responded more cautiously by setting up a Royal Commission on the Constitution the following year. In 1973, after the Conservatives had been returned to power, the Royal Commission issued its report in favour of devolution. The SNP lost Hamilton at the 1970 general election but won the remote Western Isles constituency and, though it achieved a creditable performance across Scotland, it was widely perceived to have suffered a setback largely because there had been a general expectation, encouraged by the nationalists, that they would achieve a spectacular breakthrough. For a brief period, it looked as if British territorial politics was returning to something like normality and Ted Heath quietly forgot his earlier promise to deliver Scottish devolution.

The winter of 1973/74 proved to be a watershed in British politics. The Royal Commission report was issued in October 1973 and about a week later the SNP won a by-election in Glasgow Govan. In November, the Heath government declared a 'state of emergency' and imposed a three-day week on the country in reaction to economic and industrial relations crises. A miners' strike and the overnight quadrupling of oil prices took their toll. When Heath called a general election for February 1974, he did so amidst turmoil and chaos across the country. The nationalists advanced and did so on the back of disaffection with government as much as support for radical constitutional change. Oil had been a crucial explanation for the rise of the Scottish Nationalists in 1974. The SNP had launched a campaign – 'It's Scotland's Oil' – arguing that Scotland would be much better off as an independent state by taking advantage of the oil resources which had recently been discovered off Scotland's coast. It was Middle East oil, however, which proved more important for the SNP. The oil-rich countries of the Middle East had taken advantage of the power they had over western states and pushed up prices on this basic commodity. Aided by other domestically-induced problems, this caused high levels of inflation and rising unemployment.

Scottish and Welsh nationalism in the 1970s was largely built on protest. Plaid Cymru failed to make much headway beyond the Welsh-language areas but at least had a firm base on which to build its support. Support for the SNP was always higher than that for Plaid, but the SNP failed to create a solid base of support. The translation of protest vote into support for major constitutional change simply did not occur. This became clear at the 1979 devolution referendums in Scotland and Wales. The Labour government which came to power in 1974 decided that the old policy of opposing Scottish and Welsh devolution was no longer sustainable. Using trade union block votes, a special conference of the party in Scotland was held in August 1974 to overturn official opposition to devolution. However, many party members refused to comply, seeing the SNP threat as a poor reason to make such a radical change of policy. The failure of the party leadership to carry party members with it proved costly, especially in Wales, where a group of anti-devolution Labour MPs campaigned vigorously against devolution in the 1979 referendum. In the event, Wales overwhelmingly rejected devolution in 1979 and although the Scots voted narrowly in favour, the 'Yes' vote fell well short of the 40% of the electorate required for devolution to go ahead (see Table 3.1).

The Thatcher Years and Devolution

No single figure did more to help the devolutionist cause in Scotland and Wales than Margaret Thatcher. Mrs Thatcher was perceived in Scotland and Wales as insensitive to Scottish and Welsh identity. The Conservatives had long been a minority force in Scottish politics and had never been anything else in Wales. The combination of a government operating with minority support in Scotland and Wales introducing often controversial policies led by a Prime Minister who was perceived to be insensitive to Scottish and Welsh concerns was a potent brew. In terms of home rule politics, it resulted in a much more ideologically coherent home rule

Table 3.1 Results of the 1979 and 1997 referendums in Scotland and Wales

1979

	Scotland (%)	Wales (%)
Voted Yes	51.6	20.3
Voted No	48.4	79.7
Electorate voted Yes	32.9	11.9
Electorate voted No	30.8	46.9
Turnout	63.8	58.8

1997

	Scotland (%)	Wales (%)
For Parliament/Assembly	74.3	50.3
Against Parliament/Assembly	25.7	49.7
For tax-varying powers	63.5	
Against tax-varying powers	36.5	
Turnout	60.4	50.1

campaign and eventually raised the issue to the forefront of Scottish politics and, if not quite to that level, at least brought devolution in from the cold in Wales.

In both Scotland and Wales, support for home rule became associated with the left and in both the issue became more significant after the 1987 general election. The third successive victory for the Conservatives across Britain as a whole while, in Wales and Scotland the Tories suffered further losses, forced many who had previously been sceptical about devolution to reconsider the issue. In Wales this took the form of campaigns against quangos. It was argued by home rulers that Wales was run by unelected quangos appointed by the Conservative Secretary of State for Wales. There was a 'democratic deficit' in Wales and a doubling in the number of quangos in the fourteen years following the Conservatives coming to power in 1979 (Morgan and Roberts, 1993). A parliament for Wales would go some way towards scrutinising the work of these bodies, widely believed to consist largely of Conservative supporters. The Labour Party argued that after the reorganisation of local government in Wales there would be more quango appointees in Wales than elected councillors (Welsh Labour Party, 1993).

It was very tempting for Labour in Scotland and Wales to adopt nationalist rhetoric in campaigning against the Conservatives. In 1984, Labour in Scotland went so far as to argue that the Conservatives had 'no mandate' to govern Scotland but the real pressure built up following the 1987 election. Robin Cook, previously hostile to devolution, explained why he had changed his mind in autumn 1987. In the 1970s, he maintained, devolution had been a 'compromise with nationalism' but a decade later it had become a means of protecting Scotland from Thatcherism (Mitchell, 1998a: 486). A coalition was emerging in Scotland and Wales consisting of supporters of home rule and opponents of the Conservatives. Home rule was being presented as an anti-Conservative bulwark and a way of protecting the welfare state.

In Scotland, no issue symbolised the new politics of devolution better than the poll tax. It was introduced in Scotland a year ahead of England and Scots were encouraged by opposition parties, and not just the SNP, to believe that they were being used as guinea-pigs to test an unpopular policy. It helped firm up support for a Parliament and it was asserted that the poll tax would never have been introduced by a Scottish Parliament. Home rule was rarely far from the front pages in Scotland during this period. In Wales, an even more dramatic change was occurring. Welsh nationalism had historically been associated with the Welsh language but in the late 1980s a growing section of English-speaking Welsh people began to see merit in a Welsh Assembly.

These processes culminated in the 1997 general election when the Conservative Party lost all of its remaining seats in Scotland and Wales. The Labour Party had committed itself to holding referendums in Scotland and Wales on devolution and these were held four months later. In Scotland, two questions were put to the electorate: whether Scots wanted a Parliament and whether they wanted it to have tax-varying powers. In Wales, Labour's proposals were not as radical and did not include tax-varying powers. People in Wales were only asked whether they wanted an Assembly. The results were very different from the referendums eighteen years before and, in large measure, the results of the 1997 referendums were produced by hostility to Conservative rule (Denver et al., 2000). Favouring devolution had come to be associated with an anti-Conservative attitude.

Certain expectations have built up around devolution. People in Wales and Scotland expect that London should not interfere too much in their affairs. Tony Blair's strong support for Alun Michael as Welsh Labour leader, following the resignation of Ron Davies in November 1998, was resented as interference. In addition, there are expectations in Scotland and, though less so, in Wales that levels of public services will improve. It has frequently been contended that Scottish and Welsh voters want more left-wing policies than voters in England and that without devolution this desire was frustrated (Curtice, 1996; Mitchell and Bennie, 1996; Osmond, 1998; Brown et al., 1999). However, neither the Scottish Parliament nor the Welsh Assembly has the power to deliver all that is expected of them, at least not on their own (Mitchell, 1998b; Curtice, 1999; Surridge and McCrone, 1999; Denver et al., 2000). A left-wing agenda would require the new institutions to have more financial autonomy. Among the elites supporting devolution, there was an additional expectation that the new institutions would result in a new, more consensual style of politics which also seems unlikely to emerge (Mitchell, 2000).

The Nature of Devolution

Devolution differs in Scotland and Wales in a number of respects. As we have seen, the level of support for devolution was very different. Scotland had narrowly voted in favour of a devolved Assembly in 1979 and Wales had overwhelmingly rejected it. By 1997, Scotland had overwhelmingly supported a Parliament and given convincing support for it to have tax-varying powers, whereas Wales had supported an

Assembly by the narrowest of margins. The symbolism surrounding devolution also differs between Scotland and Wales. This is encapsulated in the terms used to describe the devolved institutions. In Scotland, a Parliament has been created while in Wales an Assembly has been created. The term 'Parliament' carries with it connotations of a more important, more powerful institution than an 'Assembly'. The Labour government's white papers, which preceded the introduction of the devolution legislation, used quite different language when discussing the two countries. In the introduction to the Scottish white paper, Tony Blair declared that, 'Scotland is a proud historic nation in the United Kingdom.' In the Welsh white paper, the Welsh Secretary stated that devolution offered the people of Wales an opportunity 'alongside other successful economic regions of Europe'. The Scottish Parliament's tax-varying powers are more significant symbolically than they are in terms of autonomous policy-making. The Welsh Assembly has no such powers.

It is not only symbols that suggest that Scotland has a more important institution. In terms of powers and responsibilities, the Scottish Parliament is a more significant body than the Welsh Assembly. The legislation setting up the Scottish Parliament sets out those matters which will be retained at Westminster, rather than outlining those matters which are devolved. Matters which were not retained would be devolved (Table 3.2). London retains control over a range of important matters, including foreign and European affairs, defence, the constitution, fiscal, economic and monetary matters and social security and pensions. There is shared responsibility or a division of responsibilities in some areas such as transport and health. This leaves the Scottish Parliament with responsibility for a broad area of domestic affairs in Scotland. Housing, most aspects of health, local government, education, law and home affairs are devolved matters. However, lists of responsibilities need to be treated with care. The Scottish Parliament is completely autonomous in few if any areas of public policy. Neither, indeed, is Westminster on a wide range of matters. Complicating the division of responsibility further is the involvement of the European Union in many of these matters, as well as local government.

Table 3.2 Division of responsibilities between the Scottish Parliament and Westminster

Reserved powers (not devolved)	Areas not reserved (responsibility of Scottish Parliament)
Common market for UK goods and services	Agriculture, fisheries and forestry
Constitution of the United Kingdom	Economic development
Defence and national security	Education
Employment legislation	Environment
Fiscal, economic and monetary system	Health
Foreign policy, including relations with Europe	Housing
Health (in some areas), medicine	Law and home affairs
Media and culture	Local government
Professional regulations (in certain cases)	Research and statistics
Protection of borders	Social work
Social security	Training
Transport safety and regulation	Transport

Devolution involves a new democratically accountable layer of politics but in terms of how policy is made, it is better understood in a different way. Policy is made across different layers, resembling a marble cake rather than a layered cake. A European Commission policy directive on the environment will require to be implemented at all levels within member states – local authorities, regional and central government may each have a part to play. Housing policy may be a matter which is the responsibility of the Scottish Parliament but important decisions affecting housing will continue to made at other levels. Interest rates, social security and economic policy all affect housing policy to a very great extent. Interest rate policy remains a matter for London although it may in time move to Brussels. Social security is a retained matter and overall economic policy is also retained. That does not mean that the Scottish Parliament can have no impact on housing policy, but its scope for autonomy will be circumscribed by other levels as well as non-government factors.

The Welsh Assembly's autonomy is much more circumscribed than that of the Scottish Parliament. The Scottish Parliament has the right to pass laws in those areas which are not retained at Westminster. The Welsh Assembly has no such powers. Its legislative powers are secondary. Westminster Acts of Parliament often give ministers the power to determine details of legislation with Parliament's consent and it is the Secretary of State for Wales's powers of secondary legislation that have been devolved to the Assembly. The degree of devolution depends on how open-ended the legislation has been. A tightly drawn Act of Parliament leaves little scope for action whereas some legislation is more broadly defined leaving considerable scope for autonomy. The range of issues over which the Assembly has some power is more limited than that of the Scottish Parliament but is still quite extensive (Table 3.3).

The funding of the two devolved bodies differs. Tax-raising powers for the Scottish Parliament had been a major source of controversy in debates prior to the establishment of devolution. In the 1970s opponents of devolution had argued that a devolved Assembly without tax-raising powers would be fiscally irresponsible. In the 1980s they argued that a Parliament *with* tax-raising powers would be irresponsible. Despite these contradictions, controversy surrounding Labour's

Table 3.3 Responsibilities of Welsh Assembly

Agriculture	Local government
Ancient monuments and historic buildings	Social services
Culture	Sport and leisure
Economic development	Tourism
Education and training	Town and country planning
Environment	Transport and roads
Heath and health services	Welsh language
Highways	
Housing	
Industry	

proposals for meagre tax-raising powers led the Blair leadership to include a separate question on tax-*varying* (part of the defence was that the Parliament also had the power to lower taxes, although voters were unconvinced that this would happen). Having voted in favour, the Scots were given a Parliament which had the right to vary the basic rate of income tax by up to 3p in the pound. In 1999, had this power been used to its full it would have raised an additional £690 million, representing just under 5% of its expenditure. The bulk of the Scottish Parliament's budget would be derived from a grant from London, determined in much the same way as the Scottish Office budget had been in the past. The sum available to the Scottish Parliament each year would be based on the previous year's budget with changes in the total determined by a formula originally introduced in the late 1970s. By the time the Parliament had been established, this had also become controversial with politicians in other parts of the United Kingdom, notably regions in England, complaining that Scotland was being subsidised. This was challenged by some Scots who argued that Scotland was subsidising the rest of the UK. The absence of reliable data broken down by region and nation and the different interpretations which could be placed on the same information has meant that this has proved an ongoing issue. This would have been an issue in British politics without devolution, but devolution has highlighted an existing area of conflict.

The First Elections

Some Labour supporters of Scottish devolution, notably George Robertson, former Shadow Scottish Affairs spokesman, argued in advance of devolution that a Scottish Parliament would 'kill off' the SNP. This proved mistaken as the results of the first elections to the Scottish Parliament in May 1999 showed. In Wales, too, the evidence points to a revived Plaid Cymru. The electoral system used in the elections was based on the same first-past-the-post (FPTP) system used in elections to the House of Commons, plus a proportional top-up element. The SNP and Plaid Cymru had suffered under FPTP, as did the Scottish and Welsh Conservatives, while Labour did very well. Under the new voting system, however, the nationalists became clearly the second-largest party in both the Parliament and the Assembly (Table 3.4). Subsequent polls have shown that this was no freak result, with the SNP competing with Labour for first place in Scottish politics. However, polls also suggest that the SNP is likely to do better in elections to the Scottish Parliament than to the House of Commons, not simply because of the electoral system but because Scottish voters are more willing to support the party in Scottish elections.

Labour failed to achieve an overall majority in both the Scottish Parliament and the Welsh Assembly. In Scotland, a deal was done with the Liberal Democrats to form a coalition, although Labour dominates the coalition and there is little evidence of Liberal Democrat policy initiatives. In Wales, Labour adopted a different approach, choosing instead to govern as a minority. One consequence of this was

Table 3.4 Elections to the Scottish Parliament and Welsh Assembly, 1999

| | Constituencies | | Regional lists | | Total |
	Votes (%)	Seats	Votes (%)	Seats	seats
Scotland					
Conservative	15.5	0	15.4	18	18
Labour	38.8	53	33.6	3	56
Lib Dem	14.2	12	12.4	5	17
SNP	28.7	7	27.3	28	35
Others	2.7	1	11.3	2	3
Wales					
Conservative	15.8	1	16.5	8	9
Labour	37.6	27	35.4	1	28
Lib Dem	13.5	3	12.5	3	6
Plaid Cymru	28.4	9	30.5	8	17
Others	4.7	0	5.1	0	0

that when Labour found itself in trouble in its first year over an issue concerning European funding it could not command a majority in the Assembly. Alun Michael, the Welsh First Minister, who had already been weakened by his association with Tony Blair, was forced to resign.

Devolutionary Dynamics

As noted above, Ron Davies, former Secretary of State for Wales, has remarked that devolution is a process:

> It is not an event and neither is it a journey with a fixed end-point. The devolution process is enabling us to make our own decisions and set our own priorities, that is the important point.
>
> (Davies, 1999: 15)

There is ample evidence to back up Davies's claim although that does not mean, as nationalists hope and unionists fear, that Scotland and Wales are necessarily heading for independence. The background to the establishment of the Welsh Assembly and Scottish Parliament suggests that the process of change may not be complete. What currently binds the UK together, and how this is affected by devolution, will be important in the state's future constitutional development. Institutions are seen as crucial by Conservative politicians, as indicated by former Conservative leader William Hague's speech, quoted at the start of this chapter. According to Labour, as indicated by Gordon Brown's comments, values are more important. Devolution will have an impact on both and these are now considered in turn to gain some understanding of the process starting to unfold.

Institutional dynamics

According to William Hague, devolution upsets the institutional arrangements of the UK. Central to this is the role of Parliament at Westminster as a common UK institution. The question is whether devolution is compatible with common central institutions. This will depend on both the devolved institutions and government in London. Other states with regional government or federalism demonstrate that it is possible to operate a system of multi-level governance. The operation of successful systems does not require the avoidance of conflict. Indeed, John Osmond, a prominent Welsh devolutionist, has argued that conflict in such situations can be creative (Osmond, 1978). However, if either level decides to be confrontational, problems can arise which no amount of institutional arrangements for managing conflict will be able to prevent. Essentially, the operation of effective intergovernmental relations requires a quasi-federal culture in which each level accepts the legitimacy of the other.

The prospect of nationalists winning control of the Scottish Parliament or Welsh Assembly cannot be dismissed. However, the proportional element of the electoral system makes it unlikely that any party on its own will win overall control. As a former general secretary of the Scottish Labour Party conceded in a radio interview in April 1997, the electoral system was adopted in order to prevent the SNP assuming power. In part, it was also adopted to get support from those who feared Labour domination of the Parliament. The cost of doing this was that Labour was also unable to win power on its own. However, even if the SNP or Plaid Cymru won a majority, this would not necessarily result in the nationalists attempting to undermine devolution or embarking on a confrontational path. The current leaderships of both parties take the view that a constructive approach to devolution would make independence more likely. The hardliners in each party who might seek to undermine devolution have become increasingly marginalised, although they could be strengthened by an electoral setback.

A quasi-federal political culture can only develop if both levels accept the new arrangements. Prior to the devolution referendums most attention focused on how the devolved institutions would operate rather than on the implications for government in London. It was only recognised after the referendums that new institutions and procedures in London would be necessary for the effective working of devolution. It was decided that the London-based Secretaries of State for Scotland and Wales, appointed by the British Prime Minister, would continue to exist. However, the roles of the respective Secretaries of State for Scotland and Wales would change. These ministers in London retain the responsibility for speaking for Scotland and Wales in the Cabinet, but the Welsh Secretary of State is able to participate, though without a vote, in debates in the Welsh Assembly. As devolution legislation was passing through Parliament at Westminster, Conservative politicians proposed amendments which would create new central co-ordinating bodies to ensure that differences which would arise between Edinburgh or Cardiff and London would be managed effectively. The Labour government acknowledged the need for new bodies though it rejected those proposed by the Conservatives. Three new arrangements were proposed instead which, it was hoped, would facilitate effective co-ordination and help avoid conflict which might undermine the integrity of the state: concordats, a Joint Ministerial Committee, and the British–Irish Council.

Concordats have been drawn up and agreed between the UK government and Scottish and Welsh Executives. These provide the framework within which discussions and co-ordination will take place. However, these are non-statutory, that is they have no legal standing and neither level of government may appeal to the courts on the basis of the agreements. Specific areas covered in the concordats are financial assistance to industry, European Union policy issues, international relations and statistics. The need for agreement reflects grey areas of responsibility. For example, London retains power in European Union affairs but the Scottish Parliament has responsibility for a range of matters over which the EU has some competence, such as agriculture and the environment. As the government in London represents the UK on EU matters, some mechanism for channelling the views of the Scottish Executive on such matters via London is required. The concordat offers a framework through which this is achieved. The EU concordats for Scotland and Wales cover the provision of information, formulation of UK policy, attendance at the Council of Ministers (the key EU decision-making body), implementation of EU obligations and infraction proceedings. The last refers to the devolved institutions' responsibilities for implementing EU regulations. If a devolved institution fails to implement an EU regulation, it will have to pay any fine or penalty even though in EU law the member state's central government is legally responsible and liable. This ensures that a devolved government does not simply choose which EU regulations it implements and leave central government to pay the cost of infraction. The concordats include both responsibilities as well as rights for devolved bodies.

While most contact between the devolved institutions and London will be conducted on a bilateral or multilateral basis between departments on a routine daily basis, it was felt that there would be a need for more formal arrangements to provide some central co-ordination. The Joint Ministerial Committee, consisting of ministers of the UK government, Scottish ministers and members of the Welsh Cabinet was proposed. Its terms of reference were set out in a Memorandum of Understanding:

a. to consider non-devolved matters which impinge on devolved responsibilities, and devolved matters which impinge on non-devolved responsibilities;
b. where the UK Government and the devolved administrations so agree, to consider devolved matters if it is beneficial to discuss their respective treatment in the different parts of the UK;
c. to keep the arrangements for liaison between the UK Government and the devolved administrations under review; and
d. to consider disputes between the administrations.

(Scottish Executive, 1999: para. 23)

The British–Irish Council was an element in the Good Friday Agreement in Northern Ireland. It creates a new forum in which ministers from UK central government, the devolved institutions and also the Irish government could meet. Its main significance is symbolic, creating a body bringing together the UK and Ireland, but some observers believe that it will be the foundation for a new, loose political entity which might at some stage replace the United Kingdom (Nairn, 1999).

In terms of institutions, therefore, new arrangements have been created alongside the devolved bodies which were designed to maintain a common UK position and compensate for the loss of power in Whitehall which devolution entails. However, these arrangements remain rudimentary and the real test will come through usage. The British–Irish Council (known as the Council of the Isles by some of those who hope it will become a more significant body) is seen as important alongside the devolved institutions as a body which might replace the UK, but it is even less developed than the other arrangements. These common institutions have been designed to facilitate the sense of common identity which William Hague believes has been undermined by devolution. As ever with the British constitution, they have been designed pragmatically and it is difficult to predict how they will develop.

Shifting values

According to Labour devolutionists a set of common values binds the UK together. From this perspective, devolution is viewed not as a means of undermining these values but of allowing some variety, particularly in the implementation of these common values across the state. If values and beliefs within the UK started to diverge following devolution, then devolution could lead to the break-up of the state and devolution would be seen to have failed. An alternative view is that devolution acknowledges that some divergence already exists. Without devolution, such divergence as exists, it is argued, would lead to frustration and possibly the break-up of Britain. The question is whether devolution will satisfy Scots by allowing for a sufficient degree of autonomy while operating within a common political culture. The question is less immediately applicable to Wales because Welsh opinion was more lukewarm about having devolution in the first place.

The perception which developed in Scotland during the eighteen years of Conservative government starting in 1979 was that Scottish political values differed from those in the rest of UK or at least in England, the dominant part of the UK. At one level, devolution can be seen to have met the criticism that Scots wanted a government of a different complexion from the one in England. If a Conservative government were returned at a future UK general election, Scots could continue to have a non-Conservative Scottish Executive in Edinburgh. The prospect of having different parties in government at different levels has, if anything, increased as a consequence of one element of the devolution legislation, the reduction in Scottish MPs. A reduction in Scottish and Welsh representation in the House of Commons is to be implemented following a review of House of Commons boundaries as part of the devolution arrangements. This makes the prospect of an English majority in the Commons overruling majority opinion in Scotland and Wales more likely in the future. From a strictly limited institutionalist perspective this might seem to create problems as conflicts would emerge, but from the perspective of those who emphasise the importance of values this need not necessarily be the case. London would be able to follow a Conservative path while Cardiff and Edinburgh would follow a Labour or non-Conservative path. So long as the different levels operate within a broad consensus and accept the need for compromise this should not create insurmountable problems.

Problems arise, however, if devolution serves to create more divergence across the state rather than reflect limited differences. It is conceivable that different parties in government at the different levels would serve to emphasise or even exaggerate differences. This may even happen when the same party is in control at different levels. Scottish and Welsh Labour might want to be seen to be different from the party in London in order to respond to nationalist pressure. However, the Conservative and Labour Parties both support the union and value this above any other difference and whichever party or parties are in government at each level, this common support for the union may ensure that agreement is reached. The new institutional arrangements discussed above would then come into their own.

Contrariwise, a gradual process of divergence might develop as those in charge of the new, devolved institutions gain confidence. In large measure, the process which led to the creation of the Scottish Parliament and Welsh Assembly was based less on the existence of divergent values than the perception that this was happening, largely accounted for by support for different parties. Various studies suggest, for example, that there is limited difference between Scottish and English political values and culture (Miller et al., 1996; Brown et al., 1999: 81). However, perceptions of difference existed and played a significant part in the development of the demand for autonomy.

Another factor which may prove important is that London retains control over a wide range of significant matters which may prove important. Redistributive policies – including taxation and welfare policies – have been retained by London. Distributive policies – policies involving spending on public services – have been devolved in Scotland but the overall amount of funds available will be set by London. This means that the scope for the Scottish Parliament cutting out a distinct role for itself and thereby developing a set of aspirations and values which are radically different from those elsewhere in Britain is contained. Whether this helps retain a broadly common set of political values across the state or leads to frustration, in much the same way as happened in Scotland prior to devolution, remains unclear.

Conclusion

Devolution involves not only the creation of new institutions in Scotland and Wales but new arrangements and procedures in London, and it is not simply about the creation of new institutions. Devolution has important implications for the development of public policy across the United Kingdom and the transmission of new and possibly divergent ideas, policies and identities. In addition, the formal institutions and policies cannot be divorced from public perceptions. William Hague was right to identify the challenge to existing institutions which devolution involves. Gordon Brown was also right in stressing the enduring importance of underlying values. However, it is the complex relationship between the new institutions and the possible development of divergent values as perceived by voters which will determine the future course of constitutional politics in the UK.

Britain has changed fundamentally. Opponents of devolution often talked about the 'slippery slope to separatism'. Whether devolution towards independence or a reform which will become the settled will of the people of Britain is impossible to predict. The role of institutions in the generation of identities, loyalties and values is not clear. All that seems certain is that Britain is no longer the centralised state that it was until very recently and that devolution is indeed a process with no fixed end-point.

Summary

- Devolution not only affects Scotland and Wales, but also how the UK is governed in London.
- Devolution is not merely a new set of institutions but a process of constitutional innovation and change.
- The potential impact on people's identities, loyalties and values is impossible to predict but it seems unlikely that these matters are as yet settled.

Discussion Questions

1. What does it mean to say that devolution is 'a process' rather than 'an event'?
2. Does devolution make the break-up of the United Kingdom more likely or less likely?
3. Why was devolution accepted more enthusiastically in Scotland than in Wales?

References

Brown, A., McCrone, D., Paterson, L. and Surridge, P. (1999) *The Scottish Electorate: The 1997 General Election and Beyond*, Basingstoke: Macmillan.

Curtice, J. (1996) 'One nation again?', in R. Jowell, J. Curtice, A. Park, L. Brook and K. Thomson (eds) *British Social Attitudes: The Thirteenth Report*, Aldershot: Dartmouth, pp. 1–17.

Curtice, J. (1999) 'Is Scotland a nation and Wales not?', in B. Taylor and K. Thomson (eds) *Scotland and Wales: Nations Again?*, Cardiff: University of Wales Press, pp. 119–47.

Davies, R. (1999) *Devolution: A Process Not an Event*, Cardiff: Institute of Welsh Affairs.

Denver, D., Mitchell, J., Pattie, C. and Bochel, H. (2000) *Scotland Decides: The Devolution Issue and the Scottish Referendum*, London: Frank Cass.

Miller, W., Timpson, A. and Lessnoff, M. (1996) *Political Culture in Contemporary Britain: People and Politicians, Principles and Practice*, Oxford: Clarendon Press.

Mitchell, J. (1998a) 'The evolution of devolution: Labour's Home Rule strategy in Opposition', *Government and Opposition*, Vol. 33, No. 4, pp. 479–96.

Mitchell, J. (1998b) 'What could a Scottish Parliament do?', in H. Elcock and M. Keating (eds) *Remaking the Union: Devolution and British Politics in the 1990s*, London: Frank Cass, pp. 68–85.

Mitchell, J. (2000) 'New Parliament, new politics in Scotland?', *Parliamentary Affairs*, Vol. 53, No. 3, October, pp. 605–21.

Mitchell, J. and Bennie, L. (1996) 'Thatcherism and the Scottish question', *British Elections and Parties Yearbook, 1995*, London: Frank Cass, pp. 90–104.

Morgan, K. and Roberts, E. (1993) *The Democratic Deficit: A Guide to Quangoland*, Cardiff: Department of City and Regional Planning, University of Wales College of Cardiff.

Nairn, T. (1999) *After Britain*, London: Granta Books.

Osmond, J. (1978) *Creative Conflict*, London: Routledge & Kegan Paul.

Osmond, J. (1998) *New Politics in Wales*, London: Charter 88.

Scottish Executive (1999) *Memorandum of Understanding*, Edinburgh: Scottish Executive.

Surridge, P. and McCrone D. (1999) 'The 1997 Scottish referendum vote', in B. Taylor and K. Thomson (eds) *Scotland and Wales: Nations Again?*, Cardiff: University of Wales Press, pp. 41–64.

Welsh Labour Party (1993) *Shaping the Vision*, Cardiff: Welsh Labour Party.

Further reading

Bogdanor, Vernon (1999) *Devolution in the United Kingdom*, Oxford: Oxford University Press. This is an updated version of a book initially published in 1979 which offers a critical but sympathetic account of debates in different parts of the United Kingdom. Bogdanor dwells on the history of debates.

Bradbury, Jonathan and Mawson, John (eds) (1997) *British Regionalism and Devolution: The Challenges of State Reform and European Integration*, London: Jessica Kingsley. This book explores many changes in recent British territorial politics.

Elcock, Howard and Keating, Michael (1998) *Remaking the Union: Devolution and British Politics in the 1990s*, London: Frank Cass. This was also published as a special issue *of Regional and Federal Studies*.

Hazell, Robert (ed.) (1999) *Constitutional Futures: A History of the Next Ten Years*, Oxford: Oxford University Press. This collection of essays offers an overview of the New Labour government's constitutional plans and outlines how they might develop over the next decade.

Websites

http://www.nio.gov.uk   The Northern Ireland website.

http://www.ni-assembly.gov.uk/   Northern Ireland Assembly.

http://www.scottish-devolution.org.uk   Website for Scottish devolution.

http://www.assembly.wales.gov.uk   Website for Welsh devolution.

The Future of the Union II: Northern Ireland

Feargal Cochrane

CHAPTER FOUR

Introduction

Northern Ireland is the most divided part of the United Kingdom. It has been the site of a low-intensity conflict since 1969 that has claimed the lives of over 3,500 people, with many more having been physically and psychologically maimed. At its height, this conflict was a 'dirty war' involving no-warning bombs that killed civilians, assassinations of perceived enemies by paramilitary organisations, bombings in Northern Ireland and Britain aimed at damaging the economy and causing disruption, dubious propaganda on all sides and allegations that a 'shoot-to-kill' policy was being operated by the British government. The region is the most militarised in Europe, having a huge police force for its size and a British army presence on the streets for the last thirty years. Politically, Northern Ireland has been a thorn in the side of successive British governments due to the intractability of the conflict, the repeated diplomatic failure to secure political compromise, the negative international publicity generated and the financial costs of the conflict, amounting to billions of pounds over the last thirty years.

Political debate in Northern Ireland has concerned two central issues. The first relates to the contested political and cultural identities within the region, while the second refers to a struggle over resources and a dispute over the exercise of power within the 'state'.[1] Northern Ireland is a deeply divided society whose very history is contested, politicised, and woven into the fabric of contemporary political issues. Unlike other countries that have emerged from violent beginnings (such as the United States of America), this historical memory plays an important role in contemporary political behaviour within Northern Ireland. It does so, because the issues surrounding ethnicity, territoriality, power and national identity, which determined the region's historical development, have not yet been resolved. Consequently, history (or, more precisely, historical myths) are invested with an importance not seen in more stable societies.

Northern Ireland contains two communities divided by their ethnicity – Protestant unionists and Catholic nationalists – who live in close proximity to one another. The relationship between the two communities ranges from an uneasy alliance at best, to outright hostility and hatred. For most of the twentieth century the central issue in the region has centred around contested nationality claims. The mainly Protestant unionists wish to remain British and an integral part of the United Kingdom, while the mainly Catholic nationalist population consider hemselves to be Irish, wish to leave the United Kingdom and live in a 'united' Irish state. Alongside this ideological issue sits the more pragmatic one of political control. Both communities are concerned to uphold what they regard as their political 'rights' and their 'civil liberties', especially when they consider these to be under attack from the other community.

This chapter will show how these two issues have woven together during Northern Ireland's recent history. Since the two communities (until very recently) have seen their interests as being mutually exclusive, questions relating to democracy, liberty, equality, nationality and power became part of a power-struggle within the region. For most of the last century, these concepts have been seen as partial rather than universal in their application. Thus, an extension of freedom for one community meant a reduction of freedom for the other; giving increased power to one community meant taking it away from the other, and so on.

Background

Approximately 1.5 million people live in Northern Ireland while the population of the Irish Republic is roughly 3.5 million. The majority of Northern Ireland people are Protestant, with most of the rest being Catholic, but the relative proportions have been changing quite dramatically over the last twenty years, as the proportion of Catholics has increased. The most recent figures from the 1991 Census suggest that the Catholic population then comprised 42% of the total and it has continued to expand. This is particularly pronounced in the younger age categories where the Protestant and Catholic communities are of roughly equal size. In political terms, most Protestants are unionists and most Catholics are nationalists, although this picture is becoming more complicated. As the religious balance changes, so too does the political balance, with the nationalist community becoming more confident and the unionist community less confident about their political futures.

It is widely believed that the conflict in Northern Ireland is about religion, that Catholics and Protestants have been fighting one another for centuries and cannot come to terms with one another's religious traditions. This is a superficial reading of the dynamics of the society, however. While the conflict is defined by religion, it is not a theological war. While there is clearly a lot of hatred between different religious groups in Northern Ireland, it is not true to say that religion is the cause of these divisions. It would be more accurate to say that religion serves as a badge of ethnic identity. Consequently, the importance of the bipolar religious division in Northern Ireland does not lie in rival theologies, but in the correlation between religious tradition and political identity.

Summary

- Northern Ireland is composed of two communities with different religious traditions and conflicting political allegiances.
- Over the last twenty years the Catholic population has grown relative to the Protestant community.
- This demographic change has had an impact on political issues in Northern Ireland.

The Stormont Regime, 1921–72

At the beginning of the twentieth century, the island of Ireland was one legal and political unit under British authority. From the end of the nineteenth century, however, there was a growth in Irish nationalism and increasing demands for self-government and independence from Britain among the majority Catholic population on the island and a corresponding campaign against independence from the Protestant community, who were geographically concentrated in the North of the island. This tug-of-war between Britain and Ireland over territory has been one of the issues at the heart of conflict in Northern Ireland ever since, while the issue of whether Northern Ireland should be part of the United Kingdom or part of Ireland has never been fully resolved. Disagreement over whether Ireland should be granted self-government led to a violent 'war of independence' between Irish nationalists and the British state from 1919 to 1921. Unionists, who were worried that this would cause Britain to grant self-government, threatened to use violence to prevent its happening. So, the government felt stuck between two rival and incompatible demands. Worried about how to prevent a civil war in Ireland, it came to the decision that the most effective compromise would be to partition Ireland, keeping as many people as possible who wanted self-government within one jurisdiction and as many as possible who were opposed to self-government in another. In pursuit of this solution, Northern Ireland was created following the Government of Ireland Act in 1920.

Under the new arrangements two separate administrations were formed, one in the six counties of Ulster (which became known as Northern Ireland) the other in the remaining twenty-six counties which was initially known as the Irish Free State and formally became the Republic of Ireland in 1949. The political system that dominated Northern Ireland from 1921 to 1972 is best understood as a by-product of the power-struggle between Britain and Ireland. It was, in the words of O'Leary and McGarry, 'Neither a nation nor a full state, its creation in 1920 was the joint by-product of British and Irish state- and nation-building failures' (1993: 107). The political architecture of Northern Ireland was designed to ensure that a stable unionist majority enjoyed sufficient autonomy to carry out devolved government responsibilities. Successive British administrations came to view Northern Ireland not as the *acme* of liberal-democratic state-building, but as an effective mechanism for removing a seemingly insoluble problem from its domestic political agenda. This dubious 'out of sight, out of mind' school of statecraft was one of the central reasons for the disintegration of the Stormont regime in 1972. Instead of assuming political responsibility for the region when it became obvious that necessary political reforms had not been introduced and that events were moving out of control, successive British governments had neither the administrative structures nor political will to take remedial action until it was too late.

The flaws inherent in the political system were not fully appreciated in 1920. Northern Ireland was given its own parliament at Stormont and a number of devolved powers were transferred to this institution from Westminster. This arrangement lasted from 1921, when the first regime came into office, until 1972, when Stormont was suspended and the devolved powers were taken back by the British government in response to rising civil disorder, violence and political breakdown. It is important to understand that the Stormont regime did not involve autonomous government or independence from Westminster. In fact, it was devolved government of the type that has recently been introduced in Scotland and Wales.

Summary

- Northern Ireland was created in 1920 by the British government as a 'least-worst' option to give the majority of Ireland its independence while allowing unionists in the north to remain within the United Kingdom.
- Due to the numerical strength of the unionists, there was no rotation of government in the new regime.
- Stormont was suspended in 1972 due to the rise in sectarian violence.

Issues of Political Culture within the New State

In a sense, then, the formation of Northern Ireland was something of a political accident. It was devised as a least-worst option, rather than the achievement of a political goal, in the search for some stability in Ireland. The problem was that Northern Ireland became too stable, with a dominant but insecure unionist majority and a Catholic community that was too large to be integrated into the new regime but too small to effect any real political influence.

Political culture during the early years of the state was dominated by fear and uncertainty. This remains a feature of the unionist psyche today, and insecurity about their political surroundings is a central dynamic of contemporary unionist political behaviour. The unionist sense of being besieged by hostile forces, translated into a desire for political domination and electoral cohesion, as it was feared that a loss of political control to the nationalist community would have imperiled the very existence of the state itself. It was believed by many Protestants that if Northern Ireland were to disintegrate, their cultural and religious freedom would also evaporate under the unyielding dogma of conservative Catholicism. While such fears were debilitating, they also became an essential element of electoral cohesion, enabling the unionists to mobilise Protestant voters.

The political culture within the nationalist community was, conversely, one of being trapped inside a polity to which they held no allegiance, and increasingly a feeling that they were second-class citizens under the law. Catholic nationalists within Northern Ireland, felt that they had been corralled within an illegitimate regime at the whim of diplomatic cartographers who had redrawn lines on a map without consultation and consigned them to exclusion from the state with which they identified. So the political cultures within both communities during the early years of Northern Ireland's existence were characterised by suspicion, fear and insecurity. These negative feelings on both sides festered for fifty years, eventually erupting into sectarian violence in the late 1960s and the destruction of the Stormont regime in 1972.

In practical terms, what passed for democracy in Northern Ireland from 1920 to 1972 was in fact little more than a one-party state. The unionists were so dominantly numerically, that they were always assured of a majority in elections. This produced arrogance within the unionist population, who knew that they were always going to win elections, and fatalism within the nationalist population, who knew that they were always going to lose them. Indeed, for much of the period 1920–72, nationalist politics were shambolic, both philosophically and organisationally, functioning as little more than the political wing of the Catholic Church hierarchy. According to one observer, 'Its basic unit of organisation was not the electoral ward but the parish. . . . Nationalist candidates were not selected, they were anointed' (McCann, quoted in Arthur, 1987: 56). The political system became more of a sectarian head-count rather than a competition between competing ideologies. As a consequence, while the state was stable in terms of its electoral politics, this disguised a regime with institutionalised inequalities and a polity harbouring 'a factory of grievances' (Buckland, 1979). The inability of successive unionist governments to address (or even admit to) the inherent inequalities within the state, led eventually to the collapse of the Stormont regime in 1972.

Summary

- Unionists have felt under siege from hostile forces since 1920. They believed that to share power would have weakened their position and destroyed Northern Ireland.
- Nationalists felt abandoned after 1920, and politically and culturally disenfranchised. Consequently, they opted out of the Stormont system as they were destined to be a permanent minority within Northern Ireland and thus permanently excluded from power.

Issues in State Breakdown

The breakdown of Northern Ireland's system of devolved government in 1972 was linked to the emergence of a civil rights movement in the 1960s. It was during this period that an increasingly impatient Catholic middle class led peaceful protests and demonstrations against poverty, unemployment and electoral abuse, and came into greater confrontation with the state and the local police force, the Royal Ulster Constabulary (RUC). Crucially, the British government was becoming increasingly embarrassed at this breakdown of law and order, within what was still a region of the United Kingdom – albeit a forgotten one – and had been pressurising the unionists during the 1960s to introduce political reforms that would address nationalist grievances and calm the situation. In 1963 Terence O'Neill became the new leader of the Unionist Party and Northern Ireland's new Prime Minister. O'Neill embarked on a campaign to reform Northern Ireland and spoke in a much more inclusive way of the Catholic/nationalist community than did his predecessors. His rhetoric failed to meet Catholic expectations for reform but went far enough to make many Protestants fear that he had conceded too much and had jeopardised the Stormont regime. Having had their expectations raised, only to be dashed by O'Neill's minor reforms, the Catholics redoubled their civil rights activities and confrontations with the police. Some Protestants saw this as an attempt to destroy the state. It was not. The civil rights movement was more concerned with social and economic issues such as poverty, high unemployment, an unfair system of housing allocation and electoral malpractice.

By the end of the 1960s, community sectarianism had escalated to the point that the British army had to be sent into Northern Ireland on 14 August 1969, to keep the two sides apart. Curfews and internment without trial were introduced in 1970 and 1971, suspects being rounded up and imprisoned without being charged or legal proceedings undertaken. Houses were raided by the army and property was often destroyed. The British government was eventually charged by the European Court of Human Rights with inflicting 'degrading and inhuman treatment' on many of the people detained, most of whom, it turned out, had no involvement in violence.

The political effect of this tide of events was enormous and led to a spiral of violence and the breakdown of the political system. After internment without trial was introduced, recruitment to the IRA soared, loyalist paramilitaries grew at a similar rate and violence rose dramatically. The final straw for the British government came on 30 January 1972, more famously known as 'Bloody Sunday', when paratroopers shot dead fourteen unarmed civilians, some of them children, in the aftermath of an illegal assembly. The international embarrassment of this event for the British government was too much and by March it had suspended Stormont, returned to Westminster the powers devolved in 1920 and brought in a Secretary of State and a team of British ministers to run the administration.

The events of 1972 marked a key turning point in Northern Ireland politics for three reasons. First, it began a slow process whereby the British and Irish governments came closer together. This resulted in joint political initiatives such as the

Anglo-Irish Agreement signed on 15 November 1985, the Downing Street Declaration signed on 15 December 1993 and eventually joint-stewardship of the peace process. Second, the relationship between unionists and the British government changed gradually after 1972. When the government finally suspended Stormont and assumed direct responsibility for the region, it felt less obliged to see unionists as being part of the machinery of government, to be defended against external criticism. Until 1972 Northern Ireland, and the Unionist Party which controlled it, was a satellite of the British administration. Critics were told that they were wrong to attack a party that was trying to introduce reforms, while the Irish government was politely told to mind its own business. After 1972 unionists became simply one of many parties in the conflict. Third, from 1972 the position of the Catholic community slowly began to improve, both economically and politically. While inequalities remain, Catholics in Northern Ireland are becoming more confident while Protestants are becoming less so. As noted above, demographic trends are contributing to this as nationalists have moved from being a sizeable but controllable minority, into a position close to parity and dominance in some areas.

When direct rule from Westminster was introduced by the British government in 1972, the political battle-lines were well established. Northern nationalism was divided into the reformist Social Democratic and Labour Party (SDLP), formed in 1970, and the revolutionary republican movement, dedicated to overthrowing British rule by means of what they referred to as 'armed struggle'. After the 1981 hunger strikes, when ten republican prisoners starved themselves to death, this evolved into what became known as the 'ballot-box and armalite strategy' – an approach involving both politics and paramilitary activity. Sinn Fein (SF) gained electoral momentum after the hunger strikes, to the point that it is now one of the four largest parties in Northern Ireland and a direct competitor with the SDLP for the nationalist vote.

Unionist forces were also split between the dominant Ulster Unionist Party (UUP) and the Democratic Unionist Party (DUP), formed in 1971 and led by Rev. Ian Paisley. This was a radical alternative to the UUP and campaigned vigorously for a return to majority (i.e. unionist) rule and the restoration of the Stormont government. Between these two imposing blocs sat the moderate centrist Alliance Party of Northern Ireland (APNI), formed in 1970, which, as it name suggests, was made up of Catholics and Protestants and was committed to a policy of compromise and reconciliation.

These parties have dominated the political arena almost exclusively until very recently when loyalist paramilitaries entered politics following their cease-fire in 1994. The largest of these is the Progressive Unionist Party (PUP), led by David Ervine. The PUP has emerged out of the paramilitary group the Ulster Volunteer Force (UVF). The other party to emerge at this time was the Ulster Democratic Party (UDP), led by Gary McMichael. This party emerged from the loyalist paramilitary group the Ulster Defence Association (UDA).

Another party to make a mark in recent times has been the Northern Ireland Women's Coalition (NIWC). This gender-specific party was formed in 1996 to highlight the lack of women in the political process and the lack of elected female representation. It has taken a moderate approach, promoting dialogue and tolerance within the political process.

Summary

- The Stormont regime collapsed in 1972 due to the rise in sectarian violence combined with British government concern at the negative international publicity this had created.
- 1972 changed the political dynamics between the British and Irish governments. The introduction of 'direct rule' also changed the unionist relationship with the British government and affected the internal balance of power within Northern Ireland between the unionist and nationalist community.

Issues in the 'Peace Process'

The genesis of the current peace process in Northern Ireland dates back to 1988 when SDLP leader, John Hume, met the President of Sinn Fein, Gerry Adams, for secret talks about how to find a way out of the political conflict. These continued sporadically for the next five years and resulted in the Hume–Adams Agreement of 1993. Hume's argument (that the most effective way of achieving republican objectives was through political rather than military means) was eventually conceded by SF and conditionally by the IRA. These talks represented a clear shift within nationalist politics from the early 1980s. After the 1981 hunger strikes the SDLP and SF were divided, while republicans were excluded from discussions in an effort to marginalise them politically. The Anglo-Irish Agreement of 15 November 1985 was the culmination of this strategy. The political logic was based on bolstering the moderate mainstream and marginalising the extreme fringe parties on both sides. The failure of this strategy substantially to damage support for SF, or produce an end to the IRA campaign, led to the internal dialogue within nationalism. The talks that began in 1988 are important to subsequent events because the republican movement was forced to present an intellectual defence of its activities. Serious questions began to be asked about the purpose of the 'armed struggle' and the republican right to pursue it. This began the long slow process of re-evaluation which eventually resulted in the IRA cease-fire of August 1994.

The British government meanwhile, initiated a series of political talks between the four main constitutional parties in 1991 and 1992 (UUP, DUP, SDLP and Alliance Party). The first set of discussions took place under the guidance of the Secretary of State, Peter Brooke, and lasted from 30 April to 3 July. It was decided that three sets of relationships were to be addressed. Strand One would be concerned with relations within Northern Ireland. Strand Two would deal with the relationship between the two parts of Ireland and Strand Three would look at relations between Ireland and the United Kingdom. Sinn Fein was not invited to participate in these talks due to its perceived links with the IRA, which had not called a cease-fire.

These multi-party talks were re-heated by Northern Ireland's next Secretary of State, Sir Patrick Mayhew, in 1992. Like the 1991 round of talks, they failed to produce any substantial agreement between the parties. If a political settlement could not be reached, then what possibility was there that the violence could be suspended to provide a new environment for political discussions? Achieving the latter became the personal goal of SDLP leader John Hume in his discussions with Gerry Adams and the issuing of a joint statement by Hume and Adams in September 1993, committing themselves to searching for an end to political conflict, had huge symbolic significance.

This agreement within northern nationalism spurred the governments into action and led a few months later to the Downing Street Declaration, unveiled by the British and Irish Prime Ministers in London on 15 December 1993. This was the most important initiative since the Anglo-Irish Agreement of 1985. It was a diplomatic triumph for both governments and appeared to open the prospect of a settlement. The British government stated in Paragraph 4 of the Declaration that it would 'encourage, facilitate and enable' agreement among the Irish people. The Irish government, by way of contrast, gave its fullest statement yet of support for the principle that the consent of people living within Northern Ireland would have to be given before any change could be made in Northern Ireland's constitutional status. This was of crucial importance to the unionist community and was vital to their confidence in the 'peace process'. Paragraph 5 accepted on behalf of the Irish government, that self-determination 'must be achieved and exercised with and subject to the agreement and consent of a majority of the people of Northern Ireland'.

However, the IRA did not welcome the Downing Street Declaration. After long-drawn-out wrangling over its terms, in which SF requested (and eventually got) clarification from the British government over specific points, they rejected it. Their attitude was that Irish Prime Minister Albert Reynolds had conceded too much ground and that the unionist veto on political change remained.

One of the biggest issues within the peace process concerns why the paramilitary organisations declared cessations of violence in 1994. The first point to make is that the IRA 'cessation of military operations', called on 31 August 1994, was a product of an Irish political consensus built by Gerry Adams, John Hume and Albert Reynolds. The establishment of this consensus led the IRA Army Council to believe that a political dynamic existed, which would overcome what they referred to as 'the unionist veto'. While they did not accept the Downing Street Declaration in its entirety, key figures within the republican movement accepted the argument that Britain no longer had a selfish strategic interest in Northern Ireland. They believed that the British government would be open to persuading the unionists to accept constitutional change, even if they would not admit this publicly.

Another key element was the role played by the United States. This was seen as an international dimension to the political consensus among nationalists in Ireland. The Clinton administration had shown its good faith in January 1994 by delivering on a promise to grant Gerry Adams a 48-hour visa into the USA, despite ferocious opposition from the British government and some members of his own administration. He was later to demonstrate this commitment again by granting a visa on the eve of the IRA cease-fire to the veteran Belfast republican, Joe Cahill, whose role was to sell the strategy to hard-line Irish-American rebublicans. The American role was important for republicans, as it provided another guarantee that the peace process would have a dynamic that would overcome unionist opposition to political change.

The IRA cessation in August 1994 was followed by a loyalist cease-fire in October the same year. These events did not signal a sudden reconciliation between the two factions, but were the result of a complex mixture of circumstances that made politics a more rational alternative to violence for the paramilitary organisations.[2]

Summary

- The origins of the 'peace process' can be traced back to the secret talks between John Hume and Gerry Adams. This evolved into secret discussions between the British government and Sinn Fein.
- The political dialogue resulted in the announcement of paramilitary cease-fires in 1994.
- The announcement of cease-fires opened the way for inclusive political negotiations between all the parties, sponsored by the British and Irish governments.

Issues after the Good Friday Agreement

Following cease-fires by the IRA and loyalist paramilitaries in 1994, negotiations between the main political parties (including Sinn Fein) eventually took place to find a political settlement during 1997 and 1998. This eventually resulted in the Good Friday Agreement (GFA), reached by unionists and nationalists on 10 April 1998.

The details of the Agreement were of little surprise to seasoned observers of politics in Northern Ireland. It sought to deal with the two central issues at the heart of community conflict in the region, namely the contested politico-cultural identities of Britishness and Irishness, and the power-struggle between unionists and nationalists for political control within Northern Ireland. In basic terms, the GFA granted devolution to Northern Ireland from the Westminster Parliament. A range of devolved powers were to be exercised through a 108-member Assembly based on power-sharing between the unionist and nationalist communities. A cabinet-style executive was to be formed from this Assembly with seats being distributed relative to the numerical strength of the parties. The Agreement also envisaged the establishment of a North/South Ministerial Council within Ireland that would develop cross-border links on matters of mutual interest. Finally, a British/Irish Council was to be set up to reflect 'the totality of relationships among the peoples of these islands'. The constitutional emphasis was placed on the consent of the people within Northern Ireland. To reflect this fact, the British government would remove Article 75 of the Government of Ireland Act, while the Irish government would seek to amend Articles 2 and 3 of its constitution, making it clear that Irish unity would only be pursued by peaceful means and with the consent of a majority of the people within both jurisdictions.

In addition to its central constitutional architecture, the Agreement promised reform on policing[3] and an accelerated release scheme for paramilitaries judged to be on valid cease-fires. While this was not an amnesty, and prisoners were to be released on licence, it was too much for many unionists, and became the biggest debating point in the subsequent referendum campaign. Some nationalists believed that the unionist concentration on the early release of prisoners was a smoke screen to hide the fact that they were politically opposed to the terms of the Agreement and the principle of sharing power with the Catholic community. The other key section in the Agreement concerned the decommissioning of illegal weapons. This was eventually to become the key sticking point in the Agreement's implementation, with First Minister Designate (and UUP leader) David Trimble refusing to implement the deal before decommissioning had begun. Sinn Fein's argument, which found sympathy within the broad nationalist community, was that this was yet another precondition imposed by the unionists, which reflected their intention to try to re-negotiate the terms of the Agreement after the event. Arguments over Sinn Fein's responsibilities with regard to the decommissioning of IRA weapons were to bedevil the implementation of the Agreement in the months and years ahead.

Following the signing of the GFA in April 1998, there were referendums (on the same day, 22 May 1998) in Northern Ireland and the Irish Republic. These produced overwhelming 'Yes' votes in favour of the Agreement – 71% in Northern Ireland and 95% in the Republic. After this, elections were held to a new Northern Ireland Assembly in June. These elections saw the UUP emerge with the largest number of seats, 28, the SDLP won 22, the DUP 20 and Sinn Fein 17. The Assembly's initial task was to form an Executive and establish the details of cross-border institutions linking Northern Ireland and the Irish Republic.

There are a number of factors that explain the Good Friday Agreement. First, both unionists and nationalists were ready to 'deal' with one another. Unionists had been scarred by twenty years of political failure and a general sense of political slippage. Nationalists and republicans meanwhile, recognised that a 'united Ireland' was out of reach in the short term and would not be achieved by physical force alone. Second, the cease-fires of 1994 and the renewed IRA cease-fire of 1997[4] had created a climate that was much more conducive to political negotiations than had existed since the outbreak of violence in 1969. Third, the British and Irish governments had refined their relationship towards one another and their respective understandings of the nationalist and unionist communities. Fourth, the negative school of unionism, personified by Ian Paisley and the DUP, was in a much weaker position than it had been in previous negotiations. In fact, the very people who were at the cutting-edge of loyalism in the 1970s, who became involved in paramilitary organisations and went to jail, were now inside the negotiations 'jaw-jawing' rather than outside 'war-warring'.

The biggest issue in the post-Agreement period has been disagreement over the timing of its implementation. This concerned, in particular, delays in the establishment of the multi-party Executive and the decommissioning of paramilitary weapons. The political consequence of this stand-off between unionists and republicans was inertia in the peace process and an evaporation of trust between the sides. This stalemate was broken temporarily on 27 November 1999, when David Trimble only just succeeded in getting a compromise through his party's ruling body, the Ulster Unionist Council. This allowed the Executive to be set up in return for limited movement on the issue of decommissioning, represented by the IRA's appointment of a representative to liaise with General John de Chastelain about beginning decommissioning. Devolved powers that were revoked in 1972 were therefore returned to Northern Ireland in November 1999.

It looked to many observers as though the peace process had finally reached a positive *denouement*, and that the obstacles that had threatened to destroy the political structures had been overcome. This turned out to be a sanguine judgement. Decommissioning of paramilitary weapons did not take place, and the British Secretary of State, Peter Mandelson, worried that David Trimble would resign as First Minister and the Executive would collapse, suspended the structures of the Good Friday Agreement on 29 January 2000, barely two months into their existence. At this point, Northern Ireland was in political limbo, with a *peace* process in existence, but a *political* process that had ground to a shuddering halt.

The deadlock over the re-institution of the Executive was finally broken in May 2000 when an agreement was brokered over the sequencing of IRA decommissioning, together with a timetable for the return of the devolved powers revoked in February. The careful choreography saw a statement from the British and Irish governments on 5 May, an IRA statement declaring their intention to begin the process of 'putting arms beyond use' on 6 May, and a decision to return to government taken at a meeting of the Ulster Unionist Council on 27 May. The Assembly met again on 5 June 2000 to pick up where it had left off the previous February. At the time of writing, the structures of the GFA remain in existence, although they are threatened regularly by the internal debate within the unionist community over whether to walk away from the settlement over the decommissioning issue and the extent of policing reforms resulting from the Patten Report.

Summary

- The Good Friday Agreement attempts to deal with the two issues at the core of political conflict in Northern Ireland, namely, how contested political identities can be accommodated, and how power can be shared between the two main communities.
- There has been a series of setbacks over the implementation of the GFA, mostly relating to unionist disenchantment with the settlement and a general lack of trust on all sides over the pace of its implementation.

Conclusion

At this stage it would be foolhardy to speculate about whether or not the issues surrounding the Good Friday Agreement will be successfully resolved. However, it would be fair to conclude that the implications of the Good Friday Agreement for politics and parties in Northern Ireland could be just as radical as the effects of direct rule after 1972. From 1921 to 1999 there has been a political and cultural stand-off between two clearly defined sides: those who wanted to remain part of the United Kingdom and those who wanted to join a united Ireland. The lines were clearly drawn and the issues were clearly understood. However, since the Good Friday Agreement in 1998 (despite the problems that have surrounded its implementation), we have a compromise agreement that may conceivably allow for a more porous sense of political and cultural identity to emerge. Within this scenario, the issues about what it means to be British and what it means to be Irish may become increasingly blurred. If the Good Friday Agreement survives and is eventually implemented properly, an administration may develop with its own form of politics based on social and economic issues such as health, education and housing. Signs of this have been apparent during the fragile existence of the Northern Ireland Executive in 2000, as resource-based issues began to dominate the political debate, while broader ideological issues slipped down the agenda. Politics became very practical very quickly. They moved seamlessly from the politics of demand to the politics of decision. If the structures of the Good Friday Agreement are cemented into place, this might lead in time to a political realignment along class lines and a more orthodox form of politics developing. We will have to wait and see.

Chronology

1920   Government of Ireland Act passed at Westminster. Northern Ireland created.
1921   Sir James Craig, leader of the Unionist Party, becomes Northern Ireland's first Prime Minister.
1963   Terence O'Neill becomes leader of the Unionist Party and Prime Minister of Northern Ireland.
1972   Following a banned civil rights march in Derry on 30 January, the British army shoots fourteen unarmed civilians dead in what becomes known as 'Bloody Sunday'. On 31 March the Stormont Parliament is suspended and 'direct rule' from Westminster is introduced. Conservative Cabinet Minister William Whitelaw becomes Northern Ireland's first Secretary of State on 1 April.
1981   Ten republican prisoners die following a hunger strike in the Maze Prison.
1985   The British and Irish governments sign the Anglo-Irish Agreement, 15 November.
1993   The British and Irish governments sign the Downing Street Declaration, 15 December.
1994   The Provisional IRA announces its 'complete cessation of military operations' on 31 July. Loyalist paramilitaries announce their cease-fire on 9 October.
1995   The British and Irish governments publish the Joint Declaration for Peace, 23 February.

1998 The Good Friday Agreement (GFA) is reached on 10 April.
1999 Devolved government returns to Northern Ireland in November.
2000 The Executive is suspended on 29 January. It is restored again in June.
2001 The Westminster general election of 7 June functions as another test of support
      for the GFA. Overall, the results did not undermine the structures of the GFA
      but did indicate a further radicalisation of the Northern Ireland electorate, as
      gains were made by Sinn Fein and by the anti-Agreement Democratic Unionist
      Party.

Discussion Questions

1. What were the reasons behind the outbreak of community conflict in Northern
   Ireland in the late 1960s?
2. Analyse the Northern Ireland 'Troubles' from the following points of view:
   (a) A Protestant unionist
   (b) A Catholic nationalist
   (c) A British government politician
3. 'The Good Friday Agreement of 10 April 1998 constitutes a real "settlement" of
   the political conflict in Northern Ireland.' Examine the arguments for and
   against this statement.

Notes

1. Northern Ireland is not, of course, a state but the word is used throughout the
   chapter as a convenient shorthand when discussing the politics of the region.
2. The Provisional IRA 'cessation of military operations' took effect on 31 July
   1994 and resulted from a combination of the following factors:
   - The IRA 'armed struggle' had not resulted in Irish unity. While they could
     not be beaten militarily, they could not win either, so they had to develop a
     more political strategy to pursue their goals.
   - Both IRA activists and the communities which supported them had grown
     old and war-weary together.
   - Since the republican hunger strike of 1981, Sinn Fein had developed a polit-
     ical platform and a substantial degree of electoral support from which to
     pursue an alternative strategy.
   - Due to initiatives such as the Downing Street Declaration of 1993 (which
     they formally rejected) and ongoing contacts with the British government, SF
     became convinced that Britain had no selfish interest in remaining in Ireland.
   - Through the building of the 'Irish national consensus' with the SDLP, link-
     ing up with Dublin and, crucially, Washington, SF believed that they could
     present an irresistible force for political change.

   The two main loyalist paramilitary groups announced cease-fires on 13 October
   1994 for a combination of the following reasons:
   - It was difficult for loyalists who professed to be British and to be engaged in
     counter-revolutionary and defensive violence, to continue killing people
     when the 'enemy' had laid down its weapons, however temporarily.

- Many of the loyalist paramilitaries had been around for as long as the republicans and were just as war-weary.
- Loyalists had developed a more intelligent tier of political leadership, represented by the PUP and UDP, which was more confident, better educated and less afraid of the future than they had been in the past.
- Loyalists called their cease-fire on the basis that the union with Britain was secure.
- The loyalist cease-fire was conditional on the absence of republican violence and contained the warning that they would respond 'blow for blow' to any IRA resumption.

3. An Independent Commission was set up (eventually to be known as the Patten Commission after its Chair, Chris Patten) to investigate police reform. When it was finally published in 1999, the Patten Report was to prove highly controversial. At the time of writing (January 2002) it has been partially implemented by the British government, with the Royal Ulster Constabulary (RUC) being replaced by a new Police Service of Northern Ireland (PSNI), with new accountability structures such as a Police Ombudsman and a new Policing Board in replace of the old Police Authority.

4. The Provisonal IRA ended their 'cessation of military operations' on 9 February 1996 with the bombing of Canary Wharf in London, alleging bad faith on the part of John Major. The cease-fire was renewed in July 1997, following the election of the Labour government and the re-energising of the peace process.

References

Arthur, P. (1987) *Government and Politics of Northern Ireland* (second edition), London: Longman.

Buckland, P. (1979) *The Factory of Grievances: Devolved Government in Northern Ireland 1921–39*, Dublin: Gill and Macmillan.

O'Leary, B. and McGarry, J. (1993) *The Politics of Antagonism: Understanding Northern Ireland*, London: The Athlone Press.

Further reading

Bardon, J. (1992) *A History of Ulster*, Belfast: Blackstaff Press.

Bew, P., Patterson, H. and Gibbon, P. (1979) *The State in Northern Ireland, 1921–72: Political Forces and Social Classes*, Manchester: Manchester University Press.

Bloomfield, K. (1994). *Stormont in Crisis*, Belfast: Blackstaff Press.

Buckland, P. (1980) *James Craig*, Dublin: Gill and Macmillan.

Catterall, P. and McDougall, S. (eds) (1996) *The Northern Ireland Question in British Politics*, London: Macmillan.

Cochrane, F. (1997) *Unionist Politics and the Politics of Unionism since the Anglo-Irish Agreement*, Cork: Cork University Press.

Cochrane, F. (1996) '"Meddling at the crossroads": the decline and fall of Terence O'Neill within the unionist community', in R. English and G. Walker (eds) *Unionism in Modern Ireland*, London: Macmillan, pp. 148–68.

Cox, M., Guelke, A. and Stephen, F. (eds) (2000) *A Farewell to Arms? From 'Long War' to Long Peace in Northern Ireland*, Manchester, Manchester University Press.

Farrell, M. (1980) *Northern Ireland: The Orange State* (second edition), London: Pluto Press.

Foster, R.F. (1988) *Modern Ireland 1600–1972*, London: Penguin.

Gordon, D. (1989) *The O'Neill Years: Unionist Politics 1963–1969*, Belfast: Athol Books.

McCall, C. (1999) *Identity in Northern Ireland: Communities, Politics and Change*, London: Macmillan.

McCann, E. (1980) *War and an Irish Town* (second edition), London: Pluto Press.

O'Dochartaigh, N. (1997) *From Civil Rights to Armalites: Derry and the Birth of the Irish Troubles*, Cork: Cork University Press.

O'Malley, P. (1990) *Biting at the Grave: The Irish Hunger Strikes and the Politics of Despair*, Belfast: Blackstaff Press.

Wilson, T. (1989) *Ulster: Conflict and Consent*, Oxford: Basil Blackwell.

Wright, F. (1987) *Northern Ireland: A Comparative Analysis*, Dublin: Gill and Macmillan.

Electoral Reform

Helen Margetts

CHAPTER FIVE

The British political system has long resisted any sort of change in its electoral arrangements. The history of the so-called 'first-past-the-post' electoral system was intertwined with the beginning of the extension of the franchise and exported to British colonies throughout the nineteenth century. The system was used throughout the twentieth century for elections to all tiers of government: local, national and European. Thus before the 1990s Britain might have been considered in line with the conventional wisdom that electoral systems rarely change. But 1993 marked a 'burst of change' across the rest of the world when Italy, Japan and New Zealand all changed their electoral systems and Russia introduced a new system (Dunleavy and Margetts, 1995: 9), while the newly emerging democracies across central and eastern Europe all chose either mixed or list systems. Britain began to look out of step internationally. At the European level Britain's resistance to change was particularly prominent, as Britain became the only country by 1994 to remain committed to the first-past-the-post system for election to the European Parliament.

This chapter investigates the arguments over electoral reform in Britain from the early 1990s, as electoral change hit the political agenda and (from 1997) British voters experienced alternative electoral systems for the first time. The first part covers the empirical background to eventual change: key events, the views of the main political parties and the various alternative electoral systems that have at one time or another been proposed for Britain. The second part considers some of the theoretical justifications for reform and offers some methods of measuring the way that electoral systems fulfil their key democratic functions. The third part covers events since 1993, when arguments both for and against change came to prominence. Finally, the fourth section looks at the key contemporary debates over electoral reform for the House of Commons and looks to the future of the issue.

Background

The fundamental idea behind the first-past-the-post electoral system is that the candidate with the most votes in a constituency is elected to the legislature. During the second half of the nineteenth century, this electoral system emerged in Britain at the same time as the extension of the franchise, although there were some two-member constituencies and some electors had more than one vote (owing to the existence of university seats up until 1950, which enabled graduates to elect university representatives by post). At the time, electoral reform was much debated. On the academic side, Thomas Hare and John Stuart Mill were among those who argued in favour of reform while Walter Bagehot defended the existing system. Politicians who supported reform included former Whig Prime Minister Russell and Disraeli, who both supported an amendment to the 1867 Reform Bill for an early form of proportional representation, called the 'limited vote' with multi-member constituencies, but this was abolished in the Redistribution of Seats Act in 1885. Kier Hardie, the first leader of the Labour Party, supported reform, along with other leading figures of the Labour movement. Labour enthusiasm was renewed after a successful pact between Liberal and Labour during 1906–10 broke down, but the Labour leader Ramsay McDonald was fiercely against electoral change. The issue re-emerged in 1918 (when a Speaker's conference recommended a hybrid electoral system which passed through the Commons but was lost in the Lords); again in 1924 (with the defeat of a private members' bill calling for reform); and again in 1930 (when another bill in favour passed through the Commons but was defeated in the Lords). But the decisive result of the 1945 election 'put the issue of electoral reform to the very bottom of the political agenda, where it stayed for the next 30 years' (Linton and Southcott, 1998: 93).

Variations on Electoral Systems

Discussion of the arguments for and against electoral reform cannot proceed without some indication of the variety of electoral systems available as alternatives to first-past-the-post. There are many ways of classifying electoral systems, but most political scientists agree that the two most important dimensions are the electoral formula (translating votes into seats) and the district magnitude (Lijpart, 1994: 10). Differences in these dimensions lead to three main categories of electoral systems:

- *Majoritarian* systems, where candidates to the legislature are elected in single-member or two-member constituencies; the candidate with the most votes wins the election and the party with most seats is elected to the legislature. Examples are first-past-the-post and the Alternative Vote, which is an example of a *preferential* system, where voters are asked to record their preferences between candidates.
- *Proportional* systems, where candidates are elected in multi-member constituencies and the electoral formula makes an attempt to match the percentage of seats gained by each party to the percentage of votes cast. Examples are the List Proportional Representation system (used in Spain and the Netherlands) and the Single Transferable Vote (used in Ireland), which is another example of a preferential system coming into this category, where seats are allocated in proportion to both voters' first and subsequent preferences.
- *Mixed-member* systems, where some candidates are elected under a majoritarian system in single-member local constituencies and other candidates are elected

under a proportional formula in 'top-up' areas. For example, the Additional Member System used in Germany.

The above distinctions provide us with an infinite variety of electoral systems, which have different advantages and disadvantages (not all of them can be described here, but see further readings for places where they can). Box 5.1 outlines the key systems that are used in liberal democracies and have at one time or another been suggested for Britain.

Support for FPTP – and majoritarian systems more generally – has rested primarily on its claim to produce 'stable government'. The system exaggerates movements of opinion, and when they are strong produces large majorities in the House of Commons. Larger parties benefit – and smaller parties are unlikely to gain a foothold, which supporters claim as a protection against extremist parties such as the far right or the far left. FPTP is an extremely simple system for voters to understand, marking one 'X' against one candidate name and the allocation of seats (winner takes all) is transparent. It offers a clear link between electors and a constituency representative, a link much prized in British political culture (although opinion polls suggest that only about half the population can name their MP and a study in 1992 found that only about one in ten people had contacted their MP in the previous five years (see Dunleavy et al., 1998: 15)). This means that each member of Parliament has a direct relationship with a given geographical area.

Arguments against FPTP – and in favour of more proportional electoral systems – rest on the way in which FPTP boosts the support of larger parties and under-represents geographically dispersed smaller parties. The system works well in two-party systems such as the USA (and Britain before the 1970s) but tends to discriminate heavily against parties whose support falls below about one-third. This means that smaller parties and in particular the Liberal Democrats in Britain have long suffered a mismatch of seats gained to votes won which has steadily worsened with time, as votes for smaller parties have increased. By 1974, the low Liberal shares of the vote (common in the 1950s when Britain could much more accurately be described as a two-party system) had grown to nearly 20% of the popular vote, but the Liberals won only 2.2% of the seats in the House of Commons. Even in 1997, when tactical voting was at a peak, the Liberal Democrats only got 7% of the seats for nearly 17% of the vote. This tendency is replicated at the local level; increasingly, FPTP returns MPs on a minority share of the vote in their constituency. In the 1950s, some 14% of MPs won their seats on less than 50% of the local vote, but in the two elections in the 1990s, the figure has risen to 44% – nearly half of all MPs (Dunleavy et al., 1998: 15). The FPTP system has also tended to create 'electoral deserts' (Dunleavy et al., 1998: 13; Jenkins, 1998). During the 1980s, Labour were almost excluded from the southern half of the UK, with only three Labour seats outside London south of a line from the Wash to the Severn Estuary in both 1983 and 1987. Conversely, in 1997 the Conservative Party gained no MPs at all in Scotland and Wales and hardly any in the large conurbations of England. Jenkins (1998) called such a geographically divisive effect 'a new form of Disraeli's two nations'.

Box 5.1 Alternative electoral systems

First-past-the-post (FPTP)

Simple plurality in single-member constituencies in which winning candidates gain more votes than any other candidate on a single count.

The Alternative Vote (AV)

A majoritarian system based on single-member constituencies. Voters indicate their preferences against the candidates on the ballot paper. Candidates who secure the support of over half the voters in a constituency are elected. If no candidate receives more than half of the votes cast on the count of first preference votes, the candidate who received the fewest first preference votes is eliminated and his/her second preferences are distributed among the other candidates. This process continues until one candidate has achieved an overall majority.

The Supplementary Vote (SV)

Similar to the Alternative Vote, but voters are limited to indicating only first and second preferences. If no candidate is elected on the count of first preferences, all bar the top two candidates are eliminated and their second preferences distributed between the top two. The candidate with the greatest share of the resultant vote will be elected.

Second Ballot

Voting takes place on two separate days. If any one candidate fails to achieve an absolute majority after the first ballot, a second ballot takes place. At this stage, the losing candidates drop out and their supporters choose between a reduced list of candidates.

Proportional List Systems

List systems are intended to translate directly a party's share of the vote into an equivalent proportion of seats in Parliament. However, constituency size and the allocation method of seats used will influence the extent to which such systems operate proportionally: the D'Hondt allocation formula, for example, tends to favour larger parties. Votes are cast for lists of candidates in large multi-member constituencies and seats are allocated across party lists according to the votes cast.

Single Transferable Vote (STV)

The STV system is essentially AV in multi-member constituencies. Voters are able to rank as many candidates both within parties and across parties, as they wish, in order of preference. Any of those candidates who reach a quota are automatically elected. The surplus of candidates elected and the votes of those with fewest votes after subsequent counts are distributed to the remaining candidates until sufficient candidates reach the quota and are elected.

Mixed Systems: the Additional Member System (AMS)

Mixed systems combine a list element with a plurality or majoritarian single-constituency system. Under AMS, voters cast two votes, one for a constituency MP and the second for a party list. The allocation of 'additional members' corrects (to varying extents) the disproportionality arising from the election of single constituency MPs.

Supporters of Reform

As noted above, for the majority of the twentieth century the leaderships of the two main parties, Labour and Conservative, have been opposed to any kind of electoral reform – FPTP has served them well. But key elections in 1951 and February 1974, when first Labour and then Conservative lost the election on a higher share of the vote, left the two major parties disillusioned with the voting system, for a period at least. After 1974, about a hundred Conservative MPs pronounced themselves in favour of electoral reform (forming the Tory pressure group Conservative Action for Electoral Reform) and Lord Hailsham spoke of 'elective dictatorship' in a Dimbleby lecture. Tory impetus for reform was soon pacified, however, by the long period of Conservative Party dominance that began in 1979. The Labour Party's periods of enthusiasm for reform have also coincided with electoral problems and the Labour Campaign for Electoral Reform was established in 1979, after Labour lost the election. In contrast, the Liberal Party have been largely in favour of electoral reform, having been strongly discriminated against by first-past-the-post. The benefits of FPTP for major parties have only rarely benefited the Liberal Democrats, in specific areas (the South West) and at the local level (Richmond Council, for example, where they reap the 'leaders' bias' effect and with near majority support gained four-fifths of the seats in 1994). However, they were indifferent to the issue during the ten years when they did hold power, at the beginning of the twentieth century and as late as 1917 the London Liberal Federation produced a pamphlet entitled *The Case Against Proportional Representation*. Thus, the three largest UK political parties have always had an instrumental approach to electoral change and 'their desire to improve the electoral system has tended to vary in inverse proportion to their ability to do anything about it' (Jenkins, 1998: 6).

The wider movement of support for electoral reform has suffered from divisions and disagreements. The key groups in favour of reform are the Liberal Democrats, the Electoral Reform Society, Charter 88 and sub-elements of the Labour and Conservative parties noted above. But the Electoral Reform Society and the Liberal Democrats have remained steadfastly wedded to change based on the Single Transferable Vote system (described in Box 5.1), a complex preferential system which has not had the support of the entire reform movement and can be difficult to explain to the electorate (for example, Dunleavy et al. (1997: 30) found that 30% of survey respondents required additional explanations of STV ballot papers), although it is popular in Ireland. Other reform groups (such as Charter 88 and the Labour Campaign for Electoral Reform) have been unable to coalesce around any particular system. This lack of decision has meant that they have never had a coherent reform programme to present to either MPs or the public more generally, whose limited appetite for discussion of electoral reform is unlikely to extend to absorbing the detailed characteristics of four or five possible systems.

During the 1990s, however, within the Labour Party moves towards change were afoot which were to have an impact after the 1997 election. After the party's third consecutive defeat in 1987, there were twenty-five resolutions at its conference calling for change and in 1990 Labour moved from 'outright opposition to an agnostic position on electoral reform' (Linton and Southcott, 1998). In 1990, after a successful conference motion for a working party on electoral reform, a Commission was established under Professor (now Lord) Raymond Plant, to consider alternatives to first-past-the-post, publishing an interim report in 1991. In the 1992 election campaign, electoral reform became a key theme in the election campaign, appearing in some counts as the second most discussed issue on television news (*Guardian*, 6 April 1992). In 1993, the Plant Commission presented its final report (Plant, 1993) to the Labour National Executive Committee, recommending List PR for the European elections and the Supplementary Vote (SV) for the House of Commons. John Smith responded with the promise of a referendum to take the final decision, to be held during the first term of the next Labour government which he claimed would be 'at a time when the Labour Government had begun the most radical programme of constitutional reform this century' (Linton and Southcott, 1998: 106).

Summary

- Electoral reform has been a subject of argument since the nineteenth century, when FPTP emerged as Britain's sole electoral system.
- FPTP is criticised for benefiting large parties and creating electoral deserts.
- FPTP is supported for constituency link, creating stable government and excluding extremist parties.
- Key characteristics of electoral systems are electoral allocation formula and district magnitude.
- Main electoral systems considered for Britain are AMS, List PR, SV, STV and AV.
- Major British political parties have an instrumental approach to electoral reform.

Theoretical Considerations

Electoral systems are at the heart of normative issues of democracy. Indeed, elections to office 'by all from among all' were described as a feature of democracy derived from the fundamentals of liberty and equality by Aristotle in around 330 BC (Held, 1987: 19). Voting is the only form of political participation that the majority of the British population undertake. How those votes are translated into seats in the legislature is obviously an important characteristic of a liberal democracy.

There can be no one electoral system, however, that embodies *the* notion of democracy, that is *the* most democratic system. Rather, different electoral systems provide different democratic qualities. Perhaps the most direct attempt to judge the British electoral system on democratic grounds was carried out by the Democratic Audit of the UK during the 1990s (Weir and Beetham, 1999). The

Democratic Audit defined its democratic criteria in terms of the basic principles which underlie the 'implicit contract' that representative democracy makes between 'state and people': 'the first is that of *popular control* over the political process of decision-making within their society; the second is that of *political equality* in the exercise of that control (Weir and Beetham, 1999: 7). Beetham identified two key democratic questions to ask of an electoral system in order to satisfy these principles:

1. How effective a range of choice and information does the electoral and party system allow the voters and how far is there fair and equal access for all parties and candidates to the media and other means of communication with them?
2. To what extent do the votes of all electors carry equal weight, and how closely do the composition of Parliament and the programme of government reflect the choices actually made by the electorate?

Some of the key arguments for and against FPTP have been noted above. But to link such arguments to normative concerns of democracy requires some method-ological development (for full discussion, see Dunleavy and Margetts, 1994). A key characteristic of electoral systems that addresses the Democratic Audit's second question is the question of proportionality – the extent to which the electoral system translates votes into seats. Proportionality is not an absolute quality of an electoral system. Rather, it is a measurable characteristic that varies according to the type of electoral system and other features such as the size of constituency, the size of the legislature and other features of a political system. Political scientists have developed many different possible indicators of electoral system perform-ance in terms of matching seats to votes, the most well known of which is the concept of deviation from proportionality. Table 5.1 shows how to calculate

Table 5.1 Deviation from proportionality in the 1997 election

Party	Votes (%) (1)	Seats (%) (2)	Deviations (1)–(2)
Conservative	31.4	25.7	–5.7
Labour	44.4	65.4	+21.0
Liberal Democrat	17.2	7.2	–10.0
Scottish National Party	2.0	0.9	–1.1
Plaid Cymru	0.5	0.6	+0.1
Referendum Party	2.7	0.0	–2.7
Others	1.7	0.2	–1.5
Total	100.0	100.0	
Total deviations (ignoring + or – signs)		42.1	
DV score = total deviations/2		**21%**	

Note: Subtract the percentage of seats a party gained in the Commons from its percentage vote share to give a deviation for each party. Then add up the deviations for all parties (discarding plus or minus signs), which would otherwise cancel each other out, and divide by 2. This gives a deviation from proportionality (DV) score of 21 for the 1997 general election.

Source: Dunleavy et al. (1998: 9)

deviation from proportionality using data from the 1997 general election in Great Britain.

Perfect proportionality in an electoral system would be indicated by a score of zero, but no electoral system achieves this. In practice, there is a lower limit to the DV score, mainly set in Westminster elections by the share of total votes which is dispersed among very small parties: 4.4% in 1997. The maximum DV score is not 100 but 100% minus the largest party's share of the vote, usually about 50. Thus the British DV score of 21% in 1997 was about two-fifths of its possible maximum. As a rule of thumb, a working electoral system for the 659-seat House of Commons can be regarded as operating proportionally if it can reliably achieve a DV score of between 4% and 8% across all elections and configurations of party support, as attained by most PR systems across western Europe (Dunleavy and Margetts, 1999: 21).

Other democratic arguments in favour of electoral reform are based on the specific advantages of particular systems and are more difficult to measure. Any system with a list element, for example, is likely to benefit the representation of women and ethnic minorities, as parties can use strategies to ensure that such candidates can be represented on the list. But this advantage is difficult to quantify and in any case, Phillips (1998) has shown that it is extremely difficult to argue for the democratic benefits of social representation in the legislature on normative grounds. Preferential systems, such as the Alternative Vote and the Single Transferable Vote, allow voters to give expression to multiple preferences which may reveal important underlying trends in popular opinion (Dunleavy and Margetts, 1994). They clearly deliver more choice than FPTP, as voters effectively have more than one vote to cast. Mixed-member systems, such as the Additional Member System, allow voters to retain a constituency link while still increasing proportionality. AMS also delivers greater choice than FPTP, because voters choose at both the constituency level and the top-up level. List PR systems, alternatively, where voters vote for party lists and are unable to choose between candidates ('closed-list' systems) clearly deliver least choice of all, although there are variants where voters can nominate their preferred candidates ('open-list' systems).

The extent to which electoral systems deliver stable government, and therefore satisfies the Democratic Audit's criteria in ensuring that 'the composition of Parliament and the programme of government reflect the choices actually made by the electorate', is perhaps the most difficult of all to quantify. FPTP does tend to deliver single-party government due to its 'leaders' bias' effect that favours large parties. Governments elected under FPTP have a party mandate which offers a mechanism for linking electoral preferences to government action through the central party role in both; such mandates are less clear for coalition governments. However, opponents of proportional representation have argued that both coalition governments have been inherently unstable (citing Italy) and too stable (citing Germany): 'the fact is that there are many different kinds of coalition in Western Europe alone' (Dunleavy et al., 1998: 20). Furthermore, research has shown that coalitions can still allow parties to keep their commitments owing to agreements among the partners which let each pursue their own differing priorities (see Budge, 1998).

Summary

- Electoral systems are at the heart of normative issues of democracy.
- Different electoral systems have different democratic qualities: voter choice, voter comprehension, social representation, delivering stable government, proportionality.
- A DV score is a key indicator of proportionality.

Update

The general election of 1997 was an important landmark of change in debates over electoral reform in Britain. Before the election, a Joint Consultative Commission on Constitutional Reform, established by the Labour MP Robin Cook and the Liberal Democrat Robert McLellan, promised a 'modern and accountable constitution . . . for the future, not the past' and laid down a number of recommendations in the 'Cook–McLellan' pact, published on 5 March 1997. The Labour Party was already committed to change, at least at the European level for the next European elections, but key figures in the leadership were known to be opposed to electoral reform for either the House of Commons or for local government. Therefore it was of some surprise to many commentators that the recommendations of the Cook–McLellan report entered Labour's manifesto the next month in a section on 'new politics', which set out the establishment of an Independent Commission on Electoral Reform, renewed the promise of a referendum made by John Smith and promised exploration of the possibilities for reform for local government. Meanwhile, Labour proposals on devolution and the work of the Scottish Constitutional Convention since the 1980s meant that elections to the proposed Scottish Parliament and Welsh Assembly looked set to be conducted under mixed-member systems.

The first term of the Labour government elected in 1997 kicked off the constitutional reform agenda straightaway, with legislation for the Scottish Parliament and Welsh Assembly followed by elections in 1998. With proposals for the London Assembly established during 1998 and legislated for during 1999, a type of 'British AMS' appeared to have emerged, in Scotland, Wales and London, summarised by Dunleavy and Margetts (1999) in Table 5.2.

Table 5.2 British versions of the Additional Member System

	Assembly size	Local: top-up seats mix (%)	Top-up areas	Top-up seats per area
Scottish Parliament	129	57:43	8 euro constituencies	7
Welsh Assembly	60	67:33	5 euro constituencies	4
London Assembly	25	57:43	Greater London	11

These versions of AMS share several characteristics. The majority of representatives are elected in local constituencies (a higher majority in Wales, representing a compromise with Labour MPs who fought to retain FPTP for electing the Welsh Assembly). The electoral formula used is the 'D'Hondt rule' which slightly favours large parties (this method was also used in the European elections under List PR in 1999). They also illustrate how one of the arguments against proportional systems can be overcome – the possibility of small extremist parties securing seats in the legislature. The Scottish and Welsh electoral systems for the new Parliament and Assembly kept down the total number of local and top-up seats elected within each top-up area so as to keep the *de facto* votes threshold (the 'effective district magnitude') needed to win a seat reasonably high. In London, ministers built in a 5% legal threshold instead of leaving the 3.5% 'effective district magnitude' level which would otherwise have applied (Dunleavy, 2000: 142). Thus the British National Party (BNP), with 2.9% of the list vote for the Assembly, received no seats (and indeed would not have done, even without the legal threshold).

In 1998, the Independent Commission on the Voting System was formed (as promised in the Cook–McLellan pact) with Roy Jenkins as its Chair, charged with the criteria that the alternative system they recommended should offer the following:

- Greater voter choice.
- Deliver stable government.
- Maintain the link between MPs and local constituencies.
- Produce broadly proportional results.

These criteria represented an attempt to link the choice of the electoral system to some of the democratic criteria noted above, as well as retaining the most popular elements of first-past-the-post. The Commission had been set a difficult task. In addition to the formal criteria, Jenkins added some of his own: that the chosen system should be intellectually acceptable; that it should represent a significant change; and that it should have a reasonable chance of being implemented. He was also determined to overcome the problem of 'electoral deserts'. And after a series of public meetings held by the Commission, they concluded that any system which increased the power of the party machine (for example, a party list system) would be unacceptable to the electorate. The Commission knew they would have to propose some modification of the constituency pattern, but that it would have to be limited if the constituency link were to be maintained. They also knew that any proposal which endangered the seats of a large number of Labour MPs would meet with formidable resistance in the Parliamentary Labour Party.

The final choice of the Jenkins' Commission (see Jenkins, 1998) was AV-plus, a mixture of the Alternative Vote at the single-member level and between 15% and 20% top-up MPs elected proportionally across seventy-eight small top-up areas (based on counties and the top-up areas in Scotland and Wales), chosen to give further local accountability (Box 5.2). This system represents a sincere desire to maximise the criteria laid down for the Commission. The link between MPs and local constituencies was clearly maintained and even strengthened through the locally accountable top-up MPs. The system undoubtedly maximised voter choice, although at the possible expense of voter comprehension, given the complex ballot

---

> ### Box 5.2 AV-plus
>
> There are two sections to the ballot paper, as under AMS. In the first section, to elect
> the member for a local single-member constituency, voters indicate their preferences
> for a list of candidates, as for AV. The local candidate is then elected using the same pro-
> cedure as for AV. In the second section, voters are offered a choice of party lists to elect
> top-up members for a larger but still geographically relevant area. Jenkins proposed
> that the proportion of local to top-up members should be between 80:20 and 85:15.

paper that would be necessary. The best available estimates (see Table 5.3) suggest
that such a system would have delivered a DV score of 12 if there were 20% top-
up MPs, suggesting 'broad proportionality' only if the words are interpreted
'broadly', but DV would have been fully proportional in 1992 with a DV score of
7.6. As noted above, the criteria of 'broad proportionality' and 'stable government'
were to some extent incompatible, except insofar that coalitions can be stable. But
AV-plus would have delivered a clear Labour majority in 1997.

The importance of the Cook–McLellan Commission after the 1997 election,
evidenced by the fact that most of its key recommendations were implemented,
caused some commentators to predict that Blair was dedicated to the idea of long-
term hegemony, through co-operation with the Liberal Democrats and with constitutional reform in general and electoral reform in particular forming the plank
of New Labour's modernising agenda. Therefore, during the following two years,
the future for supporters of electoral reform looked bright. However, an apparent
desire for democratisation realised through the creation of the new assemblies was
mitigated by the Blair leadership's controlling approach to reform. In Wales, after
the resignation before the election of the 'Labour leader elect' to the new Assembly
(Ron Davies) following an indiscretion on Clapham Common, the Labour leadership used the electoral college to impose its own candidate (Alun Michael) on to
the Welsh Labour Party in place of the more popular Rhodri Morgan. Later, Alun
Michael resigned and Morgan won the leadership. With no lessons learnt, in London, the Labour leadership again employed the electoral college in the age of 'one
member one vote' to elect their chosen candidate, Frank Dobson, instead of the
vastly more popular Ken Livingstone. After a narrow defeat in the electoral college,
Livingstone stood as an independent and won the election to become the first
elected Mayor of London; the leadership contest, widely perceived as unfair, must
have played a role in ensuring Dobson's defeat. Meanwhile, the Jenkins' report
seemed to have been 'kicked into the long grass' after its publication in October
1998.

Evidence of the performance of alternative electoral systems

Thus, after the excitement of the 1990s, the implications of electoral reform for the
House of Commons remain a subject for speculation rather than empirical evidence. What would be the impact of reform? Establishing how alternative electoral
systems would perform under British conditions is difficult; comparisons across

Table 5.3 Comparing the seats won by the parties in Britain under alternative electoral systems, 1997

Voting method	Con	Lab	Lib Dem	SNP/PC	Other	DV
FPTP	165	419	46	10	1	21
Supplementary Vote	110	436	84	10	1	24
Alternative Vote	110	436	84	10	1	21
STV	144	342	131	24	0	13
AV-plus: 80:20 version	175	359	91	15	1	12
AMS: Welsh version	191	340	93	17	0	9
AMS Scottish version	198	319	105	19	0	6
AMS: 50:50 version	203	303	115	20	0	2
Pure proportionality	202	285	110	16	18	0

Source: Dunleavy and Margetts (1998); Dunleavy et al. (1998)

countries are problematic, as the electoral system is so inextricably intertwined with the rest of the political system. Research by Dunleavy, Margetts and Weir during the 1990s tried to get as close a possible to how a new system might work. Results of this research are probably the best evidence we have of the implications of a different system, and the research informed both the Independent Commission on the Voting System, the new systems for electing the London Mayor and the London Assembly. The research involves asking respondents in a large-scale survey (10,000 in 1992, 8,400 in 1997) to complete alternative ballots for the rival systems, immediately after they have voted in a general election. Regional responses are then combined with the actual election results to simulate the alternative systems. The results of this research is summarised in Table 5.3.

These results have had an important impact on the debate over electoral reform. They show that in 1997 and 1992 the most clearly and consistently proportional voting method was AMS (with half of the MPs elected locally and half elected regionally using the top-up method). Variants of AMS which gave more local seats and fewer top-up seats would be less proportional, but the Scottish version, for example, would still come into the 4–8% category required for proportional representation. The proposed AV-plus system of the Jenkins Commission, with a DV of 12, could only 'broadly' be described as 'broadly proportional'. STV, the favoured system of the Liberal Democrats, did not achieve a consistently close fit between parties' seats and their first preference votes. In both 1997 and 1992 STV produced an apparent over-representation of Labour in the Commons, for example giving Labour 53% of seats in 1997 on the basis of 44% of votes. The Supplementary Vote and the Alternative Vote were markedly less proportional than first-past-the-post in 1997; in 1992 the results of both systems were slightly more proportional than first-past-the-post in 1997. While this research can never replicate a real election (and supporters of STV would claim that the system does not purport to be proportional to first preferences and therefore cannot be judged under the same criteria as other electoral systems), it is probably the best evidence we have of how British voters would behave under alternative electoral systems.

Summary

- The Cook–McLellan pact acts as a key roadmap for Labour's constitutional reform plan, but is hampered by the leadership's controlling attitude to democratisation.
- 'British AMS' emerges, with variants for Scotland, Wales and London.
- The Jenkins Commission produces further variant (AV-plus) for the House of Commons, maximising democratic criteria, but is complex and only 'broadly' proportional.
- All new systems currently operating in Britain offer more proportional alternatives to FPTP, but some systems (AV and SV) can operate less proportionally.

Debate

Electoral reform has always been viewed as the area of the chattering classes, a suitable topic for debate at Charter 88 meetings and Islington dinner parties, but of little interest to the majority of the population. Polling questions on electoral reform are notoriously difficult to frame, with apparently contradictory answers emerging. Curtice and Jowell (1998) found, in an analysis of the British Election Study, a different distribution of answers to two questions in different parts of the questionnaire. When respondents were asked how much they agreed or disagreed with the statement 'Britain should introduce proportional representation so that the number of MPs each party gets matches more closely the number of votes each party gets', just under a half agreed with the proposition while around one in five disagreed. However, different responses were recorded to the question: 'Some people say we should change the voting system to allow smaller parties to get a fair share of MPs. Others say we should keep the voting system as it is to produce effective government. Which view comes closest to your own?' Then three in five respondents were in favour of keeping the existing system while only around one in three said they wanted to change it (Curtice and Jowell, 1998: 68). Such inconsistencies in the public's attitudes to electoral reform undoubtedly reflect the complexity of the issue. The public, quite rationally, prize different elements of different voting systems.

However, the most detailed questioning during the 1990s seems to reveal a majority in favour of reform, with notable differences between systems. An ICM poll carried out as part of the Dunleavy, Margetts and Weir (1992) research showed a non-conservative coalition of reformers strongly and consistently in favour of reform. In their 1997 survey, Dunleavy, Margetts and Weir asked a sub-sample of 1,900 respondents who had just been asked to 'vote again' using the ballot papers of alternative systems how much they would like to 'vote this way in the future'. Small majorities of respondents said that they would 'like to vote' under SV and AMS (which both use X voting) – percentages of respondents who would not like to vote this way were 21% and 22% respectively. Attitudes towards AV were mixed with nearly equal numbers liking (35%) and disliking (37%) the system. More than half the respondents disliked filling in the STV ballot paper by a margin of 2:1. Respondents were also asked to vote in a 'mock referendum', explaining in neutral terms on a show card the advantages and disadvantages of first-past-the-post and its most likely proportional rival – the Additional Member System. The outcome was evenly balanced: 41% chose first-past-the-post and 44% AMS, with 14% 'don't knows' (Dunleavy et al., 1997: 30–1). By 2000, when the same mock referendum was put to 2,401 survey respondents in a State of the Nation poll commissioned by the Joseph Rowntree Reform Trust, a clearer majority of respondents opted for change, by 53 to 27% (Dunleavy et al., 2001).

Although the evidence outlined above suggests a majority in favour of change, it is unlikely to result in any kind of popular uprising. Change has to come from the top – meaning that the attitudes of the major parties will remain crucial and, given the consistently instrumental approach to reform noted in the first two sections, electoral reform will therefore indirectly depend upon their electoral fortunes.

With regard to the political parties, the Liberal Democrats' role will depend upon the extent to which they are involved in power-sharing arrangements, as they were in the Joint Consultative Committee. However, in 1999 they elected a new leader, Charles Kennedy, who was known to be resistant to coalition agreements with Labour. The research on the performance of alternative electoral systems under British conditions (Dunleavy et al., 1997, 1998) contained some important results for the Liberal Democrats in their loyal support of STV. The Liberal Democrats' seats would almost have doubled under even SV or AV in 1997, and they would have gained 130 seats under STV. But in 1992 STV would have been slightly less favourable for the party than AMS.

In spite of both the 1997 and 2001 election results, which introduced obvious incentives for them to refocus their views, the Conservative Party have remained steadfastly opposed to electoral reform for the House of Commons, although they accepted with equanimity the 18 seats they won in the new Scottish Parliament and the 9 seats they won in the Welsh Assembly.

Meanwhile the Labour Party seem to have withdrawn from earlier enthusiasm for reform as a key theme of their modernising government. Initially, after publication of the Jenkins report, the *Guardian* reported that the Prime Minister had 'signalled his determination to accelerate New Labour's modernisation project' by telling pro-PR Labour 'to go out and evangelise about the merits of electoral reform to pave the way for a referendum after the next general election' (*Guardian*, 19 February 1999). But Blair remained personally 'unpersuaded' of the case for reform and declined to endorse the Jenkins report, while crediting it with making a 'well-argued and powerful case for the system it recommends'. Several key Cabinet members, including the Chancellor, have all publicly expressed opposition for electoral reform. By July 2000, the most likely alternative to be offered in a referendum looked like the Alternative Vote (that is, AV-plus without the 'plus'), a system which certainly would not even broadly have met the Jenkins Commission's criteria of being 'broadly proportional'. Some commentators were asking if the government had 'put the Jenkins report and its modest move towards political pluralism in Downing Street's capacious bin' (*Guardian*, 24 July 2000).

The deputy Prime Minister, John Prescott, further dimmed the hopes of the reformers in a radio interview in which he declared his opinion of demand for the introduction of proportional representation: 'Put it in a boat and send it away along with the Lib Dems' (*Guardian*, 25 September 2000). However, the radical drop of Labour support in the polls after the fuel crisis of autumn 2000 seemed to suggest another turnaround in the fortunes of the electoral reform movement: 'Now that victory no longer looks at all certain, cutting off the party's potential life-line to a deal with Charles Kennedy after the next election no longer looks so smart' (*Guardian*, 27 September 2000).

Aside from the crucial approaches of the political parties, public opinion may yet play a role. Some commentators have pointed to underlying evidence of polit-ical undercurrents in favour of increased choice in voting. Investigation of evid-ence of split-ticket voting at the synchronous 1997 general and local elections found clear evidence of many individuals casting their available votes for different parties. Tabulations from constituency results in 1997 showed at least 5% and up to 20% of electors ticket-splitting in this way, a level higher than that observed in 1979 according to both survey and aggregate data (Rallings and Thrasher, 1998: 123).

Recent elections held under alternative systems highlight and confirm such long-held and significant voter inclinations. Experience of proportional repres-entation in action in Scotland and Wales appears to have pleased voters. The State of the Nation poll noted above, suggested strong regional variations in the 26% of respondents in favour of a change to the voting system; the lead in favour of elec-toral reform in Scotland was 44% (Dunleavy et al., 2001). Curtice et al. (2000) found that a clear majority of voters in both Scotland and Wales consistently support the use of proportional representation for the devolved institutions. They found that 66% of Scottish voters and 58% of Welsh voters agreed that their new legislature should be elected using proportional representation, while 58% of Scottish voters and 56% of Welsh voters agreed that they preferred the new way of voting. Significantly for the debate over voting reform for Westminster, 59% of Scottish voters and 55% of Welsh voters agreed with the statement that the UK should introduce PR so that the number of MPs each party gets in the House of Common matches more closely the number of votes that each party gets. Inconsistencies were still present, as fewer voters agreed with a less normatively charged statement, but still, with around one-fifth unable to decide, a majority were in favour of change.

What is clear from Scottish and Welsh evidence is that support for alternative systems rises among voters who have experienced some kind of reform. In Scotland, for example, support for proportional representation for the Scottish Parliament rose from 53% in 1997, to 75% after the election in 1997 (immedi-ately after the referendum), falling (but not back to its initial level) to 66% in 1999 (Curtice et al., 2000: 17). Such trends are likely to increase as Londoners, for example, experience an independent Mayor, freed from the constraints of party representation. They may be resistant to being provided with only the major parties to choose from in the future. The rise of smaller parties in British politics is another driver for change that predates actual electoral system change. In the 1997 election, the vote for smaller or 'other parties' doubled to 4.5% from 2.7% in 1992. In 2001, the figure was 3.9%. In the May 2000 elections in London, 26% of voters voted for parties outside the three major parties in the list element of the Assembly elections. The quite distinctive party systems that emerged during the 1980s and 1990s in Scotland and Wales, now given expression through new electoral systems, could be a further impetus to change, as a similarly distinctive party system emerges in the regions of England.

Summary

- Constitutional reform is no longer a key plank of Labour's modernising agenda.
- But Labour's wavering electoral fortunes will keep the issue alive.
- Public opinion shows a majority of support for reform, especially where reforms have already been implemented.
- The increasing pluralistic nature of the British political system may provide a further push for reform.

Conclusion

Electoral reform is an argument with a long history in Britain. The end of the twentieth century, with new electoral systems in action for Scotland, Wales, London and Europe, seemed to indicate that the balance had shifted in favour of reform. But at the beginning of the twenty-first century, there is everything to play for. If the Labour government faces possible defeat in its second term, we might visualise it turning to the Liberal Democrats and implementing a referendum on reform in exchange for co-operation. For some, electoral reform would represent the end of a long battle, bringing Britain at last in line with the more modern electoral systems of its European partners. For others, it will be what a leading Conservative minister once called a 'pact with the devil'. For the British public, however, it may just be the inevitable consequence of an increasingly pluralistic political system.

Chronology

1832 Limited male franchise of property holders, total electorate 720,000.
1867 Male franchise extended, total electorate 2,231,000.
1884 Male franchise extended to all over the age of 21 who had a home, total 4,965,000.
1917 All-party Speaker's conference recommended STV in cities and large towns, AV in the counties (failed in the House of Commons).

1918 Male franchise extended, women enfranchised at the age of 30.

1928 Women enfranchised at the age of 21.

1931 Bill for the introduction of AV passed in the House of Commons, rejected in the Lords.

1948 Last remaining dual-member seats abolished.

1951 Conservative won 26 more seats than Labour with 230,684 fewer votes.

1969 Voting age reduced to 18.

1974 February general election: Conservative Party had lead of 0.7% over Labour but secured fewer seats.

1993 Publication of the report of the Plant Commission.

1997 (March) Publication of report of Joint Consultative Committee on Constitutional Reform: adopted in the Labour manifesto.

1997 (May) General election: landslide majority for Labour.

1998 (June) Elections to the new Northern Ireland Assembly, under STV.

1998 (October) Report of the Independent Commission on the Voting System.

1999 Elections to the Scottish Parliament and the Welsh Assembly under AMS.

1999 European elections under List Proportional Representation.

2000 (May) Elections for the London Mayor (Supplementary Vote) and to the Greater London Assembly (Additional Member System).

Discussion Questions

1. Which electoral system is the most democratic?
2. 'Public opinion will never be in favour of electoral reform in Britain; therefore there are no democratic gains to change.' Discuss.
3. You are appointed Chair of a new Independent Commission on the Voting System. Which electoral system would you propose for the House of Commons and why?

References

Budge, I. (1998) *Stability and Choice: A Review of Single Party and Coalition Government*, Democratic Audit Paper No. 15, London: Democratic Audit.

Curtice, J. and Jowell, R. (1998) 'Is there really a demand for constitutional change?', in *Scottish Affairs: Understanding Constitutional Change*, Edinburgh: Edinburgh University Press.

Curtice, J., Seyd, B., Park, A. and Thomson, K. (2000) *Wise after the Event? Attitudes to Voting Reform following the 1999 Scottish and Welsh Election*, London: Constitution Unit.

Dunleavy, P. (2000) 'Elections and party politics', *Developments in British Politics*, Vol. 6, Basingstoke: Macmillan.

Dunleavy, P. and Margetts, H. (1994) 'The experiential approach to auditing democracy', in D. Beetham (ed.) *Defining and Measuring Democracy*, London: Sage, pp. 155–82.

Dunleavy, P. and Margetts, H. (1995) 'Understanding the dynamics of electoral reform', *International Political Science Review*, Vol. 16, No. 1 (January).

Dunleavy, P. and Margetts, H. (1998) 'Remodelling the 1997 general election', in D. Denver, J. Fisher, P. Cowley and C. Pattie (eds) *British Elections and Parties Review. Volume 8: The 1997 General Election*, London: Frank Cass.

Dunleavy, P. and Margetts, H. (1999) 'Mixed electoral systems in Britain and the Jenkins Commission on electoral reform', *British Journal of Politics and International Relations*, Vol. 1, No. 1 (April), pp. 12–38.

Dunleavy, P., Margetts, H. and Weir, S. (1992) 'How Britain would have voted under alternative electoral systems in 1992', *Parliamentary Affairs*, Vol. 45, No. 4, pp. 640–55.

Dunleavy, P., Margetts, H. and Weir, S. (1997) *Making Votes Count: Replaying the 1990s General Elections under Alternative Electoral Systems*, London: Democratic Audit.

Dunleavy, P., Margetts, H. and Weir, S. (1998) *The Politicos Guide to Electoral Reform in Britain*, London: Politicos.

Dunleavy, P., Margetts, H., Smith, T. and Weir, S. (2001) 'Constitutional reform, New Labour in power and public trust in government', *Parliamentary Affairs*, forthcoming.

Held, D. (1987) *Models of Democracy*, Oxford: Polity Press.

Jenkins, R. (1998) *The Report of the Independent Commission on the Voting System*, London: HMSO.

Lijpart, A. (1994) *Electoral Systems and Party Systems*, Oxford: Oxford University Press.

Linton, M. and Southcott, M. (1998) *Making Votes Count: The Case for Electoral Reform*, London: Profile Books.

Phillips, A. (1998) 'Democracy and representation: or why should it matter who our representatives are?', in A. Phillips (ed.) *Feminism and Politics*, Oxford: Oxford University Press.

Plant, R. (1993) *Democracy, Representation and Elections*, Report of the Working Party on Elections (Labour Party) (the Plant Report).

Rallings, C. and Thrasher, M. (1998) 'Split-ticket voting at the 1997 British General and local elections: an aggregate analysis', in D. Denver, J. Fisher, P. Cowley and C. Pattie (eds), *British Elections and and Parties Review. Volume 8: The 1997 General Election*, London: Frank Cass.

Weir, S. and Beetham, D. (1999) *Political Power and Democratic Control in Britain*, London: Routledge.

Further reading

R. Taagepera and M. Shugart (1989) *Seats and Votes: The Effects and Determinants of Electoral Systems*, (New Haven, CT: Yale University Press), remains the best book on the detailed operation of various types of electoral systems. A. Lijphart (1994) *Electoral Systems and Party Systems* (Oxford: Oxford University Press), contains valuable comparative data and analyses the relationship between electoral systems and party systems. A. Reynolds and B. Reilly (eds) (1997) *The International IDEA Handbook on Electoral Systems Design* (London: International Institute for Democracy and Electoral Assistance) is an excellent summary of key elements of electoral systems across countries. A. Reeve and A. Ware (1992) *Electoral Systems: A Comparative and Theoretical Introduction* (London: Routledge) and D. Farrell (1997) *Comparing Electoral Systems* (Hemel Hempstead: Prentice Hall/Harvester Wheatsheaf) give good comparative introductions to the theoretical and empirical foundations for various electoral systems. S. Weir and D. Beetham (1999) *Political Power and Democratic Control in Britain* (London: Routledge) endeavour to 'audit' the British electoral system in democratic terms. The yearly *British Elections and Parties Review*, published by Frank Cass, contains many important and interesting articles on the subject as well as electoral statistics. The *Developments in British Politics* series generally has a chapter on electoral systems: P. Dunleavy (2000) 'Elections and party politics' is an excellent update. A special issue of the *International Political Science Review* (Vol. 16, No. 1, 1995), entitled *The Politics of Electoral Reform*, gives a good summary of international developments in the mid-1990s. The Jenkins report (1998), *The Report of the Independent Commission on the Voting System* (London: HMSO), is elegantly written and gives a good outline of both normative and practical considerations of the Commission. The report and likely implications of the Jenkins' proposals is summarised in P. Dunleavy, H. Margetts and S. Weir (1998) *The Politicos' Guide to Electoral Reform in Britain* (London: Politicos). M. Linton and M. Southcott (1998) *Making Votes Count* (London: Profile Books) provides a full history of electoral reform in Britain, from a clearly pro-reform perspective; D. Leonard (1996) *Elections in Britain Today* (Basingstoke: Macmillan) gives a more traditional version. The journals *Electoral Studies* and *Representation* analyse issues of electoral systems and electoral reform in detail.

Referendums

David Denver

CHAPTER SIX

Background

Referendums on matters of national importance are rare in the United Kingdom. All of those that have been held so far are listed in Table 6.1. During the 1970s there were only three significant examples.[1] The first (and so far only) UK-wide referendum, on membership of the European Community (as it was then known), was held in 1975 and this was followed in 1979 by referendums in Scotland and Wales on devolution proposals made by the government. Thereafter, with the Conservatives in office from 1979 to 1997, the use of referendums was avoided. After the election of a Labour government in 1997, however, referendums began to be used again. During the first twelve months of the new Parliament there were four significant sub-national referendums – on a devolved Parliament for Scotland, a representative Assembly for Wales, the Good Friday Agreement (also involving devolution) in Northern Ireland and the government of London. Future referendums on the electoral system to be used for the Westminster Parliament, membership of the European single currency, and devolution to the English regions are also promised.

All of the past and possible future referendums concern what might be broadly described as constitutional issues: whether the UK should remain a member of the European Community; whether a Parliament should be established in Scotland and assemblies in Wales and Northern Ireland; whether London should have a directly-elected mayor. A kind of unspoken convention has arisen that major constitutional innovations should be submitted to a referendum vote.

Table 6.1 United Kingdom referendums

Year	Electorate	Issue	Turnout (%)
1975	United Kingdom	EC membership	64.5
1979	Scotland	Devolution	63.8
1979	Wales	Devolution	58.8
1997	Scotland	Devolution	60.4
1997	Wales	Devolution	50.1
1998	London	London government	34.1
1998	Northern Ireland	Good Friday Agreement	81.0

Summary

- Referendums are rare in the UK.
- Those held or planned concern constitutional issues.

Theoretical Considerations

As the constitutional commentator Geoffrey Marshall has remarked, the new-found enthusiasm for referendums after the 1997 general election is 'a curious turn of events' (Marshall, 1997). It is curious because most British politicians and most experts on the British Constitution have, in the past, been hostile to the use of the referendum, seeing it as inconsistent with parliamentary democracy and an abdication of responsibility by elected representatives. The theory of representative government emphasises that citizens elect representatives to take decisions on their behalf. This is preferable to 'populist democracy' because representatives are more skilled at making decisions, more likely to pursue the national interest rather than simple self-interest, more likely to take the interests of unpopular minorities into account and to seek compromises which will satisfy as many people as possible. It might also be argued that referendums appear to undermine a fundamental element in the British Constitution – the sovereignty of Parliament. It is Parliament which is the final authority on all matters and turning that authority over to the people in the form of a referendum would raise serious questions about the role of Parliament in the British system of government. To avoid this criticism, all referendums held in the United Kingdom have been, in theory, advisory only, leaving the final decision on the matter concerned to Parliament. In practice, however, Parliament has never legislated in defiance of a referendum result conforming to agreed rules, and the chances of its ever doing so must be very slim.

The theoretical case for using referendums is relatively straightforward – they are democratic (see Butler and Ranney, 1994: ch. 2). Indeed, proponents of direct or participatory democracy suggest that decision-making by referendums is preferable to decision-making by elected representatives since it fulfils two democratic ideals – popular sovereignty (final authority rests with the people as a whole) and popular participation in decision-making. In this view, 'the only truly democratic way to make decisions on matters of public policy is by the full, direct, and unmediated participation of all citizens' (Butler and Ranney, 1994: 12) and referendums allow this. A less extreme view sees referendums as useful supplements to the normal workings of parliamentary democracy. In certain circumstances and under certain conditions a referendum, because it allows the public to participate in decision-making, can confer a greater legitimacy on a policy than would be the case if the decision were made by elected politicians alone. Thus in Britain, where there are no special procedures for changing the Constitution, it is always possible that an incoming government will reverse any constitutional changes made by its predecessor. When the changes have been approved in a referendum, however, they have a greater chance of being permanent since few politicians would dare to challenge the clearly-expressed will of the people.

Summary

- Opponents believe that referendums subvert parliamentary democracy and can make for 'bad' decisions.
- Proponents believe that referendums improve democracy as they allow citizens to participate in decision-making.
- Others suggest that they can be a useful occasional supplement to parliamentary democracy.

Referendums in the UK

The trigger

By 'the trigger' is meant the circumstances which prompted the referendums held so far. In many political systems referendums are mandatory if it is proposed to alter the Constitution and many also give governments authority to call referendums as they think fit. In a few cases (Italy, Switzerland and some states of the United States being the best-known examples), citizens themselves can take the initiative and set the referendum process in motion. In Britain only the government can initiate a referendum which has legal standing (which it does by Act of Parliament) and it can do so on any issue that it chooses. Why then have governments opted for referendums in the seven cases listed in Table 6.1?

In most of these cases, the decision to hold a referendum owed more to political expediency than to any concern with extending participatory democracy. The 1975 referendum on membership of the EC was forced upon an unwilling Labour Prime Minister, Harold Wilson, by opponents of membership and accepted by him as a means of coping with deep divisions on the issue in the Labour Party. As another leading Labour figure, James Callaghan, had foreseen, a referendum on the issue was 'a rubber life-raft into which the whole party may one day have to climb' (quoted in Butler and Kitzinger, 1976: 12). Callaghan was himself Prime Minister in 1979 when the first Scottish and Welsh devolution referendums were held. Once again the decision to hold referendums was forced upon the government by opponents of the policy on Labour's own backbenches and had to be conceded to keep the party together. Moreover, the government had to accept an amendment (put forward by a Labour MP) that for the devolution proposals to go ahead they would have to be supported by at least 40% of the eligible electorate, not just a majority of those voting. This is the only instance of a 'qualified majority' condition being attached to a British referendum.

The decision to hold further referendums on devolution in 1997 also owed much to political expediency. By the 1990s Labour's commitment to devolution had strengthened and the devolution scheme adopted included giving a Scottish Parliament the power to vary income tax. It was intended that the plans would be implemented by an incoming Labour government without recourse to referendums – an electoral victory would be sufficient to give the government a mandate to pursue its plans – but practical politics intruded to force a change of tack. The intention to give the new Parliament tax-varying powers came under serious attack from the Scottish Conservatives and Labour strategists feared that the carefully cultivated image of New Labour as a low-tax party might be tarnished in the run-up to the 1997 election. Moreover, caution on devolution also had the advantage of reassuring erstwhile Conservative and 'middle-England' voters to whom New Labour's electoral appeal was pitched. In the face of considerable controversy among the pro-devolution forces in Scotland, therefore, Tony Blair announced in 1996 that a referendum would be held consisting of two questions, one on the principle of establishing a Parliament and the other on tax-varying powers. This effectively neutralised the taxation issue during the forthcoming general election campaign. Having determined that devolution would be put to the electorate in Scotland, it would then have been illogical not to do the same in Wales. However, the decision to fix the date for the Welsh vote for one week after that in Scotland reflected a political calculation that the expected good result (for the government) in Scotland would help to convince waverers in Wales.

In the case of the 1998 London referendum there seems no reason to suspect that political or tactical considerations were involved – all the major parties supported the changes proposed. It seems that this referendum arose from a genuine desire to involve and consult the public on their preferences with respect to local government and it could be a forerunner to similar votes in other cities. Contrariwise, the Good Friday Agreement – which involved, among other things, re-establishing a legislature in Northern Ireland and setting up cross-border, all-Ireland institutions – was controversial within the Province. In a deeply divided society it was clearly important to establish whether there was some sort of consensus over the proposals which could then form the basis of a way forward and in these circumstances a referendum provided the ideal mechanism for doing so.

Participation

A major claim of proponents of referendums is that they enhance democracy because they allow the people to participate in making important decisions. In fact, across the world the turnout of the electorate in referendums is almost always lower than in national elections (see Butler and Ranney, 1994: 16–17). In general, voters appear to ascribe more importance to the general question of who governs their country than to specific constitutional or other issues. With the exception of Northern Ireland in 1998, the same is true of the United Kingdom (see Table 6.1). Nonetheless, despite being lower than in general elections, participation in the EC and devolution referendums can be described as 'respectable' (although Wales in 1997 was clearly disappointing) – turnout was greater than is normal in local or European Parliament elections, for example. By the same token, the London referendum clearly did not excite much interest among the electorate.

In general, the data suggest that reasonable levels of participation can be anticipated when the electorate thinks that the question at issue is an important one but not when it is seen as insignificant or peripheral. It might be suggested, however, that the infrequency with which referendums have occurred in Britain (seven in different parts of the country in twenty-five years) might have encouraged even more interest when they do come around. Certainly any expectations held by those who advocate more direct democracy that referendums would energise an electorate eager to participate have not been fulfilled.

Referendum voting

The relative rarity of referendums in Britain means that they are unfamiliar experiences for voters. Elections, by contrast, come round regularly and voters build up a fund of experience on which to draw. In referendums, the terrain is different. Whereas elections are multi-issue events structured by party competition and by candidates, referendums are one-off votes concerned with a single issue on which parties may not be united, or may be co-operating with erstwhile 'enemies', and in which there are no candidates. For the most part, however, the parties have taken clear positions in referendum votes and the choices made by voters have been structured by party. Table 6.2 shows some data on voting in four referendums which illustrate this tendency.

In 1975 a large majority of Conservative supporters and two-thirds of Liberals supported retaining UK membership of the EC. In contrast, reflecting divisions within the Labour Party, Labour voters were almost evenly divided. In the two Scottish referendums, devolution was almost unanimously supported by SNP supporters but opposed by most Conservatives. Among Labour supporters pro-devolution sentiment, already strong in 1979, increased markedly in 1997 and they were firmly behind government policy. In Wales, however, while Plaid Cymru

Table 6.2 Party support and voting choice in four referendums (% Yes)

	Con (%)	Labour (%)	Lib (Dem) (%)	SNP/Plaid Cymru (%)
Stay in EC (1975)	83	53	67	–
Scottish Assembly (1979)	21	66	–	91
Scottish Parliament (1997)	19	93	73	97
Welsh Assembly (1997)	10	59	29	93

Notes: The third column refers to Liberal supporters in 1975 and 1979 and Liberal Democrats in the 1990s. There were too few Liberals for analysis in 1979. The figures for Scotland in 1997 relate to the first referendum question, on the principle of establishing a Scottish Parliament.

Sources: Gallup (1978); Bochel and Denver (1981); author's survey of Scottish electorate, 1997; CREST survey of Welsh electorate 1997

supporters recorded a huge 'Yes' vote, Labour supporters were relatively lukewarm. Conservatives were strongly opposed and less that one-third of Liberal Democrats voted for an Assembly, despite the fact that their party campaigned strongly for devolution.

There is evidence, then, that referendum voting is frequently related to party preference. This is not to say that voters simply fall into line behind their parties and follow their advice about how to vote. Rather, it is the case that the positions adopted by parties are in tune with the previously-established preferences of their supporters on the issue concerned. Voting on party lines is far from the whole story, however. In Scotland and Wales in 1997, for example, the more Scottish or Welsh and less British people felt themselves to be, the more likely they were to support the devolution proposals (see Pattie et al., 1999). Moreover, opinion poll evidence from the 1975 EC referendum suggests that voters were quite well informed about the issues involved and seem to have based their vote on the merits of the case, as they saw them (Butler and Kitzinger, 1976: 253–5). In the case of the Scottish and Welsh 1997 referendums there is more soundly-based evidence that, independently of party supported, voters cast their ballots on the basis of their judgements concerning the pros and cons of devolution (Surridge and McCrone, 1999; Denver, 2000). This is good news for proponents of referendums since what the device is supposed to do is reveal the genuine preferences of the electorate based on careful consideration of the issue concerned.

Referendum outcomes

The results of United Kingdom referendums are summarised in Table 6.3. The three cases in the 1970s resulted in no change to the *status quo*. The decisive 'Yes' victory in the EC referendum was a vote to *remain* in the Community; the small majority for devolution in Scotland was not enough to overcome the qualified majority condition noted above; Wales rejected devolution by a huge majority. In contrast, the most recent referendums all produced majorities for radical change. It is sometimes suggested that referendums are essentially conservative devices

Table 6.3 Results of United Kingdom referendums

Year	Question	Yes (%)	No (%)	Result	Government preference
1975	Remain in EC?	67.2	32.8	Yes	Yes
1979	Establish Scottish Assembly?	51.6	48.4	No	Yes
1979	Establish Welsh Assembly?	20.3	79.7	No	Yes
1997	Establish Scottish Parliament?	74.3	25.7	Yes	Yes
1997	Tax-varying power for Scottish Parliament?	63.5	36.5	Yes	Yes
1997	Establish Welsh Assembly?	50.3	49.7	Yes	Yes
1998	Elect Mayor for London?	72.0	28.0	Yes	Yes
1998	Approve Good Friday Agreement	71.1	28.9	Yes	Yes

since the mass of voters are cautious about endorsing change. A nineteenth-century opponent of referendums argued, for example, that if popular opinion had its way, then there would have been:

> no reformation of religion, no change of dynasty, no toleration of Dissent, not even an accurate calendar. The threshing machine, the power loom, the spinning jenny and possibly the steam engine would have been prohibited.
> (cited in Marshall, 1997: 307)

The results of recent British referendums flatly contradict this view. However, the generalisation that governments usually win government-sponsored referendums (see Butler and Ranney, 1994: 261) applies in Britain since the government position has been supported in all but two cases.

A more subtle version of the last generalisation suggests that referendum outcomes have little to do with the merits of the issue concerned but, when instigated by governments, simply reflect the current popularity of the government. Thus, Franklin et al. (1995) suggest that, when governments take a position on referendum issues, voters use their referendum vote simply to indicate their approval or otherwise of the government. Evidence on this point from the British experience of referendums is mixed. In the run-up to the June 1975 referendum the government, led by Harold Wilson, was becoming more unpopular. At the start of the year, according to Gallup, 37% of voters approved of the government's record to date and 38% disapproved but in subsequent months the net approval rating (percentage approve minus percentage disapprove) declined from −1 to −29 in May. Similarly, the Prime Minister's rating (percentage satisfied minus percentage dissatisfied) was +11 in January but −9 in May (Gallup, 1975). This hardly mattered, however, as the campaign for a 'Yes' vote was supported not just by the government but also by the opposition parties, the Conservatives and Liberals. Contrariwise, the referendums on devolution in 1979 were held at a time of extreme government unpopularity and resulted in rejections of government policy. Bochel and Denver (1981: 144) argued that support for devolution in Scotland fell away dramatically in the months before the referendum because the Labour government and the Prime Minister, James Callaghan, became very unpopular for reasons quite unconnected with devolution, namely industrial unrest associated with the 'winter of discontent'. In complete contrast, the referendums of the 1990s took place while the new government and Prime Minister, Tony Blair, were enjoying an unprecedented 'honeymoon' with the electorate. This may help to account for the sweeping victory for devolution in Scotland, but there is no reason to suppose that Blair and the government were any less popular in Wales and this was not enough to avert a very close shave. All the major parties were on the same side in the Northern Ireland and London referendums so that, once again, it is difficult to argue that government popularity played any part in the outcomes.

A strong argument in favour of the use of referendums, as noted above, is that they confer greater legitimacy on the decision reached than is the case with a decision made by politicians through the normal channels. Decisions made by elites can be contested endlessly but once the people have spoken, as it were, then that is the end of the matter – for some time, at least. For example, the referendum decision to remain in the European Community was taken – decisively – more than twenty-five years ago and during that time there has been little support among mainstream politicians, including Eurosceptics, for raising the question of withdrawing entirely. Similarly, the impressive level of support for devolution in the second Scottish referendum ensured that the result was widely accepted. In the debate in the House of Commons on the bill to implement the devolution proposals, the Conservative spokesman, Michael Ancram, announced that his party would not oppose the principle of the bill since they accepted and respected 'the democratically expressed view' and 'clear decision of the Scottish people' (quoted in Denver et al., 2000: 188). In addition, the result of the referendum in Northern Ireland clearly settled the question of whether the proposals agreed by the negotiating parties should be pursued and, in subsequent debates, citing the result proved an effective way of countering the arguments of die-hard opponents of change.

However, referendums can backfire in this respect. Perhaps the most significant message of the London result was that voters did not care very much about reforming the system of local government while the result in Wales in 1997 was almost an embarrassment for the government. Barely half of the Welsh electorate voted and only just over half of them supported devolution. This was not a ringing endorsement. The referendum failed to give very much added legitimacy to the Welsh Assembly, which clearly rests on much shakier ground than the Scottish Parliament.

Summary

- Only governments can call referendums in the United Kingdom.
- Most referendums have been called for party-political reasons.
- Participation rates in referendums have varied but have almost always been lower than in general elections.
- Voting in referendums is frequently structured by party support but in some cases is clearly based on evaluations relating to the issue in question.
- Recent referendums have initiated radical changes.
- Referendums frequently, but not always, give greater legitimacy to the decisions made.

Debate

The use of referendums in Britain raises two important issues of debate. First, should we have more of them and, if so, on what subjects? Second, if further referendums do take place, what rules should be laid down concerning how they should be run?

More referendums?

As we have already seen, there have been only seven significant referendums in the UK and they have been restricted to broadly constitutional issues. Contrariwise, other constitutional issues – such as the major reform of the House of Lords carried out in 1999 and the introduction of proportional representation for the 1999 European Parliament elections – have not been subject to a referendum. British referendums have, therefore, been on *selected* constitutional issues. There is little doubt that the electorate approve of referendums on these sorts of matter. The 1997 British Election Study (BES) survey asked respondents whether decisions on joining the European single currency and introducing proportional representation for Westminster elections should be made by elected politicians or by means of a referendum. Only 14% and 15% respectively preferred politicians to decide compared with 76% and 67% opting for a referendum (the remainder being unable to state a preference). More generally, two MORI polls in the 1990s asked respondents whether Parliament should decide all important issues or there should be referendums putting certain issues to the people. In both cases large majorities (75% and 77%) opted for referendums (Constitution Unit, 1996).

In addition, the electorate appears to favour extending referendums to other sorts of issue. As far back as 1978, Gallup reported that large majorities wanted a referendum held on the re-introduction of capital punishment (83%), immigration policy (74%), the power of trade unions (64%) and further nationalisation of industries (60%) (Gallup, 1978). In the 1990s, opinion polls found that between 60% and 80% of the electorate would like to see a referendum on the death penalty (Constitution Unit, 1996).

The views of the political parties are less clear-cut. In the past, the Conservatives in government have been generally hostile to referendums (all of those held so far have been instigated by Labour governments), viewing them as unnecessary constitutional innovations. Some Conservative politicians occasionally call for referendums on issues on which the public is presumed to be more conservative than politicians (such as capital punishment or policy towards asylum-seekers), but the party leadership, fearing that holding referendums on issues such as these would open a Pandora's box, has not been keen on the idea. Nonetheless, like the other parties, the Conservatives have agreed to hold a referendum on any move to take Britain into the single European currency.

Among the major parties the Liberal Democrats are perhaps most closely identified with the values of participatory democracy. Nonetheless, the party does not have a firm view about the use of referendums and certainly has not advocated that they should be used more widely. The ideas of participatory democracy have also influenced recent thinking in the Labour Party. Within the party attempts have been made to widen participation by extending voting rights to all members (in the selection of candidates, for example) and having ballots of the membership on key issues (such as the revision of Clause Four of the party constitution in 1995). In addition, there has been a concern to increase participation in relation to local government and a government consultation paper implied support for a greater degree of direct democracy at a local level (DETR, 1998). Nonetheless, the exigencies of practical politics have had more to do with triggering British referendums than theoretical considerations related to participatory democracy. Even so, New Labour under Tony Blair has a greater interest in constitutional change than either 'Old Labour' or the Conservatives, and as long as they remain in power further referendums are likely. It should be emphasised, however, that no party has considered allowing referendums to be held on the initiative of anyone other than the government.

The questions of whether or not there should be greater use of referendums in the UK, and on what subjects, are clearly normative. That is, the answers given depends on making value judgements about the nature of democracy. As suggested above, the issues are fairly straightforward. On the one hand, those who emphasise popular sovereignty, majority rule and the widest possible participation would be likely to lean towards having more referendums on a wider range of issues than hitherto. On the other, those who fear majority tyranny and argue that government works best when citizens delegate their authority over day-to-day decisions to elected representatives would take a more restrictive view. The idea that referendums allow decisions to be made by ignorant and uncomprehending voters who fail to think through the consequences of their actions is not an essential element of this point of view but it worth noting that, with the exception of the vote on the London Mayor, there is no evidence that the electorate were anything but perfectly well informed about the issues which have been the subjects of referendums in the UK.

Clearly there can be extreme views on these questions – ranging from wanting no referendums at all to favouring votes on everything under the sun – and a variety of positions in between. Vernon Bogdanor, for example, argues that under certain circumstances wider use of the referendum 'could offer real benefits in the operation of British politics. It would prove a powerful weapon against . . . "elective dictatorship"' (1981: 93). He is one of those who subscribes to the view that referendums on subjects of major importance are useful supplements to the operation of parliamentary democracy, which is probably also the view of most citizens and politicians.

Summary

- There is strong public support for more frequent use of referendums.
- Although there are differences between them, political parties are generally less enthusiastic, preferring occasional use on constitutional issues only.
- Attitudes to greater use of referendums vary and depend on the importance ascribed to different elements of democratic theory.

Referendum rules

The rules under which British referendums have been conducted have been drawn up, hitherto, in an *ad hoc* way. In 1975 the rules and procedures for the first national referendum were drawn up by civil servants in the space of two months and incorporated into the Referendum Act. Butler and Kitzinger suggest that this was 'an administrative triumph for a small group of civil servants who were charged with devising clear and acceptable rules to cope with a situation that had no precedent' (1976: 66). Rules were agreed which covered technical matters such as the voting rights of service personnel and the areas within which votes should be counted and for which results should be announced (eventually counties in England and Wales and regions in Scotland), as well as more political issues – the wording of the referendum question, campaign finance, the role of the government and broadcasting policy. The most salient points to note about the conduct of the referendum are as follows:

- 'Umbrella groups' (Britain In Europe and the National Referendum Campaign) were formed to campaign for a 'Yes' and 'No' vote respectively. Each received a government grant of £125,000 and a free leaflet delivery.
- A government leaflet was delivered to every household advocating a 'Yes' vote.
- At the suggestion of the government, the broadcasting authorities gave each side four free referendum broadcasts on television during the campaign.
- No limits were fixed for campaign expenditure.

In the 1979 devolution referendums different rules applied. In addition to the imposition of the '40% rule' referred to above, there were no financial grants or free leaflet deliveries for campaigning organisations, and no official leaflet setting out the government's position was distributed. These referendums also threw up problems in relation to broadcasting. It was originally planned to allow each party to make a referendum broadcast but, following a court case, this was abandoned. The problem centred on the question of 'balanced' political coverage which the broadcasters are obliged to provide. Since three of the four major parties in Scotland and Wales supported devolution, with only the Conservatives advocating a 'No' vote, it was argued that allowing party broadcasts would unduly favour the 'Yes' campaign. Since there were a number of non-party and cross-party campaigning groups, it was impossible to allocate broadcasts to 'umbrella' groups and so there were no referendum broadcasts at all. Despite broadcasters' pleas for government guidance on the issue, it remained unresolved and the problem recurred in the 1997 referendums.

Devising rules and procedures for referendums in this *ad hoc* way is clearly unsatisfactory and in anticipation of further referendums the Constitution Unit and the Electoral Reform Society set up an independent commission on the conduct of referendums in April 1996. In its report (Constitution Unit, 1996) the commission proposed a number of guidelines for future referendums, including the establishment of an Electoral Commission to oversee the process, government finance for 'umbrella' organisations, equal access to the broadcast media for both sides and a ban on the use of government (as opposed to party) resources to promote one side or the other. These sorts of issue were raised again in the fifth report of the Committee on Standards in Public Life (the Neill Committee) (HMSO, 1998). Although the committee's brief was to consider the funding of political parties, it turned its attention to referendums and made a series of proposals about how they should be conducted. These were largely accepted by the government and in November 2000 an act was passed (the Parties, Elections and Referendums Act). Among other things, this provided a regulatory framework for the conduct of British referendums. An independent Electoral Commission was established to oversee the referendum process (as well as elections). Parties, individuals and organisations which wish to participate in a referendum campaign are now required to register as 'permitted participants'. They can then apply to be 'designated' as the official campaign group for one side or the other and the Commission will select 'whichever of the applicants appears to them to represent to the greatest extent those campaigning for that outcome'. Designated organisations will receive a grant (not more than £600,000) plus a free delivery of leaflets, the free use of schools for public meetings and an equal number of campaign broadcasts. Campaign expenditure will be limited and the government (*qua* government) will not be allowed to participate in the campaign other than to provide factual information.

In general, these rules and regulations represent a first attempt to ensure a level playing field for the two sides in a referendum campaign. The authors of the bill clearly hope that one large 'umbrella' group will emerge on each side and be the obvious candidate for 'designation'. If, however, there are a number of groups seeking designation – as would have been the case in Scotland in 1979 – then the Commission could find itself in a politically-sensitive position. In addition, it might be suggested that the rules are too generous to minority opinion. In Scotland in 1997 and in the referendum on the London Mayor public opinion was overwhelmingly on one side. Giving those who opposed devolution and did not want an elected mayor equal finance, television coverage and so on would confer unwarranted status on minorities. Finally, if a government calls a referendum in pursuit of its own policy – as all to date have been – it might be argued that it is unduly restrictive not to allow the government to use its resources to make its position clear to the electorate. There is, then, room for debate about the details of the regulations but what is significant is that we now have a set of referendum rules and they reflect a view of referendums as being mechanisms allowing genuine decision-making by the electorate rather than simply instruments of government policy.

Summary

- The rules governing referendums in Britain have until now been developed in an *ad hoc* way.
- Future referendums will be conducted according to a new set of regulations designed to ensure a level playing field for both sides in referendum campaigns.

Conclusion

Referendums in the UK have partially fulfilled the hopes of those who advocate their greater use. They have made a contribution to the opening up of the policy process by allowing popular participation on important constitutional issues and have bestowed greater legitimacy on the decisions made than might have been the case if politicians alone had made them. In addition, they have helped to resolve issues which governments found difficult to handle. Representative democracy does not appear to have been undermined and, rather than weakening the party system, as some critics anticipated, may have helped to hold parties together when internal divisions could have led to splits. With new permanent arrangements for conducting referendums now on the statute book, there seems little doubt that further referendums will be called. Indeed, there seems now to be an expectation among both voters and politicians that major constitutional changes should be submitted to a vote by the people. To that extent it may be said that, on a limited range of constitutional issues and as a valuable supplement to the normal operations of parliamentary democracy, the referendum is becoming an accepted part of the British Constitution.

Discussion Questions

1. Do referendums enhance democracy?
2. What arguments can be advanced for and against holding a referendum on the restoration of capital punishment in the UK?
3. Should public funds be granted to campaigning organisations in referendums?

Note

1. In addition to those listed, there was also a referendum in Northern Ireland in 1973 relating to the constitutional status of the Province. This was boycotted by nationalists, however, and was not, therefore, very meaningful.

References

Bochel, J. and Denver, D. (1981) 'The outcome', in J. Bochel, D. Denver, and A. Macartney (eds) *The Referendum Experience: Scotland 1979*, Aberdeen: Aberdeen University Press, pp. 140–6.

Bogdanor, V. (1981) *The People and the Party System: The Referendum and Electoral Reform in British Politics*, Cambridge: Cambridge University Press.

Butler, D. and Kitzinger, U. (1976) *The 1975 Referendum*, London: Macmillan.

Butler, D. and Ranney, A. (1994) *Referendums around the World: The Growing Use of Direct Democracy*, Washington, DC: American Enterprise Institute.

Constitution Unit (1996) *Report of the Commission on the Conduct of Referendums*, London: Constitution Unit.

Denver, D. (2000) 'Voting in the 1997 Scottish and Welsh referendums', paper presented at the 2000 IPSA world congress, Quebec.

Denver, D., Mitchell, J., Pattie, C. and Bochel, H. (2000) *Scotland Decides: The Devolution Issue and the Scottish Referendum*, London: Frank Cass.

DETR (1998) *Modernising Local Government: Local Democracy and Community Leadership*, London: DETR.

Franklin, M., van der Eijk, C. and Marsh, M. (1995) 'Referendum outcomes and trust in government: public support for Europe in the wake of Maastricht', *West European Politics*, Vol. 18, No. 3, pp. 101–7.

Gallup (1975) *Political Index*, Reports 174–9.

Gallup (1978) *Political Index*, Report 219.

HMSO (1998) *Fifth Report of the Committee on Standards in Public Life: The Funding of Political Parties in the UK*, cm. 4057, London: HM Stationery Office.

Marshall, G. (1997) 'The referendum: what, when and how?', *Parliamentary Affairs*, Vol. 50, No. 2, pp. 307–13.

Pattie, C., Denver, D., Mitchell, J. and Bochel, H. (1999) 'Settled will or divided society? Voting in the 1997 Scottish and Welsh referendums', in P. Cowley, D. Denver, J. Fisher and A. Russell (eds) *British Elections and Parties Yearbook*, Vol. 9, pp. 136–53.

Surridge, P. and McCrone, D. (1999) 'The 1997 Scottish referendum vote', in B. Taylor and K. Thomson (eds) *Scotland and Wales: Nations Again?*, Cardiff: University of Wales Press.

Further reading

A useful account of the theory relating to referendums and the history of debates over their use in Britain up to 1981 is given in V. Bogdanor (1981) *The People and the Party System: The Referendum and Electoral Reform in British Politics* (Cambridge: Cambridge University Press). Studies of individual British referendums include D. Butler and U. Kitzinger (1976) *The 1975 Referendum* (London: Macmillan, reprinted 1996); J. Bochel, D. Denver and A. Macartney (1981) *The Referendum Experience: Scotland 1979* (Aberdeen: Aberdeen University Press); B. Taylor and K. Thomson (eds) (1999) *Scotland and Wales: Nations Again?* (Cardiff: University of Wales Press); D. Balsom, and J.B. Jones (eds) (2000) *Road to the National Assembly for Wales* (Cardiff: University of Wales Press); and D. Denver, J. Mitchell, C. Pattie and H. Bochel (2000) *Scotland Decides: The Devolution Issue and the Scottish Referendum* (London: Frank Cass).

For comparative accounts (which also include material on the UK), see D. Butler and A. Ranney (1994) *Referendums around the World: The Growing Use of Direct Democracy* (Washington, DC: American Enterprise Institute) and M. Gallagher and P.V. Uleri (eds) (1996) *The Referendum Experience in Europe* (Basingstoke: Macmillan).

Change in Parliament

Peter J. Laugharne

CHAPTER SEVEN

Background

The British Parliament at Westminster is not a legislature renowned for undergoing change. During the twentieth century it underwent sporadic periods of change interspersed by longer periods of institutional inertia or only minimal development. This reflects the fact that in the British political system the executive is drawn from the legislature and the executive normally controls the most politically significant chamber, the House of Commons (the Lower House). Given this, change usually only occurs with the support or at least the acquiescence of government, but the executive is invariably wary of making any precipitate changes that might strengthen the hand of Parliament in the balance of power between executive and legislature. It is seldom in the executive's interest to initiate fundamental change as it is often controversial, time consuming and reduces the opportunities to legislate in other areas.

Nevertheless, the advent of the New Labour government in 1997, after the party had spent eighteen years pondering change in opposition, promised much in relation to redressing the historic power imbalance between legislature and executive, and in addressing the ongoing anomaly in a liberal democratic polity of an entirely unelected second legislative chamber: the House of Lords (the Upper House):

> The . . . election for the first time created the political conditions for either some genuine first steps in a coherent strategy of both modernization and reform, or for the need to create the appearance thereof. The secure majority promised a fundamental stability to the Government, but the majority would itself feel much less need for self-restraint. Many cynics murmured that there was need to beat the Devil to the task of finding time-consuming work for idle hands. For these idle hands were remarkably able and well-trained hands, not all absorbable in the Government, but nearly all likely to be restive if treated simply as lobby fodder. The most effective opposition might well come from within the Government's own Party.
>
> (Crick, 1968: 209–10)

Bernard Crick's observations could easily relate to the return of Tony Blair's Labour government in 1997. A government elected with an overwhelming majority, promising radical change predicated on the knowledge that it would retain its parliamentary supremacy for an entire term, was in sharp contrast to the vicissitudes and uncertainty of the Major years. A majority of 179 could pose problems however, and might inspire dissent if the backbenchers could not be kept sated, particularly as many had significant experience of senior office in local government or were professionally employed in politics. Yet Crick was writing not about 1997 but the 1966 general election. *Plus ça change* . . .

As this illustrates, many of the circumstances of British politics, and arguments concerning parliamentary reform are not new but have existed for a very long time. Aspects of the British political system are positively ancient in comparison to those of many other states. It is also a corollary of the fact that reforms that have been introduced tend to be relatively minor intra-institutional changes that have not addressed the fundamental constitutional settlement. The powers of the executive, legislative and judicial branches of government have not significantly altered, although since the nineteenth century the executive has undoubtedly increasingly dominated the entire political system.

Parliament is currently going through a period of what appears superficially to be significant change, as there now are material differences in its composition and procedures in comparison to earlier periods (such as prior to the 1997 general election). However, these changes need to be set in the context of relative institutional continuity. Parliament has comprised three constituent parts for centuries: the House of Commons, the House of Lords and the monarch (the queen or king in Parliament), and this constitutional triumvirate remains. Consequently, change in Parliament, when located in systemic context, is normally less than a constitutional rollercoaster but on occasion can be more than a placid legislative carousel.

Contrary to popular mythology, Westminster is not frozen in aspic, but is a dynamic legislature (see the chronology on p. 117 for some of the key changes to Parliament). The climate for reform in the period since 1997 has been as positive as any during the twentieth century, with the incoming Labour government wedded to the concept of modernisation and committed to constitutional reform. Whether that climate has precipitated fundamental reform is quite another matter.

Key Issues Concerning Change in Parliament

The composition and representativeness of the House of Commons

The House of Commons is a representative assembly in the sense that voters elect an individual MP to participate in proceedings at Westminster, and to represent a constituency and constituents, rather than directly participating in the legislative process themselves. In recent years the notion of representation has engendered significant debate. This especially relates to the social composition of the House of Commons, and increasingly the House of Lords, and also to the representation of women and ethnic minorities.

Reform of the House of Lords

The House of Lords is one of the oldest and certainly the largest second chamber of any legislature, having, until recently, a membership well in excess of 1,200. Its composition has, however, been a source of great political argument for more than a century, especially in relation to the majority of peers who held hereditary titles by accident of birth rather than obtained on personal merit. Numerous schemes for reform have been advocated over the years and now the argument is about how, rather than whether, to change the Upper House. Disagreements among reformers have played into the hands of conservatives who favour the *status quo*, and have contributed to change being incremental, though not insignificant, in the twentieth century. These include the reforms contained in the Parliament Acts of 1911 and 1949, circumscribing the powers of the Upper House and thus confirming the status of the House of Commons as the pre-eminent legislative chamber of the British Parliament. The crucial issue now relates to whether the Lords should be democratised and to what degree. The resolution of this issue will affect the legitimacy and inevitably the powers of the second chamber in relation to the Commons.

In many respects Labour has a vested interest in reforming the Upper House since it has been defeated in the Lords more times than Conservative governments, by a ratio of 8:1 since 1970. The changes that have taken place under the Blair government since 1997 are some of the most far-reaching and at the same time least radical to have been considered.

Modernisation of parliamentary procedures and practices

The procedures and practices of Parliament reflect its history, composition and constitutional position. For centuries, being a parliamentarian was regarded as a part-time interest rather than a full-time occupation. Many MPs had other calls on their time in the mornings, so the legislative day started in the afternoon and often extended late into the early hours of the following day. Little change occurred in this regard until recently, with demands, particularly from the growing number of women MPs and those with young families, to put the parliamentary day on a comparable footing to those of other professional occupations. Additionally, the legislature's involvement in law-making and scrutinising the policy and administration of government still owes a great deal to the nineteenth century, and it seems inadequate and ill-suited to the task of dealing with a powerful executive. This problem is compounded when one considers that the executive itself is attempting to keep pace with the demands of an increasingly dynamic, sophisticated society and global economy.

Redressing the imbalance of power between the executive and legislature

Since the advent of modern British government at the end of the nineteenth and beginning of the twentieth centuries, there has been a recognition, and in some quarters concern, over an increasing inequality in the distribution of political power between the legislature and executive in favour of the latter. In recent times attempts have been made to redress this, principally via the greater use of parliamentary committees.

The existence and use of committees in the work of Parliament can be traced back to medieval times (Laugharne, 1994: 21). The committee stage of the legislative process where a bill is considered in detail, normally by a standing committee, has long been an important part of the law-making process. However, in the past twenty years it is select committees not standing committees that have come into their own. In particular the Commons departmental select committees created in 1979 to 'shadow' government departments have obtained a high public profile and not inconsiderable power. Originally, there were fourteen departmental committees, but this has fluctuated as a consequence of modifications to the structure of government and the number of departments to be shadowed. The committees have the power to scrutinise the expenditure, policy and administration of government departments in a far more systematic manner than their predecessors. Yet there are continued demands to strengthen their powers and the resources at their disposal, and arguments concerning their efficacy and relationship to the floor of the House.

Parliamentary sovereignty, the European Union and globalisation

A basic principle of Britain's part-written but uncodified Constitution is that Parliament is sovereign. An Act of Parliament can make or repeal any law and a Parliament cannot bind its successors. Britain's retreat from empire, its membership of the European Union (EU), globalisation and the information and communication technology revolution all challenge this principle.

Britain joined the European Economic Community in 1973 and this was reaffirmed by a majority of two to one in the referendum of 1975. One of the key issues surrounding Britain's membership of what is now the European Union relates to Parliament's sovereignty over laws and public policy affecting the United Kingdom. Although Parliament is still theoretically sovereign in that it can repeal the legislation committing Britain to the EU (or even legislation granting colonies independence), in practice this is unlikely to occur. However, there appears to be popular unease, fuelled by Eurosceptic elements of the media, concerning what appears to be *Diktat* from Brussels, and this extends to a significant part of the Parliamentary Conservative and Labour parties.

Globalisation presents another challenge. There is strong evidence to suggest that governments across the world, let alone legislatures, have little sovereignty in practice over economic matters and transglobal communication. The drivers of the modern age are thus in the business rather than the political arena. Yet legislators are expected to shape public policy and hold the executive to account in areas over which they have marginal control.

Devolution of power from Whitehall and Westminster

Britain has one of, if not the, most centralised political systems of any liberal democratic polity. Yet at the same time it is a multinational state with many historic and cultural differences. Recognising this territorial dimension to British politics, various institutional arrangements and constitutional accommodations have been constructed by Westminster and Whitehall. These include territorial ministries, national parliamentary committees and dedicated debates. However, the rise of nationalism in Scotland and Wales and the lack of a political settlement in Northern Ireland have presented ongoing problems to government at the centre. Devolution of power to Scotland, Wales and Northern Ireland was one of the main planks of the 1997 Labour government's modernisation agenda. The impact on Westminster has been commensurate with the importance of these areas in legislative matters. Devolution has led to considerable and often heated argument about who should debate issues at Westminster.

Summary

The key arguments about parliamentary change concern:

- The composition and representativeness of the House of Commons.
- Reform of the House of Lords.
- Modernisation of parliamentary procedures and practices.
- Redressing the imbalance of power between the executive and legislature.
- Parliamentary sovereignty, the European Union and globalisation.
- Devolution of power from Whitehall and Westminster.

Theoretical Considerations

Westminster's position in the British constitutional settlement remains largely static. Theoretically, Parliament is sovereign but British government is government *through* Parliament not *by* Parliament. However, the British political system does not enjoy a neat Lockean separation of governmental branches such as exists in the United States. Rather, the Westminster system fuses elements of all three, personified in the office of the Lord Chancellor, who is a legislator, being a member of the House of Lords, head of the judiciary and a member of the executive as a Cabinet minister. Inevitably, there have been calls to separate the functions of the Lord Chancellor, which some regard as an affront to notions of judicial independence and executive accountability. The upshot of the fusion is that a government with a majority can, in normal circumstances, control the Commons sufficiently for the majority of its programme to be passed by the Lower House, though not necessarily in detail by the House of Lords.

In addition to being theoretically omnicompetent, Parliament continues to be a multi-functional legislature. It is a recruiting and training ground for ministers of the Crown drawn from the two Houses. It plays a role in the creation, scrutiny and review of public policy. It legislates. Additionally, it scrutinises the executive and the administration of government. Indeed, some authorities suggest that 'Central government's life is dominated by Parliament', ministers and officials being both preoccupied by, and apprehensive of, the legislature for the three-quarters of the year that it sits (James, 1999: 7; see also Ingham, quoted in Wright, 2000: 196). Nevertheless, in relation to the policy-making process, within a tri-partite typology of legislatures, Westminster falls between 'policy-making' and 'those with little or no policy effect' as a 'policy-influencing' body (Norton, 1993: 50–1). Policy-making is predominantly a function of the executive with individual legislators having only a marginal role.

Parliamentary reform is a perennial topic of argument in the drawing rooms of the political class, and has spawned a vast literature over the years. But, as Crick has mused, it '. . . is one of those things, as Mark Twain remarked about the weather, which everybody talks about, but nobody does anything about' (Crick, 1968: xv). What, then, is required for the talking to stop and the reform to begin? For ideas to become reality a number of conditions need to exist. Norton has suggested that dramatic change or paradigmatic reform in Parliament, such as the creation of the system of departmental select committees in the House of Commons in 1979, can be explained in terms of a hypothesis that it requires a combination of three independent variables:

1. A *window of opportunity*. This has two separate components, namely time and substance. The beginning of a new Parliament is the most opportune time to introduce structural and procedural change. Once a Parliament has commenced 'the likelihood (but not certainty)' is that the demands of the parliamentary process, constituency, interest group and other legislative business 'will take precedence over consideration of structure and procedures'. Once the meat of parliamentary activity is encountered, legislators will not have the leisure to be able to cogitate about the mechanics of the legislative process. Substantively, for change to occur there have to be proposals for change that normally originate in the Procedure Committee. There may be other sources of ideas for change, but that Committee has a head start given that it is an organ of the Commons, and can straightforwardly bring forward a report suggesting reform.
2. *Political will*. A window of opportunity is a necessary but insufficient condition for change. Legislators have to possess the political will so that proposals for reform are on the agenda, are debated and enacted. Mere approval of reforms emanating from the executive, as the experience of the Crossman specialist select committee experiments in the 1960s demonstrates, is not an expression of genuine political will, and reforms may therefore prove to be ephemeral.
3. A *facilitative Leader of the House*. The Leader of the House of Commons should assist in the utilisation of the window. Norton suggests it is unclear whether this need be voluntary or involuntary. Persistent cross-party pressure may result in a normally unfacilitative Leader in a weak legislative position, acquiescing to a debate and vote on proposals for change. Conforming to this scenario, Michael Foot, Leader of the House in the minority Callaghan government and proponent of the supremacy of the floor of the House over committees, acceded to a debate

challenging that view in 1978. This led to the creation of the departmental committees in 1979. A concession by a Leader assists, but advocacy of reform markedly improves, the climate for change. The Leader of the House arguably has a dual role as the Cabinet's representative in the Commons, and the Commons' mouthpiece in the Cabinet. If the latter role is favoured over the former, then the Leader is in a prime position to facilitate change (Norton, 1998).

Norton suggests that in 1979 all these conditions pertained, hence the departmental select committee reform introduced by Foot's Conservative successor, Norman St John Stevas. Between 1980 and 1997 the conditions were never entirely fulfilled and only Tony Newton, Leader of the House in the 1992–97 Parliament, oversaw any change, which was merely incremental (Norton, 1998). We shall apply Norton's theory to the 1997 Parliament in the next section.

The relationship between Parliament and the public is central in terms of its legitimacy and ability to mobilise public consent (Beer, 1966; Packenham, 1970). This has been a cause for concern in recent times, as public disquiet has increased over the impropriety of certain parliamentarians. It led Parliament to attempt to improve and regulate the conduct of its members, through the appointment of the Parliamentary Commissioner for Standards after heated debates in 1995.

At the heart of legislative legitimacy is the notion of representation. We can conceive of representation in three senses: first, as involving the election of an MP to represent the views of constituents in and to Parliament; second, in the Burkean sense of an MP representing the best interests of the constituency in a way that may or may not correspond with the views of constituents themselves; third, in a socio-economic sense, involving the MP personally reflecting the social and economic characteristics of constituents. It is this third conception that has given rise to demands for change at Westminster in recent times, with the invocation in some quarters of a normative view that for Parliament to possess legitimacy, MPs should reflect the social composition of the electorate and/or the population at large.

Political parties are the predominant determinants of the social composition of the legislature, since it is their members and selection procedures that produce candidates for election, and form the pool from which electors choose their MP. If parties and the candidates they select are not socially representative, then neither will be the House of Commons. Similarly, with a now predominantly appointed Upper House, the social characteristics of party appointees increasingly shape its composition.

Summary

- British government is government *through* Parliament not *by* Parliament.
- The Westminster system fuses all three branches of government.
- Parliament is a multi-functional legislature.
- Westminster is a policy-influencing legislature.
- Parliament's relationship with the public conditions and is conditioned by its legitimacy and ability to mobilise consent.

- Change requires a window of opportunity, political will and a facilitative Leader of the House.
- The normative theory of socio-economic representation has increasing public resonance.

Update

The 1997 general election, which saw the return of a Labour government with an overwhelming majority in the House of Commons (see Table 7.1), is viewed by many as a watershed in British politics. Parliament has been perceived as a male-dominated, white, middle-aged, middle-class institution and there remains much truth in that characterisation. Table 7.2 shows the make-up of the House of Commons in terms of previous occupation after the 2001 general elections. The changes required for the legislature to reflect British society in terms of age, gender, occupation, race, religion, sexuality or even ability are immense, and in practice an impossibility, given the legal barriers that exist. Four per cent of the electorate is disqualified from membership of the Commons by dint of their profession. These include civil servants, members of the armed forces, police officers, judges and clergy of the Church of England, the Church of Scotland and the Roman Catholic Church (Silk and Walters, 1998: 11). Peers who are members of the House of Lords, prisoners sentenced for more than one year, and those less than 21 years of age are similarly debarred.

The main change in the composition of the Commons as a result of the 1997 general election was the markedly increased number of women MPs (Table 7.3). The election produced the largest-ever representation of women, with 120 returned in total, compared to only 19 in 1979. However, the distribution across

Table 7.1 Party strengths in the Commons after the 1997 and 2001 general elections

Party	1997	2001
Labour	418	412
Conservative	165	166
Liberal Democrats	46	52
Ulster Unionists	10	6
Scottish National Party	6	5
Plaid Cymru	4	4
Social Democratic and Labour Party	3	3
Ulster Democratic Unionist Party	2	5
Sinn Fein	2	4
United Kingdom Unionist	1	0
Independent	1	1
The Speaker	1	1
Total	659	659

Source: http://www.parliament.uk

Table 7.2 Occupation of candidates for the three largest parties elected members of Parliament at the 2001 general election

	Labour	Con	Lib Dem
Professions			
Barrister	13	18	2
Solicitor	18	13	4
Doctor/dentist/optician	2	3	3
Architect/surveyor	1	4	1
Civil/chartered engineer	5	1	1
Accountant	2	3	1
Civil service/local government:	30	2	3
Armed services	1	11	0
Teachers:			
University	18	1	2
Polytechnic/college	31	0	1
School	49	6	9
Other consultancies	3	2	0
Scientific/research	6	0	0
Total	179	64	27
	(43%)	(39%)	(52%)
Business			
Company director	5	18	6
Company executive	10	31	7
Commerce/insurance	2	6	0
Management/clerical	12	2	1
General business	4	3	0
Total	33	60	14
	(8%)	(36%)	(27%)
Miscellaneous			
Misc. white collar	73	2	1
Politician/political organiser	44	18	4
Publisher/journalist	32	14	4
Farmer	0	5	1
Housewife	0	2	0
Student	0	0	0
Total	149	41	10
	(36%)	(25%)	(19%)
Manual workers			
Miner	11	1	0
Skilled worker	37	0	1
Semi/unskilled	3	0	0
Total	51	1	1
	(12%)	(1%)	(2%)
Grand total	412	166	52

Source: Butler and Kavanagh (2001)

Table 7.3 Women MPs elected at the 1997 and 2001 general elections

	1997	2001
Labour	101	95
Conservative	13	14
Liberal Democrats	3	5
Scottish National Party	2	1
The Speaker	1	0
Sinn Fein	0	1
UUP	0	1
DUP	0	1
Total	120	118

Source: Butler and Kavanagh (1997, 2001)

parties was highly uneven, with 101 Labour and only 13 Conservatives, a pattern maintained in 2001. In part this reflected Labour's parliamentary candidate selection procedures that originally designated half of all vacant winnable seats for women candidates before being deemed unlawful. To address this problem, Labour introduced the Sex Discrimination (Election Candidates) Bill in the autumn of 2001, to exclude from the operation of the Sex Discrimination Act 1975 certain matters related to the selection of candidates by political parties. In contrast, although Conservative Central Office attempted to put more women on its candidate list, local parties were reluctant to select them (Criddle, 1997). Notwithstanding the increased number of female MPs, women remain under-represented. The black and Asian communities also continue to be under-represented with a total of only nine MPs from these groups being elected in 1997 and 12 in 2001 – all for Labour. There are likely to be renewed demands for improved representation of ethnic minorities.

We examined earlier Norton's theory on change and can now apply it to the Blair government. The large Labour majority in 1997 certainly provided a window of opportunity and, with the new government committed to modernisation, there also seemed to be political will. However, with a whole raft of changes being implemented in areas ranging from relative autonomy for the Bank of England in monetary policy to devolution, perhaps the political will for change was dissipated. Additionally, Ann Taylor, the new Leader of the Commons in 1997, though initially seemingly open-minded and operating in a House where there appeared to be a climate favouring substantial change, proved in the final analysis to be rather conservative, rather than facilitative in relation to fundamental reform. That pattern was largely replicated by her immediate successor, Margaret Beckett, as has been the case with the majority of holders of that Cabinet portfolio. Robin Cook, demoted from Foreign Secretary to Leader of the Commons following the 2001 general election, has an opportunity to harness support from the Labour backbenches and bring about genuine radical transformation.

One of the potentially key drivers of change is the House of Commons Select Committee on Modernisation established in June 1997. Box 7.1 lists the topics of the Committee's reports. It has produced change in a number of areas, perhaps

Box 7.1 Modernisation of the House of Commons select committee reports

Session 1997–98

29 July 1997   First Report, The Legislative Process, HC 190
29 July 1997   First Special Report, HC 191
9 December 1997   Second Report, Explanatory Material for Bills, HC 389
9 March 1998   Third Report, Carry-over of Public Bills, HC 543
9 March 1998   Fourth Report, Conduct in the Chamber, HC 600
29 April 1998   Fifth Report, Consultation Paper on Voting Methods, HC 699
5 June 1998   Sixth Report, Voting Methods, HC779
17 June 1998   Seventh Report, The Scrutiny of European Business, HC 791

Session 1998–99

7 December 1998   First Report, The Parliamentary Calendar: Initial Proposals, HC 60
13 April 1999   Second Report, Sittings of the House in Westminster Hall, HC 194
19 July 1999   Third Report, Thursday Sittings, HC 719
1 November 1999   First Special Report, Work of the Committee: Second Progress Report, HC 865

Session 1999–00

10 April 2000   First Report, Facilities for the Media, HC 408
6 July 2000   Second Report, Programming of Legislation and Timing of Votes, HC 589
6 November 2000   Third Report, Thursday Sittings, HC 954
13 November 2000   Fourth Report, Sittings in Westminster Hall, HC 906

Session 2000–01

2 April 2001   First Report, Programming of Legislation, HC 382

Session 2001–02

12 December 2001   Modernisation of the House of Commons: A Reform Programme for Consultation, HC 440

Source: http://www.publications.parliament.uk

most notably in relation to an additional chamber inaugurated on 30 November 1999, known as Westminster Hall, although in fact it occupies the Grand Committee Room at the side of the Hall. This parallel chamber, which is semi-circular in shape, is based on the model of the Australian legislature and is intended to deal with uncontroversial matters encompassing bills, committee reports, government papers, private members' debates and adjournment motions. It sits on Tuesdays from 10 am to 1 pm and on Wednesdays from 9.30 am to 2 pm for adjournment debates and on Thursdays from 2.30 pm for up to three hours to debate select committee reports and deal with other parliamentary business.

Procedures and all the rights and privileges relating to debates in the Commons apply to the new forum. Orders and resolutions agreed in the Hall are reported to the House by the Deputy Speaker and then designated an order or resolution of the House. The quorum for proceedings is only three and at the termination of each sitting the Deputy Speaker adjourns debate without putting any question, thereby lapsing any unfinished matters. Four members have been appointed as additional Deputy Speakers who may take the Chair in Westminster Hall, as may the existing Commons Deputy Speakers. The key difference is that the new office holders are not required to relinquish their political identities, as is the case for the Commons Speaker and deputies (House of Commons, Public Information Office, 1999). The new chamber proved to be an instant success with backbench members in the sense that they have been extremely eager to get issues accepted for discussion. However, attendance at debates has been sparse. Nevertheless, Westminster Hall provides a further forum for interchange between legislators and considers matters that would almost certainly not otherwise be discussed.

Another change implemented in recent years relates to the business hours of the Commons that, as discussed earlier, for centuries reflected the part-time nature of legislative activity. Following the 'Jopling' reforms of December 1994, and the proposals of the Select Committee on Modernisation agreed in December 1998 and implemented from January 1999, the Commons now normally sits (begins business) at 2.30 pm on Mondays, Tuesdays and Wednesdays, 11.30 am on Thursdays and 9.30 am on Fridays. The hour for 'rising' (terminating proceedings) is 10.30 pm from Monday to Wednesday, 7.30 pm on Thursdays and usually 3 pm on Fridays. However, frequently from Monday to Thursday a motion is passed to extend the length of the sitting (House of Commons, Public Information Office, 1999). Prime Minister's question time has also changed. Whereas it previously took place for fifteen minutes each Tuesday and Thursday, it now occupies a thirty-minute slot on Wednesday afternoons. The Modernisation Committee also recommended that bills be permitted to roll over from one session to another, a good example being the consideration of the lengthy and extremely complex bill that eventually became the Financial Services and Markets Act 2000. Timetabling of legislation is another area in which the Committee's views have been put into practice.

The departmental select committees have also been an area of change. Currently, there are fifteen committees that scrutinise major government departments and these are shown in Table 7.4. Additionally, there are seven that may be regarded as 'cross-cutting' select committees: Deregulation, Environmental Audit, European Scrutiny, Public Accounts, Public Administration, Science and Technology and Statutory Instruments. The committees have powers to send for people, papers and records although a committee cannot order the attendance of members of either House of Parliament. The departmental committees are much improved over their predecessors, which were unsystematic in their scrutiny of government activity. However, senior backbench members have frequently expressed concern regarding the need to shift the balance of power from the executive to the legislature by increasing committee powers, enhancing resources and providing an alternative career path for backbenchers as chairs of committees (Laugharne, 1994). Most recently these demands have been re-articulated in a

Table 7.4 House of Commons departmental select committees

Committee	Principal department	Membership	Quorum
Culture, Media and Sport	Department of Culture, Media and Sport	11	3
Defence	Ministry of Defence	11	3
Education and Skills	Department for Education and Skills	11	3
Environment, Food and Rural Affairs	Department of the Environment, Food and Rural Affairs	17	5
Transport, Local Government and the Regions	Department of Transport, Local Government and the Regions	17	5
Foreign Affairs	Foreign and Commonwealth Office	11	3
Health	Department of Health	11	3
Home Affairs	Home Office; Lord Chancellor's Department; Attorney General's Office; Treasury Solicitor's Department; Crown Prosecution Service; Serious Fraud Office	11	3
International Development	Department for International Development	11	3
Northern Ireland Affairs	Northern Ireland Office; Crown Solicitor's Office	13	4
Scottish Affairs	Scottish Office; Lord Advocate's Departments	11	3
Trade and Industry	Department of Trade and Industry	11	3
Treasury	HM Treasury; Board of Inland Revenue; Board of Customs and Excise	12	3
Welsh Affairs	Welsh Office	11	3
Work and Pensions	Department of Work and Pensions	11	3

Source: http://www.parliament.uk/commons/selcom/ctteesys.htm

report from the committee of select committee chairmen (Select Committee on Liaison, 2000).

There have been attempts to integrate the standing and select committee processes. For example, the Commons Select Committee on European Legislation can recommend that European proposals be tabled for debate at special standing committees where ministers may be questioned, prior to their being discussed in the EU Council of Ministers. Similarly, it is possible to send bills to special standing committees or for them to be considered by select committees in the pre-legislative phase. One particular change consistent with the New Labour concept of 'joined-up government', though not itself entirely novel, is to have thematic select committees. One such is the Environmental Audit Select Committee which examines the impact on the environment of public policies from the full range of government departments (Wright, 2000: 218).

Labour committed itself to reform of the House of Lords in its 1997 election manifesto. Arguably, the Upper House has experienced the most significant change ever to its composition, with the removal of 666 hereditary peers, including those of royal blood. The 'Weatherill' amendment to the government's proposals gave a lifeline to 92 hereditaries to be preserved *ex officio* or via a ballot of the outgoing hereditaries. This represents a reduction by over half in the number of members of the Lords. Table 7.5 shows the composition of the reformed Upper House following the changes made by the House of Lords Act 1999.

In response to demands to state the form that stage two of reform of the Lords would take, the government appointed a twelve-member Royal Commission, chaired by the former Conservative Cabinet minister, Lord Wakeham. The Commission reported in January 2000, producing a cautious blueprint for reform that rejected the option of a totally elected chamber which might act as a rival to the Commons (HMSO, 2000). It published three options for further debate between interested parties, including the two existing Houses in a joint committee, with legislation likely only after a general election. Option A proposed 65 elected members, option C 195, but a majority of the Commission supported option B, which entailed only a small democratically-elected component in the revised chamber – just 87 out of 550 proposed members. These would be elected on regional lists similar to those of MEPs in the 1999 European Parliament elections, with one-third being elected every five years to serve a single fifteen-year term of office. A possible date for the election, subject to legislation, could be simultaneous with the next European elections in June 2004. Box 7.2 details the main proposals of the Commission's report. Notwithstanding changes to its composition, the Lords sought to reassert itself by continuing to inflict defeats on the government (Box 7.3).

Another area of fundamental change that has impacted on Westminster is devolution. The Scottish Parliament and the Welsh Assembly were created in the

---

Box 7.2 Key proposals of the Royal Commission on Lords Reform, 2000

- A new second parliamentary chamber of approximately 550 members.
- A majority of members to be chosen by an independent commission.
- The remaining, 65, 87 or 195 to be elected from the twelve regions of the UK.
- Composition of the chamber to be regularly adjusted to reflect voting patterns.
- Targets for composition will reflect the UK's gender, ethnic and faith mix.
- The link between honours and membership of the chamber will be abolished.
- The chamber should be 'at least as powerful as the present House of Lords'.

Source: *The Guardian*, 21 January, 2000

Table 7.5 Composition of the reformed House of Lords, 3 December 2001

By party strength

Party	Life peers	Hereditary peers			Bishops	Total
		EP	EOH	AROH		
Conservative	173	40	9	1		223
Labour	196	2	2			200
Lib Dem	60	3	2			65
Cross-bench	149	29	2	1		181
Archbishops ⎫					2 ⎫	26
Bishops ⎭					24 ⎭	
Other	9					9
Total	587	74	15	2	26	704

Notes: EP – hereditary peers elected by party; EOH – hereditary peers elected as office holders; AROH – appointed royal office holders – The Duke of Norfolk, The Earl Marshall (Conservative) and the Marquess of Cholmondley, The Lord Great Chamberlain (Cross-bencher).

The table excludes nine peers, eight of whom are on leave of absence and one of whom is bankrupt and may not attend.

By peerage type

		Total
Archbishops and bishops	2+24	26
Life peers under the Appellate Jurisdiction Act 1876 (Law Lords)		28
Life peers under the Life Peerages Act 1958	(113 women)	567
Peers under the House of Lords Act 1999	(4 women)	92
Total		713

By peerage rank

	Total
Archbishop	2
Duke	2
Marquess	1
Earl	25
Countess	1
Viscount	17
Bishop	24
Baron/Lord	525
Baroness	115
Lady	1
Total	713

Source: http://www.publications.parliament.uk

> **Box 7.3 Government defeats in the House of Lords, November 1999–March 2000**
>
> - November 1999 – two amendments passed to the Welfare Bill relating to Incapacity Benefit.
> - January 2000 – government defeated over proposed changes to the right of defendants to jury trial.
> - February 2000 – rejected government attempt to repeal 'Section 28' banning schools from promoting homosexuality.
> - February 2000 – defeated government on Greater London Authority (Election Expenses) Order which would have denied candidates a free mailshot.
> - March 2000 – a further narrow defeat of the government on sex education.

aftermath of the referendums held in September 1997. They took over responsibility for the respective powers of the Secretaries of State for Scotland and Wales in July 1999. These include agriculture, fisheries and food; economic development matters; education; the environment; health and social services; housing; local government; sport, the arts and transport; with the addition of criminal and civil law in Scotland. The chief difference between the two bodies is that the Scottish Parliament has full powers in relation to primary legislation (including the ability to vary the rate of income tax by plus or minus 3% of that set in London), whereas the Welsh Assembly can only operate within the existing statutory framework, and is empowered to deal only with the rules and regulations of secondary legislation. Crucially, however, these matters, and the consequent expenditure of £15 billion in Scotland and £7 billion in Wales, are no longer the preserve of the British Parliament at Westminster, though the Secretaries of State still participate in ministerial questions and are theoretically accountable there, albeit in a necessarily circumscribed form. The Scottish and Welsh Grand Committees (attended by each respective nation's MPs) at Westminster are also pale shadows of their former selves, notwithstanding the fact that they were seldom in the limelight.

In Northern Ireland, following the positive result of the referendum on the Good Friday Agreement, a new devolved Assembly was established under the Northern Ireland Act 1998. The Assembly possesses primary powers in similar areas to the other two devolved bodies, such as agriculture; economic development; education, health and social services. Despite devolution, Westminster retains responsibility for the macro policy areas, including foreign affairs; defence; the economy; social security; trade; employment and the media; together with overall constitutional affairs.

Summary

- The composition of Parliament is changing but is still predominantly male, white, middle aged and middle class.
- The three preconditions for fundamental change have not been fully met since 1997.

- The Select Committee on Modernisation has produced modest internal reform.
- Departmental select committees have been modified but arguably require a fundamental overhaul.
- The composition of the House of Lords has been substantially changed.
- Devolution has changed the scope of day-to-day oversight and legislation at Westminster.

Debate

The three main parties at Westminster each have their own perspective on parliamentary reform. The most radical view is held by the Liberal Democrats who wish to modernise Westminster within the context of a fundamental set of constitutional reforms, including a change to the electoral system for the Commons and an elected second chamber linked to a federal political structure. The Conservative Party has historically opposed fundamental change, though it has introduced incremental and occasionally more substantial reforms, such as the Life Peerages Act and departmental select committees. However, initially through the Commission to Strengthen Parliament, established by William Hague in 1999, and then in response to the Labour government's reform proposals, the Conservatives showed themselves as not averse to considering more fundamental change (*The Guardian*, 24 June 2000; *The Sunday Times*, 13 January 2002). Labour has usually fallen some way between the other two parties. It has at various times been committed to radical structural change but, paradoxically, when in office has tended to prioritise other aspects of its policy agenda over parliamentary reform. Given the historic disposition of the Conservatives, and since most governments have been either Conservative or Labour, the reasons why Westminster has been a highly conservative institution in the twentieth century are readily apparent.

As we have seen, the executive normally commands a majority in the Commons, thus any substantial changes must receive the support or at least the acquiescence of the government of the day. Ministers jealously guard their powers and, in what is regarded as a zero sum game, are wary of any increases in those of the legislature. This is equally true of their opposition counterparts. As Crick commented more than a generation ago, ' "The executive mind" on both sides of the House has little patience with even the existing opportunities of Parliamentary participation in the process of government' (Crick, 1968: 263).

Change, therefore, usually occurs at the margins and seldom challenges the pre-eminence of the government in the balance of power between executive and legislature. The reforms proposed by the Select Committee on Modernisation have consistently reflected this orthodoxy. Ministers have poured cold water over proposals to strengthen accountability to the legislature. These include granting the Commons and its select committees a veto over senior public appointments, as proposed by the Treasury Select Committee, and proposals from the Procedure and Public Accounts Committees on the consideration of public expenditure.

Norton argues that Westminster has undergone 'significant institutionalisation in the last quarter of the twentieth century'. The greater use of parliamentary committees has bred specialisation among members and within the legislature as a whole. The departmental select committees, for example, provide forums for extensive scrutiny of executive activity that did not occur hitherto. He further contends that the truly significant changes in the last quarter-century have been in intra-committee relations and in the interrelationship between committees and the floor of the House. For most of its history Parliament has been a chamber-oriented legislature and this was true for both Houses. In the past twenty-five years both the number of committees and the breadth of their activities have increased markedly. However, legislative scrutiny of bills in the Commons is still performed by *ad hoc* standing committees that continue to militate against specialisation as their membership is transient (Norton, 1998).

Other observers, such as Peter Riddell, acknowledge that many reforms have been introduced since 1997, but argue that they are minor in scope and none really addresses the power balance. Some are welcome, such as the overhaul of scrutiny of European legislation and the chamber in Westminster Hall, but the only reforms that have truly mattered are in the handling of legislation, with greater scope for early scrutiny and amendment. Be that as it may, only a few bills are examined in draft and ministers determine how individual measures are dealt with. The government has not been keen to repeat attempts to improve legislation, such as the Public Administration Committee's examination of the draft Freedom of Information Bill.

Riddell suggests that backbenchers are as complicit as ministers. The reality of life at Westminster is that the majority of opposition – as much as government – back-benchers want to serve on the front bench rather than on committees. 'The dogs are not prepared to bark, so Mr Blair can afford to ignore the pleas of reformers' (Riddell, *The Times*, 13 April 2000). Liberal critics such as Charter 88 have been equally disappointed by the slow pace of reform, which they suggest is partly the product of a commitment to consensus in the Modernisation Committee that has engendered caution.

Arguments continue over stage two of reform of the Lords, the Royal Commission report and the government's proposals. The Labour view, articulated by Lady Jay, is that 'any proposal totally to elect the second chamber – under the mistaken view that it would increase the democratic base of Parliament – would in fact undermine democracy'. Labour has, however, conceded the principle of a minority of elected members increasing over time 'in number and importance'. Unsurprisingly, it also subscribes to the retention of the Salisbury Convention, whereby the Lords do not reject legislation contained in a government's manifesto (*The Times*, 8 March 2000).

The Liberal Democrats criticised the Royal Commission's proposals as neither predicated on principle nor strengthening the legislature's capacity to oversee the executive, while the Conservatives were also critical but acknowledged that the parties would have to work together to implement them. The independent Constitution Unit, while welcoming many of the detailed proposals, argued that the report was 'too timid in its placement of the Upper House in the new con-stitutional settlement. The failure to link the chamber adequately to devolution, or to give it new constitutional powers, would leave Britain out of step with many other Western democracies' (*The Times*, 8 March 2000).

Academics such as Shell have drawn the distinction between modernising Parliament to make it more efficient and reforming it to make it more effective. 'Removing hereditary peers clearly fitted with modernisation: thinking about how the limited effectiveness of the present House could be enhanced was not a matter much in [ministers'] minds' (Shell, 2000: 309). The way in which the Lords has been reformed, he argues, owes more to short-term political tactics than long-term citizens' rights.

Labour finally brought forward its stage two proposals in the white paper, *The House of Lords: Completing the Reform*, in November 2001. The proposed reforms, largely in accord with the Royal Commission's report, met with near universal hostility, not only from the opposition parties, but also from within the ranks of Labour MPs, well over a hundred of whom signed an early day motion favouring a mainly elected Upper House. The proposals entail a chamber of 600 members, only 120 (20%) of whom would be directly elected by proportional representation probably at a general election; 120 members would be appointed by an independent commission; with the remaining 60% being made up of 332 party appointees, sixteen Anglican bishops and twelve Law Lords (see Box 7.4). There are also further limits on the powers of the House. The plans seem unlikely to proceed in their current form, so the final outcome of the process remains uncertain, but what is apparent is that there is no turning back.

Devolution, as we have seen, has led to changes at Westminster and there is a widespread feeling that ministers with an explicitly territorial remit are in a state of limbo, as the new institutions assume control. Additionally, the asymmetrical institutional landscape, and uneven nature of the process, has given rise to demands from the Conservatives for the government to address the West Lothian question (essentially, English MPs being prevented from participating in devolved matters while MPs from Scotland, Wales and Northern Ireland continue to have a say in those of England determined at Westminster). There have also been calls for

---

Box 7.4 Key proposals of the House of Lords white paper (2001)

- The hereditary peers will finally cease to have any privileged rights of membership.
- A majority of the members of the new House will be nominated by the political parties, in proportions intended to reflect the shares of the national vote in the previous general election. There will also be about 120 appointed members with no political affiliation, 120 directly elected members to represent the nations and regions, and a continuing role for Law Lords and bishops of the Church of England.
- An independent statutory Appointments Commission will have substantial powers. It will appoint the independent members and decide – within certain bounds – how many seats each major political party is entitled to, thereby substantially reducing government patronage.
- The size of the House will be capped at 600 in statute, with an interim House as close as may be to 750 members to accommodate existing life peers.
- There will be formal commitments to achieving balance and representativeness in the House.
- The link with the peerage will be dissolved.

Source: *The House of Lords: Completing the Reform*, Cm 5291, London: HMSO, 2001

regional assemblies in England (now a distant government manifesto commitment); for an English Grand Committee; for the creation of an English Parliament; and for full-blown federalism. Each of these would have a concomitant impact on the UK legislature. Whatever the final upshot of devolution for Westminster, the process has been in the best British constitutional tradition: incremental and unsystematic.

Summary

- The three main political parties hold divergent views on the reform of Parliament.
- The history of parliamentary reform in the twentieth century is the history of incrementalism.
- Modernisation of the Commons has been extremely tentative since 1997.
- Reform of the Lords has been substantial but is incomplete.
- Devolution has produced an asymmetry in how Parliament deals with issues in different parts of the British state.

Conclusion

The history of parliamentary reform in the twentieth century is the history of incrementalism. Although change in Parliament, particularly since 1997, has not fully satisfied the most ardent of reformers, it has certainly been as, if not more, rapid than in earlier periods. The last century produced a progressive diminution in the powers of the Lords and a consequent increase in those of the Commons, itself elected for the first time on a democratic, universal franchise. The essential imbalance of power between executive and legislative branches of government has not been adequately addressed, and remains an issue of debate. Since 1997, in a number of important areas, such as reform of the composition of the Lords and devolution, the changes are politically significant and may prove to be far-reaching.

The challenges on the horizon for all legislatures, not least Westminster, are immense. There are question marks over whether archaic parliamentary practice can keep pace with the information and communication technology revolution. Public policy decisions are becoming increasingly complex and need to be made ever more rapidly. Additionally, an educated electorate may become less satisfied with mediated representative democracy, and seek more participative modes of decision-making that new technology can facilitate. The diffusion of power to the Celtic periphery, Europe and possibly the English regions in time may produce a more compact legislature at Westminster with a revised focus. Parliament is an institution that helps shape, and is in turn itself shaped, by an increasingly dynamic British society. Undoubtedly, that process will produce further change in the future.

Chronology

1876 Appellate Jurisdiction Act introduces Law Lords.
1911 Quinquennial election rule prescribed; Parliament Act limits the role of the Lords.
1918 Franchise extended to most men, and to women over the age of 30; women allowed to become MPs.
1928 Minimum voting age reduced to 21 for all electors.
1949 Parliament Act further circumscribes the powers of the Lords.
1958 Life Peerages Act introduces life peers; women permitted to sit in the Lords.
1963 Peerage Act permits hereditaries to disclaim title; women hereditary peers allowed to take seats in the Lords.
1966 Crossman specialist select committee reforms introduced.
1969 Minimum voting age further reduced to 18.
1973 Britain joins the European Economic Community.
1978 Radio broadcasting introduced to both chambers and committees.
1979 Margaret Thatcher becomes the first woman Prime Minister; departmental select committees introduced.
1984 Televising of Lords introduced.
1988 Televising of Commons introduced.
1992 Betty Boothroyd MP becomes the first woman Speaker of the House of Commons.
1993 Hansard Commission on legislative process reports.
1996 Labour's women-only parliamentary candidate short-lists deemed illegal.
1997 Labour wins general election returning largest-ever number of women MPs.
1999 Introduction of backbench debates in Westminster Hall.
1999 House of Lords Act removes majority of hereditary peers from membership of Upper House.
2000 Royal Commission on Reform of the House of Lords reports.
2001 House of Lords white paper details Labour's reform proposals.

Discussion Questions

1. Should all members of the House of Lords be democratically elected?
2. 'Radical reform of Parliament will only occur when legislators collectively assert themselves against the interest of executives.' Discuss.
3. Is the 'modernised' Westminster well placed to face the political challenges of the twenty-first century?

References

Beer, S.H. (1966) 'The British legislature and the problem of mobilizing consent', in E. Frank (ed.) *Lawmakers in a Changing World*, Englewood Cliffs, NJ: Prentice Hall.

Butler, D. and Kavanagh, D. (eds) (1997) *The British General Election of 1997*, Basingstoke: Macmillan.

Butler, D. and Kavanagh, D. (eds) (2001) *The British General Election of 2001*, Basingstoke: Palgrave.

HMSO (2000) *A House for the Future*, Cm. 4534 London: http://www.parliament.uk.

HMSO (2001) *The House of Lords: Completing the Reform*, Cm. 5291 London: http://www.parliament.uk.

Crick, B. (1968) *The Reform of Parliament* (second edition), London: Weidenfeld & Nicolson.

Criddle, B. (1997) 'MPs and Candidates', in D. Butler and D. Kavanagh (eds) *The British General Election of 1997*, Basingstoke: Macmillan.

House of Commons, Public Information Office (1999) *Factsheet No. 28, Sittings of the House*, London: House of Commons.

House of Lords Act 1999, London: http://www.parliament.uk.

James, S. (1999) *British Cabinet Government* (second edition), London: Routledge.

Laugharne, P.J. (1994) *Parliament and Specialist Advice*, Liverpool: Manutius Press.

Norton, P. (1993) *Does Parliament Matter?*, Hemel Hempstead: Harvester Wheatsheaf.

Norton, P. (1998) 'Nascent institutionalisation: committees in the British Parliament', *The Journal of Legislative Studies*, Vol. 4, Spring, No. 1, pp. 143–62.

Packenham, R. (1970) 'Legislatures and political development', in A. Kornberg and L.D. Musolf (eds) *Legislatures in Developmental Perspective*, Durham, NC: Duke University Press.

Select Committee on Liaison (2000) *Shifting the Balance*, London: http://www.parliament.uk.

Sex Discrimination (Election Candidates) Bill 2001, London: http://www.parliament.uk.

Shell, D. (2000) 'Labour and the House of Lords: a case study in constitutional reform', *Parliamentary Affairs*, Vol. 53, No. 2, April.

Silk, P. and Walters, R. (1998) *How Parliament Works* (fourth edition), London: Longman.

Wright, T. (ed.) (2000) *The British Political Process: An Introduction*, London: Routledge.

Further reading

Three concise and readable introductions to Parliament are Andrew Adonis (1993), *Parliament Today* (second edition, Manchester: Manchester University Press); Philip Norton (1993), *Does Parliament Matter?* (Hemel Hempstead: Harvester Wheatsheaf); and Paul Silk and Rhodri Walters (1998) *How Parliament Works* (fourth edition, London: Longman). Donald Shell (1992) *The House of Lords* (second edition, Hemel Hempstead: Harvester Wheatsheaf) and Donald Shell and David Beamish (1993) *The House of Lords at Work* (Oxford: Clarendon Press) are illuminating studies of the Upper House. On parliamentary reform, see Peter Riddell (1998) *Parliament under Pressure* (London: Victor Gollancz). Two now slightly dated but still useful specific works are Gavin Drewry (ed.) (1989) *The New Select Committees* (second edition, Oxford: Oxford University Press) and Michael Rush (ed.) (1990) *Parliament and Pressure Politics* (Oxford: Oxford University Press). *The Journal of Legislative Studies*, *Parliamentary Affairs* and *The House Magazine* provide a wealth of up-to-date articles and information about developments at Westminster and legislatures generally. Parliament's own website can be accessed at http://www.parliament.uk.

Europe and the European Union

Roger Scully

CHAPTER EIGHT

Introduction

The 'European issue', in various manifestations, has become one of the perennial arguments within British politics. Disputes about Britain's relations with Europe are long-running and have been highly consequential for the country and its politics over the last fifty years. These disagreements, whether between Britain and its continental neighbours, or in the form of conflicts within Britain about the country's proper role in Europe, have been one of the major features of the British political scene for most of the post-war era. 'Europe' has generally remained an issue that excites passions within the political elite rather than the mass public, however: even today, after almost thirty years of British membership, few in the British public know much about the European Union (EU), and many freely confess to being bewildered by it. And yet, on at least one occasion, public opinion has exercised a decisive influence over British relations with Europe; moreover, there is every prospect of the public being called upon to issue a similar judgement in the future over the question of whether the UK should join the European single currency.

Background

At the heart of disputes about Europe within British politics are different visions of Britain itself – its place in the world, and the sort of country it is. As one Labour politician has put it:

> If you ask the question 'What is Europe about? What kind of Europe do we want?' . . . you're really asking a much more fundamental kind of question, which is 'What kind of *Britain* do you want?' It's really the same question. I think the reason why the Conservatives are so divided is this fundamental failure to bring together, to stitch together, these two different ends about what they think Britain is about.
> (Labour member of the European Parliament, interview with the author, 17 July 1998)

Whether or not one agrees with this representative's view of the problems experienced by his political opponents, what is certain is that arguments about Europe within

British politics are not trivial – they concern fundamental issues of identity, as well as political strategy, that should be of interest to all students of modern British politics.

For much of the last fifty years, the UK has appeared to co-exist with the process of European unification only with considerable unease. It has become a commonplace view among scholars that Britain's long-standing ambivalence towards the process of European unification has had its roots in British history. *Where* in that history the problems originate, however, is much more disputed. Some have seen the legacy of Britain's global empire and long-standing semi-detachment from the political affairs of continental Europe as lying behind a characteristic reluctance to become closely involved in European projects (Kaiser, 1996); others have focused more on the immediate legacy of the Second World War, which left the UK still a world power but with much of the rest of Europe in ruins and apparently with little to offer the UK. (One work on the subject (Charlton, 1983) famously concluded that a lack of understanding of post-war moves towards European unity was, for Britain, *The Price of Victory*.) Yet other scholars have come to the conclusion that the failure of the UK to join in efforts at European co-operation was primarily driven by economic considerations – that with still substantial trading ties to its imperial possessions and former colonies, the UK had little immediate economic incentive to participate in an experimental European venture with doubtful prospects of success (Milward, 1992; Moravcsik, 1998). But whatever may be the *origins* of British unease with European unity, perhaps the most remarkable thing is how this difficult relationship has generally persisted right up until the present.

The British government had been willing to join some international groupings and alliances in the years after 1945 (such as the Council of Europe and NATO), but baulked at anything that appeared to involve any substantial delegation of sovereign powers to new European centres of authority. Thus, the UK refused to sign up to the *Schuman Plan*, which launched the first, tentative steps towards what is now the European Union (EU) by creating a *European Coal and Steel Community*. The Prime Minister of the time, Clement Attlee, told the House of Commons that 'We refuse to accept the principle that the most vital economic forces of this country should be handed over to an authority that is utterly undemocratic and is responsible to nobody' (cited in Urwin, 1995: 46).

Despite some Conservative criticism of the Labour government's decision at the time, the Tories did nothing to reverse British non-membership when they returned to government shortly thereafter in 1951. Under their leadership the UK also opted out of (ultimately abortive) attempts in the early 1950s to create a *European Defence Community* and disdained the talks that ultimately led to the signing of the Rome Treaties and the founding of a broad *Economic Community* in 1957. The British were not entirely negative towards European co-operation, as they demonstrated through taking the leading role in creating a *European Free Trade Association* (EFTA) in 1960. But EFTA was distinguished from the EC by the more limited scale of its immediate policy goals (free trade between members but not common policies on external trade and agriculture, as signed up to at Rome), the absence of any longer-term objectives (where the Rome Treaties spoke of an 'ever closer union'), and by having no strong central institutions (where the EC established a Court, quasi-executive Commission, and putative Parliamentary Assembly).

The EC surprised many in the UK government by not only going ahead but by proving to be a considerable success in its early years. As the 1960s dawned, not only were the Community countries proving to be the most economically vibrant area of Europe, but their political relations had also improved – as shown by a highly symbolic 1963 Treaty of Friendship between France and Germany. It was, nonetheless, a dramatic reversal in British government policy when, in 1961, the UK government applied to join the EC. The Labour Leader of the opposition at the time, Hugh Gaitskell, famously attacked the UK's 'turning its back on a thousand years of history' but the point remained moot for some years. French President Charles de Gaulle vetoed the British application in 1963; he then repeated his action when the UK (now under a Labour government led by Harold Wilson) tentatively applied once more in 1967.

Only in the 1970s, with de Gaulle now departed from the scene, was the UK government (led now by the Conservative Edward Heath, probably the most consistently pro-European British Prime Minister since the war) able to take the country into the EC. Yet by then, with the UK joining a long-established grouping of countries, and with the British economy long since overtaken in prosperity by those of its new partners, Britain was in a poor bargaining position, and many in the UK criticised the terms of Britain's accession to the Rome Treaties. The return of a Labour government in 1974 prompted a re-negotiation of the accession terms; this new deal was then put before the British population in a referendum. After a contentious campaign that divided the Labour Party in particular, the outcome was a clear 2:1 majority for continued British membership.

The referendum result did not resolve either Britain's long-term relationship with its European partners or disputes regarding Europe within British politics. Within the Community, the UK soon acquired the reputation of an 'awkward partner' – reluctant to support new initiatives (such as currency co-operation in the European Monetary System (EMS), launched in 1979 without full UK involvement) and, from the late 1970s until a 1984 settlement at Fontainebleau, pursuing a grievance over its net contribution to the Community budget.

Meanwhile, back in the UK, both of the main parties have gone through periods of Europhobia. In the late 1970s and well into the 1980s, the Labour Party, as part of its more general move towards the left, became increasingly hostile to continued EC membership. The Community was attacked by many on the left for being a 'capitalist club', and the party's 1983 manifesto advocated complete British withdrawal. However, as Labour moved gradually back to the centre after its catastrophic 1983 election defeat, and as the party began to be aware of the possibility that a developing EU 'social agenda' on matters like workers' rights was sympathetic to the party's own outlook, Labour's hostility diminished.

Yet, curiously, as Labour gradually moved to a reconciliation with Britain's European involvement, the Conservatives have increasingly come into internal conflict on the issue, and a broadly 'anti-European' strand within the party has gradually grown in strength. Mrs Thatcher's strident and overtly nationalistic style had never fitted particularly easily with the compromise-ridden world of European co-operation. Nonetheless, she had never flirted with the policy of withdrawal, and even, in 1986, signed the Single European Act (SEA), which promised to deepen substantially the economic integration of Europe and strengthen the Community's decision-making institutions. In the late 1980s, however, friction increasingly developed between Thatcher on the one hand and, on the other, those – such as Chancellor Helmut Kohl of Germany, President François Mitterrand of France, and European Commission President Jacques Delors – wanting to use the SEA as a launching pad for advancing economic and political unity yet further. The particular issue that most clearly symbolised the broader conflict was the argument about possible progress towards a single Community currency. For Thatcher, as for many others, a single currency managed by a European central bank struck to an unacceptable degree both at the symbol and the reality of national economic independence.

Mrs Thatcher's increasingly vocal hostility towards attempts to advance European unity helped provoke the resignations of senior colleagues (Chancellor Nigel Lawson in 1989, and Deputy Prime Minister Sir Geoffrey Howe in 1990) and was, in turn, a significant factor in her own downfall. John Major, her successor, consistently sought to achieve a balance between the pro- and anti-European factions within his party. Thus, while Major spoke of putting Britain 'at the very heart of Europe' and signed the 1992 Maastricht Treaty, which enfolded the EC into a new entity, termed the *European Union* (see Box 8.1 for the institutions of the EU), he also ensured that the UK had 'opt-outs' from both the single currency and a Social Chapter concerned with workers' rights in the labour market. The anti-European faction in the Conservative Party, however, emboldened by the strong opposition to the treaty revealed in other countries (in particular in referendums held in Denmark and France) and with their suspicion of European involvements heightened by the humiliating exit of the pound sterling from the EMS forced on Britain by currency markets in September 1992, proved unwilling to accept the Maastricht compromise, and fought a long and bitter parliamentary

---

Box 8.1 The main institutions of the European Union

European Council – Meetings held 2–3 times a year by national leaders of EU member countries. Focus is on major issues and big decisions, including treaty changes.

Council of Ministers – Main law- and policy-making arena of the EU. National governments are each represented by a minister from the government department concerned with the particular issue under discussion. Some decisions are taken by unanimity/consensus, others by weighted (or 'qualified') majority.

European Parliament (EP) – The only *directly-elected* European institution: 626 members (87 from UK). Charged with overseeing the Commission, the EP (increasingly) has a major role in the passage of European legislation, along with Council of Ministers.

European Court of Justice (ECJ) – Main court of the EU: interprets treaties governing the EU in a similar manner as national supreme courts use a written constitutional document; thus it is able to judge whether policies and actions are 'constitutional' or not.

European Commission – 20 commissioners (two from the UK) head an organisation of 16,000 civil servants charged with proposing new legislation and implementing agreed policies.

campaign against the ratification of the treaty (Baker et al., 1994; Cowley and Norton, 1999). Moreover, over the following years, attacks on the alleged intrusions of the EU into British life and on the ambitions of some for the EU to become some form of federation, won increasing popularity among Conservatives. Responding to this trend in opinion, and to the decision in 1996 of the European Commission to ban exports of UK beef in the midst of concern about the spread of BSE (or 'mad cow disease'), Major launched the 'beef war', under which the UK obstructed EU business in an attempt to win re-consideration of the Commission decision. But these tactics brought little immediate pay-off for Britain on the beef issue and, while temporarily sating the anti-European mood increasingly prevalent in much of his party and the popular press, won little but contempt for Major among fellow EU countries. Major's 'heart of Europe' ambition had long since fallen by the wayside.

Thus, there was deep relief among Britain's European partners when, after the May 1997 election, the now openly pro-European Labour Party was returned to office under Tony Blair. This created an immediate improvement in Britain's relations with its partners. The UK signed up to the Amsterdam Treaty, which included some increases in the powers of the EU institutions, when any agreement would probably have been impossible under the Conservatives. However, on the biggest issue now facing the EU – the single currency – the UK remained on the outer fringes of the Union. Eleven EU member states went ahead and joined the Eurozone when the new currency was launched in January 1999; the UK was one of only four countries to stay outside (with the other three, Denmark, Sweden and initially, Greece, all giving signals that they would probably sign up to the single currency within a few years). In the Conservative Party, with the anti-European strand of the party increasingly dominant, new leader William Hague promised to stay out of the single currency for at least ten years – a prominent policy in the party's 2001 election campaign. Supporters of entry (including former Chancellor Kenneth Clarke, whom Hague had beaten for the party leadership in July 1997 and who was beaten again by the more Eurosceptic Iain Duncan-Smith in 2001) became increasingly marginalised. The Labour government publicly favoured entry but promised a national referendum before taking the UK in. Yet while few would doubt the importance of the issue, the Euro is in many respects the most recent manifestation of arguments about the appropriate relationship for the UK within 'Europe'. One thing alone seems sure, and that is that the arguments about Europe in British politics are far from over.

Summary

- There has been a long-standing ambivalence in the UK towards closer European unity.
- After the UK joined, it had an uneasy relationship with the EC/EU.
- There have been numerous disputes within the UK about the appropriate relationship with Europe.

As the next section discusses, arguments about Europe have persisted not least because of the extent to which 'Europe' matters for British politics.

Theoretical Considerations

The famous British judge, Lord Denning, wrote in the 1970s of the future impact of EU law on the British legal systems as being like 'an onrushing tide' that could not be held back and would penetrate deep into the country's body of law, legal culture and law-making process. Few legal scholars today would argue that Denning was overstating the case; moreover, his sentiment could apply with equal force to many other areas of the British polity. 'Europe' has become an all-pervasive influence – whether for good or ill – at all levels of British politics and government, from the Constitution, through major political institutions and actors, right down to ordinary voters.

The EU has had a considerable impact on perhaps *the* fundamental constitutional principle of British government in recent centuries, parliamentary sovereignty. The doctrine that, in the absence of a written constitutional text, Parliament may 'make or unmake any law', and that it can do anything except bind the similar freedom of movement of a successor Parliament, has been rendered, for many immediate practical purposes, obsolete by British membership of the Union. EU member states are obliged to conform to treaties and a body of European law that significantly impinges upon their potential freedom of action. This was made crystal clear to the UK in the 1990 *Factortame* case, when a British law passed to try to prevent the practice of 'quota-hopping' by non-British (mainly Spanish) fishing fleets was struck down because it contravened European legal and treaty requirements on the freedom of movement of workers. Parliamentary sovereignty remains intact in the ultimate sense that the British Parliament could, conceivably, pass a law revoking UK membership of the EU; barring that ultimate step, however, the doctrine is substantially compromised.

The EU also imposes significant burdens on the daily organisation and operation of the central government in the UK. At one level this is simply a workload matter – much of the time of the government is now taken up with managing the implications of EU membership. These implications include overseeing the operation of existing EU policies and laws, and engaging in the more or less constant diplomacy that now occurs, largely in Brussels, between EU member states. A large proportion of the workload of the UK's civil service now focuses on EU-related matters. As a result of the growing policy scope of the EU, a greater number of ministers are now involved in what might once have been thought of as 'foreign affairs', through negotiations with their counterparts from other Union countries. But as well as more work, this creates significant problems of policy co-ordination – making sure that ministers are all 'singing from the same song-sheet' and that different areas of government are informed of policy agreements reached by others at the European level. In addition, governments have significant constraints on their freedom of policy choices, imposed by existing European policies and also by the requirement to get wide consensus across EU member countries for major policy changes in the Union.

Most British political institutions and actors have been and are affected by EU membership. Parliament is affected not only through the impact of the EU on parliamentary sovereignty, but also at a more practical level. Parliament's role as the law-making body for the UK is increasingly honoured in the breach rather than the observance, as EU law is passed by European-level institutions without any need for subsequent ratification by national Parliaments. These Parliaments still have a potentially important role to play in scrutinising government ministers' actions at the EU level, and through analysing the longer-term impact of EU laws and policies. However, most observers would not judge Westminster to have carried out this role very effectively. For various reasons, which include the secrecy of Council of Ministers' meetings, but also ignorance about the details of EU politics on the part of most MPs, parliamentary scrutiny of national government behaviour in the EU has been limited and erratic (Norton, 1996; Riddell, 1998). The House of Commons has proved adept at conducting dramatic debates on major European treaties, but much less skilful at the dedicated scrutiny of detailed European policy work. House of Lords' committee reports on the details of EU policy are often commended, but they have rarely, if ever, captured wider political attention.

The EU also has substantial implications for major political actors in the UK, including those basic organisations of a functioning democracy, political parties. 'Europe' has often been, as indicated in the historical review above, a key focus of dispute between and within the parties. The Liberal Democrats, and their Alliance and Liberal predecessors, are the only major political movement to be consistently, and staunchly, pro-European in their outlook. Other parties have veered dramatically on the issue, perhaps because it is far from obvious how European integration relates to the traditional left–right political spectrum. Should Conservatives see the EU as being about expanding the spread of free-market, free-trade economics (something they would largely favour), or as challenging the integrity and independence of the UK (which strikes at the heart of Conservative patriotism)? Similarly, should socialists regard the EU as being about internationalism and co-operation (good) or about the expansion of capitalism (much less good)? Even the nationalist parties in Scotland and Wales went through a long process of agonising about the EU before adopting their current 'independence in Europe' positions in the late 1980s. But in addition to these ideological questions, the EU also poses more mundane questions of political organisation to parties. Most notably, the EU (and in particular, its increasingly influential Parliament) adds to the problems of co-ordination now being experienced by many parties. UK parties have traditionally focused on Westminster as *the* key centre of power. The introduction of Scottish and Welsh devolution, possible English regional devolution, when added to the British and European Parliaments, means parties having elected representatives in important institutions at different levels. How are they to co-ordinate actions across these different arenas, and how should the different parliamentary parties relate to each other? The answers to these questions remain unclear.

Last, and in some senses least, are the voters of the UK. There appears to be less enthusiasm for the EU and European unity in the UK than in many other

European countries, and concomitantly greater support for national independence. But there is also much evidence that UK voters share with their counterparts
in most EU countries considerable confusion about, and a growing alienation
from, the Union. The institutions and practices of the EU are not exactly a model
of clarity and simplicity, while media coverage of the EU does little to help educate the public. Voters can participate in the EU directly through their right (available since 1979) to vote in elections to the European Parliament. The degree of
enthusiasm that this has raised in voters was demonstrated by the 24% turnout in
the UK in the 1999 poll, the lowest turnout ever for a nationwide election. Voting
for largely unknown candidates to a little-understood chamber has, not surprisingly, failed to inspire a sense of public connection to 'Europe'; rather, increasing
numbers of people seem to regard government as having become further away
than ever.

Summary

- The EU is a challenge to the basis of the British constitution – parliamentary
  sovereignty.
- The EU poses significant practical challenges for governing institutions and
  major political actors.
- The EU may contribute to increased public alienation from politics and the
  political system.

Update

Debates and arguments about Europe within British politics remained highly
contentious. As before, specific disputes were intertwined with fundamental differences regarding what the EU should be, and the role that Britain should play
within it. An intergovernmental conference (IGC) was called by EU member states
at the beginning of 2000, with the intention of resolving institutional and other
problems standing in the way of the Union allowing membership for many of the
new democracies of central and eastern Europe. Yet the issues at stake – such as
national representation in the European Commission and the voting rights of
a country in the Council of Ministers – were not simply about institutional
efficiency. They raised fundamental questions about how a country understood
the EU and its place within the Union. For instance, restricting further the ability
of a country to exercise a veto over unwelcome policy proposals in the Council of
Ministers is, in one respect, merely a sensible change in decision-making procedures to accommodate the fact that in a twenty-five-member Union, extensive
availability of veto powers could lead to policy stagnation. However, attitudes to
such a change depended largely on how different people saw their country's membership of the EU. Those in Britain who viewed the Union in a positive light, with

many benefits to offer the UK, could see much sense in improving the speed of European decision-making. Thus, the government white paper on the IGC *Reform for Enlargement* (which began with a statement from Tony Blair that 'Unlike its predecessors, this Government is unwaveringly pro-European') favoured the extension of majority voting. The Conservative response, emanating from a party where Eurosceptics, who expect the UK to be disadvantaged by much of what EU does, were increasingly dominant, remained much more publicly concerned about retaining Britain's veto – its ability to *stop* things happening.

The ongoing debate about potential British participation in EMU and the single currency also raised concerns that went far beyond what might have seemed, immediately, to be at stake. At one level, the UK faced a purely economic decision: was moving into the single currency area likely to be beneficial for the UK economy? Potential economic benefits for business from the elimination of currency fluctuations and conversion costs had to be balanced against the rigidities implied by a 'one-size-fits-all' single monetary policy. But, perhaps inevitably, political considerations loomed large in the debate. The symbolism of 'surrendering the pound' has been used effectively by opponents of British membership of EMU. Although polls indicated that much of the public remained open to persuasion on the matter, by early 2000 public opinion polls were indicating roughly a 2:1 majority against the UK joining the Eurozone (a situation that has not changed). The pro-Euro case had not been helped by a considerable decline in the value of currency during the first year of its life or by the inability of the cross-party 'Britain in Europe' campaign to find an effective focus. Despite William Hague's official policy only being to delay possible British entry into the single currency zone for some years more than Blair, the former opposition leader embarked in early 2000 on a nationwide speaking tour on the subject; it was undoubtedly the case that the otherwise still unpopular Conservative leader hoped to use the emotional weight of a campaign to 'save the pound' as a means to generating greater public support.

The all-pervasive nature of the EU was also shown by its effects on politics in Scotland and Wales, still in the early days of operating their newly-devolved powers. Much of Wales had been granted 'Objective One' status under the Union's Regional Development Fund: this offered substantial sums for the regeneration of the area's economic infrastructure. However, the money only came with strings – 'matching funds' from the government for any European money were required for all major spending initiatives. The apparent inability of the Labour First Secretary, Alun Michael, to guarantee provision of sufficient money to Wales from the Treasury to match EU spending led to his resignation under the threat of a no-confidence motion in February 2000. Meanwhile, in Scotland, attempts to resolve a dispute about university tuition fees (the Liberal Democrats had entered a coalition with Labour in the new Scottish Parliament on the understanding that the system of student fees would be reviewed, the Lib Dems having campaigned to abolish fees in the 1999 parliamentary elections) became caught up in EU law preventing discrimination against citizens from other Union countries. A proposal that tuition fees be abolished for Scottish students only, had to be adjusted to allow students from other EU countries to benefit in a similar way. Devolution had already proved to be a highly complex process; EU obligations and policies promised to make it yet more so as the UK, as had many of its European partners before it, experienced the complicated realities of 'multi-level governance'.

Summary

The current debate on Europe in the UK includes disputes about:

- The extent to which the UK needed to retain national veto powers over EU laws and policies.
- Whether the UK ought to join the single European currency.
- How the newly devolved chambers in Scotland and Wales related both to the rest of the UK and the wider European context.

Debate

The root of many of the debates over Europe in British politics continues to be a fundamental disagreement about the implications of the EU for the UK. Is European integration compatible with British interests and the continued integrity of the UK as a country?

Those who believe that it is often advance arguments along the following lines:

- The EU brings about a welcome process of co-operation between the governments of Europe, and that this improves trust in an area with a history of conflict.
- The EU is fundamentally about co-operation between governments for their mutual benefit – any ideas about a fundamental transformation to some sort of all-embracing federal European structures are not a serious part of today's agenda. As *Reform for Enlargement* argues, 'The Eurosceptics try to portray every difference as if it called into question our fundamental relationship with Europe; and to portray every step towards co-operation as a step towards a superstate. There is not going to be a superstate. There will always be arguments between Member States precisely because they are Member States and not members of a superstate' (Foreign and Commonwealth Office, 2000: 5).
- The UK government retains its power to say no to major changes contrary to its wishes: it has a formal right of veto on new treaties and over many major European initiatives. (For instance, in late 1999, the British government vetoed plans for an EU-wide savings tax proposal which it argued might damage the bond market based in the City of London.)
- Most practically, the UK gains economically from access to the EU's single market, from any improvements in foreign and defence co-operation that the EU can bring about, and from growing European co-operation in fighting cross-border crime.

Those taking the contrary view may advance some or all of the following arguments:

- There remain important figures in the EU who do have federal ambitions for the Union of a type that threatens elements of the independence of the UK. The UK should either: say 'thus far and no further' in terms of the development of integrated European policies and institutions; try to roll back the tide of integration, with certain powers being returned to the member states of the EU; or it should leave EU altogether. The last of these three positions is that adopted by the small UK Independence Party. In recent times the Conservatives have oscillated between the first two positions.
- Many of the specific policies of the EU have been established in a form that is inimical to UK interests – either because they were set up prior to the UK joining in 1973 (the Common Agricultural Policy might be the prime example here) or because British views have been fundamentally different from those of our EU partners (for example, the Social Chapter of the Maastricht Treaty).
- Some nationalists in Scotland and Wales view the EU as implying the end of the UK as a single country but welcome this. In their view, we are increasingly moving towards a 'Europe of the Regions'. The EU certainly means that the smaller countries of the UK no longer need to belong to a single, large state for security or for economic sustainability and so the EU is to be welcomed as it makes independence viable. Others fear the influence of the EU for similar reasons, or see the UK under attack from a 'pincer' movement at the European and sub-UK levels (Redwood, 1999).

The debate on the single currency is undoubtedly influenced by broader views of the EU. Those who view the EU negatively, or who fear the 'drift to Federalism', are highly unlikely to favour British membership of the Eurozone. However, there are also a number of specific arguments, both political and economic in nature, that tend to be advanced about the single currency.

Among the arguments in favour of the UK joining the Euro are the following:

- Politically, it is suggested, joining the Euro would be a major positive signal of British commitment to the EU; it would thus help to set aside the legacy of past British ambivalence and awkwardness, and thereby allow the UK to be taken more seriously by its European partners as a major player in the EU. British influence throughout the EU would therefore increase.
- Economically, the Euro offers potential long-term benefits for the UK. Both businesses and tourists would benefit from the elimination of costs on changing currency. More fundamentally, export businesses would benefit greatly from exchange rate stability and certainty within the EU market, enabling them to plan for the future more effectively. It is no accident, for instance, that every company with a significant car-manufacturing capability in the UK wishes the UK to join the Euro.
- Joining the Euro might also help to secure the long-term position of the City of London as Europe's major financial centre, and ensure that the UK continues to attract a significant share of inward investment by multinational companies looking for a base in the EU marketplace.

However, there are also potentially powerful arguments against British membership of the Euro:

- Politically, it is argued, signing up to the Euro would be a significant loss of British independence, with numerous symbolic overtones (including losing the Queen's visage from British money).
- Economically, there could be a substantial loss of flexibility in the management of the economy. The UK would be operating under a single interest rate for the whole of the Eurozone, and would thus lose its ability to set interest rates purely for the good of the British economy.
- There might well be short-term changeover costs of converting to the new currency. The financial burden on small businesses, in particular, might be large; there could also be considerable inconvenience as numerous machines were changed over to accept the new currency, and as people struggled to accustom themselves to an entirely new set of notes and coins.

Both of the major British parties have chosen to take a 'wait-and-see' approach: officially, at least, they differ only on how long they want to wait, and what they are waiting to see. However, noises from the Labour Party are much more favourable.

Voters may well get their say on single currency in few years time. But what drives voter opinions on the EU?

- There does appear to be a significant degree of general scepticism about Europe among the British electorate. *Eurobarometer*, which conducts regular surveys of the public in EU member states, finds that whatever the general trends in public support for the EU (and for most of the 1990s the trends were downwards, after a period of rising support for integration in the late 1980s) the British public tends towards lower levels of support than most other countries (Niedermayer and Sinnott, 1995).
- Some argue, however, that this scepticism reflects primarily a lack of leadership. Many analysts of public opinion perceive a significant ability for political leaders to shape public attitudes if the public are presented with a clear vision or viewpoint that they can rally behind (Zaller, 1992). Britain, however, to a much greater degree than many of its EU partners, has lacked national leaders willing to promote a strong, positive European message. Tony Blair is the first Prime Minister since Edward Heath in the early 1970s consistently and clearly to state his pro-European credentials. But Blair is battling against an accumulated tide of public doubt, reinforced by a press, much of which is hostile to the EU. Furthermore, despite his undoubted communication skills, the Prime Minister still seems to find it difficult to develop a clear, simple and appealing message on Europe.
- The one occasion on which the people have had the opportunity to issue a judgement on Britain's involvement with Europe did seem to support the idea that voters' views can be changed by a strong and clear message from respected political leaders. The 1975 referendum on continued UK membership of the EC suggested considerable malleability to public opinion in that a near 2:1 majority *against* UK membership in opinion polls a few months prior to the vote changed in a few months to slightly more than 2:1 support *for* continued UK

membership at the time of the vote. What appears to have been most decisive in prompting this turnaround was the strong 'Yes' campaign – a campaign that united the clear majority of mainstream politicians, as well as the overwhelming majority of business interests and many trade unions.

- But is such a scenario likely to be repeated over the single currency? It remains the case that something dramatic may have to occur to move British public opinion behind supporting membership of the single currency. The balance of public opinion (see Table 8.1) is clearly against the Euro; while polls suggested that more people would support it if the government campaigned for it, the balance of opinion is still generally hostile. In addition, while Labour, the Liberal Democrats and the nationalist parties, as well as the trade unions, all seem likely to line up behind the Euro in any future vote, business views seems much more split than in 1975, with the economic case for Euro membership far less widely accepted than that for EC membership had been. While any future 'no to the Euro' campaign faces the potential problem of lacking the support of any significant mainstream non-Conservative politicians, it seems likely to be able to call on an emotional resonance in 'saving the pound' that the 'Yes' camp would struggle to achieve.

Table 8.1 Trends in recent British public opinion over membership of the Euro

Voting intentions in a referendum on joining the single currency

	Yes (%)	No (%)	Don't know (%)
Average: 1997–99	30	53	16
March 1999	32	52	15
May 1999	31	53	15
July 1999	27	58	15
September 1999	30	56	14
November 1999	27	56	17
January 2000	29	56	14
March 2000	26	58	15
May 2000	25	60	14
May 2001	24	70	7

Source: MORI – www.mori.co.uk

Chronology

1945 War ends in Europe.
1950 Launching of Schuman Plan.
1951 Treaty of Paris to form European Coal and Steel Community signed; Pleven plan for European Defence Community launched.
1954 European Defence Community Treaty rejected by French National Assembly.
1957 Rome Treaties signed to form Economic Community.

1960 Britain forms European Free Trade Association with six other countries.
1961 Prime Minister Harold Macmillan announces British application for membership of EC.
1963 French President Charles de Gaulle announces veto of British application for EC membership.
1967 Second British application for EC membership – again vetoed by de Gaulle.
1971 Third British application for EC membership made by government of Edward Heath.
1973 UK (along with Ireland and Denmark) enter the EC.
1975 UK referendum on continued EC membership: 2:1 majority vote 'Yes'.
1977–84 Prolonged dispute about British contributions to the EC budget.
1986 Single European Act signed.
1990 Mrs Thatcher's resignation (in part provoked by disputes over the EC).
1992 Maastricht Treaty on European Union signed; European monetary crisis with UK dropping out of EMS; Danish and French referendums on Maastricht Treaty showing strong public opposition.
1996 'Beef war'.
1997 Amsterdam Treaty signed.
1999 Launch of single European currency.
2002 Euro becomes legal tender.

Discussion Questions

1. Would Britain's relations with Europe have been easier if the UK had joined in the European unification process at the beginning, in the 1950s? Why or why not?
2. Why have the two major political parties alternated in their periods of greater/lesser hostility towards British involvement in Europe?
3. How important do you judge the EU to be in increasing support for devolution and/or independence in Scotland and Wales?

References

Baker, David, Gamble, Andrew and Ludlam, Steve (1994) 'The parliamentary siege of Maastricht', *Parliamentary Affairs*, Vol. 47, No. 1.

Charlton, Michael (1983) *The Price of Victory*, London: BBC Books.

Cowley, Philip and Norton, Philip (1999) 'Rebels and rebellions: Conservative MPs in the 1992 Parliament', *British Journal of Politics and International Relations*, Vol. 1, No. 1.

Foreign and Commonwealth Office (2000) *IGC: Reform for Enlargement*, London: HMSO.

Kaiser, Wolfram (1996) *Using Europe, Abusing the Europeans: Britain and European Integration, 1945–1963*, London: Macmillan.

Milward, Alan S. (1992) *The European Rescue of the Nation State*, London: Routledge.

Moravcsik, Andrew (1998) *The Choice for Europe: Social Purpose and State Power from Messina to Maastricht*, London: UCL Press.

Niedermayer, Oskar and Sinnott, Richard (eds) (1995) *Public Opinion and Internationalized Governance*, Oxford: Oxford University Press.

Norton, Philip (1996) *National Parliaments and the European Union*, London: Frank Cass.

Redwood, John (1999) *The Death of Britain? The UK's Constitutional Crisis*, London: Macmillan.

Riddell, Peter (1998) *Parliament under Pressure*, London: Gollancz.

Urwin, Derek (1995) *The Community of Europe* (second edition), London: Longman.

Zaller, John (1992) *The Nature and Origins of Mass Opinion*, Cambridge: Cambridge University Press.

Further reading

Baker, David and Seawright, David (1998) *Britain for and against Europe: British Politics and the Question of European Integration*, Oxford: Clarendon Press.

Brivati, Brian and Jones, Harriet (eds) (1993) *From Reconstruction to Integration: Britain and Europe since 1945*, Leicester: Leicester University Press.

George, Stephen (1991) *Britain and European Integration since 1945*, Oxford: Blackwell.

George, Stephen (1997) *An Awkward Partner: Britain in the European Community* (second edition), Oxford: Clarendon Press.

Gowland, David and Turner, Arthur (2000) *Reluctant Europeans: Britain and European Integration 1945–1998*, London: Longman.

Young, Hugo (1998) *This Blessed Plot: Britain and Europe from Churchill to Blair*, London: Macmillan.

Young, John W. (2000) *Britain and European Unity*, London: Macmillan.

PART THREE **Representation**

Political Parties: Organisational Change and Intra-Party Democracy

Justin Fisher

CHAPTER NINE

Introduction

British political parties have different organisational origins which are still reflected in their current structures. The organisational differences between the Conservative and Labour parties, for example, have frequently been explained by the fact that the Conservatives were a party in Parliament before they acquired a mass membership, whereas the Labour Party was formed by extra-parliamentary organisations. As a consequence, Labour has traditionally been more concerned with grass-roots opinion – a 'bottom-up' party – while the Conservatives have been more elitist – a 'top-down' party. In the past this explanation had much to commend it, but it requires re-examination because in the period since the 1997 general election both parties have made significant organisational changes and, over a longer time-span, the composition of the parties has changed. Similarly, while the old Liberal Party might have shared an organisational heritage with the Conservatives, the current Liberal Democratic party is very different and merits separate consideration.

This chapter is concerned, therefore, to evaluate the current structures of the major parties in the context of party organisational models and, more specifically, to address the question of internal party democracy.

Background

The Conservative Party

The Conservative Party is, and always has been, a hierarchical party. All party efforts are directed towards assisting the parliamentary party and especially the leader. This, in part, is a reflection of its origins. The party was established in Parliament before extra-parliamentary organisations and activities began to develop in the mid- to late nineteenth century. The parliamentary party was thus paramount from the start. A tendency to hierarchy and the pre-eminence of the leader are also reflections of the party's broad political thought, which involves approval of authority and status and a willingness to serve, as well as one of the party's key objectives which itself helps to shape party thinking: the pursuit of governmental power.

Until the reforms of 1998, two features dominated Conservative Party organisation: the lack of formal internal democracy and its divided nature. The reforms made were to some extent a challenge to these traditional features and to understand the importance of the changes a summary of the pre-1998 position is necessary.

Lack of formal internal democracy

Policy-making. The party conference has never had any formal policy-making powers in the Conservative Party. The standard interpretation has long been that the annual conference is little more than a public relations exercise at which senior party members address, and receive rousing approval from, a compliant and passive party membership. This interpretation has been challenged by Kelly (1989), who argues that it is misleading to focus on the main party conference in isolation. Rather, the many regional and sectional conferences of the party, which are held throughout the year, should also be considered. It is here, Kelly suggests, that issues are debated in a much more democratic manner and the views expressed will frequently be taken up in speeches by senior party figures at the main conference. The level of support accorded to leading spokespeople at the conference is conditioned by how extensively they articulate demands coming from the grass-roots via the other conferences. Kelly concludes that the Conservative Party is in fact far more consultative, albeit in this informal way, than has often been imagined. *Election of the party leader.* Prior to Edward Heath's election as leader in 1965, when leaders of the party resigned or died, new leaders 'emerged'. Resignation was not always wholly voluntary. In some cases 'the men in grey suits' – a loose group of senior people in the party – are alleged to have advised leaders to resign. A successor would emerge to assume the leadership by a similar process – an individual would emerge after discussions among senior party figures.

In 1965 this system was changed. Leadership candidates now had to be nominated and seconded by Conservative MPs and the latter then participated in an election. In order to secure victory, a candidate required an overall majority of votes plus a 15% lead over his/her nearest rival. If these conditions were not satisfied, a second ballot was held in which only an overall majority was required. Finally, if this had not resolved the issue, a third ballot would be held involving the most popular three candidates, using the Alternative Vote method of election. This system was amended in 1991 such that the third ballot (if required) would be confined to the top two candidates.

Divided party organisation

Before 1998, at national level there were three principal foci of power in the party: the leader, the parliamentary party and Central Council of the National Union of Conservative and Unionist Organisations. The leader had sole responsibility for the drafting of the election manifesto and direct control over Conservative Central Office, the organisational centre of the party. Local constituency associations gained representation through the Central Council but were independent of the centre. In particular, although associations were supposed to submit a proportion of their income to the centre, not all did. Moreover, there was no concept of cross-subsidy between local parties. Some local parties remain notably wealthy, others notably poor (Fisher, 2000).

The selection of parliamentary candidates

Procedures for candidate selection have not changed dramatically. In the initial stage prospective candidates apply to Conservative Central Office and officials undertake an intensive interviewing process in order to define a 'pool of eligibles' for vacant seats (Norris and Lovenduski, 1995: 35). Those approved can then apply to constituencies looking for a candidate. The constituencies themselves select candidates in three stages: a selection committee and then the constituency executive committee whittles down applications to a short-list from which the constituency members choose a candidate at a special general meeting of the constituency association. Ordinary party members, therefore, have the final say on the choice of candidate. It is worth noting, in addition, that party members now have additional roles in candidate selection as a result of the introduction of new electoral systems. Members have now voted on the ordering of candidates on party lists (e.g. for the European Parliament elections) as well as on the selection of a candidate for the election of the London Mayor.

The Labour Party

In terms of its constitution, the Labour Party has always appeared to be less hierarchical and more democratic than the Conservative Party. On the face of it, the party leadership in Parliament was accountable to its membership, even if indirectly, through the annual conference. Appearances can be deceptive, however. In his classic study in the 1950s, Robert McKenzie (1955) argued that in terms of the distribution of power within the party there was little difference between Labour and the Conservatives. Both were subject to 'the iron law of oligarchy' (Michels, 1911). Despite the constitutional position, power in the Labour Party was concentrated in the hands of the Parliamentary leadership.

Like the Conservatives, Labour has made organisational changes since the 1997 election, largely in the field of policy-making. As before, it is useful to outline the prior position for comparison.

Policy-making

The party conference has traditionally been seen as the ultimate source of authority in the party. In relation to policy-making, resolutions for debate could be put to conference by unions or Constituency Labour Party (CLP) representatives and votes on these, in theory, determined party policy. In addition, conference elected the National Executive Committee (NEC) and still does so. Technically, this makes the NEC subservient to conference but the NEC has clearly had the leading role in policy-making. Before recent changes most aspects of party policy originated from within the NEC and most of the main conference debates focused upon proposals put forward by the NEC. Since the 1980s, the NEC has also had joint responsibility, with the Parliamentary leadership, for drawing up the party's manifesto. Even before recent changes, however, its influence over the manifesto contents was in decline as more attention was given to the advice of the Shadow Communications Agency (1986–92) and its successors, which were intended to help improve the party's public image but gradually took a stronger role in policy initiation. Nonetheless, the NEC could clearly act as a check upon the power of the leadership and this certainly posed problems for Labour leaders in the past. Since the late 1980s, however, the NEC has been increasingly loyal to the leader and critics on the NEC have become increasingly marginalised.

The prominent role played by trade unions in the Labour Party has been a frequent subject of criticism by opponents. Unions affiliate to the party and acquire voting strength on the basis of the number of members affiliated. In the past, unions provided the bulk of the party's finance and had the great majority of votes at the conference – 90% until 1992. To compound matters, each union cast a 'block vote' – all of its votes being cast on one side, usually without reference to the views of union members and whether or not there were divisions in a union's conference delegation. Nonetheless, it has been argued that the power of trade unions in the party has been overstated, whether due to union restraint (Minkin, 1991), the absence of a single union view (Taylor, 1989; Minkin, 1991; Rosamund, 1992), or the fact that there is no political alternative to involvement in the Labour Party.

In 1992, the union share of the votes at conference was reduced to 70% and in the following year conference recommended that unions should be able to split their votes in future, thus ending the block voting system. Further reductions in the proportion of union votes to 50% at conference followed.

Election of the leader

Formerly, the party leader was elected by members of the Parliamentary Labour Party (PLP) alone, but in 1980 a new system was introduced. The leader and deputy leader are elected by an electoral college comprising the PLP, affiliated organisations (largely trade unions) and individual members. The votes are calculated so that one-third of the votes are allocated to each of the three components of the electoral college. A candidate must obtain more than 50% of the vote or a second ballot is held. However, before a contest can take place a challenger for the leadership must have the support of at least 20% of the PLP (this was increased from 5% in 1988). Moreover, if the Labour Party is in government, this requirement must be accompanied by the approval for the contest by at least two-thirds of the annual conference. These stipulations have led many to observe that despite Labour's stronger democratic credentials, it is easier to unseat a Conservative leader than it is to unseat a Labour one.

The contests for the deputy leadership have proved to be politically significant. The first such contest in 1981, for example, saw a very narrow victory for Denis Healey, identified with the right wing of the party, over Tony Benn, the standard bearer of the left. In subsequent contests, the deputy leadership has been seen as a way of uniting different wings of the party. Thus, Roy Hattersley, elected deputy in 1983, formed, it was said, a 'dream ticket' with the more left-wing Neil Kinnock; John Prescott's trade union connections and 'old Labour' credentials are seen to balance Tony Blair's modernising approach.

Controversially, however, this system has also been used to elect the leader of the party in the Welsh Assembly and for the Labour mayoral candidate in London. This was controversial because, in the first place, some unions chose not to split their vote and, in the second place, because some argued that the mayoral contest was essentially a candidate election. If that were the case, ordinary candidate selection procedures were more appropriate. The result of these elections was that the candidates preferred by the leadership both won, but at the price of creating division. And, of course, the Welsh Assembly leader subsequently resigned, while the Labour mayoral candidate was beaten by his former rival, who stood as an Independent.

Selection of parliamentary candidates

Since 1993 parliamentary candidates have been selected on the basis of one member, one vote (OMOV). Previously selections were made by local electoral colleges in which trade unions had up to 40% of the votes.

Until the current round of selections any party member could apply for selection. A local committee then compiled a short-list from those who had acquired a nomination. Constituencies do not have a free hand, however. The most obvious limitation was a decision taken in 1993 that, in half the parliamentary seats where Labour was the incumbent or where it stood a good chance of victory, there should be all-women short-lists of candidates. This represented a developing trend within the Labour Party to attempt to increase the number of women in Parliament. This proved to be a very successful innovation in that 101 of Labour's 1997 MPs were women, but it caused some resentment among CLPs. As a result, the policy was challenged in the courts and found to be illegal. In the Scottish and Welsh elections of 1999 a new approach to achieving the same end was introduced – 'twinning' constituencies and requiring one to select a woman and one a man.

Formerly the NEC played a minor role in candidate selection. It had the power to approve a candidate after selection and rarely withheld approval. Since the mid-1980s, however, the NEC has displayed a far greater willingness to exercise its power of veto and formally took a much greater role in the selection of by-election candidates. Currently, aspirants for candidature have to be approved before being able to apply and CLPs can only select from the panel of approved candidates. Thus while OMOV has extended democracy in the party, central control over candidate selection has increased. It is worth noting also that the introduction of party lists for election to the European Parliament, as well as in Scotland, Wales and London, further increased central control since the centre determined the ordering of lists, thus influencing substantially which individuals were elected.

The Liberal Democrats

The organisational structures and procedures of the Liberal Democrats have not changed very much in recent years. On paper, the party appears to be very democratic, members have participatory rights in policy-making, leadership elections and candidate selection. The party conference, to which party members send representatives, is sovereign in policy-making. Members are also able vote on part of the composition of the Federal Policy Committee, which drafts manifestos. That said, the party leader still chairs and directs the work of this important committee. A national postal ballot on the basis of one member, one vote elects not only the leader, but also the head of the extra-parliamentary party (the Party President).

Candidate selection in the Liberal Democrats is broadly similar to that in the Conservative Party, although with a greater devolution of responsibilities. Aspirants apply to their state party (England, Wales or Scotland), which then filters out those deemed unsuitable and creates an approved list of candidates. Anyone who passes this first stage can then apply for selection in local constituencies, where selected members of the local party draw up short-lists. At this stage, the party insists on quotas of women. The final decision rests with a ballot of all the members of the constituency. The policy of promoting women candidates was also reflected in the party's lists for the European Parliament election (but not in the Scottish, Welsh or London elections), with the party insisting upon 'zipping' by gender – most regional lists were headed by a woman, followed by a man, then another woman and so on.

The generally democratic nature of Liberal Democrat organisation is partly explained by fact that the party has relatively few MPs and needs to develop a strong membership base, particularly since few have institutional sources of income. Since they need to retain members, the Liberal Democrats have a clear incentive to maximise membership influence.

Summary

- The Conservative Party has always had a hierarchical organisation.
- Constitutionally, Labour has appeared to be more internally democratic than the Conservatives.
- The Liberal Democrats appear to be the most internally democratic of the major parties.
- Internal democracy can be evaluated by examining policy-making, leadership elections and candidate selection.

Theoretical Considerations

It is useful to outline some theories relating to party organisation at this point, because they help to explain why parties have the structures that they do. Broadly speaking, the principal theories of party organisation can be categorised into two types: those which focus mainly on the composition of the party membership; and those which focus broadly on the ways in which parties adapt to electoral competition. A summary appears in Table 9.1.

Table 9.1 Broad theories of membership roles in party organisations

	Role of members
Duverger (1954)	• Differentiation between cadre and non-cadre parties. • Cadre parties – limited role for members. • Mass parties – extensive role for members. Limited leadership discretion. Members actively sought.
Strom (1990)	• Differentiation between capital and non-capital parties. • Small role for members in parties representing capital. • For non-capital parties, active role for members in policy-making. Strong focus on leadership accountability. Overall, emphasis on satisfying members rather than maximising votes.
Kirchheimer (1966)	• Strengthening of leaders, downgrading of members. Growth of party professionals. New role for interest groups in party programme. Demand for intra-party consensus.
Epstein (1967)	• Differentiation between electoral and non-electoral parties. • In non-electoral parties, satisfaction of members secondary to votes. Once non-electoral parties become electoral parties, members' interests become secondary. • In electoral parties, vote-catching renders all other interests secondary. Demand for flexibility and limited role for members.
Katz and Mair (1995)	• Members largely irrelevant due to capital-intensive approach. Members required for three reasons: resources in internal party power struggles, leadership elections and to maintain the party myth.

Party composition

The most famous advocate of this approach is Maurice Duverger (1954). According to Duverger, there are essentially two types of party – *cadre parties* and *mass parties*. Cadre parties are more elitist. These are likely to be parties that existed at the elite level prior to extensions of the franchise to the broad mass of citizens. These parties had little need or desire to seek a large membership, relying instead on a few individuals – it was quality rather than quantity of members that mattered. Moreover, there was little financial incentive to recruit members, because such parties usually had wealthy financial backers.

Duverger also argued that there were two main types of cadre party. One grouped around aristocrats, prominent industrialists, bankers and influential churchmen; the other grouped around lesser industrialists, trades peoples, teachers, civil servants, lawyers and writers. Such organisation as existed at the local level was a *caucus*. This was run by local *notables*, who had expert knowledge of running election campaigns.

According to Duverger, mass parties were more commonly found on the left. The left would want to educate the newly-enfranchised voters politically and so leftist parties had an incentive to recruit as many members as possible. Also, there was a financial rationale in membership recruitment since leftist parties would be less likely to be the beneficiaries of large financial backing. Mass membership would also involve some elements of internal party democracy since individual members would expect some influence in return for their commitment to the party. While Duverger's view was that cadre parties would be more likely to be right wing and mass parties left wing, he recognised that rightist parties might ultimately seek to become more like mass parties in order to extend their appeal.

A second advocate of the party composition approach is Kaare Strom (1990). Like Duverger, he argued that left- and right-wing parties could be differentiated. Right-wing parties are likely to be wealthier, can therefore pay for campaign services and consequently have little incentive to extend participatory rights to members. In contrast, parties representing labour are less wealthy and cannot afford professional campaign help. They must rely upon active members and so must provide activists with participatory incentives. As a consequence, members become involved in policy-making as well as holding leaders to account. However, Strom argues that members will have less regard for the views of the electorate than leaders do. In short, members are likely to be policy-oriented as opposed to leaders, who are vote maximisers (Strom, 1990: 577). Since leaders have to involve the membership in policy-making, this is likely to run the risk of electoral failure.

Electoral competition

There are three principal theories to summarise here. What unites them is a view that party support on the basis of social cleavages is in decline. Consequently, parties have become electoral maximisers, seeking support for all sections of society. Otto Kirchheimer (1966) argued that this led to their becoming what he described as 'catch-all' parties. The organisational consequences of this development were that party leadership was strengthened and party members played a declining role in policy-making and candidate selection. The logic was that members would become increasingly insignificant, in terms of their number, their financial importance to parties and their participation in campaigns, since parties would become increasingly professional in both campaigning and organisation, a point later reinforced by the analysis of Pannebianco (1988). This process would be aided by a growth is state financial assistance to parties. In addition, parties would seek more support by incorporating interest groups' demands into party programmes and generally seeking consensus in order to seek an advantage among voters.

Leon Epstein (1967) offers a second variation on this theme. Parties should be differentiated, in his view, according to whether they sought primarily to advocate a cause or to win votes. Epstein describes the former as 'non-electoral parties' and the latter as 'electoral parties'. In non-electoral parties, exemplified by traditional European left-wing parties, membership participation was likely to be more extensive. However, if such parties became more concerned with vote maximisation, the participatory rights of members would become secondary to the goal of securing votes. Moreover, Epstein argued, the vote-seeking strategy would demand a flexible approach to party management whereby the party leadership could operate fairly autonomously. It would become desirable to limit members' influence so that no inconsistency was apparent between the vote-seeking leadership and the cause-oriented members.

A third variation is offered by Richard Katz and Peter Mair (1995). Their conception of the cartel party was essentially driven by the growth of state subsidies to political parties which enabled parties to sustain their organisations. Although direct state subsidy is not a feature of the UK system, Katz and Mair offer some insights which are useful in the UK context. They argue that as parties become wealthy, members will become increasingly irrelevant. However, parties will still require members for two main reasons. First, members can become a resource, via internal elections, in intra-party battles. Second, by retaining members a party can continue to propagate the myth that it is a representative mass party.

Summary

- Theoretical models focus either upon the composition of the party or upon electoral maximisation.
- The role of members will tend to be greater under party composition models.
- The role of members is seen to be in decline in electoral competition models.

Update

Conservative Party

Following the 1997 general election defeat, *Blueprint for Change* was issued the Conservative Party. It proposed significant changes in Conservative Party organisation. The perceived need for change was a product of five factors (Webb, 2000: 195–6). First, the scale of defeat in 1997 was bound to lead to an examination of the organisational as well as the political failings of the party. Second, the new party leader, William Hague, needed to make his mark on the party and in the light of the rancour that had preceded the 1997 defeat, organisational change was likely to ignite less fervent passions than major policy change. Third, there had been for some considerable time a number of internal critics (such as the *Charter Movement*) who had called for greater democracy within the party. Many party members agreed – 43% of members felt that the party did not pay attention to their views (compared with 39% of Labour members) and only 57% had a strong sense of political efficacy (compared with 74% of Labour members) (Fisher, 1996: 153). Fourth, the central party had encountered considerable financial difficulties during the 1990s and yet had frequently been frustrated in attempts to alleviate these problems by gaining access to the funds of some wealthy local Constituency Associations. Finally, there was a broad feeling within the party that it had fallen a long way behind the Labour Party in terms of organisation and management. The Conservatives, too, needed to modernise.

The party's consultation exercise on reform produced *Fresh Future*. The *Fresh Future* proposals were overwhelmingly endorsed by the party membership (80% in favour) in 1998. These created, for the first time, a 'single and unified' party in the sense that its 'voluntary, professional and parliamentary pillars were drawn together into a single structure' (Webb, 2000: 196). Second, the party devised a new and binding codified constitution. Third, a new *Board of Management* was formed as the 'supreme decision-making body on all matters relating to party organisation and management' (quoted in Webb, 2000: 196).

One of the most notable features of the new party constitution is the disappearance of the autonomy of the Constituency Associations, which are now formally subject to the authority of the central party. Formal control includes the requirement for annual reports and criteria for local party performance in areas such as membership, fund-raising and campaigning. Failure to meet performance targets can result in the centre effectively taking over a 'failing' local party (Webb, 2000: 196–7).

The Conservative Party's system of conferences is maintained and the status of conference deliberations and decisions remains consultative rather than binding. As a result, while members may retain informal influence over policy, as Kelly (1989) suggests, they continue to lack any formal input.

Election of the leader

The new constitution introduced a system in which the parliamentary party now only has the right to act as the preliminary selectorate in the choice of leader. Through a system of ballots, the MPs reduce the number of candidates to two and the final choice is then in the hands of the party's mass membership, who cast their votes in a one member one vote postal ballot. The procedure, which was used to elect Ian Duncan-Smith in 2001, is outlined in Figure 9.1. Importantly, it will now be more difficult to challenge an incumbent leader since a vote of no confidence is required before a contest can take place. Previously, a challenger needed the support of only 10% of MPs to mount a challenge.

Plebiscitary democracy

Recent changes have involved an extension of internal party democracy, not just in relation to leadership elections but also in relation to other party matters. While the exercise had no formal status, the National Union undertook a process of consultation during the last party leader election under the old system in 1997. Peers, MEPs, constituency chairs and members of the Nation Union Executive were consulted at each round of the contest, the results being presented to the 1922 Committee before MPs voted. Significantly, every group preferred Clarke to Hague (Denver et al., 1998: 281) although Hague was elected.

There have also been two internal party referendums, both in 1998. First, the party membership was balloted on the *Fresh Future* reforms. This produced a vote of 80% in favour. Second, the membership was balloted on the leadership's stance on the single European currency (a policy of opposition to British membership in the next election manifesto) and 84% supported the leadership.

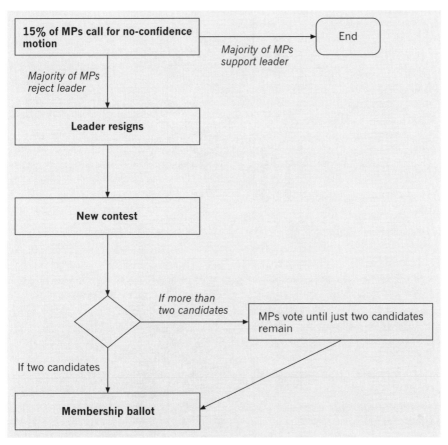

Figure 9.1 Conservative leadership election process

Labour Party

Policy-making

Labour, too, has undergone radical organisational change. While organisational reforms had been ongoing for the previous decade, *Partnership in Power*, first issued as a consultation document in January 1997, represented an attempt to re-define internal policy-making with a view to the likely election of a Labour government. These changes were approved at the 1997, post-election conference. The purpose was to create more stable relationships between future Labour governments and the rest of the party, as well as to strengthen intra-party democracy. There was a strong desire on the part of the leadership to avoid highly visible and damaging conflicts between Labour governments and the extra-parliamentary party. It was hoped to achieve this through a new system of policy-making, based upon the idea of a two-year 'rolling programme' of policy formulation. A diagram of the process is shown in Figure 9.2 and Table 9.2.

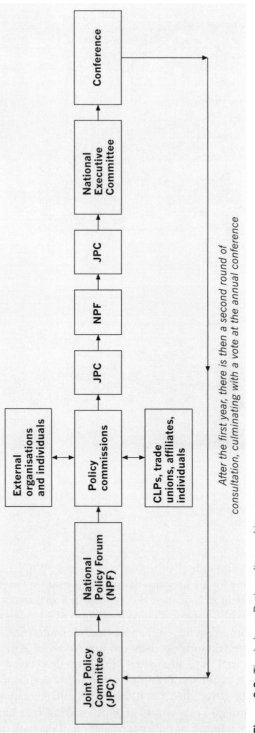

After the first year, there is then a second round of consultation, culminating with a vote at the annual conference

Figure 9.2 The Labour Party policy-making process

Table 9.2 Membership of various parts of the Labour policy-making process

Joint Policy Committee	National Policy Forum	Policy commissions	National Executive Committee
Chaired by the party leader	175 members drawn from all parts of the party	Eight individual policy commissions initially established	Elected members by conference, non-elected members marked*
Composition: 8 Ministers 8 NEC members 3 Elected from NPF	*Composition:* 54 CLP representatives 19 Regional party representatives 20 Trade union representatives 9 MPs 6 MEPs 8 Ministers 9 Local government representatives 9 Socialist Society representatives All NEC members	*Composition:* 3 Ministers 3 NEC members 4 NPF members	*Composition:* 12 Trade union representatives 1 Socialist Society representative 6 CLP representatives 2 Local government representatives 3 PLP/MEP representatives 1 Youth representative* 3 Ministers* Leader* Deputy leader* Leader of MEPs* Treasurer* General secretary*

The main vehicle for the leadership in the policy-making process is the *Joint Policy Committee* (JPC) (Webb, 2000: 204). The JPC provides 'strategic oversight' of the process and sets the initial agenda and terms of reference for detailed consideration by the National Policy Forum (NPF). Its first task in year one of the two-year cycle is to establish a number of *policy commissions* and their precise terms of reference. These commissions invite, receive and consider submissions from a variety of sources (including individual members) before producing reports with comments and proposals for the JPC to consider. The JPC is then able to add its own comments before passing it in turn on to the NPF for deliberation. It then returns to the JPC for consideration before the NEC prepares a document for discussion at conference. The consequence of this model is that while individual members have an input into the process via submissions and the NPF, the leadership has several opportunities to offer counter-proposals. This input is further enhanced by the fact that a second year-long round of consultation and modification then occurs before conference votes on the final policy recommendations (Webb, 2000: 203–4).

The intention is to create a system of policy-making that is consensual, and avoid conference being the scene for electorally-damaging party conflicts. Conference remains sovereign, but its agenda is fundamentally determined by the new process in which the leadership takes a very strong role. Indeed, Seyd and Whiteley argue that the whole process is demonstrably dominated by the leadership since, in particular, ministerial participation is much better resourced than that of ordinary members of the National Policy Forum (Seyd and Whiteley, 2000: 80).

Plebiscitary democracy

Like the Conservatives, Labour has also employed plebiscitary democracy. This was first used in 1995, when Tony Blair balloted individual members to approve changes to Clause Four of the party's constitution. In 1996, the leadership held another referendum on proposals for the forthcoming election manifesto. In both ballots, the leadership position was overwhelmingly endorsed by the membership.

Summary

- Both the Labour and Conservative parties have undergone significant organisational reform since the 1997 general election.
- Conservative reforms have focused upon a consolidation of existing party structures into one structure and reforms to the election of the leader.
- Labour reforms have focused primarily upon the policy-making process.

Debate

The first question to consider is the extent to which current party organisations reflect the theoretical models introduced above. In the case of party composition models, Duverger's model provides a reasonable historical fit. The Conservative and Liberal parties fit well as cadre parties. In addition, both demonstrated the influence of the mass party by extending their organisation on the ground. In the case of Labour, the evidence is more mixed. The initial organisation of the Labour Party owed less to mass parties and more to a form of cadre – with the trade unions acting as notables.

Strom's analyses fits Labour well until 1983. As Seyd and Whiteley note, the view of the leadership was that the heavy defeat at the 1983 election was a consequence of the party having been hijacked by extremists. The election was fought on a programme that reflected these activists' priorities rather than those of the electorate and the result was humiliation at the polls. However, the leadership response was not to reduce individual members' involvement but to increase it, and also increase the number of members. In this way, it was hoped that the party would reflect the desires of the electorate more closely (Seyd and Whiteley, 2000: 75–6).

Electoral competition models fare rather better. In line with Kirchheimer's thesis, in both the Labour and Conservative parties, the leader has been strengthened and there has been a growth of party professionalism. Moreover, Labour's new policy process involves interest groups in making submissions to policy commissions and explicitly seeks consensus. However, members remain important to the parties. Involvement in decision-making has increased and the parties have also acknowledged the important role that party members play in campaigning. Epstein's thesis fits well for the Conservatives. The party has always sought to allow the leadership maximum flexibility and the continued lack of formal policy involvement for members continues this tradition. In the case of Labour, the model certainly fits the pre-1980s period, when membership participation was limited and membership recruitment half-hearted (Seyd and Whiteley, 2000: 75). However, membership involvement has increased more recently, thereby reducing flexibility in theory, and of course membership is now sought more vigorously. Katz and Mair's analysis is also useful. While their view of the irrelevance of members is not borne out, the idea of members as a resource is instructive. Both the Conservative and Labour parties have used plebiscitary democracy to fight intra-party battles. The use of referendums has allowed the leadership to claim greater legitimacy for its position. Moreover, the Conservative reforms mean that the membership will now be used as a resource in the final round of leadership contests. Finally, all parties continue to seek members in order to extend the myth of the mass party.

Overall, we can argue that British parties are now characterised by elements of Duverger's, Kirchheimer's and Katz and Mair's theses. Leaders still dominate the parties, but the continuing role of members has generally been understated. Of course, the electoral competition models were largely conceived with extensive state subventions in mind – something that does not exist in Britain. However, as we have seen, the assumption that parties only require members for financial input is clearly flawed.

The next question to consider is the extent of internal democracy in the parties. We can evaluate this be examining three components of party decision-making where members may become involved – policy-making, leadership elections and candidate selection. The details are summarised in Table 9.3. At first sight, it seems clear that the Liberal Democrats are most internally democratic. Members are involved in all three aspects, and in choosing leaders and selecting candidates their views are paramount. In policy-making, the principal check is the leadership domination of the manifesto-drafting Federal Policy Committee. In part of this strong membership is an inheritance from the Social Democratic Party (SDP) (which united with the Liberals to form the Liberal Democrats in 1988). The leaders of the SDP had broken away from Labour and were anxious to remove power from large groups like the unions. However, what must also be borne in mind is the Liberal Democrats' electoral position. The party is unlikely to gain power at Westminster in the near future. In that sense, the Liberal Democrats appear as a 'non-electoral' party in Epstein's terminology and thus a greater membership role is more appropriate. It is the case, however, that the party is in power (at least in coalition) in Scotland and in Wales. It remains to be seen whether extensive membership participation will survive the party's new-found status in the devolved institutions.

Comparing the Labour and Conservative parties, it would appear that Labour is more internally democratic. On the one hand, Conservative members have a

Table 9.3 Party organisational roles

	Labour			Conservatives			Liberal Democrats		
	Role of members	Role of centre	Balance of power	Role of members	Role of centre	Balance of power	Role of members	Role of centre	Balance of power
Policy-making	Submissions to policy commissions. Membership of National Policy Forum. Annual conference.	Membership of all policy-making bodies. Key role agenda-setting via Joint Policy Committee.	Dominated by the centre, though enhanced role for members.	No formal role.	Determines all party policy.	Centre.	Sovereign annual conference. Election of Federal Policy Committee.	Party leader chairs and directs Federal Policy Committee.	Slightly in favour of members, but leadership role on Federal Policy Committee is important.
Selection of candidates	All members have a vote (OMOV) from panel of approved candidates.	Drawing-up of approved panel. Determining of position on party lists.	Relative balance, though central panel vetting important.	All members have a vote. Local elites draw up a short-list. Additionally, members vote on ordering of party lists.	Initial vetting of all potential candidates. Technical veto over local choices (not used).	Members and especially local party elites.	All members have a vote. Local elites draw up a short-list, subject to quota requirements.	Initial vetting of all potential candidates. Use of quotas on short-lists. Determining of party lists for Euro elections.	Members and local party elites, though quotas significant.
Election of leader	All members have a vote in the membership section of the electoral college (each section carries one-third of the votes in the college).	Parliamentarians have one-third of the electoral college votes. Ability to draw up short-list for non-leadership contests where electoral college is used.	For leadership elections, a relatively even balance. For non-leadership contests, centre has greater power.	All members have vote, but vote is restricted to just final two candidates.	All MPs have a vote on whether to retain the leader. MPs decide (through voting) which are the final two candidates.	Slightly towards the centre, since MPs frame the membership ballot. But, members have the final say.	All members have a vote.	None.	Members.

greater role in candidate selection and, arguably, now in leadership elections. But, they continue to have no formal role in policy-making. There are democratic elements of consultation within the party but these are largely informal. The party in that sense is like a family: discussion may take place and even be heeded, but it is always clear that the head of the family is in charge. Moreover, just as informal democratic expression can be extended, so it can easily be withdrawn. Labour members, by way of contrast, are involved in various stages of its new policy-making process. Members can either become involved or be represented in the National Policy Forum, through submissions to policy commissions and at the party's conference, which remains supreme. Yet while the party is constitutionally democratic, it is clear that the leadership plays a much stronger role than the constitution suggests. Partly through control of bodies like the NEC and the NPF, and partly through the compliance of the party, the Labour leader clearly plays a vital role in the party's affairs.

Summary

- Electoral competition models of party organisation describe British parties best, although they fail to explain the growth, rather than the decline, in scope for membership participation.
- The reforms in the Conservative and Labour parties have done little to diminish leadership power.
- The Liberal Democrats remain the most internally democratic party.

Conclusion

British political parties have made significant organisational changes in recent years. In the case of Labour and the Conservatives, these have been in part a result of the shock of electoral defeat. In the case of the Liberal Democrats, the formation of a new party has itself been the impetus. Importantly, while traditional electoral cleavages have declined, the parties have extended the role of members rather than marginalised them. This has been for three principal reasons. First, in keeping with Duverger's thesis, there has been more of a convergence around the idea of a mass party (even though membership numbers have rarely been impressive). Second, parties have acknowledged that members play an important role, and one that has hitherto been understated. Finally, party leaderships have seen that members can also perform an excellent resource role in settling intra-party disputes. Thus far, the use of members in this way has favoured the leadership.

Yet despite this growth of participation, leaderships arguably remain just as dominant as ever. In the Conservative Party, members still have no formal role in policy-making, and William Hague, like Tony Blair, realised the potential enhancement of leadership power that can arise from party referendums. In the Labour Party's new policy-making process, the leadership has plenty of time to avoid disputes and set agendas, while in the Liberal Democrats the leaders control the committee that drafts the manifestos. In short, it seems doubtful that recent changes have fundamentally altered the oligarchic tendencies in parties that Michels predicted in 1911 and McKenzie observed in Britain in the 1950s.

Chronology

1867 National Union of Conservative and Constitutional Associations formed.
1870 Conservative Central Office established.
1877 National Liberal Federation formed.
1900 Labour Representation Committee (LRC) established.
1906 LRC becomes the Labour Party.
1918 Category of individual members created by the Labour Party.
1965 Conservative leadership rules changed. Formal elections by the parliamentary party introduced.
1980 Labour leadership election rules changed. Elections now by electoral college.
1981 Formation of the Social Democratic Party (SDP).
1983 SDP/Liberal Alliance established.   .
1988 Liberal Democrats formed from a merger of the SDP and the Liberal Party.
1992 Trade union vote at Labour Conference reduced from 90% to 70%.
1993 OMOV introduced for Labour candidate selection.
       Trade union vote at Labour Conference begins to reduce to 50%.
1996 'All-women short-lists' for Labour parliamentary candidates ruled illegal.
1997 *Partnership in Power* issued and approved by the Labour Party.
       Blueprint for Change issued by the Conservative Party.
1988 *Fresh Future*, a result of consultation following *Blueprint for Change*, approved by the Conservative Party.
       Alun Michael elected leader of the Labour Party in Wales.
2000 Frank Dobson selected as Labour candidate for the London mayoral election.
2001 Iain Duncan-Smith elected leader of the Conservative Party under new rules.

Discussion Questions

1. Discuss the view that the recent reforms in the Conservative and Labour parties are largely cosmetic exercises designed simply to enhance the power of the leadership.
2. If you were forming a new political party, how much influence would you give members in terms of policy-making, the election of the leader and the selection of candidates?
3. In terms of organisation, are British parties closer to Duverger's model or those such as Kirchheimer's?

References

Denver, D., Fisher, J., Cowley, P. and Pattie, C. (1998) *British Elections and Parties Review.* Vol. 8: *The 1997 General Election*, London: Frank Cass.

Duverger, M. (1954) *Political Parties: Their Organisation and Activity in the Modern State*, London: Methuen.

Epstein, L. (1967) *Political Parties in Western Democracies*, London: Pall Mall Press.

Fisher, J. (1996) *British Political Parties*, Hemel Hempstead: Prentice Hall.

Fisher, J. (2000) 'Small kingdoms and crumbling organisations: examining the variation in constituency party membership and resources', in P. Cowley, D. Denver, A. Russell and L. Harrison, *British Elections and Parties Review* (Vol. 10), London: Frank Cass.

Katz, R. and Mair, P. (1995) 'Changing models of party organization and party democracy: the emergence of the cartel party', *Party Politics*, Vol. 1, No. 1, pp. 5–28.

Kelly, R. (1989) *Conservative Party Conferences*, Manchester: Manchester University Press.

Kirchheimer, O. (1966) 'The transformation of west European party systems', in J. LaPalombara and M. Weiner (eds) *Political Parties and Political Development*, Princeton, NJ: Princeton University Press.

McKenzie, R. (1955) *British Political Parties*, London: Heinemann.

Michels, R. (1911) *Political Parties: A Sociological Study of the Oligarchical Tendencies of Modern Democracy*, New York: Collier Macmillan.

Minkin, L. (1991) *The Contentious Alliance*, Edinburgh: Edinburgh University Press.

Norris, P. and Lovenduski, J. (1995) *Political Recruitment*, Cambridge: Cambridge University Press.

Pannebianco, A. (1988) *Political Parties: Organisation and Power*, Cambridge: Cambridge University Press.

Rosamund, B. (1992) 'The Labour Party, trade unions and industrial relations', in M. Smith and J. Spear (eds) *The Changing Labour Party*, London: Routledge.

Seyd, P. and Whiteley, P. (2000) 'New Labour and the party: members and organisation', in S. Ludlam and M. Smith (eds) *New Labour in Government*, Basingstoke: Macmillan.

Strom, K. (1990) 'A behavioural theory of competitive political parties', *American Journal of Political Science*, Vol. 34, No. 2, pp. 565–98.

Taylor, A. (1989) *Trade Unions and Politics*, London: Macmillan.

Webb, P. (2000) *The Modern British Party System*, London: Sage.

Further reading

Given that both Labour and the Conservatives have made radical changes to their organisations, up-to-date material is fairly limited. Of that which is available, P. Webb (2000) *The Modern British Party System* (London: Sage) is the best, though R. Garner and R. Kelly (1998) *British Political Parties Today* (Manchester: Manchester University Press) is also useful. P. Seyd (1999) 'New parties/new policies? A case study of the British Labour Party', *Party Politics*, Vol. 5, No. 3, pp. 383–405, offers an interesting study of changes in the Labour Party. On theories of party organisation, A. Ware (1996) *Political Parties and Party Systems* (Oxford: Oxford University Press) and M. Maor (1997) *Political Parties and Party Systems* (London: Routledge) provide useful summaries. The best book on candidate selection is P. Norris and J. Lovenduski (1995) *Political Recruitment* (Cambridge: Cambridge University Press), though some of the detail is now out of date. J. Bradbury J. Mitchell,

L. Bennie and D. Denver (2000) 'Candidate selection, devolution and modernization: the selection of Labour Party candidates for the 1999 Scottish Parliament and Welsh Assembly elections', in P. Cowley, D. Denver, A. Russell and L. Harrison, *British Elections and Parties Review* (Vol. 10) (London: Frank Cass) offer a detailed examination of candidate selection in the newly-devolved Assemblies.

Elections and Voting

David Denver

CHAPTER TEN

Background

General elections in the United Kingdom are, undeniably, major events in the life of the nation. They involve almost the whole adult population in one way or another and precipitate a period of greatly increased political activity, interest, discussion and media coverage. They determine who governs – in practice which party's leader and leading figures form the government and control public policy for the next few years – and thus affect the lives of everyone. As David Butler has observed, 'History used to be marked off by the dates of Kings. . . . Now it is marked by the dates of (general) elections' (1998: 454). The precise dates of general elections are decided by the Prime Minister, the only constraint being that a Parliament must have ended exactly five years after the date of its first meeting. In fact, since 1950 the average time between general elections has been about three and a half years, ranging from just over seven months between February and October 1974 to just over five years between 1992 and 1997. Since 1979 the gap has always been four years or more.

In addition, however, citizens are regularly called upon to vote in other types of election (sometimes referred to as 'second-order' elections). Almost every year there are elections for local councils in England and there is a fixed cycle of local elections in Scotland and Wales. Once every five years (1994, 1999, 2004, etc.) there are elections to the European Parliament and in Scotland, Wales and Northern Ireland, from 1999 there has been a further cycle of elections to the devolved Parliament and Assemblies. 'Elections galore!', one might say – and certainly more than enough to satisfy the keenest enthusiast for elections and to keep electoral analysts busy.

Theoretical Considerations

Elections are, of course, a central element in democratic theory or at least in the theory of representative democracy. It is elections which allow citizens to participate directly in politics – even if it is only every so often – and ultimately to determine the personnel and policies of governments. Exactly how and how much elections affect what governments do is a matter of some debate and one influential view (Schumpeter, 1943) suggests that they merely allow voters to choose between competing elites. Nonetheless, in a democracy only a government which is elected by the people is thought to be legitimate. There is more to democracy than elections, of course – there are other channels of citizen influence, for example – but it is the existence of free, competitive elections which remains the essential difference between states which are widely recognised to be democratic and those which are not. It is through elections that citizens can hold their governors accountable. At least once every five years the British electorate can pass judgement on the government and either allow it to continue in office or 'throw the rascals out' and try another lot.

Summary

- Elections allow citizens to participate in politics.
- They confer democratic legitimacy on governments.
- They make governments accountable to citizens.

Electoral Systems

One of the key areas of current debate relating to elections in Britain concerns electoral systems. Up to about twenty years ago interest in electoral systems was confined to a relatively small number of enthusiasts, but discontent with the traditional first-past-the-post British system began to increase and, as part of its modernising agenda, the Blair government introduced new electoral systems for the Scottish and European Parliaments and Welsh and Northern Irish Assemblies. In addition, a debate and referendum on the Westminster system was promised. These developments have led politicians, commentators and others to think more carefully about what an electoral system is supposed to achieve, the effects of different systems and whether some might be more 'democratic' than others. These and other questions are considered in Chapter 5, however, so they are simply noted here.

Participation in Elections

One of the key theoretical claims made on behalf of elections in the context of democracy is that they are the primary means whereby citizens participate in politics. In fact, it appears that citizens have become increasingly unwilling to participate in this way. Figure 10.1 charts the level of turnout at each general election since 1950. Turnout in 1950 and 1951 was unusually high – easily the highest since women gained the vote – and it fell quite sharply in 1955. From 1955 to 1992 there was no clear trend but 1997 saw the lowest turnout of the series to that

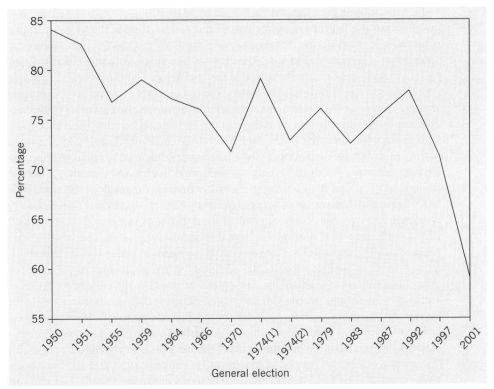

Figure 10.1 Percentage turnout in general elections in Great Britain, 1950–2001

point and it was followed by a truly catastrophic slump in 2001, to just 59.2% – the worst turnout in any general election since 1918. Moreover, increased non-voting was not confined to general elections. After 1997 turnout in local elections was very poor (averaging 30% in 1998, 32% in 1999 and 29.5% in 2000 – well below the levels achieved in the 1970s and 1980s). The same was true of turnout in parliamentary by-elections – in only four of the sixteen held between 1997 and 2001 was turnout greater than 50% and in six it failed to reach 30% (and was below 20% in one case). In the European Parliament elections in June 2000 only 23% of the British electorate bothered to vote. These are certainly worrying statistics for those who believe that participation in elections is a hallmark of democracy and concern over the issue prompted the government to allow experiments with various arrangements for voting in the 2000 round of local elections. Normally voters have to present themselves on a specific day at a designated polling station (usually schools, church halls, community centres and the like) between designated hours and cast their vote in person, with special arrangements being allowed for limited categories of person to vote by post or proxy. In the 2000 local elections, however, in different experimental areas, polling stations were sited in supermarkets, voting was extended over a few days, electronic voting was permitted, the rules about postal voting were relaxed and an all-postal ballot was conducted. Only all-postal ballots appeared to make any significant difference to turnout levels.

In order to evaluate electoral participation in Britain more fully, however, it is useful to put the figures into some sort of theoretical, historical and comparative contexts. A theoretical context is provided by Downs (1957), who arrestingly argued that it is irrational to vote. The chances of a single vote making any difference to the outcome of the election – in the country as a whole or even in a single constituency – are infinitesimal. Since voting has costs – going to the polling station – and few obvious benefits, why should we expect the electorate to bother? The surprising thing is that so many people do vote, especially given that most seats are safe for one party or another. They do so, however, largely out of a sense of duty or to express their support for a party or candidate rather than to affect the election outcome. We would expect electoral participation to be greater, however, when voters feel that their vote matters, either because the result of the election is likely to have important consequences or because the result (locally or nationally) is expected to be close. Thus, turnout in local elections is lower than in general elections because local authorities have few significant powers and whether one party or another controls local councils does not seem to make a great deal of difference to what happens locally. In addition, many authorities are always (or almost always) controlled by the same party so there is little incentive to vote. Similarly, why should people vote for representatives in the European Parliament – a remote institution with few powers about which they know little and care less?

In historical terms, it is worth noting that analysis of turnout trends over time suggests that it is higher when the result of the election is expected to be close and lower when one party is expected to win easily. Thus the 1950 and 1951 elections were expected to be (and were) very close in terms of the final result. In 1997 and 2001, however, the results were widely thought to be foregone conclusions. Although this cannot entirely explain the turnout slump in 2001, it does suggest that a more closely-fought election in future might see some recovery in turnout. In a comparative context, there are two points to consider. First, electoral participation in Britain has usually been far from the worst internationally. Comparing thirty-seven countries over the period 1960–95, Franklin (1996) finds that Britain comes twenty-seventh. Second, the decline in turnout in the UK is mirrored elsewhere. Lijphart notes that 'in western Europe average turnout went down by about 5 percentage points from the early 1960s to the late 1980s, and it declined even further in the 1990s, by more than 4 percentage points in twenty-three western democracies plus Japan' (2000: 316).

As well as varying over time, electoral participation in Britain varies geographically – from constituency to constituency – and also from person to person. Constituency variations are largely explained by two types of factor. The first is the social structure of the constituency. In broad terms, constituencies which are more middle class, contain more owner occupiers and are generally more affluent than average tend to have higher turnouts. Contrariwise, more deprived and more working-class constituencies with large numbers of council tenants and/or people who rent their homes from landlords tend to have lower turnouts, especially in inner-city areas. Second, varying electoral contexts – in particular the marginality or safeness of the seat concerned – affect turnout levels. Probably because parties campaign harder in them, more marginal seats tend to have higher turnouts than safer seats. An analysis of turnout in the 1997 election showed that just three variables (percentage of households with no car (an indicator of relative affluence/deprivation), percentage of manual workers and degree of marginality) together explained almost 70% of the variation in constituency turnouts (Denver and Hands, 1997: 220). In 2001 just two of these (percentage with no car and marginality) accounted for 68% of the turnout variation across constituencies. Social structure and marginality are not the whole story, however. In some areas, Wales being a good example, there appears simply to be a tradition of high turnout. However, in inner cities turnout is even worse than would be expected on the basis of social structure and marginality. This is likely to be caused by the fact that these areas tend to have very large transient populations.

To describe the participation patterns of individuals we need to move from examining election results to looking at the results of surveys of the electorate. Three main conclusions can be drawn from survey studies of non-voting in the 1970s and 1980s (see Crewe et al., 1977; Swaddle and Heath, 1989). First, very few people deliberately or consistently abstain from voting. When non-voters are asked why they failed to turn out they overwhelmingly give 'circumstantial' reasons – being ill, away on the day and so on. Second, only four overlapping social groups are regularly found to have participation rates that are significantly lower than 'average – those aged 18–24, unmarried people, those who live in privately-rented accommodation and those who are residentially mobile. In more recent elections, however, analysts have found that there is also a class effect with working-class electors having a lower turnout than more solidly middle-class groups (Heath and Taylor, 1999). Third, those who are strong supporters of a party (strong 'party identifiers') are much more likely to vote than those who are only weakly committed or do not see themselves as party supporters. Being a strong supporter of a party gives a person a reason for voting over and above any sense of citizen duty. There has been a marked decline in the strength of party identification in Britain since the 1960s to the 1990s (Crewe and Thomson, 1999) and this seems likely to be an important underlying cause of the downward trend in turnout.

Table 10.1 shows the turnout of different groups in the 2001 election. Although turnout was much lower than usual, the differences between the groups discussed above were again clearly evident (data on residential mobility are not available).

Summary

- In recent elections turnout has declined sharply.
- In terms of costs and benefits it is voting rather than non-voting that needs to be explained.
- Declining turnout appears to be an international phenomenon.
- Constituency variations across the UK are related to social structure and marginality.
- Young, mobile, single people with a weak party identity are the least likely to vote.

Table 10.1 Percentage turnout in the 2001 general election

Category	(%)	Category	(%)
Sex		*Marital status*	
Male	58	Married	66
Female	59	Widowed	72
		Separated/divorced	54
		Cohabiting	38
Age		Never married	43
18–24	35		
25–34	40	*Occupation*	
35–44	53	Professional/managerial	66
45–54	64	Other non-manual	61
55–64	67	Skilled manual	57
65+	76	Other manual	52
Housing tenure		*Party identification*	
Owner occupier	67	Very strong	81
Renter	48	Fairly strong	72
		Not very strong	50
		None	28

Note: Data are weighted to actual turnout.

Source: British Election Study 2001, cross-section survey

Influences on Party Choice: A Dealigned Electorate

Over the past forty years or so there has been a marked change in how political scientists have sought to explain how people come to vote for a particular party. In the 1950s and 1960s they emphasised long-term, 'background' characteristics such as occupational class, age, sex, religion and family tradition. By the 1990s much more attention was being paid to electors' opinions, attitudes and judgements, and the processes helping to form them (political communication). This reflects a change among the electorate itself, from being broadly and consistently aligned with one party or another to being 'dealigned'.

'Dealignment' refers to two related but conceptually distinct processes. Early voting studies, in the 1950s and 1960s, had suggested that party support was a product of major social cleavages. There was a clear alignment between the social groups to which voters belonged (especially their social class) and the party they voted for. From the 1970s, however, on most measures, class voting declined (see Table 10.2). On the Alford index it reached an all-time low in 1997 and increased only slightly in 2001; the level of 'absolute class voting' continued to decline in 2001. There has been, then, a 'class dealignment' and no new social cleavage has emerged to replace class as the primary social basis of party support. Region of residence has become more important but within-region variations remain very substantial. Ethnic minority voters are a strongly Labour-supporting group but, since they constitute only about 5% of the electorate, ethnicity fails to discriminate among the vast majority of voters. The second aspect of dealignment relates to party identification. Just as they acquire a national identity – being Scottish,

Table 10.2 Class voting, 1964–2001

Election	Alford index	Absolute class voting
1964	42	63
1966	43	66
1970	33	60
1974 (Feb)	35	55
1974 (Oct)	32	54
1979	27	55
1983	25	47
1987	25	49
1992	27	54
1997	20	46
2001	23	45

Note: The 'Alford' index is calculated by subtracting Labour's percentage share of the vote among non-manual (middle-class) workers from its share among manual (working-class) workers. Thus, if there were no difference between classes in terms of Labour support, the score would be zero; if all of the working class and none of the middle class voted Labour, the score would be 100. Absolute class voting is measured as the number of non-manual workers voting Conservative plus manual workers voting Labour as a percentage of all voters.

Table 10.3 'Very strong' party identifiers, 1964–2001

Election	(%)	Election	(%)
1964	43	1983	20
1966	43	1987	19
1970	41	1992	19
1974 (Feb)	29	1997	16
1974 (Oct)	26	2001	14
1979	21		

English or whatever – many people also acquire a party identity – being Conservative, Labour or whatever. In the past, party identity was mainly a consequence of socialisation into family and community traditions, and voters rarely deviated from supporting their party. As noted above, however, the strength of British voters' attachment to parties has steadily declined. By 2001 only 14% described themselves as 'very strong' party supporters as compared with more than 40% in the 1960s (see Table 10.3). This is evidence of a 'partisan dealignment'.

Dealignment would be expected to have important electoral consequences. Strong party identification and the class–party link bound voters securely to their party and thus ensured stability in party support over lengthy periods. The dealigned electorate is more likely to be affected by short-term forces, more open to persuasion by the parties and the media, more indecisive about which party to vote for, and more likely to switch parties. Rather than party choice being stable and predictable (as with the aligned electorate of the 1950s and 1960s) we should expect the dealigned electorate of the 1980s and after to be volatile and unpredictable.

We can sum up these expectations by suggesting that the change from an aligned to a dealigned electorate involves a move from 'habitual' to 'judgemental' voting. When the electorate was aligned by class and party identification, it would be fair to describe the party choice of voters as being a matter of habit rather than anything else. For most voters, indeed, the idea that they made a 'choice', in the sense of a conscious decision about which party to support as election day drew near, is misleading. Rather, they had a 'standing decision' derived from class, family tradition and so on, which made voting for the appropriate party almost automatic. In the dealigned era, however, the prevalence of this kind of habitual voting decreased.

Most commentators agree that this is the case but there is some disagreement about what has replaced aligned or habitual voting. Some have suggested that 'issue voting' is now much more important, with electors making up their minds on the basis of the parties' policies on important contemporary issues, such as taxation, defence, the National Health Service and education. Others argue that it is voters' opinions about the performance of the government in office that is important, and in particular the success or failure of the government in running the economy, and yet others that it is the more general political values, principles or ideologies of voters which lead them to support one party or another. There is also a widespread impression that the electors' reactions to the party leaders are now more influential in determining party choice than they used to be.

What ties these various strands together, however, is the idea that, as compared with the period of alignment, voters have become increasingly likely to base their choice of party on judgements – whether about current issues, ideologies, party leaders, government performance or the state of the economy. We might say, then, that habitual voting, which predominated in the 1950s, has declined and in more recent elections has given way to what we might term judgemental voting.

This picture of the modern electorate drawn by dealignment theory might appear to be contradicted by the results of elections from 1979 to 1992. In one very important respect these displayed striking stability – the Conservatives won all four and their share of the vote in Great Britain varied only slightly, from 44.9% in 1979 to 43.5% in 1983, 43.3% in 1987 and 42.8% in 1992. The vote shares gained by Labour and the Liberal Democrats (and their predecessors) varied much more and it is also the case that in the periods between elections the Conservatives experienced lengthy periods of unpopularity and suffered spectacular losses in parliamentary by-elections and local elections. Nonetheless, when a general election came round voters appeared to forget their mid-term misgivings and regularly returned the Conservatives to power. If dealignment theory was correct, there was a paradox – an allegedly volatile electorate regularly produced stable election outcomes.

It can be argued, however, that the outcomes of general elections in this period were in line with what would be expected of a dealigned electorate. In this view, it is a mistake to regard the roughly 40% of the vote that the Conservatives consistently garnered from 1979 to 1992 as constituting a solid bloc of core supporters. Data on party identification from the relevant British Election Study (BES) surveys show that the true Conservative core – those who identified very strongly with the party – never amounted to more than 9% of the electorate in this period. Rather, at successive elections, the Conservatives were able to put together a temporary coalition of voters, which then dissolved in the inter-election periods. These coalitions were based on electors' short-term judgements concerning such political issues as taxation, welfare and defence policy, the overall performance of the government, the parties' leaders and prospects for the economy. In addition, for most of the 1980s the main opposition party, Labour, was deeply divided and was perceived by voters as having moved too far to the left and having unappealing leaders.

The 1992 election

We can take the unexpected Conservative victory in 1992 as an example of this argument. Having won the 1987 election decisively, the Conservatives under Margaret Thatcher fell behind Labour in the opinion polls in June 1989. By March 1990, with the furore over the introduction of the poll tax in full swing, Labour had a huge lead (54% of voting intentions compared to 30% for the Conservatives). Parliamentary by-elections in this period told the same story. Between May 1989 and November 1991 the Tories defended seven seats in by-elections and lost them all – four to Labour and three to the Liberal Democrats. Nonetheless, the Conservatives' position improved after John Major replaced Mrs Thatcher as Prime Minister in November 1990 and they went on to win the 1992 election fairly comfortably (see Table 10.4).

This victory was not a straightforward consequence of the electorate's preferences on issues, however. Polls showed that the three issues that were most frequently mentioned by voters as being important in helping them decide how to vote were the National Health Service, unemployment and education, and on these issues most voters thought that Labour had the best policies. The Conservatives had large leads on prices, taxes and defence, but these were rated as less important by the voters. When it came to polling day, however, 49% of respondents to the Harris exit poll said that they would be worse off under Labour's tax and benefit policies while only 30% said that they would be better off. Only 7% of the former voted Labour compared with 82% of the latter. This suggests that the Tories unremitting attacks on Labour's tax proposals during the campaign eventually paid off.

Most commentators argue that the state of the economy is the central issue in determining whether or not voters support the governing party. The economy is

Table 10.4 General election results, 1992–2001

	1992		1997		2001	
	Vote share (%)	Seats	Vote share (%)	Seats	Vote share (%)	Seats
Conservative	41.9	336	30.7	165	31.7	166
Labour	34.4	271	43.2	418	40.7	412
Liberal Democrats	17.8	20	16.8	46	18.3	52
Others	5.9	24	9.3	30	9.4	29

Note: Figures refer to the United Kingdom as a whole.

not a 'position' issue on which people take sides, such as the privatisation of publicly-owned industries, for example. Everyone wants economic prosperity and the issue is how well the parties have performed, or might perform in future, in delivering it. In general, during the lengthy period of Conservative domination, the electorate adjudged them to be the party which was more competent at handling the economy. In the twelve months before the 1992 election, for example, when asked by Gallup which party was best able to cope with Britain's economic difficulties, an average of 45% of respondents opted for the Conservatives and 30% for Labour. In April 1992, just before the election, 52% opted for the Conservatives and 31% for Labour. Similarly, during the 1992 campaign, 42% believed that Britain as a whole would be worse off under Labour, and 44% that they and their families would be worse off, compared with 38% and 30% respectively who thought that things would be better.

The question of the effect of economic performance on party popularity has received a good deal of attention from academic specialists. Sanders (1995) argues that between 1983 and 1992 the level of support for the Conservatives was closely related to the level of personal economic optimism – how people viewed the financial prospects of their household. In turn, economic optimism was influenced by the performance of the 'real' economy. On this basis, explaining the series of Conservative victories after 1979 is not difficult. Once in government, the Conservatives were able to manage the economy in such a way as to ensure that when an election came round personal economic optimism outweighed pessimism among the voters, even if only temporarily, and thus reaped the expected electoral reward. This also happened in 1992.

A further factor helping to explain Conservative electoral successes in this period is the relative popularity of the party leaders. The traditional view of the effect of leaders on voting, when aligned voting was the rule, was that their competence, character and personality counted for little with the electorate. With the erosion of the influence of long-term factors on party choice, however, party leaders have come to figure more prominently in voters' calculations and at three of the four elections from 1979 to 1992 Conservative leaders have been far more popular than their Labour counterparts (see Table 10.5). Margaret Thatcher became very unpopular after 1987 and was replaced by John Major. In 1992 Major was the favoured choice as Prime Minister, having a slightly larger lead over Neil Kinnock than Mrs Thatcher had had in 1987. It is not possible to attach a precise weight to the influence of party leaders on the electorate, but it is hard not to believe that the significantly greater electoral appeal of John Major goes some way to explaining the failure of an electorate which was Labour-inclined on issues to switch their votes to the Conservatives in significant numbers.

A final point of significance in explaining the Conservatives' electoral hegemony after 1979 and their victory in 1992 is that during this period they enjoyed the overwhelming support of the British national press. When strong party identification and class voting underpinned party choice, these were generally enough to ensure that voters were unaffected by the blandishments of newspapers. As noted above, however, dealignment theory suggests that a dealigned electorate is more open to persuasion and influence. During the 1980s support for the

Table 10.5 Best person for Prime Minister, 1979–2001

	1979 (%)	1983 (%)	1987 (%)	1992 (%)	1997 (%)	2001 (%)
Conservative leader	33	46	46	47	28	20
Labour leader	44	35	22	22	38	52
Liberal, etc. leader	24	13	12	21	15	15
SDP leader	–	6	11	–	–	–

Note: The percentages of people who were unable to make a choice are not shown.

Source: Gallup

Conservatives and opposition to Labour, became strident to the point of hysteria in the mass-circulation 'Tory tabloids' and on election day 1992 *The Sun*, the paper with the largest readership of all, famously printed on its front page a caricature of Neil Kinnock's head in a light bulb, with a headline saying: 'If Kinnock wins today will the last person in Britain please turn out the lights.' Evidence that voters are influenced by the papers that they read remains somewhat patchy partly because researching the question is extremely difficult, but the weight of opinion among analysts is that the Conservatives derived some electoral advantage from the strong press backing that they received (see Curtice and Semetko, 1994).

The elections of 1997 and 2001

Any doubts that the electorate had become dealigned were swept away by the 1997 election. The results compared with 1992 (Table 10.4) show that the electorate displayed high levels of volatility. The swing from Conservative to Labour (10%) was almost double the previous post-war record (5.2% in 1979) and the vote share of 'other' candidates was also a record. According to the BES post-election survey, about 30% of 1992 Conservative voters switched parties (compared with 10% of 1992 Labour voters) and, overall, about one-quarter of those who voted in both elections did not support the same party. There was also evidence of more tactical voting than ever before. Underlying these patterns, as we have seen, class voting and strong party identification reached new lows for the modern period. In addition, as far as issues were concerned Labour was the preferred party – often by huge margins – on all except defence, which hardly figured in the campaign.

The basis of Labour's victory was laid in the period between 1992 and 1997 when the Conservatives had a terrible time in office (see Denver, 1998). In particular, in this period they lost four short-term electoral advantages. First, they lost the enthusiastic support of most of the national press. In general Conservative papers were much more lukewarm (at best) in their support for the party while *The Sun*, which had been violently anti-Labour in 1992, caused a sensation at the start of the 1997 campaign by announcing that it now backed Tony Blair and New Labour. On election day its front cover had a picture of Tony Blair and the head-line 'It Must Be You'. As noted above, the extent to which newspapers influence their readers is a matter of some debate but at the very least the changed attitude of the national press – especially that of *The Sun* – cannot have helped the Conservatives or harmed Labour. Second, the open divisions in the Conservative Party after 1992, especially over the question of Europe, took a heavy toll. Traditionally, the Conservatives have been seen as a largely united party – which is a plus for voters – with Labour being prone to fratricidal struggles. In 1992, for example, 72% of voters thought that the Conservatives were united with only 33% saying the same of Labour. Divisions within the governing party were evident after 1992, however, and by 1997 the normal situation was reversed: now 59% thought that Labour was united and only 16% thought that the Conservatives were. Third, the Conservatives lost their long-established reputation for being able to manage the economy effectively. Within six months of the 1992 election, the UK was forced to withdraw from the European Exchange Rate Mechanism in humiliating circumstances, which involved an effective devaluation of the pound and, eventually, tax increases, and the government never recovered from this. From October 1992, polls consistently showed the public believing that Labour was better able to handle Britain's economy and support for the parties was closely related to this perception. An improved economic performance and cuts in personal taxation in the latter part of the government's tenure failed to erase memories of earlier problems and tax increases. In March 1997, just before the election was called, when asked whether the Conservatives or Labour were the better party to handle economic difficulties, 49% opted for the latter and 35% for the former (the remainder could not answer or said that there was no difference between them). Finally, the voters' assessments of the major party leaders were dramatically different from what they had been in the three previous elections (Table 10.5). From the moment he took over as Labour leader in 1994, Tony Blair was preferred as Prime Minister by a wide margin over John Major and he never lost this ascendancy. By the time of the 1997 election no less than 90% of electors thought that he would make a very or quite good Prime Minister compared with only 45% thinking the same of Major (BES cross-section survey). When asked who would make the best Prime Minister, Blair was preferred by 47% of exit poll respondents, Major by 33% and Ashdown by 20%. It is hard to avoid the conclusion that the electorate's judgements about the relative merits of the party leaders importantly influenced voting in the election. All of this evidence suggests that in 1997 the British electorate made its decision on the basis of judgements about party policies, the record of the government in office and the capabilities of the party leaders, rather than falling back upon traditional loyalties.

Little changed at the 2001 general election (see Denver, 2002). Once again Labour held all the short-term advantages. The national press was even more favourably disposed towards Labour, Tony Blair had a commanding lead over William Hague as the most preferred Prime Minister (Table 10.5), Labour had a clear lead as the party preferred on the most important issues and the voters had a favourable view of Labour's handling of the economy. The Conservatives had never recovered from the disaster of 1992. Besides having a leader who failed to impress the electorate, they were still perceived as divided and, according to Gallup data, large majorities of the voters thought that they did not have a strong team of leaders (81%), were out of touch with modern Britain (69%) and went on too much about Europe (65%). With all that stacked up against the Opposition, it is no surprise that, even if voters were not all that enthusiastic about Labour, they proved unwilling to vote the government out of office.

Conclusion

There are still some strong party identifiers among British voters, providing each party with a core vote which they are unlikely to lose. But there are now more voters than ever who can be characterised as 'dealigned' and 'judgemental'. This renders electoral politics fluid and much more unpredictable than formerly. As a consequence, we should expect more elections to be like 1997, with a large turnover of votes and short-term factors having a decisive impact. This implies that despite two successive hammerings at the hands of the voters, the Conservatives are far from dead. Under Iain Duncan-Smith they are seeking to renew their image and it is always possible that the Labour government will run into heavy weather or that Tony Blair's electoral appeal will decline.

An illustration of what is possible was given in the autumn of 2000. After the 1997 election Labour – unusually for a governing party – easily led the Opposition in voting intentions for more than three years. In August 2000 the average figures for all polls were Labour 48%, Conservative 33% and Liberal Democrats 15% (meaning that Labour was even further ahead than they had been at the general election). In seven polls taken between 14 and 23 September, however, following the blockading of oil terminals to protest about petrol prices, the average figures were Labour 35%, Conservative 38% and Liberal Democrats 20%. There could hardly be a clearer illustration of the fickleness and volatility of the modern, dealigned British electorate.

Discussion Questions

1. Why are voters less committed to parties than they used to be?
2. Does low turnout represent a 'crisis of democracy' in Britain?
3. Can the Conservative Party win the next election?

References

Butler, D. (1998) 'Reflections on British elections and their study', *Annual Review of Political Science*, Vol. 1, pp. 451–64.

Crewe, I. and Thomson, K. (1999) 'Party loyalties: dealignment or realignment?', in G. Evans and P. Norris (eds) *Critical Elections*, London: Sage, pp. 64–86.

Crewe, I., Fox, T. and Alt, J. (1977) 'Non-voting in British general elections 1966–October 1974', in C. Crouch (ed.) *British Political Sociology Yearbook*, Vol. 3, London: Croom Helm.

Curtice, J. and Semetko, H. (1994) 'Does it matter what the papers say?', in A. Heath, R. Jowell and J. Curtice, with B. Taylor, *Labour's Last Chance? The 1992 Election and Beyond*, Aldershot: Dartmouth, pp. 43–63.

Denver, D. (1998) 'The government that could do no right', in A. King (ed.) *New Labour Triumphs: Britain at the Polls*, Chatham, NJ: Chatham House, pp. 15–48.

Denver, D. (2002) 'The results: how Britain voted (or didn't)', in A. Geddes and J. Tonge (eds) *Labour's Second Landslide: The British General Election 2001*, Manchester: Manchester University Press.

Denver, D. and Hands, G. (1997) 'Turnout', in P. Norris and N. Gavin (eds) *Britain Votes 1997*, Oxford: Oxford University Press, pp. 212–24.

Downs, A. (1957) *An Economic Theory of Democracy*, New York: Harper.

Franklin, M. (1996) 'Electoral participation', in L. Leduc, R.G. Niemi and P. Norris (eds) *Comparing Democracies: Elections and Voting in Global Perspective*, Thousand Oaks, CA: Sage, pp. 216–35.

Heath, A. and Taylor, B. (1999) 'New sources of abstention?', in G. Evans and P. Norris (eds) *Critical Elections*, London: Sage, pp. 164–80.

Lijphart, A. (2000) 'Turnout', in R. Rose (ed.) *International Encyclopedia of Elections*, London: Macmillan, pp. 314–21.

Sanders, D. (1995) '"It's the economy, stupid": the economy and support for the Conservative Party, 1979–94', *Talking Politics*, Vol. 3, pp. 158–67.

Schumpeter, J. (1943) *Capitalism, Socialism and Democracy*, London: Allen & Unwin.

Swaddle, K. and Heath, A. (1989) 'Official and reported turnout in the British general election of 1987', *British Journal of Political Science*, Vol. 19, pp. 537–51.

Further reading

Lengthy and detailed accounts of the 2001 election can be found in David Butler and Dennis Kavanagh (2001) *The British General Election of 2001* (Basingstoke: Palgrave); Anthony King (ed.) (2001) *Britain at the Polls 2001* (Chatham, NJ: Chatham House); Pippa Norris (ed.) (2001) *Britain Votes 2001* (Oxford: Oxford University Press). The volume edited by Andrew Geddes and Jon Tonge (2001) *Labour's Second Landslide: The British General Election 2001* (Manchester: Manchester University Press) is pitched at a lower level and is readable and useful. For more details on voting behaviour in Britain, see David Denver (2002) *Elections and Voters in Britain* (Basingstoke: Palgrave) and Pippa Norris (1997) *Electoral Change since 1945* (Oxford: Blackwell).

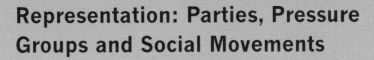

Representation: Parties, Pressure Groups and Social Movements

Paul Webb

CHAPTER ELEVEN

Introduction

It is by no means uncommon to encounter the argument that 'political parties and pressure groups are competitors' (Grant, 2000: 214). This is chiefly because of the notion that parties have been challenged in respect of their role as conduits of representative linkage, given the evidence that political participation through parties has declined at broadly the same time it has increased through pressure groups and social movements. Jeremy Richardson, for instance, argues that west European societies such as Britain's constitute a changing 'market for activism', and 'parties as traditional opportunity structures for activism are now subject to strong challenges' (Richardson, 1995: 117).

In general, those perceiving such a challenge by pressure groups in the 'market for activism' are often purveyors of the theme of party decline. This is a multi-dimensional argument based on the view that political parties are in some sense 'failing' in the essential tasks they perform in a democratic political system – for instance, as mechanisms of accountable government, as channels of political communication, as means of representation and participation, or some combination of these (Lawson and Merkl, 1988). In this chapter, I shall argue that there remain a number of political functions to which parties remain absolutely central, especially political recruitment, governance and the aggregation of interests. This notwithstanding, however, they have been challenged by the ineluctable rise of pressure groups and new social movements in respect of other functions, such as the mobilisation of political participation and the articulation of interests. In short, democratic politics everywhere is characterised by a necessary and increasingly rich blend of party life and non-partisan group activity.

Seen in this light, it is clear that while there may be tensions between different types of political entrepreneur, there can be little doubt that democracy requires *all* of them – parties, pressure groups and social movements – to function effectively. In any event, it is certainly the case that western democracies such as Britain clearly enjoy the input of each, in spite of the indisputable decline of party membership and the further possibility of a parallel erosion of activism among the remaining party faithful. Therefore, notwithstanding the various challenges to party, it seems to remain the case that, as E.E. Schattschneider once said, 'modern democracy is unthinkable save in terms of political parties' (1942: 1). Consequently, this chapter will seek to review the roles of representative agents in modern Britain by exploring the limits of what they can achieve and where they are in tension with one another.

Theoretical Considerations

First, let us clarify the nature of the political actors we are concerned with in this chapter. Parties, pressure groups and social movements are all part of the rich complexity of political activity in a liberal democracy. However, while observers readily (and in my view justifiably) discuss these as distinct entities, close examination reveals how the boundaries between them can often become blurred. Take, for instance, Alan Ware's definition of a *political party* as an organisation that '(a) seeks influence within a state, often by attempting to occupy positions in government, and (b) usually consists of more than a single interest in society and so to some degree attempts to "aggregate interests"' (Ware, 1996: 5). That this is a less than airtight definition is indicated by the way it fudges a number of issues through the use of words like 'often' and 'usually'; even so, it is as effective a definition as any and has a number of strengths.

First, it points to the centrality of the state as a focal point for party activity. Parties are interested in public policy questions which carry implications for the allocation of resources; to put it more succinctly, parties focus on the business of the state. This distinguishes them from organisations which work entirely or primarily within the domain of private interests and activities. Second, it recognises the central importance of office-seeking motivations for party action; this is one of the key factors which helps distinguish parties from pressure groups and social movements. That said, pressure groups may occasionally compete for office in an attempt to further their cause. Wyn Grant (2000: 13) cites the example of 'The Valley Party', an organisation of Charlton Athletic supporters formed to contest the local elections in the London Borough of Greenwich in the early 1990s, whose purpose was to pressurise the borough into aiding the football club's return from exile to its long-standing home ground ('The Valley'). However, it is rare for pressure groups to adopt an office-seeking strategy such as this.

A further problem with this aspect of the definition is conceded by Ware himself, namely that organisations commonly recognised as parties do not *always* seek governmental office: there are a number of examples of parties refusing to contest elections for fear of legitimising a political system to which they are opposed (Ware, 1996: 4). Note that a key implication of their office-seeking strategy is that parties must render themselves formally accountable to the electorate, a requirement rarely faced by pressure groups or social movements. What is more, modern political parties are generally prepared to accommodate, to some degree or other, a demand for internal organisational accountability; even the Conservative Party, whose pre-democratic origins have continued to shape its internal procedures and structures into the modern era, has seen fit to enhance the participatory rights of its members in respect of activities such as candidate selection and the election of leaders in recent years (Webb, 2000: 192–9). The pressure to be internally and externally accountable in this way is a consequence of parties' direct control of the state, and is not something encountered by interest groups or social movements (which is not to say that the latter always lack systems of internal accountability).

Third, in pointing to the way in which parties usually attempt to 'aggregate' a coalition of social interests and groups behind a programme covering a broad range of policy issues, Ware's definition further distinguishes parties from pressure groups which tend to focus on single issues, or clusters of closely-related issues. Finally, it also avoids the pitfall of the classic Burkean definition of party (1906) as a body of men united in 'some particular principle on which they are all agreed', because not all parties actually do share a great deal of common ground over basic principles. Once again, though, we should qualify this statement by conceding that this is relatively unusual; most political parties are based on some reasonably distinctive set of values or issue preferences.

A *pressure group* can be defined as an organisation which seeks to influence the formulation and implementation of public policy in respect of a specific field of policies or issues, without usually seeking governmental office. Once more we find ourselves falling back on words like 'usually', which is not surprising for this definition is essentially the reverse of that set out for party. The narrowness of the range of policy concerns emphasised in it serves to distinguish pressure groups from most parties, as already suggested; that is, pressure groups do not generally seek to *aggregate* a variety of interests, though they undoubtedly seek to *articulate* specific group interests (a point to which we shall return in due course). The second clause in this definition further distinguishes pressure groups from parties, since the former rarely, if ever, seek positions in government, whereas the latter often do. More succinctly, while both parties and pressure groups may be policy-seeking organisations, the latter seek to achieve their policy aims through wielding influence, but the former aim to fulfil their policy goals through both influence and the occupation of office. To reiterate, however, this is not an absolutely water-tight definition, for we know that parties sometimes prefer not to seek office, while pressure groups occasionally do contest office.

A *social movement* can be defined as a collective entity that seeks diffuse cultural influence, while lacking the definite organisational structure of a pressure group. For instance, it is common to speak of 'the feminist movement', but an individual could consider herself (or himself) part of this movement without actually joining any specific organisation. A social movement is essentially a widespread body of opinion rather than an institution enjoying a definite organisational structure or membership; its goal is to change popular attitudes (hence the reference to 'diffuse cultural influence' above), and perhaps ultimately public policies. However, when direct policy influence is sought, it is likely to be through a particular pressure group or network of pressure groups which constitute a subset of the broader social movement. Thus, while many people may be considered adherents of the environmentalist 'movement' by virtue of the opinions to which they subscribe, only some of them will join specific environmentalist pressure groups which have relatively precise organisational structures, rules and public policy aims (Byrne, 1997: 15). A final noteworthy feature of social movements is that they are primarily associated with protest politics, perhaps precisely because they lack the institutionalised channels of political access to decision-making that parties and interest groups often enjoy (Rucht, 2000: 97).

In the nexus of representative linkages between state and society, each of these types of actor – party, pressure group and social movement – plays an important role. The relative importance of each in fostering such linkage depends critically on the theoretical perspective of the observer, however. Debate is therefore shaped by underlying (and not always explicit) normative theories of democracy and/or analytical theories of policy-making and political behaviour. A few examples should serve to make this clear.

One of the best-known models of democracy developed in the twentieth century was proposed by Joseph Schumpeter in his classic work *Capitalism, Socialism and Democracy* (first published in 1942). His was an elitist conception of how democracy worked, emphasising as it did the cognitive limits of most citizens and the consequent need for political leadership. For instance, he questioned how far it was possible to attribute a rational and independent political will to the citizenry, and he pointed to the lack of political interest that many display: 'Without the initiative that comes from immediate responsibility, ignorance will persist in the face of masses of information, however complete and correct.' Consequently, he suggested that:

> . . . the typical citizen drops down to a lower level of mental performance as soon as he enters the political field. He argues and analyses in a way that he would readily recognize as infantile within the sphere of his real interests. He becomes a primitive again. His thinking becomes associative and affective.
>
> (Schumpeter, 1952: 262)

His conclusion was that the business of politics should be restricted mainly to elected elites. The political participation of most citizens should be limited to voting in order to choose between competing teams of leaders, legitimise their rule and ensure, through holding them to account, that such rule did not become tyrannical. Once voted into power leaders should be left to conduct the business of politics unimpeded by 'back-seat driving' from the electorate. Schumpeter's model is both analytical and prescriptive and places the political party in an important position as a key mechanism in the process of choosing ruling elites (or 'political recruitment', to use functionalist language). However, Schumpeter does not see party as playing an important role in fostering participation, or even in feeding back grass-roots demands to ruling elites. Rather, it is to be understood as motivated primarily by office-seeking imperatives and therefore as central to the critical function of recruiting political elites. In short, elitist conceptions of democracy such as Schumpeter's tend to privilege the role played by competitive political parties, but critics would contend that such conceptions only sustain an impoverished vision of party and democracy.

Among the critics would be those maintaining participatory visions of democracy. From Rousseau on, there have been thinkers arguing that political participation is valuable for the way in which it fosters cognitive and moral development among individuals, enriches the quality of civic life and helps build communities. In their modern guise (Pateman, 1970; Barber, 1985), such arguments generally coincide with the view that parties should not hold an especially privileged position in the political system. Although parties (along with other institutions of representative democracy) might remain an inevitable part of participatory democracy, they should be supplemented and even by-passed by other, often more innovatory, mechanisms of political participation, such as referendums, public initiatives, voter juries, works councils, and so on. It is especially notable that apologists for participatory democracy often regard social movements and their attendant pressure groups as a vital ingredient in this participatory mix. Indeed, such bodies are themselves often suffused with participatory values; this has been a particular feature, for instance, of environmentalist, pacifist and feminist movements (Byrne, 1997: 132).

It is not only overarching normative visions of democracy such as the Schumpeterian or participatory ones which shape perceptions of the roles played by political actors like parties, pressure groups and social movements; analytical models of policy-making have a similar effect. In particular, it is clear that classic models of group behaviour and policy-making, such as pluralism and corporatism, place great emphasis on the importance to democratic politics of pressure group activity. Pluralism suggests that power is dispersed between a multitude of social interests, some more powerful than others, but none accumulating a concentration of power across a multiplicity of different policy arenas (Dahl, 1971). Access to politics is facilitated by the many interest groups which exist and which seek to influence policy-makers in government. While party politics remains important to governmental decision-making according to the pluralist conception of things, the influence of pressure groups is accorded far greater prominence than under elitist democracy. Corporatism, however, is characterised by a greater willingness to locate pressure groups at the centre of policy-making processes to the detriment of political parties. Deriving from pluralist theory, (neo-)corporatism was highly voguish in the 1970s and stressed the way in which policy often emerged as a result of highly institutionalised forms of bargaining between government and key interest actors. These interest groups occupied a privileged position and in some instances were virtually co-opted by the state (Schmitter, 1974). This was taken to imply that, while parties in Parliament may still be required to ratify government decisions, real power lay with those engaged in corporatist arenas of representation and policy-making.

In truth, it should be said that neither pluralism nor corporatism offers an entirely persuasive account of politics in contemporary Britain. While the former is shaped predominantly by American experience, the latter bears the strong imprint of politics in other parts of western Europe (such as Scandinavia, the Netherlands, Germany and Austria). In recent years, far greater currency has been accorded to notions of policy community and policy network (Richardson and Jordan, 1979). These refer to more or less insulated arenas of policy-making activity in which key actors interact in a stable and continuing fashion. Policy is disaggregated by sector though, so that, rather as in pluralism, power is somewhat dispersed. Thus, different actors operate in different sectoral networks or communities. Networks and communities are similar but the latter implies a closer, more integrated relationship between the various participants involved. In either case, it is clear that interest groups are, once again, accorded a central role in representative and policy-making processes, although party politicians are not, in principle, excluded from playing a part within networks.

Summary

- While it is admittedly difficult to draw clear boundaries between political parties, pressure groups and social movements as agents of representation, there is little doubt that there are obvious basic distinctions between them.
- Thus, parties generally seek to aggregate a coalition of support across a wide range of interests, and tend to seek elective public office, thereby laying themselves open to processes of external and internal accountability; pressure groups usually focus on a far narrower range of issues, and rarely seek elective office, thus avoiding the requirements of external electoral accountability; and social movements seek diffuse cultural or attitudinal influence, but lack definite organisational basis.
- Evaluations of the relative importance for representative politics of these different actors tend to depend on the observer's theoretical stance. Thus, elitist democrats usually emphasise the centrality of parties because of their role in recruiting political elites and providing accountable government, while participatory democrats prefer to stress the importance of pressure groups and (especially) social movements in enabling ordinary citizens to take an active and influential part in politics. Analytical theories of policy-making such as pluralism and (especially) corporatism emphasise the significance of pressure groups for shaping policy outcomes, while models of policy communities and networks leave greater scope for influence by party politicians.

Debate

We have seen, then, how different theoretical perspectives shape the observer's perception of the relative importance of parties, pressure groups and social movements for representative politics in modern Britain. It is useful to assess the debate about this subject from a functionalist perspective. That is, the question of which type of actor is more central to politics and how effectively each performs really depends on the systemic political functions one is discussing. The following discussion is structured around three of the classic political functions which are performed in any political system, and which are directly relevant to the provision of representation: articulation, aggregation and the fostering of participation.

The articulation and aggregation of interests

The related functions of the articulation and aggregation of interests constitute key elements of representative activity. The *articulation of interests* refers to the representative role played by actors such as parties, interest groups and social movements in publicly expressing and pursuing the political demands of particular social groups. The *aggregation of interests* refers to a related but broader process by which parties bundle together the demands of a variety of social groups; a modern left-wing party, for instance, might seek to express the interests of the working class, women, immigrants and ethnic minorities, environmentalists, and so on. The aggregation of social group interests in this fashion is not quite so straightforward as the articulation of a narrower set of interests, since it requires the prioritisation of demands. Where all social group demands which a party seeks to aggregate are compatible, this will be relatively unproblematic, but this is by no means always the case. It is quite possible, for example, that the pursuit of certain environmental policies designed to restrict pollution and the over-exploitation of natural resources could conflict with other policies aimed at maximising industrial output and job opportunities. Under such circumstances, a left-wing party will be obliged to make the difficult decision about which set of group interests it should prioritise – those of the environmental lobby or those of the working classes who could be expected to benefit if output were maximised and unemployment minimised.

Processes of social and political change have almost certainly confronted all representative actors with new challenges and opportunities as articulators and aggregators of group interests. This is notably so in respect of the process of European integration; while parties have found it difficult to adapt to the new institutional context of European Union politics, pressure groups have been increasingly active in seeking to exercise influence at this level. Although it would be a gross exaggeration to suggest that party politics has no role to play in the EU (Bardi, 1994; Gaffney, 1996; Hix and Lord, 1997), it is clear that its idiosyncratic institutional framework does not readily lend it to any straightforward model of party government or representation. EU citizens are not able to elect (via the European Parliament (EP)) a European executive which can then be held to account (via the EP). The intergovernmental aspects of the EU imply, moreover, that policy outputs at this level reflect far more than the programmatic impact of a party government (or even a coalition government) – complex bargaining between national governments of varied partisan hue lie behind much European public policy. It would hardly be surprising, therefore, if citizens tended not to seek representation on European-level issues through parties. Indeed, this is all the more likely if it is true that 'the failure of parties to identify and/or respond to the emergence of new concerns sufficiently early created market opportunities for those unwilling to be constrained by the complexities of party coalitions' (Richardson, 1995: 124), for cross-party coalition-building is all the more complex at the European level. This matters little for the general influence of pressure groups, however. They focus on specific issues (or sets of similar policy issues closely connected by an underlying theme) and face few obstacles in organising themselves to lobby the Commission of the EU directly. With the gathering speed of European integration, therefore, it is no surprise to discover that pressure group organisation and activity at the EU level has burgeoned (Mazey and Richardson, 1992, 1993). Such developments tend to provide grist to neo-pluralist perspectives for they suggest that parties are less central to the process of interest articulation than interest groups.

Within the UK, the Labour government's desire for institutional 'modernisation' and reform has further impacted on the major agencies of representative politics. In particular, the attempt to relocate state power away from central government via devolution and reform of metropolitan local government has complicated matters for parties more than it has for pressure groups. As in the case of the EU, organised interests find it relatively straightforward to exploit the opportunities of new channels for lobbying in order to fulfil the articulation function. For parties, however, it is not always so easy. In particular, the remarkable success of Ken Livingstone in wresting the London mayoralty away from any of the established parties suggests that candidate-centred strategies may render normal patterns of party politics irrelevant, at least at this level of political jurisdiction. That said, in the newly devolved regimes in Scotland and Wales, parties are adapting and it would be an exaggeration to suggest that party politics has been seriously undermined by these new institutional structures, though they may have generated extra layers of intra-party dissonance (that is, the potential for conflict between the national party leaderships in London and their Scottish and Welsh wings). Thus, party democracy remains highly relevant to the devolved arenas of politics in the UK, but it has become more problematic.

At least as significant as processes of European integration and institutional reform of the state has been the growing heterogeneity of British society, since this has brought new social group demands and issues on to the agenda of politics to which the parties have sometimes struggled to respond. Thus, as new issue cleavages, such as environmentalism, and the rights of women and sexual minorities and ethnic minorities, have become prominent, those concerned have often felt that single-issue groups and social movements have articulated their particular demands more quickly and effectively than parties (Byrne, 1997). This argument is akin to the view sometimes propounded in comparative research that, when parties 'fail' (or perhaps just falter) in this way, alternative organisations emerge to link state to society (Lawson and Merkl, 1988). In essence, the emergence of social heterogeneity and new cleavages has generated a number of more or less simultaneous effects, including partisan dealignment, the decline of party memberships and the rise of single-issue group activity (Webb, 2000: ch.2, 226–7).

If social heterogeneity poses a direct challenge to the capacity of political parties to articulate interests, however, it also complicates their task of interest aggregation, though it does not render it obsolete. For, notwithstanding the challenge of growing societal complexity, it is hard to see an alternative vehicle to the political party for the aggregation of political demands in a country like the United Kingdom. Though in principle demands can certainly be aggregated into coherent legislative programmes by other actors (individual politicians in candidate-centred presidential systems like the USA's, bureaucrats in non-democratic systems), really only parties can do so legitimately in parliamentary democracies, and there is little doubt that the citizenry look overwhelmingly to the parties to fulfil this function in Britain. Single-issue groups or social movements may be challenging parties as articulators of particular group demands, but by definition they are not in the business of bundling together a multiplicity of interests into ordered and coherent programmes of legislative action. Interest aggregation, then, remains a core party function. Even so, this task has become more complex given the growing number of cross-cutting political cleavages in society. In effect, the major parties have been challenged to build increasingly broad coalitions of support at a time when such as task has become inherently more difficult. Moreover, not only have major parties struggled to aggregate interests as effectively as hitherto, but their attempts to do so may even have undermined their ability to articulate traditional group demands. For Labour at least, the adoption of a more broadly aggregative inter-class appeal – the catch-all strategy (Kirchheimer, 1966) – has probably weakened its role as a working-class tribune. In short, in attempting to develop its aggregative capacity, Labour may well have weakened its ability to articulate demands on behalf of certain social constituencies.

Nevertheless, while it is undoubtedly true that social and political changes have complicated parties' traditional tasks of articulating and aggregating social group demands, it would be a gross exaggeration to suggest that British political parties are generally failing to match the agendas or respond to the demands of the electorate. In fact, contemporary British parties are more likely to be criticised for pandering to the vagaries of public opinion, given the development of 'political marketing' techniques (Franklin, 1994; Scammell, 1995). That is, modern electorally-motivated parties are often derided for moulding their policies and candidate appeals to what their opinion researchers suggest voters want, but looked at in another light, this might be regarded as just another way of saying that parties are increasingly responsive to citizens.

Even so, parties cannot always provide programmes which are wholly acceptable to the electorate and it therefore seems obvious that group activity and political protest must be regarded as vital supplementary channels of preference-articulation, and, indeed, these channels of expression occasionally reveal enormous pressure for change in public policy. This was apparent, for instance, in the poll tax affair (Butler et al., 1995); this generated a startling campaign of protest and civil disobedience which suggested that the government had not only misread popular preferences on the issue, but had also fatally overestimated the public's capacity for passively indulging even a powerfully-placed administration. Ultimately, this episode almost certainly contributed to Margaret Thatcher's replacement by John Major and the rescinding of an unpopular law. It could be said that this demonstrated the remaining capacity of the party system to respond to the public agenda, although plainly it did not do so without the 'assistance' of demands which were articulated in channels quite external to the party system – that is, a broad movement of social protest which sustained a number of more specific pressure groups. It is possible that the remarkable fuel tax protests which afflicted the Blair government in 2000 (note once again that we refer to a government enjoying an unassailable parliamentary majority) are significant in a similar way. On the whole, then, it seems clear that while parties remain central to the complex task of aggregating interests, the function of articulating group demands is one they are increasingly compelled to share with single-issue groups and new social movements. Indeed, their representative capacity can be rendered more effective when they work in conjunction with these other actors. These are developments which tend to be seized on by those inclined to argue for the growing importance of pressure groups and social movements generally, be they pluralists, corporatists or participatory democrats.

Political participation

Recent evidence certainly indicates that more British citizens are prepared to participate in single-issue group activity than to join a political party: thus, whereas some 13.8% of respondents surveyed in the mid-1980s declared that they had 'got together with other people to raise an issue' in the previous five years and 11.2% had 'supported or worked in an organised group to raise an issue', only 7.4% claimed to be party members and only 5.2% had helped raised funds on behalf of a political party. Even fewer had actually offered their services as canvassers or clerical workers to parties (Parry and Moyser, 1990; Parry et al., 1992: 44). Table 11.1 reports membership of a variety of associational groups in 1990, confirming that activity in party politics ranks fairly low in such a league table. These data do not tell us anything about change over time, of course, but evidence which bears upon change can also be cited. For instance, Kees Aarts reports that the proportion of Britons involved in social organisations increased from 48% to 61% between 1959 and 1990 (Aarts, 1995: 232). Similarly, Peter Hall has calculated that 'the average number of associational memberships among the adult population grew by 44% between 1959 and 1990, rising most rapidly in the 1960s but subsiding only slightly thereafter' (Hall, 1998: 4). By contrast, the membership of parties in Britain has plainly declined since the 1960s, not only in absolute terms but also as a proportion of the registered electorate. This is so notwithstanding a temporary upturn in Labour Party individual membership in the mid-1990s (see Table 11.2).

   The decline of party membership and activism is a cross-national phenomenon (Katz et al., 1992), but it is not one which is easily explained. In truth, there are a number of competing explanatory factors, some of which are very hard to measure and whose impact is therefore well nigh impossible to gauge (Webb, 2000: ch. 8). For instance, it is equally possible that citizens have become less inclined to join political parties as generalised disillusionment with their performance spreads. In

Table 11.1 Membership of various types of political and social organisation, 1990

Type of organisation	Percentage of sample reporting membership
Sports or recreation	16.9
Religious or church organisation	16.6
Trade unions	14.4
Professional associations	9.8
Education, arts, music or cultural	9.3
Conservation, environment, ecology	5.0
Political parties or groups	4.9
Women's groups	4.8
Youth association work	4.6
Local community action groups	2.7
Animal rights	1.9
Peace movement	1.1
Average	7.7

Source: Budge, et al. (1997: 163); derived from European Values Study data, 1990

Table 11.2 Major parties' individual memberships in Britain (election years only)

Year	Labour	Conservative	Lib/Lib Dem	Total	Membership/electorate
1964	830,116	2,150,000	278,690	3,258,806	9.36
1966	775,693	2,150,000	234,345	3,160,038	9.12
1970	680,191	2,150,000	234,345	3,064,536	8.03
1974	691,889	1,500,000	190,000	2,381,889	5.97
1979	666,091	1,350,000	145,000	2,161,091	5.26
1983	295,344	1,200,000	145,258*	1,640,602	3.89
1987	288,829	1,000,000	137,500*	1,426,329	3.30
1992	279,530	500,000	100,000	879,530	2.03
1997	405,000	400,000	100,000	905,000	2.09

Note: * Includes SDP membership figures. 'Membership/electorate' reports the percentage of the registered electorate who were individual party members.

Sources: Labour Party NEC annual reports; National Union of Conservative and Unionist Associations; Liberal Democrats Information Office; Berrington and Hague (1997: 48)

particular, the problems which all western governing parties have faced in managing economies and public sector budgets since the 1970s may well have negatively influenced the popularity of parties in general (Webb, 1996). Then again, the supply of willing recruits in advanced industrial society could be affected by the process of cognitive mobilisation of voters, since greater access to higher education and non-partisan sources of political information might reduce the relative importance of parties as political communicators and serve to enhance the sense of political efficacy which citizens need to become active in interest groups (Katz, 1990: 144–5). A further possibility is that party membership has fallen as the value of the non-political benefits provided by parties has diminished. For instance, party membership has always been a form of social as well as political activity, and all of the main parties have traditionally recruited from their associated social clubs (the Conservative clubs, Liberal clubs and various working men's and trades and labour clubs affiliated to Labour), which provided relatively cheap and congenial sources of entertainment and leisure for members. However, it seems probable that the attractiveness of such benefits has declined considerably with the expansion of alternative (non-partisan) sources of entertainment and leisure in British society. Alternatively, it could be that the roots of both party membership decline and pressure group emergence may lie in a common phenomenon such as the erosion of the class cleavage, as writers such as Otto Kirchheimer suggested as long ago as the 1960s (Kirchheimer, 1966). More pertinently from our point of view, there is the argument that the decline of participation in party politics is caused by the challenge posed by the emergence of alternative forms of representative agency which better articulate group interests – pressure groups and social movements. This position, for instance, is central to Richardson's contention that Britain constitutes a changing 'market for activism' (Richardson, 1995: 117).

In fact, while this is a difficult issue to get to the bottom of, it seems most likely that the decline of party membership is a concomitant of the broader process of partisan dealignment which has characterised mass political behaviour in the country since 1970. A variety of factors have contributed to partisan dealignment, including the strategic decisions of the parties themselves, the emergence of new cross-cutting cleavages, social mobility and weak policy performance by governing parties (see Webb, 2000: 221–7). What is clear, though, is that advocates of participatory democracy frequently seize on declining party membership and activism and contrast this with evidence of burgeoning single-issue groups and social movement activity in order to suggest that parties represent an outmoded institutional impasse: as Geoff Mulgan puts it, they are stuck in the nineteenth century – 'centralized, pyramidal, national with strictly defined rules of authority and sovereignty' (1994a: 16; see also Mulgan, 1994b).

Summary

- While parties, pressure groups and social movements can all play their part in articulating group interests and fostering political participation, only the former can perform the vital function of aggregating demands.
- Developments such as European integration, reform of the British state and growing social heterogeneity have in their different ways all tended to complicate the tasks before political parties while offering interest groups and social movements new 'markets for activism'.

Conclusion

We have seen that in a liberal democracy such as contemporary Britain political parties, interest groups and social movements are all key actors in the provision of representative linkage between state and society. Moreover, the position that one takes on the relative merits of these different types of actor depends in no small part on the observer's theoretical predilections, both normative and analytical. Social and political changes, including the emergence of a social heterogeneity, European integration and reform of the UK's institutional structures, have all impacted on the main agencies of representation, and often in ways that appear to render the effectiveness of political parties diminished while enhancing that of pressure groups and social movements. This perception seems to be underlined by changing patterns of citizen participation in politics.

However, such a reading is simplistic and misleading, for parties, interest groups and social movements are not necessarily engaged in some kind of zero sum game in which only one can gain at the expense of the others (Rucht, 2000: 104). Thus, the growth of group politics and participation in social movements does not necessarily imply the decline or failure of parties. This is illustrated by the fact that citizens themselves do not seem to regard participation via these various types of agency as mutually exclusive. For instance, across a range of west European countries, including Britain, supporters of new social movements are significantly *more* likely to express a positive party preference than those not involved with new social movements (Aarts, 1995: 251). Commitment to group activity appears to be – as research on political participation has often pointed out – a stimulant to partisanship.

In truth, the representative roles of parties, single-issue groups and social movements overlap, and can reasonably be seen as complementing rather than challenging each other. Parties may perhaps be less strongly anchored in society than their two counterparts in the provision of representation, but they reach far more deeply into the state itself, where they perform functions which single-issue groups and social movements cannot. We have already seen that this is particularly true of the aggregative function, but it is possible to go further. In respect of the functions of governing and recruiting political elites, parties remain pre-eminent almost everywhere in the democratic world (Webb et al., November 2002). Indeed, consideration of the governing function makes it virtually impossible to speak of party decline, for it is in government that party effects are most clearly discernible. Notwithstanding the many and varied constraints which undoubtedly limit the scope for governmental action, there is abundant serious evidence to confirm that, in a variety of ways, political parties do 'make a difference' to public policy outcomes once they have the opportunity to hold governmental office for a reasonable period of time (Rose, 1980; Hogwood, 1992; Klingemann et al., 1994; Schmidt, 1996; Boix, 1998; Webb, 2000: 259–67). The demise of the neo-corporatism since the 1970s only serves to reinforce the enduring importance of political parties in this respect.

Nevertheless, to argue that parties remain far too central to a number of key political functions to be credibly regarded as 'failing' is not to overlook the fact that they have shortcomings as articulators of group demands and as conduits of mass political participation. Since 1960 advanced industrial societies such as Britain's have simultaneously experienced both a notable increase in the dissemination of non-partisan political information via the mass media and the expansion of higher education. These are the twin engines driving a process of 'cognitive mobilisation' which in turn has fed a greater sense of political efficacy among citizens and a correspondingly augmented desire for active involvement in politics (Barnes and Kaase, 1979; Dalton, 1996: 21–7). Parties alone seem unable to meet this growing demand, but pressure groups and social movements have proved important vehicles on which the cognitively mobilised can hitch a ride.

Discussion Questions

1. How do analytical and normative theories impact on debates about representation?
2. How have social developments like cognitive mobilisation and growing social heterogeneity affected patterns of representation in contemporary Britain?
3. What are the respective roles of parties, pressure groups and social movements in fostering articulation, aggregation and participation?

References

Aarts, K. (1995) 'Intermediate organizations and interest representation', in H.D. Klingemann and D. Fuchs (eds) *Citizens and the State*, Oxford: Oxford University Press.

Barber, B. (1985) *Strong Democracy: Participatory Politics for a New Age*, Berkeley, CA: University of California Press.

Bardi, L. (1994) 'Transnational party federations, European parliamentary party groups and the building of Europarties', in R.S. Katz and P. Mair (eds) *How Parties Organize: Change and Adaptation in Party Organizations in Western Democracies*, London: Sage, pp. 357–71.

Barnes, S.H. and Kaase, M. (1979) *Political Action: Mass Participation in Five Western Democracies*, Beverly Hills, CA: Sage.

Berrington, H. and Hague, R. (1997) 'The Liberal Democrat campaign', in P. Norris and N.T. Gavin (eds) *Britain Votes 1997*, Oxford: Oxford University Press, pp. 47–60.

Boix, C. (1998) *Political Parties, Growth and Equality*, Cambridge: Cambridge University Press.

Budge, I. et al. (1997) *The Politics of the New Europe: Atlantic to the Urals*, London: Longman.

Burke, E. (1906) 'Thoughts on the cause of the present discontents', in H. Frowde (ed.) *The Works of the Right Honourable Edmund Burke*, London: Oxford University Press, pp. 1–88 (first published, 1770).

Butler, D., Adonis, A. and Travers, T. (1995) *Policy Failure in British Government: The Politics of the Poll Tax*, Oxford: Oxford University Press.

Byrne, P. (1997) *Social Movements in Britain*, London: Routledge.

Dahl, R. (1971) *Polyarchy, Participation and Opposition*, New Haven, CT: Yale University Press.

Dalton, R. (1996) *Citizen Politics: Public Opinion and Political Parties in Advanced Western Democracies* (second edition), Chatham, NJ: Chatham House.

Franklin, B. (1994) *Packaging Politics*, London: Edward Arnold.

Gaffney, J. (1996) *Political Parties in the European Union*, London: Routledge.

Grant, W. (2000) *Pressure Groups and British Politics*, Basingstoke: Macmillan.

Hall, P.A. (1998) 'Social capital in Britain', paper presented to the Annual Meeting of the American Political Science Association, Boston, September.

Hix, S. and Lord, C. (1997) *Political Parties in the European Union*, Basingstoke: Macmillan.

Hogwood, B. (1992) *Trends in British Public Policy*, Buckingham: Open University Press.

Katz, R.S. (1990) 'Parties as linkage: a vestigial function?', *European Journal of Political Research*, Vol. 18, pp. 143–62.

Katz, R.S., Mair, P., Bardi, L., Bille, L., Deschouwer, K., Farrell, D., Koole, R., Morlino, L., Muller, W., Pierre, J., Poguntke, T., Sundberg, J., Svasanad, L., van de Velde, F., Webb, P. and Widfeldt, A. (1992) 'The membership of political parties in European democracies, 1960–1990', *European Journal of Political Research*, Vol. 22, pp. 329–45.

Kirchheimer, O. (1966) 'The transformation of west European party systems', in J. LaPalombara and M. Weiner (eds) *Political Parties and Political Development*, Princeton, NJ: Princeton University Press.

Klingemann, H.-D., Hofferbert, R. and Budge, I. (1994) *Parties, Policies and Democracy*, Boulder, CO: Westview Press.

Lawson, K. and Merkl, P. (1988) *When Parties Fail: Emerging Alternative Organizations*, Princeton, NJ: Princeton University Press.

Mazey, S. and Richardson, J. (1992) 'Pressure groups in the European Community', *Parliamentary Affairs*, Vol. 45, pp. 95–127.

Mazey, S. and Richardson, J. (1993) *Lobbying in the European Community*, Oxford: Oxford University Press.

Mulgan, G. (1994a) 'Party-free politics', *New Statesman & Society*, 15 April.

Mulgan, G. (1994b) *Politics in an Anti-Political Age*, Cambridge: Polity Press.

Parry, G. and Moyser, G. (1990) 'A map of political participation in Britain', *Government & Opposition*, Vol. 25, pp. 147–69.

Parry, G., Moyser, G. and Day, N. (1992) *Political Participation and Democracy in Britain*, Cambridge: Cambridge University Press.

Pateman, C. (1970) *Participation and Democratic Theory*, Cambridge: Cambridge University Press.

Richardson, J. (1995) 'The market for political activism: interest groups as a challenge to political parties', *West European Politics*, Vol. 18, pp. 116–39.

Richardson, J. and Jordan, G. (1979) *Governing under Pressure*, Oxford: Martin Robertson.

Rose, R. (1980) *Do Parties Make a Difference?* (second edition), Chatham, NJ: Chatham House (London: Macmillan, 1984).

Rucht, D. (2000) 'Political participation in Europe' in R. Sakwa and A. Stevens (eds) *Contemporary Europe*, Basingstoke: Macmillan, pp. 85–108.

Scammell, M. (1995) *Designer Politics: How Elections Are Won*, Basingstoke: Macmillan.

Schattschneider, E.E. (1942) *Party Government*, New York City: Rinehart & Co.

Schmidt, M. (1996) 'When parties matter: a review of the possibilities and limits of partisan influence on public policy', *European Journal of Political Research*, Vol. 30, pp. 155–83.

Schmitter, P.C. (1974) 'Still the century of corporatism?', *Review of Politics*, Vol. 36, pp. 85–131.

Schumpeter, J.A. (1952) *Capitalism, Socialism and Democracy* (fifth edition), London: George Allen & Unwin.

Ware, A. (1996) *Political Parties and Party Systems*, Oxford: Oxford University Press.

Webb, P.D. (1996) 'Apartisanship and anti-party sentiment in the UK: correlates and constraints', *European Journal of Political Research*, Vol. 29, pp. 365–82.

Webb, P.D. (2000) *The Modern British Party System*, London: Sage.

Webb, P.D., Farrell, D.M. and Holliday, I. (November 2002) *Political Parties in Advanced Industrial Societies*, Oxford: Oxford University Press.

Further reading

Byrne, P. (1997) *Social Movements in Britain*, London: Routledge.

Grant, W. (2000) *Pressure Groups and British Politics*, Basingstoke: Macmillan.

Richardson, J. (1995) 'The market for political activism: interest groups as a challenge to political parties', *West European Politics*, Vol. 18, pp. 116–39.

Rucht, D. (2000) 'Political participation in Europe', in R. Sakwa and A. Stevens (eds) *Contemporary Europe*, Basingstoke: Macmillan, pp. 85–108.

Schmidt, M. (1996) 'When parties matter: a review of the possibilities and limits of partisan influence on public policy', *European Journal of Political Research*, Vol. 30, pp. 155–83.

Webb, P.D. (2000) *The Modern British Party System*, London: Sage.

Webb, P.D., Farrell, D.M. and Holliday, I. (November 2002) *Political Parties in Advanced Industrial Societies*, Oxford: Oxford University Press.

The Media and Politics

Ralph Negrine

CHAPTER TWELVE

Background

It is inconceivable to imagine politics without the medium of television. Our first glimpses of actors in the political arena are essentially derived from this visual medium: the men – and increasingly, women – in suits sitting on green benches in the House of Commons and arguing is a particularly potent image of what politics has come to signify in this day and age. But a mere half-century before, the medium of television had not yet had any impact on the conduct or organisation of politics. In fact, in the immediate post-war period, it was the press and, to a lesser extent, radio which were the channels of political communication. Neither provided the simultaneity or created the mass audience of the kind that television was to bring about, and bring about so rapidly! In 1950 only 10% of households had television. By 1959 the figure had climbed to 75%, reaching 90% by 1966 (Butler and Stokes, 1971: 269). More critically, television had moved rapidly to centre-stage for political communication. According to Butler and Stokes, by 1964 – less than a decade after commercial television began – 'fully 65 per cent of those who followed the [election] campaign at all said that they had relied on television, and only 28 per cent that they had relied more on the press' (1971: 270).

Looking back at these changes, one is struck not only by the rapid displacement of one medium by another, but also by the multiplication of media, and hence news, outlets. In the period between 1945 and 1955, the press and BBC radio (three services) dominated, with BBC television (one channel!) slowly adding to the menu of choices. Subsequent additions – commercial television from 1955, BBC2 in 1963, commercial radio in the early 1970s, Channel Four in 1982 – increased the diversity of outlets even further. In the 1980s, cable and satellite television exploded the idea of 'scarcity' in television, and in the late 1990s digital broadcasting promised a range of services that would have been unthinkable in the period immediately after the Second World War.

It is tempting to see this growth as part and parcel of technological progress and as a means of liberation from the strictures of the early years of broadcasting. There is no doubt that the success of commercial television in the 1950s forced the BBC to re-think its programme output, as well as its manner of address, just as the pirate radio stations forced the BBC to set up its own popular music services. But such developments also brought about changes in *political communication*. Jay

Blumler and Dennis Kavanagh (1999) have described the immediate post-war period as the First Age of political communication, in which there is scarcity of outlets and a clear subservience of the media to politics. One exemplar of this subservience was the existence of the Fourteen-Day Rule, which prevented broadcasters from dealing with any matters of controversy that were to be debated in Parliament within a fortnight (see Negrine, 1998b).

In the Second Age of political communication, the 1960s, 'limited-channel, nation-wide television became the dominant medium of political communication, while the grip of party loyalty on voters was loosening' (Blumler and Kavanagh, 1999: 212). In this period, according to Blumler and Kavanagh, 'the core features of the professional model of modern campaigning emerged' (ibid., 1999: 213). The Third Age, the present, 'is marked by the proliferation of the main means of communication, media abundance, ubiquity, reach, and celerity. . . . New patterns and adaptations ensue for all involved in the political communication process' (ibid., 1999: 213).

The growth in the number of outlets has thus significantly altered the processes and flows of political communication. The image of the 1950s family huddled together around the radio or television set has given way to an image, and a reality, of a family whose members are dispersed around a house, with each having access to his/her preferred media outlets. Media abundance thus means not only a greater choice of media and news outlets, but also an opportunity *not* to choose news outlets. Hence the concern about the changing media landscape generally, the general increase in the number of entertainment channels, and the decline in the range of news and current affairs vehicles on both the existing terrestrial and satellite (Barnett and Seymour, 1999). Moreover, as such services begin to serve a more fragmented audience, there may be fewer opportunities for all citizens to come together as a political and civic community. However, when citizens do come together – for instance when mourning Diana, Princess of Wales, or watching a football match involving a national team – they often come together in large numbers.

But it is not so much the onward march of the medium of television *per se* that is significant, but its centrality as a medium for communicating politics. David Butler and Donald Stokes neatly captured the moment of transition in their work when they wrote that in the 1960s, 'the experience of following politics by print and broadcast is in many ways more alike than different', but that such differences may:

> become a good deal larger as parties and producers develop new arts in the
> presentation of political television. It seems that television has at times had
> a sharp impact on the public's evaluation of politics and politicians, as it
> probably did while 'That Was the Week That Was' gathered its audience in
> 1962–3 or while the 'Army–McCarthy' hearings held the American public
> transfixed nine years earlier. If dramatic confrontations of party leaders, as in
> the Kennedy–Nixon debates, were to become a feature of British elections,
> television's potential might become more apparent.
>
> (Butler and Stokes, 1971: 281)

For those in politics, television's potential was indeed very apparent, even in this early stage of its development. In his history of the relationship of television and politics, Michael Cockerell (1988: 88) illustrates the growing realisation of television's potential through the example of Harold Wilson (Prime Minister, 1964–70, 1974–77). Marcia Williams, Wilson's secretary, tried at all times to ensure that his appearances conveyed an image of youth, sincerity and simplicity. In making efforts to 'manage' the appearances of Wilson, Marcia Williams was already showing an appreciation of the need for politics, and politicians, 'to adapt to broadcasting' (Seymour-Ure, 1991: 167).

Television, then, was to become the new terrain on which political battles would be fought, and those who sought to survive in the era of television had to learn how it worked and, more importantly, how to use it. At a more general level, though, political systems were transformed from ones in which the media – principally, the press – were central to the conduct and practice of politics to ones in which television has moved to centre-stage. Such political systems became known as 'media-centred democracies' or 'videocracies' (Mazzoleni, 1995: 315) (see Box 12.1). The implications of this change for the conduct of contemporary politics will be discussed more fully later. Next, we will explore some of the ways in which the mass media have had an impact on politics, including during election campaigns. Then we will focus on the press and politics. In summary, therefore, the insertion of the media into the political system has led to a situation in which it is not possible to think, discuss or consider politics as a process or as an activity independently of what the media do or say.

Box 12.1

Videocracy – 'democracy *by* media. It is the extreme consequence of . . . 'mediatization'. . . . It is the media (as a whole) who are thought to decide who should be the actors, what are the rules, what are the messages, what are the issues at stake, and who are the winners and the losers in elections, and in the common political domain (Mazzoleni, 1995: 315).

Mediatization – 'refers to the changes in the party form and in its communication patterns with the electoral market' (Mazzoleni, 1995: 307).

Summary

- There has been an explosion in the number of media outlets in the post-war period.
- The development of television – and other media – has led to a different set of relationships between politicians and the media.
- Politicians have been forced to adapt to the needs and practices of the medium of television.
- The medium of television has given rise to 'media-centred democracies'.

Theoretical Considerations

The absence of any conclusive empirical evidence in support of specific media effects, such as on voting behaviour (but see below), should not detract from a more general discussion of the ways in which the media have contributed to contemporary forms of modern life, including political life. Much depends on how 'effects' are perceived and 'impacts' are defined, and, indeed, on which medium and on which audiences the discussion focuses. As Colin Seymour-Ure observed in his study of 'the political impact of mass media', we need to ask broad questions such as 'what kind of effect?' and 'upon whom', and 'how far and in what ways are the political relationships and individuals affected by the communication between them?' (Seymour-Ure, 1974: 42). In this way, we can avoid the 'assumption that the effect of the media is limited to the potency of their messages' (Seymour-Ure, 1974: 43).

When exploring 'the media and politics', then, one should not simply think in terms of such effects as on voting behaviour – and it is immensely difficult to provide evidence of such direct effects anyway given the methodological problems of identifying one single source of influence only – but on the ways in which the existence and presence of the media have altered relationships, re-drawn the boundaries of the political system and even re-defined the nature of politics itself. The Internet, for instance, creates the possibility of moving away from a representative form of democracy to a more direct form of citizen involvement. For example, it is now considered important for key political actors to try to speak directly to the public at large via the Internet, rather than to allow journalists to filter the message they want to get across; and the current view among key political advisers is that in contemporary politics 'every day is election day' and that there needs to be 'a permanent campaign to keep a permanent majority' (Wintour, 2000). The importance of these examples is that they point to a form of politics, and a way of thinking about politics and political activity, that is different from any era in which the media did not exist, or in which other media were dominant.

In this respect, it is the medium of television that has had an enormous 'impact' on politics in the last century. Indeed, television's visual and linguistic properties make it difficult to identify only one simple message or only one single set of messages for an audience (or audiences) to decode its 'effects'. Its 'cumulative effects' are related to the ways in which it 'transmits reality and affects the imagery of politics and political figures' (Lang and Lang, 1982: 220). It follows, therefore, that it matters how things appear.

The realisation that 'how things appear matter' has had tremendous consequences. It has meant that political actors and their consultants have had to learn how to use television in order both to minimise its unpredictability and/or to manage the images which it conveys. This has meant much more than simply dressing-up in appropriate colour tones or becoming more 'telegenic'. It has meant thinking strategically about how to use the settings in which political actors would be presented on the television screen to advantage. But adapting to the medium of television has been only one reaction to the realisation of its importance; a more complex reaction has been to begin to tailor political activity – speeches, visits, the release of information – so as to elicit the desired media reaction, that is, favourable rather than critical publicity. At election times, it has meant creating a more sophisticated and effective communication strategy (see below).

Unfortunately, media traditions and routines have their own peculiar practices, and requirements (i.e. their own 'logic'), which often run counter to the wishes of political actors, and this immediately sets up a difficult relationship between the two. Nevertheless, both co-exist, sometimes in co-operation, sometimes in conflict: journalists want news from political actors, while political actors want publicity from journalists; journalists want sound-bites, and politicians have learned to provide these; journalists want interesting and controversial news from politicians, and politicians are often able to comply with this. As Timothy Cook has argued, news is indeed:

> a coproduction of sources (usually officials) and journalists, but . . . sources cannot simply push their fingers and make news in their own terms. Instead, not only is news a reworking of official actions, events and statements with production values in mind. These production values favour particular kinds of news and information over others, and thereby end up endowing the news with particular politics.
>
> (Cook, 1998: 114)

A good example of this 'co-production' is the so-called 'sound-bite', namely, a brief statement or sound-clip made for inclusion in a television news item. As political actors came to appreciate television producers' need for snippets of speech in a short news item, they soon learned to deliver what was expected of them. Television producers got what they wanted for their news items, and politicians ensured that they got what they wanted to say on air.

But there are numerous occasions when the media are at the receiving end of a well-structured and highly controlled set of political 'messages'. Writing about the 1995 Labour Party conference, Patrick Wintour (1995) neatly anticipated the hallmarks of the then Labour government-in-waiting's media strategy:

> The presence of the media patrolling for the slightest sign of any split is slowly killing debate in the conference hall. . . . The professionalism in the communications operation is also now quite frightening. [The Party Organisation has] made sure everybody's singing from the same song-sheet. . . . In the Labour Party now, nothing is left to chance.
>
> (Wintour, 1995: 25)

As we shall see below, this media strategy became a key characteristic of the Labour government under Alastair Campbell, its media overlord. So, while it is correct to see 'the political–media complex (as) a constantly evolving relationship between media institutions and the institutions of politics and government and the way in which both relate to the public' (Swanson, 1997: 1265–6), it is also important to appreciate the enormous efforts that one side of that relationship increasingly puts into controlling the outcome.

Often, this aspect of the relationship is not highlighted enough. Even Jay Blumler's definition of 'the modern publicity process (as involving) a competitive struggle to influence and control popular perceptions of key political events and issues through the major mass media' (1990: 103) does not introduce the sort of historical analyses which would question whether the two institutions in this relationship were, or are, ever equal partners. He is undoubtedly correct in suggesting that once 'the modern publicity process takes over' other things follow on. For example, there is a greater attention to how policy decisions 'will play in the arena of media-filtered mass *perceptions*' (1990: 106), and there is a greater degree of professionalisation on the part of sources (1990: 104), but these consequences are the result of a greater effort at controlling communication by those in power and the media can do little to fight back. They may be critical, show up the government's activities, even be cynical, but these are minor responses to the onslaught of professional publicity aimed at them and the public.

In 1998, when the Select Committee on Public Administration took evidence from Alastair Campbell, Tony Blair's then Chief Press Secretary, it became clear that it was his intention to get the Prime Minister's messages across to government, the media and the public. One of his roles was, he noted, to manage 'the Strategic Communication Unit and that is really about being involved in the taking of a strategic overview of how government should communicate the policies and its activities' (Select Committee on Public Administration, 1998: 51) Later on he also observed that his job involved 'trying to make sure that the whole of Government is aware of the strategic messages that the Prime Minister wants delivered' (ibid., 1998: 52).

Other examples, some historical, also suggest an unequal partnership. At a very general level, it is the British Parliament, through its various Acts and licensing mechanisms, which has ensured that broadcasters' coverage of controversial material is 'presented with due accuracy and impartiality' (Broadcasting Act 1990, Section 6(1)(b)). While few would disagree with such a requirement, its very existence suggests that one institution (the political one) is superior to the other (the broadcast media). A more obvious illustration of this point is the Broadcasting Ban of 1988–94, which prohibited broadcasters from broadcasting words spoken by members of proscribed organisations, notably the IRA. This could be imposed on the broadcasters because, according to the Broadcasting Act 1990, the 'Secretary of State may at any time by notice require the (Independent Television) Commission to direct the holders of any licences . . . to refrain from including in the programmes . . . any matter or classes of matter . . .' (Broadcasting Act 1990, Section 10(3), p. 11).

The struggles over the coverage of the Suez crisis in 1956, the problems over the coverage of the politics of Northern Ireland, the concern over the transmission of Duncan Campbell's *Secret Society* series in 1987, and the furore over the *Death on the Rock* programme in 1988 are perhaps also indicative of a set of broadcast institutions that are more constrained in their coverage than one would initially assume (see Negrine, 1998b). Interestingly, many of these examples refer to particular programmes rather than everyday political news coverage. It may be, therefore, that an interdependent relationship of more or less equals does exist between the political and media institutions at an everyday level, but that at times of 'crisis' or deeper critical questioning, the broadcasters are more severely constrained (Tracey, 1978). Finally, one possible reason why none of these examples relates to the 1990s may be that there has been a general downward shift in the quality and range of the sorts of current affairs programme which used to adopt a critical stance (Barnett and Seymour, 1999).

A more recent, and curious, illustration of the peculiarity of the 'political–media complex' is the concern over the disappearance – but later reappearance – of newspaper coverage of parliamentary debates. Before 1991, these were a regular feature of most broadsheet newspapers and the space devoted to debates and other parliamentary activities sat alongside the usual mix of political and other coverage. In 1991, *The Times* abandoned its coverage of parliamentary debates on the grounds that they were not read, that they were not newsworthy enough and that they merely reproduced a charade. They did not, in other words, deal with politics and power. Other newspapers followed the example of *The Times*, leaving Parliament without regular coverage (see Negrine, 1998a).

Members of Parliament were generally unhappy about this development and saw it as a fundamental questioning of the relevance and importance of Parliament itself within the British political system. Other, related concerns were also highlighted: had the media interpretation of speeches become more important than the actual speech? Had parliamentary debates given way to off-the-record comments by 'sources'? Was Parliament no longer worthy of its own dedicated space? Was Parliament now no longer different from other institutions in the land?

Similar concerns came to the fore in 1997 when the BBC's Radio 4 *Today* programme announced that it would no longer carry the 'Yesterday in Parliament' slot at 8.50 am. The BBC argued that 'Yesterday in Parliament' did not fit in well with the *Today* programme as a whole. It would be moved – banished, some would say – to long wave. Not surprisingly, audience figures for the new programme slot were extremely disappointing, and after much criticism of the BBC, including one debate in Parliament, the BBC announced that it would review its decisions about parliamentary coverage. In July 1999, the BBC reintroduced 'Yesterday in Parliament' into the *Today* programme but in a shortened form and at an earlier time.

It took *The Daily Telegraph* and *The Times* until the autumn of 1999 to re-introduce the parliamentary page, albeit in a more truncated form. Although commercial and competitive considerations may have played a part in these decisions, it is also worth noting that it is *parliamentary coverage* that is accorded sufficient status to warrant its re-introduction. Parliament is thus re-affirmed as an institution that is fundamental to British political life; overlooking it – as the press had done – was both an oversight and a mistake. The BBC had to bear that in mind, just as it had to note the Culture Secretary's comments that it had a 'duty as a public service broadcaster, not only to entertain but also to educate and inform' (BBC Online, 1999).

But if the media and political institutions are in a continuous struggle to 'influence and control public perceptions of events', is the public relegated to a spectator role only? Does it play no part over the processes of political communication? One simple answer to this question must clearly be that the public is there to be influenced by, say, those seeking office or, conversely, by those who wish to alert the public to the machinations of those seeking office. This helps explain, in part, the efforts at control over the communications process by political actors and the apparent cynicism, verging on disdain, often found in news reports.

A more complicated answer to the question about the role of the public in the generation of political communication would suggest that the public is anything but an empty vessel into which information is poured. A number of different approaches to the study of the media audience (see, for example, Neumann et al., 1992) have in fact argued very strongly that the audience/public is an active one, interpreting or decoding information from within particular class, regional, national, ethnic or personal locations. The idea of the active audience thus makes it difficult to adopt any position which suggests the media have an 'effect' even on such specific acts as voting.

Added to this is the attention that must be paid to the many forces that come into play when an individual votes. There are considerations of class, gender and ethnicity, as well as economic and regional ones. Personal histories also contribute to this one single act. All these sit alongside media considerations. No wonder, then, that it is so difficult to be precise about the effects of the media. Even when there is a clear instance of changed conditions, for example *The Sun* backing the Labour Party in the 1997 election, the problem of identifying effects remains. Pippa Norris et al. concluded their chapter on 'the effects of newspapers' as follows:

> *The Sun*'s conversion did not evidently bring the Labour Party new recruits. Equally Labour's new recruits did not prove particularly keen to switch to *The Sun*. At best we have found . . . that newspapers have but a limited influence on the voting behaviour of their readers. Where they can make a difference is in mobilizing their more faithful readers by playing them a familiar tune, readers who indeed may well have chosen that paper precisely because it plays a tune they have long considered an old favourite.
>
> (Norris et al., 1999: 169)

The absence of convincing empirical evidence in support of a 'powerful media' does not detract from the fact that political actors continue to put considerable effort into controlling public perceptions. At election times, those efforts increase, just as, in fact, the media's efforts to resist those efforts also increase.

Summary

- It is difficult to identify the media's effects on politics. Such 'effects' or 'impacts' may be both direct and indirect, short term and long term, intended and unintended.
- The media, particularly television, have had 'impacts' on the ways in which the activity of politics is carried out.
- Politicians continue to want to control the media agenda; the media continue to try to evade those controls.
- In studying how the public understands politics and political activity, it is best to see the public as an 'active audience'.

Update

Although the 'effects' of the media on politics and on political activity need to be seen as complex and long term, the study of the media, and their part in the conduct of elections, has tended to be seen as providing instances where shorter-term 'effects' can be studied comparatively easily. In practice, as we have seen, this has not been the case. Nevertheless, the study of the forms and effects of political communication during election times continues to generate considerable interest and it attracts much more attention than the broader agenda identified earlier in this chapter.

However, even within the study of 'the media and elections' there has been evidence of a greater interest in bigger issues than simply whether or not the media have had an 'impact' on voting behaviour. For example, there is now an interest in such ideas as 'the media–political complex' and 'modern publicity process'. These ideas represent an appreciation of the ways in which the presence of the media, particularly television, alter the nature of politics and political activity. Similarly, the interest in the idea of 'the permanent campaign', in 'political marketing' and in 'Americanisation' (see Box 12.1) shows how students of political communication are moving away from limited studies of 'the media and elections' and are beginning to look at larger issues, concerning the 'hows' and 'whys' of such processes of political communication, sometimes drawing in comparative analytical frameworks to look at changes that have a global resonance. These sorts of approach, and the questions that they pose, are briefly sketched below.

Box 12.2

Americanisation – The 'patterns of modern electoral campaigning and their consequences' include 'personalization of politics, expanding reliance on technical experts and professional advertisers, growing disenchantment of political parties from citizens, development of autonomous structures of communication, and casting citizens in the role of spectators ... (Swanson, 1997: 249)

Debate

The 'permanent campaign' is now probably a feature of all pre-election periods, at least in Britain. Political parties are continually assessing their standing and aligning themselves in such a way as to occupy pole position in forthcoming elections. The Labour Party victory in 1997, for example, was preceded by a period of modernisation of the party which included a programme of reform to make it appear less of a threat to a large part of the potential electorate. As Philip Gould (1998) relates in his account of the period up to that election, a concerted effort was made to seek out, through a variety of research methods (focus groups, surveys, etc.), those things that needed to be emphasised and those that needed to be played down. This strategy, and the attendant principles, became part of the so-called 'War Book' which analysed meticulously the strengths and weaknesses of the major contenders for office and how best to exploit them. Those seeking office must therefore see themselves as if in a permanent campaign to win, and presumably retain, office.

The professional attention now paid to elections contrasts starkly with what is often taken to be the older and more traditional form of campaigning, namely, the making of speeches in church halls or town squares, and the unco-ordinated and unsophisticated running of campaigns. The greater professional attention found in contemporary electioneering has been described as part and parcel of 'political marketing' (Maarek, 1995). This refers to the modern, co-ordinated, professionally slick, centralised communication strategy that has clear aims and objectives and that is said to characterise modern political communication. With political marketing nothing is left to chance – colours are made to co-ordinate with platforms, suits with backgrounds, and all speakers must speak with the same voice, and so on. The lessons and tools of marketing are thus used to 'package' and 'sell' politics. Citizens become more like consumers in that they are forced to choose between political parties in the same way as they would choose between products. There are, however, three points worth considering in relation to political marketing:

- Were campaigns, in the past, as unsophisticated as their caricature suggests?
- Is political marketing part of the general commercialisation of society and part of the 'promotional culture' which has infected many areas of contemporary activities? (Wernick, 1992)
- Is political marketing something to be abhorred, or is it beneficial?

Views differ on this last point, but Maggie Scammell has suggested that there is a positive side to political marketing. She claims that it can 'bring real democratic benefits by improving two-way communications between voters and politicians and, theoretically at least, allowing both parties and voters to be better informed and to make more rational choices' (1995: xv).

This assumes a great deal about the way in which the process of communication is conducted, and the implicit intentions of the communicators. Focus groups of voters, for instance, may give political parties a better insight into how their policies will play in the public arena, but does this reduce politics to an exercise in satisfying voters and potential voters, and does it eliminate ideology from political parties? Put differently, is political marketing also, in some undefined way, related to the emergence of political parties that are less ideological than their predecessors?

Another theme which emerges from recent studies is that of 'Americanisation'. Many definitions of this can be found and these, one way or another, play up or play on the fear that British politics is following the same path as that travelled by American politicians and the American media. Americanisation is seen as 'a gradual assimilation . . . of US campaign practices' with a particular emphasis on television, personalisation and the professionalisation of political actors (Kaid and

Holtz-Bacha, 1995: 8–9; see also Mancini and Swanson, 1996). However, because differences between the political systems survive – Britain has no direct equivalent of a President, the political parties are not identical in structure or organisation, and so on – it is difficult to be more precise about the nature of the process by which practices are imported and political communication practices and political systems become similar.

This does not mean that practices that have an American pedigree have not been adopted and/or adapted into other political systems, but that the meaning of this process of adoption and/or adaptation is much more difficult to grasp. What does the term 'Americanisation' actually mean? At a more complex level, are we looking at changes at a global level, at changes that can be related to issues of 'modernization', or what? (see Negrine, 1996).

Summary

- Political parties currently adopt strategies that involve close attention to media activity, for example, the 'permanent campaign'.
- Election campaigns are highly professional and tightly organised activities.
- Politics is now 'marketed' in a professional and careful way.
- Many of the practices now adopted in Britain have their origin in USA, thus leading to fears of 'Americanisation'.

The Press

Since 1945, the newspaper industry has gone through a great many changes. A series of title closures in the 1950s and 1960s (e.g. *The News Chronicle* in 1960, *The Sunday Citizen* in 1967) and major industrial disputes in the 1970s, appeared to threaten its future survival, yet at the beginning of the new millennium, it is now in relatively healthy shape. It could be argued, therefore, that rather than undermining the industry, the changes may have led to its consolidation as weak titles were allowed to perish and older industrial practices were abandoned in the face of new technologies in printing and publishing. Paradoxically, while the industry shunned the newer technologies of publishing for most of the late twentieth century, that very same industry is fully embracing the technology of the twenty-first century, the Internet. Clearly, this is partly an attempt to ward off competition, but it must also be seen as a determined effort to re-position the print media alongside the electronic ones.

The cumulative effect of all these changes can be seen in Table 12.1, which contrasts the number of national titles presently available to those available immediately after 1945. The data in this table reveal two points which deserve further

Table 12.1 Circulation (in 000s) of national daily and Sunday newspapers, 1947–1999 (ownership in 1999 in brackets)

	1947	1961	1976	1987	1999 (Oct)
The Daily Telegraph (1855)	1,015	1,248	1,308	1,147	1,034 (Black, C.)
The Times (1785)	268	253	310	442	735 (News International – Murdoch)
The Guardian (1821)	126*	245	306	494	403 (Scott Trust)
The Financial Times (1888)	71*	132	174	280	426 (Pearson)
The Independent (1986)				293	230 (O'Reilly, T.)
Daily Mail (1896)	2,076	2,610	1,755	1,759	2,378 (Associated Newspapers)
Daily Express (1900)	3,855	4,328	2,594	1,697	1,069 (United Media)
Daily Herald (The Sun from 1964)	2,134	1,394	3,708 (as The Sun)	3,993	3,608 (News International – Murdoch)
News Chronicle (1930)	1,623	absorbed by Daily Mail in 1960	–	–	–
Daily Worker (from 1966 Morning Star)	118	60	*	*	*
Daily Graphic (later Sketch) (1908)	772	981	merged with Daily Mail in 1971	–	
Daily Mirror (1903)	3,702	4,561	3,851	3,123	2,307 (various institutional investors)
Today (1986)				closed in 1995	–
Daily Star (1978)				1,289	613 (United Media)
The Sunday Telegraph (1961)	–	688	759	693	824 (Black, C.)
The Sunday Times (1822)	568	967	1,382	1,314	1,374 (News International – Murdoch)
The Observer (1791)	384	715	670	722	414 (Scott Trust)
The Independent on Sunday (1990)	–	–	–	–	262 (O'Reilly, T.)
News of the World (1843)	7,890	6,643	5,138	5,360	4,151 (News International – Murdoch)
Reynolds News (1850)	720	310	later Sunday Citizen, died 1967	–	–
Sunday Express (1918)	2,577	4,457	3,451	2,033	979 (United News)
Sunday Chronicle (1855)	1,178	–	–	–	–
Sunday Dispatch (1801)	2,061	–	died 1961	–	–
Sunday Pictorial/ Sunday Mirror (1915)	4,006	5,306	4,101 (with Mirror)	2,953	2,037 (various institutional investors)
Sunday Graphic (1915)	1,185	died 1960	–	–	–
The People (1881)	4,670	5,450	4,094	2,743	1,578 (various institutional investors)
Mail on Sunday (1982)	–	–	–	1,919	2,332 (Associated Newspapers)

* The 1947 Royal Commission did not treat either of these newspapers as 'national' qualities.

Source: Royal Commissions on the press, 1947–49, 1962, 1977; Seymour-Ure (1991); The Guardian, 1997

comment. The first point relates to the general decline in the circulation of the national and Sunday tabloid newspapers. The broadsheet newspapers have not suffered a similar fate but have, in fact, seen their circulation rise over the same period. The reasons for these trends are undoubtedly complex and must include such things as the impact of television generally, the availability of news via television, a better-educated population, and the increase in magazine titles. How the industry will fare in the twenty-first century in the face of competition from more television channels and the Internet – in which they all have a presence – is an intriguing question, to which we shall return in the concluding section of this chapter. The second point is the concentration of ownership in the newspaper industry. The fact of concentration, though, is perhaps less an issue than its consequences on the range of views available through the British press. These consequences can be illustrated with two examples: newspaper allegiances during general elections, and allegiances during the 1999 European election.

Newspapers, unlike the electronic media, are not required to remain impartial in respect of matters of controversy. The history of the press has been one of struggle against control. This has given rise to a press which operates in the free market and without any limitations which affect its ability to cover controversial subjects. Consequently, the press can align itself with political parties and/or political actors at will.

At election times, these allegiances are not only clearly articulated and freely advertised, but they also colour the coverage. The *Daily Mail*, for example, has always supported the Conservative Party and it has often carried what can only be described as propaganda on its behalf. Between 1945 and 1992, those allegiances were fairly constant and predictable, but in 1997 there were some significant changes which overturned the balance of support between the two major parties: the overwhelming Conservative support up to and including 1992 vanished, a trend that continued in 2001 (see Table 12.2).

There may have been specific reasons for this change: the newspapers despaired of John Major's leadership of the Conservative Party in government (1992–97) and there was a list of policy failures – the coal dispute in 1992, leaving the Exchange Rate Mechanism (ERM) in 1992, divisions over Europe, 'sleaze' – that further alarmed them. The press, like the country, turned against the Conservatives. But were the newspapers leading, or following, public opinion? More critically, did newspapers such as *The Sun* – but incidentally not *The Times* – align themselves with Tony Blair and New Labour because *their proprietors* had abandoned John Major and supported Blair? There were three concerns here. First, if newspapers could switch allegiances so easily, they could also switch back. Second, what price would political parties have to pay to guarantee continued support from newspapers? Third, what did such shifts tell us about the power of the proprietor? While such concerns were clearly inflamed by rumour and gossip, they did touch on the much larger question of proprietorial control over content and its translation into political power.

A very similar set of concerns arose in the course of the 1999 European elections. Some newspapers, like *The Guardian*, approached the election with a general

Table 12.2 Daily newspaper partisanship and circulation (in 000s) during general elections in 1979, 1983, 1992, 1997 and 2001

	1979	1983	1992	1997	2001
Daily Express	2,458	1,936	1,525	1,220	929
	Con	Con	Con	Con	Lab
The Sun	3,942	4,155	3,571	3,842	3,288
	Con	Con	Con	Lab	Lab
Daily Mail	1,973	1,834	1,675	2,151	2,337
	Con	Con	Con	Con	Con
Daily Mirror	3,783	3,267	2,903	3,084	2,056
	Lab	Lab	Lab	Lab	Lab
Daily Telegraph	1,358	1,284	1,038	1,134	989
	Con	Con	Con	Con	Con
The Guardian	275	417	429	401	362
		Not Con landslide	Lab victory, more Lib Dem	Lab	Lab
The Times	Not published	321 Con	386 Con	719 Eurosceptic	667 Lab
The Financial Times	–	–	290 Not a Con victory	307 Lab	176 Lab
The Independent	–	–	390 No endorsement	251 Lab	197 Not Con
Today	–	–	533 Con	–	–
Daily Star	880 Neutral	1,313 Con	806 Con	648 Lab	585 Lab
Total circulation	14,669	14,527	13,546	13,757	11,586
Total Conservative circulation	9,731 (66%)	10,843 (75%)	9,534 (70%)	4,504 (33%)	3,326 (29%)
Total Labour circulation	4,058 (28%)	3,267 (22%)	3,332 (25%)	8,533 (62%)	8,063 (70%)

Source: I. Crewe and M. Harrop (1986); C. Seymour-Ure (1997); M. Scammell and M. Harrop (2002)

commitment to the European cause. Others, such as the *Daily Mail, The Daily Telegraph* and *The Sun* showed their antipathy towards the European cause in many ways, ranging from the sorts of story they selected to cover to the vehemence of their attacks on matters European. With the then Conservative Party leader, William Hague, taking up the anti-European stance, there seemed to be room for the creation of a partnership of convenience. But what also emerged during these elections was the fact that the proprietors of these newspapers – one naturalised American, one Canadian – were themselves anti-European and favoured stronger ties across the Atlantic. Once again, did their particular political preferences feed into editorial processes, and how did it impact on coverage? (See, for example, Miller, 1991; Curtice, 1997; and Norris et al.)

Summary

- The newspaper industry has changed considerably since 1945 – in organisation, consolidation and in its circulation.
- Newspapers continue to display strong political allegiances.
- Newspapers continue to play an important part in the conduct of politics, for example, in respect of the pros and cons of the European Union.
- Empirical evidence relating to the impact of newspapers on voting behaviour is still somewhat contradictory.

Conclusion

This chapter has focused on a series of issues which were very much current in the immediate post-war period – a period which has been described as the Second Age of political communication by Blumler and Kavanagh (1999). New developments will bring about some changes that are likely to complicate the relatively simple set of concerns identified above. The main changes to note relate to the growth in the variety and range of media services that are rapidly coming on-stream. Digital television, newspapers on the Internet and the Internet itself are all likely further to fragment the audience that was once available for political communication. The more choices there are, the greater the opportunities to avoid watching, reading or accessing political content. How this will impact on questions of the 'effects' of political communication we still do not know. What may remain unaffected by these changes are the continuing efforts of the powerful to colonise the means of political communication and to fight for their preferred message to be disseminated to the wider public. Journalists will continue to confront politicians, as they have traditionally done, but they will be doing so in a changed media environment.

As for the public, it will tune in and out of political communication in a more selective and erratic way. On occasions the nation may still come together, but it is likely that such occasions will diminish in frequency.

Chronology

1944 Fourteen-Day Rule drawn up.
1951 First television party election broadcast (PEB) by Lord Samuel.
1954 Television Act, which established television, is passed.
1955 First commercial television company broadcasts.
1955 ITN starts broadcasting.
1956 Fourteen-Day Rule temporarily withdrawn.
1956 Suez crisis.
1957 Robin Day interviews Prime Minister Harold Macmillan – the first major political interview.

1963   BBC2 starts broadcasting.
1964   *Daily Herald* becomes *The Sun*.
1969   Rupert Murdoch acquires *The Sun*.
1982   Channel 4 launched.
1982   Sky Channel, a satellite service, begins broadcasting across Europe.
1985   *Real Lives: At the Edge of the Union* BBC programme held up. One-day strike of journalists in broadcasting.
1986   *The Independent* newspaper launched.
1986   News International moves to Wapping.
1988   Broadcasting Ban introduced.
1989   Television cameras enter the House of Commons.
1990   Broadcasting Act published.
1990   BSkyB formed.
1991   ITV franchises awarded for ten years.
1994   Broadcasting Ban lifted.
1996   Broadcasting Act published.
1997   Channel 5 launched.
1997   New Labour government elected.
1997   Alastair Campbell becomes Press Secretary to Prime Minister Tony Blair.
2001   Alastair Campbell becomes Director of Communications and Strategy to Tony Blair.

Discussion Questions

1. What are the main theoretical and methodological problems that need to be considered when studying the political impact of the mass media?
2. How have political actors adapted to the medium of television?
3. Consider the ways in which the Internet could change politics and the conduct of politics in this century?

References

Barnett, S. and Seymour, E. (1999) *'A Shrinking Iceberg Travelling South . . .'* – *Changing Trends in British Television: A Case Study of Drama and Current Affairs*, London: The Campaign for Quality Television.

BBC Online (1999) 'BBC attacked for "goobledegook managers"', 30 March, http://www.bbc.co.uk/hi/english/uk_politics/newsid_307000/307120.stm.

Blumler, J. (1990) 'Elections, the media and the modern publicity process', in M. Ferguson, (ed.) *Public Communication. The New Imperatives*, London: Sage, pp. 101–13.

Blumler, J. and Kavanagh, D. (1999) 'The third age of political communication: influences and features', *Political Communication*, Vol. 16, Taylor & Francis, pp. 209–30.

Butler, D. and Stokes, D. (1971) *Political Change in Britain*, London: Pelican.

Cockerell, M. (1988) *Live From Number 10*, London: faber & faber.

Cook, T.E. (1998) *Governing with the News: The News Media as a Political Institution*, Chicago, IL: Chicago University Press.

Curtice, J. (1997) 'Is the *Sun* shining on Tony Blair?', *Press/Politics*, Vol. 2, No. 2.

Gould, P. (1998) *The Unfinished Revolution*, London: Little, Brown and Co.

Kaid, L. and Holtz-Bacha, C. (eds) (1995) *Political Advertising in Western Democracies*, London: Sage.

Lang, K. and Lang, G. (1982) *Television and Politics Re-Viewed*, London: Sage.

Maarek, P. (1995) *Political Marketing and Communication*, Luton: John Libbey.

Mancini, P. and Swanson, D. (eds) (1996) *Politics, Media and Modern Democracy*, Westport, CT: Praeger.

Mazzoleni, G. (1995) 'Towards a "videocracy": Italian political communication at a turning point', *European Journal of Communication*, Vol, 10, No. 3, pp. 291–320.

Miller, D. (1991) *Media and Voters: The Audience, Content, and Influence of Press and Television at the 1987 General Election*, Oxford: Clarendon Press.

Negrine, R. (1996) *The Communication of Politics*, London: Sage.

Negrine, R. (1998a) *Parliaments and the Media*, London: Pinter.

Negrine, R. (1998b) *Television and the Press since 1945*, Manchester: Manchester University Press.

Neuman, W.R., Just, M. and Crigler, A. (1992) *Common Knowledge*, Chicago, IL: University of Chicago Press.

Norris, P., Curtice, J., Sanders, D., Scammell, M. and Semetko, H. (1999) *On Message: Communicating the Campaign*, London: Sage.

Scammell, M. (1995) *Designer Politics*, Basingstoke: Macmillan.

Select Committee on Public Administration (1998) *The Government Information and Communication Service: Report and Proceedings*, Sixth Report, HC 770, July.

Seymour-Ure, C. (1974) *The Political Impact of Mass Media*, London: Methuen.

Seymour-Ure, C. (1991) *The British Press and Broadcasting since 1945*, Oxford: Blackwell.

Swanson, D. (1997) 'The political-media complex at 50', *American Behavioral Scientist*, Vol. 40, No. 8, pp. 1265–6, 1264–82.

Tracey, M. (1978) *The Production of Political Television*, London: Routledge & Kegan Paul.

Wernick, A. (1992) *Promotional Culture*, London: Sage.

Wintour, P. (1995) 'How the party fixed the show', Guardian Outlook, *The Guardian*, 7–8 October, p. 25.

Wintour, P. (2000) 'Every day is election day, politicians are told', *The Guardian*, 22 July.

Further reading

Blumler, J. and Kavanagh, D. (1999) 'The third age of political communication: influences and features', *Political Communication*, Vol. 16, pp. 209–30. London: Taylor & Francis.

Mancini, P. and Swanson, D. (eds) (1996) *Politics, Media and Modern Democracy*, Westport, CT: Praeger.

Mazzoleni, G. (1995) 'Towards a "videocracy": Italian political communication at a turning point', *European Journal of Communication*, Vol. 10, No. 3, pp. 291–320.

Negrine, R. (1996) *The Communication of Politics*, London: Sage.

Negrine, R. (1998) *Television and the Press since 1945*, Manchester: Manchester University Press.

Scammell, M. (1995) *Designer Politics*, Basingstoke: Macmillan.

Swanson, D. (1997) 'The political-media complex at 50', *American Behavioral Scientist*, Vol. 40, No. 8, pp. 1265–6, 1264–82.

Citizenship

Keith Faulks

CHAPTER THIRTEEN

Introduction

Citizenship bestows upon the individual legitimate membership of a political community. In the modern world, this normally means membership of a nation state, although in recent times international organisations such as the European Union (EU) have employed the language of citizenship when seeking to legitimise systems of governance that reach beyond individual states.

Modern citizenship carries with it a set of rights and responsibilities, the exercise of which express a two-way relationship between the individual and a particular community. In liberal countries, such as Britain, the state is obliged to uphold the basic rights of the individual and in return citizens are required to exercise certain responsibilities in order to maintain the conditions for stable governance. Following T.H. Marshall's (1992) classic text, it is common to divide citizenship rights into three types:

1. *Civil rights*: free speech, freedom of worship, freedom of association, the right to protest peacefully, the right to a fair trial and property rights.
2. *Political rights*: the right to vote and stand for office.
3. *Social rights*: social benefits, health care, education and state pensions.

Responsibilities can be usefully divided into two kinds:

1. *Legal duties*: paying taxes, jury and military service, obeying the law.
2. *Moral obligations*: to participate in the wider community, to help vulnerable members of society, to maintain the environment, to develop one's own potential and encourage others to do the same.

What rights citizens should enjoy and what responsibilities they should be expected to perform are questions of great controversy. In Britain, our thoughts on these issues have been greatly influenced by T.H. Marshall, whose *Citizenship and Social Class*, first published in 1950, is the most famous work written on British citizenship in the post-war period. Marshall's theory provides us with a useful framework with which to analyse how citizenship has been understood for two main reasons. First, Marshall developed a useful typology of rights, which he used to analyse the progress of citizenship in Britain since the eighteenth century. In contemporary debates, many commentators therefore begin with Marshall's ideas even if they seek to go beyond the limitations of his theory in suggesting new forms of rights or in emphasising the importance of citizens' responsibilities. Second,

Citizenship and Social Class is a classic expression of the post-war settlement in British politics, sometimes known as Butskellism or the period of 'consensus politics'. Marshall's argument that social rights, guaranteed by the state, are essential to a rounded sense of citizenship was largely accepted by the main political parties up until the election of Margaret Thatcher's government in 1979. Perhaps the main aim of the Thatcherite governments of 1979–97 was to reconfigure the relationship between the individual and the state by transforming citizenship as it had been understood by Marshall and by advocates of the post-war settlement generally. A key issue in this chapter will therefore be how recent social and political changes have challenged the foundations of this broad Marshallian consensus.

Having summarised Marshall's theory in section one, the second part of the chapter explores some issues his argument raises for rights, responsibilities and social membership. In section three, I outline the Thatcherite alternative to Marshall's model of citizenship. Finally, I analyse the impact New Labour has had upon citizenship, and briefly comment on the current perspectives of the other two main political parties.

It should be noted that some issues of relevance to citizenship in modern Britain are not discussed in detail in this chapter. For example, the language of citizenship, and particularly its stress upon equal civil, political and social rights is of direct relevance to the conflict between Catholics and Protestants in Northern Ireland, where the equality of these rights has been disputed by the Catholic minority. It is hoped that the theoretical overview of citizenship presented here may enhance the reader's understanding of such issues. This is because the ongoing struggle for rights, the extension of political participation to previously excluded groups and the willingness among citizens' to exercise their responsibilities are all crucial factors in analysing the nature of governance in contemporary Britain at local, regional, national and supranational levels.

Background

In his *Citizenship and Social Class*, Marshall focused upon the rights of citizenship and in particular the development of social rights in the twentieth century. As a liberal, Marshall had a strong commitment to market mechanisms as the most efficient distributor of resources. However, he understood that the market, left unregulated, could create damaging inequalities as well as great wealth. The main problem Marshall was concerned with, then, was how the inherent inequalities of a capitalist economy could be reconciled with the egalitarian status of citizenship. In order to explore how this tension had been managed in modern Britain Marshall set about examining the roots of citizenship.

For Marshall, citizenship can be understood as progressing in three main historical stages. In the eighteenth century, the rights of citizenship were primarily civil in character. Marshall correctly identifies how civil rights such as the protection of property were essential to capital accumulation and thus at this stage citizenship was a supportive mechanism for the free market. In the nineteenth century, political rights were gradually extended to the working class. Marshall recognises that unlike civil rights, 'the political rights of citizenship . . . were full of potential danger to the capitalist system' (1992: 25). The widening of the franchise created the potential for the labour movement to increase greatly its influence over the management of the economy, through the use of the vote as well as the strike. This growing influence of the labour movement was institutionalised in the form of the Labour Party in 1900 and the extension of citizenship into the social sphere was a central goal of Labour in government.

Marshall was delivering the lectures upon which *Citizenship and Social Class* was based in 1949, at a time when Attlee's Labour government was laying the foundations of the modern welfare state. Marshall saw this as the institutional basis for social rights. He observed that the welfare state had largely resolved the tension between capitalism and citizenship by effectively civilising and legitimising the inequalities that the market produced. By this Marshall meant that although equality of income was an impossible and undesirable objective, the rights embodied in the welfare state would ensure that income differentials would not prevent lower income groups from enjoying a decent standard of living.

In the post-war period in Britain there was a broad consensus among the main political parties that the maintenance of the Marshallian model of citizenship was a desirable end for government. Social rights were seen as an essential element of stable governance because they provided all citizens with a stake in the country's prosperity and thus restricted calls for more radical reform of the capitalist system. Marshall has been criticised, however, for failing to analyse fully the conditions upon which such a consensus rested. This criticism highlights a more fundamental weakness in his theory: Marshall fails satisfactorily to explain why citizenship rights were extended in Britain. It is important to address this question, however, if we are to understand why rights are not as secure as Marshall implied.

Giddens (1985) theorises the relationship between class and citizenship in a very different way from Marshall. Giddens rejects Marshall's contention that citizenship necessarily reduces class hostilities. Instead, Giddens stresses that class struggle is best understood as the key medium for the extension of rights. Certainly, popular struggle for rights is an important factor in explaining the spread of citizenship. However, such struggle is wider in character than Giddens implies. Social movements that have extended rights include the women's liberation movement, anti-racist campaigners, and the disability movement as well as workers.

In contrast to theories that stress the role of social struggle, Michael Mann (1996) has argued that rights are largely the products of political expediency on the part of elites. In particular, the ruling classes of the eighteenth and nineteenth centuries were faced with the task of modernising their societies in ways that prevented the revolutionary overthrow of their privileged position. In this reading, rights are useful tools of social control, which are extended by elites to purchase the loyalty of the working class and other groups that may threaten social order.

Any sophisticated theory of the development of citizenship must in fact take into account both struggle and political expediency. In the case of Britain, it would be a mistake to underplay the active role campaigners for equality and social justice have played in extending rights. It is difficult, for example, to see how political and civil rights would have been extended to women and sexual minorities without the efforts and sacrifices of individuals such as Sylvia Pankhurst or Oscar Wilde. Citizenship cannot therefore be understood as resulting purely from the cynical manipulation of elites.

Nonetheless, the likely success of these struggles is largely determined by the context in which they take place. It is clear that certain historical circumstances have proved favourable to the extension of citizenship, making the effective resistance of elites less tenable. Many scholars have pointed to the role war has played in the extension of citizenship. In her analysis of the development of British nationhood, Colley shows how the passing of important laws that extended rights, such as the Catholic Emancipation Act in 1829, were 'intimately bound up with the impact of war' (1992: 361–2), demonstrating how the growing involvement of British people in the wars against Napoleon gave the masses considerable leverage in widening rights and political participation (ibid.: 371). Demands from elites for greater military duties have more recently created a climate wherein citizenship could further be enhanced. The extension of the vote to some women in 1918 and the creation of the welfare state in 1945, for example, were directly related to the 'total wars' of 1914–18 and 1939–45. These conflicts demanded not just widespread male conscription, but also a much greater role for women in the domestic war effort as whole societies were mobilised. More recently, professional, highly technological armies have replaced the mass conscript armies of the past, which did so much to increase citizenship rights indirectly. It is unlikely therefore that in the future warfare will be an important factor in extending rights.

The connection between social changes associated with warfare and citizenship suggest a more general observation: citizenship rights can usefully be understood as a series of trade-offs between conflicting social groups which are nonetheless tied into reciprocal relationships within the state. The nature of these relationships, and the balance of power that exists between social groups, shifts over time according to the coherence of these groups and the resources available to them. This approach helps us to understand why the rights Marshall identifies have been subject to dilution in recent years (Faulks, 1998).

Since the 1980s, there has been a significant weakening in working-class organisation. This is illustrated by the rapid decline in trade union membership and in the continuing decline in class voting. Consequently, the coherence of the working class has decreased; as have the number of resources workers can draw upon to bargain for greater rights and social protection. The Fordist techniques of mass industrial society, which did much to increase the bargaining power and organisation of the working class, have given way to more 'flexible' forms of industry (Lash and Urry, 1987; Faulks, 1998: ch. 6). Britain's industry is now concentrated in the service sector rather than manufacturing, where the bastions of working-class power, such as mining and steel production, were found in the past. The mass unemployment of the 1980s and 1990s further decreased labour's ability to disrupt the production process and arguably removed some of the supporting pillars for the maintenance of rights.

It is these kinds of social change that have formed the backdrop to the neo-liberal approach to citizenship that has dominated British politics since the 1980s (see Box 13.1). In particular, it can be argued that the reduction in the influence

---

> ## Box 13.1 Theories of citizenship
>
> Two main approaches, both with their roots in classical liberalism, have been particularly significant in shaping citizenship in Britain during the post-war period.
>
> ***Social liberalism:*** associated with the writings of T.H. Marshall, who, in his essay *Citizenship and Social Class*, argued that with the development of the welfare state in the 1950s capitalism had been modified. Citizens now enjoyed social, as well as civil and political rights. Marshall's ideas expressed a general consensus on citizenship between the major political parties up until the election of Margaret Thatcher.
>
> ***Neo-liberalism:*** associated with the Austrian philosopher Hayek. Neo-liberals rejected the notion that social rights enhanced citizenship. Instead, neo-liberals advocated the reduction of public spending on welfare benefits and emphasised market rights that facilitated innovation and personal initiative. It was highly influential on the Thatcher and Major governments, as witnessed by policies such as privatisation, council house sales and the Citizen's Charter of 1991, which defined citizenship primarily in terms of market choice and consumer rights.

of the labour movement facilitated the removal of social rights in the 1980s such as the payment of social security benefit to under-18 year olds and the scrapping of the social fund in 1986, which had provided one-off grants to benefit claimants to purchase essentials such as a cooker or heater (see Faulks, 1998: 151–2). Before examining this challenge to the Marshallian model in more detail, I shall first explore some other limitations of Marshall's account of citizenship.

Summary

- The most influential theory of citizenship in Britain is associated with T.H. Marshall (1992). He argues that civil, political and social rights have gradually developed since the eighteenth century in ways which have 'civilised' the inequalities of capitalism.
- Marshall's advocacy of state-funded social rights was generally endorsed by the main political parties up until 1979.
- Marshall failed, however, to account for why rights had developed in Britain. Other theorists have stressed the role of social struggle and political expediency, both of which can lead to the contraction as well as the extension of rights.

Theoretical Considerations

A number of theoretical issues, in addition to the question of historical development, are raised by Marshall's theory. I shall briefly consider three of the most important in this section. Each of the issues discussed here has been central to recent debates in the citizenship literature and has also been directly relevant to public policy. First, there is the question of the relationship between rights and responsibilities. Second, Marshall has been criticised for overlooking the barriers that impede women's and minorities' citizenship rights. Finally, I explore Marshall's assumption that the boundaries of the nation state set the appropriate limits for citizenship.

Rights and responsibilities

Marshall wrote comparatively little on the question of responsibilities. Somewhat vaguely, Marshall contended that citizens do have a general responsibility 'towards the welfare of the community' (1992: 41). He notes, however, that the history of citizenship in Britain could generally be understood as 'a shift of emphasis from duties to rights' (Marshall, 1992: 7). For social conservatives like Selbourne (1994), as well as for communitarian thinkers such as Etzioni (1995), this shift marks the decline rather than the enhancement of citizenship. According to these critics of liberalism, responsibilities should be given much more prominence in the citizenship equation than they are afforded in Marshall's approach. Selbourne believes that an emphasis upon social rights has actually undermined citizenship. By making the state responsible for citizens' income, many individuals have become dependent upon benefits and have lost the sense of self-reliance that is so central to encouraging the obligations upon which the community depends. Selbourne holds that the raise of social rights in post-war Britain has undermined 'the citizen's sense of co-responsibility for the condition of the civic order to which he belongs' (Selbourne, 1994: 63). In a similar vein, Etzioni (1995) advocates a freeze on the creation of new rights in liberal societies, which he sees as having encouraged a culture of self-interest and introspection. He stresses the need for policies that will enhance the individual's sense of obligation. Among such policies are compulsory national service, a greater stress on civic education and the promotion of family values, which Etzioni considers to be the cornerstone of moral obligation.

The attraction of such arguments is that they do identify some real problems in liberal democracies generally. A major oversight in Marshall's theory is the lack of emphasis he places upon the active performance of both responsibilities and rights. In fact it could be argued that it is an ethic of participation that distinguishes citizenship from mere subjecthood. Extensive rights can in theory be enjoyed by those who have no active part in deciding how they will be governed. Citizenship, contrariwise, necessarily implies democracy. Marshall says little about this aspect of citizenship but in recent years there has been something of a participation crisis in Britain, as both voting turnout (particularly in local elections) and the willingness of citizens to involve themselves in formal politics has declined sharply (Dalton, 1996). Apathy towards conventional political institutions generally is on the increase. A British Cohort survey conducted in 1997 found that a large majority of citizens born in 1970 had 'no interest' or were 'not very interested' in politics (*Sunday Times*, 1997). More generally, indicators of anti-social behaviour, such as crime and public disorder, are increasing and levels of public concern over these problems is also growing (Benyon and Edwards, 1997).

It is probable that these developments are an aspect of what Beck (1997) has christened *individualisation*. By this Beck means that modern liberal societies like Britain are witnessing a decline in deference and sense of attachment to established authorities and collectivities such as religion and class. An objective for politicians and reformers is therefore to find new ways to bond diverse individuals together so as to avoid the further erosion of civil society caused by social fragmentation and alienation. For communitarians, the promotion of an active citizenship that stresses individual and social responsibilities is one possible path towards this objective (Etzioni, 1995).

While there is strong case for increasing the number of duties citizens are required to undertake and for trying to create a supportive climate for the development of obligations through citizenship education, it would be a mistake to accompany such reform with a restriction on rights. A dilution of social rights, for example, would be likely to lessen rather than increase the commitment marginalised groups feel towards the community. In fact there is strong argument to suggest that social changes, particularly those associated with rapid technological innovations, require new forms of rights. Ravetz, for example, has highlighted the potential threat to the exercise of citizenship posed by new inequalities of access to information and communication technologies. He argues that 'for an active citizenry to contribute, government must have a policy to manage the distribution of information, founded upon the goal of maximising the range and quality of information available to individuals and civic associations' (Ravetz, 1999: 91). The challenge for government generally is to re-think citizenship in ways that close the gap between the passive receipt of benefits and the active participation that any successful system of governance requires.

Social exclusion and citizenship

In a powerful critique of Marshall's theory, Walby (1994) has shown how the development of rights for women has taken a very different path from the one described by Marshall. In reality, important civil rights are still being fought for and won today. For example, married women's rights not to be raped by the husband or to be taxed separately from their spouse have only been achieved in the 1990s. Such ongoing struggles make Marshall's assertion that civil rights had been achieved by the end of the eighteenth century seem complacent. Walby also points out that women did not achieve equal political rights until 1928, calling into question Marshall's identification of political rights with the nineteenth century. Finally, it is clear that social rights have been gendered in Britain. Beveridge's model of social rights, upon which the welfare state is based, was founded upon the assumption that women's major duty would be to reproduce and care for future citizens rather than being active in the public sphere themselves. Consequently, women have often been unable to make sufficient contributions to the National Insurance Scheme so as to enjoy full state pensions or to access the highest levels of unemployment benefit.

Women, ethnic minorities and other marginalised groups, such as sexual minorities and the disabled, have also found that the possession of formal rights does not necessarily guarantee equality of opportunity. Sometimes this is due to direct discrimination; often it can be explained by problems with the organisation of political and social institutions. Thus legislation on equal pay for women or against racial and sexual discrimination is often thwarted in practice by the deep structures of inequality that penalise women and minorities. It may be, for instance, that women have formal equality with men to apply for powerful jobs or to stand as MPs. However, the lack of adequate state-funded childcare or the failure of men to undertake equal childcare responsibilities often makes this right an empty one in practice. Up until recently, for example, the House of Commons had a large number of bars, but no childcare facilities! Institutional racism is another example of how in practice the rights of minorities can be infringed. The Macpherson Report of 1999 (which investigated the highly publicised murder of the black teenager Stephen Lawrence in 1993) defined institutional racism as an 'unwitting and unconscious prejudice' against ethnic minorities that was ingrained within the police force and which prevented the effective investigation of the Lawrence murder (Johnston et al., 1999).

The main aim of this sub-section has been to highlight how struggles for citizenship can never be complete. Inconstitencies in laws or social discrimination will always be exposed by groups who wish to assert their equality of worth with the rest of population. Recently, the controversial debate over the lowering of the age of consent for gays and the proposed repeal of Section 28, which bans the 'promotion' of homosexuality in schools, demonstrates how minorities still face deeply-rooted prejudice in their struggle for equal rights. Citizenship is therefore a dynamic rather than a static concept that can be restricted as well as extended through the actions of a diverse range of social movements.

Citizenship and the nation state

Marshall takes as given the idea that citizenship only makes sense within the context of the nation state. This assumption, however, hides a deep tension within liberalism between its acceptance of the state on one hand, and its embrace of universal rights which apply to all humans regardless of nationality on the other. This contradiction is played out in practice through the complexities of immigration legislation. Despite Britain's apparent commitment to human rights, citizenship often acts as an exclusionary concept, denying rights to foreigners and even to those who might be legally resident but are not British nationals.

In a series of Immigration Acts since the Second World War, successive British governments have attempted to manage the 'problem' of immigration. Often this legislation has discriminated on the basis of colour. The 1971 Immigration Act, for example, introduced restrictions on the granting of work permits which had the effect of favouring immigrants from white members of the Commonwealth, such as Canada and Australia, over Britain's former colonies populated primarily by black and Asian peoples (Faulks, 1998: 49). The application of immigration policies which are not scrupulously fair is a particular problem for any government that stresses its commitment to human rights abroad. On coming to power in 1997, the Labour government pledged that it would adopt an 'ethical foreign policy'. However, critics have pointed to how Labour's approach to refugees, for example, has been draconian and has fallen short of the respect for human rights to which it claims to be committed. Such problems lend considerable weight to those who have argued that citizenship status should be based purely on residence (see Faulks, 2000).

The limits of a purely state-centred view of citizenship has further been highlighted by globalisation. Elsewhere I have defined globalisation as 'the intensification of global risks, which necessitate greater co-operation between states' (Faulks, 1999: 2). This definition stresses how problems such as the threat of nuclear war, ecological crises such as global warming, international migration, global crime and terrorism challenge the basis of our rights and freedoms but cannot be managed successfully by any one state acting alone. States have begun to recognise this fact and the post-Cold War period has witnessed a growth in the influence of international organisations such the United Nations and regional bodies like the European Union. The increasing power of these organisations can be interpreted as collective responses to the insecurities associated with globalisation.

The most significant development in terms of citizenship rights for Britons has been the extension of 'European citizenship' as part of the provisions of the Maastricht Treaty of 1992 (Meehan, 1993). As well as granting basic civil freedoms, such as free movement and diplomatic protection via any member state's embassies, most importantly EU citizenship gives the individual the ability to vote and stand in local and European elections in any member state. As such, EU citizenship does mark an important break with Marshall's state-centred model. However, EU institutions still lack a significant participatory dimension. Moreover, there are dangers in the EU's approach to the question of immigration and identity, which has tended to mirror the worst aspects of exclusion as practised by nation states (O'Leary, 1998).

Summary

- Social conservatives and communitarians have insisted that greater emphasis be placed upon the responsibilities of citizenship. However, there is also a strong case for extending citizens' entitlements in areas such as information rights.
- Citizenship is no guarantee of equality in practice. Deep structural inequalities such as sexism and institutional racism continue to restrict the opportunities of women and minorities to enjoy their rights and perform their responsibilities.
- Globalisation is leading to the extension of citizenship beyond the state, through such developments as European Union citizenship.

Update

Since the 1980s, there has been a proliferation of works exploring the concept of citizenship (Andrews, 1991; Heater and Oliver, 1994). This period of academic interest can be contrasted with the three decades after the publication of *Citizenship and Social Class* when little was written on the subject. This relative neglect can be accounted for by the general consensus on citizenship in post-war Britain. Recent interests in the concept can in large part be explained by the desire among commentators, particularly in the centre and on the left of British politics, to explain and contest the rejection of the Marshallian model by the Thatcher and Major governments. There can be little doubt that these governments transformed citizenship in modern Britain (Faulks, 1998).

Ian Gilmour (1992: 128), a minister in Margaret Thatcher's first Cabinet in 1979, has argued that while the Conservative Party has never embraced a notion of citizenship that stressed equality 'it has seldom gone out of its way to heighten inequality'. Thatcherism, in contrast, saw inequality as a desirable mechanism for encouraging personal effort and promoting entrepreneurship. Thatcherism, which I take to include the Major as well as Thatcher government, marked a profound break with the post-war consensus on citizenship by pointing to the dangers of extensive social rights and by stressing the importance of a limited conception of civil rights, or as I have called them, market rights (Faulks, 1998: 147–8). These rights were concerned with the ownership of property, consumer rights, and the right to choose between competing providers of public services. In asserting individuals' market rights, the government identified several major barriers to these rights. First, social rights were seen as requiring excessive levels of taxation, reducing freedom of choice, as well as fostering a dependence upon the 'nanny state'. Second, welfare rights were seen as part of a wider problem of government overload where the state had grown too powerful and the bureaucracy self-serving and inefficient. Third, extensive trade union rights, and particularly the 'closed shop', were seen as an infringement of citizens' market rights.

The Thatcherites made both direct and indirect use of the language of citizenship to legitimise their attempts to tackle the roots of these problems. Trade union reform was justified in terms of increasing the individual's right to choose not to be a member of a union and to decide for themselves whether to work or not. The introduction of the 1991 Citizen's Charter was portrayed as enhancing consumer rights. The lowering of direct taxation was aimed, it was argued, at giving citizens greater choice and personal freedom. As well as aiming to enhance market rights, the Thatcherites employed the language of responsibilities. Letwin (1992) has coined the useful phrase 'vigorous virtues' to encapsulate the Thatcherite aim of increasing self-reliance and individual autonomy. In 1988 the Conservatives articulated this objective by seeking to encourage 'active citizenship'. Citizens were asked to mix an ethic of self-help with a sense of obligation to the wider community. Other citizenship responsibilities were also stressed in this period. Home ownership was seen as an expression of self-help and as forming the basis for active citizenship by providing a stake in society. The poll tax, introduced in 1990, expressed the duty all citizens have to contribute to the up-keep of local services. Reform of social security, in particular the introduction of the Job Seeker's Allowance in 1996, stressed welfare claimants' duty actively to seek work. Great emphasis was also placed on the individual's responsibility to make provision for their own future through private insurance against illness or unemployment.

As a result of these policies, however, 'government was not tamed but became more authoritarian and, so far from market forces proving benign in social matters, citizenship was devalued and society damaged' (Gilmour, 1992: 131). The Thatcherite crusade to transform the citizen's relationship to the state led to greater social inequality. A extensive study into wealth and income distribution by the Joseph Rowntree Foundation (1995) showed how the wealth gap between rich and poor had grown significantly in the 1980s. This had the negative result of preventing many citizens from successfully exercising their rights or performing their responsibilities.

The Conservative governments' failure to modernise the Constitution and their centralisation of state power, which was arguably an inevitable part of removing those 'vested interests' that stood in the way of economic deregulation, also demonstrated a lack of commitment to enhancing political and civil rights (see Gilmour, 1992). As I have argued in *Citizenship in Modern Britain* (1998), through the implementation of policies such as the poll tax, trade union legislation and the Criminal Justice Act of 1994, basic rights such as the right to vote, the right of association and the right to silence were undermined. In short, the Thatcherite model of citizenship was one that played up the freedom of the individual and the market, expressed through a commitment to market rights, and played down political, social and certain civil rights such as protest and assembly.

Summary

- The recent popularity of citizenship in the social science literature is largely a by-product of the attack on the Marshallian model of rights by the Thatcherite governments of 1979–97.
- Thatcherism stressed the promotion of market rights and the 'vigorous virtues' of independence and self-help, as opposed to social rights guaranteed by the state.
- Inequalities in Britain grew under Thatcherism, however, and several key rights, such as those of association, were undermined.

Debate

The 1997 general election marked the end of the eighteen-year-long dominance of central government by the Conservative Party. Whether this defeat marked the end of Thatcherism as a pervasive influence upon citizen–state relations in Britain is debatable, however. In the person of Tony Blair, Labour has a leader who has openly praised the achievements of Thatcherism. Through his desire to re-write the Labour Party's Clause Four, which had previously committed the party (at least theoretically) to public ownership, Blair showed his determination to embrace an economic policy that had at its heart the 'rigours of the market' (Blair, 1996). Since Neil Kinnock began a series of policy reviews in the 1980s, however, Labour has been a party in search of an ideological coherence that makes it distinctive from both the old left and the neo-liberal right. Among the concepts and theories it has flirted with under Blair have been communitarianism, the idea of 'stakeholding', ethical socialism, and most recently the idea of the 'Third Way'.

The Third Way, expressed most fully by Anthony Giddens (1998), attempts to articulate a system of governance that moves beyond the limits of both neo-liberalism and state socialism. At the heart of this philosophy lies a conception of citizenship that stresses the mutual interdependence of rights and responsibilities. Giddens has suggested that 'a prime motto for the new politics [is] no rights without responsibilities' (1998: 65). This idea is echoed in the Labour's new Clause Four, which states that 'the rights we enjoy reflect the duties we owe'.

The attractions of citizenship to those who seek a fresh politics that moves beyond the old left and new right are obvious. On the one hand, the rights side of the citizenship equation is an important component of the government's proposed modernisation of Britain's political system (Labour Party, 1997: 32–5). Labour's commitment to a bill of rights, devolution, the reform of the House of Lords, freedom of information and the possible introduction of proportional representation are all concerned with enhancing political citizenship in ways which transcend the 'old politics'. In contrast to New Labour, the neo-liberal right generally advocates the maintenance of the *status quo* on constitutional issues, while the old left, it is argued, prioritises issues of economic control and distribution over constitutional matters.

The fact that citizenship entails responsibilities as well as rights has also been useful rhetorically for New Labour. An increase in the duties of citizenship is seen as necessary to offset the over-emphasis Thatcherism placed upon individualism. New Labour has been able to argue, with much justification, that the Thatcherites stressed individual success and material gain at the expense of the networks of responsibilities within civil society that are necessary to hold the community together. New Labour also claims that its willingness to embrace responsibilities as well as rights distances it from the old left, which has tended to defend a very statist and passive approach to welfare issues. On this question of social rights, Labour has taken up calls by people like Giddens (1998: 111–18) for 'positive welfare'. Labour's New Deal, which aims to get young people back into employment, and incentives to work, such as the minimum wage and the family tax credit, are policies aimed at shifting the model of welfare from a 'hand out' to a 'hand up'. Political rights have also certainly been enhanced by Labour's programme of devolution and the reform of the House of Lords. Labour has shown itself to be sensitive to some of the issues of exclusion raised in section two of this chapter, with the appointment of a Minister for Women and the creation of a Social Exclusion Unit, which attempts to co-ordinate government policy across departments to address material and cultural marginalisation. Perhaps most importantly, civil rights are likely to be enhanced by Labour's introduction of the European Convention on Human Rights into the British Constitution in 1998. This allows courts to declare government laws to be in violation of citizens' rights (see Ewing, Chapter 24 in this volume).

Despite these positive developments, however, we cannot afford to be too optimistic about Labour's commitment to enriching citizenship. Its approach to constitutional reform has seemed piecemeal and contradictory. The Labour leadership's stage-managing of devolution in Wales, Scotland and London and the leadership selection procedures adopted (see Fisher, Chapter 9 in this volume) is in tension with the democratisation to which Labour says it is committed. Labour has also drawn criticism over its failure to significantly reverse the erosion of trade union rights, the exclusionary implications of its asylum legislation, and its apparent acceptance of the denial of basic civil freedoms such as the right to remain silent, which was a victim of the 1994 Criminal Justice Act. Moreover, Labour's Freedom of Information Act, though representing some progress in enhancing civil rights, is a far from comprehensive defence of the open government that is crucial to the informed performance of rights and responsibilities by citizens. In an age of growing technological inequalities, information rights need to be considered core rights of citizenship now. The government's introduction of citizenship education, to be compulsory in secondary schools from 2002, must be regarded as a positive move in this regard. However, there is arguably little point in teaching children the values associated with citizenship if a more comprehensive approach to information rights is not developed.

Regarding Britain's membership of the European Union, the government's policy towards European Monetary Union in particular looks to be driven largely by economic considerations. This is to ignore the huge implications a single currency has for democratic citizenship. The low level of turnout in the last election to the European Parliament show that even the one European Union body which has some democratic accountability has hardly captured the imagination of Britain's citizens. The development of citizenship in the European context has been created by elitist decision-making bodies and has been concerned overwhelmingly with legitimising the Union through minimal rights provisions. The ethic of participation that is central to citizenship has been missing from the EU.

Perhaps the main barrier, however, to the enhancement of citizenship under Labour is its essentially neo-liberal approach to the economy. Important services that are crucial to social rights, such as education and health, are comparatively underfunded when compared to Britain's European partners. Labour has, however, committed itself to lowering taxes where possible and keeping a tight check on public spending. There is so far little evidence to suggest therefore that Labour is fully committed to tackling the major impediment to citizenship in Britain, namely the vast levels of material inequality which have actually been widening since the 1980s (Joseph Rowntree Foundation, 1995). Opinion polls have shown that Labour may have got the public mood wrong on these issues. Even at the height of Thatcherism, a large majority of British citizens expressed support for more public spending on a large range of services, including health, education and welfare (see Edgell and Duke, 1991: ch. 4).

What of the other main political parties? The Liberal Democrats are in the strange position of watching many of their policies, on constitutional reform in particular, being implemented by another political party and now remain distinctive only in their commitment to raise more taxes to enhance social rights and in their firm support for democratic citizenship to reach outwards to embrace the institutions of EU government. In contrast to both the Liberal Democrats and Labour, the Conservatives remain highly sceptical of the merits of constitutional reform both at home and in Europe. Under William Hague's and now Iain Duncan-Smith's leadership, the legacy of Thatcherism's approach to citizenship seems secure. Citizenship for the Conservatives remain a strictly national issue and Britain should not, for example, give up important controls on immigration to the institutions of the EU. On the question of social rights, the Conservatives in opposition have committed themselves to lowering income tax and have asserted the merits of a mixed form of welfare with a greater role for private insurance. Any future Conservative government under Duncan-Smith is therefore likely to re-employ the Thatcherite strategy of enhancing market rights for some but demanding greater responsibilities from all.

Summary

- New Labour, through its advocacy of a 'Third Way' of governance, has placed the modernisation of citizenship at the heart of its public policy.
- By reforming the constitution and by beginning to tackle the exclusion caused by unemployment and low pay, Labour has enhanced citizenship to some extent. Labour's neo-liberal economic policy, however, remains the main barrier to the further enrichment of citizenship rights.
- The Liberal Democrats remain supportive of many of Labour's reforms, while advocating the extension of social rights and European Union citizenship. The Conservatives have continued to draw upon the legacy of Thatcherism and stress the importance of market rights and personal responsibility.

Conclusion

Since Marshall wrote his famous work, the debate surrounding citizenship has widened considerably. Issues such as the exclusion of women and minorities, the advocacy of new rights and responsibilities not envisaged by Marshall and the implications of globalisation for citizen–state relations have highlighted the fact that citizenship is a dynamic status that is subject to dilution as well as extension. The attack by the Thatcherite governments upon the Marshallian model that underpinned a broad post-war consensus on citizenship has, in particular, underlined the vulnerability of social rights. Thatcherism's assertion of market rights and personal responsibility did create opportunities for some but at the cost of greater inequality and the erosion of basic rights for many. The New Labour government has made some attempt to provide greater protection for rights through its constitutional reforms. It has also been more ready than the Conservatives to acknowledge the damaging effects inequalities can have upon citizenship. Nonetheless, arguably it remains doubtful whether New Labour can successfully combine its stated commitment to enriching citizenship with its stress upon economic prudence and relatively low rates of taxation.

Chronology

1950 Publication of T.H. Marshall's *Citizenship and Social Class*, which defends publicly-funded social rights as an essential component of citizenship.

1950–1979 Period of broad consensus between the three main political parties on citizenship that embraces the need for the state to protect civil, political *and* social rights.

1979 Election of first Thatcher government. Begins an eighteen-year period of radical change where neo-liberal perspectives on citizenship come to dominate. Great emphasis is placed upon personal responsibilities and the promotion of 'market rights'.

1988 Thatcher government promotes the idea of 'active citizenship'. Citizens are encouraged to take more responsibility for their own lives and the social cohesion of their communities through voluntary acts of good citizenship such as membership of neighbourhood watch schemes, for example.

1991 John Major launches his Citizen's Charter which aims to ensure choice and quality for users of public services. However, it contains no provision for constitutional change to enhance civil, political or social rights.

1992 The European Union's Maastricht Treaty creates the concept of EU citizenship which grants all citizens of member states additional civil and political rights, including the right to vote in local and European elections when resident in *any* member state.

1994 The Labour Party re-writes its Constitution that now stresses the need to balance citizenship rights with responsibilities.

1997 Election of the New Labour government committed to renewing citizenship in Britain, particularly through constitutional reform such as devolution, reform of the House of the Lords and the adoption of the European Convention of Human Rights into Britain's Constitution.

2002 Citizenship is introduced as a compulsory subject into secondary schools at Key Stage 3.

Discussion Questions

1. How can we best account for the development of citizenship in Britain?
2. What impact did Thatcherism have upon citizenship?
3. Should the rights we enjoy reflect the duties we owe?

References

Andrews, G. (ed.) (1991) *Citizenship*, London: Lawrence and Wishart.

Beck, U. (1997) *The Reinvention of Politics*, Cambridge: Polity Press.

Benyon, J. and Edwards, A. (1997) 'Crime and public order', in P. Dunleavy, A. Gamble, I. Holliday and G. Peele (eds) *Developments in British Politics* (Vol. 15), Basingstoke: Macmillan, pp. 326–41.

Blair, T. (1996) *New Britain*, London: Fourth Estate.

Colley, L. (1992) *Britons: Forging the Nation 1707–1837*, London: Pimlico.

Crewe, I. and Harrop, M. (1986) *Political Communications: The British General Election of 1983*, Cambridge: Cambridge University Press, p. 139.

Dalton, R. (1996) *Citizen Politics* (second edition), Chatham, NJ: Chatham House.

Edgell, S. and Duke, V. (1991) *A Measure of Thatcherism*, London: Harper-Collins.

Etzioni, A. (1995) *The Spirit of Community*, London: Fontana Press.

Faulks, K. (1998) *Citizenship in Modern Britain*, Edinburgh: Edinburgh University Press.

Faulks, K. (1999) *Political Sociology*, Edinburgh: Edinburgh University Press.

Faulks, K. (2000) *Citizenship*, London: Routledge.

Giddens, A. (1985) *The Nation-State and Violence*, Cambridge: Polity Press.

Giddens, A. (1998) *The Third Way*, Cambridge: Polity Press.

Gilmour, I. (1992) *Dancing with Dogma*, London: Pocket Books.

Heater, D. and Oliver, D. (1994) *The Foundations of Citizenship*, Hemel Hempstead: Harvester/Wheatsheaf.

Johnston, P., Steele, J. and Jones, G. (1999) 'We must change as a nation', *Electronic Telegraph*, 25 February (www.telegraph.co.uk).

Joseph Rowntree Foundation (1995) *Inquiry into Income and Wealth*, York: Joseph Rowntree Foundation.

Labour Party (1997) *Because Britain Deserves Better*, London: Labour Party.

Lash, S. and Urry, J. (1987) *The End of Organised Capitalism*, Cambridge: Polity Press.

Letwin, S. (1992) *The Anatomy of Thatcherism*, London: Fontana.

Mann, M. (1996) 'Ruling class strategies and citizenship', in M. Bulmer and A. Rees (eds) (1996) *Citizenship Today*, London: UCL, pp. 125–44.

Marshall, T.H. (1992) 'Citizenship and social class', in T.H. Marshall and T. Bottomore, *Citizenship and Social Class*, London: Pluto Press, pp. 1–51.

Meehan, E. (1993) *Citizenship and the European Community*, London: Sage.

O'Leary, S. (1998) 'The options for the reform of European Union citizenship', in S. O'Leary and T. Tiilikainen (eds) *Citizenship and Nationality Status in the New Europe*, London: IPPR, pp. 81–116.

Ravetz, J. (1999) 'Information communication technology: a barrier to citizenship?', *New Technology in the Human Services*, Vol. 12, Nos 3/4, pp. 87–94.

Scammell, M. and Harrop, M. (2002) 'The press disarmed', in D. Butler and D. Kavanagh (eds), *The British General Election of 2001*, Basingstoke: Palgrave, pp. 158–9.

Selbourne, D. (1994) *The Principle of Duty*, London: Sinclair-Stevenson.

Seymour-Ure, C. (1997) 'Editorial opinion in the national press', *Parliamentary Affairs*, Vol. 50, pp. 586–608, 591.

Sunday Times (1997) 'Thatcher's children to boycott polling booths', 23 March.

Walby, S. (1994) 'Is citizenship gendered?', *Sociology*, Vol. 20, No. 6, pp. 379–95.

Further reading

For broad conceptual overviews of the concept see K. Faulks (2000) *Citizenship* (London: Routledge) and D. Heater (1999) *What is Citizenship?* (Cambridge: Polity Press). On citizenship in Britain, T.H. Marshall's (1992) 'Citizenship and social class', in T.H. Marshall and T. Bottomore, *Citizenship and Social Class* (London: Pluto Press) remains a good starting point. Bulmer and Rees's (1996) *Citizenship Today* (London: UCL Press) brings together a set of interesting essays that examine the contemporary relevance of Marshall's theory. D. Heater and D. Oliver (1994) *The Foundations of Citizenship* (Hemel Hempstead: Harvester Wheatsheaf) and K. Faulks (1998) *Citizenship in Modern Britain* (Edinburgh: Edinburgh University Press) discuss many of the issues raised in this chapter in more detail. D. Selbourne (1994) *The Principle of Duty* (London: Sinclair-Stevenson) advances a controversial theory of citizenship that stresses the incompatibility of social and political rights. The best feminist approach to citizenship is R. Lister (1997) *Citizenship: Feminist Perspectives* (Basingstoke: Macmillan). Useful collections that illustrate the diversity and range of the citizenship debate today include G. Andrews (ed.) (1991) *Citizenship* (London: Lawrence and Wishart), B. Turner (ed.) (1993) *Citizenship and Social Theory* (London: Sage) and B. Van Steenbergen (ed.) (1994) *The Condition of Citizenship* (London: Sage).

PART FOUR Executives and Governance

Prime Minister and Cabinet

Martin J. Smith

CHAPTER FOURTEEN

Introduction

Most discussion of the role and relationships of the Cabinet and the Prime Minister have been conducted within the confines of an argument over whether prime ministerial government (and more recently presidentialism) has replaced Cabinet government. This chapter will outline this discussion, highlighting that it is essentially flawed because it is both irresolvable and fails to understand the operation of the core executive. The chapter will suggest that in order to understand how the Prime Minister and Cabinet work we have to recognise that both have resources and therefore are dependent on each other. Consequently, the operation of the core executive is not about competition between the core and the centre, but about structures of dependence which both enable and constrain the Prime Minister and Cabinet ministers. The chapter will begin by outlining the traditional debate and its problems. It will then describe an alternative way of examining the Prime Minister and Cabinet and review the implications that this model has for understanding the role of the Prime Minister.

Prime Ministerial versus Cabinet Government

The latter half of the last century saw the relatively rapid accrual of new institutional resources to the Prime Ministers (see Table 14.1). This growth in the Prime Ministers' institutional support, combined with a declining role of the full Cabinet in policy-making, led to a long and in the end inherently sterile debate over whether prime ministerial government had replaced Cabinet government (Hennessy, 1994). The essence of the argument of those who support the notion of prime ministerial government is that Prime Ministers have been accruing increasing powers over time and their control of patronage, the agenda and key policy areas means that they can rarely be challenged by the Cabinet. In the modern executive the notion of *primus inter pares* is untenable because the Prime Minister dominates. In the 1980s, Thatcher was presented as the apotheosis of prime ministerial government. She was seen as dictating much of what went on in government, undermining the role of the cabinet and intervening directly in a range of departmental policies (see Crossman, 1972; King, 1985a; Burch, 1988; Kavanagh, 1990; Madgwick, 1991; Hennessy, 1994; Thomas, 1998 for a discussion). Contrariwise, authors like Jones

Table 14.1 Institutional change and academic debate

Institutional change	Academic debate
Wilson (1964–70): establishes political office and enlarges press office.	Mackintosh (1963) initiates a debate about the history of the Cabinet. The decline of Cabinet government is further supported by Crossman (1966).
Heath (1970–74): establishes central policy review staff.	Brown (1968) and Jones (1975) argue that Cabinet government continues and point to constraints on Prime Minister.
Wilson (1974–76): creates formal policy unit.	
Thatcher (1979–90): denudes the role of the Cabinet; intervenes increasingly in decisions; works through *ad hoc* groups, special advisors and bilateral meetings with cabinet.	A large body of literature highlights the style and dominance of Thatcher and questions the degree of prime ministerial government (King, 1985b; Hennessy, 1986; Burch, 1988; Kavanagh, 1990; Foster, 1997).
Major (1990–94): attempts to increase the role of Cabinet in policy-making but Policy Unit retains central role.	Literature by those involved in government under Thatcher and Major suggests that the Cabinet is still important (see Lawson, 1994; Wakeham, 1994; Hogg and Hill, 1995).
Blair (1997–): increases the size and centrality of the Policy Unit; establishes the position of Cabinet enforcer; and uses 'joined-up' government in an attempt to impose prime ministerial will on departments.	Literature on presidentialism (Foley 1993; Pryce 1997) is developed, with some analysis of Blair suggesting a shift to Bonapartism and increased one-person control (Hennessy, 2000).

(1975) highlight the limits on the Prime Minister and the need for Cabinet support. The case is highlighted by Thatcher's fall and Major's difficulty in achieving
policy goals. In recent times the argument has been developed further by those
who argue that we have moved beyond prime ministerial government to presidentialism (Foley, 1993; Pryce, 1997). (See Box 14.1).

Under Attlee, Churchill, Eden and Macmillan, the Prime Minister's Office was
a small unit made up of permanent civil servants in the private office, supplemented with a small number of special policy advisors who provided particular
policy advice (Lee et al., 1998). However, with the election of Harold Wilson in
1964 there was a move to increase the resources of No. 10 and he established for
the first time a political office which was supplemented by an enlarged press office
(Pryce, 1997). Since then nearly all Prime Ministers have increased the size of the
Policy Unit, its centrality and their role in detailed policy-making (see Lee et al.,
1998; Kavanagh and Seldon, 1999). The predominant interpretation is that the
whole Cabinet system lost influence during the 1980s and that Thatcher effectively
moved away from a system of formal Cabinet committees (Foster, 1997). These
changes have only been reinforced by Blair's premiership (see Box 14.2).

Box 14.1 The end of Cabinet?

Lady Thatcher developed a practice, which she carried through by force of personality, by which *ad hoc* groupings of ministers were frequently used instead, often because they were known to be favourable to the outcome she wanted. In more recent years departmental ministers had a choice: they might ask the prime minister to put it on the cabinet agenda or for him or for the deputy prime minister to set up such a grouping or himself set up such a grouping; or he might believe it enough to persuade the prime minister with minimal consultation with other ministers affected. (Foster, 1997: 5)

Box 14.2 The maintenance of Cabinet government

Wakeham (1994), a minister in the Thatcher government, argues that, despite her style, Cabinet government continued. Prime Ministers need the support of the Cabinet. They are often greatly constrained by the party and the Cabinet, and are severely limited in the extent to which they can sack colleagues (Brown, 1968: 35; Jones, 1975; Alderman, 1976; James, 1999: 117–24). As Lawson points out, 'There is a limit to the number of resignations that a prime minister can wear sensibly' (1994: 444). In addition, the Prime Minister often cannot control the agenda and is often severely limited in the degree to which he/she can exercise patronage (see Alderman, 1976). Could Blair conceivably have appointed anyone other than Gordon Brown as his Chancellor?

The prime ministerial versus Cabinet government debate is essentially sterile, simplistic, irresolvable and an unhelpful discussion of central government. It focuses too much on the personality of an individual; it sees power as an object rather than something that is fluid and relational; it ignores the constraints on actors; and it simplifies the way decisions are made in central government. In particular, it ignores the fact that departments in Britain have considerable autonomy and therefore there are important resource, institutional and time constraints on what the Prime Minister can do (see Daintith and Page, 1999; Marsh et al., 2001). Essentially neither position can help us to understand central government because they misconceive the nature of power and the institutional make-up of the core executive.

While the Prime Minister is the most visible aspect of the core executive, he or she is not the only important actor. Any complex evaluation of the operation of central government needs to understand the interaction of myriad institutions and the multiple interconnections that allow the system to function. Government is complex and society is complex, and no individual has the capabilities to control either.

It is important to recognise that actors beyond the Prime Minister and the Cabinet also matter and affect the way they operate. Indeed, despite the growth of the institutions of the Prime Minister's Office, the Prime Minister still does not have all the necessary resources and mechanisms for policy-making, is often dependent on the support of the Chancellor and the Treasury, lacks the institutional means for intervention in a whole range of policy areas and is often constrained by events completely beyond his/her control (see Box 14.3). Moreover, the weaknesses and failures of the mechanisms for collective agreement, the Cabinet

---

Box 14.3 The Prime Minister's dependency

Lawson's experiences of the Cabinet provide some recognition of this variability in the Prime Minister's power and how the Prime Minister needs support:

> I suspect that the power of the Prime Minister does vary from Prime Minister to Prime Minister, and perhaps it also varies according to the political strength that a particular Prime Minister has at a given time. What was certainly observable during Margaret Thatcher's very long period in office . . . was that there was a steadily widening gulf between her and her Cabinet colleagues, which made the process of Cabinet government more and more difficult to achieve in a satisfactory way.
>
> (Lawson, 1994: 441–2)

and the Cabinet Office, even make it difficult for the Prime Minister to impose order through consensus.

One of the peculiarities of the British core executive is that it is a strange blend of institutions, formal and informal rules, cultures and personalism. There are sets of rules defining the powers of certain actors but more effective regulation often develops through the inculcation of values and norms which affect the behaviour of officials and ministers. However, while officials are in many ways extremely rule bound, ministers and the Prime Minister in particular are given the space to act. The Prime Minister can change the nature of the Prime Minister's Office or the role of Cabinet or create and abolish new departments at will. However, all Prime Ministers, from Churchill and his overlord experiment to Blair and the desire for joined-up government, have found how difficult it is to break down the institutional power of departments and their day-to-day control over policy-making.

Summary

- The institutional resources of the Prime Minister increased greatly in the second half of the twentieth century.
- This increase in prime ministerial resources led to a debate over whether Cabinet government had been replaced by prime ministerial government.
- The debate was inherently sterile because it could not be resolved, and it misunderstood both the nature of central government and that of power.

Analysing the Core Executive

The work of a number of authors (Bruce-Gardyne and Lawson, 1976; Dunleavy and Rhodes, 1990; Burch and Holliday, 1996; Smith, 1999) have suggested that the traditional understandings of the relationship between Cabinet and Prime Minister are oversimplified. In order to appreciate the complexities of the policy-making within the core executive it is necessary to recognise the following:

- All actors within the core executive have resources (see Table 14.2).
- In order to achieve goals resources have to be exchanged.
- Notions of prime ministerial government, Cabinet government or president-ialism are irrelevant because power within the core executive is based on dependency not command.
- In order to understand the operation of the core executive we need to trace the structures of dependency.
- These structures of dependency are often based on overlapping networks. Frequently these networks do not follow formal organisational structures and this can lead to fragmentation and conflict over responsibility and territory.
- Even resource-rich actors, such as the Prime Minister, are dependent on other actors to achieve their goals. Therefore, government works through building alliances rather than command.
- Actors operate within a structured arena. Traditional approaches to central government have placed too much emphasis on personality. Prime Ministers, officials and ministers are bound by external organisation, the rules of the game, the structures of institutions, other actors and the context. Therefore, the nature and form of the core executive does not change with personality.
- The degree of dependency that actors have on each other varies according to the context. As the political and economic situation changes, actors may become more or less dependent. Economic success may provide the Chancellor with more freedom, electoral success may provide the Prime Minister with greater room for manoeuvre. Economic failure means the Chancellor needs more sup-port from the Prime Minister. Political failure means the Prime Minister needs more support from the Cabinet.
- Because of the distribution of resources, the strength of departments and over-lapping networks, the core executive is fragmented and central co-ordination is extremely difficult.

The relationships between ministers, between ministers and officials, and between ministers and the Prime Minister do not primarily depend on per-sonality. They are structured relationships which are shaped by the rules of the Whitehall game, the institutions of government, past policy choices and by the external political and economic context. Asking whether there is prime minis-terial government does not take us far in understanding the operation of central government.

Table 14.2 Resources of Prime Ministers, ministers and officials

Prime Minister	Ministers	Officials
Patronage	Political support	Permanence
Authority	Authority	Knowledge
Political support/party	Department	Time
Political support/electorate	Knowledge	Whitehall network
Prime Minister's Office	Policy networks	Control over information
Bilateral policy-making	Policy success	Keepers of the Constitution

Different actors and institutions need each other. Cabinet minister and Prime Ministers have resources but in order to achieve goals they need to exchange resources. The process of exchange – the alliances – that are built to some extent depends on the particular context. If a Prime Minister has just won an election, he or she is less dependent than one who is very unpopular in the polls and is therefore less dependent on the tactics and strategies that ministers and Prime Ministers use. The Prime Minister has no authority if it is not recognised by ministers, and the continual overriding of the wishes of the Cabinet will undermine that authority. Therefore even dominant Prime Ministers need to exchange resources (see Figure 14.1).

Clearly, the Prime Minister has resources that are unavailable to other ministers, as well as the traditionally-cited formal resources of patronage, control of the Cabinet agenda, appointment of Cabinet committees and the Prime Minister's Office. The Prime Minister also has the less tangible resources of the ability to intervene in any policy area and authority. Only the Prime Minister really has any collective oversight; most ministers lack the interest, time, ability or institutional support to be involved in other areas of policy. This oversight enables Prime Ministers to involve themselves in any area of policy-making they choose. Crucially, the Prime Minister does have a degree of authority that is greater than any other minister.

Authority is the acceptance of power without needing to exercise formal capabilities (Wrong, 1988). A crucial rule of the Whitehall game is that ministers and civil servants accept the authority of the Prime Minister. Nevertheless, unlike other

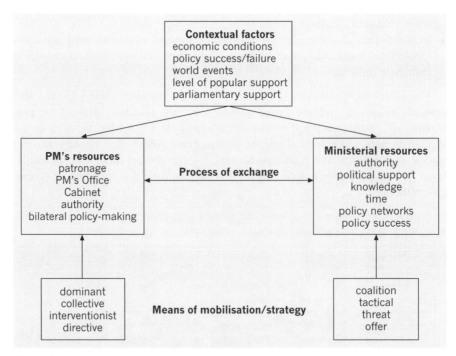

Figure 14.1 A model of prime ministerial power

resources which are fairly objective, prime ministerial authority is largely relational and will depend on the position of the Prime Minister. In particular, the
Prime Minister has greatest authority after an electoral victory, and particularly if
it is an unexpected one such as that of Heath in 1970 (Campbell, 1993: 289).

Thatcher's authority was greatest after the Falkland's victory and the subsequent
landslide election victory in 1983, which allowed her to remove most of her critics
from the Cabinet and, according to King (1985b), it allowed her 'to put her stamp
on an extraordinarily wide range of policy decisions'. Major's problem in 1990 was
a lack of authority. Although he had authority from his win in the Conservative
election leadership, he was not always seen as his own man. His electoral mandate
was won by Thatcher and she initially constantly reminded the new Prime
Minister that he was there to implement her agenda. The absence of independent
authority limited his Cabinet and policy options. For a long period Major was
in a position of reacting to problems such as the poll tax and Exchange Rate
Mechanism (ERM) membership, rather than setting his own agenda. Conversely,
the size of Labour's victory in 1997, which was largely attributed to Tony Blair,
meant the new Prime Minister had tremendous authority to force through new
policies despite some veiled criticism among MPs.

Despite formal and informal resources, to understand prime ministerial power
it is necessary to examine resource exchange that results from dependency. Even
with an array of institutional resources and the authority of the office, a Prime
Minister can achieve nothing on her/his own. In order to translate capabilities
into power, she/he is dependent on others for advice, information, support, and
assistance in making policy. Ministers and civil servants clearly have their own
resources, as we will see in the next chapter. Perhaps most importantly, ministers
have their own sources of authority. Many senior ministers have such high authority
that it is almost impossible for a Prime Minister to dismiss them. For example, in
the period around 1987/1988 Nigel Lawson was in an exceptionally strong position.
As Chancellor of the Exchequer he controlled significant institutional resources,
not least the Treasury, which effectively gave him control of economic policy.
Moreover, he was seen as architect of Britain's economic revival and subsequently
he had tremendous authority within the Tory Party (Watkins, 1991: 96). As he had
little ambition to be Prime Minister he could take political risks. Lawson's stock
rose further with his radical tax-cutting 1988 budget which delivered a balanced
budget and cuts in taxation. Consequently, despite major disagreements between
Thatcher and Lawson, he was, in the Prime Minister's word, 'unassailable'.
Thatcher admitted to Kenneth Baker that she could not have sacked Lawson
because 'I might well have had to go as well' (Thatcher, quoted in Baker, 1993:
315). Likewise, because John Prescott has an independent power base in the party,
it seems highly unlikely that Blair could remove him from Cabinet.

Not only is a Prime Minister confronted with ministerial resources, he or she is
also highly dependent on the Cabinet for his/her authority. Authority, because it
is based on legitimacy, exists only while it is recognised, and therefore a Prime
Minister's authority can only extend as far as the Cabinet will allow. The limits of
authority are illustrated starkly in the case of Thatcher's resignation where the
Cabinet effectively removed the Prime Minister's authority. Thatcher would have

gone on to a second ballot in the leadership contest had she not realised that Cabinet support was slipping away. She admits in her memoirs that once she was convinced that she had lost Cabinet support she decided not to stand in the second round:

> A prime minister who knows that his or her cabinet has withheld its support is fatally weakened. I knew – and I am sure that they knew – that I would not willingly remain an hour in 10 Downing Street without the real authority to govern.
> (Thatcher, 1993: 851)

This process of exchange is also affected by the particular context. The degree of dependency and the need to exchange resources will depend on the context. If the external context is favourable to the Prime Minister in terms of economic policy or electorally, then the Prime Minister has less dependence on the Cabinet. If the external context is less favourable, the Prime Minister requires more support.

Success in achieving policy goals for both ministers and the Prime Minister will depend on tactics. How resources are deployed is an important aspect in power and it means that in certain situations ministers with relatively low resources can defeat the Prime Minister or more highly resourced ministers. The three most recent Prime Ministers have had very different strategies and tactics. Thatcher's strategy was generally interventionist; Major was more collectivist; and Blair's strategy appears directive (see Table 14.3).

Thatcher wanted to intervene in the work of departments. As Lord Young confirmed in an interview, Thatcher's impact on the department was:

> Absolutely enormous. I used to be in fear and trembling when I went to see her as she somehow knew more about my department than I did. She worked incredibly hard and had an incredible capacity for detail. It was very difficult to get anything over her, very difficult.

Patrick Jenkin also accepted that Thatcher had an enormous effect on departments, especially when compared to Edward Heath. One former official in the Department of Education said that: 'There were occasions in my time in education when policy pronouncements emerged from No. 10 of which we were totally unaware.' But she was often highly tactical in her approach, creating the right

Table 14.3 Strategies and tactics of Prime Ministers

	Thatcher	**Major**	**Blair**
Strategy	Interventionist	Collectivist	Directive
Tactics	Using small groups of ministers to build support for her goals.	Working with the Cabinet to build consensus.	Using the PM's Office and Cabinet Office to develop strategic direction.
	Bilateral meetings with ministers.	Delaying decisions until support.	Use of a 'Cabinet enforcer' to ensure ministers follow direction.

Cabinet committees, building the necessary alliances or working bilaterally with ministers to by-pass Cabinet opposition. Even a dominant Prime Minister like Thatcher is dependent on colleagues if she wants to intervene and in the first phase of her administration Thatcher was effective at building alliances in order to achieve her goals. She was also effective at using relatively independent figures like Lord Whitelaw and John Wakeham as conduits between her and the Cabinet so that compromises could be worked out without direct confrontation or capitulation.

Later, when she found increasing opposition in the Cabinet, Thatcher's tactic was to operate, to some degree, outside the Cabinet system. She depended on her political advisors for support and influenced policy by operating bilaterally with ministers who were not in a position to resist her demands. In Lawson's view, after her defeat over Westland:

> The lesson that Margaret took from it was that her colleagues were troublesome and her courtiers loyal. From then on she began to distance herself from colleagues who had been closest to her – certainly those who had minds of their own – and to retreat to the Number 10 bunker, where the leading figures were Charles Powell and Bernard Ingham.
>
> (Lawson, 1992: 680)

With ministers like Whitelaw, Walker and, at certain times, Lawson, Thatcher was more dependent on them than they were on her, and so they had considerable freedom and, in Whitelaw and Lawson's case, influence. Consequently, even a Prime Minister with a dominant style who wants to intervene needs to understand the lines of dependence and work out tactics accordingly. For the first half of her period in office, Thatcher's tactics worked relatively well and she was effective at achieving her goals.

Major was clearly in a different structural position from Thatcher, coming into office without his own electoral mandate and with the economy in recession. Consequently, he adopted a different strategy. Thatcher was seen to have been removed from office because she would not listen and ignored her lines of dependency. Therefore the new Prime Minister was expected to be more collegiate and Major obliged. He was concerned with reasserting Cabinet government. In Anthony Seldon's (1997: 738) assessment:

> Major, by temperament and choice, was a conciliator. Before he became prime minister, he had found Mrs Thatcher's style of 'macho leadership' personally distasteful. His chairmanship of cabinet and cabinet committees, in contrast, allowed ministers to express their views, and guided them to a conclusion in line with his intentions. Rather than have dissent in the cabinet, he preferred to delay decisions until he could reconcile differences.

These changed tactics were not solely determined by personality but were what the circumstances required. As Seldon suggests, 'Major's leadership could be argued to have been exactly what was required for the times' (Seldon, 1997: 742). With the removal of Thatcher, the party and the Cabinet had different visions of

Conservatism, and Major had to try to keep the Cabinet together. Baker records in his memoirs:

> John's style of chairing the Cabinet was quite different from Margaret's. John encouraged discussion and elicited colleagues' views. . . . One of John's great talents is his skill in handling difficult meetings and teasing out a consensus.
>
> (Baker, 1993: 427)

Although it is too early to be definitive, Blair's strategy appears to be one of setting an overall policy direction with the Cabinet under his leadership and then ensuring that the departments follow the broad policy outline, although it seems he was willing to become closely involved in certain policies, such as education, Northern Ireland and even the issue of the 'millennium bug'. The role of the 'Cabinet enforcer' seems to be to ensure that departments are acting in the collective interest of the government. The Cabinet enforcer is useful for the Prime Minister because he can seem not to be interfering directly himself.

However, it also appears that Blair is aware of his dependencies. Two ministers, Gordon Brown and John Prescott, are in strong positions. Brown agreed not to challenge Blair for the leadership of the party and so Blair owes his position, to some extent, to Brown, who probably is the one Cabinet minister who could challenge Blair. As a result of Brown's support for Blair, he has been given control of the government's economic strategy (Draper, 1997: 30). According to Draper:

> Blair knows that his relationship with Brown is a key factor when it comes to the government's success. It is much closer than usual relationship for a Prime Minister and Chancellor, and the two heavyweights regularly discuss matters that go well beyond the Treasury remit.
>
> (Draper, 1997: 29)

Labour's position on membership of European Monetary Union (EMU) is a result of policy worked out between Blair and Brown.

Prescott also has a strong position because he was elected by the party as deputy leader and is seen as protecting the compassionate heart of 'old' Labour. He also provides a useful function for Blair in that he can often convince the party membership that key policy changes such as trade union reform and not renationalising the railways are not at odds with Labour's principles. Prescott has too much party support and is too important in that position for Blair to be able to remove him.

It is also the case that minister can win battles with the Prime Minister through clever tactics. Virginia Bottomley saved a threat to the Department of Heritage budget by releasing a letter from the Chancellor saying lottery money would be in addition to, and not a replacement of, existing expenditure. One of the best examples of ministerial tactics is when Lynda Chalker was faced with a large cut in the Overseas Development Agency's expenditure. The department sent out a press release outlining how the proposed cuts in the budget would mean a 5% cut in ODA expenditure and the lowest level of expenditure ever on overseas aid. Indeed, the department pointed out that with the Fundamental Expenditure Review, the real cut in expenditure would by 16%. The department then encouraged the NGOs to lobby the Treasury and the Prime Minister, pointing out how many projects would be affected by these cuts. As a consequence of the lobbying, the cuts were restored.

Prime Ministers undoubtedly have more resources than other ministers. However, ministers are in a strong position because they are the head of departments and it is only departments that have the capability both to make and implement detailed policy. Therefore departments are a crucial site of power within the central state. This means that the relationship between Prime Minister and Cabinet is a fluctuating mediation between a Prime Minster who has authority and an overseeing capacity and departmental ministers who have their own varying levels of authority and a departmental machine. If a Prime Minister wants to make an impact, he or she often needs the departmental machine and the support of the minister. Thatcher lost the ability to influence economic policy when she lost the support of Lawson. Blair can only have an impact on home affairs policy by working with David Blunkett.

Summary

- All actors within the core executive have resources.
- While the Prime Minister has more resources than others, he or she does not have all the resources necessary to achieve goals and therefore is dependent on others to change resources.
- The degree of freedom the Prime Minster has to exercise resources depends on the political and economic context.
- It makes little sense to talk of prime ministerial or Cabinet government because power is fluid and the influence of the Prime Minister changes according to issues, circumstances and relationships.

The Prime Minister as Entrepreneur and Risk Manager

Despite the emphasis on dependency and a recognition that actors within the core executive operate within a structured context, we also need to recognise that the Prime Minister is an exceptional individual within the core executive. The Prime Minister has more authority than any other actor and has the ability to change the structure of the core executive and, of course, the make-up of the Cabinet. Two examples illustrate the particular position of the Prime Minister. The first is the way in which the Prime Minister can re-draw the boundaries of government without consultation. In 1974 Harold Wilson decided to split the Department of Trade and Industry into two departments in order to prevent Tony Benn having a significant economic power base. This change was made without consultation either in Cabinet or with senior officials. The Prime Minister can make changes in the machinery of government almost at whim and all Prime Ministers have done so. Tony Blair has made significant changes in the centre with the creation of the Cabinet enforcer and bodies such as the Social Exclusion Unit which have an important impact on the way that the Prime Minister interacts with the rest of the core executive.

The second is the way in which prime ministerial signals are read within Whitehall as these can have an immediate and dramatic impact on the direction of policy. Hennessy (2000: 6) suggests that the two most important words in Whitehall are 'Tony wants'. The Scott Report provides an example of how a relatively informal comment by the Prime Minister can reverberate through Whitehall. The report reveals that on 4 December 1984 Thatcher met Tariq Aziz, the Iraqi Foreign Secretary. She told Aziz that Britain had terminated the supply of weapons to Iran and even items which may have a military application. In her comments Thatcher had gone further than the rule specified on the guidelines for arms sales (Scott, 1996: 215). Thatcher's statement was then discussed by the Inter-departmental Committee dealing with arm sales. Scott reports the summary record as concluding:

> There was some discussion as to how this [i.e. the Prime Minister's statement to Tariq Aziz] might affect the Ministerial Guidelines. It was concluded that the guidelines were the prime source of policy on defence sales to Iran and Iraq and that the Prime Minister's comments as reported in the Private Secretary's letter were compatible with these Guidelines. However, the IDC took the view that the Prime Minister's comments meant that the IDC should err on the side of strictness when deciding on cases where the evidence was inconclusive.
>
> (quoted in Scott, 1996: 215–16)

A comment by the Prime Minister in effect resulted in a policy change without the Prime Minister directly suggesting any change. Indeed, the Prime Minister had been wrong in her interpretation.

It is important to acknowledge that the Prime Minister is an actor who can make a difference. However, the problem is how we conceptualise the agency of the Prime Minister. The traditional approach focuses on the Prime Minister's personality or style. This is problematic, not least because the relationship between personality and action is not specified; it is often difficult to ascribe personality traits and while personality is constant, the power and the impact of the Prime Minister changes. A more analytical approach to agency is provided by rational choice theory. This approach sees actors as utility maximisers who act in their own self-interest. While there are clearly examples of Prime Ministers acting as rational self-interested actors, the constraints on, and the visibility of, their actions can make this difficult. A concept developed within rational choice theory is the notion of political entrepreneurs who can use their power and selective incentives to overcome collective action problems (see Dunleavy, 1991). Essentially the Prime Minister is surrounded by ministers who are concerned with protecting their own self-interests or more precisely the departmental interest (see Castle, 1980; Ponting, 1986). The pursuit of self-interest can undermine the collective goods/goals of government and so the role of the Prime Minister is to act as an entrepreneur who provides the leadership and benefits to ministers to persuade them to act for the common, rather than personal, good. The Prime Minister can use his control of patronage, his authority and control over resources like time and money to persuade ministers to act in certain ways. Moreover, the Prime Minister is an entrepreneur who not only creates incentives for certain choices but can also use leadership authority to shape preferences so that Cabinet members choose collective goods (Dunleavy, 1991: 143).

The notion of the Prime Minister as a political entrepreneur is a useful way of understanding Prime Ministers. Thatcher and Blair have both attempted to set collective policy goals which they expect Cabinet ministers to follow and have emphasised the need to break down selective benefits. One element of the modernising government programme is to provide incentives for officials and ministers to deal with cross-cutting problems in a co-ordinated way rather than stick to departmental silos.

While the notion of the Prime Minister as a political entrepreneur may be useful, it is limited by its rational choice underpinnings and the notion that agency is based on assumption of utility maximisers (for a discussion, see Ward, 1995). An alternative way of conceiving agency is as risk managers. People have the compulsion both to achieve security but also to take risks as a means of progress. Much of the role of the Prime Minister can be seen as an attempt to manage risk to him- or herself and the government. An example of risk management is apparent in the Labour government's strategy towards economic policy. Blair and Brown's fundamental concern was to remove the risk that previous Labour governments faced of sterling crises which have thrown the government off course and undermined their governing competence. Consequently, they have followed the strategy of essentially continuing the Conservative policy of fiscal conservatism as a mechanism for reassuring the markets. The next step in this strategy would be to join the Euro, locking Britain into a potentially strong currency area that is less prone to currency speculation, with the added benefits that economic decisions would be made in the European Union, removing the dangers of the government's economic competence being undermined. However, membership of the Euro depends on a referendum, which creates the risk that the government may lose. Consequently, the Prime Minister is in the difficult position of having to balance the economic risks of Euro membership with the political risks of a lost referendum. This analysis helps to explain some of the conflicts and ambiguities in Labour's approach to monetary union. It also provides a motivation for prime ministerial actions and helps to explain why the Prime Minister may shift from a collective to an individualist form of government.

Summary

- The personalism of the British political system means that the Prime Minister can have an impact as an individual. There is a need to conceptualise the Prime Minister beyond personality.
- One way to do this is to see the Prime Minister as a rational actor who is a political entrepreneur, using the control of resources as a mechanism for ensuring collective action.
- An alternative notion is to see the Prime Minister as a risk manager attempting to assess ways of managing risks to himself/herself and the government as a whole.

Conclusion

The traditional arguments concerning prime ministerial and Cabinet government provide a rather narrow understanding of this key relationship within the core executive. If we are to understand how the Prime Minister and Cabinet interact, we have to see them as interdependent. Both the Prime Minister and the Cabinet have resources and in order to achieve policy and political goals they need to exchange resources. However, the degree of resource exchange and dependency varies according to circumstances. The freedom that the Prime Minister has depends on his/her political situation, the wider economic conditions and the authority and resources of the colleague that he/she is dealing with. This means that power within the core executive is fluid and cannot be simply ascribed either to the Prime Minister or the Cabinet.

Nevertheless, the Prime Minister is not the same as any other Cabinet minister. He/she is an agent who can affect what goes on in government. This means that we need a theory of agency which is based on more than the style or personality of the premier. The Prime Minister is a political entrepreneur who attempts to induce his/her colleagues to act in certain ways and at the same time having to assess and manage risk to himself/herself and the government. Personality may affect risk management strategies and the tactics that the Prime Minister uses but it is not the main determinant of the operation of the core executive.

Discussion Questions

1. Does the growth of prime ministerial resources mean we now have a presidential Prime Minister?
2. How do conceptions of power influence our understanding of the relationship between the Prime Minister and the Cabinet?
3. How useful is it to see the Prime Minister as a political entrepreneur or risk manager?

References

Alderman, R.K. (1976) 'The Prime Minister and the appointment of ministers: an exercise in political bargaining', *Parliamentary Affairs*, Vol. 29, pp. 101–34.

Baker, K. (1993) *The Turbulent Years: My Life in Politics*, London: faber & faber.

Brown, A.H. (1968) 'Prime ministerial power (Part I)', *Public Law*, Spring, pp. 28–51.

Bruce-Gardyne, J. and Lawson, N. (1976) *The Power Game*, London: Macmillan.

Burch, M. (1988) 'British Cabinet: a residual executive', *Parliamentary Affairs*, Vol. 41, pp. 34–47.

Burch, M. and Holliday, I. (1996) *The British Cabinet System*, Hemel Hempstead: Prentice Hall.

Campbell, J. (1993) *Edward Heath: A Biography*, London: Jonathon Cape.

Castle, B. (1980) *The Castle Diaries 1974–76*, London: Weidenfeld & Nicolson.

Crossman, R. (1966) 'Introduction' to W. Bagehot, *The English Constitution*, London: Fontana.

Crossman, R. (1972) *Inside View*, London: Jonathon Cape.

Daintith, T. and Page, A. (1999) *The Executive in the Constitution*, Oxford: Oxford University Press.

Draper, D. (1997) *Blair's Hundred Days*, London: Faber.

Dunleavy, P. (1991) *Bureaucracy, Democracy and Public Choice*, Hemel Hempstead: Harvester Wheatsheaf.

Dunleavy, P. and Rhodes, R.A.W. (1990) 'Core executive studies in Britain', *Public Administration*, Vol. 68, pp. 3–28.

Foley, M. (1993) *The Rise of the British Presidency*, Manchester: Manchester University Press.

Foster, C.D. (1997) *A Stronger Centre of Government*, London: Constitutional Unit.

Hennessy, P. (1986) *Cabinet*, Oxford: Blackwell.

Hennessy, P. (1994) 'Cabinet government: a commentary', *Contemporary Record*, Vol. 8, pp. 484–94.

Hennessy, P. (2000) *The Blair Revolution in Government*, Leeds: University of Leeds, Institute for Politics and International Studies.

Hogg, S. and Hill, J. (1995) *Too Close to Call*, London: Little Brown and Co.

James, S. (1999) *British Cabinet Government*, London: Routledge.

Jones, G. (1975) 'Development of the Cabinet', in W. Thornhill (ed.) *The Modernisation of British Government*, London: Pitman.

Kavanagh, D. (1990) *Thatcherism and British Politics*, Oxford: Oxford University Press.

Kavanagh, D. and Seldon, A. (1999) *The Powers behind the Prime Minister*, Oxford: Oxford University Press.

King, A. (1985a) 'Introduction: the textbook Prime Minister', in A. King (ed.) *The British Prime Minister*, Basingstoke: Macmillan.

King, A. (1985b) 'Margaret Thatcher: the style of a Prime Minister', in A. King (ed.) *The British Prime Minister*, Basingstoke: Macmillan.

Lawson, N. (1992) *The View from No. 11*, London: Bantam Press.

Lawson, N. (1994) 'Cabinet government in the Thatcher years', *Contemporary Record*, Vol. 8, pp. 440–7.

Lee, J., Jones, G. and Burnham, J. (1998) *At the Centre of Whitehall*, London: Macmillan.

Mackintosh, J.P. (1963) *The British Cabinet*, London: Stevens and Sons Limited.

Madgwick, P. (1991) *British Government: The Central Executive Territory*, London: Philip Allen.

Marsh, D., Richards, D. and Smith, M.J. (2001) *Reinventing Whitehall? The Changing Role of Central Government Departments*, Basingstoke: Macmillan.

Ponting, C. (1986) *Whitehall: Tragedy and Farce*, London: Hamish Hamilton.

Pryce, S. (1997) *Presidentializing the Premiership*, London: Macmillan.

Scott, R. (1996) *Report of the Inquiry into the Export of Defence Equipment and Dual Use Goods to Iraq and Related Prosecutions*, London: HMSO.

Seldon, A. (1997) *Major: A Political Life*, London: Weidenfeld & Nicolson.

Smith, M.J. (1999) *The Core Executive in Britain*, Basingstoke: Macmillan.

Thatcher, M. (1993) *The Downing Street Years*, London: HarperCollins.

Thomas, G. (1998) *Prime Minister and Cabinet Today*, Manchester: Manchester University Press.

Wakeham, J. (1994) 'Cabinet government', *Contemporary Record*, Vol. 8, pp. 473–83.

Ward, H. (1995) 'Rational choice theory', in D. Marsh and G. Stoker (eds) *Theory and Methods in Political Science*, London: Macmillan.

Watkins, A. (1991) *A Conservative Coup*, London: Duckworth.

Wrong, D. (1988) *Power*, Oxford: Blackwell.

Further reading

J.P. Mackintosh's (1963) *The British Cabinet* (third edition, 1977, London: Stevens and Sons Ltd) is a magisterial study of the history of Cabinet and still worth reading. The prime ministerial government argument is clearly outlined by R. Crossman (1966) 'Introduction', in W. Bagehot, *The English Constitution* (London: Fontana), and dismissed by G. Jones (1975) 'Development of the Cabinet', in W. Thornhill (ed.) *The Modernisation of British Government* (London: Pitman). Presidentialism is advocated by M. Foley (1993) *The Rise of the British Presidency* (Manchester: Manchester University Press). The debate is summarised by G. Thomas (1998) *Prime Minister and Cabinet Today* (Manchester: Manchester University Press) and A. King (1985) *The British Prime Minister* (Basingstoke: Macmillan). The history of the Prime Minister's Office is recounted in J. Lee, G. Jones and J. Burnham (1998) *At the Centre of Whitehall* (London: Macmillan) and D. Kavanagh and A. Seldon (1999) *The Powers behind the Prime Minister* (Oxford: Oxford University Press). The first sophisticated analysis of the core executive is in R. Rhodes and P. Dunleavy (1995) *Prime Minister, Cabinet and Core Executive* (London: Macmillan). M. Burch and I. Holliday (1996) *The British Cabinet System* (Hemel Hempstead: Prentice Hall) and M.J. Smith (1999) *The Core Executive in Britain* (Basingstoke: Macmillan) apply the term. Details on the importance of departments are provided in T. Daintith and A. Page (1999) *The Executive in the Constitution* (Oxford: Oxford University Press) and D. Marsh, D. Richards and M.J. Smith (2001), *Reinventing Whitehall?* (Basingstoke: Macmillan).

Ministers, Civil Servants and Advisors

Robert Pyper

CHAPTER FIFTEEN

This chapter focuses on the functioning of, and changing relationships between, a set of key actors operating at the very heart of the British system of government. To a very considerable extent, the interactions between ministers, civil servants and advisors determine the ebb and flow of politics in this country, as well as influencing the content and style of public policy. The shifting relationships in this field have been subject to considerable debate, comment and analysis in recent years. Debates and arguments have focused on issues of civil service power and influence, the nature and extent of official and ministerial accountability, the appropriateness of managerial reform in government, and the specific policy advice requirements of ministers. The purpose of this chapter is to chart the key developments and examine the main issues surrounding ministers, civil servants and advisors in British central government.

Background

The conventional, traditional view of working relations at the top level of British government was deceptively simple – ministers made policy, while senior civil servants offered advice on its framing and execution. At lower levels of the departmental hierarchies, officials implemented policy by delivering government services to the public. In fact, matters were always slightly more complicated than this. The ministerial role could be described in terms of the five components set out in Box 15.1. The work of civil servants could similarly be viewed in terms of a set of roles, some of which overlap with those of their ministers. The four key components of civil service work are also displayed in Box 15.1.

Although modern government has become increasingly complex, the numbers of government ministers and the work they carry out have barely changed. For example, the first administration of Harold Wilson in October 1964 contained a total of 112 ministers in thirty-three departments of state. The government of Margaret Thatcher which took office in May 1979 consisted of 104 ministers in twenty-six departments. Tony Blair's administration, formed in June 1997, contained 108 ministers in twenty-one departments. Overall, therefore, while there has been some rationalisation of the departmental configuration over this period, there has been relatively little alteration in the numbers of British government ministers during the past forty years (House of Commons, 1964; House of Commons, 1979; Cabinet Office website, February 2000).

Box 15.1 Job descriptions

Ministers

1. *Policy leadership*: giving a clear direction to the overall policy stance of the department. As Secretary of State, the senior minister has a particularly important role to play here.
2. *Departmental management*: running the organisation in an efficient and effective fashion.
3. *Legislative steering*: piloting bills for which the department has primary responsibility through the various parliamentary stages.
4. *'Ambassadorship'*: representing the interests of the department in the Cabinet and its committees (in the case of the Secretary of State), in meetings with key client groups, in the councils of the European Union, and in public.
5. *Accountability*: within the context of collective and individual ministerial responsibility, accounting for departmental policies and actions to the Prime Minister and the government as a whole, to Parliament (via the full range of mechanisms of scrutiny) and to the public.

Civil servants

1. *Policy advice*: the provision of detailed policy advice to ministers, carried out primarily by the most senior Whitehall civil servants.
2. *Departmental administration and management*: while ministers have overall responsibility for the management of departments, the day-to-day functions associated with this are carried out by civil servants.
3. *Implementation*: at the middle and lower levels of the official hierarchy, civil servants are primarily concerned with executing policy, delivering services.
4. *Accountability*: in simple terms, civil servants are accountable for their work upwards to their own official superiors and to ministers, and, in certain strictly limited circumstances, to Parliament (for example, the accounting officer of a department to the Public Accounts Committee of the House of Commons).

Specific aspects of the ministerial role have assumed greater prominence in more recent times. In particular, Britain's membership of the European Union has had significant implications for ministers in the sense that their policy leadership and 'ambassadorial' roles involve considerable liaison and interaction with their EU counterparts and the institutions of the European Union. Beyond this, some commentators argue that the accountability dimension of ministers' work has changed because the conventions of ministerial responsibility have loosened over the years. However, it might be that they are harking back to a 'golden age' of constitutional purity that never really existed. Both collective and individual ministerial responsibility are, and have always been, fairly malleable concepts which respond to the imperatives of political reality. The bounds of collective responsibility have always been strained by the propensity of powerful ministers, such as Tony Benn and Michael Heseltine, to challenge the policies of their own governments. This convention's requirement that ministers respect the secrecy and confidentiality of discussions within government has been repeatedly breached by leaks and the publication of ministerial diaries and memoirs. Similarly, the operation of the 'sanctions' clauses of individual ministerial responsibility have been shown to be susceptible to political factors. The lesson we can draw from an array of cases, including the failure of policy towards the Falkland Islands, mismanagement of prisons, the 'arms for Iraq affair' and countless instances of 'sleaze' and questionable personal behaviour, is that ministers may or may not resign when failures have occurred in aspects of their work or private lives, depending on the political circumstances surrounding the case (for coverage of the key cases, see Pyper, 1993, 1994; Woodhouse 1993, 1994, 1997).

In contrast with the relative lack of change in the basic ministerial roles, civil servants have found their roles affected by staff cuts, coupled with substantial managerial and structural change. The civil service has been reduced in size from over 1 million in the early 1950s to around 750,000 in 1979 and to 480,000 in 2000 (see Table 15.1). 'Europeanisation' had an impact on the working of civil servants, at first in the so-called 'Euro-elite' corners of Whitehall (the Cabinet Office, the Foreign Office, and the Ministry of Agriculture, Fisheries and Food, for example), but steadily across the full range of departments and executive agencies. Framing policy with a view to European Union requirements and implementing EU legislation and directives became an increasingly common feature of the work of civil servants at all levels of the system.

While the organisation continued to carry out the full range of roles described in Box 15.1, increasing emphasis came to be placed on matters of departmental management, policy implementation and accountability. At the same time, as we shall see, senior civil servants found that their responsibility for policy advice was being encroached upon due to a developing ministerial penchant for special policy advisors and think tanks.

The civil service was subjected to a measure of change as a consequence of the Fulton Report in 1968. Fulton represented the first serious, in-depth examination of the organisation and strategic purpose of the civil service since the Northcote–Trevelyan Report of 1854. The great Victorian inquiry laid the foundations for a modern civil service based on recruitment through competitive examinations, promotion on merit, and a rational division of functions. Fulton recommended a programme of reform designed to equip the civil service for the challenges of the late twentieth century. This included the establishment of the Civil Service Department (CSD) as a force for strategic management (the CSD was abolished by Margaret Thatcher in 1981 as she sought more direct control over

Table 15.1 The decline of the mandarins

Year	Total numbers of civil servants in post
1979	747,940
1984	634,480
1989	586,650
1994	559,400
2000	480,000

Source: Cabinet Office website (February 2001)

Whitehall reform), the Civil Service College as a forum for the training and education of new breeds of manager, and the inculcation of new management methods at all levels of the system. However, for a variety of reasons (including lack of sustained political support and elements of official intransigence), Fulton ultimately failed to transform the civil service. The major, lasting manifestations of civil service reform would be seen in the combination of structural and managerial reforms spearheaded from Downing Street during the 1980s and 1990s.

Initially based on the work of Derek Rayner's Efficiency Unit, managerial changes swept through Whitehall during this period. Many reforms were implemented under the umbrella of the Financial Management Initiative, including management and financial information systems, devolved budgets, value-for-money testing, performance indicators and rational budgeting techniques. Under Robin Ibbs, Rayner's successor, the managerial changes were consolidated and then expanded through the structural reforms which led to the creation of the Next Steps executive agencies.

Next Steps transformed the basic structure of the civil service. The creation of executive agencies, from 1988 onwards, was based on the idea that certain key departmental functions could be carried out by offshoots of the Whitehall departments. For example, the full range of social security benefits would be delivered to the public through an executive agency of the Department of Social Security rather than by the traditional branch offices of the Department itself. Other agencies might focus on the provision of in-house services, such as information technology or property management. The whole point of this structural reorganisation was to improve service delivery while modernising the management of the civil service itself (for details of the origins and implications of Next Steps, see Greer, 1994; Pyper, 1995). Under Next Steps, every government department was obliged to conduct ongoing analyses of their detailed activities and programmes. A decade after publication of the Next Steps Report, UK central government had been fundamentally restructured to the point where over 76% of the civil service was in executive agencies, of which 138 were Next Steps agencies. Next Steps served as a catalyst for broad-ranging managerial and structural change within the civil service. Pay, recruitment and promotion 'flexibilities' were developed around the Next Steps agency model, and subtle alterations were gradually made to established parliamentary procedures in order to facilitate the accountability of the chief executives.

Although Next Steps was broadly supported by all of the political parties, the initiative aroused controversy in some respects. The possible loss of coherence, corporate identity and shared public service values seriously concerned some observers (see Chapman, 1997). While the establishment of the new agencies seemed to bring greater transparency to the work of the civil service, there were debates about the overall implications for accountability. When introducing Next Steps, the Thatcher government had declared that this would have no implications for accountability. The officials working in executive agencies would be subject to scrutiny by select committees and the Parliamentary Ombudsman in the same way as other civil servants. As in the past, this would be deemed to be indirect accountability in the sense that the officials would merely be helping their ministers to be properly accountable to Parliament. However, in practice, ministers were gradually forced to move away from this position and tolerate the increased accountability of civil servants to Parliament. Although there was no formal recognition of a

constitutional change to the doctrine of ministerial responsibility, subtle alterations were made to established parliamentary procedures in order to facilitate the
accountability of the chief executives (their answers to Parliamentary questions
were published in Hansard and the Public Accounts Committee was allowed
access to the chief executives in their capacity as accounting officers). Recurring
crises surrounding the work of some agencies, including the Child Support Agency
and the Prison Service Agency indicated that serious flaws remained in the system
of accountability, but these cases should not be allowed to detract from the fact
that Next Steps, taken as a whole, brought about increased 'visibility' of senior civil
servants and helped to change at least some elements of the system of official
accountability.

The Major government continued the process of civil service reform, introducing market testing (competitive tendering) across a wide range of civil service activities and processes, launching the Private Finance Initiative as a mechanism for
involving the private sector in public capital spending projects, and proffering the
Citizen's Charter as a means of enhancing the quality of service delivery. As we
shall see, these themes of civil service managerial reform would be carried forward
by the Blair government in the period after 1997.

One of the key civil service roles identified in Box 15.1 concerns the provision
of policy advice to ministers. Traditionally, this was the preserve of the Whitehall
mandarins, the most senior officials working at the top levels of the departments of
state. Historically, Prime Ministers had made some use of special policy advisors.
For example, Winston Churchill appointed Professor Frederick Lindemann as
his 'Personal Advisor in Scientific Matters' and other Premiers relied to a greater
or lesser degree on specialist policy advice from 'experts' of one description or
another. However, from 1964 onwards there was a marked trend towards the use
of special policy advisors by increasing numbers of ministers. The impact of this
was to be quite significant for the traditional civil service role in the provision of
policy advice to ministers. Viewed positively, the role of special policy advisors
would be to offer ministers tailored, expert advice and support which are not available within the conventional civil service framework. A more negative interpretation would see the special advisors as a malign influence, second-guessing and
undermining the civil service from a constitutionally unorthodox position.

An inherent suspicion of the conservative nature of the civil service, coupled
with doubts about the capacity of the most senior officials to serve a Labour
administration after thirteen years of Conservative government, led some of the
more senior Cabinet ministers in the Labour government of 1964–70 to rely on
the services of political advisors. For example, Richard Crossman brought the
academic Brian Abel-Smith into the Department of Health and Social Security. In
its official evidence to the Fulton Committee on the Civil Service in 1966, the
Labour Party recommended a significant increase in the numbers of political
appointments within government departments, together with the development of
a European style *cabinet* system for departmental ministers. This would have allowed
for the creation of small teams of advisors, partly drawn from relevant policy
experts within the civil service and partly from the outside world (academia, business and commerce, the party). The Fulton Report concluded that there might be
a case for the appointment of relatively small numbers of political advisors, but

the concept of the ministerial *cabinet* was rejected on the grounds that the existing civil service structures were still best suited to the task of providing high-level policy advice (for a discussion of the *cabinet* concept, see Neville-Jones, 1983).

Nonetheless, by the later 1960s the *cabinet* idea was also being considered in Conservative Party circles. Under Edward Heath, the Conservatives set up a 'businessmen's team' headed by Richard Meyjes from Shell and including Derek Rayner from Marks & Spencer. In government from 1970, Heath was advised by his businessmen to conduct a major review of ministerial private offices, with a view to establishing a *cabinet* system. Senior civil servants resisted this proposal, and Heath was reluctant to carry the project forward. The Central Policy Review Staff (CPRS), a government 'think tank', was perhaps the nearest the British system of government would come to embracing the *cabinet* concept, but the CPRS was really designed to provide strategic policy advice to the Cabinet collectively, and the Prime Minister in particular, rather than to ministers individually (for full details of the rise and fall of the CPRS, see Blackstone and Plowden, 1990). Nonetheless, by the end of the Heath government in 1974 the trend for ministers to use special political advisors had become entrenched.

Labour's return to office in 1974 heralded a quite remarkable increase in the numbers of special advisors used by ministers. No fewer than thirty-eight were appointed within months of the election victory. In part, at least, this was a response to the emerging view in some Labour circles that senior civil servants had sabotaged much of the reforming zeal of the 1964–70 governments (for example, see Benn, 1982). The Prime Minister, Harold Wilson, issued guidelines to govern the appointments of ministerial advisors. Although some ministers chose not to make use of the scheme, the norm was for government departments to have one or two special advisors, working closely with the Secretary of State.

In some cases, the advisors had a significant impact. For example, the Home Secretary, Roy Jenkins, appointed the barrister and QC Anthony Lester and he was credited with playing a major part in shaping the law on sex equality and race relations. Lester worked well in tandem with Home Office civil servants. The same could not be said for Tony Benn's special advisors at the Departments of Industry and Energy between 1974 and 1979. Frances Morrell and Francis Cripps were credited with making significant policy contributions, including drafting white papers and providing the research which opened up the whole issue of Britain's future nuclear energy policy. There was considerable friction in the working relationships between Morrell and Cripps and the senior officials in the Departments of Industry and Energy (see Benn, 1990).

By the late 1970s, the number of special advisors in Whitehall was starting to fall, partly because many of the appointments had been short-term ones, and partly due to the antipathy felt by the new Prime Minister, James Callaghan, towards the scheme. Callaghan was deeply suspicious of political advisors, and blamed them for leaks of information from within the government. There was also some speculation to the effect that senior civil servants had neutered the effect of the political advisors (see Young, 1976). It became steadily more difficult for ministers to make these appointments, advisors' conditions of service were tightened up and their access to Cabinet documents strictly restricted.

The arrival of Margaret Thatcher in Downing Street in 1979 brought a dramatic strengthening of the Prime Minister's system of policy advice, but Thatcher's departmental ministers found it more difficult to make use of special advisors. Some ministers were given the opportunity to appoint advisors, normally bringing them in from the Conservative Party's Research Department. However, it was clear that the Prime Minister was prepared to monitor very closely the number and type of advisors chosen by her ministers. By this stage, an increasingly important advisory role was being assumed by external think tanks. At earlier stages in the twentieth century bodies like Political and Economic Planning and the National Institute of Economic and Social Research fed policy advice into government. During the 1980s a series of 'new right' think tanks established close working relations with senior members of the Thatcher governments. Although it is very difficult to be precise about the specific role played by the Institute of Economic Affairs, the Centre for Policy Studies and the Adam Smith Institute in the development of government policy, it is clear that these bodies influenced the broad agenda within which many of the policy debates of that time took place. Close observers of the most powerful think tanks have expressed serious reservations about their democratic legitimacy. Denham and Garnett cast doubt on the extent to which these policy bodies genuinely contribute to an effective pluralist society. They ask serious questions about the relationship between ministers and 'think tanks inside the charmed circle which become transmission belts for news and advice which pleases the government' or function as devices which facilitate the floating of ideas in the pretence that they have emerged from outside Whitehall (Denham and Garnett, 1998: 204).

The whole issue of policy support for ministers came under consideration again in the mid-1980s, when a report from the House of Commons Treasury and Civil Service Select Committee favoured the idea of special political advisors and came out in support of the *cabinet* concept. The Committee proposed that a *cabinet* type of body, to be called the 'Minister's Policy Unit' should be established on an experimental basis in a number of departments, in order to gauge its effectiveness. However, this recommendation was not followed up, and the rather *ad hoc* arrangements and intermittent use of policy advisors by ministers continued.

As we shall see below, the arrival of the Blair government in 1997 signalled some significant developments in the use of special advisors by ministers, the continued use of external think tanks and the emergence of 'task forces' as drivers of policy change.

Summary

- The key aspects of the ministerial role in British government have remained largely unchanged in modern times. However, the work of the civil service has been affected by two developments.
- Structural and managerial reform impinged upon the civil service roles in departmental administration and management, and had some implications for accountability.

- The increasing use of special policy advisors by ministers served to supplement the traditional role of the civil service in the realm of policy advice.

Theoretical Considerations

A range of theoretical considerations impinge upon the major themes of this chapter. Although it is impossible to do justice to all of these in the space available, some comments can be offered on some of the main theoretical and conceptual approaches which can shed light on our areas of concern.

Our understanding of the changes which have taken place in recent years to the shape and structure of the civil service and to the roles of civil servants in organisational management and policy implementation can be enhanced through engaging with the developing literature on the New Public Management (NMP). Themes, including the significance of private sector managerial approaches in government, the conceptual and practical differences between traditional public administration and NPM, the separation of policy creation and implementation, the pros and cons of consumerist approaches to accountability, and the performance management and value for money agendas, are set out in a range of sources (see, for example, Metcalf and Richards, 1990; Foster and Plowden, 1996; Flynn, 1997; Hughes, 1998).

Civil service power can be examined from a number of different, sometimes competing perspectives. The perspective of Tony Benn, for example, was informed by a Marxist analysis of the class backgrounds of senior civil servants. The tendency for those with shared educational and social experiences to act as an elite and defend established interests within the British state was argued in some detail by Ralph Miliband (1969). By contrast, new right interpretations of the power of the civil service stress the tendency for bureaucracies to expand, maximise budgets and defend their own interests against those of the elected politicians. Public choice theory, largely derived from Downs (1957, 1967) and Niskanen (1973) has given an intellectual gloss to this political perspective.

Students can steer a path between these perspectives, and seek to view ministerial–civil service relationships and the management of public policy through the prism of policy networks (see Rhodes, 1997) and theories of power-dependency (see, for example, Smith, 1999). These approaches highlight the complex nature of policy-making and implementation, set out the key resources available to ministers and civil servants as they engage in power struggles over policy, and bring home the need to look beyond the rather closed world of Whitehall and Westminster in order to understand the part played by the full range of governmental and non-governmental policy actors.

Light can be shed upon the issues surrounding ministerial and official accountability by contrasting constitutional norms with practical reality. Theories and analyses of accountability proliferate. Gray and Jenkins (1985) link accountability with the concept of stewardship; Elcock (1991) favours a directional model of accountability ('upwards, outwards and downwards'); Lawton and Rose (1991) deploy a typology ('political, managerial, legal consumer and professional accountability'); and Pyper (1996) argues for an approach which differentiates between weaker ('answerability') and stronger forms of accountability (the latter encompassing explanations of actions or policies, amendatory actions, redress of grievances and sanctions on political and official actors).

Summary

Theoretical perspectives and concepts which can aid our understanding of this topic include:

- New Public Management.
- Power theories (including elite and public choice).
- Policy network analysis.
- Concepts of accountability.

Update

In the wake of the 1997 general election the civil service was given seven 'challenges' by the new Prime Minister (see Box 15.2). It was clear that the process of managerial change which had started in the 1980s would continue under New Labour. Furthermore, Whitehall would be required to play a major part in the implementation of the government's programme.

In order to do this, modernisation of the civil service was a vital prerequisite. Thoroughgoing reform was fully supported by a set of relatively younger mandarins, led by Sir Michael Bichard, then the Permanent Secretary at the Department for Education and Employment and Sir Richard Mottram, Permanent Secretary at the Department of the Environment, Transport and the Regions. The modernisers argued that the managerial reforms which had engulfed the lower reaches of the civil service should now spread to the top levels. Senior appointments should go

Box 15.2 Blair's challenges for the civil service

1. **Implement constitutional reform** in a way that preserves a unified civil service, ensures a close working relationship between the UK government and the devolved administrations.
2. Staff in all departments are to **integrate the EU dimension into policy-making**.
3. **Public services are to be improved**, be more innovative and responsive to users, and be delivered in an efficient and joined-up way.
4. Create **a more innovative and less risk-averse culture** in the civil service.
5. **Improve collaborative working** across organisational boundaries.
6. **Manage the civil service so as to equip it to meet these challenges**.
7. **Think ahead strategically** to future priorities.

Box 15.3 Ethnic and gender issues in the civil service

Looking forward to the shape of the civil service in the new millennium, in May 1999 the Head of the Service, Sir Richard Wilson identified cultural challenges:

> We have far too few women, people from black and ethnic minority backgrounds and people with disabilities in the senior parts of the Civil Service. We must be part of, not apart from, the society we serve. This is a top priority. We want a Civil Service which values the differences that people bring to it. We need to have the benefit of those differences. We must not only reflect the full diversity of society but also be strengthened by that diversity.

The problem: In 1999 only 18% of civil servants were women and only 1.6% of civil servants came from ethnic minorities.

The target: By 2005 at least 36% of civil servants are to be women and at least 3.2% of civil servants are to be from ethnic minorities.

Some progress?   In 1999 Opportunity 2000 rated the civil service top from 14 employment sectors in investing in women's progress.

---

to those with 'operational' experience (rather than those with more arcane 'policy' backgrounds), and the entire social and educational mix of the civil service should be transformed to give a fairer reflection of society at large. Although he often appeared to be trailing in the wake of the modernisers, the new Head of the Civil Service, Sir Richard Wilson, put his full weight behind the need to make the organisation reflect the wider society (see Box 15.3).

During the latter stages of the extended period of Conservative government some concerns had emerged about the extent to which senior civil servants would be able to adapt to meet the demands of a Labour administration. Labour's traditional suspicion of the mandarins had not been entirely overcome during the relatively cordial informal briefings which took place in the period leading up to the general election. Labour's worries had less to do with any overt politicisation of Whitehall during the eighteen years of Conservative rule, but were related to the natural development of a particular 'mind-set' among officials who had worked for so long within a Conservative policy environment. Additionally, the new government ministers had become accustomed, while in opposition, to the efficiency of the party's Millbank policy machine, and they quickly began to draw unfavourable comparisons between the party's responsiveness and Whitehall lethargy.

Some senior civil servants appeared to fall victim to these types of concern. The most high profile of these came when the merger of Environment and Transport in Deputy Prime Minister John Prescott's new 'super-department' saw the departure of Sir Patrick Brown, Permanent Secretary at Transport, who was a leading implementer of the previous government's privatisation programme (although it was not entirely clear that this was a causal factor). Matters were smoother when Richard Wilson was appointed to succeed Sir Robin Butler as Cabinet Secretary and Head of the Civil Service from January 1998, and this was generally welcomed within Whitehall (Butler, 1997).

However, rather than brutally replace large numbers of civil servants and risk the accusation that it was politicising the civil service, Labour attempted to counterbalance the effect of any entrenched 'mind-sets' by bringing into Whitehall an unprecedented number of special policy advisors. The implication of this will be assessed below. In the meantime, together with his senior ministers, Blair started to draft a framework for governance, built around the theme of 'modernisation'. The result was a white paper, *Modernising Government*, published in the spring of 1999 (see Box 15.4).

The white paper encapsulated many of the civil service management and service delivery themes which had been developing piecemeal during the life of the Blair administration, and indeed before. The document's glossy image, short PR-style phraseology and avowedly 'modern' approach were, nonetheless, typically New Labour. An implementation programme was put in place to take the *Modernising Government* agenda forward. A Modernising Public Services Group was set up within the Cabinet Office and, together with the *Modernising Government* Project Board (containing external and civil service members), this body drew up an action plan. The early priorities were categorised as 'responsiveness', 'effectiveness and efficiency', 'joined-up government' and 'quality'.

It seems likely that *Modernising Government* will bring about further significant change to the culture and management of the civil service. One senior academic analyst believed that the long-term impact of this white paper 'is likely to be comparable to that of the Next Steps Report' (Chapman, 1999: 8). It should be clearly understood, however, that while its rhetoric emphasised 'newness' and 'modernisation', the Blair government's basic approach to issues of service delivery and civil service management built upon the foundations laid by the Conservatives during the 1980s and early 1990s. This can be illustrated with reference to the fact that Labour rebranded and repackaged, rather than abolished, market testing, the Private Finance Initiative and the Citizen's Charter. Whatever the roots of the reform agenda might have been, Labour ministers expected their civil servants successfully to manage change on a continuous basis.

In opposition, Labour had criticised what it saw as the dogmatism of market testing, which forced government departments and agencies to expose categories of their work to competitive tendering within a system of strict timetables and targets. After the 1997 election, the new government adopted a different approach. Its stated objective was to ensure that all departments reviewed the full range of their services and functions over a five-year period starting in 1999. The aim was to identify the 'best supplier' of each service and function, while improving quality and value for money across government. Under this Better Quality Services (BQS) initiative, departments were required to have plans in place for the programme of reviews by the autumn of 1999.

BQS focuses on end results and service standards while attempting to secure the best quality and value for money for the taxpayer. The 'best supplier' of a service is identified through considering the possibility of competition but, unlike the market-testing programme, there is no compulsion to set up a tendering process. The government made it clear that if internal restructuring or managerial 'reprocessing' results in quality improvements, no competition is necessary. However, it

Box 15.4 Modernising government

Summary of the white paper *Modernising Government*, published in March 1999.

Central objective

To provide 'better government to make life better for people'.

Aims

To ensure that policy-making is more 'joined up' and that the strategic focus on public service users, not providers, delivers high-quality and efficient public services.

New reforms

'Government direct':   Public services to be available 24 hours a day, seven days a week, where there is a demand.

'Joined-up government':   The co-ordination of public services and more strategic policy-making.

Removal of unnecessary regulation: The requirements that departments avoid imposing new regulatory burdens and submit those deemed necessary to Regulatory Impact Assessments.

Information age government: Targets for all dealings with government to be deliverable electronically by 2008.

'Learning labs':   To encourage new ways of front-line working and suspend rules that stifle innovation.

Incentives: For public service staff, including financial rewards for those who identify savings or service improvements.

New focus on delivery within Whitehall: Permanent secretaries to pursue delivery of key government targets, recruit more 'outsiders', promote able young staff.

Key commitments

Forward-looking policy-making:

- Identify and spread best practice via a new Centre for Management and Policy Studies (which will incorporate the Civil Service College).
- Joint training of ministers and civil servants.
- Peer review of departments.

Responsive public services:

- Remove obstacles to joined-up working through local partnerships, one-stop shops and other means.
- Involve and meet the needs of different groups in society.

Quality public services:

- Review all government department services and activities over five years to identify the best suppliers.
- Set new targets for all public bodies, with a focus on real improvements in quality and effectiveness.
- Monitor performance closely to strike a balance between intervention when things go wrong and allowing successful organisations freedom to manage.

Box 15.4 (continued)

Information age government:

- An IT strategy for government to co-ordinate development of digital signatures, smart cards, websites and call centres.
- Benchmark progress against targets for electronic services.

Public service:

- To be valued, not denigrated.
- Modernise the civil service (including the revision of performance management arrangements); tackle under-representation of women, ethnic minorities and people with disabilities; build capacity for innovation.
- Establish a public sector employment forum to bring together and develop key players across the public sector.

is stressed that these internal reviews must be 'robust' and in order to ensure this they are subject to close scrutiny by the Cabinet Office, the Treasury and the Cabinet's public expenditure committee.

The Private Finance Initiative (PFI), launched by the Major government in 1992, was designed to allow public authorities, including central government departments and agencies, to commission major capital projects such as schools, hospitals, roads and bridges, without incurring an initial outlay. Private sector contractors would provide the initial capital and take on the risks associated with construction, in return for operating licences for the resulting facility, which would enable them to recoup their costs. At the end of the contracted period for leasing-back the facility from the private company (which might be thirty years), it would revert to the public sector body. In many respects, the PFI symbolised certain aspects of civil service change. Across Whitehall, officials were required to develop new skills and techniques in order to manage this process and conduct effective business with the private sector.

Labour criticised the PFI in opposition, although as the 1997 general election approached it became increasingly clear that the initiative would survive in some form. Once in government, Labour immediately ended the requirement that all public sector capital projects should be tested for PFI potential. However, ministers committed themselves to a revised and refocused version of the initiative. By 1999 some £4.7 billion worth of PFI deals had been approved by Labour (making a total of £13 billion since the launch of PFI) with another £11 billion worth projected for the period 1999–2002. Within the National Health Service alone, PFI deals would underpin the building of thirteen new hospitals (see HM Treasury website for details).

Labour's repackaging of the PFI involved attempting to address the managerial problems surrounding the initiative by commissioning reports from financial experts. As a result, in the summer of 1999 the government launched a new body, Partnerships UK, to supplement the established role of Treasury officials in running the PFI. The new body was to improve the central co-ordination of the initiative by acting as the overall project manager for PFI deals and enforcing a greater standardisation of the bidding and contractual process. The government's hope was that this would prevent any repetition of the disastrous problems associated with the large PFI computer contracts, symbolised by the Passport Agency's disastrous deal with the electronics corporation Siemens, which produced massive backlogs in the passport application system in 1999 and acute embarrassment for the government.

Nonetheless, critics remained unconvinced by the whole PFI project. The former senior Treasury and Cabinet Office civil servant, Sir Peter Kemp (1999), raised serious questions about the 'hidden spending' and unconventional 'value-for-money' studies surrounding PFI projects and argued that the rationale for this kind of public–private partnership was 'pretty thin'.

If schemes like Better Quality Services and the Private Finance Initiative focused on improving the management of government departments and agencies, the Citizen's Charter was designed to enhance the accessibility and accountability of civil servants and, indeed, public servants generally. When the Charter was launched by the Major government, Labour made it clear that it supported the idea of improved answerability and better service delivery. Within the Charter scheme, 'mini-Charters' were published to cover the full range of public service users, including those seeking employment, Benefits Agency customers, NHS patients, rail passengers, taxpayers, parents of school children, students in higher education and people using the courts. However, Labour persistently questioned the extent to which the Charter was a substantive initiative rather than a political gimmick whose objectives could never be achieved without extra expenditure.

The Blair government was committed to 'relaunch' and 'refocus' the Charter. Renamed as *Service First*, the intention was to replace the 'top-down' system inherited from the Conservatives with a 'bottom-up' approach. This meant that the existing Charters were viewed as having been the property of the service providers, drawn up with little or no consultation with those who use the services. Civil servants would devise the new Charters in consultation with the public and the rather vague statements and low service targets would be replaced with clear information about the 'outcomes' service users should expect, together with meaningful indicators of service quality (Cabinet Office, 1998). Under the *Service First* programme, new principles of public service delivery were published, building upon the existing Charter principles, while all of the existing Charters were to be reviewed and replaced with new versions. The quality of the new Charters was to be monitored centrally, while the Charter Mark award scheme was to be made more rigorous. There was a clear indication of increased rigour when, in the summer of 1999, the Passport Agency, which had held a Charter Mark since 1992, was stripped of its award following prolonged chaos in its operations and a backlog of around 500,000 passport applications. In the past some organisations had voluntarily given up their Charter Marks, or failed to have them renewed after the initial three-year period, but this was the first instance of award-stripping.

While the Blair government pushed on with its civil service reform agenda, a new set of dynamics came to play upon the ministerial–civil servant relationship. The Labour government retained reasonably close relationships with some centre-left external think tanks, including Demos and the Institute for Public Policy

Research. However, a more significant impact on policy was to come from the ranks of policy advisors. The arrival of unprecedented numbers of policy advisors in Whitehall raised important questions about the respective policy roles of ministers, civil servants and 'irregulars'.

The policy advisors came in two types. The so-called 'policy wonks' worked directly with ministers or within the burgeoning taskforces (some estimates reckoned over forty of these existed). They were given responsibility for developing cross-cutting policies in spheres such as social exclusion. The 'spin doctors' took up media liaison roles. At the end of the Major government there had been around thirty-five special advisors in Whitehall. There was an immediate influx of fifty-three under New Labour, and the number rose steadily, to reach seventy-four by the end of 1999 (Richards, 2000: 6). A special civil service pay system operates for these advisors (see the Cabinet Office website) but they are not regular civil servants. Their avowedly political roles give them freedoms denied to normal civil servants, and they are best described as Whitehall 'irregulars'. The influx of special advisors led to tensions and strains between the government and some elements of the civil service (Draper, 1997: 118–19), largely due to the fact that their functions seemed to overlap significantly with those of civil service information officers. As a consequence, seven civil servants (including the senior information officer in the Treasury) left their posts within weeks of the general election. By June 1998 twenty-five Heads or Deputy Heads of Information had been replaced and by August 1999 only two of the Whitehall Directors of Communications who were in post when Labour came to power still remained (Select Committee on Public Administration, 1998; Oborne, 1999: 216).

An even more high-profile departure was that of Sir Terry Burns, Permanent Secretary at the Treasury, in the summer of 1998, following reports about his marginalisation and the increasing weight being given to the advice of Treasury special advisors led by Ed Balls. A well-informed source noted that relationships between Treasury ministers and advisors on the one hand, and civil servants on the other, improved markedly after the arrival of Sir Andrew Turnbull as Permanent Secretary (Hennessy, 1999: 12). Nonetheless, there could be no masking the strains between the civil service and the special advisors. The most graphic illustration of the tensions emerged within the Department of Transport, Local Government and the Regions. In September 2001, the Secretary of State, Stephen Byers, came under pressure to dismiss his special advisor, Jo Moore, when it became known that she had advised 'burying' some bad news by issuing press releases in the immediate wake of the 11 September terrorist attacks. Although Byers resisted this pressure, Moore was obliged to make a public apology for her behaviour. During the following months, further details of the poor working relationship between Moore and the department's career officials came to light. Finally, in February 2002, the tensions came to the surface in dramatic fashion when further allegations against Byers's special advisor were leaked, resulting in an announcement that both Moore and Martin Sixsmith, the department's Communications Director (although a recent recruit to the civil service, he was a 'permanent' official rather than a special advisor) were resigning. Sixsmith later challenged the official version of events, and denied that he had resigned. As a result, the Permanent Secretary of the department, Richard Mottram, was obliged to issue an extraordinary public statement setting out a rather sorry tale of infighting between Moore and the civil servants (see Ward, 2002). The key issues and debates surrounding the current use of special advisors, and their relationships with ministers and civil servants, will be pursued in the next section.

Summary

- In power, New Labour has rolled on the civil service reform agenda it inherited from the Conservatives, while refining, relaunching and refocusing key features of the programme.
- The Blair government has continued to emphasise the need for developments and modernisation in the civil service roles of organisational management and policy implementation and delivery.
- The entire *Modernising Government* agenda is geared to meet this requirement for ongoing improvements in the performance of civil servants.
- At the same time, the civil service and ministerial roles in policy advice and policy leadership have been impinged upon by the increased numbers and prominence of special policy advisors.

Debate

Any observer is bound to be struck by the relative lack of debate and dispute between the political parties on many of the central issues relating to the civil service and ministers. Neither, with the notable exception of ministerial 'sleaze', are these matters which seem to resonate significantly with the electorate. A consensus has emerged on the core civil service issues. This was largely formed during the extended period of Conservative government after 1979, when the policy of one party was distinctly proactive, took the policies of the other parties along in its wake, and played a central role in shifting state policy, public opinion and the parameters of political debate. By the time of the 1997 general election, none of the parties devoted space in their manifestos to civil service issues (with the exception of a small section in the Conservative Manifesto devoted to the Citizen's Charter), or indeed to the relationships between ministers and civil servants.

This was hardly surprising. As noted above, the Labour Party's attitude towards Next Steps was always broadly supportive. Criticisms, when they came, tended to focus on the *causes célèbres* associated with the Prison Service Agency and the Child Support Agency, but while the opposition attacked on the issues of ministerial conduct or lack of accountability, the general principles and impact of Next Steps were praised. While in opposition, Tony Blair's senior policy advisors on the civil service freely admitted that executive agencies '. . . have improved the delivery of government services through better management and delegation' (Mandelson and

Liddle, 1996: 251). We have seen that even in the spheres where Labour initially opposed the approach taken by the Conservative government, such as market testing, the Citizen's Charter and the Private Finance Initiative, the party's stance gradually changed, to the point where the Blair government placed the emphasis on 'relaunching' and 'refocusing' these initiatives.

None of this should be taken to imply that there are no debates on any of the matters we have examined. Analysts and commentators dispute the overall impact and implications of civil service reform. For some, the changes in civil service structures, management and service delivery mechanisms have failed to alter the fundamental character of an institution which still bears the imprint of Northcote and Trevelyan. John Garrett, erstwhile management consultant and former Labour spokesman on the civil service, remains sceptical about his party's attempts at reform. This stems from his belief that the modernisers have failed to wrest the top Whitehall posts away from traditionalists:

> New Labour's white paper promises 'joined-up government', 'joined-up policy-making', 'joined-up working' and 'joined-up public service delivery'. It proposes to open up the 'senior' Civil Service of 3,000 top jobs to women, ethnic minorities and people with disabilities. But, crucially, it intends to keep a fast-stream programme for generalist mandarins headed for the top jobs. Sir Humphrey has secured the future for his clones.
>
> (Garrett, 1999: 15)

Other observers dispute this perspective, and argue that the general impact of change has been very significant. Some believe that the overall effect has been negative. This interpretation of events sees the Next Steps programme, market testing and associated developments as an effective 'Balkanisation' of the civil service. It is argued that breaking the service up into increasingly independent components inevitably dilutes the cohesiveness, character and even the ethical base of civil service work (for a cogent exposition of this view, see Chapman, 1997). It might be argued that the additional long-term impact of devolution on the concept of a unified British civil service could create fresh tensions which will have to be managed properly if cohesiveness is to be retained (see Pyper, 1999).

However, other analysts adopt a more relaxed perspective. Hennessy (1993) and Butler (1993), for example, see the modern reforms in the context of an evolutionary tradition, within which the civil service has always been prepared to adapt to change. To some extent this is borne out by the approach of the Head of the Civil Service, Sir Richard Wilson. Although in many respects a traditionalist, Wilson has been keen to embrace change, albeit while emphasising that this should not be to the detriment of 'our core values' (Wilson, 1999).

More overt party and public debates have developed around some of the issues relating to the policy advice and leadership roles of civil servants and ministers. Although numerous illustrations of this could be cited, the Scott Inquiry and subsequent report into the 'arms for Iraq' affair (Bogdanor, 1996; Norton-Taylor et al., 1996; Adams and Pyper, 1997) was symbolic. This raised serious questions and initiated debates about the apparent cynicism shown by senior officials in their dealings with Parliament, and the extent to which they had colluded with ministers to mislead MPs. The opposition parties linked the behaviour of senior civil servants in this affair to the negative impact of an extended period of Conservative government upon the civil service as a whole. For academic observers, blatant politicisation was seen to have been less of a problem than the creation of a particular, unquestioning 'mind-set' which limited policy advice options and led officials to tell ministers what they wanted to hear rather than what they needed to know.

In some senses, these debates have become even more acute, albeit with a different focus, under the Blair government. The influx of special policy advisors created ripples of controversy. At one point, the level of concern was such that the Civil Service First Commissioner (who oversees the appointments system) asked the Prime Minister to curtail political appointments. An internal inquiry into the effect of the 'spin doctors' on the Government Information and Communication Service was set up under Cabinet Office official Sir Robin Mountfield. His implicit conclusion was that the civil service had much to learn from Labour's media relations system and as a result of his report a new Strategic Communications Unit containing a mixture of career officials and party appointees was set up in Downing Street (Oborne, 1999: 217–18).

Debates were further fuelled by an investigation by the House of Commons Select Committee on Public Administration (1998), part of which focused on the behaviour of Alastair Campbell, the Prime Minister's Official Spokesman and effective chief of the spin doctors. Campbell, together with the Number 10 Chief of Staff Jonathan Powell, has been allowed (following a special Order in Council) to combine the status of civil servant and special policy advisor, thus straddling the political/official divide (Oborne, 1999: 151). Campbell's role, and that of the spin doctors more generally, was said to undermine the civil service and, indeed, even in some instances to limit the powers of ministers. The Select Committee took a particular interest in the fact that Campbell had ordered the Social Security ministers to clear all of their press communications with him in advance (for more on this, see Oborne, 1999: 156–7). Instances of aggressive and negative briefings by some ministerial spin doctors against other ministers were also examined. The context of all of this became clear during the open disputes which were taking place between the spin doctors of Gordon Brown, Peter Mandelson and Tony Blair, and again during the Byers/Moore affair in the Department of Transport, Local Government and the Regions, when open warfare seemed to have broken out between a spin doctor and the civil service.

The arguments that all-powerful special advisors serve to politicise the civil service and even relegate democratically-elected politicians to the margins have to be placed in context. 'Politicisation' of the civil service is a recurring theme in the modern civil service. It is customary for opposition parties to accuse the party in government of abusing the traditional neutrality of the civil service. Counter-arguments tend to be made by those in charge of the civil service at any given time (for current examples, see Box 15.5). It can be argued further than special political advisors might actually insulate the civil service from politicisation since these appointees are explicitly not civil servants (Campbell's position admittedly blurs this distinction) and they will return to the outside world at some point.

Box 15.5 Policy wonks, spin doctors, ministers and mandarins – some views

What the mandarinate got wrong about the transition [from Major to Blair] was the degree to which they [Labour ministers] would carry on as they had in opposition. Usually people put that behind them when they get the car and the red box. Not this lot. They have brought their own people with them and they still work through their familiars.

(anonymous source, quoted by Peter Hennessy, 1999)

In the Blair government the spin doctor counts for more, much more, than the policy boss.

(Peter Oborne, 1999)

I took the view that it was not reasonable to ask people who had worked closely with some advisers, on whom they relied to a considerable extent reasonably and rightly, to have the support completely removed from them when they came to office. I am also comforted by the knowledge that the odds are stacked in favour of the civil service.

(Sir Robin Butler, former Head of the Civil Service, in evidence to the Select Committee on Public Administration, 1998)

I do not think the senior civil service of 3,700 people is in danger of being swamped by 70 special advisors.

(Sir Richard Wilson, Head of the Civil Service, quoted by Steve Richards, 2000)

The job of Cabinet ministers in Tony Blair's government is to do what they are told by Campbell, Miliband and one or two others at the heart of government.... The fact that so much power is concentrated in the hands of a clique of unelected officials causes unease with many MPs and ministers. But that is one of the simple things which New Labour is all about: exercising power from the centre.

(Peter Oborne, 1999)

Recent events have made it increasingly clear that the time has come to limit the number of special advisers, and to define with unmistakable clarity the duties and responsibilities that are proper to special advisers and those which are not, and their proper relationship with ministers and with civil servants. I have never been in favour of a Civil Service Act or of statute legislation to define and limit the responsibilities of special advisers. ... But I recognise that there are many people who think that codes of conduct are no longer sufficient.

(Lord Armstrong, former Head of the Civil Service, 2002)

A compromise position was occupied by Lord Neill and his Committee on Standards in Public Life when it reported in January 2000. Keen to preserve the traditional civil service roles in policy advice, and protect ministers against vindictive briefings by the spin doctors of rivals within a government, Neill recommended that limits (set out in a code of conduct) should be placed on both special advisors and policy taskforces. He concluded that the civil service had not been politicised, but argued that it was time to 'take stock' of a developing situation (Neill, 2000). The Byers/Moore affair forced the issue even further, and restarted the debate about the need for a Civil Service Act to clarify the respective roles and responsibilities of permanent officials and special advisors.

Summary

- While there has been a relative dearth of debate between the political parties about certain elements of this topic, expert analysts and observers have disputed the implications and impact of civil service reform.
- Party political (and to some extent public) debate has focused on the issue of politicisation.
- This has been brought to the fore in the period since 1997 due to the Labour government's wholesale utilisation of political advisors, although there is considerable room for debate about the precise impact of this development.

Conclusion

If we have to identify a single major theme which has run like a thread through this chapter it must be 'modernisation'. The working relationships, modes of operation and roles of ministers, civil servants and advisors have shifted and changed to greater or lesser degrees over recent years. As ever in the context of United Kingdom governance, attempts are made to strike a reasonable balance between adherence to tradition and continuity of approach on the one hand, and giving the agents of change and modernisation their opportunities on the other. No part of the UK polity has been left untouched by the impact of membership of the European Union and, as we noted, ministers and civil servants have been at the forefront of the policy interface with the EU. Social trends have also had an impact on this topic, in the sense that the civil service has had to face up to the need for a fairer and more representative ethnic and gender balance. Although these matters are being addressed, one might argue that this is happening quite belatedly and perhaps only partially. On the ministerial front, however, it should be noted that while the 'progressive' Blair administration contains a greater number of female Cabinet ministers than any previous government, the overall representation of women and people from ethnic minority backgrounds in ministerial ranks is not overwhelmingly impressive.

Chronology

1854   Northcote–Trevelyan Report on the civil service.
1968   Fulton Report on the civil service.
1974   The Labour government begins a major experiment with special advisors.
1976   Prime Minister James Callaghan limits the scope and use of special advisors.
1979   Prime Minister Thatcher expands the use of external think tanks but limits ministerial use of special advisors.

1988 Next Steps Report and launch of executive agencies.
1991 Citizen's Charter is launched by the Major government.
       Competing for Quality white paper launches market testing.
1992 The Private Finance Initiative is launched by the Major government.
1997 The Blair government relaunches the Private Finance Initiative.
       Significant use of special advisors ('policy wonks' and 'spin doctors') by New
       Labour ministers.
       Mountfield Report on Government Information and Communication Service.
1998 Sir Richard Wilson succeeds Sir Robin Butler as Cabinet Secretary and Head of
       the Civil Service.
       The Public Administration Select Committee Report on Government Information
       and Communication Service.
       Market testing is 'refocused' as *Better Quality Services*.
       The Citizen's Charter is relaunched as *Service First*.
1999 *Modernising Government* white paper is published.
2000 The Neill Committee on Standards in Public Life urges limits on the use of
       special advisors and policy taskforces.
2001 Resignation of special advisor Jo Moore sparks fresh debate about the
       relationship between civil servants, ministers and advisors.

Discussion Questions

1. Identify and comment upon two issues of debate relating to the work of UK
   civil servants in the early twenty-first century.
2. What have been the major developments in relations between ministers, civil
   servants and special advisors in the Blair government?
3. To what extent have the theories and concepts associated with the New Public
   Management informed civil service reform in the UK?

References

Adams, Juliet and Pyper, Robert (1997) 'Whatever happened to the Scott Report?', *Talking Politics*, Vol. 7, No. 2.
Armstrong, Robert (2002) 'Daylight jobbery', *The Spectator*, 2 March.
Benn, Tony (1982) *Arguments for Democracy*, London: Penguin.
Benn, Tony (1990) *Against the Tide. Diaries 1973–76*, London: Arrow Books.
Blackstone, Tessa and Plowden, William (1990) *Inside the Think Tank. Advising the Cabinet 1971–1983*, London: Mandarin.
Bogdanor, Vernon (1996) 'The Scott Report', *Public Administration*, Vol. 74, No. 4.
Butler, Sir Robin (1993) 'The evolution of the civil service – a progress report', *Public Administration*, Vol. 71, No. 3.
Butler, Sir Robin (1997) 'The changing civil service', unpublished paper, *Future Whitehall* Conference, Church House, London, 24 September.
Cabinet Office (1998) *Government's Response to the Consultation on the Future of the Citizen's Charter Programme*, London: Cabinet Office.

Chapman, R.A. (1997) 'The end of the civil service', in P. Barberis (ed.) *The Civil Service in an Era of Change*, Aldershot: Dartmouth.

Chapman, R.A. (1999) 'The importance of "modernising government"', *Teaching Public Administration*, Vol. 19, No. 1.

Denham, Andrew and Garnett, Mark (1998) *British Think Tanks and the Climate of Opinion*, London: UCL Press.

Downs, Anthony (1957) *An Economic Theory of Democracy*, London: Harper & Row.

Downs, Anthony (1967) *Inside Bureaucracy*, London: Little, Brown and Co.

Draper, Derek (1997) *Blair's Hundred Days*, London: faber & faber.

Elcock, Howard (1991) *Change and Decay? Public Administration in the 1990s*, London: Longman.

Flynn, Norman (1997) *Public Sector Management* (third edition), Hemel Hempstead: Prentice Hall/Harvester Wheatsheaf.

Foster, Christopher D. and Plowden, Francis J. (1996) *The State Under Stress*, Buckingham: Open University Press.

Garrett, John (1999) 'Not in front of the servants', *New Statesman*, 4 October.

Gray, Andrew and Jenkins, William I. (1985) *Administrative Politics in British Government*, Hemel Hempstead: Harvester Wheatsheaf.

Greer, Patricia (1994) *Transforming Central Government. The Next Steps Initiative*, Buckingham: Open University Press.

Hennessy, Peter (1993) 'Questions of ethics for government', *FDA News*, Vol. 13, No. 1.

Hennessy, Peter (1999) *The Blair Centre: A Question of Command and Control?*, London: Public Management Foundation.

House of Commons (1964) *HC Debates*, 5th Series, Vol. 702, Session 1964–65.

House of Commons (1979) *HC Debates*, 5th Series, Vol. 967, Session 1979–80.

Hughes, Owen E. (1998) *Public Management and Administration* (second edition), Basingstoke: Macmillan.

Kemp, Sir Peter (1999) 'Please stop fiddling the books', *New Statesman*, 18 October.

Lawton, Alan and Rose, Aidan (1991) *Organisation and Management in the Public Sector*, London: Pitman.

Mandelson, Peter and Liddle, Roger (1996) *The Blair Revolution. Can New Labour Deliver?*, London: faber & faber.

Metcalf, Les and Richards, Sue (1990) *Improving Public Management*, Buckingham: Open University Press.

Miliband, Ralph (1969) *The State in Capitalist Society*, London: Quartet.

Neill, Lord (2000) *Reinforcing Standards Report from the Committee on Standards in Public Life*, London: HMSO.

Neville-Jones, Pauline (1983) 'The continental *cabinet* system: the effects of transposing it to the United Kingdom', *The Political Quarterly*, Vol. 54, No. 3, July–September.

Niskanen, W.A. (1973) *Bureaucracy: Servant or Master?*, London: Institute of Economic Affairs.

Norton-Taylor, Richard, Lloyd, Mark, Cook, Stephen (1996) *Knee Deep in Dishonour: The Scott Report and its Aftermath*, London: Victor Gollancz.

Oborne, Peter (1999) *Alastair Campbell, New Labour and the Rise of the Media Class*, London: Aurum Press.

Pyper, Robert (1993) 'When they have to go . . . why ministers resign', *Talking Politics*, Vol. 5, No. 2 (winter).

Pyper, Robert (1994) 'Individual ministerial responsibility: dissecting the doctrine', *Politics Review*, Vol. 4, No. 1 (September).

Pyper, Robert (1995) *The British Civil Service*, Hemel Hempstead: Prentice Hall/Harvester Wheatsheaf.

Pyper, Robert (1996) 'The parameters of accountability', in R. Pyper (ed.) *Aspects of Accountability in the British System of Government*, Eastham: Tudor.

Pyper, Robert (1999) 'The civil service: a neglected dimension of devolution', *Public Money and Management*, Vol. 19, No. 2.

Rhodes, R.A.W. (1997) *Understanding Governance: Policy Networks, Governance, Reflexivity and Accountability*, Milton Keynes: Open University Press.

Richards, Steve (2000) 'The special advisers are here to stay', *New Statesman*, 17 January.

Select Committee on Public Administration (1998) *Sixth Report: The Government Information and Communication Service*, HC 770, Session 1997–98.

Smith, Martin J. (1999) *The Core Executive in Britain*, Basingstoke: Macmillan.

Ward, Lucy (2002) 'Press chief accused over resignation', *The Guardian*, 26 February.

Wilson, Sir Richard (1999) 'The civil service in the new millennium', unpublished lecture, May.

Woodhouse, Diana (1993) 'When do ministers resign?', *Parliamentary Affairs*, Vol. 46, No. 3 (July).

Woodhouse, Diana (1994) *Ministers and Parliament: Accountability in Theory and Practice*, Oxford: Oxford University Press.

Woodhouse, Diana (1997) 'Ministerial responsibility: something old, something new?', *Public Law* (summer).

Young, Hugo (1976) 'How Whitehall's mandarins tamed Labour's 38 special advisers', *The Sunday Times*, 19 September.

Further reading

Students seeking to explore the topic of ministers, civil servants and advisors in more detail have at their disposal a wide range of sources. The list of references contains the key works in this field. Simon James (1999) *British Cabinet Government* (second edition, London: Routledge) offers a sound outline of the work of government ministers, Robert Pyper (1995) *The British Civil Service* (Hemel Hempstead: Prentice Hall/Harvester Wheatsheaf) covers the developing reforms in the civil service and Nicholas Jones (1999) *Sultans of Spin* (London: Victor Gollancz) and Peter Oborne (1999) *Alistair Campbell, New Labour and the Rise of the Media Class* (London: Aurum Press) provide invaluable insights into the world of special advisors within the Blair government.

When seeking to understand a topic which is subject to continuous change, it is important to look beyond books. The following journals and periodicals provide regular articles and features on the themes discussed in this chapter: *New Statesman, Parliamentary Affairs, Public Money and Management, Public Policy and Administration, Politics Review* and *Talking Politics*.

Keeping up to date with developments in central government has become considerably more straightforward since the development of the Internet. The following websites merit regular visits:

The Cabinet Office: http://www.cabinet-office.gov.uk
Downing Street: http://www.number-10.gov.uk
The Government Information Service: http://www.open.gov.uk

New Local Governance

David Wilson

CHAPTER SIXTEEN

Introduction

During the last two decades elected local government in Britain has had a rough passage. On the one hand, it has seen a loss of powers and responsibilities and on the other, it has seen the rise of a range of powerful unelected local quangos. Local authorities now 'share the turf' with a wide variety of agencies (e.g. health authorities, police authorities, primary care groups, action zones, partnerships), none of which is directly elected. Elected local government is now but one part of a complex mosaic of organisations concerned with community governance. Stoker provides a useful summary of the situation:

> What happened to British local government during the period of Conservative government from 1979 to 1997 was in many respects a brutal illustration of power politics. The funding system was reformed to provide central government with a considerable (and probably unprecedented) level of control over spending. Various functions and responsibilities were stripped away from local authorities or organised in a way that obliged local authorities to work in partnership with other public and private agencies in the carrying out of the functions.
>
> (Stoker, 1999: 1)

There has been a shift from local government to local governance with local authorities now sharing more than ever before the provision of services. Indeed, the very term 'local government' has become somewhat passé; 'local governance' is currently in vogue. This recognises elected local authorities as but one element of community governance alongside the increased involvement of quangos, voluntary sector agencies and private sector organisations. Indeed, quangos are responsible for over £40 billion of public funds. As Loughlin observes, 'Local councils have been stripped of governmental responsibility for certain services which continue to be public services but which are now provided by agencies which are funded directly from the centre' (Loughlin, 1996: 56). The shift from government to governance is at the heart of this chapter.

Background

It is not possible to understand the present system of local governance properly without some appreciation of how it came about. It is a system that has evolved gradually, in a piecemeal manner, over the centuries. There is no codified constitutional document setting out the rights and responsibilities of local authorities and their relationship with the centre. The Municipal Corporations Act 1835 can be seen as the foundation of present-day local government. The powers of the seventy-eight multi-purpose elected local authorities which this Act created were limited, but the principle of elected local self-government had been established. See the Chronology (p. 278), which begins with this piece of legislation, for an outline of the development of local government in England and Wales.

Despite the dilution of local authority service provision through the advent of alternative providers, Midwinter reminds us of the continuing importance of service provision: 'Despite the welter of rhetoric, the image of radical reform, the language of the new public management, the glitz of marketing and public relations, the central role of a local authority remains – municipal provision of services' (Midwinter, 1995: 131). Wilson and Game (1998: ch. 6) show the continued importance of service delivery by elected local authorities despite responsibility for certain services being removed. Elected local government is still big business. Classifications abound; Box 16.1 provides one possible picture of activities.

While local authorities still have a substantial role in service delivery at the local level almost all the services mentioned in Box 16.1 have undergone significant transformation during the past few years. Sometimes the council's role is being shared with a range of other providers, but while partnership and collaboration are becoming increasingly common, elected local authorities still remain big players in the world of community governance. Councils in the UK spend some £80 billion each year, around a quarter of all public expenditure;

Box 16.1 Elected local authorities – provision of services

1. **Need services**: For example, education, personal social services, housing benefit.

2. **Protective services**: For example, fire and rescue, and, most obviously, the police until the creation of the new independent police authorities in April 1995.

3. **Amenity services**: For example, highways, street cleaning, planning, parks and open spaces, environmental health, refuse disposal, consumer protection, economic development.

4. **Facility services**: For example, housing, libraries, museums and art galleries, recreational centres, refuse collection, cemeteries and crematoria.

Source: Adapted from Wilson and Game (1998)

this is more than a 'bit' part, even if attrition rather than growth has become the watchword.

Alongside a diminution in service delivery, local authorities have been subject to significant structural changes, the thrust of which has been the creation of fewer, larger authorities. In the early 1970s there were 1,855 principal local authorities in Britain. By the mid-1970s this was cut back to 521. Today there are 441. Compared with much of Europe, Britain now has significantly bigger authorities and far more inhabitants per elected member, as Table 16.1 indicates. The rationale for this strategy has invariably been economic in origin and has focused upon economies of scale. From the standpoint of ordinary citizens, however, this is frequently said to represent a 'democratic deficit' in that larger authorities and fewer councillors can result in increased remoteness from local decision-making.

Scotland currently has thirty-two all-purpose unitary authorities and Wales twenty-two. The position in England is much more complex, comprising a combination of two-tier and unitary authorities, as indicated in Figure 16.1.

Table 16.1 Britain's large-scale local government

	Inhabitants per elected member	Average population per council
France	116	1,580
Iceland	194	1,330
Germany	250	4,925
Italy	397	7,130
Norway	515	9,000
Spain	597	4,930
Sweden	667	30,040
Belgium	783	16,960
Denmark	1,084	18,760
Portugal	1,125	32,300
UK	2,605	118,400

Source: Council of Europe, *Local and Regional Authorities in Europe*, No. 56 (1996)

Summary

- Contemporary local governance is the product of history; it has evolved gradually.
- Local authorities are increasingly 'sharing the turf' with other non-elected agencies in service delivery.
- While the functional role of elected local authorities has been eroded, it still remains big business.
- Numbers of elected local authorities have declined dramatically since the early 1970s; they have become larger and potentially more remote from ordinary citizens.

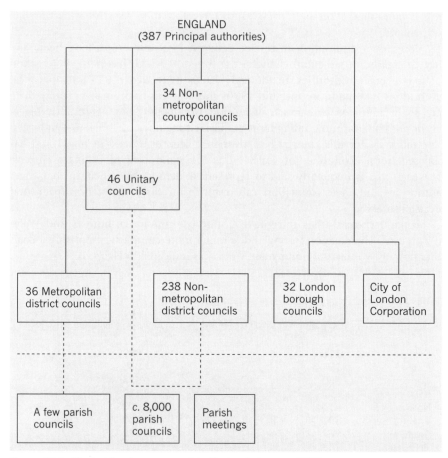

Figure 16.1 Elected local government in England, January 2000

Theoretical Considerations

There is no normative general theory from which we can deduce what local governance ought to be. Debate has focused around concepts such as account-ability, responsiveness, representativeness, participation and pluralism. Much of the thinking about theories of local government is rooted in the nineteenth century with John Stuart Mill, in his *Considerations on Representative Government* (1861), presenting a series of arguments in favour of elected local government. Mill argued that local political institutions are an essential element of a democratic society because they widen the opportunity to participate and provide the means of educating citizens in the practice of politics. He also argued that more efficient and effective service provision was likely because services will be closer to the people and hence more user-sensitive. The five concepts cited above will now be discussed.

Accountability of decision-makers to those who elect them is widely perceived as a lynch-pin of local democracy. In the world of local governance, direct account-ability to the electorate in some policy sectors (e.g. health) is missing, but, arguably, other forms of accountability are not. The picture of accountability painted by advocates of elected local government often exaggerates the virtues of that particular form of government. Most notably it underplays the poor turnouts in local elec-tions in the last few years. Average turnouts of 29% in 1998, 32% in 1999 and barely 30% in 2000 do little to strengthen the case of those who call for elected local government to extend its functions and pull back some of those services handed over to non-elected bodies. Table 16.2 provides information on declining turnout levels in six metropolitan boroughs during the years 1994–98. In an attempt to try to improve turnout the government passed a Representation of the People Act in early 2000 which allowed councils to experiment with new electoral arrangements such as voting on different days and electronic voting. The govern-ment permitted 32 councils to pilot new schemes in the May 2000 local elections but of the experiments only blanket postal voting yielded significant results. For example, Gateshead Metropolitan Borough Council's (MBC's) all-postal voting in two wards saw turnout rise from 30% to 63% in one and 19% to 46% in the other.

Turnout at local elections in Britain compares unfavourably with most other European countries. This means that accountability via the ballot box has become increasingly tenuous. In any event, some would argue that local elections are simply national elections writ small – essentially judgements on the performance of national governments rather than individual local authorities. As Jim Bulpitt (1993) has shown, too idealistic a model of accountability via multi-functional elected local authorities can all too easily emerge, particularly given the fragmenta-tion of service delivery at local level.

Ken Young (1994) has argued that the actual activities, priorities and motiva-tions of non-elected bodies such as Technical Enterprise Councils (TECs), health trusts, etc. need to be carefully examined before dismissing them (simply because they are not directly elected) as inherently inferior to, or less desirable than, elected local government. For example, the 'accountability' associated with elected local government needs to be set against the 'accountability' associated with the publication of accounts or glossy annual reports, circulated with local newspapers, which characterise parts of the 'quango' sector. For Beetham, the crucial point is that 'wherever policy decisions are taken affecting the use and distribution of

Table 16.2 Metropolitan boroughs: turnout levels

	1994	1996	1998
Barnsley	39.0	23.3	20.3
Knowsley	32.8	23.4	18.5
Rotherham	37.0	23.6	20.8
Salford	31.9	24.3	18.9
Sunderland	30.5	23.0	17.8
Wigan	30.4	25.0	17.4

Source: C. Rallings and M. Thrasher, *Local Election Handbooks* for 1994, 1996, 1998

public resources, there should be a transparent and effective form of accountability to the relevant public. No system of political accountability is perfect. But it is only those with an interest in monopolising executive control at the centre who can be satisfied with arrangements as imperfect as those we currently have' (Beetham, 1996: 42). As King observes, 'the lines of accountability between voters and quangos are murky' (1996: 216); unfortunately, the representative system is hardly a role model of accountability in action.

Like accountability, *responsiveness* is a strand of theory frequently applied to local government. Being on the spot, councils are able, so the argument goes, to identify faster and better than central government the most appropriate response to any local situation. Sharpe terms this ability the 'knowledge value' of local government:

> Central government is not equipped to grasp the inimitable conditions of each locality. Local government is preferable precisely because locally elected institutions employing their own specialist staff are better placed to understand and interpret both the conditions and the needs of local communities.
>
> (Sharpe 1970: 155)

Diverse solutions also provide scope for local innovation and experimentation, and for different models of good practice. A centralised system of administration would be unlikely to foster such values. The increased use by local authorities in recent years of opinion polls, referendums, customer satisfaction surveys and the like has enhanced this responsiveness dimension.

While elected councillors are our *representatives*, they are certainly not representative of the population as a whole. A census by the Local Government Management Board (1998) showed that 76% of councillors in England and Wales were male and that almost 97% were white; the average age was 56. A later survey published in the *Municipal Year Book 2000* showed a ratio of 2:8 male councillors to every one female among the 17,832 councillors from the 388 councils in the UK who responded. The range varied from just 12% of the councillors in Northern Ireland's 26 districts being women, to a peak of 28% of councillors in the 46 English unitaries and 238 English districts. Table 16.3 presents a profile of councillors, emphasising the lack of social representativeness among our elected representatives.

Aggregate data such as those presented in Table 16.3 provide useful numerical measures about the extent to which certain social groups are over- or under-represented in the population of councillors. They can, however, prompt misleading generalisations by obscuring significant contrasts between different parts of the country. For example, the number of ethnic minority councillors in both Leicester and Birmingham approximates to their position in the overall population of the two cities. There is also a danger in seeing representative government purely in terms of producing a socio-economic cross-section or statistical reflection of the electorate, rather than the representation of ideas and ideals. The latter as well as the former need to be incorporated into discussions about the representative nature of local governance.

Representative democracy, the Labour government argues, needs to be supplemented by participatory democracy. *Participation* is a theoretical strand frequently

Table 16.3 Councillor profiles

	England	Wales
Average age	55.4	57.8
Male	72.1%	79.6%
Female	27.8%	20.4%

	England and Wales
Retired	32.9%
Employed full time	29.6%
Employed part time	8.2%
Self-employed	15.2%
Not working	11.9%
White	96.9%
Indian	0.7%
Black Caribbean	0.5%
Pakistani	0.5%
Other	2.4%

Source: Local Government Management Board (1998)

espoused by advocates of local democracy; it has received greater emphasis under Labour, largely because of the perceived deficiencies of representative democracy. It is important to remember, however, that more participation is not the same thing as more democracy.

The mode of participation most assiduously developed by Conservative administrations was in relation to service use: in terms both of assessing service quality (through satisfaction surveys and charter initiatives) and contributing to service management (e.g. through more powerful school-governing bodies and forms of tenant management). The customer was sovereign. The empowerment of customers was also seen as a means of disciplining self-interested politicians.

While the current Labour government sees the value of public participation in relation to service quality, enhanced participation is also part of an explicitly political agenda, incorporating broader issues of democratic renewal. Given the intermittent nature of local elections, public involvement is seen as crucial to the health of local democracy. A raft of new methods of consultation have emerged, such as citizens' juries, citizens' panels, visioning exercises, to work alongside more traditional mechanisms, such as public meetings. Participatory schemes abound but in themselves, no matter how innovatory they may appear, they do not necessarily result in policy impact. Such schemes guarantee nothing; indeed, they might even be counter-productive in raising expectations among participants that are then not met.

Participation also has an important educative role, notably its contribution to citizen education. Beetham (1996) reminds us, however, that the term 'participation' is far too vague a concept to serve as an equivalent for 'democracy' in the absence of any specification of participation in what form, by whom, or to what effect. He recalls that the most 'participatory' political regimes of the twentieth century 'were communist systems, so-called people's democracies; yet that participation delivered little popular control over the personnel or policies of government' (Beetham, 1996: 33). Likewise, Parry and Moyser emphasise:

> A participatory democrat will not look merely to maximising participation but to equalising it. Participation and democracy are inextricably and conceptually linked but the relationship is far more complex than might be implied by a simple equation between greater participation and greater democracy.
>
> (Parry and Moyser, 1990: 169)

It is ironic that while the Labour government is keen that councils promote public participation initiatives, the same government is imposing local executive leadership and increasing the scope of central government inspectorates. Linked to the massive financial powers still retained by the centre, enhanced public participation needs to be seen in context.

Perhaps the most frequently cited theoretical justification for local government is *pluralism*. As the Widdicombe Report put it: 'The case for pluralism is that power should not be concentrated in one organisation of state, but should be dispersed, thereby providing political checks and balances, and a restraint on arbitrary government and absolutism' (Widdicombe, 1986: 48). Ten years earlier, another government report, the Layfield Committee (1976) had seen local government's role in almost identical terms:

> By providing a large number of points where decisions are taken by people of different political persuasion . . . it acts as a counterweight to the uniformity inherent in government decisions. It spreads political power.
>
> (Layfield Committee, 1976: 53)

Yet while local government allows some diffusion of power, it always needs to be remembered that local institutions are established and can be abolished by the centre – hence any diffusion of power is relative. Again, as Stoker emphasises, smaller communities do not necessarily behave in a more democratic way: 'They can be stifling or disabling in reinforcing relationships of subordination and narrow parochialism' (Stoker, 1996: 24). Somehow, local choice needs to be reconciled with concerns about equal treatment for all. In this context theoretical perspectives are helpful, but they can only provide a framework for politicians and practitioners to deliver the goods.

Summary

- There is no theory of local government in the sense of a normative general theory from which we can deduce what local government ought to be.
- Transparent and effective forms of *accountability* should be central to local governance.
- *Responsiveness* to the public has assumed greater importance in recent years.
- Local governance needs to address issues of *representativeness* given existing problems about social mix.

- *Participation* schemes abound at local level but it must be emphasised that more participation is not the same thing as more democracy.
- *Pluralism* needs to be set in the context of central government power.
- A major challenge for government is to square local choice with the need for equality of provision.

Update

As we have seen, elected local authorities now 'share the turf' with a wide range of agencies, zones and partnerships, none of which is directly elected. 'Joined-up government' at the local level is a central theme of the Labour government. It is an integral part of the 'modernisation' process which is underway. In a nutshell, central government's agenda for local authorities is: modernise or perish. Tony Blair uses the language of 'rewards' for local authorities prepared to embrace the Labour government's new policy agenda, especially in the context of developing modern organisational structures and effecting more participatory democracy: 'where councils embrace this agenda of change and show that they can adapt to play a part in modernising their locality, then they will find their status and power enhanced'. At the same time he emphasised: 'If you are unwilling or unable to work to the modern agenda, then the government will have to look to other partners to take on your role' (Blair, 1998: 20, 22). This is the context within which contemporary local government is operating. Sticks and carrots are the order of the day.

Lowndes has encapsulated the prevailing tension between central government and local authorities:

> Local authorities feel they have only limited opportunities to change their ways of working without the loosening of central controls (particularly over finance). At the same time, central government argues that local authorities must 'earn' such increased autonomy through demonstrating their willingness and ability to work in new ways.
>
> (Lowndes, 1999: 116)

Given the partial demise of what was once near-monopolistic direct service provision, elected local government is increasingly being judged not solely by the services it delivers but by its ability to lead the social, economic and political development of their communities. Central to this role is the development of partnerships and networks.

'Joined-up government'

As we have seen, the once dominant position of local authorities as service providers has been challenged both by the rise of local quangos, zones, and the increased involvement of private sector organisations and voluntary bodies. The continued development of holistic, or joined-up, government was a central feature of the Labour government's white paper, *Modernising Government* (Cabinet Office,

1999). Partnerships between elected local government and both the private and voluntary sectors are here to stay. There is to be no return to local authorities being near-monopolistic service providers.

The advent of Employment Zones, Health Action Zones and Education Action Zones clearly demonstrated the new Labour government's commitment to working through a mixed economy of local provision. The establishment of an £800 million 'New Deal for Communities' programme for the regeneration of some of the country's poorest housing estates reflects the same thinking. Likewise, the 'Sure Start' project was established to support pre-school children and their families; again, the focus was on the socially disadvantaged and it involved co-operation between education, health and social service agencies. These and similar initiatives reflect the Labour government's desire to embrace collaboration between agencies as a way of joining up hitherto fragmented services in order to meet community needs more effectively.

The 1998 white paper, *Modern Local Government: In Touch with the People*, argued that 'effective local partnerships are fundamental to the success of councils' strategic role. It is essential that councils work with a wide range of agencies and organisations that operate locally' (DETR, 1998: 82). Partnerships, however, are not problem-free; they frequently bring difficulties of co-ordination and fragmentation. The problem, as Benyon and Edwards (1999: 166) point out in the context of local governance and crime control, is that resources are usually gained for specific projects with different time scales which frustrate co-ordination, thereby undermining the attainment of policy goals.

Partnerships frequently emerge as a result of legislation. For example, the Crime and Disorder Act 1998 placed a duty on district councils to liaise with the relevant county council and police authority to prepare a strategy in the three-year period from 1 April 1999. The Health Act 1999 introduced a new duty of partnership between health and local authorities and provides for greater flexibility in joint budgeting and services. It emphasises the need to work in partnership in commissioning and delivering care as well as at the strategic planning level. There are new powers, including primary care trusts and local authorities being able to transfer parts of their budgets to each other for expenditure on health-related issues. However, legislative frameworks are one thing; cultural change is quite another. In practice, partnerships and networks require a considerable investment of time and effort if they are to maximise their potential and deliver better-quality services.

Partnership, then, is seen by the Labour government as crucial to the successful delivery of quality services at a local level. Tony Blair made this very clear:

> The days of the all-purpose authority that planned and delivered everything are gone. They are finished. It is in partnership with others – public agencies, private companies, community groups and voluntary organisations – in which local government's future lies. Local authorities will deliver some services but their distinctive leadership role will be to weave and knit together the contribution of the various stakeholders.
>
> (Blair, 1998: 13)

Central–local relations

Soon after becoming Minister for Local Government, Hilary Armstrong articulated her vision of the new pattern of relationships with local authorities: 'It is vital we lose the skills of battle and find the skills of organisation and partnership' (Armstrong, 1997: 18). The major lesson of the Conservative years had been that change imposed across the board, without consultation, 'is prone to considerable implementation failure and the production of a range of unintended effects' (Stoker, 1999: 17). In November 1997 the government and local authorities signed a concordat setting out the terms of the working relationship between central and local government – a document which recognised the 'independent democratic legitimacy of local government'. Yet despite the spirit of reconciliation between central and local government, the following was included in the accompanying schedule:

> Where the Government considers that a local authority (or a local authority service) is falling below an acceptable standard it will work with the authority concerned to secure improvements. The Government reserves its powers under statute to intervene in cases of failure.
>
> (Lowndes, 1999: 134)

The retention of such regulatory powers by central government – especially the special improvement teams or 'hit squads' to address serious failings in education and social services standards – has caused much concern among local authorities. As Len Duvall, chair of the newly-formed Improvement and Development Agency, put it: 'death by inspection and hit squads lie in wait for authorities not up to scratch' (*Municipal Journal*, 30 July–5 August 1999). Indeed, the government has formed new inspectorates, for example a new Best Value Inspectorate (incorporating a Housing Inspectorate), established from 1 April 2000 under the auspices of the Audit Commission. This sits alongside established inspectorates such as the Benefit Fraud Inspectorate, HM Fire Services Inspectorate, HM Inspectorate of Constabulary, the Social Services Inspectorate and the Office for Standards in Education (OFSTED).

The new Best Value Inspectorate is designed to ensure that local authorities review their services in accordance with the legislation and have set 'challenging' and 'realistic' performance targets. Audit Commission Controller, Andrew Foster estimated that in the year starting April 2000 there would be around 1,000 best value inspections – a substantial addition to the already extensive inspection regime.

It is clear that the Labour government sees inspectorates as being of central importance in its quest for the continuous improvement of local services. In this context the potential for 'fall out' with individual local authorities is clear (e.g. Hackney London Borough Council over education in 1999 where, following an adverse OFSTED report in March, the Secretary of State maintained that two functions – school improvement and language support – were so far below standard that they should be contracted out). The government's commitment to further developing and co-ordinating the network of inspection agencies was emphasised in July 1999 when it established a co-ordinated Best Value Inspectorate Forum for

England, the composition of which is presented in Box 16.2. Inspectorates are an integral part of the government's modernisation agenda; the establishment of the Best Value Inspectorate, which has operated from April 2000, is but the latest variation on a theme.

Lowndes (1999) argues that the government's increasingly trenchant tone in demanding change is seen by many in local government to be at odds with the acclaimed spirit of partnership in central–local relations. The two levels of government have competing expectations and priorities. For central government, greater autonomy and increased powers will only follow:

> after local authorities have proved their commitment to change, particularly
> in terms of renewing relationships with local communities. For its part,
> local government wants the government to grant it greater autonomy and
> new powers as an expression of a shared commitment to the principle of
> local self-government.
>
> (Lowndes, 1999: 134)

In particular, local authorities will continue to look for some restoration of financial discretion. Despite the different agendas, local and central government are, as Lowndes observes, engaged together in building new institutions for governance – in work on best value, cross-cutting issues, democratic renewal and constitutional change – and it is out of this day-to-day interaction that greater trust can be rebuilt. Nevertheless, the 'modernise or perish' message so clearly articulated by the centre, plus the development and extension of inspectorates and the reluctance of the centre to devolve greater financial freedom to local authorities, means that tensions in central–local relations are unlikely to be dissipated quickly.

Box 16.2 Best Value Inspectorate Forum

- The Benefit Fraud Inspectorate
- HM Fire Services Inspectorate
- HM Inspectorate of Constabulary
- The Social Services Inspectorate
- The Office for Standards in Education (OFSTED)
- The Best Value Inspectorate (incorporating a Housing Inspectorate)

Summary

- 'Joined-up' or holistic government is a central plank of the Labour government's thinking at the local level. 'Zones' are but one part of the government's partnership strategy.
- Elected local authorities now increasingly work with a wide range of public, private and voluntary organisations in providing community services.
- The 'modernise or perish' message from the Labour government to local authorities is clear and unmistakable.

- Inspectorates have expanded and developed under New Labour.
- Tensions between central government departments and local authorities are far from being resolved, notably in the sphere of finance.

Debate

While the Blair government is keen that councils actively promote public participation, that same government is arguably encouraging more elitist local leadership and has retained extensive powers for itself at the centre, especially in the financial sphere. Significant policy initiatives have been discussed in the previous two sections of this chapter. Here the focus will be upon what is probably the most contentious area of all, namely the replacement of a traditional service-based committee system by new forms of executive government. New organisational patterns are, of course, shaped by ideologies and values. The Labour government's modernisation agenda has been particularly influential in this context.

The 1998 white paper, *Modern Local Government: In Touch with the People* came up with three models of executive leadership. These are presented in Box 16.3. They were also included in the Local Government Bill which was announced in the Queen's Speech in November 1999. The Local Government Association (LGA) welcomed the inclusion in the November 1999 bill of a power to promote the social, economic and environmental well-being of the local area. This was not in the draft bill published in March, and the change followed intense LGA lobbying. The power provides protection against *ultra vires*, encourages councils to provide community leadership and can also help cut down the maze of regulations restraining council actions.

The three models of executive leadership became part of the Local Government Act 2000, but in order to get the legislation through the House of Lords the government made a number of concessions, one of which was that small shire districts with a population of 85,000 or less were to be given a fourth option, namely a 're-vamped' committee system which could come into force *if* councils

---

Box 16.3 New models of political management

Option 1: *A directly elected mayor with a cabinet.* The mayor will be directly elected by the whole electorate and will appoint a cabinet drawn from councillors.

Option 2: *A cabinet with a leader.* The leader will be elected by the council, and the cabinet will be made up of councillors either appointed by the leader or elected by the council.

Option 3: *A directly elected mayor with a council manager.* The mayor will be directly elected by local people, with a full-time manager appointed by the council, to whom both strategic policy and day-to-day decision-making could be delegated.

Source: *Modern Local Government: In Touch with the People* (DETR, 1998)

could demonstrate that they had the backing of the local community. Hence some 86 councils (21% of local authorities) were free to begin consulting in autumn 2000 on whether or not they wanted to reject the three options presented in the 1998 white paper. Despite opposition (much of it from backbench councillors fearful of losing power to a small elite of senior councillors), the government has moved ahead on executive leadership, the first direct elections for mayor being held for the new Greater London Authority (GLA) on 4 May 2000. Ken Livingstone, standing as an independent after the Labour Party had selected Frank Dobson as its candidate, was elected. The 25-member Greater London Assembly was elected at the same time with Conservatives and Labour each winning nine seats, the Liberal Democrats four and the Greens three, so that no party had over-all control. Turnout for the mayoral elections (34%) was very disappointing; time will tell how many other British cities follow suit.

Debate has been intense about the advantages and disadvantages of executive leadership at local level. The 1998 white paper argued that the existing committee system was inefficient and opaque:

> It results in councillors spending too many hours on fruitless meetings. . . .
> Above all, the committee system leads to real decisions being taken elsewhere,
> behind closed doors, with little open, democratic scrutiny and where many
> councillors feel unable to influence events.
>
> (1998: para. 1.15)

The origins of the elected mayor option (favoured by the Blair government) can be traced back to Michael Heseltine some ten years ago. The idea made little headway until, in 1995, the report of the independent Commission for Local Democracy (CLD) put elected mayors centre-stage with its first recommendation:

> Local authorities should consist of a directly elected Council and a directly
> elected Leader/Mayor. Both Council and Leader/Mayor should be voted in
> for a term of three years, but the elected Leader may only serve two full terms
> in office.
>
> (CLD, 1995: 54)

The CLD believed that a directly-elected mayor was an important means of enhancing democracy in local government, which would then be highly visible and thus highly accountable. The Labour government's 1998 white paper was similarly enthusiastic about prioritising the elected mayor solution but admitted it would not suit every locality. Jones and Stewart, however, reflect the scepticism which many then had (and still have) about directly-elected mayors:

> It is as if the Commission regards it as a piece of magic which will
> automatically increase turn-out and build a vibrant local democracy. But the
> magic does not seem to work in the US. In 1991 in Phoenix – an authority
> with a city manager and directly elected mayor – only 17% of the electorate
> voted, and that is of the electorate who bothered to register as voters.
>
> (Jones and Stewart, 1995: 8)

Debate about the virtues of directly-elected mayors is fierce. Opponents argue that elitism would be rife, yet the incumbent would be directly elected by the people – there is little elitist in that! Mayors would create a leader with some political 'clout', someone who would be well-known and clearly accountable. They could also become a vehicle for influence beyond the locality. French mayors and German *Bürgermeister* are significant players in their national political systems: such 'big-hitters' are currently lacking in Britain. Surveys show that while the insiders (councillors) are overwhelmingly hostile to new forms of executive leadership, outsiders are overwhelmingly enthusiastic. The insiders, notably backbenchers, are fearful of being marginalised; outsiders have no such vested interest in maintaining the *status quo*. Miller and Dickinson (2000) show that the public have a fairly jaundiced view of the way local democracy works at the moment and give strong support to reforms such as elected mayors and local referendums which will increase the direct say of people in decision-making. Their survey showed that while 78% of the public believed that the council leader should be directly elected, only 18% of councillors held this opinion (Miller and Dickinson, 2000: 142). Under executive government, backbench councillors would become scrutineers of policy and community representatives. Indeed, the latter role could flourish given the reduction in time spent in committees, but councillors still remain sceptical.

Advocates of elected mayors argue that this form of executive leadership works well in other countries where local democracy is in a much healthier state than it is in Britain. Opponents argue equally strongly that we need to beware of uncritically adopting practices from elsewhere. All political systems have their own values, cultures and legal contracts; what works well in one country is not necessarily appropriate elsewhere. As Page has observed: 'Valid lessons from cross-national experience can only be drawn on the basis of the systematic application of knowledge about how policies and institutions work' (1998: 1). The Labour government, as we have noted, sees executive leadership as a major plank in its modernisation programme. Such a development would undoubtedly raise the profile of local authorities but this could be at the expense of democratic values and grass-roots needs.

Summary

- The advent of new patterns of local political leadership means the end of the traditional pattern of service committees.
- In all but the smallest local authorities three models of executive leadership are on offer (see Box 16.3).
- There are widespread fears by councillors that their policy-making role will be drastically curtailed in the new world of executive government, although they will have important scrutiny and community representative roles.
- Executive leadership could give a badly-needed boost to the profile and impact of local government; at the same time the propensity towards elitism needs to be acknowledged.

Conclusion

Recent years have witnessed a shift from local government to local governance; local authorities now share service delivery with a wide range of other agencies. Yet despite its direct service role being eroded, elected local government still remains big business. All this change has taken place during a period in which the numbers of authorities and the number of councillors have declined drastically.

There is no theory of local government in the sense of a normative general theory from which we can deduce what local government ought to be. There are, however, a number of theoretical strands which permeate debate about local government. The most important of these are: accountability, responsiveness, representativeness, participation and pluralism. There remains the challenge of, on the one hand, encouraging local distinctiveness and choice, and on the other hand, espousing the need for equality of provision. The circle is not easily squared.

In the new world of local governance, joined-up or holistic government is centre-stage; partnership strategies abound at local level. There is little doubt that the 'modernise or perish' message has registered with even the most traditional local authorities; the further development of inspectorates will help to ensure that minimum levels of service delivery are provided at the local level, albeit within a context in which tensions between central and local government have far from disappeared.

The Labour government is ushering in executive leadership for local councils despite fears by backbench councillors that they will be marginalised by such a development. While the advent of directly-elected mayors and Cabinet government could give local government a badly-needed boost to both profile and impact, it potentially heralds a move towards elitism which could mean local leaderships losing touch with grass-roots opinion.

To conclude, fewer people than ever seem interested in representative democracy at the local level; the centre has strengthened and developed its inspection regimes; attempts to enhance public participation in decision-making have not effectively drawn in the socially excluded; there is little indication that, apart from modifying the payment of grants, central government is prepared to relax its financial stranglehold on local authorities. Perhaps most crucially of all, we need to recognise that democratic local government is vulnerable. Is there going to be local democracy in the twenty-first century? It is a survival issue.

Chronology

1835 Municipal Corporations Act establishes directly-elected corporate boroughs in place of self-electing and frequently corrupt medieval corporations.

1888 Local Government Act establishes 62 elected county councils and 61 all-purpose county borough councils.

1894 Local Government Act, within county council areas, establishes 535 urban district councils, 472 rural district councils and 270 non-county borough councils.

1899 London Government Act sets up 28 metropolitan borough councils plus the Corporation of London.
1929 Local Government Act abolishes the Poor Law Guardians Boards and transfers functions to local government.
1963 London Government Act creates 32 London boroughs and a Greater London Council (GLC).
1972 Local Government Act removes county borough councils, reduces the number of county councils in England and Wales to 47, establishes six Metropolitan County Councils and 36 metropolitan district councils.
1985 Local Government Act abolishes the GLC and the six Metropolitan County Councils with effect from April 1986.
1992 Local Government Finance Act replaces 'poll tax' with Council Tax.
1992 Local Government Act supports further structural reorganisation to create some new unitary councils.
1997 Local Government and Rating Act supports new opportunities for parish council formation.
1999 Greater London Authority Act establishes an elected assembly and a separate directly-elected mayor for the capital. First elections are held on 4 May 2000.
2000 Local Government Act supports new models of local executive leadership.

Discussion Questions

1. What do you understand by 'local governance'? Explain its major features.
2. How accountable is local governance?
3. Will the advent of executive forms of government lead to the development of governance by a local elite?

References

Armstrong, H. (1997) 'Five sides to a new leaf', *Municipal Journal*, 4 July, pp. 18–19.

Beetham, D. (1996) 'Theorising democracy and local government', in D. King and G. Stoker (eds) *Rethinking Local Democracy*, Basingstoke: Macmillan, pp. 28–49.

Benyon, J. and Edwards, A. (1999) 'Community governance of crime control', in G. Stoker (ed.) *The New Management of British Local Governance*, Basingstoke: Macmillan, pp. 145–67.

Bulpitt, J. (1993) 'Review' in *Public Administration*, winter, pp. 621–3.

Blair, T. (1998) *Leading the Way: A New Vision for Local Government*, London: Institute for Public Policy Research.

Cabinet Office (1999) *Modernising Government*, London: HMSO.

CLD (1995) *Taking Charge: The Rebirth of Local Democracy*, London: Commission for Local Democracy/Municipal Journal Books.

Council of Europe (1996) *Local and Regional Authorities in Europe*, Brussels: European Commission.

DETR (1998) *Modern Local Government: In Touch with the People*, London: Department of the Environment, Transport and the Regions.

Jones, G. and Stewart, J. (1995) 'Directly elected nightmayor', *Local Government Chronicle*, 7 July.

King, D. (1996) 'Conclusion', in D. King and G. Stoker (eds) *Rethinking Local Democracy*, Basingstoke: Macmillan, pp. 214–23.

Layfield Committee (1976) *Report of the Committee of Enquiry into Local Government Finance*, Cmnd 6543, London: HMSO.

Local Government Management Board (1998) *Census of Councillors*, Luton: LGMB.

Loughlin, M. (1996) 'The constitutional status of local government', in L. Pratchett and D. Wilson (eds) *Local Democracy and Local Government*, Basingstoke: Macmillan, pp. 38–61.

Lowndes, V. (1999) 'Rebuilding trust in central/local relations: policy or passion?', *Local Government Studies*, Vol. 25, No. 4, pp. 116–36.

Midwinter, A. (1995) *Local Government in Scotland: Reform or Decline?*, London: Macmillan.

Mill, J.S. (1861) *Considerations on Representative Government*, London: J.M. Dent.

Miller, W. and Dickinson, M. (2000) 'Local governance: the assessments of councillors, quango members and the public', in G. Stoker (ed.) *The New Politics of British Local Governance*, Basingstoke: Macmillan, pp. 130–49.

Municipal Journal Books (2000) *Municipal Year Book 2000*, London: Municipal Journal Books.

Page, E. (1998) *Future Governance: Lessons from Comparative Public Policy*, Draft proposal to ESRC (University of Hull).

Parry, G. and Moyser, G. (1990) 'A map of political participation in Britain', *Government and Opposition*, Vol. 25, No. 2, pp. 147–69.

Rallings, C. and Thrasher, M. (1994, 1996, 1998) *Local Election Handbooks*, London: Local Government Chronicle Publications.

Sharpe, L.J. (1970) 'Theories and values of local government', *Political Studies*, Vol. 18, pp. 153–74.

Stoker, G. (1996) 'Introduction: normative theories of local government and democracy', in D. King and G. Stoker (eds) *Rethinking Local Democracy*, Basingstoke: Macmillan, pp. 1–27.

Stoker, G. (ed.) (1999) *The New Management of British Local Governance*, Basingstoke: Macmillan.

Widdicombe, D. (Chairman) (1986) *The Conduct of Local Authority Business: Report of the Committee of Inquiry into the Conduct of Local Authority Business*, Cmnd 9797, London: HMSO.

Wilson, D. and Game, C. (1998) *Local Government in the United Kingdom*, Basingstoke: Macmillan.

Young, K. (1994) 'Rethinking accountability: an issue paper', QMC Public Policy Seminar, 28 April.

PART FIVE Policy

The Economy

Jim Tomlinson

CHAPTER SEVENTEEN

Introduction

Since 1945 all governments in Britain have attempted to manage the economy and secure electoral support on the basis of demonstrating their effectiveness in that management. In turn, the electorate have used judgements of the economic competence of governments as an important factor in their voting decisions. Much of post-war politics has therefore been about national economic management. From a political point of view the key questions are: what have been the goals of such management? How can those goals best be achieved? And, perhaps most fundamentally, can national governments really deliver these desirable outcomes, or has their power to do so been seriously weakened by the process of international economic integration?

Background

The great figures of nineteenth-century British politics fought elections on matters of foreign policy, constitutional change and social reform. In the twentieth century the extension of the franchise (achieving universal suffrage in 1928), the rise of the Labour Party (founded in 1900 and forming its first government in 1924), and the economic depression of the 1920s and 1930s combined to bring economic issues to the forefront of politics. The evident ability of the wartime coalition government (1940–45) to manage the war economy successfully led to the politically irresistible demand that this management be continued in peacetime.

In the 1940s the key aim of economic management was the achievement of full employment, following the mass unemployment and its attendant miseries in the 1930s. The wartime coalition committed future governments to pursue a 'high and stable' level of employment, and all parties endorsed this goal. It proved quite easily deliverable in the early post-war years. By the early 1950s previous pessimism about Britain's post-war economic prospects had given way to the belief that full employment would be a permanent fixture, and that the key aim of government should now be to increase the standard of living, usually interpreted as increasing the growth rate of Gross Domestic Product (GDP). However, by the end of that decade the failure of Britain to grow as fast as its continental neighbours was increasingly used as a reason for damning British performance, and early in the

1960s a wave of criticism swept across British politics, suggesting that the country was suffering from a chronic economic 'decline'. Promising to reverse that 'decline' and carry through a radical programme of modernisation secured Labour a narrow victory in the 1964 general election (Butler and King, 1965). High hopes were raised by this administration about the ability of governments to increase the growth rate by new policies. But while the rate of economic expansion in the 1960s was quite respectable by historic standards, it did not accelerate to match the performance of countries like West Germany, France and Italy. Probably such a rapid acceleration was an impossibility; these countries were catching up with Britain (and America), having ended the war with much lower living standards than Britain, and once they had caught up their own growth inevitably slowed down (Crafts, 1995). Nevertheless, British governments, having raised expectations, found the electorate unsympathetic when these expectations were disappointed. After the defeat of the Wilson government in 1970, the Conservatives under Heath tried their own brand of modernisation (including entry into the EEC), only in turn to disappoint in office and be rejected by the electorate in 1974.

These failures to deliver economic improvement became more evident in the mid-1970s. The collapse of the Bretton Woods system (see Box 17.1) early in that decade destabilised exchange rates, and the quadrupling of oil prices in 1972/73 by the Organisation of Petroleum Exporting Countries (OPEC) sent a wave of both deflation and inflation around the world, affecting especially countries like Britain which were substantial oil importers. The inflation, unemployment and balance of payments problems which followed threw into question the whole post-war regime of national economic management – its aims, means of delivery, and the idea of a 'national economy' on which it rested.

In the 1950s and 1960s most policy attention was on employment and growth, the latter, as we have noted, growing in significance as the period wore on. Unemployment in these decades averaged less than 2%, and while there was much discontent with the growth rate, by historic standards it was highly respectable at around 2.5% per annum (GDP per person). Understandably this period is often, in retrospect, regarded as a 'Golden Age' for Britain as well as the other major industrial economies. It was punctuated by periodic worries about the balance of payments, but again, by comparison with what was to follow in later decades,

Box 17.1 Bretton Woods

The Bretton Woods agreement, named after a town in New Hampshire, USA, was signed in 1944, and was based on ideas put forward mainly by the Americans and the British. It established the International Monetary Fund (IMF), and down to the early 1970s created an international monetary regime whose main feature was fixed exchange rates. Many economists have seen these as establishing stability by providing a constraint on domestic expansionary policy, but also allowing full employment to be achieved in the 'Golden Age' (Eichengreen, 1994). The end of Bretton Woods in the early 1970s inaugurated a period of floating and highly unstable exchange rates that has lasted until the present day.

these worries seem highly exaggerated. Britain was basically 'paying its way' in the world. The Conservatives in the 1950s also expressed worries about inflation, but these fears were muted, not least because Britain's inflation rate, though high by historic standards, was below that of other major industrial countries until the late 1960s (Wright, 1979: 173–81).

Whatever the precise balance of policy concerns, all governments in these years assumed that they had extremely powerful levers with which to control the economy. When in 1956 the social democrat and Labour MP Anthony Crosland published his landmark book, *The Future of Socialism*, he saw Britain as having a new type of 'post-capitalist' society, characterised by a powerful state that, within limits, could deliver whatever it had the political will to achieve. Such views were shared widely across the political spectrum. This did not mean the state was viewed as all-powerful, and in particular it was accepted that there were trade-offs between achieving low inflation and high levels of employment, but the idea that the state could and should effectively shape economic performance was largely taken as read.

Such optimism was challenged by the simultaneous economic problems of the 1970s. In particular, the combination of high inflation (which was on an upward trend from 1968) and high unemployment (which rose to over one million in 1971) seemed fatally to undermine the idea that there was a trade-off between these two policy aims. The Golden Age was associated with Keynesian ideas, which suggested that the manipulation of the level of demand in the economy was the means by which this trade-off could be made; a little more demand would lower unemployment, a little less would reduce inflation. The simultaneous occurrence of high inflation and unemployment was therefore not just an immediate political problem for government policy, but a challenge to the fundamental ideas on which policy had rested. Increasingly the 'Keynesian consensus' was challenged by those who argued that government was much less powerful than previously assumed, and that in trying to do too much it could actively harm economic performance (Thompson, 1996).

Such ideas were not to come to full flowering until after Mrs Thatcher's election victory in 1979. The preceding Labour government (1974–79) tried to achieve the combination of low inflation and low unemployment primarily by striking a deal with the trade unions (the 'Social Contract'), within which the government would attempt to deliver the unions policy wishes and in return the unions would ease pressure for wage increases. This policy, after initially failing to prevent inflation rising to an all-time high of 25% in 1975, did eventually aid a fall in the rate of price increase without any increase in unemployment over the 1975–78 period. But the (eventual) success of the Labour government in grappling with the inflation/unemployment issue was offset by difficulties in coping with another aspect of the economy, the 'loss of confidence' that led to huge outflows of capital from the country and a decline in the international value of the pound. This loss of confidence had no simple cause. In part it was due to the international financial markets' general dislike of Labour governments, especially one that was in such close alliance with the trade unions, but more especially it reflected the rise in public borrowing (the Public Sector Borrowing Requirement or PSBR) that was such a striking feature of the mid-1970s. In the Golden Age, governments had run current budget surpluses and borrowed only on a small scale for investment. But in the 1970s, beginning under the Heath government, public spending began to rise sharply without a parallel rise in taxation. The result was that the PSBR rose to an unprecedented level in peacetime, at its peak almost 10% of GDP in 1975/76. The Labour government came under pressure almost from the time it took office to cut back on spending and borrowing, and eventually it did so, beginning in a small way in 1975, and much more radically the year after. In fact, 1976/77 saw the biggest fall in public spending ever except in the aftermath of war, and that year also saw the end of the long-term trend of rising share of state spending in national income that had been a striking feature of the post-war period (Heald, 1983: ch. 1).

But it was on the borrowing side of the government accounts that even more attention was focused because of the belief, held increasingly widely in the 1970s, that such borrowing, by causing an expansion of the money supply, fed directly into the rate of inflation. For international financial markets, therefore, a Labour government that presided over large-scale public borrowing and high inflation was combining almost all possible sins. The crunch came in 1976 when the pound fell to an all-time low of $1.55 (the rate had been $2.40 from 1967 to 1972). By the time the bottom was reached, the government had already set in motion big cuts in public spending, inflation was past its peak, and the economy was recovering. But to secure itself against the loss of confidence the government had to gain a 'seal of approval' for its policies from the International Monetary Fund. In return for a loan, the government agreed with the IMF to further cuts in both public spending and the PSBR. This deal with the IMF was extremely humiliating for the government, but much more than that immediate effect, it brought into question the power of the government to manage the economy. How far could a British government effectively control the economy if, as the experience of the mid-1970s suggested, international investors could exert such pressures upon its policies (Artis and Cobham, 1991)?

This sense of a loss of governmental ability to run the national economy was greatly reinforced by a famous speech by the Prime Minister James Callaghan at the Labour Party conference in September 1976, when he said that the option of spending the way out of recession 'no longer exists, and that insofar as ever it did exist it only worked on each occasion since the war by injecting a bigger dose of inflation into the economy' (Labour Party Annual Conference Report, 1976: 188). Taken at face value this statement was a repudiation of the post-war Keynesian consensus about the ability of governments to manage the economy, especially in the pursuit of full employment. Some commentators, then and subsequently, saw it as recognition by Labour of the limits of government in the face of the growth of international economic integration, evident in the growth in trade in goods and services but especially in the rise in volume of capital flows. Contrariwise, it is clear that the speech was given at a time when the Labour leadership's overwhelming anxiety was to placate international capital markets, stop the capital outflow and stabilise the value of the pound. Repudiation of Keynesianism was what these markets wanted to hear. However, policies pursued by Labour *after* this speech suggest that the government had not given up on attempts to manage the economy in order to achieve high levels of employment. Once the crisis of 1976 was past, the government again expanded the economy to reduce unemployment, and public spending started to edge back up. Nevertheless, the crisis of 1976 can reasonably be seen as marking a watershed between a period when national governments of both parties believed they could effectively manage their economies and one in which that belief was, at best, highly qualified by recognition of the scale of international economic interconnections.

While the Labour government of the 1970s came to speak a language attuned to the prejudices of international capital markets without necessarily fully believing what they said, the Conservatives under Mrs Thatcher shared those prejudices about the desirability of reducing the role of government in the economic field. Thatcherite Conservatism explicitly asserted that governments should limit their ambitions to controlling inflation and providing a stable financial framework in which the private sector would be best able to maximise output and employment. The Conservative government's Medium Term Financial Strategy (MTFS, introduced in 1980) emphasised this point by giving priority to cutting inflation by aiming to reduce public borrowing and the rate of growth of the money supply.

While the Thatcher government's economic approach explicitly argued that governments could and should not be directly responsible for the level of employment, they were extremely wary of the electoral effects of any major increase in unemployment. The evidence suggests that neither they nor anyone else anticipated that their MTFS would bring about the huge increase in unemployment which occurred in 1979–81 when the numbers out of work doubled, and continued to rise until 1986. This unexpected collapse in the labour market was brought about by the impact of the new government's economic policies, which (along with the discovery of North Sea Oil) drove the exchange rate up with unprecedented rapidity. This rise in the exchange rate rendered large parts of the economy, especially in manufacturing, uncompetitive, bringing a major slump in output and employment (Keegan, 1984).

Since the Second World War a key assumption of British politics had been that any government presiding over mass unemployment would be severely punished by the electorate. The 1983 general election showed this was not necessarily so. While the share of the Conservatives in the poll was only 42%, the key feature of the election was the split in the non-Conservative vote, with Labour only just beating the Liberals and Social Democrats into third place with 28%. In addition, while unemployment was still rising at the time of the election, output (and therefore living standards) were increasing again from 1982 (Tomlinson, 1990: 334). The government had survived the slump its policies had brought about, and the message was that if other factors were right, mass unemployment need not be fatal to a government's chances of re-election. The same message could be seen in the result of the 1987 election when, with the economy in a sharp recovery phase but unemployment still around the 3 million mark, the Conservatives were once again re-elected.

The Thatcher years were ones of bust and boom. An unsustainable boom followed the slump of the early 1980s later in the decade, which by 1989 was causing rising inflation. To reassert their anti-inflationary credentials the Conservatives entered the European Exchange Rate Mechanism (ERM) in 1990 at a very high exchange rate, only to be forced out two years later by the belief in financial markets that the deflationary impact of that policy was becoming intolerable. The result was one of the most humiliating policy reversals ever ('Black Wednesday') when in September 1992 Britain left the ERM amidst confusion. This policy reversal was economically beneficial in allowing a sharp recovery of output and employment that was to endure into the new millennium, but its political implications were even greater. The Conservatives' reputation for economic competence was destroyed, and this was to prove a reputation impossible to recover before the 1997 election (see Figure 17.1), or, indeed, even after Labour had been in power for four years.

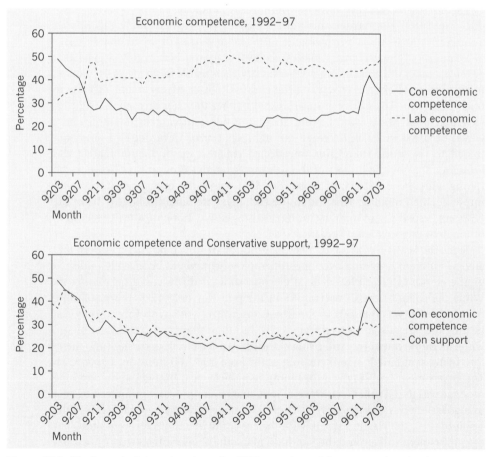

Figure 17.1 The impact of departure from the ERM on voters, giving approval to the Conservative government's record

Source: Gallup

Summary

- Since the Second World War electoral success has been closely related to governments' success in running the economy.
- Until the 1970s governments seemed to achieve a large measure of success in achieving their aims, although from the 1960s there was a widespread belief that governments should deliver faster growth.
- From the 1970s the ability of governments to achieve their economic goals was widely questioned.
- While governments have at times retreated from claims about their ability to deliver economic goals, the electorate still punished perceived incompetence in this area.

Theoretical Considerations

A Marxist economist has asserted that the idea of a national economy in Britain as elsewhere is a 'Keynesian myth' (Radice, 1984). It is certainly true that the modern British economy has always been highly integrated with the rest of the world; more integrated, in fact, than any other major economy. Measured by the volume of trade, capital, and labour flows relative to British national income, this integration reached very high levels before the First World War. At that time the policy of free trade, the fact that London was the world's leading capital market, and the almost complete absence of controls over movements of people meant that integration was at a peak, which was not to be even approached until sixty or seventy years later. The result of the First World War and the inter-war slump was to put this process of integration into reverse, and it was only after 1945, and initially very slowly, that economies were opened up once again. By the 1970s the process of trade liberalisation, which was ratcheted up by the Kennedy Round (see Box 17.2) of trade talks in the 1960s and the liberalisation of capital markets, coupled with the growing role of multinational companies with their ability to shift capital around the world, was leading to growing questioning of the ability of national governments to determine the fate of their economies.

Box 17.2 The Kennedy Round

Under the General Agreement on Tariffs and Trade (GATT) of 1947 the major western countries committed themselves to the progressive liberalisation of international trade. This was achieved by successive 'rounds' of negotiation. The Kennedy Round, named after the US President elected in 1960, was highly protracted but eventually led to industrial tariff reductions of 35–40% (see Brett, 1985: 77).

The belief that governments could and should manage their economies is commonly associated with the work of Keynes, who emerged in the 1920s as an apostle of national economic management and lived to see that idea embodied in the 1944 white paper on employment policy. But Keynes was extremely conscious in all his policy work that management of the British economy would have to be undertaken within an international environment that would necessarily limit what national governments could achieve. That indeed was why he spent the last years of his life (in the mid-1940s) trying to design and negotiate a set of *international* economic institutions that would enable governments to pursue their domestic goals without being thrown off-track by external events (Skidelsky, 2000). In the Golden Age the institutions that he was involved in designing seemed to have worked. Despite the growth of international integration, governments were able to secure domestic aims, especially full employment, without being undermined by external forces. However, this congenial situation was highly contingent. Above all, in a country like Britain, full employment did *not* require large budget deficits; as noted above, in this period budgets were close to balance. A buoyant world economy, driven above all by unprecedentedly high investment levels, meant that full employment was compatible with public finances that did not undermine financial confidence. The boom supplied the taxes to pay for the higher public spending. It was only in the 1970s, when the underlying economic situation deteriorated so markedly, that there was a conflict between using the budget for domestic purposes and the desire of international financial markets for fiscal conservatism (Heald, 1983: ch. 3).

Those arguments begun in the 1970s have become extraordinarily widespread by the beginning of the twenty-first century. Much of this discussion has been conducted under the heading of 'globalisation', which may be defined as the idea that international economic integration has now become so widespread that the ability of individual national governments to manage their economies is disappearing. In this theory, governments that pursue policies uncongenial to international investors will be punished by the loss of capital and will be forced to reverse their policies. The existence of globalisation is very widely taken for granted; yet the empirical foundations for believing in that existence is far from sure. Of course, there are difficulties in judging those foundations. One problem is that the term is often used in a very vague way, with the political intention, as some commentators have argued, to 'frighten the children'. By this is meant the desire, especially on the part of New Labour, to use the alleged existence of globalisation to persuade Labour supporters that what can be done by a Labour government in the economic field is highly constrained. Globalisation in this context is about talking down expectations. Another problem in the discussion of globalisation is that accounts of it are commonly highly ahistorical, seeming to assume that international economic integration is a recent phenomenon. In fact, by most measures, its development is best thought of as having a 'U-shape', with a peak in 1914, a sharp decline thereafter, bottoming out in 1945 to be followed by an upwards movement that accelerated from the 1960s.

So does globalisation exist? Serious empirical work in the area suggests that any extreme version that suggests that governments are powerless in the face of 'global forces' needs to be highly qualified (Hirst and Thompson, 1999). Capital does indeed flow readily between countries, but rather than being 'global' most of these movements are in narrow channels between the world's rich countries. As far as multinational companies are concerned, they are far from 'footloose', so although they may leave a country where they consider policy disadvantages them, this happens far less often than theorists of globalisation suggest. It is not the case that, for example, a rise in corporate taxes is likely to cause a major exodus of productive capital. It is also true that the effectiveness of fiscal policy is constrained by the ability of international investors to shift funds out of a country they consider 'irresponsible'. This is especially so where the political colour of the government is uncongenial to financial markets, as was shown in Britain in 1975/76 and, for example, during the 'socialist experiment' in France in the early 1980s. But this needs to be put into historical perspective. There is nothing new in this process, as is clear from the experience of the Labour government in Britain in 1931, when the government's policy of subsidising the Unemployment Insurance Fund (see Box 17.3) from the budget, and the deficit that followed, led to a sharp loss of financial confidence, the flight of capital, and the collapse of the government.

A further aspect of the globalisation thesis, that governments like the British one are confronted by serious problems because of the need to be competitive with goods produced in low-wage countries, also needs to be highly qualified. On the one hand, low wages are not necessarily a competitive advantage for a country; that depends on the level of productivity. On the other, the pattern of world trade is overwhelmingly one in which the rich trade with the rich (e.g. Britain with the European Union and the USA), so that low-wage countries find it very hard to exert any competitive pressure that their wage levels may suggest. The belief that rich countries operating in a globalised world economy will see huge job losses and major unemployment as economic activity flees to the third world has little basis in reality.

Finally, while it is true that short-term monetary flows are larger now than ever before, like longer-term capital flows these are mainly regional in character rather than 'global'. This does not of course mean that such flows do not act to constrain

Box 17.3 The National Insurance Fund

National Insurance against unemployment began in Britain with an Act of 1911. It was based on contributions from employers, employees and the state. It was planned to be self-financing as long as unemployment was not too high. During and just after the First World War the scheme was greatly expanded, and in the heavy unemployment from 1921 the Fund became financially unbalanced as contributions fell but claims increased. Under the Labour government of 1929–31 the problem became much worse. The government subsidised the Fund from the ordinary budget, but this was regarded in financial and Conservative circles as unacceptable, and eventually the government fell, as it was unable to agree to cut unemployment benefit to placate financial opinion (see Tomlinson, 1990: ch. 4).

government's discretion in economic policy, and proposals such as that for the 'Tobin Tax' (see Box 17.4) would help to reduce such destabilising movements. But such constraints on national policies should not be exaggerated; it is usually only in crisis conditions, when countries depart markedly from international norms of economic behaviour (such as Britain in the 1970s), that this constraint really bites.

In summary, many of the processes of internationalisation of economic flows associated with 'globalisation' are long-standing features of the modern world, not part of some recent trend. Second, the patterns of these economic flows are much more regional than global, and the impact of the developing countries thereby much reduced. Third, national governments have *always* been constrained by international factors, especially in big trading, financial and capital-exporting countries like Britain, but these constraints are much less tight than commonly believed. A good example of this is the development of the welfare state. Proponents of the globalisation thesis commonly assert that high levels of state welfare would be eroded by globalisation, as financial capital would flow out of countries which financed such welfare by borrowing, while multinational companies would flee from countries which financed it from high taxes. It is true that welfare states cannot be financed to any substantial extent from borrowing, but that has never been the normal pattern. Only in the highly particular and fleeting circumstances of the 1970s was that true on any scale in Britain. But, since that decade, and financed by taxation, spending on welfare has grown in almost every year (including under Mrs Thatcher) despite alleged 'globalisation' (Callaghan, 1999).

Box 17.4 The Tobin Tax

Named after a Nobel prize-winning American economist, this tax would fall on short-term international capital movements. Its aim would be to put 'some grit in the wheels' of international finance and thereby stabilise exchange rates. The revenue from the tax would be used to aid developing countries (see Tobin, 1994).

Summary

- Britain has been highly integrated in the world economy since the nineteenth century, and this has always limited the power of the government to manage the economy.
- The weakening of the power of national governments by recent international economic integration is much exaggerated in popular discussion.
- 'Globalisation' is a highly political term, often used more as part of a political polemic than as an accurate description of the world.

Update

The Labour government that came to power in 1997 explicitly aimed to reduce expectations about what government could deliver in the economic field. It did not promise a return to full employment, and endorsed the Conservative priority of keeping inflation low by giving the Bank of England autonomy to pursue a 2.5% inflation target. Labour also committed itself to tight control of government spending and borrowing for the first two years in office, and not to raise the rates of income tax (although other taxes did rise to help reduce the budget deficit inherited from the Conservatives). These policy priorities were underpinned by an explicit claim about the relative weakness of national governments to achieve their economic goals in a world characterised as undergoing a rapid process of 'globalisation', which was said to render governments highly vulnerable to international forces. In this framework the prime responsibility of government in the economic field was to prepare the workforce for effective competition in global markets, above all by improving skills and training. It was from this perspective that the government's claim that its priorities were 'education, education and education' fitted into its understanding of the limited capacities of governments.

Labour's economic policies in office were highly 'responsible', and they had no difficulty in sustaining the confidence of international financial markets. Uniquely for a Labour government, they suffered from upward rather than downward pressure on the exchange rate, as Britain continued to be a highly attractive destination for international capital flows (flows which masked weaknesses on the current side of the balance of payments). After two years of tight restraint, the continuing upswing of the economic cycle enabled the government to promise big rises in public spending without breaching the rules of 'sound finance' (i.e. that borrowing would be for investment purposes only, and any budget deficits in the downswing of the cycle would be offset by surpluses in the upswing). The effects of this spending were just starting to be felt in the run-up to the 2001 election. At the same time, the continuing fall in unemployment made talk of full employment once again acceptable in Labour circles as it became clear that, barring a world recession, this goal might be achievable without any threat of increasing inflation. By the time of the 2001 election Labour seemed to have secured a reputation for competence in economic management, which was a key reason for their re-election.

On the Conservative side, the emphasis was on a reassertion of liberal economic positions. Much criticism was made of Labour's higher taxes on business and savings, increased regulation of business, and alleged penchant for intervention in the economy. There was a great deal of emphasis on the higher ('stealth') taxes imposed since 1997, and promises of big tax cuts if the Conservatives were to be returned to power. By the same token, the Conservatives promised to match Labour spending on the health and education systems, and there was no serious suggestion of 'rolling back the state' in these areas, where public support for higher spending seemed to be at its strongest. The Conservative's electoral position was undoubtedly weakened by the financial stability and continuing upswing in the economy under Labour, while the legacy of the 'boom and bust' of the 1980s and 1990s had not yet worn off with the electorate. Economic conditions and the party's perceived abilities to manage the national economy continued to be key electoral issues.

Debate

Arguments about the role of government in managing the economy are based on disagreements about what the aims of policy should be and how those aims should be achieved. But they are also arguments about how far government management of the economy is in principle either possible or desirable.

There has been convergence between the two major political parties on the aims of policy, though these have never been the main area of contention. In the 1960s and 1970s Labour gave a lower priority to reducing inflation than the Conservatives. This partly reflected the Conservative emphasis on the destabilising effects of inflation for social and political order. Labour, as the party representing those who sell their labour to live, was traditionally more concerned with unemployment, as was shown by the heated party debates about the government's seeming willingness to tolerate one million unemployed in the 1970s. The Conservatives, in contrast, have occasionally been led to articulate the view that unemployment might be 'a price worth paying' to achieve other goals, especially the defeat of inflation. But this difference was more one of emphasis than of fundamental disagreement. At least until the 1980s both parties believed mass unemployment would be electorally disastrous for the party in power. Since then both parties seem to have played down the employment issue, though this has been much more contested in Labour than in Conservative circles, and Labour has never disputed the intrinsic desirability of full employment as opposed to the ability of governments to deliver it.

On inflation there has been a notable conversion of Labour to the anti-inflation cause. This has been driven by an acceptance of the electoral damage done to Labour being thought to be 'the party of inflation' after the experience of the 1970s, coupled with the recognition that low inflation is necessary for financial confidence.

In the case of economic growth there has never been much difference between the parties. Since the 1950s both have consistently promised to deliver a more rapid growth of living standards than their opponents. So strong is the belief that the electorate is, above all, interested in higher money incomes that environmental arguments, seen as threatening growth, have found it very hard to make a serious impression on the main parties. The fact that the Conservatives in the 2001 election could put so much emphasis on cutting petrol taxes without Labour emphasising the environmental costs of such a policy, suggests how a narrow conception of the growth of the standard of living dominated both parties' thinking.

The parties have in the past been significantly divided on the means to achieve policy aims, even where they shared those aims. On unemployment, Labour has tended to favour fiscal policy to expand the economy, the Conservatives placing more weight on monetary measures insofar as it has believed macro-economic measures are at all effective. On inflation, Conservatives again traditionally favoured monetary measures, Labour traditionally having more belief in incomes policy because of their belief in their ability to 'get along' with the unions. However, Conservative governments until the 1970s tried incomes policies, and generally the difference between the parties on how to control inflation has never been central to economic debates. In recent years Labour has been converted to the emphasis on monetary policy, partly because the institutional basis for incomes policy has weakened with the decline of trade unions, and partly because of recognition that tight monetary policy is required for financial confidence.

In terms of policy instruments, the parties up until the 1990s were most divided on the ways of delivering faster growth. This division in turn reflected broader ideological differences between left and right. Labour broadly believed that the state had a major role to play in shaping the behaviour of industry, including stimulating and often financing investment and research and development. By way of contrast, especially from the 1970s, the Conservatives believed that better incentives, deregulation and generally rolling back the state were the main paths to improved performance. Here again there has been convergence in recent years, with Labour after 1997 continuing with the policies it inherited of weak regulation of the private sector, low direct taxation, and a focus on allowing the maximum freedom to business rather than seeking to control its activities.

This convergence is also evident in attitudes to the European Union. While once Labour was predominantly hostile, today both parties' leaderships are supporters of membership. Euroscepticism in the Conservative Party mainly concerns the politics of the Union, not the idea of a 'common market' in which the British economy is open to competition from other member states, and conversely has free access to their markets. Labour was converted to the EU in large part because a similar views about the benefits of competition and a large potential market. The belief that the EU could function as a substitute for weakened national governments in regulating the economy in a globalising world is one sometimes to be found on the left of the Labour Party, but is not a view endorsed by the leadership – at least not explicitly.

How is such a recurrent pattern of convergence in economic policy to be explained? In part the answer is that both parties, albeit following different routes, have come to accept that government action on the economy is limited in effect and potentially damaging if carried too far.

The Conservatives were converted to a brand of economic liberalism under Mrs Thatcher, and there has been no retreat from this position since her departure from the leadership. This liberalism is characterised by a highly sceptical attitude to the efficacy of state action in the economic field, and a belief that market forces usually deliver efficient outcomes. From this perspective, arguments that suggest the world economy is becoming more integrated, and that governments will have to pursue business-friendly policies in order to compete in a globalised world present no problem. Indeed, they enable Conservatives to convert an ideological preference for free markets into an alleged necessity for national survival in this new world order. Conservatives have generally bandied the word 'globalisation' around much less than those on the left, but to most Conservatives its existence is taken for granted, and indeed welcomed, as a further extension of the free market in which they so strongly believe.

For Labour, by contrast, the term 'globalisation' is much more politically important because arguments about its existence and implications go to the heart of the Old/New Labour divide. If globalisation is a fact of life, then radical modernisation of policy towards a low tax/low regulation regime, with pro-business policies, appears the only viable route to electoral popularity. If, however, globalisation is greatly exaggerated, the options available to Labour in government are much wider, and the argument becomes less one of 'recognition of necessity' and more one about what is desirable, subject to much looser constraints.

Summary

- Since the 1970s there has been convergence between the parties on economic policy, though this only became very explicit in the 1990s.
- This convergence is predominantly around economic liberal or 'Thatcherite' views about, for example, the importance of low inflation and the limits of state action. However, the amount of change in Labour views is exaggerated by comparing the policy views of New Labour with the crisis-driven policies of the 1970s. On the welfare state, and its associated high levels of public spending, there is little evidence of the triumph of liberal policies.

Conclusion

In its second term the emphasis by Labour on globalisation may fade because the term will have served its function in 'massaging down' public expectations about what governments can deliver. (Such massaging has been a feature of all governments since the 1970s as public expectations have outrun governments' capacity to deliver.) The limitations on the powers of national governments are likely to be played down, compared with, for example, the continuing responsibility of national governments to move towards full employment (the 2001 Manifesto promised this would be achieved 'in all regions' by 2010), and to expand public spending in order to rebuild the economic infrastructure. This latter prospect was combined with renewed promises not to raise the standard or higher rate of income tax. Such a combination relies on continuing economic growth to deliver tax revenues. If this did not occur, the prospect of a large budget deficit would undermine the hard-won reputation for fiscal 'responsibility' and at the same time conflict with the prospect of joining the Euro, which requires adherence to small budget deficits. The latter conflict would once again illustrate the useful adage that it is in the bad times that national governments are most constrained by international forces.

Chronology

1944 Wartime coalition government publishes the white paper on employment policy, committing future governments to pursue a 'high and stable' level of employment.

1954 Recognising that full employment seems here to stay, the Conservative Chancellor of the Exchequer, R.A. Butler says the British can look forward to 'doubling their standard of living every twenty-five years'.

1957 Prime Minister Harold Macmillan tells the British public they have 'never had it so good'.

1960–63 Michael Shanks's *The Stagnant Society* sells 60,000 copies and stimulates widespread cross-party debate on why the British economy is 'declining'.

1964 Harold Wilson wins an election dominated by the issue of modernising the British economy.

1973–74 OPEC I signals an end to the long boom, and high inflation and unemployment and low growth follow.

1976 Prime Minister James Callaghan pronounces the end of the Keynesian era.

1979 Mrs Thatcher is elected and promises to 'roll back the state', including its role in economic management.

1979–81 Unemployment doubles and manufacturing output falls by 20%.

1983 Mrs Thatcher wins a second term with unemployment at 3 million and rising.

1992 The Conservative government under Major is forced out of the ERM in humiliating circumstances.

1997 Labour is elected. The government is committed to low inflation and tight controls on public spending.

2001 Labour is re-elected, promising full employment by 2010.

Discussion Questions

1. How closely have the electoral fortunes of the two main parties been the result of the economic policies they have pursued?
2. What do you understand by the term 'globalisation'? What is the political significance of the term?
3. What economic goals should the political parties try to focus the attention of the electorate upon?

References

Artis, M. and Cobham, D. (1991) *Labour's Economic Policies 1974–79*, Manchester: Manchester University Press.

Brett, A. (1985) *The World Economy since the War*, London: Routledge.

Butler, D. and King, A. (1965) *The British General Election of 1964*, London: Macmillan.

Callaghan, J. (1999) *The Retreat of the State?*, Manchester: Manchester University Press.

Crafts, N. (1995) 'The golden age of economic growth in Western Europe, 1945–73' *Economic History Review*, Vol. 48, pp. 429–47.

Crosland, A. (1956) *The Future of Socialism*, London: Cape.

Eichengreen, B. (1994) *International Monetary Arrangements for the Twenty-First Century*, Washington, DC: Brookings Institute.

Heald, D. (1983) *Public Expenditure: Its Defence and Reform*, Oxford: Martin Robertson.

Hirst, P. and Thompson, G. (1999) *Globalization in Question* (second edition), Cambridge: Cambridge University Press.

Keegan, W. (1984) *Mrs Thatcher's Economic Experiment*, Harmondsworth: Penguin.

Labour Party (1976) *Labour Party Annual Conference Report 1976*, London: London Labour Party.

Radice, H. (1984) 'The national economy: a Keynesian myth?', in *Capital and Class*, No. 22, pp. 111–40.

Shanks, M. (1961) *The Stagnant Society*, Harmondsworth: Penguin.

Skidelsky, R. (2000) *John Maynard Keynes: Fighting for Britain 1937–1946*, London: Macmillan.

Thompson, N. (1996) 'Economic ideas and the development of economic opinion', in R. Coopey and N. Woodward (eds) *Britain in the 1970s*, London: UCL Press, pp. 55–80.

Tobin, J. (1994) 'Speculators' tax', *New Economy*, Vol. 1, pp. 104–9.

Tomlinson, J. (1990) *Public Policy and the Economy*, Oxford: Oxford University Press.

Wright, J. (1979) *Britain in the Age of Economic Management*, Oxford: Oxford University Press.

Further reading

Gray, J. (1997) *False Dawns: The Delusions of Global Capitalism*, London: Granta.

Hirst, P. and Thompson, G. (2000) 'Globalization in one country? The peculiarities of the British', *Economy and Society*, Vol. 29, pp. 335–56.

Martin, P. and Schumann, H. (1997) *The Global Trap: Globalization and the Assault on Democracy and Prosperity*, London: Zed Books.

Middleton, R. (2000) *The British Economy since 1945: Engaging with the Debate*, London: Macmillan.

Tomlinson, J. (2000) *The Politics of Decline: Understanding Post-war Britain*, Harlow: Longman.

Health Care Policy

Michael Moran

CHAPTER EIGHTEEN

Background

Arguments about health care policy are right at the centre of British politics, and no wonder. In personal terms, health is something we all value immensely; and since at least the Second World War governments in Britain have accepted a large measure of responsibility for the health of the population. Many measures show the importance of health. Every year Britain now spends around 7% of its Gross National Product (the standard measure of national wealth) on health care and the figure has nearly doubled in the last generation (see Table 18.1). Most of that money comes from the public purse – over 80% of spending on health care comes from the taxpayer. The National Health Service is one of the biggest components of the welfare state in Britain and takes a large slice of public spending. The sheer size of the National Health Service is awesome: more than one million people work in the NHS, ranging from the most highly-paid consultants and managers to the most poorly-paid cleaners and porters. The Service is the equivalent of a giant industry, and those who work in it form a large and well-organised section of the electorate. What is more, this 'industry' helps support other important parts of the economy. About 100,000 people are estimated to work in the pharmaceutical industry in the UK, for example, and the NHS is a major customer of that industry.

Expense, scale and economic importance all make health care a central feature of British politics. But something more intangible is also at work: the feelings of the people at large. Over the last generation popular attachment to many import-ant institutions in British life has come under strain but one of the remarkable

Table 18.1 Spending on health care as a percentage of Gross National Product

	1960	1997
United Kingdom	3.9	6.7
Canada	5.5	9.0
France	4.2	9.6
Germany	4.8	10.4
Italy	3.6	7.6
Japan	3.0	7.3
United States	5.2	13.5

Source: OECD (1998)

features of health care is that the National Health Service and the values it embodies have not lost their hold over the popular imagination. People worry about the effectiveness of the service (Donelan, et al., 1999) but its central historical purpose – to deliver health care free to everyone at the point of treatment – still commands overwhelming support.

Health care in Britain, therefore, consists of a very complex political cocktail: huge cost; a large slice of the electorate with a vested interest in spending on the Health Service; and a mix of popular support for the Health Service's basic principles coupled with worries about whether those principles are being realised in practice. This cocktail, we shall see, is not only complex; for politicians who have to win elections it is potentially explosive.

This state of affairs originates in one historical event: the foundation of the National Health Service by the Labour government in 1948. Although much of what was then established had been anticipated both before and during the Second World War, the NHS was nevertheless a unique achievement. It committed the state to paying for almost all the cost of health care with money raised by taxation. It gave virtually everybody in the community their own source of health care in the family doctor, the general practitioner (GP). It practised the principles of 'universalism'. That is, it gave everybody in the community the same access to a wide range of free, or nearly free, health care services. For the first time in the history of the British people everyone could be assured of free health care and advice from their family doctor, and free hospital treatment if their doctor thought it necessary.

Theoretical Considerations

The National Health Service was a great achievement, unique in British history and virtually unique in the world when it was established. (Only New Zealand could by 1948 claim a similar system.) What is more, it turned out to have one quite unexpected achievement. From the very beginning of the Service there were anguished debates about its expense, but as other countries began to provide similarly universal health care in the 1950s and 1960s it became possible to compare the cost of the NHS with the health care systems of other nations. The single most striking feature of the Service, viewed in this light, is that it has been extraordinarily cheap. Britain spends a smaller proportion of national wealth on health care than any other obviously comparable nation (see the figures in Table 18.1). What is more, while there is room for argument about the quality of some of the clinical care delivered by parts of the Service, there is no convincing evidence that the British are less healthy than other peoples as a result of this economy. In short, the NHS turns out not only to have been a striking historical achievement; it has also been exceptionally good value for money.

The root of this achievement – and also the root of some of the key arguments about health care – lies in a key organising principle of the Service. The NHS was what is sometimes called a 'command' system. It is so called because resources were raised and distributed by command of the state: the money came from taxation raised by the coercive power of the state and it was allocated, not at the demand of patients, but as a result of administrative decisions taken by those who ran the Service. 'Command' allowed the NHS to deliver in two very different areas. The fact that the central state commanded resource raising through taxation meant that it could keep a comparatively tight grip on spending; hence the history of economy in the Service. It also meant that the Service was highly successful at delivering on the principle of equity – that all citizens, irrespective of their wealth or social standing, should have equal entitlements to treatments. In practice there was inequality in access to the resources of the NHS, but comparative studies show that Britain's Health Service, while not perfect, was better than most at realising the equity principle (see Box 18.1).

The theory and practice of equity explains the affection in which the Service is held, since 'equity' seems to match everyday notions of fairness to which most of us are deeply attached. But the virtues of economy and equity were bought at a price and that price could be summarised in one word: rationing. The Health Service was cheap and it spread its resources widely (and therefore thinly) around the community. Yet the very principle on which it was founded – free health care as an entitlement for all – inevitably raised high expectations. There was, and there remains, a big demand for health care. That demand can only be met by some very tough rationing decisions. The history of the NHS as a source of political debate can be seen as the history of how to come to terms with rationing problems.

Box 18.1 Two principles of the NHS

Command: Resources are raised by command of the state (taxation).

Equity: All have equal entitlement to health care resources irrespective of occupation, locality or personal characteristics.

Update

When the NHS was founded in 1948 Britain was still running an economy of scarcity. Almost everything of importance was rationed. Consumption of much food, fuel and consumer goods was subject to state controls that had originated in the Second World War. The NHS was a product of this era of austerity, yet oddly one of its central principles – rationing at the command of the state – was never mentioned. It was only in the 1980s that the language of 'rationing' began to be openly used. Neither is this difficult to fathom. Making rationing choices in health care is an almost uniquely sensitive business. Even rationing food in wartime and post-war Britain did not involve more than imposing discomfort on some people. Rationing health care, by contrast, causes more than discomfort. Withholding treatment – which is what rationing involves – causes fear, pain and, at the extremes, death. It is small wonder that open political debate about this was avoided at all costs.

Almost from the beginning of the history of the Service, governments developed two ways of coping with resource scarcity. One involved trying to control the demand for health care, while the other involved controlling its supply. Controlling demand almost from the beginning involved imposing some charges for health services. Charges could simultaneously achieve two things: imposing a cost for a hitherto free service could deter people from demanding it and the charges themselves could obviously raise money that would otherwise have to come out of taxation. Almost from the beginning governments levied some charges, and almost from the beginning experienced their limitations. The fact that charges contradicted one of the Service's founding principles made them an explosive subject of argument. The fall of the Labour government in 1951, after six years in office, was partly due to ministerial resignations over the imposition of charges for some dental and optical services. Successive governments, therefore, tried to avoid the stigma of being seen to undermine the founding principles. They targeted services that might be thought to be beyond the core of health care (some dental and opticians' services) or else they exempted the sick and poor from charges. But exemptions only illustrated the dilemmas faced by politicians trying to curb demand for care. To control demand effectively required imposing costs on the big consumers of health care, who are the long-term sick. But these are also the most vulnerable people in the community and charging them exposed politicians to criticism that was potentially catastrophic electorally. Exempting the sick and the poor helped rebut these charges, but exemptions destroyed the very purpose of charging. The history of the levy on prescriptions for medicine, one of the commonest means of trying to raise funds and suppress demand, makes the point. By the 1990s over 80% of all prescriptions consumed were exempted from charges.

In short, elected politicians who tried to suppress demand by charging for health care were offered a small return for a great deal of blame – exactly the reverse of what the sensible politician looks for. This explains why, for most of the history of the Service, governments tried to cope with the rationing problem by controlling, not the demand, but the *supply* of care. In this they had a powerful ally – the medical profession. Stripped of the rhetoric of citizenship, the National Health Service in practice actually offered something quite modest: the right to register with a family doctor, to consult that doctor, and to receive any health care that the doctor might think appropriate (or none at all). General practitioners were 'gatekeepers' to the hospital system. The only direct routes into hospital were drastic and unique – becoming pregnant, for instance, or being run over in the street. Otherwise the only route into the expensive world of the hospital was by reference from the family general practitioner. Moreover, once in the hospital decisions about treatment – and thus decisions about who was to be allocated resources – were made by medical specialists. From the beginning of the Service, therefore, there developed what Klein memorably called 'the politics of the double bed'. Governments decided what total resources should be available for health care and doctors made the hard decisions about who was to be allocated those scarce resources (Klein, 1990). The authority of the doctor meant that patients did not usually challenge rationing decisions, while politicians were spared potentially explosive choices. A famous study of health care rationing graphically described what went on in the treatment of kidney disease with the expensive technology of dialysis machines:

> Confronted by a person older than the prevailing unofficial age of cut-off for dialysis, the . . . GP tells the victim of chronic renal failure that nothing can be done except to make the patient as comfortable as possible in the time remaining. The . . . nephrologist tells the family of a patient who is difficult to handle that dialysis would be painful and burdensome and that the patient would be more comfortable without it.
>
> (Aaron and Schwartz, 1984: 101)

The division of labour between politicians and doctors worked as long as two things existed – deferential patients and a stable alliance between doctors and the state. In the 1980s, however, neither of these conditions could be sustained. When the NHS was established the British were used to rationing – after all, they had experienced nearly ten years during which most of the necessities of life were controlled by the state. But by the 1980s almost nothing was rationed any more, except through markets. Rationing by the state, which in 1948 had been the norm, now looked like a historical peculiarity. Doctors found that patients, used to their role as consumers in the marketplace, were increasingly restive in the face of health care rationing by medical professionals. One sign of this was the way in which the more affluent began to use private health care insurance to buy treatment or at least to buy speedier treatment (see Mohan, 1995: 160).

The stable alliance between doctors and the state was destroyed by the state's constant pressure to husband resources. Doctors are effective gatekeepers because their clinical choices overwhelmingly affect how resources are spent in a modern health care system. But for this very reason, government, desperately trying to rein in spending, intruded more and more deeply into the domain of clinical choice. Over the first forty years of the Service there was a gradual growth of control by non-clinical managers, especially in hospitals. The terms of the division of labour between medicine and the state were thus violated by the state. This culminated in a great spending crisis towards the end of the 1980s. Government, anxious to control spending, imposed caps on budgets. As the money ran out, so did the resources to treat patients in hospitals. The hidden secret of the National Health Service – that it rested on life and death rationing decisions – was out in the open. The Prime Minister (Mrs Thatcher) established a small senior review group to consider reform options. There is little doubt that the Prime Minister would have preferred to abolish the 'command' system and replace it with a market in health care, but the deep popular attachment to the NHS made that impossible. The reforms that were eventually implemented in the early 1990s thus tried to combine 'command' and the market through the device of what is usually called the 'internal market' in health care. A separation was enforced between the providers of health care – for example, big hospitals – and purchasers of health care (for instance, a reorganised system of family doctors.) The theory was that this new system would make providers compete and therefore act in a more responsive and efficient way to the needs of both purchasers and patients.

Debate

The single biggest consequence of the 'internal market' reforms of the early 1990s was political. They transformed the politics of the National Health Service in Britain. They did this by turning issues that had rarely been debated publicly into central points of contention. The hidden secrets of the Service were no longer secret; the genie escaped from the lamp. Three changes should be emphasised.

Rationing

This was the single biggest change, and one we have already anticipated. The word rationing has become commonplace for the first time in health care debates, and the use of the word signifies that the old system – where doctors rationed, and patients deferred to the clinical authority of medicine – has vanished. Unfortunately, it has proved impossible as yet to replace it with any stable alternative. Rationing health care involves often agonising choices and the victims of those choices (for instance, patients with diseases treatable only with very expensive therapy) make good 'copy' for tabloid newspapers (Harrison and Moran, 1999). Elected politicians want to distance themselves from such explosive debates. In principle, the internal market should accomplish this because 'purchasers' should make rationing choices in the light of the claims on their budgets, but the evidence is that the rationing debate is too difficult even for 'non-partisan' purchasers. Studies of explicit rationing suggest that attempts to develop systematic rationing rules have been confined to excluding a few marginal cosmetic procedures, like tattoo removal (Klein, et al.: 1996). Rationing in the new millennium is more open than ever in the NHS, but it is also as improvised as ever.

Equity

The notion that everyone in a similar medical condition should be treated the same was a central principle of the NHS from foundation, as we have seen. In practice there was a great deal of inequality in the allocation of health care resources between classes and regions, but the centralised 'command' system nevertheless made the NHS more effective at securing equity than other health care systems. The internal market reforms were an attempt to cope with the problems of the old 'command' system while preserving equity. Yet the very principle of competition in markets – albeit tightly-controlled markets – ran contrary to the principle of a common standard for all. The point of competition was that some would emerge with a better service than others. So far there is little evidence of the emergence of a 'two-tier' Service in the core areas of health care, but there is substantial evidence of the decay of the equity principle in fields conventionally viewed as not concerned with life-threatening conditions. The most obvious case is dentistry. Originally a core service freely available, National Health Service dentistry is now recognised to have disappeared over large parts of the country, leaving patients to make their own private arrangements.

Power

The Health Service founded in 1948 was successful at delivering free health care to the whole population at bargain basement prices because it rested on a particular set of power relations between three sets of actors: the state, doctors and patients. The state decided what total package of resources the country could afford. Doctors used their clinical authority to make the hard life-and-death rationing choices about the allocation of scarce resources. Patients deferred to the clinical authority of the medical profession, rarely thinking of what was happening to them as an act of rationing. By the 1980s, as we have seen, this power system was highly unstable and in the 1990s it fell completely apart. The state, desperate to squeeze more efficiency out of the system, invaded the clinical domain, subjecting doctors to ever tighter scrutiny. It also swept aside the traditional understanding that no major reform of the Service would happen over the head of the medical profession: the internal market reforms pushed through in the early 1990s did exactly that. The medical profession, once the centrepiece of the power system in health care, found itself under siege from two sides. The state was squeezing it from the top, and patients were squeezing it from below. Patients increasingly organised themselves into pressure groups, especially groups catering for those suffering 'chronic' (long-term) illnesses (Wood, 2000b). In the surgeries and hospital wards doctors found themselves confronting patients who bore little resemblance to the deferential citizens of the 1940s. Rather, having become increasingly accustomed to a competitive economy where the emphasis was on service to the consumer, patients were decreasingly likely to abide by the injunction 'trust me, I'm a doctor'. This injunction began to sound as unconvincing as 'trust me, I'm a professor'. At the same time, doctors were faced with the rise of other important groups in the health care workforce. In the 1940s, for instance, health care managers were virtually an unknown breed. By the 1990s they were a distinct cadre, challenging the traditional clinical expertise of the doctor with their own expertise in budget control and human resource management. At the start of the new millennium doctors still retain important sources of power and authority, of course, but the key feature of power relations in the Health Service now is their unstable, contested nature. Nobody is dominant, and there is no settled power system.

Themes

It will be obvious that the ferment of reform in the 1990s left many issues about health care open to debate – indeed, more open than at any time in the history of the Service. The adversarial two-party system in Westminster might be thought the perfect place for these debates. Yet when we look at the positions of the parties we encounter a paradoxical state of affairs. Labour and Conservative abuse each other as never before about the National Health Service. Yet they have fundamentally the same interests and face fundamentally the same problems. Meanwhile, debate about the key issues facing the Service – rationing, equity and power – takes place outside the party arena.

Since the foundation of the Service the behaviour of the two main parties has been conditioned by one overwhelming consideration. They know that they share a common political fate: as long as Labour and Conservative dominate general elections to Parliament, they know that they will have to spend some time in government and some in Opposition. For the first forty years or so of the life of the Service this meant that they had to live with the secret of the NHS, namely that it was a system that delivered cheap health care by covert rationing. Periods in government imposed the necessity of living with this fact; periods in opposition offered the possibility of exploiting it. Both Labour and Conservative in office imposed charges on patients – for instance for prescriptions – and both destroyed the effectiveness of charges by exempting the vulnerable from those charges. When the party in office imposed charges it was abused by Her Majesty's Opposition, which was abused in turn when it did the same thing in government.

It is the case that the parties had some differences in their social support and in their philosophies and that this produced some differences of nuance. Labour, after all, established the National Health Service. It drew electoral support from some of the very poor who were most vulnerable to policies like charging for services. It also had some connections with trade unionism in the health service and, not unexpectedly, those who work in the Service always lobby for more spending. The Conservatives, by contrast, not only claimed to be the party sympathetic to the market – and therefore sceptical of the command nature of the NHS – but also, as the party of the professional middle classes, were the natural political home of doctors. These facts combined to make the Conservatives mildly sceptical of the introduction of the Service in 1948, and committed the party to undoing some of the command elements of the system on their return to office in 1951.

In practice, the success and the limits of the NHS swept these party differences aside. The Conservatives, faced with overwhelming popular support for the NHS, soon retreated from their early reform plans. Labour in office, needing the doctors to do the hard job of rationing, soon settled down to live in peace with the medical profession. Hard debates about priorities and management took place, but they took place inside government, as elected politicians were faced with the need to make choices. The last place any rational politician wanted a debate about priorities or rationing was on the electoral hustings or on the floor of the House of Commons.

This need to avoid the central and most contentious issues became still more acute in the 1990s as the old power arrangements in the Service fell apart. Labour denounced the Conservative reforms of the early 1990s, but merely tinkered with them on return to government in 1997 (Wood, 2000a). The governing party has to confront the issues of rationing, equity and power in making policy for the Service, but it does not want to confront them publicly in partisan debate. One important result has been to focus partisan debate about the Service on what are essentially symptoms of its problems, rather than the underlying problems themselves. The most important instance of this is the way in which debate between the parties now turns so much on arguments about waiting lists. How long we have to wait for an operation is a very important matter for us as patients, but for the Service as a whole waiting lists are only a symptom of the wider rationing and power problems. Nevertheless, arguments about who is best or worst at 'reducing' waiting lists takes centre-stage, and for some very good reasons. Waiting lists are indicators whose interpretation is infinitely malleable. They are also easily manipulable by the party in office. Any particular waiting list can be shortened or even eliminated completely simply by diverting resources in that direction. Both parties have routinely done this when in office, especially as general elections neared. For opposition parties, waiting lists provide human drama: the statistic can easily be converted into the heart-rending story of a sick child or a terminally ill and frail person. Finally, those who work in the Service routinely feed such stories to the press as part of their continuing campaign for more resources.

The unstable nature of power relations in the 1990s was a great help to politicians in health debates. The most important task of any rational politician in the health care arena is to arrange matters so as to take credit for the many good things done by the Health Service and to lay off the blame for its failings elsewhere: to centralise credit and decentralise blame. The very instability and institutional complexity of the world created in the wake of the Conservative reforms of the early 1990s was a great help to politicians in achieving this.

Prospects

The National Health Service occupies a unique place in post-war British politics: it is a success. The British have had cheap, cost-effective health care for over half a century, spending less than other comparable countries on health care. Everybody has had access to care. For the most part nobody has had to worry about ability to pay. The scourge of the poor in earlier generations – sickness compounded by poverty – has been eliminated. Standard indicators of health outcomes – like life expectancy – suggest that this cheap service has not damaged the health of the citizens and, indeed, the evidence suggests that many higher-spending countries have poorer results (the United States being the most spectacular and catastrophic example.) Measured by some obvious standards – economy, equity, effectiveness – the Service has been far from perfect, but it has been better than the obvious available alternatives.

This does not mean that there have been no issues to debate, but the way in which the NHS achieved success made it difficult to argue about some key questions, at least in the partisan political arena. As we have seen, the Service worked because it was able to ration brutally, but at the same time was able to 'depoliticise' rationing. Shifting the tricky rationing decisions to the domain of the doctor worked in an era when medical authority was unquestioned and doctors were happy to do the rationing. For a generation politicians were able to evade hard rationing choices. But the conditions of the 1950s obviously do not exist fifty years on. We have lost our covert mechanisms of rationing but have yet to replace them with the results of open, considered debate about health care priorities. Politicians, wary of being damaged electorally, find it immensely difficult to debate these issues so they focus instead on side issues such as waiting lists. The

Service nevertheless needs a considered rationing philosophy. That is going to be a tall order. Essentially, there are three possibilities, and all pose big problems.

Market-based rationing

In Britain most goods and services are rationed by the market: you get what you pay for and that includes necessities of life that are just as basic as health care, such as food and shelter. Markets seem to be outstanding at producing an abundance of supply and at creating suppliers who are responsive to customers. But markets allocate resources unequally. At the extreme, the very poorest get nothing at all. The popularity of the NHS is undoubtedly due to the fact that it rests on the principle of equity – the very principle which the market violates. Whether the British are ready to abandon this principle is doubtful.

Technocratic rationing

This means using systematic measuring techniques to ensure that resources are allocated where they do most good. Most of us, if we were forced to choose between treating a 30-year-old and a 90-year-old with the same life-threatening medical condition, would probably intuitively feel that it was better, regrettably, to treat the 30-year-old because the younger patient will have more years of life to look forward to. Technocratic rationing tries to systematise that intuition into measurable policy choices, but it faces big problems. Can we measure in this way? And even if we can, are we prepared to face the human consequences of making such choices? Can we look the condemned 90-year-old in the eye? These problems lead some to the third solution.

Rule of rescue rationing

This approach says that we are morally bound to assist those in trouble, irrespective of calculations about resources. Many highly-regarded rescue services in our society (consider the lifeboats or mountain rescue services) operate on this principle. They go when called, irrespective of the cost or the merits of the distressed person. The idea that we have a duty simply to give aid to the suffering is one that is deep in all of us. The problem with this rule in health care is also obvious, however, even if we just try to aid the suffering. There is so much to do that we will still be forced to make some choices about priorities.

Summary

This chapter has:

- Explained how the original success of the National Health Service depended on a system of covert rationing which suppressed arguments about how to allocate health care resources.
- Described why that covert system became untenable.

- Analysed what the change has done to the character of arguments about policy.
- Summarised some of the terms of the arguments that should now take place about health care priorities.

Discussion Questions

1. What would be the best system of rationing resources in the National Health Service?
2. Can politicians who have to fight elections ever openly argue about health care rationing?
3. What have been the main successes, and the main failures, of the National Health Service?

References

Aaron, H.J. and Schwartz, W.B. (1984) *The Painful Prescription: Rationing Hospital Care*, Washington, DC: Brookings Institute.

Donelan, K., Blendon, R., Schoen, C., Davis, K. and Binns, K. (1999) 'The cost of health system change: public discontent in five nations', *Health Affairs*, Vol. 18, No. 3, pp. 206–16.

Harrison, S. and Moran, M. (1999) 'Resources and rationing: managing supply and demand in health care', in G. Albrecht, R. Fitzpatrick and S. Scrimshaw (eds) *The Handbook of Social Studies in Health and Medicine*, New York: Sage.

Klein, R. (1990) 'The state and the profession: the politics of the double bed', *British Medical Journal*, Vol. 301, pp. 700–2.

Klein, R., Day, P. and Redmayne, S. (1996) *Priority Setting and Rationing in the National Health Service*, Buckingham: Open University Press.

Mohan, J. (1995) *A National Health Service? The Restructuring of Health Care in Britain*, Basingstoke: Macmillan.

OECD (1998) *OECD Health Data 98: A Comparative Analysis of 29 Countries*, machine-readable CD Rom, Paris: Organisation for Economic Cooperation and Development.

Wood, B. (2000a) 'Health policy', in D. Coates and P. Lawler (eds) *Labour into Power*, Manchester: Manchester University Press.

Wood, B. (2000b) *Patient Power? Patients' Associations in Britain and America*, Buckingham: Open University Press.

Further reading

The classic study of the NHS which explores in a beautifully clear way all the issues of authority and resource allocation surveyed here is R. Klein (1995) *The New Politics of the NHS* (third edition, Harlow: Longman). It is essential reading. H.J. Aaron and W.B. Schwartz (1984) *The Painful Prescription* (Washington, DC: Brookings Institute), a study of rationing in the USA and UK, though based on now dated evidence, is still the single best study of this subject. J. Mohan (1995) *Governing the Health Care State* (Manchester: Manchester University Press) is a radical interpretation of health policy since 1979. B. Wood (2000b) *Patient Power?* (Buckingham: Open University Press) is a pioneering study of the rise of patient power. M. Moran (1999) *Governing the Health Care State: A Comparative Study of the United Kingdom, United States and Germany* (Manchester: Manchester University Press) sets the British system in an international context.

Foreign and Defence Policy

Paul G. Harris

CHAPTER NINETEEN

When we study British politics, we tend to look inward – at party politics and parliamentary affairs, at public policies on the environment and the economy, at governmental services like health care and criminal justice. But the British government is responsible for much more. It must also ensure national security and promote Britain's national interests, and it must take decisions and implement policies that allow Britain to benefit from the processes of economic interdependence and globalisation that are eroding national sovereignty. It also arguably has the responsibility to promote Britain's values abroad.

In this chapter we briefly examine Britain's foreign and defence policies. By foreign policy we mean the combination of national and governmental values and preferences towards the world, the goals the government seeks to achieve to promote those preferences and the means by which it implements those goals. In simplest terms, the goals of foreign policy are to protect British territory and protect and promote Britain's economic vitality and (at least by example) the British way of life – the culture, language, type of government, economic system, legal system, and the like. We begin with a short survey of the history of British foreign and defence policy. We then look at how foreign and defence policies are made in contemporary Britain. That is followed by a summary of the principles underlying British foreign policy. Finally, we introduce some of the key contemporary issues in British foreign and defence policy.

Background

For most of its history Britain was a great power, with colonies spread across the globe. Its naval power in particular was able to extend British influence to other continents and was a key guarantor of maritime access to the colonies and the instrument of *Pax Britannica* (which refers to the country's willingness and ability to foster international peace and stability, and to enforce common international standards, such as those of trade and freedom of movement on the high seas). Closer to home, Britain acted as a stabilising influence on the European continent, stepping in as events required to maintain the European balance of power. Thus, for example, Napoleon's efforts to control Europe were thwarted in large measure by British power. In time, however, acting as the guarantor of stability on the European continent while managing and controlling the Empire, led Britain to over-extend its national capabilities and resources. By the turn of the twentieth century Britain's global influence was about to be dealt a decisive setback. With the outbreak of the First World War, no doubt the government expected once again to restore the balance of power in Europe. However, the war did not go as planned and, instead of imposing order on Europe, Britain found its power – and the blood and treasure underlying it – sapped by a long war. Hence, when Britain once again was at war with Germany and its allies in the Second World War, it allied itself with the United States, at first tacitly, due to US reticence, but eventually in the most robust fashion. Nevertheless, by the end of the Second World War Britain's global influence was in its twilight (Barnett, 1972; Northedge, 1974). In its weakened state Britain had limited capacity to prevent restive colonies from seeking and securing their independence, which was, in the end, in keeping with the wave of decolonisation and formation of new states that spread around the world in the decades following the Second World War. In the place of Empire Britain was forced to settle for a more equal relationship with its former colonies in the Commonwealth.

The key feature of history in the second half of the twentieth century was the emergence of a Cold War between the new post-war superpowers: the United States and the Soviet Union. Winston Churchill warned the Americans in particular of the necessity to confront the Soviet Union and he was arguably instrumental in early efforts by the western world to prepare for the long confrontation. Britain joined with the United States and other western countries in an Atlantic Alliance, manifested in the North Atlantic Treaty Organisation (NATO). There were times when Britain was unsure whether to favour its European allies or the Americans, as indicated by its ill-fated effort in 1956 to secure the Suez Canal, with the help of France and Israel. But it would not be until after the Cold War that Britain would again seriously question its close relationship with the United States in the security environment. Beyond just security, however, Britain slowly turned towards Europe, finally joining the European Economic Community in 1973. Its integration with western Europe would, alongside the slow denouement of the Cold War, characterise much of Britain's foreign policy in the final decades of the twentieth century.

Thus from its heyday in the nineteenth century to the present, Britain's place in the world has shifted from that of a global power to that of a 'middle power'. This does not mean that it is without international influence, however. Britain is not an ordinary country. It is a leading member of prominent international organisations, including the European Union, NATO and the United Nations, where it holds a permanent seat – and a decisive veto – on the Security Council. It has a relatively large economy and an important role in global trade, and the City of London remains a hub of international finance. And it has one of the more powerful defence forces in the world, with the ability to project those forces abroad, as well as a nuclear arsenal which arguably acts as a deterrent against those who might want to use weapons of mass destruction against Britain or otherwise intimidate it. Thus, while Britain is no longer a superpower, which some might say it was in the nineteenth century, it is still a 'great' power with substantial ability to shape international events.

Summary

- Britain was one of world's greatest powers, particularly during the period of *Pax Britannica* before the First World War.
- The First and Second World Wars and the Cold War required Britain to ally itself with the United States to secure peace on the European continent.
- Britain remains a great 'middle' power, with ongoing ability to project its power and influence abroad.

Theoretical Considerations

Explaining and understanding British foreign policy usually requires us to consider very many factors. How can we get our minds around what are sometimes complex cases of foreign policy? How can we organise and manage all the possible variables and explanations? Just as understanding domestic politics can be aided by the use of theory, so too can international relations and foreign policy. Theory is a way of making the world or some part of it more intelligible or better understood. More rigorously, it can be defined as 'an intellectual construct that helps one to select facts and interpret them in such a way as to facilitate explanation and prediction concerning regularities and recurrences or repetitions of observed phenomena' (Viotti and Kauppi, 1999: 3). Thus theory helps us to understand British foreign policy by simplifying reality and focusing our attention on the actors and institutions that may be most useful for explaining specific events.

Three approaches to foreign policy

Theoretical approaches to foreign policy can be organised into three categories: systemic theories, which emphasise the influence of the international system and the distribution of power within it; societal theories, which focus our attention on British politics, society and culture; and state-centric theories, which find answers to questions about foreign policy within the state and the individuals who work therein. How might these theoretical approaches help explain British foreign policy? We can take Britain's participation in European integration as an example. From the perspective of systemic theory, one could argue that Britain has participated in the European Union and its predecessors because its global power was waning. It recognised that the most effective way to compete economically with the Americans and Japanese was to join 'Fortress Europe'. And European integration was seen as a way of cementing the interests of Britain and the continent in the Cold War with the Soviet Union and its eastern European allies. From the perspective of societal theory, one could argue that businesses pressurised the government to join the European Economic Community (EEC). Subsequently, citizens began to feel a kinship with the organisation and pressed government to continue integration, and in turn the Labour and Liberal Democratic Parties supported closer relations with Europe. From the perspective of state-centric theory, we might argue that the government pushed EEC membership. Whitehall collectively supported European integration and British participation, and once it joined the organisation bureaucrats endeavoured to maintain the *status quo*. These three approaches are simplified versions of existing theoretical approaches, but they illustrate how theory helps to illuminate key aspects of British foreign policy (see Smith and Smith, 1988).

Summary

- Just as understanding politics requires theory, so too does understanding international relations and foreign policy.
- Theory helps make the world or some part of it easier to understand by explaining the relationships between important actors and forces.
- Some scholars identify three broad theoretical approaches to foreign policy: systemic theories, societal theories, and state-centric theories.

Underlying Principles of British Foreign Policy

Several principles permeate British foreign policy (Martin and Garnett, 1997), most of which have endured for decades.

Britain should play a major role in international relations. While Britain must accept a diminished role in the world relative to its imperial past, no government has tried to withdraw from an active and robust role in international affairs. Some have argued that Britain should let other countries take on global responsibilities, but the post-1997 Labour government chose an active role. Indeed, despite its attractions, according to Martin and Garnett the notion of withdrawing from the world 'does not seem a realistic proposition for a major power, strategically located, with global interests and commitments and a recent "great power" history' (Martin and Garnett, 1997: 84).

Foreign policy should promote Britain's economic interests, notably by promoting international trade. Indeed, without a strong economy, it is impossible to maintain more traditional power resources, such as military strength, that protect vital national interests.

Related to economic interests is the continuing British commitment to promoting free trade, whether regionally in the EU or globally under the rubric of the World Trade Organisation. This is a long-term goal. Governments see free trade as the best guarantor of Britain's long-term economic interests. Hence they have been less willing in recent years to engage in mercantilist policies that seek to promote short-term interests of British industries at the expense of foreign countries and long-term British economic goals. More broadly and contemporaneously, foreign policy will have to meet the challenges of economic globalisation.

Support for a strong conventional and nuclear military capability to protect British territory and national interests, and to project British power beyond the British Isles. *Britain is essentially part of Europe and its interests require a safe and prosperous Europe.* Hence Britain's commitment to NATO and European economic integration.
Commitment to close relations with the United States because of shared interests and international goals, and because of US ability to project those interests globally.
Responsibility towards fellow members of the Commonwealth and particularly towards Britain's dependent territories (for example, the Falkland Islands, Gibraltar and Hong Kong before its return to China).
A realistic recognition that *Britain must engage the world beyond Europe* to promote the stability and free trade upon which its future prosperity will increasingly rely.
What has of late been referred to as *an 'ethical' foreign policy* (see Box 19.1), but which has in the post-war period been manifested as a consistent commitment to

---

Box 19.1 An ethical foreign policy? The case of Kosovo [speech by Tony Blair supporting NATO intervention in Kosovo]

Tony Blair, Statement to the House of Commons, Tuesday, 13 April 1999

Madam Speaker, I would like, with your permission, to bring the House fully up to date with events in Kosovo.

Milosevic's action in Kosovo – the murder, rape and terror he has visited on innocents – is ample justification for military action. To those who wanted more negotiation, I say: we struggled for a year to find a solution for Kosovo by peaceful means, despite Milosevic's brutality on the ground. We intervened when the diplomatic avenue was exhausted, and when the hideous policy of ethnic cleansing was under way. For make no mistake: this brutality was planned well in advance.

Even as the Rambouillet talks were continuing, Serb troops were massing in Kosovo and a new offensive was getting under way – 40,000 troops and 300 tanks assembled. We now know that Belgrade was making detailed plans for ethnic cleansing as early as February. Five days before NATO dropped a single bomb, Serb forces began a massive new offensive aimed at clearing Kosovo of its ethnic Albanian majority, wiping out their political class and even destroying evidence that Albanians had ever lived there.

NATO must remain united and resolute. There can be no compromise on the terms we have set out. They must be met in full. We shall continue until they are. Ethnic cleansing must be defeated, and seen to be defeated. Milosevic's policies in Kosovo must be defeated, and seen to be defeated. I believe we have a clear strategic interest in peace in the Balkans. But this is now military action for a moral purpose as much as a strategic interest. This barbarity perpetrated against innocent civilians in Kosovo, simply on the grounds of their ethnic identity, cannot be allowed.

The conflict we now face in Kosovo is a test of our commitment and our resolve to ensure that the twenty-first century does not begin with a continuing reminder in Europe of the worst aspects of the century now drawing to a close. I urge the House to continue to give its unfailing support to the men and women of our armed forces and to the values they are striving to uphold on behalf of us all.

Excerpted from: Tony Blair, 'NATO must remain united and resolute', *Guardian Unlimited*, 13 April 1999, http://www.guardianunlimited.co.uk/Kosovo/Category/0,7768,206611,00.html

what former Foreign Secretary Douglas Hurd called 'a safer and more decent international order' (cited in Martin and Garnett, 1997: 85). This has never meant, even lately, that the British government would try to perfect the world, but has meant a willingness to give relatively generous aid for development assistance (although not nearly as much per capita as some of its European counterparts) and for humanitarian aid projects, to join or even *lead* multilateral peacekeeping efforts, and recently to use force to end gross and widespread abuses of human rights.

Compared to most domestic issues, differences between Britain's political parties over foreign policy are relatively few. There is a general consensus on the above principles, although this is relatively new. Before the 1990s there were many differences between Labour and the Conservatives, particularly in the area of security. It was not long ago that Labour advocated renunciation of Britain's nuclear forces. However, since the end of the Cold War around 1990 there has been general consensus on basic principles, although this does not mean that there are no differences over how robustly policies should be implemented, or by what means. Neither does it mean that there are not often differences *within* the parties. While there is general agreement among the parties that Britain should be an active participant in the EU, the Liberal Democrats want much more integration with Brussels, while the Conservatives have been using opposition to British involvement in the Euro as a way to garner support. 'New' Labour, which generally now agrees with the Conservatives on most foreign policy principles, is in the middle. Not surprisingly, it has said that the degree to which Britain will integrate with its EU partners will be a function of British national interests.

Summary

- Several enduring principles underlie British foreign and defence policies.
- The most fundamental principle is that Britain should play a major role in international relations in order to protect its interests and ideals.
- Politicians and policy-makers from different points on the political spectrum tend to support these principles, although they do debate how best to implement them.

Major Actors in British Foreign Policy

Many actors and forces shape British foreign policy. Here we look briefly at six of them (see Clarke, 1988; Seldon, 1998). While the actors we expect to see involved in foreign policy – the Prime Minister, Foreign Secretary and the Foreign and Commonwealth Office (FCO) – are important, even a cursory look at most foreign policy situations shows that these are by no means the only ones involved. Other actors within Britain, from minor government departments to the courts and the media, and actors outside the country, from the EU to powerful foreigners, also play sometimes key roles in foreign policy-making.

The Prime Minister, Foreign Secretary and Cabinet

The Prime Minister is the final arbiter of foreign policy. In crises requiring fast action, he or she may consult very few people. Ordinarily, however, he or she will consult the Cabinet and work with the Foreign Secretary. The degree to which he or she does so may depend on personality. Few Prime Ministers hesitate to take an active role in foreign policy, however, regardless of their qualifications for doing so. Sometimes they can be decisive, as happened with Margaret Thatcher's leadership in the 1982 Falkland Islands War and with Tony Blair's leadership during NATO's 1999 humanitarian intervention to end ethnic cleansing in Kosovo. The Foreign Minister, too, can be an arbiter of foreign policy in his or her own right. If he or she has a strong personality, he or she may be able to persuade the foreign policy bureaucracy, notably the Foreign and Commonwealth Office (FCO), to follow his or her lead enthusiastically, and he or she may be able to pull the Prime Minister and Cabinet along.

Government departments

While all government departments have some role to play in foreign and defence policy, five are arguably the most important: FCO, Ministry of Defence, Treasury, Department of Trade and Industry and Department for the Environment, Food and Rural Affairs. The first two are most important (see Boxes 19.2 and 19.3), and in everyday foreign affairs the FCO is central. It conducts British diplomacy, administers most of Britain's official relations with other countries, and runs Britain's embassies around the world. These departments are nominally subservient to the country's political leaders, but in reality career civil servants handle the day-to-day business of foreign policy and rivalries between departments can mute the influence of government ministers.

Parliament

Parliament usually has the role of hearing and debating government policy, and it is increasingly active in overseeing the ways in which foreign and defence policy are implemented. It rarely initiates policy, but it does on occasion force the government to look again at its decisions. It is in Parliament, particularly the Commons, where government policy is publicly challenged. This is done routinely on issues surrounding Britain's role in Europe, although most often the debate is about the details of foreign and defence policy – in this case, how *closely* Britain should be tied to Europe, not *whether* it should be – and rarely about the general direction of policy. This is because the parties agree that national interests must be protected and they frequently agree on how to define those interests.

Box 19.2 The Foreign and Commonwealth Office website

The Mission of the Foreign and Commonwealth Office is to promote the national interests of the United Kingdom and to contribute to a strong world community. We shall pursue that Mission to secure for Britain four benefits through our foreign policy:

- Security. We shall ensure the security of the United Kingdom and the Dependent Territories, and peace for our people by promoting international stability, fostering our defence alliances and promoting arms control actively;
- Prosperity. We shall make maximum use of our overseas posts to promote trade abroad and boost jobs at home;
- Quality of Life. We shall work with others to protect the World's environment and to counter the menace of drugs, terrorism and crime;
- Mutual respect. We shall work through our international forums and bilateral relationships to spread the values of human rights, civil liberties and democracy which we demand for ourselves.

To secure these benefits for the United Kingdom we shall conduct a global foreign policy with the following strategic aims:

- To make the United Kingdom a leading player in a Europe of independent nation states;
- To strengthen the Commonwealth and to improve the prosperity of its members and cooperation between its members;
- To use the status of the United Kingdom at the United Nations to secure more effective international action to keep the peace of the world and to combat poverty in the world;
- To foster a people's diplomacy through services to British citizens abroad and by increasing respect and goodwill for Britain among the peoples of the world drawing on the assets of the British Council and the BBC World Service;
- To strengthen our relationships in all regions of the world.

Excerpted from: Foreign and Commonwealth Office website, 12 May 1997, http://www.fco.gov.uk/directory/dynpage.asp?Page=26

The Courts

The courts act as checks on government policies. They assess them in light of existing law, both domestic and international (the latter including, importantly, EU laws that increasingly restrict the government's range of action). The most visible example of this came at the turn of the century, when the Blair government detained former Chilean dictator Augusto Pinochet, who was receiving medical treatment in Britain, after a request for extradition from Spain on charges of atrocities committed while he was leader of Chile. Following an early decision saying that Pinochet had sovereign immunity and thereby could not be extradited, the Courts concluded that the government had the legal authority to send him to Spain. However, he was allowed to return home to Chile on medical grounds.

Box 19.3 The Ministry of Defence website

Defence Mission

The purpose of the Ministry of Defence, and the Armed Forces, is to:

- defend the United Kingdom, and Overseas Territories, our people and interests;
- act as a force for good by strengthening international peace and security.

To achieve this, we:

- make a vital contribution to Britain's security policy and its promotion at home and abroad;
- direct and provide a defence effort that meets the needs of the present, prepares for the future and ensures against the unpredictable;
- generate modern, battle-winning forces and other defence capabilities to help prevent conflicts and build stability;
- resolve crises and respond to emergencies;
- protect and further UK interests;
- meet our commitments and responsibilities;
- work with Allies and partners to strengthen international security relationships.

Excerpted from: United Kingdom, Ministry of Defence, 'About the MOD: Mission', 2000, http://www.mod.uk/aboutus/mission.htm

Interest groups and the media

Interest groups of all sorts endeavour to pressurise government to implement policies that promote their particular objectives. Thus businesses reliant on exports or imported components will push for free trade and further integration with Europe, while those who are threatened by imports will oppose such policies. Non-governmental organisations, such as those interested in the environment, health, human rights, or land mines, will press the government to promote their causes in international negotiations. The media can pressurise government by publicising the views of interested groups and the business community, and can be an independent force in shaping public opinion, to which the government must then attend. The media can also be instruments of foreign policy (as can interest groups), projecting British preferences and values abroad. The BBC World Service is the most visible example of this.

Foreign and international actors

The foreign policies of Britain can also be influenced by foreign and international actors. The most important is now the European Union. Britain's international economic policies have for some time been closely connected with those of its EU partners, but increasingly it is joining with European countries (often *leading* them) in areas as diverse as collective security policy, global environmental change and human rights. Britain is also affected by more universal international organisations. It is part of the World Trade Organization, and almost always complies with its norms and rules, and it seeks to fulfil the broad objectives of the United Nations objectives which it is active in shaping as a prominent UN member state and permanent member of the Security Council. British foreign policy can also be influenced by other countries. The Blair government, like some of its predecessors, was often accused of following the lead of the United States, although this is mostly appearance, as the two countries' objectives often coincide. And British foreign policy can be influenced by decisions of powerful individuals, such as Rupert Murdoch, who owns several British newspapers, and Bill Gates, head of Microsoft, whose decisions influence the course of electronic commerce and the use of microelectronics in global business.

Summary

- A very large number of different and often competing actors endeavour to influence British foreign and defence policies.
- Importantly, while they often lead on policy, the Prime Minister and the key ministries are seldom the only important actors.
- Much of British foreign policy is decided and implemented by actors and forces beyond Whitehall, such as individual citizens, Members of Parliament, businesses and foreign actors.

Debate

British foreign policy is characterised, to a very great degree, by continuity. However, some issues are subject to debate. Other chapters have demonstrated the importance of British involvement in European integration. Here we look at some other key issues that concern the foreign policy and defence establishments in Britain.

How involved should Britain be in international trade and economics?

British governments are faced with new challenges arising from economic globalisation. Britain's economy has for centuries been more open than most, but now we are even more dependent for our economic vitality on what happens in the rest of the world. Making British exports competitive is not a simple matter when faced with global competition. Hence one of the main goals of the FCO is to promote British economic interests. Indeed, 'today the criterion of successful foreign policy is not physical security but material prosperity' (Martin and Garnett, 1997: 3). To that end, British foreign policy has been increasingly devoted to fostering free trade and, more specifically, British exports. But economic globalisation – the permeability of national borders, the global ripple effects of economic decisions by producers and consumers, and the increasing inability of national governments to determine the vitality of the domestic economies – is making it more difficult for the British government to protect and preserve the home economy. Rather than fighting globalisation independently, one could argue, the British government has in recent decades instead chosen to join with other countries, particularly other countries in western Europe, to manage and compete collectively in the global economy. Britain is also involved in the World Trade Organization, successor to the General Agreement on Tariffs and Trade, which endeavours to lower tariffs and barriers to trade; the Organisation for Economic Cooperation and Development, a grouping of the twelve largest economies, which seeks to negotiate norms of international economic exchange; and the Group of Seven industrialised countries, which co-ordinates the preferences of most of the largest economies of the world. By participating in these international economic organisations Britain seeks to promote one of its most enduring foreign policy objectives: free trade and the benefits that accrue from it. As such, there is relatively little debate about British involvement in the global economy and arguments tend to revolve around how deeply to integrate Britain into a common European foreign economic strategy. In this respect, however, Britain arguably has little room to manoeuvre – despite the anti-EU activists' calls for it to quit the European Union and join the North American Free Trade Agreement.

Should Britain have an independent defence policy?

Reputable countries with experienced diplomats can achieve most of their objectives without resorting to force. However, many would argue that having a strong military to support the diplomats increases their rate of success. Thus the 1930s' assertion of one observer of British foreign policy sometimes still holds true: 'The weight of Great Britain in diplomatic bargaining is, in the last resort, proportionate to the strength of her armaments, and her influence for peace is measurable in terms of the force she can muster to prevent the overthrow of the political equilibrium by armed force' (Chaput, 1935: 372). And, of course, it is still sometimes necessary to use force to promote British interests and ideals. Witness the numerous actions of British forces in both the Persian Gulf and the Balkans over the last decade.

The military exists to fulfil three goals of the government: defence of national territory (particularly Britain itself), defence of allies (particularly European and NATO allies) and, as far as possible, the promotion of international order (Martin and Garnett, 1997: 84). Since the Second World War, Britain has favoured collective measures to defend itself, its interests, and its allies. This has been manifested most profoundly in NATO. With some glaring exceptions (for example the Suez crisis of 1956) NATO has received strong support from Britain. During the Cold War NATO was seen as a bulwark against potential Soviet aggression. Indeed, thousands of soldiers from the United States were stationed in Britain during the Cold War. In the last decade, Britain has continued to support NATO and the trans-Atlantic ties it engenders. However, at the same time it has joined with other European countries to form closer military bonds and to attach a stronger military capability on to the EU, either working alongside or instead of NATO (we do not yet know).

Britain spends a larger proportion of its wealth on its military than any other country in western Europe, signifying the continued importance it is deemed to play in promoting Britain's international objectives. Defence spending fell after the Cold War, putting pressure on the Ministry of Defence (MOD) to allocate funds where they were needed most. The MOD and defence contractors argue that Britain's large weapons export industry helps lower the cost of weapons. Some analysts debate this contention, suggesting instead that subsidies to the weapons industry could be spent more wisely elsewhere. In any case, Britain is among the world's greatest arms exporters, and there is little likelihood that this will change soon – particularly since the current government seems unwilling to do much about it, despite the contradiction between arms exports and its stated 'ethical foreign policy' (see below and Box 19.1).

Events during the final two decades of the last century – the Falklands War, the Gulf War, the wars in the former Yugoslavia – have reminded policy-makers of the need for military forces. More money is being spent on sea and airlift capacity and the MOD is making its forces more mobile to enable Britain to project forces to potential hotspots abroad more easily. Nevertheless, the Cold War still affects Britain's defence posture. It still maintains a force of nuclear missiles stationed aboard submarines. While these have little utility in most areas of defence policy, the government maintains them largely because it believes that they act as a deterrent against governments or terrorists who might be tempted to threaten Britain with weapons of mass destruction (nuclear, biological or chemical).

Today the definition of 'defence' is more fluid than it once was. Britain faces few direct threats to its most vital interests. It is in the fortuitous position of being able to 'choose' its conflicts. This can free resources for other defence-related concerns. These are increasingly conflicts related to humanitarian issues, although there are usually implications for more vital long-term national interests. For example, especially since the end of the Cold War, and particularly since the advent of the Blair government, the military has been used to protect human rights, as British participation in the NATO intervention in Kosovo demonstrated. And peacekeeping has become a normal task for British forces.

The changing post-Cold War threat environment, where true threats are few, has heightened the debate among those who wish to see Britain give strong support to NATO and US involvement in European security, on the one hand, and those who advocate an independent European military 'rapid reaction' force that could act independently of NATO – and which would naturally be subject to substantial British influence given the size and importance of its defence forces – on the other. With the exception of Labour's left wing, what is much less debated is the continued commitment to maintaining Britain's ability to use force independently to promote its interests abroad.

Should Britain be a leader in international environmental protection?

In addition to traditional concerns about national defence and economic vitality, British foreign policy has devoted more resources to new issues that have gained salience in recent decades. Among these issues are changes to the natural environment which, in recent years, have been recognised by governments as important topics of international concern. Environmental issues were launched on to the international agenda in the early 1970s. Among the concerns was acid rain in northern Europe, which was caused in large part by the burning of coal in Britain. This demonstrated that what Britain did could affect the environment of other countries. But in the last decade the most pressing concerns for Britain have been, among other environmental issues, stratospheric ozone depletion and global warming (and the climatic changes that are expected to result from it). Britain was at first opposed to action to ban the use of chemicals causing ozone depletion. Eventually Margaret Thatcher joined other governments in that effort, however, and the international treaty to protect the ozone layer was strengthened at a meeting in London in 1990, reportedly at her behest.

More recently, the government of Tony Blair has been active in pushing for stronger international efforts to limit the effects of global warming. It was instrumental in forging consensus at the conference of the parties to the climate change convention at Kyoto in 1997. That meeting resulted in an agreement by developed countries to start reducing their emissions of pollutants that are believed to cause global warming and climate change. Britain pledged to reduce its own emissions well below the targets set for other developed countries. Arguably, however, this was somewhat disingenuous because that apparently difficult target was made easy by the shift from coal to gas energy in Britain – a result of gas deposits in the North Sea and Thatcher's crackdown on the coal miners. Environmentalists argue that Britain is still not doing enough, and that the government is too protective of industrial interests. In contrast, some conservatives think it has already done too much to force reductions in polluting emissions, thereby stifling economic growth. This is a debate that is likely to be influenced in coming years by continuing signs of environmental decline.

Should Britain's foreign policy be guided by ethics?

Upon taking office in 1997 the Labour government headed by Tony Blair argued that values and ethics would play a larger role in foreign policy (see Boxes 19.1 and 19.4). According to the then Foreign Secretary Robin Cook, Britain's foreign policy 'must have an ethical dimension and must support the demands of other peoples for democratic rights on which we insist for ourselves' (Cook, 1997). The Blair government would, he said, 'put human rights at the heart or our foreign policy' (Cook, 1997). Indeed, there were new efforts to make humanitarian assistance and modern development strategies visible parts of British foreign policy, and the government supported efforts to end conflict in the Balkans. Most notable was its participation in the 1999 NATO intervention in Yugoslavia to end ethnic

Box 19.4 Promoting Britain's values abroad: the Foreign Secretary's debate [excerpt from Foreign Secretary Robin Cook's 2000 speech]

Diplomacy for Democracy

We have done much to promote British values of democracy and freedom.

- We have given a new priority to human rights. We now run projects to give practical support to human rights from developing village democracy in China to fighting sexual exploitation in the Philippines.
- We have launched a global programme to challenge torture and to help its victims.
- We have dropped the previous government's refusal to lobby against the use of the death penalty. We now consistently oppose its use.
- We have turned the UK into a leading advocate for the International Criminal Court.
- We have been robust in detaining war criminals in Bosnia, and we give wider support to the War Crimes Tribunals than any other single nation.
- We have introduced tough new criteria on arms sales and secured a European Code of Conduct which extends similar standards to our partners, and competitors, in the European Union. We have also introduced a detailed annual report which makes the UK more transparent on arms exports than any other European nation.

But the clearest contrast is between the long years of temporising with Milosevic, which marked the response to ethnic cleansing in Bosnia, and our defeat of his attempt to do the same in Kosovo. The Kosovar Albanians may have witnessed many appalling scenes. But at least they were spared the sight of the international community tolerating the oppression which produced the massacre of Srebrenica. And they have been spared the long-term consequences of such temporising: six months after the Kosovo conflict, most Kosovar refugees have returned home; four years after Dayton, the majority of Bosnian refugees still have not.

I am content to leave the last word on our record to Amnesty, whose recent report concluded that this Government 'has made a genuine and active commitment to human rights'. Not many governments can quote with satisfaction the verdict of Amnesty International.

Promoting Human Rights

Curiously, it is our pursuit of Diplomacy for Democracy that has proved the most controversial part of our foreign policy. The proposition that there should be a place for promoting human rights within foreign policy is one that would produce consensus not controversy in North America or most other European countries. There is no need for this to be a matter of partisan politics in Britain either. Let me therefore deal with the two most common lines of attack.

My reply to them is not a fresh invention. I anticipated both of them when I set out our commitment on human rights within a month of taking office.

The first line of attack is that our democratic values and our national interests are doomed to conflict in foreign policy so that we must choose between promoting our values or pursuing our interests. Whether that was ever true in the past I leave to historians to debate. But those who advance that view are still living in the past. In the global age it is in Britain's national interest to promote British values of freedom and democracy.

Along with authoritarian government come corruption and arbitrary government. What trade and investment require is competition, transparency and the rule of law. All are more easily built on an open society and accountable government.

Box 19.4 *(continued)*

Governments which respect freedom of expression are more likely to provide the transparency to be secure trading partners. Countries which observe the rule of law at home are more likely to accept their international obligations to fight the drugs trade or halt weapons proliferation.

Promoting our values enhances our prosperity, and reinforces our security.

The second line of attack is even more specious. It claims that, because we cannot put everything right, it is inconsistent to try to put anything right. This is not a maxim which we follow in any other walk of life, else we would be reduced to permanent paralysis. Nor should we let it bring foreign policy to a halt.

I flatly reject the cynical view that, because we cannot make the world perfect, we should give up on trying to make it better. The obligation on us is not to put everything right, but to do what we can to make a difference. We will therefore take every realistic, responsible step to pursue diplomacy for democracy.

Excerpted from: 'Foreign policy and national interest', Speech by the Foreign Secretary, Robin Cook, to the Royal Institute of International Affairs, Chatham House, London, 28 January 2000, http://hrpd.fco.gov.uk/news/keyspeech.asp?Speech=interest

cleansing and other atrocities committed by Serbian leader Slobodan Milosevic and his forces. NATO was divided over the intervention, especially as it dragged on and civilian casualties mounted. But Prime Minister Blair and his foreign and defence ministers were forthright and vocal in their denunciations of Serbian atrocities and in their support for ending the atrocities and punishing those responsible. Blair's public statements and behind-the-scenes cajoling arguably contributed greatly to holding NATO together until Milosevic agreed to permit ground forces to enter Kosovo (see Box 19.1).

Although Cook called only for an ethical *dimension* to foreign policy, this was interpreted as meaning a foreign policy based on ethics and, as such, has been subject to criticism (see Box 19.4). Britain continued to export arms to countries using them for highly dubious purposes (that is, not for self-defence) and such exports diverted poor countries' resources from essential basic human needs. The Blair government supported economic sanctions against Iraq and was alone in joining US air strikes against that country, while it defied UN sanctions that were imposed following its invasion of Kuwait in 1990. And the Blair government was subjected to intense criticism when it prevented peaceful demonstrators from protesting publicly during the state visit of Chinese President Jiang Zemin in 1999, whose government was committing human rights abuses across China and suppressing the indigenous people of Tibet. In contrast, conservatives criticised the government for trying too hard to inject ethics into foreign policy, and in so doing threatening more vital interests, such as relations with other great powers and important trading states.

Summary

- There is consensus that Britain has little choice but to remain actively engaged in the world economy, although there is debate about how best to do this to the benefit of the national economy.
- While there is still consensus on maintaining a strong independent military capability, forces within the Labour government are pushing to have Britain lean more towards Europe and less towards the United States.
- Britain is now actively engaged in new foreign policy issues, particularly with regard to the environment and the promotion of human rights, but some critics think these issues ought not be primary foreign policy goals.

Conclusion

This chapter has sought to introduce only some of the most evident and important features of British foreign and defence policy. Most obvious from this discussion, perhaps, is myriad actors and forces shaping policies and the many important considerations faced by British policy-makers in the past and future. While it is not possible accurately to predict all of the foreign and defence challenges that will face future governments, we can assume that Britain will remain actively engaged in the world. It will continue to maintain a large military establishment to protect vital interests and, increasingly, to project force in sometimes far away places. It will do this in concert with other powers but it will continue its historical willingness to act alone if necessary. It will remain highly integrated with the European and world economies and it will use its diplomatic influence to foster trade that benefits Britain. And it will likely remain committed, within limits and depending on who is in power, to protecting and promoting British ideals of democracy and human rights in other countries, at least insofar as doing so does not threaten more vital national interests. In short, Britain is an internationalist 'middle' power committed to protecting its interests, which almost always coincide with promoting a stable and just international order. Politicians and students of their work will always debate how best to implement these principles, but they rarely challenge them on fundamentals.

Summary

- Much as it has been for centuries, Britain remains a great 'middle' power with the ability to influence international affairs through diplomacy and, where necessary, the use of military force.
- The key principles underlying all British policies towards the outside world are: (1) active engagement in the world; (2) promotion of vital national interests,

particularly free trade; (3) support for a strong defence capability; (4) integration with Europe and continued close relations with the United States; and (5) where possible, an increasing interest in promoting ethics in international affairs.

Discussion Questions

1. When analysing British foreign and defence policies, what actors should we focus on – the Prime Minister, government departments, international organisations or other actors? Should the public have more direct influence on foreign policy decisions?
2. Should British foreign policy be restricted to protecting vital national interests, or should it also be devoted to promoting humanitarian objectives?
3. What should British military forces be used for? Should Britain maintain its nuclear arsenal?

References

Barnett, C. (1972) *The Collapse of British Power*, London: Eyre Methuen.

Chaput, R. (1935) *Disarmament in British Foreign Policy*, London: Allen & Unwin.

Clarke, M. (1988) 'The policy-making process', in M. Smith, S. Smith and B. White (eds) *British Foreign Policy: Tradition, Change and Transformation*, London: Unwin Hyman, pp. 71–95.

Cook, Robin (1997) 'Robin Cook's speech on the government's ethical foreign policy', *Guardian Unlimited* website: http://www.newsunlimited/co.uk/indonesia/Story/0,2763,19238,00.html.

Martin, L. and Garnett, J. (1997) *British Foreign Policy*, London: Royal Institute of International Affairs, pp. 82–6.

Northedge, F. (1974) *The Descent from Power*, London: Allen & Unwin.

Seldon, A. (1998) 'Foreign and defence policy', in D. Cavanagh, A. Gray, B. Jones, M. Moran, P. Norton and A. Seldon (eds) *Politics UK*, London: Prentice Hall, pp. 488–91.

Smith, S. and Smith, M. (1988) 'The analytical background: approaches to the study of British foreign policy', in M. Smith, S. Smith and B. White (eds) *British Foreign Policy: Tradition, Change and Transformation*, London: Unwin Hyman, pp. 3–23.

Viotti, Paul R. and Kauppi, Mark V. (1999) *International Relations Theory*, Boston, MA: Allyn and Bacon.

Further reading

Baker, David and Seawright, David (eds) (1998) *Britain For and Against Europe: British Politics and the Question of European Integration*, Oxford: Clarendon Press.

Bartlett, C.J. (1989) *British Foreign Policy in the Twentieth Century*, London: Palgrave.

Chamberlain, Muriel E. (1988) *Pax Britannica?: British Foreign Policy, 1789–1914*, London and New York: Longman.

Hennessy, Peter (1990) *The Intellectual Consequences of the Peace: British Foreign and Defence Policy-making in the 1990s*, Glasgow: University of Strathclyde.

Laurence, Martin and Garnett, John (1997) *British Foreign Policy: Challenges and Choices for the Twenty-first Century*, London: Royal Institute of International Affairs/Pinter.

Smith, Michael, Smith, Steve and White, Brian (eds) (1988) *British Foreign Policy: Tradition, Change and Transformation*, London: Unwin Hyman.

Environmental Policy

Robert Garner

CHAPTER TWENTY

Considered as a separate and unified branch of public policy, concern for the environment is a relatively new player on the political stage. Of course, governments in Britain and elsewhere have always taken decisions affecting the environment, but it is only since the 1970s that the issue has emerged as a distinct policy area, and only since the late 1980s that concerted popular demand for action has been evident. One of the key dimensions of the environment as a political issue is its technical core. Much of the action imperatives surrounding the issue, therefore, have their roots in scientific evidence that a problem exists. Equally, however, there is a scientific debate about the nature, causes and consequences of particular environmental problems, and this makes decision-making particularly difficult and often contentious.

This chapter has four main sections. The first seeks to document the emergence of the environment as an important political issue in Britain, and describe the two major environmental policy arenas. The second section seeks to outline the key empirical and normative contexts to the environmental debate, serving as a framework for the third and fourth sections. The third seeks to provide an update of environmental policy-making in Britain and, in particular, an assessment of the environmental record of the Labour government elected in 1997. In the fourth section, competing interpretations for the rise of the environment as a political issue are recorded and discussed and, finally, an attempt is made to identify the major determinants of environmental policy.

Background

In Britain, public policy designed to improve the natural environment dates back at least as far as the nineteenth century. Indeed, Britain is credited with having the oldest pollution control machinery in the world and by the end of the 1940s had developed the world's most comprehensive land-use planning system (Vogel, 1986: 44). For much of the post-war period, however, environmental issues, with very few exceptions, played little part in British political discourse. From time to time, individual issues with an environmental flavour hit the headlines. However, the publicity surrounding these incidents quickly died down and there was no perception that they were in some way connected, with common causes and solutions. In particular, little criticism was heard of the environmental consequences of an intensive agricultural regime that had dominated after the Second World War, and even less was directed at the secrecy inherent in the system for regulating industrial emissions (O'Riordan and Weale, 1989: 278–9).

The climate began to change in the 1970s, at least internationally. Amid dire academic predictions of imminent environmental catastrophe (see below), world leaders met in Stockholm in 1972 (proceedings published as Ward and Dubos, 1972). Out of this meeting, among other things, came a new United Nations agency – the United Nations Environment Programme – created to promote and oversee international action. However, the environment stubbornly refused to move up the political agenda in Britain. Environmental ginger groups were formed in all the major political parties during this period (Flynn and Lowe, 1992: 10–11), but as a whole the main parties showed little interest in, and were certainly not divided significantly on, environmental issues. The one exception was the Liberal Party, whose interest in the environment came earlier and went further than the two main parties. The greater willingness of the Liberal Party to consider tackling environmental problems can perhaps be, at least partly, explained by the party's distance from power. It is much easier for a party to offer radical proposals, possibly requiring economic sacrifices, when it knows this is not going to determine whether the party wins an election or not. For the two major parties, mention of the importance of the environment had, by the late 1970s, become an established element of party programmes, but it existed as 'nothing more than a "token" declaration, there to look good, but achieving little' (Robinson, 1992: 24–5). Throughout the 1970s the economy in general, and industrial relations in particular, took centre-stage.

During the early years of the Thatcher period, there was not only indifference, but also hostility, to environmentalism. The worsening economic climate made environmental concern, often seen as existing in a conflict relationship with economic growth, a luxury. Moreover, the neo-liberalism of the Thatcher government was inevitably ideologically hostile to the active state and the limits to freedom associated with an effective strategy to protect the environment.

By the end of the 1980s, however, a dramatic sea-change had taken place. Opinion polls began to reveal growing environmental concern, green consumerism became widespread, and the Green Party, which had previously made little impact, won 15% of the vote in the 1989 European Parliament elections. As a result, the government responded. Thatcher announced her 'conversion' to environmental protection (McCormick, 1991: 58–60) and this was accompanied by significant government action, to which the other major parties had to respond by strengthening their own environmental programmes (Carter, 1992: 126–30).

Major institutional changes with environmentally beneficial results were made (see below), the government accepted Britain's responsibility for acid rain, and played a leading role in the international negotiations leading to action on ozone-depleting chemicals. In addition, a more sympathetic Environment Secretary, Chris Patten, was appointed and the first comprehensive white paper on the environment, *This Common Inheritance*, was published (Department of the Environment, 1990). This action was accompanied, and at least partly influenced by, international political developments such as the granting of a greater environmental role to the

European Union and the meeting of world governments in Rio for the so-called Earth Summit, in 1992.

The environment has not retained the level of high-profile political importance it gained in the late 1980s, although this is at least partly a product of the issue's normalisation as a regular and common concern of government. Environmental concerns now occupy a much more important place in British political discourse than they did in the 1970s, but they are still usually dwarfed by traditional economic issues. The Major administration, by common consent, did very little to further environmental protection. Its main achievement was the formation of an Environment Agency (see below), which began work in 1996, but there was little else. The road-building programme was cut, but this was more to do with economic retrenchment, and a reaction to the direct action pursued by a new breed of road protestors, than environmental commitment. One issue that might usefully be classified under the environmental umbrella, not least because it focuses on the relationship between humans and another part of nature, is animal welfare. During the Major government, the key animal welfare issue involved widespread opposition to the export of live animals, and the significant fact was that the government was able to do little to pacify this opposition, partly because of a lack of political will and partly because of the constraints of EU membership (see below).

In the post-Rio era, old-style 'first-generation' environmental problems, such as general pollution control, have been dwarfed by so-called 'second-generation' problems, focusing in particular on global warming and biodiversity. The Major government published a number of post-Rio documents and set up an advisory panel on sustainable development (Dodds and Bigg, 1995: 13–15), but few new firm commitments emerged, the exceptions being an increase in VAT on domestic fuel, an increase in road fuel duty, the introduction of various energy-efficiency schemes and a landfill tax. Most environmentalists regarded these proposals as inadequate, and the first was not even primarily driven by environmental considerations, as opposed to being a general tax-raising measure. It is true that, by the time of the 1997 election, the Major government had already met the carbon dioxide (CO_2) reduction targets – a return to 1990 levels by the year 2000 – agreed at Rio, but this was a relatively easy target achieved primarily as a product of declining economic activity, coupled with the general decline of the coal industry and, more specifically, a switch from coal to gas-fired power stations, rather than through the implementation of a coherent strategy.

In the run-up to both the 1997 and 2001 elections, and the campaigns themselves, the environment was largely ignored. The Liberal Democrats, as usual, produced the most far-reaching proposals. Labour's strategies to tackle global warming were based on a shift to renewable energy sources, the creation of an environmental task force from the unemployed and, most importantly of all, the introduction of an integrated transport system. As both elections approached, however, largely as a result of the fact that voters tend to prioritise bread-and-butter issues over those such as the environment, traditional economic issues were at the forefront of the campaigns of both major parties, and the environment was barely mentioned.

Environmental policy arenas

British environmental legislation has grown up in a haphazard fashion. It is useful to identify the two main systems within which this legislation can usually be located – the land-use planning and pollution control systems (Blowers, 1987: 279). The former system effectively takes the development of private property under public control. All developments require the permission of local planning authorities. In the event of permission not being granted, the applicant has the right of appeal to the Secretary of State of the Department of Environment, Food and Rural Affairs (DEFRA) (or the relevant Welsh or Scottish authorities), who will often set up a public inquiry to consider the appeal.

In making planning decisions, attention has to be paid to wider government objectives (often the product of supranational agreements) and the existence of areas designated by the state conservation agencies (now known as English Nature and the Countryside Agency) as environmentally important. The former agency, together with the equivalents in Scotland, Wales and Northern Ireland, is responsible for identifying areas which have a particularly important flora, fauna or geology, and then recommending to the Secretary of State that these areas be designated as sites of special scientific interest (SSSI), or national nature reserves. One of the most important functions of the Countryside Agency is to identify areas which can be designated as areas of outstanding natural beauty (AONB), national parks, countryside parks and heritage coasts.

While the land-use planning system has remained pretty much unaltered since the 1940s, the pollution control system has been subject to a great deal of change in the past two decades or so. The traditional British approach to pollution control was based on a number of different inspectorates. Their operating procedures, however, were indistinguishable (Hawkins, 1984; Smith, 1997: ch. 3). Rather than having a uniform system of controls, inspectors negotiated with industrial plants before coming to an agreement on the nature and amount of the pollution that would be permitted. The system was therefore flexible, informal and remained largely secretive. Prosecutions for exceeding the agreed level of emissions were extremely rare.

In the past two decades or so, there have been numerous changes to this system. The Royal Commission on Environmental Pollution, formed in 1969 to advise governments, regularly recommended the streamlining of pollution control mechanisms, but it was not until the 1980s that fundamental change began to occur. Three main institutional developments are worth noting. These came about not primarily because of the Conservative government's interest in environmental issues but because of external pressures, particularly from the European Union (EU). In 1987, Her Majesty's Inspectorate of Pollution (HMIP) – an amalgam of the separate pollution inspectorates – was created with the aim of integrating pollution control (see below). In addition, in 1989, responsibility for water quality was transferred from ten separate Regional Water Authorities to a newly created National Rivers Authority (NRA). These two bodies were then later amalgamated into a separate Environment Agency, which began its work in April 1996. These institutional changes accompanied and, to some degree, presaged some change in operational principles. The most fundamental aim was to encourage the greater integration of pollution control and of environmental policy-making in general (see below). In addition, there was a shift away from regulatory control towards the introduction of economic instruments (so-called 'green taxes'), and a shift away from granting site-specific pollution permits towards the introduction of uniform standards.

It should be noted that the distinction between the two systems described above is somewhat artificial. In the first place, they are not entirely separate administratively since they are both centred on the Department of the Environment, Food and Rural Affairs, originally created in 1970 as the Department of the Environment. Second, the distinction is artificial because environmental problems are characterised by their interdependence, a fact reflected in the increasingly recognised need to create a holistic strategy in order to achieve sustainable development. A decision to allow planning permission for a road or an industrial development will have consequences for pollution levels and, if it also results in the destruction of flora, will contribute to global warming since it represents the loss of sinks for CO_2 emissions. The complexity, and apparent catastrophic consequences, of climate change means that most of the environmental issues facing governments in the world relate to it in one way or another.

Summary

- Before the 1970s, the environment as a distinct area of public policy was rarely considered by politicians or the public.
- By the late 1970s, there had been international concern about the environment. Although all British parties had environmental commitments in their manifestos by late 1970s, there was little practical interest in the issue and some hostility by Thatcherites and many trade unionists concerned about the economic effects of environmental measures.
- The environment burst on to the political stage in the late 1980s, provoking a governmental response.
- Throughout the 1990s the environment remained on the political agenda but at a lower level than the late 1980s.
- There are two main environmental policy arenas – the land-use planning system and the pollution control system. The latter has changed considerably over the past two decades or so.

Theoretical Considerations

A competent assessment of environmental policy in Britain requires some wider understanding of the nature of the issue. Three areas are focused on in this section. First, the nature of environmentalism as an ideology is considered; second, the two main environmental policy arenas are critically examined; and finally, a comment is made about the inevitability of the supranational dimension of environmentalism.

Environmental ideology

Environmental thinkers make competing economic, philosophical and political claims of an empirical and normative nature. Very crudely, it is possible to make myriad claims manageable by distinguishing between a radical (or 'dark' green) perspective on the one hand, and a reformist (or 'light' green) perspective on the other. As Table 20.1 reveals, the radical approach is uncompromising. Economically, the approach took its impetus from the *Limits to Growth* report written by a group of American academics in the early 1970s (Meadows et al., 1972). It suggests that there is a trade-off between economic growth and environmental protection, and that the only way of achieving the latter is by severely constraining the former. Often accompanying a limits to growth perspective is a suspicion of scientific and technological 'fixes', and an ecocentric ethic, which holds that the natural world has intrinsic value, and does not exist just for the benefit of humans. Moreover, dark greens also argue that radical social and political change, whether decentralised and egalitarian or centralised and authoritarian, is necessary to achieve the sustainable society.

For radical greens, there is no reformist route to sustainability. Indeed, the ideology of ecology is often seen as distinct from, and incompatible with, the main western ideologies of socialism and liberalism which are regarded by many greens as irredeemably productivist and anthropocentric (or human-centred). This separateness has been used to justify the creation of green political parties with their own programme of policies based on the distinct ideology. There is, however, an alternative reformist perspective which, its proponents argue, offers a realistic, but still worthwhile, route to sustainability, and which can be used to judge the environmental record of modern governments. This approach is anthropocentric, but recognises that environmental protection is in the enlightened self-interest of the

Table 20.1 Reformist and radical approaches to environmentalism

Reformist	Radical
1. Modified sustainable economic growth/ecological modernisation	Limits to, and undesirability of, economic growth.
2. Large role for technological development as a provider of solutions for environmental problems.	A distrust of scientific and technological 'fixes'.
3. Environmental solutions can co-exist with existing social and political structures.	Radical social and political change necessary: either authoritarian (for 'survivalists') or decentralised and democratic political organisation.
4. Anthropocentrism and a commitment to intragenerational and intergenerational equity.	Intrinsic value of nature or, at least, a weaker version of anthropocentrism; a commitment to social justice within human society and between humans and non-human nature.

Source: Garner (2000: 11)

human species. It also suggests that environmental protection can be effectively incorporated within the political and economic structures of modern industrial society, without fundamentally threatening economic growth, material prosperity or liberal democracy. Those governments concerned about the environment follow this light green route.

The fundamental tenet of this reformist position is the proposition that economic growth and environmental protection are not necessarily incompatible objectives. This approach has been defined as 'ecological modernisation' (Weale, 1992: 66–92; Dryzek, 1997: 137–52; Hajer, 1997; Barry, 1999: 113–18). Ecological modernisation is based on a number of related arguments. It is argued that:

- Through the use of renewable resources, and greater energy conservation, economic growth need not necessarily be synonymous with the utilisation of non-renewable resources.
- The production of low-polluting goods, designed to be environmentally less damaging, can also be a source of economic growth.
- Acting on environmental problems now may save costs to future generations.
- Although more stringent environmental measures may disadvantage some parts of the economy, overall there will be economic benefits, in terms, for instance, of the tourist industry, better public health, and less road congestion.

The key point about ecological modernisation is that, if accepted, governments can be much more proactive, and take action even when doubts, even though minor, about the causes and consequences of environmental problems remain, since they recognise there will be few economic costs of doing so. Hajer (1997: 104–74), for one, argues that decision-maker's failure to recognise the force of ecological modernisation at least partly explains why Britain's environmental record is not as good as in other countries, particularly Germany, where ecological modernisation has been adopted.

An assessment of British environmental decision-making

The strengths of the land-use planning system are that it allows for a considerable amount of participation, which environmental groups, whether permanent national organisations or local *ad hoc* groups, have been able to take advantage of. Local authorities have to take into account central government environmental orders and, indeed, many have their own sustainable development plans (known as Agenda 21s after the relevant chapter agreed at the Rio Summit) in any case (see Rydin, 1997). The weaknesses are that environmentalists cannot appeal against a decision to grant planning permission, and there is also a perception that the public inquiry process tends to be biased against those who want to protect the environment, not least because of the financial clout required to put a case effectively (Vogel, 1986: 135–7). Perhaps the most significant weakness is the limited powers of the state conservation agencies, particularly in relation to the farming community. Neither English Nature nor the Countryside Agency has the power to insist that designated areas are protected, only the right to persuade and cajole planning authorities and farmers to take the environmental importance of land into account. Farmers have traditionally been excluded from the planning system, on the grounds that it was assumed they would automatically conserve the country-side. Unfortunately, intensive agricultural practices have severely damaged flora and fauna, and the state conservation agencies do not have the resources to pay farmers to use more extensive systems or even to stop farming land all together (Vogel, 1986: 140–2; Pearce, 1993: 111–13).

Three areas of debate can be identified in pollution control policy. First, there is a consensus among environmentalists that a move towards *integrated pollution control* is desirable, if not essential. Two types of integration can be identified. One relates to the integration of the environmental efforts of government departments. This is regarded as essential because a number of policy areas, and therefore government departments, have an impact on the environment. Effective environmental decision-making, therefore, requires that a number of government departments be made aware of their environmental responsibilities. Another form of integration relates to the combining of the work of those agencies respons-ible for regulating emissions into the air, water or soil. By contrast, a fragmented regulatory system is likely to be inefficient and unlikely to produce an optimal distribution of emissions (Dryzek, 1987: 10–13; Weale, 1992: 93–5).

There are two other main debates in pollution control policy. The first concerns the choice between the traditionally pragmatic British regulatory system and the imposition of rigorous uniform standards on the other. The advantages of the latter is that it avoids the dangers of what has been described as an implementa-tion deficit whereby the regulators 'go native' by becoming too close to the regulated (Weale, 1992: 17, 87). By way of contrast, the enforcement of uniform standards may well lead to greater corporate resistance and much time-consuming and expensive litigation (Vogel, 1986: 23).

The second debate concerns the use of economic instruments as a means of replacing or supplementing regulatory standards (see Connelly and Smith, 1999: 159–71). Advocates of economic instruments argue that the best way of making the polluter pay is not through a system of permits and the stick of prosecution, but through the use of a system of economic incentives whereby the stick is pro-vided by the market. This approach is particularly associated with so-called 'green taxes' whereby an extra cost for the consumer or producer is added for activity which causes environmental damage. Britain has only gone a short way down the road towards the introduction of economic instruments, although the current Labour government has shown some interest (see below). The previous Conservative government created a price differential between leaded and unleaded petrol, increased VAT on domestic fuel, and introduced a landfill tax which charged local authorities for the amount of waste they deposited in landfill sites, thereby encouraging them to set up re-cycling schemes.

Economic instruments are cheaper to enforce than a traditional regulatory approach, encourage producers to keep improving their pollution control proced-ures, and do not involve the implementation deficit associated with regulatory regimes. However, it has been argued that economic instruments legitimise pollut-ing activities, they are difficult to set at an optimal level and, since they involve additional taxation, are difficult for liberal democratic governments to sell to the voters. The recent protests against fuel duty, the levying of which, at least in part, had an environmental function, is a classic example of this difficulty.

Sovereignty and the environment

We have been focusing on British environmental decision-making, but it should be emphasised that the environment is increasingly a supranational, rather than a national, issue. At an empirical level, much of Britain's environmental policy is, at the very least, influenced by international commitments made at the Rio Summit or at the more recent meeting of world governments in 1997 at Kyoto. Moreover, the European Union has become increasingly involved in environmental policy and, as the only international organisation 'with the power to agree environmental policies binding on its members' (McCormick, 1991: 128), its influence has been substantial both in terms of the style of policy-making, and in particular the move towards integrated pollution control and the imposition of rigid, uniform standards of pollution control, and the substance of policy-making, particularly in areas such as wildlife conservation and emission controls (see below for more detail).

The supranational dimension of environmentalism is clearly justified. Environmental problems are multinational, if not global, and therefore require the involvement of as many of the affected states as possible. Persuading states to act is much easier if they know that other states will also act, therefore sharing the burden. In particular, the long-term protection of the environment depends upon the active participation of the developing world in global environmental agreements. Unless development in the third world is sustainable, the environmental costs could be catastrophic. It is for this reason that the international community has sought to link environmental issues with other pressing concerns – such as poverty and debt – in the developing world. To this end, a United Nations Environment Programme (UNEP) organised conference in 1987 sought to operationalise the principle of 'sustainable development' (World Commission on Environment and Development, 1987), and the Rio Summit sought to take this process further.

Summary

- Radical and reformist perspectives on the environment exist, with distinctive political, economic and philosophical positions.
- The reformist view, associated with the concepts of sustainable development and ecological modernisation, offers the prospect of reconciling environmental protection and economic growth.
- An effective reformist strategy in Britain requires improvements to the land-use planning and pollution control systems.
- Greater controls on intensive agricultural practices are required, along with greater powers for the state conservation agencies to enforce the protection of designated areas.

- There is a consensus that integrated pollution control is desirable, and some support for uniform standards (as opposed to a pragmatic case-by-case approach) and economic instruments (as opposed to a traditional regulatory approach).
- Environmentalism is an issue which has become increasingly supranational in orientation and, normatively, this is desirable.

Update

It is too early to provide a comprehensive assessment of the Labour government's environmental record, but a provisional account identifies, not surprisingly perhaps, strengths and weaknesses. On the plus side is the following:

- *There have been steps towards a more integrative approach to environmental decision-making.* There have been no more changes to the pollution control institutional structure. However, it does appear that the Environment Agency, after an uncertain beginning, has become tougher on polluters under the auspices of the Labour government. Environment Agency prosecutions, for instance, have increased by about 30% since 1997 (*Guardian*, 22 March 1999). Moreover, there has been some progress in ensuring that a range of policy areas has an environmental dimension. An important first step was the incorporation of the transport portfolio into the Department of the Environment, a crucial prerequisite for an integrated transport policy (see below), although since 2001, transport has again been separated as part of the newly-formed Departments of Transport, Local Governments and the Regions. The government also established a new all-party House of Commons Environmental Audit Select Committee, designed to scrutinise the environmental claims made by government departments, and has continued, and expanded, the previous Conservative government's introduction of 'green' ministers, responsible for environmental policy, in every department.
- *The government has made significant commitments to cut greenhouse gas emissions.* The Labour government played a leading role in the Kyoto summit in December 1997, encouraging the United States administration to agree to cuts in greenhouse gas emissions, and agreeing to a higher than average cut for Britain (a 20% cut in CO_2 emissions and a 12.5% cut in total greenhouse emissions as part of an overall EU target of 8%).
- *Substantive policy initiatives to meet the Kyoto commitment have been introduced.* A significant increase in the use of renewable energy sources (10% of electricity needs must be produced from renewable sources by 2010) has been demanded, and there has also been a major cut in the previous administration's road-building programme. The use of green taxes, too, has been increased. The landfill tax scheme has been expanded, car excise duty has been adjusted to benefit cars with smaller engines, and fuel continues to rise above the rate of inflation. Potentially of greatest importance was the government's announcement, in the 1999 budget, of its intention to introduce an industrial energy tax

whereby organisations will pay a surcharge on purchases of electricity, gas and coal, the proceeds of which will be used to reduce employers' national insurance contributions by 0.5% (*Guardian*, 10 March 1999).

- *The government published its promised white paper on an integrated transport policy in July 1998 and passed a bill in the 1999–2000 session of Parliament* (see Box 20.1).

Some of the main weaknesses of Labour's environmental record are as follows:

- *Environmental integration has been limited.* Many key environmental responsibilities remain with departments other than DEFRA and yet these other departments are not noticeably 'greener' than before. Moreover, there was a conspicuous absence of environmental themes in the government's 1998 comprehensive spending review (HMSO, 1998). The level of importance attached to the environment in government is, perhaps, best illustrated by the fact that the Environment Minister (currently Michael Meacher) is not deemed worthy of a seat at the Cabinet table.
- *There are doubts about the government's ability to meet the ambitious targets agreed at Kyoto.* In particular, the green tax schemes can be criticised as inadequate. The graduated vehicle duty scheme is very moderate and is unlikely, because of motorists' ability to afford the increases, to change behaviour significantly. Similarly, the government has already moderated its plans for an energy tax after complaints from the manufacturing sector. Moreover, the estimate is that the scheme will only produce a 2% saving on CO_2 emissions anyway. Considerable additional cuts have to be made and yet it is not clear where they are going to come from. One possibility of action is on transport policy, but the government has so far achieved very little. Some road-building commitments have been retained, although it should be noted that road-building, in the form say of by-passes that reduce congestion and fumes, is not automatically bad, and action on the integrated transport white paper was delayed amidst claims that Blair regarded it as too anti-car. Even though a transport bill was included and passed in the 1999–2000 parliamentary session, the legislation leaves a great deal to be desired (see Box 20.1).

Summary

- An initial analysis of the Labour government's environmental record reveals both strengths and weaknesses.
- On the positive side, there have been steps towards a more integrative approach to environmental decision-making, the government has made significant commitments to cut greenhouse gas emissions, and there have been some substantive policy initiatives designed to meet the Kyoto commitment, including an extensive transport policy.
- On the negative side, environmental integration has been limited, and there are doubts about the government's ability to meet the ambitious targets agreed at Kyoto.

Box 20.1 An integrated transport policy

Until Labour introduced its white paper in 1998, no government had been prepared to risk the wrath of those interests – including car drivers and manufacturers – who stand to lose out from the introduction of an integrated transport policy. Constraints on car use, however, is a crucial part of any strategy to reduce carbon dioxide emissions, as well as reducing pollution, congestion and the destruction of the countryside. In line with the ecological modernisation approach, which denies there is a conflict between economic growth and environmental protection, there are also economic costs of an unsustainable transport policy – in terms of the constraints on business caused by congestion, the health costs of pollution and the costs of road repairs (Pearce, 1993: 152–8).

The white paper was finally published in July 1998 (Department of the Environment, Transport and the Regions, 1998). Its major provisions are:

- A Commission for Integrated Transport to provide government with impartial advice.
- A requirement that local authorities produce a long-term transport plan.
- A national minimum concessionary bus fare for pensioners.
- The creation of a Strategic Rail Authority to oversee the privatised rail companies.
- The establishment of a national public transport information system.

The most innovative proposal is the granting to local authorities of the power to raise revenue through the levying of charges for driving into city centres and for workplace parking. Known as 'hypothecation', this is a major shift in Treasury policy since it has long been opposed to earmarking taxation revenues for particular purposes.

After a substantial delay, allegedly due to Blair's concern that the proposals might upset the voters of 'Middle England', the bill was included, and passed, in the 1999–2000 session of Parliament. There are a number of weaknesses in the legislation. While environmentalists welcomed the congestion and parking taxes in the white paper, it will be up to individual local authorities whether or not to implement them and some of them may think that the economic costs – in terms, for instance, of lost trade – may not be worth paying. One can be forgiven for thinking that the government has denied its responsibilities on this issue since it will be local authorities that are blamed by those motorists who find themselves out of pocket. Moreover, environmentalists also criticised the proposals for their failure to include targets for traffic reduction.

Source: Adapted from Garner (1999: 28). See also *Guardian*, 6 August 1999

Debate

In this final section, two important questions are considered. First, why has the environment emerged as an important policy issue; and second, what are the major factors determining the nature of environmental policy?

Explaining the emergence of environmentalism

It is tempting to assume that the emergence of environmentalism as an issue of considerable public import can be explained simply by reference to environmental deterioration. Such a correlation, however, is difficult to establish conclusively, not least because it can be shown that the strongest environmental movements do not necessarily occur in those countries with the worst environmental problems.

Indeed, as we shall see, some scholars have argued that the objective state of the environment is not as important as other factors.

Martell (1994: ch. 4) provides us with a useful starting point here when he distinguishes three possible explanations for the emergence of environmentalism:

- Cultural or structural factors.
- Mediating influence of the environmental lobby, the media and scientists.
- Objective environmental problems.

The last two require little comment. Clearly, the means by which environmental information reaches the public is of considerable importance. This is particularly the case where environmental problems, such as global warming, ozone depletion and resource depletion, cannot be readily visualised. More contentious is the view that the growth of environmental concern is a by-product of cultural and structural factors happening independently of the actual objective state of the environment.

The cultural approach is associated above all with the work of Ronald Inglehart (1977, 1990), who shows how those born after 1945 are more likely to espouse post-material values (see Table 20.2). He suggests that more and more people have adopted this value system as a result of increasing affluence and a guarantee of economic security provided by the welfare state. Thus, as economic needs are met, people are able to turn their attention to meeting non-material goals, one of which is the desire for a quality environment within which to live and work.

The cultural explanation for the rise of environmentalism does, though, have some strengths. In particular, *the development of the environmental movement does appear to be linked to the economic climate.* Concern for the environment tends to increase during periods of economic expansion (1890s, 1920s, late 1950s and early 1970s), and drops off when recession bites (the classic example being the early 1990s). This is further confirmed by Worcester's research (1997: 162–3), which reveals that support for environmentalism is 'correlated negatively with the Economic Optimism Index, which measures people's expectations of future economic prosperity'. There are also some problems with the cultural approach:

- *Why does the satisfaction of material needs lead to post-materialism as opposed to additional material wants?*

Table 20.2 Materialist and post-materialist value types in six western European nations by age group, 1970

Age group	65+	55–64	45–54	35–44	25–34	15–24
%						
Materialist	48	45	36	35	31	20*
Post-materialist	3	7	8	12	14	25*

* The generation born after 1945.

Source: Adapted from Inglehart (1990: 49)

- *Post-materialism might not be a product of affluence.* The evidence suggests that the social composition of the environmental movement is varied and not, as one would expect if Inglehart were right, dominated by the more affluent. Other factors, therefore, such as occupation, the role of the media and the environmental movement in promoting post-material issues, or the impact of the expansion of higher educational opportunities in the post-Second World War period, might be responsible.

One alternative is provided by Stephen Cotgrove and Andrew Duff (1980, 1981). Their structural explanation for rising environmental concern suggests that the increasing incidence of post-material values can be explained, not by reference to affluence, but as a reflection of the ideological disposition of a new occupational grouping which has emerged in the post-war period. Post-material values, Cotgrove and Duff argue, are particularly prevalent among those who work in the non-productive service sector – doctors, social workers, teachers and so on – the very occupational groupings which have expanded since 1945. Those who work in the non-productive service sector are insulated from the dominant values of industrial society. It is not being claimed that the environmentalism of those who work in the non-productive service sector is an expression of class interests, in the sense that the pursuit of post-material values benefits them more than it does other sections of society. Rather, the structural explanation suggests that changing values derive from ideals rather than class interest.

Even though Cotgrove and Duff's approach is more consistent with the social composition of the environmental movement than Inglehart's, a number of weaknesses with the theory are evident:

- *It is not entirely clear why the ideals of the non-productive service sector are more likely to be post-material.* In particular, as Lowe and Rudig (1986: 522) point out, why should those working in the public sector espouse the end of economic growth when it is precisely that which ensures the continued existence of the welfare state?
- *The social profile of the environmental movement is more mixed than the structural approach would suggest.*
- *Causality is problematic.* It may be the case that those with post-material values choose occupations which are consistent with their value system. If so, it cannot be shown that the occupation is the cause of the adoption of post-material values and therefore the whole theory is undermined.

As pointed out above, those theories which emphasise the importance of structural or cultural factors in the rise of environmentalism completely ignore the possibility that it is the deterioration of the environment, and those agents seeking to draw attention to it, which has played a key role in bringing the issue on to the political agenda. This might be criticised on the grounds that to 'effectively divorce . . . environmental concern from ecological problems' (Lowe and Rudig, 1986: 518) is surely to lose sight of much that is important.

Determinants of environmental policy

As well as describing and assessing environmental policy the political scientists must also seek to explain why the policy is as it is. Trying to identify the major determinants of public policy, however, is no easy task. In western liberal democracies, policy decisions come about as a result of the national, supranational and maybe even subnational interaction between elected politicians, bureaucrats working within public authorities, interest groups and public opinion. There is also a case for saying that constitutional arrangements, such as the type of electoral system employed, can have an impact on the nature of public policy in general, and environmental policy in particular. It is argued, for instance, that the existence of a system of proportional representation in Germany, accompanied by a federal system of government, has made it much easier for the German greens to influence decision-making.

Political scientists have attempted to build theories or models of the policy process in order to make sense of the mass of empirical evidence generated by research (see Garner, 2000: ch. 9). Probably the most popular category of approach focuses on the distribution of power between political actors. The classical pluralist model, which emphasises a rough balance of power between competing interests, is often the starting point for the power approach, with some scholars defending its applicability while others seek to criticise it from alternative elitist or Marxist positions.

It is useful to start an examination of policy determinants by focusing on political parties since they are peculiarly central to the British political system. As we have seen, all of the major British parties took on a greener hue from the 1980s onwards. As Robinson (1992) suggests, the environmental policy adopted by political parties might be explained in 'pressure' or 'intentional' terms; the former referring to externally applied pressure and the latter to internally generated factors. Internal factors, encouraging or limiting the development of environmental policy, have been evident in all of the main British parties. These can be based on the role of key individuals, ideology or interests.

Individual politicians in key positions can be obstructive or provide a force for change. Mrs Thatcher, for example, played both roles in the environmental debate in the 1980s. More significantly, the interests served by political parties can be an important determining factor. Traditionally, for instance, it has been suggested that Labour's links with the trade unions has provided limits to the party's environmental policy because unions have often assumed an economic cost of environmental protection. More recently, by contrast, as Labour's institutional links with the unions has loosened, and as the union movement has ceased to be dominated by the old-style manufacturing unions, this previous constraint has begun to unravel, and this may help to explain Labour's adoption of a more comprehensive environmental programme. The Conservative's links with big business have played a similarly restricting role (Robinson 1992: 193–7). Conversely, the Liberal Democrats remain 'greener' than the other two main parties at least partly because they remain independent of important economic interests.

The interests promoted by a political party are closely linked with its ideology. In the 1980s, for instance, Conservative environmental policy should be seen in the context of the ideological split between the so-called 'wets' and 'dries', with the former much more likely to be sympathetic to the protection of Britain's natural heritage than the latter (Flynn and Lowe, 1992: 20). The implication here is that when the free market faction is predominant there is likely to be greater hostility to environmental policy.

Likewise, Labour's environmental policy is partly a product of ideology. Traditionally, the party's working-class socialist ethos tended to regard environmentalism as, at worst, a middle-class irrelevance which denied the fruits of economic growth to the rest of society or, at best, a justification for improving the quality of the urban environment for the benefit of the working class rather than the protection of nature for its own sake. As a corollary to organisational change, Labour's dominant ideology has now been largely shorn of many elements of class-based and socialist politics and, as a result, the prospects for more emphasis on environmentalism in the party's programme would seem to be enhanced (see, for instance Giddens, 1998: 54–68). By contrast, it might be suggested that the 'New' Labour emphasis on inclusivity and consensus militates against effective environmental policy since it precludes taking action which causes dissent from significant sections of society. The failure to introduce quickly an integrated transport policy for fear of upsetting sections of society who would have to make sacrifices is one classic example of this limiting effect at work. Clearly, the adoption of an ecological modernisation approach, which denies the conflict between environmental protection and economic growth, would be extremely useful for a Labour government intent on building consensus.

While political parties provide one determinant of environmental policy, there are other, undoubtedly more important, external factors that have to be considered. The public mood puts electoral pressure on political parties and this, in turn, is accompanied, and often shaped by, the role of experts and the dissemenation of knowledge (which plays a particularly important role in environmental policy-making), organised interests and international treaty obligations. The limits to environmental policy-making are to a large extent determined by the nature of the so-called 'policy communities', consisting of ministers, officials and relevant organised interests, surrounding issue areas (Marsh and Rhodes, 1992). The failure to integrate environmental concerns into fully a range of policy areas, for instance, can be explained by the influence of economic interests within various policy communities, the role of the farmers within the agricultural community being a prime example (Grant, 1989: ch. 7). Similarly, the scope and powers of the Environment Agency, as well as the stringency of green taxes, should be seen in the context of those powerful industries affected.

Organised interests now increasingly operate at the supranational level, reflecting the internationalisation of environmental policy-making. Some obligations entered into by the British government, such as those on climate change and ozone depletion, are global but, most important of all, it is the European Union which has a significant impact on British environmental policy. This has particularly been the case since the 1986 Single European Act which established the EU's legal competence to tackle environmental issues, and made it more difficult for one member state to veto proposals in the Council of Ministers, a development which was enhanced by the provisions of the Maastricht Treaty in 1991.

It is difficult to determine the precise nature of the EU's influence on British environmental policy, with some scholars suggesting it has been greater than others (see Lowe and Ward, 1998). Clearly, conflict between British governments and the EU was endemic for much of the 1980s and the early 1990s – particularly over issues such as acid rain, radioactive contamination of the Irish Sea, road construction and falling standards of water and air quality – and Britain gained the never wholly justified reputation as the 'dirty man of Europe'. However, since then, the relationship has become more co-operative and two dimensional and there is now a recognition that in some areas, such as land-use planning and animal welfare, Britain has more effective measures in place than many other member states (Haigh and Lanigan 1995; Jordan, 1998).

It is easy to point to specific areas of both environmental policy outcomes and changes to the decision-making structure where the EU has been influential; a great deal of the emphasis on integrated pollution control and the imposition of uniform standards, for example, has come primarily from the EU and other member states which have adopted the approach. Moreover, the National Rivers Authority was created because the original intention, to incorporate responsibility for water quality in the privatised water companies, was found to be illegal under EU law (McCormick, 1991: 96–8). Nevertheless, it is possible to exaggerate the degree of change in British environmental policy, the degree to which the EU has been responsible for these changes and the EU's force for environmental good. In this context, it is important to remember that one of the biggest causes of environmental degradation in the countryside has been the Common Agricultural Policy.

Summary

- Explanations for the rise of environmentalism centre either on the impact of environmental degradation and the way it is portrayed or on cultural or structural changes to society occurring independently of objective environmental conditions.
- Cultural changes focus on affluence as the cause of a growing post-material culture, while structural explanations focus on the existence of a new service sector occupational group associated with the post-war expansion of the welfare state.
- Political parties provide one obvious determinant of environmental policy but their influence is relatively limited.
- Of greater importance is the role of public opinion, experts, organised groups and, most important of all, supranational treaty obligations and organisations, most notably the European Union.

Conclusion

Environmental politics has come a long way in the past three decades or so. Growing public concern, the product, according to competing explanations, of worsening environmental degradation or fundamental structural or cultural change, has resulted in a sustained national and, even more important, supra-national response. The dominance of piecemeal initiatives has been diminished in favour of recognition that environmental problems are interdependent and require a holistic response from decision-makers. The interdependence of environmental problems has been reinforced by the identification of genuine global problems such as ozone depletion and climate change. As a result, even though it still makes sense to distinguish between land-use planning and pollution control policy in Britain, there is a significant technical and administrative overlap. Put simply, land-use planning determines what sort of development is permitted and the decisions taken impact on levels of pollution in general and greenhouse gas emissions in particular.

From a radical perspective, the changes required in order to make sustainability a reality look prohibitively difficult for pluralistic, liberal and capitalist societies such as Britain. The development of a convincing reformist perspective, however, offers some hope. For it to succeed, the integration of environmental concerns into a wide variety of governmental responsibilities is essential. The increasingly fragmented and sectorised character of modern government militates against such an outcome. In addition, while it helps to have political parties, or at least their leaderships, committed to sustainable policies, they are largely impotent in the face of those powerful economic interests which stand to gain from inaction, and a general public jealously protective of the freedoms which seem threatened by more stringent environmental measures. In the light of this, a wider acceptance of the ideology of ecological modernisation – which denies there is necessarily a conflictual relationship between economic growth and environmental protection – would seem to be long overdue. It would be wrong to assume, however, that no economic dislocation will result, at least in the short term, from sustainable policies. Unfortunately, it seems unlikely that the present Labour government, with its preference for inclusion and consensus, will be prepared to take the difficult choices necessary if a sustainable future is to be assured.

Chronology

1863 Alkali Act – created the Alkali Inspectorate, the forerunner of the general Industrial Air Pollution Inspectorate.

1947 Town and Country Planning Act – the major post-war planning legislation requiring that all proposed development be subject to planning permission.

1949 National Parks and Access to the Countryside Act – created a system of national parks and the administrative machinery to run them.

1954 Protection of Birds Act – a statute up-dating earlier legislation on the protection of birds which, in turn, was superseded by the 1981 Wildlife and Countryside Act.

1956 Clean Air Act – passed in response to the infamous smogs, particularly in London.

1968 Agriculture (Miscellaneous Provisions) Act – the first specific legislation providing protection to farm animals.

1969 Creation of the Royal Commission on Environmental Pollution.

1970 Creation of the Department of the Environment.

1972 Stockholm Conference on the Human Environment.

1973 Water Act.

1981 Wildlife and Countryside Act.

1986 Animals (Scientific Procedures) Act.

1987 Creation of Her Majesty's Inspectorate of Pollution.

1988 Agriculture Act.

1989 Water Act (created the National Rivers Authority).

1990 Environmental Protection Act.

1990 (September) white paper, *This Common Inheritance*, published.

1992 (June) UN Conference on Environment and Development (the Earth Summit) held in Rio de Janeiro.

1995 Environment Act (among other things, created the Environment Agency and the Scottish Environmental Protection Agency).

1998 Scotland Act – devolved environmental responsibilities to a new Scottish Parliament and Executive.

1998 Government of Wales Act – devolved some secondary environmental responsibilities to the Welsh Assembly and its committees.

Discussion Questions

1. Account for the emergence of the environment as an important issue of public concern.
2. Critically examine the reformist approach to environmentalism.
3. What or who has been the most important determinant of environmental policy in Britain?

References

Barry, J. (1999) *Rethinking Green Politics: Nature, Virtue and Progress*, London, Sage.

Blowers, A. (1987) 'Transition or transformation? Environmental policy under Thatcher', *Public Administration*, Vol. 65, pp. 227–94.

Carter, N. (1992) 'The "greening" of Labour', in M.J. Smith and J. Spear (eds) *The Changing Labour Party*, London: Routledge.

Connelly, J. and Smith, G. (1999) *Politics and the Environment: From Theory to Practice*, London: Routledge.

Cotgrove, S. and Duff, A. (1980) 'Environmentalism, middle-class radicalism and politics', *Sociological Review*, Vol. 28, pp. 333–51.

Cotgrove, S. and Duff, A. (1981) 'Environmentalism, values and social change', *British Journal of Sociology*, Vol. 32, pp. 92–110.

Department of the Environment (1990) *This Common Inheritance: Britain's Environmental Strategy*, Cmnd 1200, London: HMSO.

Department of Environment, Transport and the Regions (1998) *A New Deal for Transport: Better for Everyone*, London: HMSO.

Dodds, F. and Bigg, T. (1995) *The United Nations Commission on Sustainable Development: Three Years since the Rio Summit*, London: UNED–UK.

Dryzek, J. (1987) *Rational Ecology*, Oxford: Blackwell.

Dryzek, J. (1997) *The Politics of the Earth: Environmental Discourses*, Oxford: Oxford University Press.

Flynn, A. and Lowe, P. (1992) 'The greening of the Tories: the Conservative party and the environment' in W. Rudig (ed.) *Green Politics Two*, Edinburgh: Edinburgh University Press, pp. 9–36.

Garner, R. (1999) 'How green is Labour?', *Politics Review*, Vol. 8, No. 4, pp. 26–8.

Garner, R. (2000) *Environmental Politics*, Basingstoke: Macmillan.

Giddens, A. (1998) *The Third Way: The Renewal of Social Democracy*, Cambridge: Polity Press.

Grant, W. (1989) *Pressure Groups, Politics and Democracy in Britain*, Hemel Hempstead: Philip Allan.

Haigh, N. and Lanigan, C. (1995) 'Impact of the European Union on UK environmental policy making', in T. Gray (ed.) *UK Environmental Policy in the 1990s*, Basingstoke: Macmillan, pp. 11–17.

Hajer, M. (1997) *The Politics of Environmental Discourse: Ecological Modernization and the Policy Process*, Oxford: Clarendon Press.

Hawkins, K. (1984) *Environment and Enforcement*, Oxford: Clarendon Press.

HMSO (1998) *Modern Public Services for Britain: Investing in Reform. Comprehensive Spending Review*, Cmnd 4011. London: HMSO.

Inglehart, R. (1977) *The Silent Revolution: Changing Values and Political Styles among Western Publics*, Princeton, NJ: Princeton University Press.

Inglehart (1990) 'Values, ideology and cognitive mobilization in new social movements', in R. Dalton and M. Kuechler (eds) *Challenging the Political Order: New Social and Political Movements in Western Democracies*, Cambridge: Polity Press, pp. 43–66.

Jordan, A. (1998) 'The impact on UK environmental administration', in P. Lowe and S. Ward (eds) *British Environmental Policy and Europe: Politics and Policy in Transition*, London: Routledge, pp. 173–94.

Lowe, P. and Rudig, W. (1986) 'Review article: political ecology and the social sciences – the state of the art', *British Journal of Political Science*, Vol. 16, pp. 513–50.

Lowe, P. and Ward, S. (1998) 'Britain and Europe: themes and issues in national environmental policy', in P. Lowe and S. Ward (eds) *British Environmental Policy and Europe: Politics and Policy in Transition*, London: Routledge, pp. 3–30.

Marsh, D. and Rhodes, R. (eds) (1992) *Policy Networks in British Politics*, Oxford: Oxford University Press.

Martell, L. (1994) *Ecology and Society*, Cambridge: Polity Press.

McCormick, J. (1991) *British Politics and the Environment*, London: Earthscan.

Meadows, D.H., Meadows, D.L., Randers, J. and Behrens III, W. (1972) *The Limits to Growth: A Report for the Club of Rome's Project on the Predicament of Mankind*, New York: Universe.

O'Riordan, T. and Weale, A. (1989) 'Administrative reorganisation and policy change: the case of Her Majesty's Inspectorate of Pollution', *Public Administration*, Vol. 67, pp. 277–95.

Pearce, D. (1993) *Blueprint 3: Measuring Sustainable Development*, London: Earthscan.

Robinson, M. (1992) *The Greening of British Party Politics*, Manchester: Manchester University Press.

Rydin, Y. (1997) 'Policy networks, local discourses and the implementation of sustainable development', in S. Baker, M. Kousis, D. Richardson and S. Young (eds) *The Politics of Sustainable Development: Theory, Policy and Practice within the European Union*, London: Routledge, pp. 152–74.

Smith, A. (1997) *Integrated Pollution Control: Change and Continuity in the UK Industrial Pollution Policy Network*, Aldershot: Ashgate.

Vogel, D. (1986) *National Styles of Regulation: Environmental Policing in Great Britain and the United States*, Ithaca, NY: Cornell University Press.

Ward, B. and Dubos, R. (1972) *Only One Earth: The Care and Maintenance of a Small Planet*, London: Andre Deutsch, pp. 221–45.

Weale, A. (1992) *The New Politics of Pollution*, Manchester: Manchester University Press.

Worcester, R. (1997) 'Public opinion and the environment', in M. Jacobs, *Greening the Millennium: The New Politics of the Environment*, Oxford: Blackwell, pp. 160–73.

World Commission on Environment and Development (1987) *Our Common Future*, Oxford: Oxford University Press.

Further reading

There are two textbooks which cover the empirical and theoretical dimensions of environmentalism: R. Garner (2000) *Environmental Politics* (Basingstoke: Macmillan) and J. Connelly and G. Smith (1999) *Politics and the Environment* (London: Routledge). There is also much of use in the journal *Environmental Politics*, published by Frank Cass. A. Smith (1997) *Integrated Pollution Control* (Aldershot: Ashgate) provides a detailed and relatively up-to-date account of pollution control policy and D. Vogel (1986) *National Styles of Regulation* (Ithaca, NY: Cornell University Press) is useful for its historical and comparative emphasis. A. Dobson (1995) *Green Political Thought* (second edition, London: Unwin Hyman) is regarded as the major text on green political thought, although J. Dryzek (1997) *The Politics of the Earth* (Oxford: Oxford University Press) and R. Eckersley (1992) *Environmentalism and Political Theory* (London: UCL Press) are also worth reading. A. Weale (1992) *The New Politics of Pollution* (Manchester: Manchester University Press) and M. Hajer (1997) *The Politics of Environmental Discourse* (Oxford: Clarendon Press) explore the concept of ecological modernisation, and D. Pearce (1993) *Blueprint 3* (London: Earthscan), includes some useful statistics to back up its claims.

The best three textbooks on international environmental politics are T. Brenton (1994) *The Greening of Machiavelli: The Evolution of International Environmental Politics* (London: Earthscan), L. Elliot (1998) *The Global Politics of the Environment* (Basingstoke: Macmillan) and G. Porter and J. Brown (1996) *Global Environmental Politics* (second edition, Boulder, CO: Westview Press). L. Martell (1994) *Ecology and Society* (Cambridge: Polity Press) is useful for a number of the issues explored in this chapter, but provides a particularly good summary of the debate about the rise of environmentalism. Those who want to read the major contributions to this debate should look at R. Inglehart (1977) *The Silent Revolution* (Princeton, NJ:

Princeton University Press) and (1990) 'Values, ideology and cognitive mobilization in new social movements', in R. Dalton and M. Kuechler (eds) *Challenging the Political Order* (Cambridge: Polity Press, pp. 43–66), and S. Cotgrove and A. Duff (1980) 'Environmentalism, middle-class radicalism and politics', *Sociological Review*, Vol. 28, pp. 333–51, and (1981) 'Environmentalism, values and social change', *British Journal of Sociology*, Vol. 32, pp. 92–110. There is a massive literature exploring the determinants of environmental policy. The best way in is to look at chapter 9 of Garner (2000) and follow up the references found there.

Dealing with Moral Issues

Philip Cowley

CHAPTER TWENTY-ONE

Background

Should capital punishment be restored? Should gay men be allowed to have sex at the age of 16? Should fox-hunting be banned? Should the state allow scientists to 'clone' from embryos? These questions, all of which were debated during the 1997 Parliament, may not be part of mainstream party political debate in Britain, but they are far from unimportant. They matter greatly to many people, including those not directly affected by them. When discussed, they tend to generate heated argument in a way that does not apply to many, or even most, other political issues.

There are also important questions about the way that this type of issue is resolved in the British political system. Traditionally, and for reasons that are not entirely clear, they are usually regarded as 'issues of conscience' on which it would be wrong for political parties to adopt a stance. Instead, the decision is left to individual MPs voting how they see fit. This has important consequences for the way in which such issues are resolved.

This chapter begins by explaining what we mean by 'moral issues', before explaining how these issues have developed over the last forty years. The second half of the chapter discusses the consequences for British politics of the way in which these sorts of issues are treated, showing how they are removed from the political arena, how, despite claims that they are above party, the role of political parties remains important and how the position adopted by the executive also remains important, despite claims that it is neutral.

Theoretical Considerations

In one of the most famous single sentences ever written on public policy, T.J. Lowi (1972) wrote that 'policy determines politics', meaning that different types of policy generate different types of political conflict. This is certainly true when it comes to issues of morality. Although what is perceived as 'moral' varies, both from country to country and over time, once a policy is so perceived it is usually dealt with in a different way other types of policy. Abortion policy, for example, is treated atypically in twenty-one out of the twenty-two countries studied by Studlar (2001).

Moral issues – most simply defined as those in which at least one advocacy coalition (for want of a better term) views the issue in terms of morality or sin – are said to have the six characteristics shown in Table 21.1. These are drawn from the considerable literature on morality policy, much of which focuses on the United States. Yet the USA is an atypical political system. It also has the highest levels of religious practice of any western democracy and is socially increasingly heterogeneous, thus generating a large number of potentially socially conflicting

Table 21.1 The six characteristics of morality politics

Characteristic	Discussion
Moral policies often involve issues of first principle, about which it is difficult to compromise.	Is it right for the state to kill? Does life begin at conception? Is homosexuality sinful? Issues such as these rarely have a comfortable middle ground.
Whereas much political debate is about means, debates about moral issues are usually about ends.	Nearly everyone wants low unemployment, or good health provision, or peace in Northern Ireland (the ends), but we disagree about how to achieve it (the means). Debates about moral issues – such as abortion – are usually about the end itself rather than the means.
Because they are about first principles, moral policies are often technically simpler than most issues – they are what have been called 'easy issues'.	This is not to deny that they frequently involve complex technical issues, but there is often an overriding issue that is easier to grasp. For example, embryo research involves extremely complex scientific issues, but for many these are secondary to more fundamental questions about the point at which life begins. As a result it is easier for people to have a position on moral issues compared to, say, taxation policy.
Because they are concerned with first principles and are easily understood, moral issues can be highly politically salient.	The debate over basic values 'is exciting and meaningful and so can grab citizen attention'.
Moral issues have a higher level of citizen participation than other policy issues.	Citizens have an incentive to participate, both because their basic values are being threatened and because the information barriers that usually limit citizen involvement do not exist.
Because of all the above, policy-makers will be more responsive to the general public when it comes to issues of morality compared to other types of policy.	Policy-makers must pay close attention to what the public wants, 'be it out of a sense of democratic duty or self-interest'.

Source: Derived and adapted from Mooney (2001)

sets of religious values. As a result, it treats more political issues as moral issues than any other established western democracy (Studlar, 2001). As will be seen, these six characteristics are not all easily applied to the British case, however.

Nonetheless, in the UK many moral issues are treated differently from normal politics, being referred to as 'issues of conscience'. These are issues on which the political parties do not take a stance, allowing their parliamentarians 'free votes' on the subjects. Although there is no agreed definition of what constitutes an issue of conscience, topics usually considered to be covered include corporal and capital punishment, abortion and embryo research, hunting, contraception, euthanasia, the punishment of war criminals, Sunday entertainment and trading, homosexuality, prostitution, censorship, divorce and (somewhat incongruously) the compulsory wearing of car seatbelts (Jones, 1995).

Yet the fit between 'morality' and issues of conscience in the UK is far from absolute. There are *prima facie* issues of morality that are generally not viewed as issues of conscience in Britain. For example, the majority of animal welfare issues go through the standard legislative process. Hunting is the exception, being seen as an issue of conscience for reasons that are difficult to identify. Issues such as single parenting, while usually acknowledged as having a moral dimension, are not treated as issues of conscience. Similarly, the then Conservative government took special care that policy on AIDS should be treated as a medical issue rather than one of morality. Moreover, even with those issues that are normally seen as being issues of conscience, there is nothing automatic about MPs having free votes. There have been occasions in recent years when MPs were not granted free votes on issues in the above list, including capital punishment, homosexuality and Sunday trading. Indeed, the 1997 Parliament saw both main parties put a whip on the vote to abolish Section 28 (see below). Free votes on these issues, therefore, may be the norm, but they are not the rule.

Update

In the space of just four years in the late-1960s (see the Chronology) capital punishment was (*de facto*) abolished, male homosexuality was legalised, and the laws on censorship, divorce and abortion were all significantly liberalised. For Roy Jenkins, Home Secretary for part of the period and facilitator of the changes, the reforms made Britain a civilised place in which to live. For many others – mainly but not solely on the political right – this was the point at which the rot set in (Hitchens, 1999).

Seen from the end of the century, however, the changes of the 1960s do not appear as dramatic as they did at the time. Most were messy compromises, riddled with caveats and exemptions. Male homosexuality, for example, may have been legalised, but the new law did not apply to Scotland or Northern Ireland or to members of the armed forces or merchant navy; the minimum age of consent was set at 21, five years higher than for heterosexuals; the definition of private (as in 'between consenting adults in private') was very strict; and the laws governing soliciting became even tighter than they were before. The Abortion Act was also a compromise measure, which pleased neither extreme of opinion. Although it has come to be interpreted in a way that provides relatively liberal access to abortion, it need not have been so. It, too, did not (and does not) apply to Northern Ireland. Neither was there divorce on demand: the 1969 Divorce Reform Act, like the Abortion Act, was also a compromise. Given the speed at which divorces are granted today – 'with conveyor-belt speed and impersonality' (Stone, 1995: 2) – it is worth remembering that the most controversial part of the 1969 Divorce Reform Act was that divorce without mutual consent would be available after five years.

This period has important consequences for our understanding of moral issues. It shows – despite the claims of the US literature – that it *is* possible to reach legislative compromises on moral issues. Such compromises may not please either side of the debate – that is, the various advocacy coalitions themselves may not compromise – but the resolution of the issues by the state can and often does involve compromise. It also shows that the reforms of the 1960s were far from the 'official endorsement of hedonism' sometimes claimed by popular historiography (the phrase is from Weeks, 1989: 263). Those who enacted the changes were not themselves spring chickens: 'The change', as Cate Haste noted, 'was not brought about, as it had appeared, by youth protest; the people who carried through the legislative reforms and institutional changes were all by then approaching middle age' (Haste, 1994: ix). Moreover, each campaign had been a lengthy process, with long reformist antecedents. Divorce, for example, had been liberalised periodically since the nineteenth century. The campaign for the reform of the death penalty similarly went back to the nineteenth century, with the campaign for abolition dating back to the 1930s (and the law overturned in the 1960s had itself only been in place for eight years). Although abortion had been a statutory offence since 1803, the first liberalisation came in 1938, as a result of a court case, *R v Bourne*. Moreover, a report or investigation of some kind, ranging from Royal Commissions to Joint Select Committees, preceded all the successful measures. For good or ill, the reforms of the 1960s did not come out of the blue.

Until 1997 there was no similar concentrated period of reform to compare to that of the late 1960s. But some of the battles fought in the 1960s continued. Arguments over abortion, for example, did not end with the passing of the Abortion Act in 1967. Indeed, if anything they grew in intensity, complicated by the arrival of questions about embryo research, a subject that gave people – usually the same people – something else about which they disagreed. There were repeated attempts to reform the abortion law, almost all attempting to limit the availability of abortion (Millns and Sheldon, 1998).

Similarly, debates about capital punishment, homosexuality and divorce continued. Capital punishment debates became a regular feature of the House of Commons, although the likelihood of reintroduction diminished steadily over time: in 1979 the Commons majority against the death penalty was 20%; in 1994, it was 43%. There were, however, changes to the laws relating to divorce and homosexuality.

Some of the battles of the 1960s continued to be fought but in new packaging. British politics no longer sees fierce debates about censorship of the theatre – as it did in the 1960s – but it has seen concern and legislative action over 'video nasties' (Durham, 1998). Similarly, we rarely have heated debates over Sunday entertainment (as we did in the 1960s), but the issue of Sunday trading has been extremely contentious.

New issues also emerged. The War Crimes Act 1991 required the Parliament Acts to force it through the House of Lords (the only time that this procedure had been invoked by a Conservative government to enact legislation). Issues of animal welfare – and in particular hunting – have moved to centre-stage, with heated debates on hunting becoming a regular feature in recent years.

So, in the years following the 1960s there was no substantial single period of reform, although the cumulative effect of changes was still substantial. This period, too, helps further our understanding of the way moral issues have been resolved in the UK. Many of the debates in this period – again despite what the US literature says – were not about first principles at all. There was, for example, no legislative attempt to repeal the Abortion Act *in toto*. The various proposed reforms merely tinkered with it at the edges – up to how many weeks of pregnancy should an abortion be allowed, or the grounds on which abortion was permitted. In 1994 the debate about the homosexual age of consent was not about whether homosexuality was wrong or sinful, but about the age at which someone could engage in homosexual sex. And debates in this period about divorce were not about whether divorce was right or wrong, but about the grounds under which it should be permitted, whether it was being made too easy, and so on. Issues of first principle underlay these debates, of course – and ones about which people felt very strongly – but the debates themselves were about more prosaic matters. Parliamentarians are rarely asked about issues in general; instead they are presented with specific legislative proposals.

The Parliament elected in 1997 will probably come to be seen as another 'reforming' Parliament, similar to that of the 1960s (albeit not quite as successful). It saw two private members' bill dealing with euthanasia and, although neither made it to the statute book, the increasing numbers of MPs participating showed that this was an issue of increasing importance. The laws relating to handguns were reformed in 1997, resulting in an outright ban on ownership of handguns. The Crime and Disorder Act 1998 removed the death penalty for the civilian crimes for which it remained on the statute book, while the Human Rights Act 1998 made it impossible for the death penalty to return, short of Britain's renouncing the European Convention on Human Rights (Judge, 1999). The divorce laws were reformed in 2001 when the Lord Chancellor announced that the government was abandoning Part II of the Family Law Act 1996, which had required couples to attend compulsory information meetings, since research had indicated that the meetings were counter-productive.

Parliament also voted to allow research on 'stem cells', the parents of all types of human tissue that can develop into any type of cell. The existing law, framed in the Human Fertilisation and Embryology Act permitted scientists to experiment on embryos up to fourteen days old for the purposes of research into fertility. The change in the law allowed experimentation for research into degenerative diseases. It also allowed researchers to carry out a limited form of 'therapeutic cloning', creating a genetically identical embryo of a patient using stem cells from that embryo to treat disease. And the issue of contraception returned to the agenda, resulting in sales of the 'morning after pill' being allowed over the counter. The two most high-profile moral issues during the 1997 Parliament, however, were those of fox-hunting (outlined in Box 21.1) and homosexuality. The latter saw three controversial issues being debated – 'gays in the military', the age of consent and Section 28.

Although controversial, the government's decision in 2000 to change the rules to allow homosexuals to serve in the military was the least contentious of the three

Box 21.1 Fox-hunting

In November 1997, the Commons, by a majority of 260, gave a second reading to a private members' bill introduced by a Labour backbencher, Michael Foster, to ban hunting with dogs. Labour's 1997 manifesto had promised a free vote on hunting but gave no specific commitment to ensure the passage of any legislation. The government, worried that if the bill reached the Lords pro-hunting peers might scupper their flagship legislation on devolution, refused to grant the bill additional parliamentary time. As a result, it went the way of many previous private members' bills on fox-hunting and was 'talked out' in the Commons.

Some members of the Cabinet were uneasy about banning hunting, both on grounds of civil liberties and because they feared the political fallout. The newly formed Countryside Alliance organised a rally opposing a ban in London in July 1997 which was attended by around 250,000 people. But the pressure for a ban from grass-roots members of the Labour Party and MPs was intense.

Jack Straw, the Home Secretary, established an official inquiry headed by Lord Burns into the costs and practicalities of any ban. The Burns inquiry reported in June 2000 (Cm 4763), stating that between 6,000 and 8,000 full-time equivalent jobs depended on hunting but that the experience of being pursued by dogs 'seriously compromises the welfare of the fox'. Straw announced that a government bill would be brought forward in the fourth session of the Parliament that would give MPs a series of legislative options: (i) for hunting to continue, with self-regulation (essentially the *status quo*); (ii) for hunting to be banned; or (iii) a compromise in which hunting would continue but hunt premises could be inspected and members of hunts would have to undergo training. The Commons voted solidly for the outright ban, rejecting the other two options, although the middle-way option was supported by several members of the Cabinet, including Straw, David Blunkett and Robin Cook.

Despite the large majority in favour of a ban, there was no chance of the bill becoming law. Although it would pass the Commons – unlike private members' bills, opponents cannot talk out a government bill – it faced certain defeat in the Lords. Because the government had introduced the bill into the fourth (and final) session of the Parliament, it was then not possible to reintroduce it in order to utilise the Parliament Acts to force the bill through. Despite the hope of the animal welfare lobby – and the fears of the countryside sports lobby – hunting managed to survive the 1997 Parliament despite an enormous Commons majority in favour of its abolition.

Following Labour's re-election in 2001, the government announced that it would give MPs another vote on the issue. With Labour MPs in the Commons almost bound to guarantee an overwhelming Commons majority for a total ban, but with the Lords equally likely to oppose an outright ban, whether hunting survives the 2001 Parliament thus depends on the will of the government to see the issue through to a conclusion.

proposed reforms. The government had little choice in the matter since in 1999 the European Court of Human Rights had found in favour of complainants on the grounds that sexuality was a private matter. Considerably more contentious were the equalisation of the age of consent – achieved in 2000 as a result of the Sexual Offences (Amendment) Act (see Box 21.2) – and the debate over Section 28 (see Box 21.3).

Debate

British politics has been described as 'post-parliamentary'. Public policy is formulated in segmented consensus-seeking policy networks, each network consisting of the relevant organised interests and executive units (Richardson and Jordan, 1979: 191). Policy thus constructed is then presented to a legislature that, as a result of high levels of party cohesion and an electoral system that gives exaggerated parliamentary majorities to the governing party, almost automatically agrees to it. It is extremely rare for government measures to be defeated in Parliament; even

Box 21.2 The homosexual age of consent

In 1998, a Labour backbencher, Ann Keen, moved an amendment to the Crime and Disorder Bill to lower the age of consent for male homosexual sex to 16. This was overwhelmingly backed by the Commons but was then (equally overwhelmingly) voted down in the Lords. The government was concerned that if the clause remained in the bill, then the Lords would vote down the entire bill. So in return for Ms Keen withdrawing her amendment, the government agreed to introduce a bill of its own (albeit with free votes) in the next session. As well as lowering the age of consent, the government's bill introduced guidelines to protect youths aged 16 and 17 in care, school or in the armed forces. That bill also passed the Commons, and was then again voted down in the Lords.

The government promptly reintroduced the bill in the third session and so for the third year running the subject of male homosexual sex came before Parliament. This time, however, the Lords did not reject the bill outright at second reading, not because of any reduction in peers' hostility towards it, but because rejection at second reading would have allowed the government immediately to invoke the Parliament Acts. Instead, in November, the Lords amended the bill in committee. They extended the number of categories of people who could be prosecuted for abusing positions of trust, and also amended the bill to allow non-penetrative homosexual sex at 16, but anal intercourse with both men and women only at 18. This, they claimed, met the desires of those who wanted equality while protecting young people against what they perceived to be harmful sexual practices. This argument failed to persuade the supporters of the clause and the government invoked the Parliament Acts to get the original measure through. Nonetheless, the Lords' action had been an effective delaying tactic. Royal Assent was finally received on 30 November 2000. In total, the Lords had delayed the reduction in the age of consent by two years. Ironically, therefore, any gay 16-year old who had been cheered by the success of the Keen amendment would have been 18 (old enough to engage in sex under the existing law) by the time that the age of consent was lowered to 16.

Box 21.3 Section 28

Included in the Local Government Bill 2000 was a clause to repeal Section 28 of the Local Government Act 1988, which prohibited local authorities from promoting 'the teaching in any maintained school of the acceptability of homosexuality as a pretended family relationship'. Although the debate over Section 28 involved a *prima facie* issue of conscience, the political parties issued whips for votes on the issue, with little or no controversy. The issue was also the first notable example of a difference in policy between Westminster and the Scottish Parliament.

In Scotland – where this was a devolved matter – there was a concerted and high-profile campaign to 'Keep the Clause', part-funded by Brian Soutar, the owner of Stagecoach. This included a privately-funded ballot of the Scottish electorate (on a turnout of around a third more than 80% voted in favour of its retention), a widespread billboard campaign and the vocal support of the *Daily Record*. But the Scottish Parliament voted overwhelmingly for the abolition of what in Scotland was called Section 2A and with no House of Lords to block the reform Section 2A has now gone (Pugsley, 2000).

At Westminster the Local Government Bill was introduced into the House of Lords. This was a tactical blunder since the Parliament Acts cannot be invoked on a bill introduced first into the Lords. The Lords therefore effectively held a veto. Rattled by events in Scotland and facing defeat in the Lords, David Blunkett, the Education and Employment Secretary, promised to place marriage at the heart of strengthened sex education guidelines. Despite this, in February 2000 the Lords voted by a majority of 45 effectively to keep Section 28. The government then attempted another compromise with the Lords, by amending the Learning and Skills Bill, so that teachers would stress the importance of family life, marriage and 'stable and loving relationships for the nurture of children'. However, Section 28's supporters in the Lords were unimpressed and again voted against the government's compromise.

Then, in July 2000, once the Local Government Bill had returned to the Lords (the Commons having voted overwhelmingly to repeal Section 28), peers again voted for its retention by an almost identical majority to that in February. The following day the government announced that it was dropping the repeal clause in the Bill in order to avoid endangering the other measures in the Bill, including the power to create locally-elected mayors. Moreover, Hilary Armstrong, the Minister for Local Government and the Regions, singularly refused to guarantee the reintroduction of repeal legislation within the lifetime of the 1997 Parliament, presaging the issue's absence from the final Queen's Speech of the Parliament. The government went into the 2001 election not having removed Section 28 from the statute book, with the promise of more lively debate ahead.

minor amendments are very unlikely unless supported by the government. According to Norton, Parliament is 'at best a proximate – at worst, a marginal – actor in determining the content of measures of public policy' (Norton, 1993: 88). In Britain, therefore, the government may not necessarily govern well, but it certainly governs.

As far as 'conscience' issues are concerned, however, this pattern does not appear to hold. The parties generally do not adopt a stance on them, the executive remains neutral and parliamentarians are left to decide according to their own consciences. As a result, rather than being peripheral, the legislature – and the legislators within it – become central to morality policy politics. If the formulation of British public policy as a whole is post-parliamentary, it remains firmly parliamentary when dealing with issues of conscience.

Therefore, although we have already identified ways in which the politics of morality policy in Britain may not fit exactly with the US model, it does appear to be atypical. This has important consequences for the British political system: in particular it removes moral issues from the electoral domain. However, despite the different way in which morality politics is handled, there are more similarities with 'normal' politics than are immediately evident. First, although parliamentarians are not instructed how to vote, party remains the key determinant of vote outcomes. Second, although the executive usually declares itself neutral, it remains an important political actor.

The electoral arena

Treating most morality politics as issues of conscience removes them almost entirely from the electoral domain. British elections rarely include more than a passing mention (if that) of such issues. Because the parties do not take stances on these issues, they are rarely mentioned in their manifestos. They are largely absent from the national campaign, not featuring in the top ten issues in the broadcast or print media (Cowley, 2001). Neither are the issues mentioned by the public as being important, either in terms of the needs of the nation as a whole or in terms of determining their own vote.

Of course, given that there are free votes on these issues, their low electoral salience is not surprising. It is, after all, difficult for a party to campaign on, or to be attacked on, an issue on which its official stance is to be neutral. However, given that a free vote leaves the decision up to the individual candidates, we might expect candidates to raise morality issues as part of their campaign and for pressure groups to target individual candidates. Yet even this happens very rarely. Analysis of candidates' election addresses shows that these issues are raised only very rarely (Cowley, 2001). Some organisations, such as the Movement for Christian Democracy, do try to publicise the stances of candidates on specific issues, but until recently they were hampered by the 1983 Representation of the People Act, which prohibited expenditure by groups of more than a total of £5 during the election period to convey information to electors with a view to promoting the election of a candidate. Such evidence as we have about the activity of such groups at election time suggests that it is very limited (see, for example, Butler and Kavanagh, 1997: 220–1).

As a result, electors' knowledge about the stances taken by candidates on morality issues is low (Crewe, 1985). There is some limited evidence that positions taken by MPs on free votes – most notably the death penalty – can have a slight effect a candidate's electoral fortunes (Pattie et al., 1994), but insofar as 'personal' votes are gained this is a result of work carried out by MPs on behalf of constituents rather than their stances on issues (Norton and Wood, 1993). British elections remain primarily national-level events in which morality issues play but a small part. Thus, the most striking feature about morality policy in general elections in Britain is its lack of importance. With one or two minor exceptions, morality issues simply do not register during elections.

This demonstrates another very important difference between Britain and the USA. Moral issues may have high salience when they are passing through Parliament, sometimes attracting significant letter-writing campaigns and/or external protests. As one MP said, 'God writes an awful lot of letters' (as do people who like foxes). In turn, this can lead to increased media coverage of the issue (Cowley and Stace, 1996). However, this increased salience remains limited to these narrow points in time. For most of the time – and especially during elections – the salience of these issues is low. Morality issues, therefore, may not automatically enjoy high salience if – as in Britain – the political environment helps to neutralise them.

In turn, this leads to another, perhaps crucial, difference between Britain and the USA. In the USA, it is argued, policy-makers will be more responsive to the general public on issues of morality compared to other policy types, 'be it out of a sense of democratic duty or self-interest' (Mooney, 2001). Yet in Britain, because these issues have been largely removed from the electoral arena, it is not especially in a politician's 'self-interest' to follow the majority of his or her constituents' preferences, because there is no cost associated with not doing so. There is, therefore, often little congruence between the views of voters and public policy. Evidence suggests, for example, that the public are somewhat less liberal than the parliamentary elite on homosexuality (although responses depend slightly on what question is asked) and it is clear that the vast majority of the British public want the reinstatement of capital punishment. Contrariwise, there is a coincidence of views between the mass and the elite on some issues. For example, the British public favours a fairly liberal abortion law (which *de facto* is what they have got). But that is all it is – a coincidence.

The Parties, Elections and Referendums Act 2000 raised the limit that any organisation can spend in any constituency to £500, which, although still not an enormous sum, is a notable increase on the previous limit and might allow active groups to achieve limited but effective coverage in a constituency. Only if that happens and only if it appears to have electoral consequences (and there were no signs of that in 2001), then British politicians may have to start to pay more attention to the views of voters on these issues.

The centrality of party

One of the main justifications for treating issues of morality as free votes and thus removing them from the political fray is that they are said to 'cut across party lines', to be 'non-party', 'above party', 'cross-party', or not to be 'issues of party politics'. This belief is understandable. When these issues come before Parliament, they tend to be supported (or opposed) by a range of MPs on both sides of the House and advocates often stress the cross-party nature of their support. This is unusual since the majority of votes see complete party cohesion, with no MPs voting against their party's line. As a result, the issues are usually reported differently in the media. Precisely because they are not the norm, the free vote and the extent of cross-party support are highlighted, as the focus of reporting is not (as it usually is) the split between government and opposition.

Despite this perception, however, conscience issues *are* essentially party issues. The media and politicians tend to concentrate on the exceptions (MPs voting against the majority of their party) and overlook the norm (the majority of MPs are not doing so). For example, when two Labour MPs voted against banning hunting and eight Conservatives voted in favour of a ban, *The Times* (29 November 1997) said that they had 'defied conventional wisdom about the politics of hunting'. Yet 374 Labour MPs (99% of those voting) supported a ban, while 128 Conservatives (94%) opposed it.

We can examine this more systematically by using a simple index to measure party unity – and the extent of divisions within parties – on a number of recent free votes. The index is calculated by subtracting the minority percentage on any vote from the majority percentage (excluding all non-voters) and then expressing the outcome as a proportion. A score of zero indicates that the party is completely split, with half voting one way and half the other. A score of 1.0 indicates that the party is completely cohesive, with all voting MPs voting the same way. A party vote, in which 90% of a party vote together (Lowell, 1908), yields an index of 0.8. A split involving one-third voting in one lobby being opposed by the other two-thirds yields a figure of 0.33. Table 21.2 shows the index scores for the three main parties for a series of important free votes between 1990 and 2000. Bold type indicates the cases in which a majority of another party voted with the majority of the Conservative MPs.

Three features of Table 21.2 merit comment and, although the exact scores vary slightly, if a different sample of votes is used for analysis, the basic message remains the same whatever votes are analysed (see, Cowley and Stuart, 1997; Cowley et al., 2000). First, in every free vote analysed here the majority of Labour MPs opposed the majority of Conservative MPs – just as in 'normal' politics. Second, although the majority of Liberal Democrat MPs usually voted with the majority of Labour MPs (there were just two votes – on abortion in 1990 and Sunday trading in 1994 – where the majority of Liberal Democrat MPs voted with the majority of Conservatives), the most striking feature of Liberal Democrat

Table 21.2 Party divisions on selected free votes, 1990–2000

	Lab	Lib Dem	Con
Abortion (1990)	0.30	**0.50**	0.89
Capital punishment (1994)	1.00	1.00	0.09
Sunday trading (1994)	0.51	**0.12**	0.78
Divorce (1996)	0.82	0.45	0.17
Gun control (1997)	0.98	0.00	1.00
Sex offences (2000)	0.96	0.68	0.80
Stem cells (2000)	0.56	0.45	0.12
Fox-hunting (2000)	0.96	0.20	0.90

Note: Bold type indicates cases where a majority of another party voted together with a majority of Conservatives.

Table 21.3 Labour and Conservative cohesion on free votes

Labour	Conservative		
	Split	Divided	Cohesive
Split	–	–	Abortion (1990)
Divided	Stem cells (2000)	Sunday trading (1994)	–
Cohesive	Capital punishment (1994)	–	Gun control (1997)
	Divorce (1996)	–	Sexual offences (2000)
		–	Fox-hunting (2000)

voting is how badly the party splits. Although the other parties split on occasions (as Table 21.2 shows, Labour scored lower than 0.8 on three votes, the Conservatives on four), the Lib Dems failed to achieve a party vote (a score of 0.8 or more) in all but one of the votes. Third, the pattern of party splits across issues is striking. Table 21.3 compares the level of division in the two main parties for the different issues. Three issues – stem cells, capital punishment and divorce – split the Conservatives (that is, an index of less than 0.33), but on these Labour was either cohesive (0.8 or more) or, at worst, divided (0.33 to 0.8). Just one issue split Labour badly (abortion), but on that the Conservatives were cohesive. Three issues – gun control, sexual offences, and fox-hunting – saw both parties largely or completely cohesive. No issue split both the parties at same time.

If we move from macroanalysis – examining how the parties behave *en bloc* – to microanalysis – examining how individual MPs behave when voting – party remains pre-eminent. Studies of MPs' voting on these issues find that their party allegiance is the only consistent factor affecting how they vote. To be sure, there are other influences. Roman Catholic MPs are more likely to vote in favour of restrictions on abortion and embryo research and are less likely to support euthanasia; women are less likely than men to vote in favour of restrictions on abortion; younger and better-educated MPs tend to be more liberal in their voting. All of these are sporadic influences, however. In general, party is the dominating factor (Pattie et al., 1998).

Given this, it is difficult to argue that these issues are non-partisan in Britain. It is rare to find an issue on which both of the major parties are significantly split. Conscience issues may split some of the parties some of the time, but they do not split all of the parties all of the time. The outcome of votes on these issues, therefore, owes much – although not everything – to the party composition of the Commons, just as it does in 'normal' politics.

The importance of the executive

Just as party remains important even when the issues are described as non-party, so the executive remains important even when the decision is left to the legislature. Sometimes this is because the executive declares itself neutral but applies pressure behind the scenes. As one Cabinet minister wryly admitted in March 1996, there are 'free votes and free votes'. Yet even when the executive is not applying such pressure, it is not divorced from the policy-making process. Rather, it remains an actor, playing an important role in facilitating the discussion and resolution of the issues. It does so in two principal ways: either by lending assistance to private members' bills – that is, bills introduced by backbench MPs – or by bringing forward government bills on which it then adopts a neutral stance, either in full or in part. The former used to be the norm. The reforms of the 1960s were all passed as a result of private members' legislation. The avowed neutrality of the government on these issues (that is, allowing free votes on the bills) and the fact that the bills emanated from backbench MPs combined to give the impression that the government was neutral. In fact, far from being a neutral bystander, the then Labour government (and in particular, Roy Jenkins) were central to the passage of these bills. This is because the rules of Parliament do not make it easy for private members' bills to succeed. It is easy for those who object to their content to obstruct and kill them, whatever the size of the bill's majority. Indeed, the ease with which these bills can be stopped is illustrated by the fact that not since 1959 has such a bill, opposed by even a single MP at either second or third reading, passed into law without the government of the day lending its support by granting the bill additional parliamentary time (Marsh and Read, 1988). In the 1960s, in particular, the Labour government gave considerable time to the various private members' bills dealing with conscience issues (Short, 1989). Had it not done so, all would have failed. The attitude of the government was vital.

Governments since the 1960s have been less willing to grant private members additional time. As a result, a series of backbench measures backed by the Commons has failed to become law, most notably those dealing with hunting and abortion. Private members' bills continue to be used by backbench MPs to enact uncontroversial pieces of legislation and to attract publicity for a topic (as we have seen, in 1997, it was a private member's bill on hunting that pushed the issue on to the agenda). But it is now more usual for conscience issues to be resolved by means of a government bill.

This can be done in one of two ways. Sometimes backbench MPs move amendments to government bills, inserting clauses concerning moral issues into bills primarily concerned with other matters. Thus, backbench MPs have attempted to insert amendments dealing with the age of consent or capital punishment into many criminal justice bills. Ann Keen's amendment in 1998 was an attempt to get an amendment on homosexuality into a bill on Crime and Disorder, for example. Alternatively, the government can choose to introduce a bill into Parliament and then adopt a neutral stance on it. This tactic is now very common and was used for the Human Fertilisation and Embryology Bill, the Sunday Trading Bill, and in this Parliament, the Sexual Offences (Amendment) Bill (both times), and the Hunting Bill. In such cases the government believes that it is important for the issue to be resolved and introduces a bill to expedite the process. The resolution of the issue appears more important for the government than the outcome.

Although the executive adopts a neutral stance on these issues, this does not mean that its role is unimportant. The very act of introducing a bill enables the legislature to come to a decision – something that might be difficult otherwise given the vulnerability of private members' legislation – and once a decision has been reached the government will ensure that the bill reaches the statute book, both by applying the whips to the rest of the bill's passage or, as in the case of both the War Crimes and Sexual Offences (Amendment) Acts, invoking the Parliament Acts to force the issue past a hostile Upper Chamber.

It could be argued that in doing this the executive is simply enabling the will of the legislature to prevail. However, the government clearly plays an important role by choosing *which* issues it will facilitate in this way. Since 1992, for example, it is likely that there was a majority in the Commons in favour of abolishing hunting with hounds. Yet the Conservative government elected in 1992 – the majority of whose members supported hunting – did not bring a bill forward to facilitate the legislature in making its decision. As a result, hunting continued to be legal. Similarly, it continues to be legal at the time of writing, because the executive did not bring forward a bill of its own until too late in the 1997 Parliament. By contrast, despite almost identical levels of support in the Commons and opposition in the Lords, the age of consent for gay men *was* lowered to 16, because the government brought the bill forward with enough time to utilise the Parliament Acts. The decision of the executive, therefore, while appearing to be neutral, was (and is) not neutral in its effect on policy – just as in 'normal' politics.

Conclusion

Moral issues are worth studying for three reasons. First, they are intrinsically interesting since they involve deeply-held principles. They are the type of issue that taxi drivers harangue passengers about; people argue and get excited about them. The question of how such issues are resolved in public policy deserves attention. Second, they involve a different style of policy-making. The majority of issues of morality are treated in Britain as a breed apart. In a political system dominated by party and executive, they are considered non-partisan and are dealt with by the legislature. That said, in practice the differences are not as great as they seem at first. Despite the perception that moral issues are non-partisan, party is key to determining the outcome of votes and the resolution of public policy, just as it is in normal politics. Similarly, just as in non-morality policy areas, the stance of the executive is important in determining the outcome. Third, despite fallacious claims that these issues are 'above' party politics, conscience issues are a classic example of party difference. In an era when many people complain about excessive party convergence – 'they are all the same' – these issues provide clear examples of the differences that remain between the political parties.

Chronology

1965 Murder (Abolition of the Death Penalty) Act suspends capital punishment for nearly all civilian crimes.

1967 Abortion Act makes abortion legal on the basis of statute law.
Sexual Offences Act legalises consenting sexual acts between two men aged 21 or over in England and Wales.

1968 Theatres Act ends theatre censorship.

1969 Divorce Reform Act liberalises divorce laws, replacing the concept of matrimonial offence with the concept of the 'irretrievable breakdown of marriage'.

1980 Criminal Justice (Scotland) Act legalises male homosexual sex in Scotland on the same basis as in England and Wales.

1982 Liberalisation spreads to Northern Ireland as a result of the Homosexual Offences (NI) Order (despite the best efforts of a wonderfully-named campaign to 'Save Ulster From Sodomy').

1984 Matrimonial and Family Proceedings Act reduces the time required to elapse before a divorce can be initiated.

1986 Shops Bill, which would have deregulated Sunday trading, is defeated at second reading, the only time in the whole of the twentieth century that a government with a secure majority has lost a bill at second reading.

1988 Local Government Act prohibits local councils from 'promoting' homosexuality – a rare example of a reform that is not in a liberal direction.

1990 Human Fertilisation and Embryology Act both legalises embryo research and lowers to twenty-four weeks the time limit for abortions.

1991 War Crimes Act, which allows British courts to prosecute British citizens for actions conducted outside the UK at a time when they were not UK citizens, reaches the statute book. The Act is forced past the House of Lords using the Parliament Acts, the only time a Conservative government has used the Parliament Acts to enact legislation.

1993 Sunday Trading Act partially deregulates Sunday trading.

1994 Criminal Justice and Public Order Act reduces the male homosexual age of consent to 18, still two years higher than for heterosexuals but three years lower than the age limit set in the 1960s.

1996 Family Law Act removes the concept of 'fault' from divorce.

1997 The House of Commons votes overwhelmingly for Foster bill to ban hunting. Firearms (Amendment) Act bans ownership of handguns.

1998 Crime and Disorder Act removes the death penalty from the civilian crimes for which it remained on the statute book.
Human Rights Act makes it impossible for the death penalty to return, short of Britain's renouncing the European Convention on Human Rights.
Ann Keen's amendment to lower the age of consent for homosexual sex to 16 is carried by the House of Commons but thrown out by the House of Lords.

1999 Government introduces Sexual Offences (Amendment) Bill, which lowers the age of consent for homosexuals to 16 and introduces guidelines to protect youths aged 16 or 17 in care, school or the armed forces. This is carried by the Commons, but rejected by the Lords.

2000 Government reintroduces Sexual Offences (Amendment) Bill, again carried by Commons. The House of Lords tries to amend, but the government uses the Parliament Acts to force the bill past the Lords and on to the statute book.
Burns Inquiry into hunting publishes its report.
Defence Secretary announces that homosexuals are to be allowed in the armed forces, as a result of the European Court of Human Rights ruling the previous year.
The Lords vote to retain Section 28. The government announces that the repeal of Section 28 is being dropped from the Local Government Bill and will not be reintroduced in the next session.

2001 Lord Chancellor announces that the government will repeal Part II of Family Law Act 1996.

Parliament votes to allow research on 'stem cells' for the purposes of research into degenerative diseases.

Government brings forward the Hunting Bill. Commons votes for a total ban, but the Bill faces certain defeat in Lords.

Lords vote to allow the 'morning after pill' to be sold over the counter.

Discussion Questions

1. What – if anything – distinguishes those issues classed as issues of conscience from other political issues?
2. How should the British political system deal with this type of issue?
3. Did the reforms of the 1960s – and those that followed – make Britain a 'civilised place to live'?

References

Butler, David and Kavanagh, Dennis (1997) *The British General Election of 1997*, London: Macmillan.

Cowley, Philip (2001) 'Morality policy without politics? The case of Britain', in Christopher Z. Mooney (ed.) *The Public Clash of Private Values: The Politics of Morality Policy*, Chatham, NJ: Chatham House.

Cowley, Philip and Stace, Nick (1996) 'The Wild Mammals (Protection) Bill: a parliamentary white elephant?', *Journal of Legislative Studies*, Vol. 2, pp. 339–55.

Cowley, Philip and Stuart, Mark (1997) 'Sodomy, slaughter, Sunday shopping and seatbelts', *Party Politics*, Vol. 3, pp. 119–30.

Cowley, Philip, Darcy, Darren, Mellors, Colin, Neal, Jon and Stuart, Mark (2000) 'Mr Blair's loyal opposition? The Liberal Democrats in Parliament', *British Elections and Parties Review*, Vol. 10, pp. 100–16.

Crewe, Ivor (1985) 'MPs and their constituents in Britain: how strong are the links?', in Vernon Bogdanor (ed.) *Representatives of the People*, Aldershot: Gower.

Durham, Martin (1998) 'Censorship', in Philip Cowley (ed.) *Conscience and Parliament*, London: Frank Cass.

Haste, Cate (1994) *Rules of Desire*, London: Pimlico.

Hitchens, Peter (1999) *The Abolition of Britain*, London: Quartet.

Jones, Peter (1995) 'Members of Parliament and issues of conscience', in Peter Jones (ed.) *Party, Parliament and Personality*, London: Routledge.

Judge, David (1999) 'Capital punishment: Burke and Dicey meet the European Convention on Human Rights', *Public Law*, Spring, pp. 6–13.

Lowell, A. Lawrence (1908) *The Government of England*, London: Macmillan.

Lowi, Theodore J. (1972) 'Four systems of policy, politics and choice', *Public Administration Review*, Vol. 32, pp. 298–310.

Marsh, David and Read, Melvyn (1988) *Private Members' Bills*, Cambridge: Cambridge University Press.

Millns, Susan and Sheldon, Sally (1998) 'Abortion', in Philip Cowley (ed.) *Conscience and Parliament*, London: Frank Cass.

Mooney, Christopher Z. (ed.) (2001) *The Public Clash of Private Values: The Politics of Morality Policy*, Chatham, NJ: Chatham House.

Norton, Philip (1993) *Does Parliament Matter?*, London: Harvester Wheatsheaf.

Norton, Philip and Wood, David M. (1993) *Back From Westminster*, Lexington, KT: University Press of Kentucky.

Pattie, Charles, Fieldhouse, Ed and Johnston, Ron J. (1994) 'The price of conscience: the electoral correlates and consequences of free votes and rebellions in the British House of Commons 1987–92', *British Journal of Political Science*, Vol. 24, pp. 359–80.

Pattie, Charles, Johnston, Ron J. and Stuart, Mark (1998) 'Voting without party?', in Philip Cowley (ed.) *Conscience and Parliament*, London: Frank Cass.

Pugsley, Robert (2000) 'Section 28: pressure groups and the power of the House of Lords', *Politics Review*, Vol. 10, pp. 24–5.

Richardson, Jeremy and Jordan, Grant (1979) *Governing under Pressure: The Policy Process in a Post-Parliamentary Democracy*, Oxford: Martin Robertson.

Short, Edward (1989) *Whip to Wilson*, London: MacDonald.

Stone, L. (1995) *The Road to Divorce*, Oxford: Oxford University Press.

Studlar, Donley (2001) 'What constitutes morality policy? A cross-national analysis', in Christopher Z. Mooney (ed.) *The Public Clash of Private Values: The Politics of Morality Policy*, Chatham, NJ: Chatham House.

Weeks, J. (1989) *Sex, Politics and Society* (second edition), London: Longman.

Further reading

Peter G. Richards (1970) *Parliament and Conscience* (London: George Allen & Unwin) is the classic study of the reforms of the 1960s. Peter Hitchens (1999) *The Abolition of Britain* (London: Quartet) is a wonderfully entertaining – if somewhat eccentric – critique of the period, and everything else that followed. Philip Cowley (ed.) (1998) *Conscience and Parliament* (London: Frank Cass) covers eight of the most contentious issues from 1970 up to 1997. Christopher Z. Mooney (2001) *The Public Clash of Private Values* (Chatham, NJ: Chatham House) consists mainly of US case studies, but it also contains several interesting theoretical and comparative chapters. Peter Jones (ed.) (1995) *Party, Parliament and Personality* (London: Routledge) is a well-argued demolition of the case for 'free votes'. David Marsh and Melvyn Read (1988) *Private Members' Bills* (Cambridge: Cambridge University Press) outlines the uses and abuses of private members' bills. The journal *Parliamentary Affairs* also regularly contains useful articles on individual moral debates in Britain.

PART SIX Regulation

Regulating Society: Quangos

David Wilson

CHAPTER TWENTY-TWO

Introduction

Quangos are a high-profile and frequently controversial part of the regulatory state. The term quango (quasi-autonomous non-governmental organisation) was originally coined for those organisations which were legally private but which performed statutory functions for government in a semi-independent way (such as the General Medical Council). Over the years, however, other organisations which were carrying out governmental functions but were deliberately set up at arm's length or semi-independently (such as the Equal Opportunities Commission) also became known as quangos (quasi-autonomous government organisations). Today the term is used to embrace both groups and the species has become of central importance in enabling government to formulate, implement and regulate public policy.

Skelcher argues that 'ideology and pragmatism have combined to reshape the British governmental system by introducing a class of organisations having considerable public significance yet remaining largely outside democratic political activity' (Skelcher, 1998: 1). Quangos are to be found playing an important role in almost every area of public policy. The 70,000 appointees to the boards of some 6,500 quangos exercise enormous influence. Possibly the major source of contention is that they are not directly elected to such positions, but appointed. This gives rise to important issues relating to the accountability of such bodies in a democratic society, a topic which will be discussed later in the chapter.

Quangos have long been politically contentious. In his Foreword to the Labour government's consultation paper *Opening up Quangos* (Cabinet Office, 1997a), David Clark, Chancellor of the Duchy of Lancaster, lamented inheriting large numbers of quangos 'whose lack of openness in appointments to their boards and in the business they were conducting attracted widespread criticism'. He advocated 'opening up quangos to public scrutiny and making them more accountable to the public that they serve' (Cabinet Office, 1997a: 1). While the Blair government committed itself to reducing the number of quangos, in its first two years in office it had created as many new quangos as it had abolished, including some major additions, such as the Low Pay Commission and Regional Development Agencies (RDAs). Quangos have become an integral part of the state; they need to be evaluated both administratively and politically. Given the complexities of the subject, a thorough understanding of the origins and nature of the species is essential at the outset.

Background

Development

While quangos have become high-profile in recent years, they are not new. Neither are they an exclusively British phenomenon. They have a long history in countries as diverse as the Netherlands, New Zealand, Denmark and Germany. Indeed, there is much to learn from trends and experiences in other countries (see Flinders and Smith, 1999: Part 2). In Britain, the Crown Agents originated in the mid-nineteenth century and the Horserace Totaliser Board (the Tote) began in 1928. Considerable numbers of single-purpose *ad hoc* boards were also created at a local level during the period of urbanisation and industrialisation in the eighteenth and nineteenth centuries (for example, turnpike trusts, boards of improvement commissioners, poor law boards). The tangle of appointed and elected bodies which operated at local level is illustrated in Box 22.1.

Although they are not new, the dominance of the new right under the Conservatives in the 1980s provided a major stimulus to the expansion of quangos. Local authorities (mostly Labour-controlled) were a particular target. The advocates of new public management, with its emphasis on market mechanisms, consumerism and single-purpose bodies, used quangos to an unprecedented extent. Often such bodies took over local authority functions. To quote Skelcher:

> There has been a spectacular growth in this appointed sector of government since the late 1980s. The creation of new types of public body and the transfer of activities from elected local government to appointed quangos has substantially increased both the number and the range of policy areas in which they operate.
>
> (Skelcher, 1998: 1, 2)

Before going further, however, it is necessary to step into the definition minefield.

Box 22.1 Administrative tangle

A selection of the bodies that constituted the local government of England and Wales towards the end of the nineteenth century:

302	municipal boroughs
31	Improvement Act districts
574	rural sanitary districts
58	port sanitary districts
2,302	school board districts
362	highway districts
6,477	highway parishes
1,052	burial board districts
618	Poor Law unions

Source: Hollis (1987: 3)

Definitions and numbers

The word 'quango' is widely used, but with considerable variation and not a little confusion as to its meaning. Given that there is no universally accepted agreement about what constitutes a quango it is hardly surprising that there is marked disagreement about numbers. These differences are interpreted by both government and opposition to serve their own purposes, namely presenting a picture of a quango state that is either contracting or expanding. The official government definition, non-departmental public body (NDPB), is very restrictive and can be termed *exclusive*. A NDPB is defined in the 1980 Pliatzky Report as: 'A body which has a role in the processes of national government, but is not a government department, or part of one, and which accordingly operates to a greater or lesser extent at arm's length from Ministers' (Pliatzky Report, 1980: 556). This restrictive definition quite deliberately produces relatively few quangos – something that is clearly desirable from the standpoint of central government. It excludes, for example, National Health Service Trusts and health authorities. Table 22.1 presents summary details of quangos from 1979 to 1999 using the official government NDPB definition.

Table 22.1 Exclusive definition of quangos: summary of non-departmental public bodies (NDPBs), 1979–99

	Executive bodies			Advisory bodies	Tribunals	Boards of visitors	Total number of NDPBs
	Number	Number of staff[a]	Total expenditure £m[b]	Number	Number	Number	
1979	492	217,000	6,150	1,485	70	120	2,167
1982	450	205,500	8,330	1,173	64	123	1,810
1983	431	196,700	9,940	1,074	65	121	1,691
1984[c]	402	141,200	7,280	1,087	71	121	1,681
1985	399	138,300	7,770	1,069	65	121	1,654
1986	406	146,300	8,240	1,062	64	126	1,658
1987	396	148,700	9,100	1,057	64	126	1,643
1988	390	134,600	9,450	1,066	65	127	1,648
1989	395	118,300	9,410	969	64	127	1,555
1990	374	117,500	11,870	971	66	128	1,539
1991	375	116,400	13,080	874	64	131	1,444
1992	369	114,400	13,750	846	66	131	1,412
1993	358	111,300	15,410	829	68	134	1,389
1994	325	110,200	18,330	814	71	135	1,345
1995	320	109,000	20,840	699	73	135	1,227
1996	309	107,000	21,420	674	75	136	1,194
1997	305	106,400	22,400	610	75	138	1,128
1998	304	107,800	24,130	563	69	137	1,073
1999	306	108,400	23,370	544	69	138	1,057

[a] Figures include civil servants at the Advisory, Conciliation and Arbitration Service and the Health and Safety Commission and Executive.
[b] Current prices.
[c] Staff and expenditure figures from 1984 exclude the English and Welsh Water Authorities which were reclassified as nationalised industries. Staff numbers in 1983 were approx. 58,000. Expenditure was approx. £2,600m.

Source: Cabinet Office, *Public Bodies* (various years)

In contrast to the above, a more *inclusive* definition is provided by others. Davis (1993) has coined NESPOs (non-elected public service organisations). This embraces the government's definition (NDPBs) plus the NHS bodies including NHS Trusts. The most frequently cited alternative definition, however, is that put forward by Weir and Hall (1994) – 'extra-governmental organisation' (EGO). EGOs are defined as 'executive bodies of a semi-autonomous nature which effectively act as agencies for central government and carry out government policies' (Weir and Hall, 1994: 2). Weir and Hall's 1994 document was updated in 1996, through a report entitled *The Untouchables* (Hall and Weir, 1996), which delineated some 6,424 EGOs, as set out in Table 22.2. Interestingly, in 1997 the annual government publication *Public Bodies* first made reference to the non-recognised local executive quangos as a collective group. According to this report there were 4,651 Local Public Spending Bodies in 1997 with 69,813 board members (Cabinet Office, 1997b: vii). Under the Labour government, therefore, the existence of what the Nolan Committee (1996: 1) called 'Local Public Spending Bodies' has at least been acknowledged, but the government is not prepared to shift from its narrow definition of NDPBs; such a shift would be politically unwise since it would provide ammunition for opposition parties to attack it for presiding over a huge proliferation of quangos.

To repeat, a variety of definitions of the term 'quango' has emerged. The government's NDPB definition is *exclusive*, having a very narrow focus and being limited to a relatively small number of national bodies. Others (such as NESPOs and EGOs) are much more *inclusive*, considering quangos to be 'any body that spends public money to fulfil a public task but with some degree of independence from elected representatives' (Flinders and Smith, 1999: 4). Looking at the exclusive definition (Table 22.1) it appears that quango numbers have steadily declined (largely through amalgamations), whereas the wider definition (Table 22.2) still

Table 22.2 Inclusive definition of quangos: summary of extra-governmental organisations (EGOs) in the UK in 1996

Organisation	1996
Executive NDPBs	309
NHS bodies	788
Advisory NDPBs	674
Non-recognised EGOs	4,653
Career service companies	91
Grant-maintained schools	1,103
City technology colleges	15
Further education corporations	560
Higher education corporations	175
Registered housing associations	2,565
Police authorities	41
Training and Enterprise Councils	81
Local enterprise companies	22
Total	**6,424**

Source: Hall and Weir (1996)

points to a proliferation of non-elected bodies. In the absence of agreement about definitions, numerical variations are likely to continue. They will undoubtedly continue to be used by both government and opposition to 'prove' different points.

The position is even more complex than that presented above because within each category there is a tremendous variety of organisations. Taking NDPBs as an example, compare the massive UK Atomic Energy Authority with the tiny Apple and Pear Research Council, or the Arts Council of Great Britain with the UK Polar Medical Assessment Committee. They are worlds apart. Diversity in terms of finance, organisation, objectives and accountability is enormous.

Quangos and policy-making

Quangos are frequently heavily criticised because they are widely perceived as being unelected, unresponsive and having an unfair and secretive appointments system. These criticisms are important and will be discussed later, but the role of quangos in shaping policy and in carrying out particular government functions also needs to be recognised. They have a number of positive attributes, some of which were outlined in the Labour government's consultative paper, *Opening up Quangos* (1997a) and which are set out below:

1. Many quangos provide expert advice to ministers on technical and specialised issues. For example, in 1996 the Human Genetics Advisory Committee was set up to take a broad view of developments in human genetics and advise government on ways to build public confidence in this highly controversial area. Other examples include the Spongiform Encephalopathy Advisory Committee (which provided briefings during the BSE outbreak among cattle), and the Expert Advisory Group on AIDS. As Skelcher notes, many advisory quangos 'play a central role in shaping government policy and legislation by virtue of the weight of authoritative opinion they contain and expert evidence they offer [and are] of major significance to an understanding of the way in which government is informed and policy is shaped' (Skelcher, 1998: 3).
2. A number of government functions need to be carried out at arm's length from ministers. These include regulation (for example, by the Health and Safety Commission and Executive, and the Environment Agency) and decisions on funding for the sciences.
3. Quangos can provide a quick and flexible response to matters of particular concern. For example, the Nolan Committee on Standards in Public Life (1996) was set up to address concerns about sleaze. There is a huge range of models of quangos which means that bodies can be set up in a way which best meets the needs of the functions they are given; in other words, there is infinite flexibility. Indeed, Weir and Beetham (1999: 196) describe quangos as the 'government's flexible friends', enabling government to fashion them to meet changing policy and management needs as required.
4. Quangos can often provide a valuable mechanism for bringing together partnerships between government and other interests. For example, the boards of

Housing Action Trusts (HATs) include nominees from local authorities and nominees elected by residents of the Trust's area.

5. Quangos can carry out a range of commercial activities when board members need a degree of independence from government to make decisions, as in the case of the Regional Development Agencies (RDAs) established in April 1999.

6. Quasi-government provides opportunities to bring a large number of ordinary people into public life as with, for example, NDPB tribunals and boards of Visitors to penal establishments. Later in the chapter this dimension will be explored further as the socio-economic backgrounds of 'quangocrats' are considered.

In addition to the above there are also management spin-offs associated with quangos. As Skelcher observes, 'notions of efficient management have constantly informed the case for appointed bodies' (1998: 48). Flinders (1999: 34) makes a similar point, arguing that executive quangos, especially Local Public Spending Bodies, have been seen as important agents for the introduction of innovative new management practices, often imported from the private sector. Single-purpose agencies such as NHS Hospital Trusts are frequently seen to have a specialised professional focus that would be less likely as part of a multi-functional organisation. For example, in 1999, the Leicester Royal Infirmary NHS Trust comprised eleven individuals including a Medical Director, a Professor of Nursing, a Medical Professor from the University of Leicester as well as financial and human resource management specialists. The chairman and five non-executive directors were appointed by the Secretary of State for Health and five executive directors are employed by the Trust. The Labour government has repeatedly emphasised, however, that where quangos are the means of delivering particular functions or services, they should be open and accountable. The Leicester Royal Infirmary NHS Trust meets monthly and members of the public are able to attend meetings to see decision-making in action. An excellent twenty-page glossy annual report is also widely circulated via local newspapers and is presented to the Trust's annual public meeting which, again, is open to all and includes a question-and-answer session with the chairman and members of the Trust Board.

Summary

- Although not new, quangos have developed apace since the 1980s, especially at the local level, often as a device to by-pass unsympathetic elected local authorities and to make government more effective and thereby less expensive.
- Definitions and numbers of quangos are fiercely contested. There is no universal agreement about what constitutes a quango or how many there are.
- The specialist nature of many quangos means that they have an important role in advising on policy formulation. Through executive agencies they also have a role in implementing policy.
- The infinite flexibility of quangos is a major attraction to central government.

Theoretical Considerations

Democratic accountability is at the heart of contemporary debate about quangos (see Wilson, 1995). There are no democratic elections to the boards of quangos. With unelected members and independence from ministers, there is no obvious mechanism by which quangos can be held to account to the public for their activities. At the local level the members of these bodies have been termed by John Stewart (1992) as the 'new magistracy', that is a non-elected elite replacing elected councillors in an increasing number of service areas. Box 22.2 outlines the growth of this so-called new magistracy.

Critics of the quango state have been particularly keen to emphasise the undemocratic nature of transferring power away from elected bodies such as local authorities to unelected quangos, as illustrated in Box 22.2. Because of this there is now less direct accountability to the electorate in policy areas such as health and education. However, the advocates of elected local government frequently exaggerate the virtues of that particular form of government. Accountability via the ballot box is wearing thin at the local level. Turnouts in local elections plummeted in 1998 when only 29% of the electorate bothered to vote. In some localities turnout levels are little short of embarrassing. Events in Westminster, Doncaster and Glasgow have also served as a reminder that elected local authorities are not immune from charges of fraud, corruption or partisan patronage. Although local

Box 22.2 The growth of the new magistracy

- Local authority representatives removed from district health authorities and family health service authorities; post-1990 health authorities have no local authority representatives as of right.
- NHS Trusts created to manage delivery by hospitals and community services.
- Training and Enterprise Councils and local enterprise companies created to exercise functions at a local level, incorporating or overlapping with some local authority activities.
- Careers service companies, formed by partnerships of local authorities, business and others, bid for contracts to deliver careers service in each locality. Formerly part of local government.
- Self-appointing boards of governors take responsibility from local education authorities for further education colleges and sixth-form colleges.
- Schools encouraged to opt out of local authority control and become grant-maintained, funded and regulated by new national NDPBs.
- Housing associations gain increased responsibility for social housing.
- Housing Action Trusts and urban development corporations created to carry out urban regeneration in specific localities, with some transfer of responsibility from local authorities.
- Police authorities with majority local authority membership abolished. Now police authorities have seventeen members: five appointed by minister after local consultation, nine by local authorities and three by magistrates.

Source: Adapted from Skelcher (1998)

government is formally accountable to the public via the ballot box, therefore, this might actually mean very little in practice. Too idealistic a picture is often painted; at the same time, too negative a picture is frequently painted of accountability in the quango sector.

Much central government activity has had the citizen as consumer as its focus. In this context the last Conservative government argued that the growth of quangos had, in fact, produced a 'democratic gain' rather than a 'democratic deficit'. Accountability, it maintained, had been strengthened by making services more responsive to consumers. The Conservatives argued that the customer culture provided increased opportunities to complain and secure redress and hence enhance accountability. The advent of Citizen's Charters, grant-maintained schools, HATs, NHS Trusts, etc., essentially focused on the citizen as a consumer of services. In such a context, is the traditional form of direct accountability through the ballot box most meaningful or can accountability emerge through, for example, contractual relationships, performance indicators, and the like?

The new thinking was encapsulated by William Waldegrave in July 1993. In reply to complaints of a 'democratic deficit' with the advent of increasing numbers of appointed bodies, he argued that the Conservative government had actually effected a 'democratic gain' in the management of public services:

> We have not in any way altered or undermined the basic structure of
> public service accountability to Parliament and hence to individual citizens.
> But we have made it useable. We have strengthened these formal lines of
> accountability by making our public services directly accountable to their
> customers.
>
> (Waldegrave, 1993: 9)

For Waldegrave and his Cabinet colleagues, the crucial point was the output, the end product, rather than intervening democratic processes. This, of course, fails to address the question of whether public services should not be both democratically controlled *and* consumer-responsive.

For commentators such as Graham Mather (1994), the search for new forms of accountability should start not with the ballot box but with the contract. He gives four reasons why this should be so. First, the contract is a form of specification, exchange and account combined in one instrument – it therefore has both precision and transparency. Second, it is the means whereby the market economy effects transactions. Third, modern forms of government are consciously borrowing from the new institutional economies. For example, the architect of New Zealand's radical administrative reforms, Graham Scott, argued that they were developed from practical experience and the literature on institutional economies, public administration, accounting, finance and management. Fourth, Mather argues that 'it is no longer easy to draw a clear boundary between market and state. In my view it is undesirable to do so. We see in Britain a healthy constant testing and probing, both intellectual and commercial, of the borders of the state in the search for potential alternative providers' (Mather, 1994: 4). Contract or market account-ability cuts across many of the long-cherished forms of electoral accountability, but it has been an important strand of Conservative political theory in recent years.

The 'accountability' associated with elected local government needs to be set against the 'accountability' associated with the publication of accounts/scrutiny by the press, public, and so on which characterises much of the quango sector. Conservative Junior Health Minister, Dr Brian Mawhinney, exemplified this strand of thought in a written parliamentary answer:

> Every year each National Health Service Trust issues a summary business plan and an annual report, makes its accounts publicly available and holds a public meeting. In addition, the trusts issue a strategic plan every three years. This is the minimum requirement that many Trusts exceed. It represents a high level of public accountability which requires no improvement.

A number of quangos (for example, the National Board for Nursing, Midwifery and Health Visiting for Scotland) do hold their meetings in public, and others, such as the Particle Physics and Astronomy Research Council, publish short summaries of the conclusions of every council meeting. English Heritage recently undertook the largest consultation ever held on a heritage issue when considering the future of Stonehenge: over 100,000 questionnaires were issued and over forty public meetings held. Additionally, a wide range of quangos are developing Internet websites.

Moving from the national stage to what the Nolan Committee called 'Local Public Spending Bodies', there are similar examples of diverse patterns of accountability. Higher education institutions (HEIs) publish their annual reports and accounts. Most of them hold meetings in public and all of them make agendas and minutes available. The same applies to further education institutions. All NHS Trusts, health authorities, Scottish health boards and most special health authorities now hold board meetings in public. The NHS Executive in England issued over 250,000 copies of its code of practice on openness in the NHS, with over 200,000 leaflets going to health service bodies for distribution for the public. Simply because accountability is not via the ballot box does not necessarily mean that it is non-existent. Neither should accountability be seen as simply a legal or contractual concept. Accountability is about the construction of an agreed language or discourse about the assessment of conduct and performance (Klein and Day, 1987). It is best seen as a multi-layered concept (see Stoker, 1999a: 49). The fact nonetheless remains that government by quangos means that many important areas of public policy involve no representative decision-making processes. This democratic deficit 'represents a fundamental weakness in the ability of citizens to be involved in the structures with which society governs itself' (Skelcher, 1998: 181).

Summary

- The stereotypical picture of elected local government being necessarily more accountable than quangos simply because it is elected needs to be treated with some caution.
- The democratic values of elected local authorities are frequently exaggerated: accountability via the ballot box is wearing thin, especially at the local level.

- The New Public Management (NPM) school of thought argues that the rise of quangos has strengthened rather than weakened accountability by making services more directly responsive to consumers.
- The proliferation of non-elected quangos limits the ability of citizens to shape government policy directly.

Update

The Labour government came to power in May 1997 committed to reforming quangos. Through its consultation paper, *Opening up Quangos* (Cabinet Office, 1997a) and the ensuing document *Quangos: Opening the Doors* (Cabinet Office, 1998a) it put forward proposals to reduce the democratic deficit. The government aimed to make quangos more accountable, more open and better understood; they also advocated better links with elected local authorities. Despite progress in this direction Flinders and Cole argue that 'the government's specific reforms are weak in both depth and coverage and the impact of the wider constitutional reforms on British quasi-government remains uncertain' (1999: 234). This viewpoint needs to be set against the real advances that have been made under the Blair government.

One area where progress certainly has been limited is in reducing the number of quangos. Flinders and Cole (1999: 235) show that in the two-year period from May 1997 the government created approximately thirty new NDPBs and announced plans to create sixteen more. In the same period twenty-four NDPBs were abolished with thirty-seven more candidates put on a hit list. But, as the same authors note, births and deaths are never simple in the world of quangos since roles and functions are frequently transferred from one body to another. For example, the Scottish Seed Potato Council has been abolished but its functions taken over by the new British Potato Council. In other areas a 'straight swap' has replaced one old body with a new one. For example, the Race Relations Employment Advisory Group has been abolished and the Race Relations Forum created. Plans have also been announced for the amalgamation of a range of smaller bodies into new 'super-quangos'. For example, in Wales it is proposed that the functions of the Development Board for Rural Wales, the Land Authority for Wales and the Welsh Development Agency are to be transferred to a new body called the Welsh Economic Development Agency.

The advent of the nine English Regional Development Associations (RDAs), however, reflects the government's concern to integrate a 'representative' dimension into the new breed of quangos. Four out of the twelve board members in each region comprise councillors drawn from that region. Positions on the boards are all openly advertised and the Commissioner for Public Appointments oversees the selection process. No appointments to RDAs are made without candidates first being scrutinised by a panel including a person independent of government.

As we have seen, the Labour government's consultation paper, *Opening up Quangos* was soon followed by *Quangos: Opening the Doors* (June 1998). Box 22.3 summarises the major proposals in this document.

Box 22.3 Labour's reform proposals: a summary

- NDPBs should hold annual open meetings where practical and appropriate.
- NDPBs should invite evidence from the public to discuss matters of public concern.
- Where practicable, NDPBs should release summary reports of meetings.
- NDPBs should aim to consult their users on a wide range of issues.
- The proposed Freedom of Information Act is expected to cover all public bodies, including NDPBs, allowing public access to their records.
- NDPBs which have direct dealings with the public should be brought within the jurisdiction of the Parliamentary Ombudsman.
- All NDPBs should produce and make publicly available annual reports.
- Executive NDPBs should produce and distribute information widely, making full use of the World Wide Web.
- All NDPBs will be reviewed every five years to establish that the functions are still required.
- The government aims to improve the representative nature of board members, especially ethnic minorities and women.

Source: Cabinet Office (1998a)

In *Quangos: Opening the Doors* (Cabinet Office, 1998a) the government drew back from suggesting the abolition of quangos or advocating the wholesale transfer of their functions back to elected local authorities. Essentially the proposals entailed refining the existing product rather than engaging in radical change. The emphasis was upon greater openness, increased accountability, greater information, broadening the base of board appointees, and (wherever possible) reducing quango numbers. Flinders and Cole expressed scepticism about the proposals:

> The key characteristic of the government's agenda is that the reform process is given to quangos. NDPBs 'should hold open meetings, release summary reports, consult their users, invite evidence' but the public will have no legal rights to force the bodies to carry through these guidelines. Furthermore, these reforms are restricted to NDPBs. All local spending bodies are, therefore, excluded. The present proposals make no recommendations designed to increase the capacity of (parliamentary) select committees to enforce accountability.
>
> (Flinders and Cole, 1999: 236)

Not all is doom and gloom, however. There have been some improvements in the representative nature of quango post holders. At September 1999, 33% of public appointments on NDPBs were held by women (compared with 23% in 1992). At the same date, 4.7% of appointments were held by members of ethnic minorities (compared with 2% in 1992). Stoker, reflecting upon the quality of local representatives, observes:

> In private conversations ministers and their advisers make comparisons between the lively, ethnically diverse and gender-balanced representation on some local quangos and police authorities and the dull, middle-aged or elderly men that dominate the politics of many elected authorities. Indeed, they argue,

appointments to local quangos open up opportunities for involvement to a whole variety of people that would not stand in local elections.

(Stoker, 1999b: 11)

In other words, quangos have democratic potential. They can be a vehicle for offering more opportunities for involvement and participation. In his Foreword to *Quangos: Opening up Public Appointments* (Cabinet Office, 1998b) the then Chancellor of the Duchy of Lancaster emphasised that the government had drawn up an action plan 'to ensure that further progress is made'. There were two commitments at the heart of government strategy: First, there was a commitment, in principle, to the equal representation of women and men in public appointments, and a pro-rata representation of members of ethnic minority groups. Second, there was a commitment to appoint on merit, using fair selection procedures which recognise non-traditional career patterns as suitable qualifications for appointments.

Each government department has drawn up plans covering the period 1998–2001 for increasing the representation of women and members of ethnic minorities on public bodies. The goals and objectives are revised annually in the light of progress made (which is monitored by the Public Appointment Unit). All will be involved in encouraging individuals in under-represented groups to apply for appointments by targeted advertising where appropriate and by setting clear job descriptions and person specifications which do not contain unnecessary requirements which might discourage or eliminate their applications. The Blair government is taking issues of representativeness seriously although it must be stressed that the above proposals apply only to NDPBs and NHS bodies and not to the vast majority of 'non-recognised' locally-appointed bodies.

Summary

- The Labour government came to power in May 1997 aiming to make quangos more accountable, more open and better understood.
- While numbers have been slightly reduced, there has been no wholesale culling of the species.
- In practice the government's reforms have been evolutionary rather than radical, with persuasion rather than direction being the dominant theme.
- While there has been some improvement in increasing the numbers of women and ethnic minorities on boards of quangos, there is still much to accomplish.

Debate

Accountability, appointments and patronage provide the main areas for debate. Accountability has been discussed earlier in the chapter; appointments and patronage will be dealt with in this section.

Concern about the party political affiliations of the quango appointments made directly by ministers and departments has long been articulated although, as we shall see, appointments have been subject to a code supervised by the Committee for Public Appointments since July 1996. It is hardly surprising, however, that every government wants to have people sympathetic to its viewpoint placed in those executive quangos which are central to the delivery of its policies, such as the Arts Council or Higher Education Funding Council. Advisory quangos, such as the Spongiform Encephalopathy Advisory Committee or British Overseas Trade Board, tend to be less subject to party political bias but according to Weir and Beetham (1999: 223) there is 'commercial penetration of advisory quangos' because many expert or specialist members have professional connections with the industries that they are overseeing. As Stott notes, without 'members representing other interests to act as a counter-balance, the decisions of these bodies may be biased to commercial interests. This undermines the argument that advisory NDPBs provide independent and expert advice for government' (Stott, 2000: 100).

Numbers of appointments to quangos remain high. In 1998, for example, the Department of Health had 3,794 public appointments under its auspices, 3,123 of which were to NHS boards and the remainder to NDPBs. The Lord Chancellor made 3,809 appointments to tribunals and 1,850 appointments to other NDPBs. Traditionally, parliamentary influence over appointments to chairs or boards of quangos has been minimal. In effect, the matter has almost entirely been one of ministerial discretion and consequently party political factors have invariably been to the fore. As we have seen, John Stewart has argued that at local level a 'new magistracy' is being created, in the sense that a non-elected elite is assuming responsibility for a large part of local governance. The elite is found on the boards of health authorities and hospital trusts, Training and Enterprise Councils (TECs), the boards of governors of grant-maintained schools, the governing bodies of colleges of further education and Housing Trusts (Stewart, 1992: 7). The partisan background of appointees is frequently lamented, yet this is essentially only an extension of the sovereignty of Parliament (which has become, invariably, the sovereignty of government). Majority governments can almost always convert their policy priorities into legislation and in the same way they can use their dominance to place supporters or sympathisers on quangos. The surprise, surely, would be if this did *not* happen given that the dominance of government is an integral part of the British political scene.

Skelcher (1998) argues that the concept of patronage has two distinct meanings that are frequently confused. He distinguishes between patronage as a *process* of appointment by an individual or small group and patronage as an intention or *motive* to place supporters in positions of power and argues that process patronage does not necessarily secure political advantage:

> The failure to separate *motive patronage* from *process patronage* results in a lack of clarity in almost all discussions about quango appointments. The confusion of the two meanings leads to an uncritical assumption that a patronage process will inevitably result in a partisan outcome. Process patronage may produce this result, and indeed is more likely to than an open appointments system, but it is not inevitable.
>
> (Skelcher, 1998: 83)

During the mid-1990s much of the debate about the extent of 'patronage' focused upon alleged Conservative 'bias' in appointments. One junior minister at the Department of Trade and Industry (Lady Denton) had responsibility in 1993 for 804 public appointments. She was reported as saying: 'I can't remember knowingly appointing a Labour supporter' (*Independent on Sunday*, 23 March 1993). In 1994 John Redwood, Secretary of State for Wales, was heavily criticised for appointing as chairman of the Welsh Development Agency a former Conservative Party fund-raiser in Monte Carlo. Partisanship, however, is at the very core of British politics; there is arguably an element of naivety on the part of those who express surprise at such appointments. With fewer and fewer local authorities remaining under Conservative control, quangos were an ideal means for Conservative central government to by-pass democratically-elected bodies, thereby ensuring that central government policy permeated through to the local level.

The attack on the Conservative government's use of quangos invariably oversimplified the debate about accountability. It created the impression that all unelected bodies were inherently bad and that everything would be transformed if they were abolished. As Hirst (1995) emphasises this is simplistic. The problem of accountability is not restricted to quangos:

> The danger in the rhetoric of the growth of 'unaccountable' government is that we tend to fall back on existing forms of political accountability as if they were unproblematic. There is now a serious issue about the degree to which representative institutions can render government in general accountable and not just quangos.
>
> (Hirst, 1995: 164)

Hirst sees quangos as 'just one, unimaginative and undemocratic, solution to a general crisis' (ibid.: 164) of representative government in Britain. The Labour government's current emphasis on enhancing public participation (via referendums, citizens' juries and the like) reflects a recognition of the deficiencies of representative democracy. Representative democracy needs to be supplemented by participatory democracy; quangos are not unique in being a problem area.

In May 1995 the Committee of Standards in Public Life (the Nolan Committee) published its first report (Cm 2850) in which it made a number of recommendations (nearly all of which were accepted by the Major government) designed to restore public confidence by injecting mechanisms to ensure greater openness and independent external scrutiny into the appointments process. As we have seen, the Blair government has extended these recommendations to advisory NDPBs and boards of visitors to penal establishments. An independent Commissioner for Public Appointments (Sir Leonard Peach) was appointed to regulate, monitor and report on the operation of the public appointments process. In his third report (1998), Peach quotes his auditors as saying 'there is no evidence of Ministers intervening to ensure advancement of their nominees and colleagues' and that 'patronage on behalf of individuals is clearly not an issue'. There are now regular advertisements in the press seeking nominees for NDPBs. These developments are important steps in the direction of more open, less secretive government but party political appointments have not disappeared.

Since coming to power in 1997 the Labour government has created a new breed of quango taskforces – composed of business people and others with relevant expertise to investigate a wide range of issues. Some of these, such as the Football Task Force, Better Regulation Task Force, Disability Rights Task Force and Skills Task Force have now become permanent advisory NDPBs and hence fall within the exclusive definition of quango. Among the issues dealt with by the Football Task Force have been racism in football, access for the disabled, ticket prices and the increasing commercialisation of football. Meanwhile, the shifting of deckchairs continues. For example, Learning and Skills Councils (LSCs) replaced TECs and the Further Education Funding Council (FEFC) in the planning and co-ordination of skills development and training for people over the age of 16 in April 2001. These councils (47 in total) have a budget of around £5 billion, potentially saving some £50 million a year by reducing duplication and bureaucracy in the TEC/FEFC system. Business has a big role to play in the new councils. The aim is for some 40% of members to have substantial recent business or commercial experience along with the national chairman and the majority of local chairmen. Democratic accountability via the ballot box does not feature.

As Stott (2000) notes, fragmentation of government is a consequence of transferring public policy and service management functions to separate single-focus quangos. Despite calls for 'joined-up' government, this precludes integration of related areas. 'Duplication, waste and reduced efficiency, which are signs of inadequate integration, can negate any benefits that arise from the use of single-purpose specialised bodies' such as quangos (Stott, 2000: 100–1). By creating quangos and by steering appointments central government can, in effect, dictate the way issues are handled. It can take issues out of the democratic arena in a way which effectively marginalises elected representatives.

Summary

- Numbers of appointments to quangos remain high but there is now greater transparency about the process.
- Given the highly partisan nature of the British political system it would be surprising if party political factors did not come into play in the appointments process.
- Taskforces have emerged since 1997 as the latest form of quangos. Meanwhile, births, marriages and deaths of quangos continue apace.
- The advent of quangos has led to increased fragmentation of both governmental structure and the policy-making process, despite the Labour government's calls for 'joined-up' or holistic government.

Conclusion

As we have seen, quangos are not new features of the regulatory state. They have been created over many years for a variety of different administrative, policy and party political reasons. What has emerged, Christopher Hood argues, is 'a largely unrationalised development in that it is something born of expediency and pragmatism rather than of conscious philosophy or strategy' (Hood, 1982: 51). Size, role and impact vary enormously. In education, for example, the creation of non-elected bodies has contributed to the centralisation of educational policy-making. To quote Johnson and Riley:

> The development of quangos as arms-length agencies of government has created scope for indirect government intervention and influence in key policy areas and has been part of a power realignment strengthening central over local government. Within education, as many other areas of the public service, quangos are now major players. Through them, the tentacles of central government now reach into increasingly complex arenas.
>
> (Johnson and Riley, 1995: 109)

As Skelcher (1998: 5) observes, from one perspective, quasi-government is the weighing of public values and the exercise of judgement – an essentially political activity – by a group of individuals appointed through a process of patronage and having no accountability or legitimacy with citizens. From another perspective it is an effective and politically astute way of governing and managing public services by drawing on the skills and experience of experts who, by virtue of being insulated from public view and party competition, are able to reach the best decisions for the community. Their non-directly-elected status nevertheless remains a particular cause of concern. As long ago as 1978 Holland and Fallon argued in a Conservative Party pamphlet that reforms were necessary. Fifteen years later (*Observer*, 4 July 1993) Sir Philip Holland maintained that the only way to curb the growth of quangos was through 'eternal vigilance'. He continued: 'The whole argument of bringing power closer to the people is bogus. Quangos are always in the interests of ministers and civil servants. They are not elected and are not answerable to the people.'

For many years the debate about quangos was couched in simplistic party political terms. Since 1996, however, there has been a more considered response to issues such as accountability, patronage and numbers. Despite all the problems associated with quangos, there are signs that greater appreciation of their role within the state now exists. It will be interesting to see whether the Blair government recognises their democratic potential (Flinders et al., 1997) and uses quasi-government to widen the circle of public participation, diffuse power and offer more active forms of citizenship, a particular challenge given the difficulties of representative democracy, especially at a local level. As yet, however, there are few signs that the government has a coherent reform agenda to clarify roles, responsibilities and relationships across quasi-government. As Flinders and Cole observe, 'without a government commitment to think strategically about the functions of quangos, limit executive patronage powers and "open up" all quangos, problems are likely to persist. The quango state will probably grow more complex and the democratic deficit remain' (Flinders and Cole, 1999: 238). Radical change does not appear imminent; quangos are here to stay.

Discussion Questions

1. Why do governments of all parties love quangos?
2. Why should there be more democratic control over quangos?
3. 'Quangos are far more accountable than is frequently maintained.' Discuss.

References

Cabinet Office (1997a) *Opening up Quangos*, London: HMSO. Also available at: http://www.open.gov.uk/m-of-g/consult97/qufore.htm

Cabinet Office (1997b) *Public Bodies 1997*, London: HMSO.

Cabinet Office (1998a) *Quangos: Opening the Doors*, London: HMSO. Also available at: http://www.cabinet-office.gov.uk/central/1998/pb/open/index.htm

Cabinet Office (1998b) *Quangos: Opening Up Public Appointments*, London: HMSO.

Davis, H. (1993) *A First Guide to Appointed Local Executive Bodies in the West Midlands*, Birmingham: City Council and University of Birmingham Partnership Paper.

Flinders, M. (1999) 'Quangos: Why do governments love them?', in M. Flinders and M. Smith (eds) *Quangos, Accountability and Reform*, Basingstoke: Macmillan.

Flinders, M. and Cole, M. (1999) 'Opening or closing Pandora's Box? New Labour and the quango state', *Talking Politics*, Vol. 12, No. 1, pp. 234–39.

Flinders, M. and Smith, M. (eds) (1999) *Quangos, Accountability and Reform*, Basingstoke: Macmillan.

Flinders, M., Harden, I. and Marquand, D. (1997) *How to Make Quangos Democratic*, London: Charter 88.

Hall, W. and Weir, S. (1996) *The Untouchables*, London: Scarman Trust for the Democratic Audit.

Hirst, P. (1995) 'Quangos and democratic government', in F.F. Ridley and D. Wilson (eds) *The Quango Debate*, Oxford: Oxford University Press, pp. 163–81.

Hollis, P. (1987) *Ladies Elect: Women in English Local Government, 1865–1914*, Oxford: Oxford University Press.

Hood, C. (1982) 'Governmental bodies and government growth', in A. Barker (ed.) *Quangos in Britain*, Basingstoke: Macmillan.

Johnson, H. and Riley, K. (1995) 'The impact of quangos and new government agencies on education', in F.F. Ridley and D. Wilson (eds) *The Quango Debate*, Oxford: Oxford University Press, pp. 106–18.

Klein, R. and Day, D. (1987) *Accountabilities in Five Public Services*, London: Tavistock.

Mather, G. (1994) 'The market, accountability and the civil service', PAC Conference, York, September.

Nolan Committee (1995) *Committee on Standards in Public Life, Local Public Spending Bodies, Vol. 1: Report*, Cm 3270–1, London: HMSO.

Pliatzky Report (1980) *Report on Non-Departmental Public Bodies*, Cmnd 7197, London: HMSO.

Skelcher, C. (1998) *The Appointed State*, Buckingham: Open University Press.

Stewart, J. (1992) 'The rebuilding of public accountability', Paper to European Policy Forum Conference, December.

Stoker, G. (1999a) 'Quangos and local democracy', in M. Flinders and M.J. Smith (eds) *Quangos, Accountability and Reform*, Basingstoke: Macmillan, pp. 40–54.

Stoker, G. (1999b) 'Remaking local democracy: lessons from New Labour's reform strategy', Paper presented at University of Manchester's Department of Government's Golden Anniversary, 10 September.

Stott, A.W. (2000) 'Quangos: are they unloved and misunderstood?', in L. Robins and B. Jones (eds) *Debates in British Politics Today*, Manchester: Manchester University Press, pp. 89–103 .

Waldegrave, W. (1993) 'The reality of reform and accountability in today's public service', Public Finance Foundation/BDO Consulting, Public Service Lecture, July.

Weir, S. and Beetham, D. (1999) *Political Power and Democratic Control in Britain*, London: Routledge.

Weir, S. and Hall, W. (eds) (1994) *EGO Trip: Extra-Governmental Organisations in the United Kingdom and their Accountability*, Colchester: University of Essex: Democratic Audit/Scarman Trust.

Wilson, D. (1995) 'Quangos in the skeletal state', in F.F. Ridley and D. Wilson (eds) *The Quango Debate*, Oxford: Oxford University Press, pp. 3–13.

Regulating Politics: The Committee on Standards in Public Life

Justin Fisher

CHAPTER TWENTY-THREE

Introduction

The Committee on Standards in Public Life was established in 1994 in response to rising concern about 'sleaze' in British politics. Disquiet over standards in public life is not a new concern. During the last century, it arose periodically and was based upon cases which were more serious than those which occurred in the 1990s. Each episode led to legislation or rules designed to remedy the individual problem and this led to patchy coverage, both in terms of scope and compliance (see Chronology). Despite this pragmatic approach to dealing with 'sleaze', the system broadly worked. In the 1990s, however, it became apparent that the previously more informal and piecemeal approaches were no longer effective and demand grew for a more coherent approach to standards in public life. The Committee (known sometimes as the Nolan, Neill or Wicks Committees, after their respective chairs) has had a prodigious work-rate. To date, it has produced seven substantial reports which have had a significant impact. It stands as the principal regulator of British political life. In this chapter, we examine why it was established, its key recommendations and the methods of regulation employed, and also attempt to evaluate how successful it has been.

Background

Sleaze is not a new phenomenon in British politics. As the Chronology shows, there have been periodic episodes throughout the last hundred years. However, the use of the term 'sleaze' *is* new (Dunleavy and Weir, 1995: 603). Definitions of sleaze vary and while broader interpretations, which include sexual misconduct, may feed into perceptions of wrongdoing, the Committee has devoted itself to questions of conduct in relation to the fulfilment of the duties of a public servant. Nevertheless, during the late 1980s and early 1990s, there were a number of factors that cumulatively led to concerns with 'sleaze' and ultimately to the establishment of the Committee on Standards in Public Life.

First, there was disquiet over the role of lobbyists. Professional lobbying, involving specialised firms, had grown considerably in the 1980s, and unease was growing at the extent of the practice. Second, there were allegations of financial wrongdoing by MPs. In some cases these were genuine attempts at self-enrichment but, crucially, in others the activities involved were not strictly forbidden, although they crossed the previously-accepted frontiers of conduct and standards in public life. Third, there were concerns that appointments to public bodies were becoming increasingly partisan – it was thought that many appointees were disproportionately supporters of the governing party. Fourth, there had been a series of appointments of former ministers (and senior civil servants) into positions within companies with which they had previously had dealings when in office. Finally, there were a series of sexually-related scandals concerning mainly Conservative MPs and ministers. These were especially embarrassing because they followed the Prime Minister's announcement that British society needed to go 'Back to Basics', which appeared to promote, among other things, a more traditional emphasis upon sexual morality and family values. In addition to these factors, questions relating to party finance and donations re-emerged (Fisher, 1994), although this was not central to conceptions of sleaze. Nevertheless, like many of the factors that contributed to the impression of sleaze, it was not so much the individual cases that were significant, but the accumulation of cases.

Essentially, it became apparent that existing legislation had failed to deal with a series of emerging problems. Three reports in 1993 and 1994 by the Public Accounts Committee and the Audit Commission illustrated the problem. The Public Accounts Committee report claimed that there were:

> a number of serious failures in administrative and financial systems and controls within departments and other public bodies, which have led to money being wasted or otherwise improperly spent. These failings represent a departure from the standards of conduct which have mainly been established during the past 140 years.
>
> (quoted in Doig, 1996: 47)

Similarly, the Audit Commission reports on local government and the National Health Service suggested that standards of public conduct were similarly under threat, and that the delegation of management and financial responsibilities was in part responsible. For Doig, the speed at which public sector organisations had been forced to change as a result of government policy had resulted in misperceptions among public servants that they were now in a quasi-private sector environment and the decline of a clear public service ethos (Doig, 1996: 47–8).

These reports attracted relatively little attention but they pointed to a problem with existing codes of conduct where the public sector ethos had diminished. This was emphasised further by reports from the Select Committee on Members' Interests, which highlighted the fact that MPs were increasingly ignorant of the rules pertaining to the Register of Members' Interests and worse, that there was 'an indifference to the spirit and letter of the rules relating to financial interests' (Doig, 1996: 49). In essence, the existing rules were failing because of both intentional and unintentional misconceptions. For some there was confusion about the culture which had hitherto sustained the rules; for others there was deliberate loophole-seeking. Little that was done actually contravened the rules, but much contravened the conventions that had emerged.

Under more favourable political circumstances, Major might have been able to 'tough it out' but the government was unpopular. When a series of scandals emerged in 1994 regarding allegations of Conservative MPs taking 'cash for questions', Major had little alternative but to act and the Committee on Standards in Public Life was established in October 1994.

The Committee on Standards in Public Life

This Committee is an independent advisory non-departmental public body (NDPB). It is a standing committee. This is important, because unlike committees created for a specific purpose, such as those that examined electoral reform or the House of Lords, the Committee is able to review and justify its actions after it has reported. For example, when the Committee makes recommendations, its permanent character means that it can continue to press for their implementation. It can also answer and clarify queries and review and assess the progress of its own recommendations. Thus, the Committee's sixth report was essentially a review of progress on its first report. The recommendations of committees that are not permanent, in contrast, are more vulnerable to non-implementation because the committees cease to exist after reporting, which makes it more difficult to respond to criticisms or press governments for action. As we shall see, its permanence is one explanation for the notable success of the Committee on Standards in Public Life.

Issues come on to the agenda of the Committee via a number of routes. In the first instance, the Committee's terms of reference determine the types of issue that can be considered:

> To examine current concerns about all holders of public office, including arrangements relating to financial and commercial activities, and make recommendations as to any changes in present arrangements which might be required to ensure the highest standards of propriety in public life.
>
> The term 'public life' includes: ministers, civil servants and advisors; Members of Parliament and UK Members of the European Parliament; members and senior officers of all NDPBs and of NHS bodies; non-ministerial office holders; members and other senior officers of other bodies discharging publicly-funded functions; and elected members and senior officers of local authorities.
>
> (Committee on Standards in Public Life, 1995: Introduction)

Tony Blair extended these terms of reference in 1997 to include issues relating to the funding of political parties.

Beyond that, the Committee determines 'current concerns' by a process of 'horizon-scanning' – Committee members and its secretariat survey the political scene and make recommendations about issues that should be examined. This process is supported by close contact with senior political journalists. The Committee then makes proposals to the government which to date have almost all been accepted by the Prime Minister.

Members of the Committee are appointed by the Prime Minister for renewable periods of up to three years. As Box 23.1 shows, its members are drawn from across the major parties and from senior positions in public life – including professors of politics!

Box 23.1 Members and former members of the Committee on Standards in Public Life

The Rt Hon the Lord Nolan of Brasted (Chair 1994 to 9 November 1997) – *Law Lord*

Lord Neill of Bladen QC (Chair 10 November 1997 to 28 February 2001) – *Former Vice-Chancellor of the University of Oxford and Chairman of the Bar Council*

Sir Nigel Wicks GCB CVO CBU (Chair 1 March 2001 to 29 February 2004) – *Former Principal Private Secretary to Margaret Thatcher and Director of International Finance at the Treasury*

Ann Abraham – *Legal Services Ombudsman for England and Wales*

Sir Clifford Boulton GCB – *Officer of the House of Commons, 1953–94*

Professor Alice Brown – *Professor of Politics, University of Edinburgh*

Sir Anthony Cleaver – *Chairman of the Medical Research Council*

Rita Donaghy OBE – *Chair of ACAS and former President of the TUC*

The Lord Goodhart QC – *Liberal Democrat peer*

Frances Heaton – *Director of Lazard Brothers*

Sir Martin Jacomb – *Chairman, Delta PLC*

Professor Anthony King – *Professor of Government, University of Essex*

The Rt Hon Tom King CH MP – *Former Conservative Cabinet minister*

The Rt Hon John MacGregor OBE – *Former Conservative Cabinet minister*

Rabbi Julia Neuberger – *Chief Executive of the King's Fund health care charity*

The Rt Hon the Lord Shore of Stepney – *Former Labour Cabinet member*

The Rt Hon Chris Smith MP – *Former Labour Cabinet minister*

The Rt Hon Lord Thomson of Monifieth KT DL – *Former Labour minister, Liberal Democrat peer*

Sir William Utting CB – *Former Chief Inspector of Social Services*

Dame Anne Warburton DCVO CMG – *Former Official at the Foreign Office*

Baroness Warwick of Undercliffe – *Chief Executive, Committee of Vice-Chancellors and Principals* (now called Universities UK)

Summary

- Sleaze in British politics is not new.
- A cumulative combination of factors led to the establishment of the Committee on Standards in Public Life, which demonstrated that existing rules were no longer effective.
- The Committee on Standards in Public Life is a standing committee with a specific remit to examine concerns and make recommendation to ensure the highest standards of propriety in public life.

Theoretical Considerations

The existence of rules and regulations in public life raises theoretical questions. These are principally concerned with the effectiveness of self-regulation *versus* written rules with an external body to devise and enforce such rules. The traditional position, as far as Parliament is concerned, is based on self-regulation. This stems from the notion of parliamentary sovereignty. If Parliament is sovereign, then another authority cannot compel it or its members to act in a particular way. Hence, MPs are protected by parliamentary privilege, which enables them to speak freely in Parliament without fear of prosecution for libel. Self-regulation of Parliament has a long tradition and is guarded very closely, but other organisations representing professions also claim a right to self-regulation. The British Medical Association, for example, has long argued that regulation of doctors is better carried out by doctors themselves than by outsiders. There is merit in this argument. To begin with, members of a profession may be best placed to evaluate arguments and disputes based upon their own specialist knowledge of the field. Moreover, many would argue that regulation within a profession has more legitimacy than that carried out from outside. Others argue that self-regulation merely leads to self-protection, or as Dunleavy and Weir (1995: 614) put it, a 'club ethos'. In addition, while few would argue against the utility of legislation, such as factory acts or health and safety measures as means of enforcing standards, it sometimes appears that professions believe that they should be above such things.

A second question that arises is one of the effectiveness of rules *versus* trust (Philp, 2000). A system of rules which must be adhered to contradicts the notions of trust and self-regulation. A system based on trust implies that practitioners or organisations can be trusted to uphold standards. The dominant political culture will influence whether rules or trust is more likely to be employed. Thus, the British system has relied more on trust and informal arrangements whereas the United States favours more regulation. This is reflected in the absence and presence of written constitutions, for example. Those who advocate trust do so in part because they view excessive regulation as creating a culture whereby compliance with standards is dictated primarily by a need to comply with rules rather than the integrity of desiring high standards. They point to four particular problems of excessive regulation.

First, rules can create 'perverse incentives' (Philp, 2000). Excessive regulation can lead people to interpret rules literally – doing no more or no less than is required. MPs opposed to establishing the Register of Members' Interests, for example, argued that it would justify behaviour falling below acceptable standards which, nonetheless, was not explicitly forbidden by the rules. Second, a regulatory mechanism must itself be regulated. In other words, if rules are imposed because some are not trusted to uphold standards, then why should those imposing and implementing the rules themselves be trusted? They too need to be regulated and the process becomes never-ending. Third, the drafting and imposition of rules can be affected by partisanship. This was an issue when the Committee's fifth report, on party finance, was being discussed. The Conservative Party was concerned that the impact of recommendations should not disadvantage it disproportionately, particularly with reference to whether corporate donations to political parties – from which the Conservatives have been the primary beneficiaries – should be permitted. Finally, regulations are more costly than trust since they involve people in drafting and enforcement. Trust involves little or no cost. Nonetheless, as Table 23.1 shows, the 'cost of standards' has been remarkably low.

There are arguments in favour of a rule-based system, however. First, and most obviously, the mechanisms of trust had seemingly become ineffective by the 1980s. Second, public confidence is an important element of the debate on standards in public life and it appears that the public did not view trust as the most effective way of ensuring that standards were upheld. Dunleavy and Weir (1995: 610) found in a 1995 survey that reliance on self-regulation by Parliament was supported by only 26% of the public while 67% preferred rules enforced from outside. Moreover, 78% felt that questions of ministerial misconduct should be dealt with either by an independent commission or the courts, rather than by the Prime Minister or Parliament (Dunleavy and Weir, 1995: 611). Their conclusion was that self-regulation was neither publicly supported nor effective.

A second general theoretical area of concern is whether a decline in public confidence in the political system may threaten the health of democracy. Certainly, the accumulation of sleaze episodes appears to have affected public

Table 23.1 The costs of standards – expenditure of the Committee on Standards in Public Life

£s	1994–95[1]	1995–96	1996–97	1997–98	1998–99	1999–2000
Total allocation	433,760	557,534	503,410	485,000	675,300	535,000
Total net expenditure	269,858	473,489	484,684	521,079	676,358	447,232
Outturn	–163,902	–84,045	–18,726	36,080	1,058	–87,768[2]

[1] October 1994–March 1995.
[2] Forecast outturn.

Source: Committee on Standards in Public Life (2000a)

opinion (see Tables 23.2 and 23.3). That is significant, because should trust in political institutions (in the broadest sense) decline, this may weaken support for democratic values and in turn threaten political stability. As Curtice and Jowell (1995: 144) point out, concerns about the decline of 'civic culture' in Britain are not new. Nonetheless, they noted in their analysis of data collected in 1994, a distinct decline in trust and feelings of political efficacy, which occurred among supporters of all the main parties, in the 1980s and early 1990s (Curtice and Jowell, 1995: 146–51).

While a decline in trust is clearly of significance, what matters more is whether this is translated into political action (or inaction). Curtice and Jowell (1995: 159–60) investigated the extent to which levels of political trust made an impact upon election turnout, partisanship, interest in politics and sense of duty regarding voting. In all aspects except the last, the level of political trust had no discernible effect. No matter what their level of trust in the system and politicians, individuals were equally likely to vote, to be partisan and to be interested in politics. Indeed, those with the lowest level of political trust were most interested in politics! Trust did make a difference to whether people thought that it was everyone's duty to vote, but only among those with the lowest level of trust. Furthermore, when Curtice and Jowell repeated their analysis following the 1997 general election, they found that trust in the political system had no discernible impact upon levels of voter registration and turnout, leading them to conclude that whatever caused low turnout at the election it was nothing to do with declining political confidence (Curtice and Jowell, 1997: 98–9).

Table 23.2 Public opinion and confidence in government

People you trust to tell the truth (%)	1983	1993	1997	1999	2000
Government ministers	16	11	12	23	21
Politicians generally	18	14	15	23	20
Civil servants	25	37	36	47	47
Journalists	19	10	15	15	15

Source: MORI

Table 23.3 Evaluations of the system of governing Britain

The system of governing Britain ...	1973	1977	1991	1994	1995	1996
...could not be improved or only improved in small ways (%)	48	34	33	29	22	35
...could be improved quite a lot or a great deal (%)	49	62	63	69	76	63

Source: Curtice and Jowell (1997: 91)

Summary

- An emphasis on self-regulation or on external control is a critical variable in terms of the kinds of recommendations made about standards in public life.
- Critics of self-regulation argue that it leads to self-protection. Advocates argue that it is more effective in enforcing standards.
- There was a decline in political trust in the 1990s but this had no discernible effect on electoral participation.

Update

The first report

The first report of the Committee on Standards in Public Life was published in 1995. It concluded that there was no conclusive evidence that standards of behaviour in public life had declined but acknowledged that procedures for maintaining and enforcing standards were weak. Consequently, it was not clear to all within public life as to what were the boundaries of acceptable conduct. This, the Committee argued, was the principal reason for public disquiet. The report set out four general recommendations that were applicable across the whole of public life. First, seven principles of conduct underpinning public life were established (see Box 23.2). These form a benchmark from which to evaluate public standards. Second, all public bodies should draw up a Code of Conduct incorporating these principles. (This has been one of the Committee's clear successes as the principles have been embedded in codes of conduct across various areas of public life, including the voluntary sector.) Third, independent systems for maintaining standards should be supported by independent scrutiny and, finally, the need to educate public officials about standards was recognised.

In total, fifty-five specific recommendations were made covering MPs, ministers, civil servants and executive quangos. Of key importance was the establishment of a Commissioner of Standards to oversee new rules on MPs' interests, the establishment of a Public Appointments Commissioner to oversee quango appointments and a requirement for former ministers to seek clearance for jobs that they wish to take within two years of leaving office. However, the Committee decided not to regulate lobbyists. The reasons for this were threefold. First, the Committee did not wish to restrict access to politicians. Second, it was deemed sufficient to regulate those who are lobbied. Third, there was a question of the difficulty of actually defining lobbyists.

Of critical importance, was the continuation of self-regulation for Parliament. The enforcement of the Code of Conduct raised serious issues concerning the Commons' privilege to self-regulate. While clarification on criminal liability for bribery was sought, the establishment of the Parliamentary Commissioner indicated that self-regulation was to be maintained. Indeed, Oliver (1995: 596–8)

Box 23.2 The seven principles of public life

Selflessness – Holders of public office should take decisions solely in terms of the public interest. They should not do so in order to gain financial or other material benefits for themselves, their family, or their friends.

Integrity – Holders of public office should not place themselves under any financial or other obligation to outside individuals or organisations which might influence them in the performance of their official duties.

Objectivity – In carrying out public business, including making public appointments, awarding contracts, or recommending individuals for rewards and benefits, holders of public office should make choices on merit.

Accountability – Holders of public office are accountable for their decisions and actions to the public and must submit themselves to whatever scrutiny is appropriate to their office.

Openness – Holders of public office should be as open as possible about all the decisions and actions they take. They should give reasons for their decisions and restrict information only when the wider public interest clearly demands.

Honesty – Holders of public office have a duty to declare any private interests relating to their public duties and to take steps to resolve any conflicts arising in a way that protects the public interest.

Leadership – Holders of public office should promote and support these principles by leadership and example.

claims that this was the only realistic option, since it was most unlikely that the House of Commons would have consented to an extra-parliamentary body supervising its standards. Overall, the bulk of the recommendations were accepted and implemented. There was, however, one notable exception. The Committee recommended that the Prime Minister should be the enforcer of the Ministerial Code of Conduct. John Major rejected this (as did Tony Blair subsequently). Consequently, there remains doubt as to who should enforce ministerial standards.

The second report

The second report was published in 1996. This dealt with local public spending bodies. Building on the general principles previously established, the report made fifty recommendations about standards of governance, accountability and propriety in further and higher education bodies, grant-maintained schools, Training and Enterprise Councils (TECs) and Registered Housing Associations. The report argued for the adoption of good practice as set out in the first report to be adopted within the sectors covered in the second. In addition, it supported the principle of unpaid voluntary service by board members; limiting terms of office; the provision of external assistance in resolving internal disputes and the establishment of codes of practice on 'whistleblowing'.

The third report

The Committee's third report, published in 1997, was concerned with local government and made thirty-nine recommendations. Among these were that local councils should develop a clear code of conduct for councillors and have a standards committee, that courts should be involved in imposing penalties for misconduct (unlike Parliament) and that a Local Government Tribunal should be established. In the light of these recommendations, changes were recommended in relation to planning, surcharges and whistleblowing. The planning proposals were of particular significance, since this was the area on which the Committee received the largest number of submissions. Importantly, the report affirmed that the process by which planning decisions were made was an administrative rather than a quasi-judicial process, thereby emphasising a political rather than a legal view of planning. By and large, the government accepted these recommendations, with the exception of local discretion over enforcing codes of conduct. The government argued that enforcement should be at regional rather than local level.

The fourth report

The fourth report, published in 1997, was a review of progress on the recommendations of the Committee's first two reports, with reference to NDPBs, NHS Trusts and Local Public Spending Bodies. Although the relevant recommendations had been accepted and were being implemented, the Committee believed that there were continuing areas of concern. These included communication of standards of conduct and whistleblowing to staff, as well as the speed of implementation and the interpretation of the earlier recommendations. Twenty-two observations, intended to improve implementation, were included in the report. This illustrates the importance of the 'standing' status of the Committee, which allows it to review the implementation of earlier recommendations.

The fifth report

Arising from the Prime Minister's extension of the Committee's terms of reference, the fifth report (1998) examined the vexed question of party finance. This report was surprisingly radical, making some one hundred recommendations which including the establishment of an independent electoral commission (see Box 23.3). Despite its radicalism, it achieved what no previous attempt to reform party finance in the last century had achieved: cross-party consensus. As a consequence, the recommendations passed relatively smoothly into law, with the government rejecting only one relatively minor recommendation – tax relief on donations to parties.

Box 23.3 Why the fifth report was so radical

Since the 1970s, political finance has been subject to periodic examination. With the exception of the introduction of financial aid for opposition parties in Parliament, what distinguishes these previous attempts from the Parties, Elections and Referendums Act 2000 (which was based on the fifth report), is their generally limited scope and failure to reform a system of political finance based largely upon the 1883 *Corrupt and Illegal Practices Act* (Fisher, 2000a).

The Neill report represented proposals for the most fundamental reform in British party finance since 1883. It was a wide-ranging report which made no fewer than 100 proposals for reform, including:

- Limits on campaign expenditure.
- The establishment of an electoral commission.
- Declaration of donations by parties.
- A ban on foreign donations.
- A modest increase in state funding.

Critically, the report was supported by all parties and was supported almost in entirety by the government when it published its response in July 1999. Subsequently, the proposals were put to Parliament in the 1999–2000 session and passed on 30 November 2000.

The sixth report

Like the fourth, the sixth Committee report was a review. Published in 2000, it reviewed progress on the recommendations of the first report as well as assessing how successful the Committee's work had been. Measuring success is no easy task but this assessment, which came to positive conclusions, was almost entirely based on the untested opinions of 'academic and editorial commentators' rather than genuine evidence. Nonetheless, the new report made forty-one further recommendations. Of key importance was a re-statement of the commitment to parliamentary self-regulation (save for those involving allegations of crime). Nevertheless, new procedures for self-regulation were recommended, including a preliminary tribunal, comprising an independent lawyer and two to four senior MPs. Regarding civil servants, the report re-stated the need to ingrain a public-sector ethos and recommended that the Civil Service Code (first established in 1996) be put on a statutory footing. The report further investigated the role of special advisors. These are ministerial advisors, who are not recruited through open competition, but are technically civil servants and are therefore paid for out of public funds. Governed by the Civil Service Code, they are exempted from provisions relating to impartiality and objectivity. The report concluded that special advisors played a valuable public function and should therefore remain as civil servants, but that a new code of practice for such civil servants should be issued. Finally, the report re-stated the opposition to a register of lobbyists expressed in the first report.

The seventh report

The seventh report of the Committee concerned conduct in the House of Lords. Published at the end of 2000, it sought to bring the House of Lords into line with procedures in the other British Parliaments and Assemblies. Specifically, the report called for the introduction of a Code of Conduct, incorporating the seven principles referred to above, as well as principles relating to the declaration and registration of interests. In conjunction with this, the report proposed moving to a mandatory register of interests in order to reassure the public and clearly define the parameters of acceptable behaviour. Similarly, with regard to lobbying, the onus was placed upon the lobbied rather than the lobbyists. Finally, as with the Commons, the report re-affirmed the Committee's belief in self-regulation.

Summary

- The Committee has produced seven reports covering a range of topics and including two reviews of the effectiveness of previous recommendations.
- Reports have favoured self-regulation rather than external control for MPs, but not for parties.
- Registration of lobbyists has been resisted.

Debate

These reports have generated a variety of reactions. Among the most visible was that of Conservative MP Alan Duncan challenging Lord Nolan in the street after the publication of the first report in 1995, over the proposed disclosure of all extra payments received as a result of services provided in his capacity as an MP. Most reactions have been more measured and the most remarkable fact is the consensus that has surrounded the vast majority of proposals. The first report, predictably enough since it was the first of it kind, aroused most debate. The most prominent source of contention has been the question of self-regulation. Initially, many backbench MPs saw the Nolan report as a threat to self-regulation, even though it had rejected external controls. They objected to what they saw as the implication in the report that they were a 'bunch of crooks' (quoted in Oliver, 1997: 550). For Berrington, complaints regarding an infringement of self-regulation were hollow: 'Sovereignty is what politicians talk about when they have nothing palpable left to say' (Berrington, 1995: 438). Yet he also argues that discouraging outside activity by MPs might *reduce* the professionalism of MPs, since their contact with the outside world would be further reduced (Berrington, 1995: 443).

Dunleavy and Weir (1995), while supporting many of the Nolan reforms, argued strongly against the continuation of self-regulation. Not only does it fail to command public support, but it continues what they see as unsatisfactory elements of the British political system in general – 'unspoken understandings, conventional limits, the self-restraint of political elites and a muddling through revisionism as a way of coping with emerging problems' (Dunleavy and Weir, 1995: 613). In short, Dunleavy and Weir call for external regulation of MPs.

Norton (1997: 370) argues that, although the regulations could have gone further, they were a significant advance and, furthermore, provide an incentive to MPs to ensure that self-regulation worked. If it did not, there would be calls for even stronger external regulation. Along similar lines, Oliver (1995) argues that any serious threat to self-regulation would have meant that the first report would have become more of a political football and that no consensus would have emerged around the recommendations. Certainly there is merit in this view. Since the proposals required parliamentary approval, it would have been politically naive to pursue proposals that would almost certainly be unacceptable to MPs. The initial hostile reaction of some MPs to the lesser issue of requiring a declaration of all payments illustrate this point. Parallels also exist with the fifth report. This rejected comprehensive state funding of political parties but by doing so, it could be argued, ensured the successful passage of what were already very radical reforms. However, Oliver remains sceptical about the effectiveness of self-regulation, largely because of the difficulties of divorcing the process from party loyalty. She argues that exercising party political advantage may not only jeopardise a fair and even-handed process for those who are to be judged, but may also undermine public confidence in the concept of self-regulation (Oliver, 1997: 553–7).

Debates on the third report largely focus on the issue of planning. As noted above, the report takes a political rather than legal view of the local planning process. In other words, there is a view that councillors should not necessarily make planning decisions simply on the basis of planning regulations but, as elected representatives, should also consider the views of those they represent. If this were not done, it is not clear why councillors should be involved in the planning process at all. This approach is supported by Stott (1998), who argues that any attempt to divorce the political role of councillors from their planning function would be undemocratic and that councillors should listen to the advice of planning officers, but not be bound by it. Darke (1997) disagrees, advocating a quasi-judicial role for planners because decisions may be influenced by partisan considerations. Citing a study of planning officers, Darke shows that 60% said that councillors made planning decisions based upon party political considerations (Darke, 1997: iv) His conclusion, similar to that of the government, is that good practice in decision-making on planning should be subject to national, rather than local guidelines, since this would overcome 'the inevitable patchiness' of leaving the process to individual councils.

Reaction to the fifth report has been largely positive. As Box 23.3 shows, it was a radical report which nonetheless attracted cross-party support. The principal debates have concerned whether comprehensive state funding for parties should have been recommended and whether national spending limits in election campaigns is the best way of reducing the effects of inequalities in parties' financial resources. The Committee rejected state funding, finding the case in favour insufficiently compelling, but proposed setting national expenditure limits at general elections. It was argued that capping expenditure would make the electoral playing field at least a little more level and that the restriction would limit the 'arms race' in campaign spending that had been developing between the two main parties. It can be argued that these two arguments are flawed. First, the argument relating to levelling the playing field seems to assume that the more money a party spends the greater the electoral payoff. While there is clear evidence that this is true at constituency level (Johnston and Pattie, 1995), Fisher (1999) demonstrates that national spending has no apparent effect on a party's popularity. He calculates, for example, that in the period 1959–94 an annual increase of £1,000 (at 1963 prices) in expenditure by the Conservatives when in government resulted in a 0.004% increase in their poll ratings (and that was the only significant relationship found).

The flaw in the argument relating to the campaign 'arms race' is the focus on campaign spending. Studies of party finance consistently show that most party expenditure is not spent on campaigns but on routine maintenance of the party infrastructure (Fisher, 2000b). Since parties are competing continually and effectively campaigning throughout the electoral cycle, limits affecting one period of expenditure (during campaigns) may not make much difference to overall expenditure. In any case, the question must surely be raised as to whether it is desirable to restrict campaigning at all. Campaigns are about political communication and, at a time when there are concerns regarding levels of political engagement on the part of the electorate, there is a case to be made that parties' attempts to engage the electorate should be encouraged rather than restricted.

Reactions to the seventh report were mixed. Labour and Liberal Democrat peers broadly supported it, while Conservatives displayed some unease. Their reservations principally concern the mandatory registration of interests, since in their view this might have the effect of turning the Lords into a house of full-time politicians.

Has the Committee been successful?

As suggested above, the Committee's own evaluations of its success have been conspicuous for their lack of serious attention to appropriate evidence (sixth report). They asked the opinions of observers and received mostly positive responses. Thus, Peter Preston, former Editor-in Chief of the *Guardian*, wrote:

> I think that the Committee and the reports . . . and the implementation of their recommendations have made a substantial difference, not only in the way in which public life in this country is perceived but to the actual practice of it.
> (Committee on Standards in Public Life, 2000b: 12)

Seeking the opinion of informed observers seems a startlingly unscientific method of evaluation, however. Three alternatives means of evaluating the success of the Committee's work suggest themselves: the extent to which its recommendations have been accepted; the extent to which public opinion has changed; and the extent to which the recommendations have been observed.

In terms of acceptance of its recommendations, the Committee has been very successful indeed. Over 90% have been accepted with outright rejections being few and far between. From the third report on local government, for example, the government did not accept that oversight of codes of conduct should be devolved to the local level but adopted devolution of this responsibility to the regional level. Tax relief on donations to parties, as proposed in the fifth report, was rejected outright since it was seen as indirect state funding. The recommendation in both the first and sixth reports that the Prime Minister should enforce the ministerial code has twice been rejected by the government. In addition, the House of Commons has rejected the recommendation to establish a tribunal procedure in contested cases of serious misconduct by MPs (sixth report: recommendation 3). Overall, however, there is no doubt that the Committee has been successful in having its recommendations accepted.

The picture is more mixed with regard to change in public opinion, partially due to a lack of relevant data. Nevertheless, the proportion of the electorate thinking that the system of governing Britain could be improved considerably has fallen since the establishment of the Committee (see Table 23.3). Feelings of personal political efficacy have also shown a minor improvement. In 1994, 28% felt they had no say in what the government did while in 1996 the figure was 24%, although this figure was still significantly higher than was the case in 1991 (16%) (Curtice and Jowell, 1997: 93). Other indicators of public trust derive from polls asking respondents to indicate their levels of trust in various professions. These data suggest a promising, if modest, trend. The percentages believing that politicians tell the truth were 18%, 14% 15%, 23% and 20% in 1983, 1993, 1997, 1999 and 2000 respectively. In addition, in those same years, ministers were judged to tell the truth by 16%, 11%, 12%, 23% and 21% (see Table 23.2). However, as a note of caution, it should be acknowledged that Curtice and Jowell (1997: 106) found that, initially at least, the change of government in 1997 had had a positive impact upon responses to these sorts of questions.

The extent to which the Committee's recommendations have been observed also indicates some success. The seven principles of standards in public life have been incorporated into codes of conduct for many public bodies and form a benchmark against which adherence to standards is evaluated. In addition, the recommendations of the first report have seen the establishment of a Public Appointments Commissioner and a Parliamentary Commissioner for Standards, whose role it is to oversee the observation of public standards. Contrariwise, scandal in British politics has not disappeared. The Committee could never eliminate scandal completely, of course. But episodes in 2001, such as that concerning Lord Irvine, the Lord Chancellor, who, despite his formally impartial role, engaged in fund-raising for the Labour Party among lawyers, suggest that there may still be a lack of clarity concerning acceptable standards of behaviour, even if, technically, individuals did nothing wrong.

A further question to be asked is which reform arising from the Committee's work has been most significant. At a general level, the widespread incorporation of the seven principles is very important since it implies a general acceptance of the standards laid out by the Committee. More specifically, the reform of party finance is probably the most significant step since it has led to most change in established practice. Previous attempts to reform party finance had been characterised by persistent failure. Following the Committee's fifth report, however, the government enacted a very wide-ranging and radical act, which has changed considerably the regulation and probably the structure of British party finance and also impacted on the conduct of election campaigns (Fisher, 2001).

Given that the Committee has, by and large, been successful, the final task is to account for this success. Two main reasons can be suggested. First, its structure as a standing committee is vitally important. By virtue of this, the Committee can clarify points within its reports, respond to criticisms and, most important, put pressure on government if recommendations are not accepted or enacted. Although the Committee cannot insist upon its recommendations being adopted, since formally it only makes recommendations to the Prime Minister, its permanence means that it is more difficult for governments to ignore recommendations or 'kick them into touch'. This contrasts with special committees such as those established to examine electoral reform and the House of Lords, or indeed, Royal Commissions. In short, it is much easier to sideline recommendations if the body that made them no longer exists.

The second reason to account for the Committee's success is, in a sense, its initial success. Since its first and subsequent early reports were almost universally accepted, a momentum has built up. It becomes more difficult to reject the recommendations of a Committee that has been seen to 'get it right' previously. In other words, if a significant proportion of the Committee's proposals had been rejected in the past, it would be easier to reject them in the future. The high level of acceptance gives the Committee greater moral authority.

Summary

- The emphasis on self-regulation has been challenged either as unworkable, or subject to possible distortion.
- Opinion is divided about the extent to which councillors should act politically rather than judicially.
- Some have argued that the fifth report could have included an greater extension of state funding for political parties.
- By a series of indicators, the Committee can claim to have been successful thus far.

Conclusion

Overall, the Committee on Standards in Public Life has been successful. Its ideas are now incorporated into many aspects of public life and in addition, its work is held in high regard both in the United Kingdom and overseas. What of the future? Where does the Committee go from here? Clearly, there are a finite number of institutions that can be examined and re-examined. One possibility is to extend the Committee's remit, as was done in case of political parties, to include areas such as the media (Philp, 2000). Yet by doing so the Committee risks both duplicating the work of others and challenging powerful actors such as the press. By examining questions such as press freedom, for example, the Committee could find itself in conflict with institutions which do not share others' views of its moral authority. A subsequent report with many rejected recommendations could therefore jeopardise the Committee's future standing. All of this is not to say that the Committee should only examine easy topics (which it clearly has not done up to now), but that moves to examine non-formal institutions could prove to be problematic. Of course, the Committee could continue to examine various aspects of public life and then make its role largely one of reviewer. Indeed, the ultimate indicator of success would be if the Committee's role were to become that minimal. In the meantime, the Committee must be wary of future threats to standards in public life. Complacency is one obvious threat. In addition, the case can be made that if the Committee recommends too many rules, rather than relying on trust, then rules will serve to highlight loopholes which, as was very apparent in the early 1990s, is a real threat to standards in public life.

Chronology

1912 Marconi Scandal. A government minister used insider knowledge for trading in shares. The Prime Minister acknowledged that existing rules of prudence may not have been observed. The result was new rules on obligation for ministers not to use public office for private gain. New rules of prudence were drafted, requiring ministers to avoid any transactions which might be construed as breaching rules of obligation.

1922 Sale of honours for party funds. A long-standing practice pursued by both the Liberal and Conservative parties was exposed. It resulted in the Honours (Prevention of Abuses) Act 1925, which formally prohibited the sale of honours in return for political funds, together with a scrutiny committee to examine the grant of honours.

1928 Internal inquiry into currency speculation by senior civil servants. It resulted in new rules stipulating both that civil servants must be honest and behave in a manner that puts them beyond any suspicion of dishonesty.

1936 Senior civil servant exposed for seeking an appointment with an airline whose activities he was responsible for regulating. It resulted in new rules on the movement of civil servants to private sector companies with whom they had official dealings.

1948 Lynskey Tribunal inquiry. It followed an attempt to bribe a junior government minister. It resulted in a parliamentary committee to establish the links between lobbying and bribery, and recommended only 'vigilance and good sense' as safeguards of standards.

1969 Select Committee inquiry into lobbying following allegations of influence-peddling by a governing party MP who also worked for a public relations firm. The resulting report proposed rules on declaring interests when representing views related to those interests. It stopped short of a register on the grounds that 'honour and self-restraint' were sufficient and that it would be an infringement of privacy.

1970   Poulson Affair concerning corruption in local government. It led to the Royal Commission on Standards of Conduct in Public Life (the Salmon inquiry) and the Prime Minister's Committee on Local Government Rules of Conduct (the Redclife–Maud inquiry). Both committees concluded that public life was generally honest. Two new select committees on MPs' conduct and interests were established.

1974   Register of Members' Interests is established as a revised version of the 1969 proposals.

1993   Scott Inquiry into 'arms for Iraq'.

1994   Series of sexual scandals involving Conservative MPs. Beginnings of the Jonathan Aitken scandal. Cash for questions scandal involving Conservative MPs Neil Hamilton and Tim Smith. Committee on Standards in Public Life is established.

1995   First report of the Committee on Standards in Public Life is published.

1996   Second report of the Committee on Standards in Public Life is published.

1997   Third and fourth reports of the Committee on Standards in Public Life are published.

1998   Fifth report of the Committee on Standards in Public Life is published.

2000   Sixth and seventh reports of the Committee on Standards in Public Life are published. Political Parties, Elections and Referendums Act, arising from the Committee's fifth report, is passed.

Discussion Questions

1. Is self-regulation sufficient to ensure appropriate standards of conduct among MPs?
2. Was the establishment of the Nolan Committee an appropriate response to perceptions of a decline in standards in public life?
3. What lessons can be learnt about the success of the Neill Committee in re-forming party finance and the apparent failure of the Jenkins and Wakeham committees to reform the electoral system and the House of Lords?

References

Berrington, Hugh (1995) 'Political ethics: the Nolan Report', *Government and Opposition*, Vol. 30, No. 4, pp. 431–51.

Committee on Standards in Public Life (1995) *First Report of The Committee on Standards in Public Life*, Cm 2850–I, London: HMSO. Also, http://www.archive.official-documents.co.uk/document/cm28/2850/285001.htm

Committee on Standards in Public Life (1996) *Second Report of The Committee on Standards in Public Life: Local Public Spending Bodies*, Cm 3270–I, London: HMSO.

Committee on Standards in Public Life (1997a) *Third Report of The Committee on Standards in Public Life: Standards of Conduct in Local Government in England, Scotland and Wales*, Cm 3701–I, London: HMSO.

Committee on Standards in Public Life (1997b) *Fourth Report of The Committee on Standards in Public Life: Review of Standards of Conduct in Executive NDPBs, NHS Trusts and Local Public Spending Bodies*, London: HMSO.

Committee on Standards in Public Life (1998) *Fifth Report of The Committee on Standards in Public Life: The Funding of Political Parties in the United Kingdom*, Cm 4057–I, London: TSO.

Committee on Standards in Public Life (2000a) *Annual Report of The Committee on Standards in Public Life 1999–2000*, London: Committee on Standards in Public Life.

Committee on Standards in Public Life (2000b) *Sixth Report of The Committee on Standards in Public Life: Reinforcing Standards*, Cm 4557–I, London: HMSO.

Committee on Standards in Public Life (2000c) *Seventh Report of The Committee on Standards in Public Life: Standards of Conduct in the House of Lords*, Cm 4903–I, London: HMSO.

Curtice John and Jowell, Roger (1995) 'The sceptical electorate', in R. Jowell, J. Curtice, A. Park, L. Brook and D. Ahrendt (eds) *British Social Attitudes. The 12th Report*, Aldershot: Dartmouth.

Curtice, John and Jowell, Roger (1997) 'Trust in the political system', in R. Jowell, J. Curtice, A. Park, L. Brook, K. Thomson and C. Bryson (eds) *British Social Attitudes. The 14th Report*, Aldershot: Ashgate.

Darke, Roy (1997) 'Viewpoint. Standards in public life,' *Town Planning Review*, Vol. 68, No. 1, pp. iii–vi.

Doig, A. (1996) 'From Lynskey to Nolan: the corruption of British politics and public service?', *Journal of Law and Society*, Vol. 23, No. 1, pp. 36–56.

Dunleavy, Patrick and Weir, Stuart (1995) 'Sleaze in Britain: media influences, public response and constitutional significance', *Parliamentary Affairs*, Vol. 48, No. 4, pp. 602–16.

Fisher, Justin (1994) 'Political donations to the Conservative Party', *Parliamentary Affairs*, Vol. 47, No. 1, pp. 61–72.

Fisher, Justin (1999) 'Party expenditure and electoral prospects: a national level analysis of Britain', *Electoral Studies*, Vol, 18, No. 4, pp. 519–32.

Fisher, Justin (2000a) 'Party finance and corruption: Britain', in Robert Williams (ed.) *Party Finance and Corruption*, Basingstoke: Macmillan, pp. 15–36.

Fisher, Justin (2000b) 'Economic performance or electoral necessity? Evaluating the system of voluntary income to political parties', *British Journal of Politics and International Relations*, Vol. 2, No. 2, pp. 179–204.

Fisher, Justin (2001) 'Campaign finance: elections under new rules', in Pippa Norris (ed.) *Britain Votes 2001*, Oxford: Oxford University Press, pp. 125–36.

Johnston, R. and Pattie, C. (1995) 'The impact of spending on party constituency campaigns in recent British general elections', *Party Politics*, Vol. 1, pp. 261–73.

Norton, Philip (1997) 'The United Kingdom: restoring confidence?', *Parliamentary Affairs*, Vol. 50, No. 3, pp. 357–72.

Oliver, Dawn (1995) The Committee on Standards in Public Life: regulating the conduct of members of parliament', *Parliamentary Affairs*, Vol. 48, No. 4, pp. 590–601.

Oliver, Dawn (1997) 'Regulating the conduct of MPs. The British experience of combating corruption', *Political Studies*, Vol. 45, No. 3, pp. 539–58.

Philp, Mark (2000) 'Neill and Nolan', Paper presented at the Constitution Unit, University College London.

Stott, Tony (1998) 'Nolan, councillors and planning', *Local Government Studies*, Vol. 24, No. 4, pp. 46–63.

Further reading

The Committee's website provides free, downloadable versions of both the full reports and report summaries. This can be found at: www.public-standards.gov.uk. In addition to the material listed in the references, a special edition of *Parliamentary Affairs* (1995) Vol. 48, No. 4, *Sleaze: Politics, Private Interests and Public Reaction* provides an excellent set of articles dealing with public standards. On related issues of political corruption, see the special edition of *Political Studies* (1997) Vol. 45, No. 3, *Political Corruption*. For a general overview of party finance and corruption, see Robert Williams (ed.) (2000) *Party Finance and Political Corruption* (Basingstoke: Macmillan). On a history of scandal in British politics, see Alan Doig (1990) *Westminster Babylon* (London: Allison & Busby). On the electoral impact of sleaze in Britain, see David M. Farrell, Ian McAllister and Donley T. Studlar (1998) 'Sex, money and politics: sleaze and the Conservative Party in the 1997 election', in David Denver, Justin Fisher, Philip Cowley and Charles Pattie (eds) *British Elections and Parties Review. Vol. 8: The 1997 General Election* (London: Frank Cass).

The Courts and the Judiciary

Keith D. Ewing

CHAPTER TWENTY-FOUR

Introduction

The courts play an important part in the political process, a role which is often underestimated. It is true that the judicial role is more important in some countries than in others, particularly where there is a written constitution which empowers the judges to restrain governmental action which is inconsistent with the terms of the constitution. This may be because legislation has been enacted contrary to protected constitutional principles, such as freedom of expression or the right to a fair trial. Or in a federal system it may be because the federal legislature has legislated on a matter which is reserved for the states or provinces. But although historically Britain has had no entrenched rights of this kind, and no division of legislative authority between constituent parts of the country,[1] this has changed significantly since the general election in 1997. As a result of the Human Rights Act 1998 and the government's programme of legislative devolution (to Scotland, Wales (albeit without primary legislative powers) and Northern Ireland) the courts have become even more prominent parts of the political landscape. Although this is not to exaggerate the role of the courts and judges, a full account of British politics cannot now ignore them (see Box 24.1).

Theoretical Considerations

The nature of the judicial role means that the courts are inevitably drawn into political disputes. As we shall see, the principles which the judges apply when dealing with these disputes are very flexible and open-textured: almost all of the cases which get as far as the higher courts could easily be decided either way. Indeed, many cases are majority decisions, further revealing that there is no such thing as certainty or predictability in the process of legal decision-making. This is a reality of the process which gives rise to some awkward questions about the extent to which judges have scope to allow personal beliefs, opinions or prejudices to colour their judgement; awkward because unlike the politician who is popularly elected and politically accountable (both to Parliament and to the people), judges are neither elected nor accountable for the decisions which they take, notwithstanding the sometimes far-reaching implications of these decisions. Curiously, this is a matter which is rarely considered by lawyers, apparently unembarrassed by the judicial role despite the fact that it has become much more significant in recent years.

Box 24.1 Courts and judges

There is a large number of judges who sit in a wide range of courts and tribunals. Different courts and tribunals perform different functions. It is necessary also to recognise that in the United Kingdom there are three separate legal systems (England and Wales, Northern Ireland and Scotland), each with its own court system which differs from the others. In England and Wales, criminal offences are tried before magistrates' courts and the Crown Court, the latter dealing with more serious offences. The Crown Court is organised on a circuit basis and will be presided over in any particular case by a High Court judge, a circuit judge, or a Recorder. The Crown Court sits with a jury for the trial of offenders, though there are currently controversial proposals to limit the right to trial by jury. Less serious offences are heard by the magistrates' court, which may consist of unpaid lay magistrates. They will be assisted by a clerk who is legally qualified, and it is possible for some cases to be heard by a legally qualified district judge. Criminal cases in Scotland are typically dealt with by the Sheriff Court or in more serious cases by the High Court of Justiciary.

Civil matters in England and Wales are tried normally before the county courts and the High Court, the former dealing with less serious cases. More important civil matters are dealt with by the High Court, normally by one judge sitting alone. An appeal lies from the High Court in civil cases (and from the Crown Court in criminal cases) to the Court of Appeal (usually a court of three judges), and from the Court of Appeal to the House of Lords (see Box 24.2). There are also a number of specialist courts and tribunals for dealing with special areas of the law, such as planning, social security and employment. An employment dispute, for example, may begin in a local employment tribunal, a panel of three with a legally-qualified chair and two persons with experience of each side of the industry. There are thought to be benefits in terms of low cost and high expertise in specialist courts and tribunals of this nature. From there an appeal lies to the Employment Appeal Tribunal, and from there to the Court of Appeal and on to the House of Lords. In Scotland, civil cases are heard in the Sheriff Court or in the Court of Session, from which there is a right of appeal to the House of Lords (though there is no right of appeal from the High Court of Justiciary in criminal matters).

In this chapter we consider the composition and powers of the judiciary. These are matters which raise fundamental questions in a representative democracy, to the extent that part of the judicial function is to police the democratic process itself. But as we have seen, judges are not elected and so cannot be removed if we the people are unhappy about the way in which they discharge their duties. It might be expected nevertheless that those who would presume to police the democratic process would themselves wear a badge of democratic legitimacy: the fact that they are not elected does not mean that they ought not to be representative of the community they serve, even if it cannot be said that they represent the community in the proper sense of the term. Neither does it mean that they cannot be accountable to the community, even if the fact that they are unelected means that the judges can be accountable only indirectly. These are matters which we consider later in this chapter. But it is important also to consider what it is that judges do: the case for a representative and accountable judiciary is all the more compelling the closer the judges are moved towards the centre of the political conflict.

Box 24.2 The House of Lords

Unlike other countries Britain does not have a Supreme Court as that term is normally understood: in England and Wales, the Court of Appeal and the High Court are collectively known as the 'Supreme Court of Judicature'. But our highest court (for all three jurisdictions except for Scottish criminal cases) is in fact the House of Lords, its decisions operating as binding precedents on the lower courts. This means that the law as laid down by the House of Lords must be followed, until it is overruled by the House of Lords itself or reversed by an Act of Parliament. Decisions of the Court of Appeal are binding on the High Court and the lower courts and tribunals, and in Scotland decisions of the Inner House of the Court of Session are binding on single judges sitting in the Outer House. The House of Lords is in a real sense an anachronism, being both a legislative chamber and the supreme judicial body in the country. The judicial business is, however, conducted only by the Appellate Committee of the House of Lords, which is composed exclusively of Law Lords, senior figures usually with many years of experience as judges in the High Court and the Court of Appeal. It is unknown in modern times for the judicial business of the House to be conducted by anyone other than a Law Lord (see Box 24.3).

Box 24.3 Separation of powers?

The Law Lords are appointed to the House for life, though they retire from judicial business at the age of 70 (though this can be extended). They may take part in the legislative business of the House, and do so particularly on legal questions. It is the case, nevertheless, that the Lord Chancellor may also sit in appeal cases and he does so from time to time. His is a truly remarkable position – perhaps without precedent in any advanced liberal democracy – being a prominent member of all three branches of government. The Law Lords normally sit in committees of five at a time, and their number is often depleted when one or more of their number is asked to chair a governmental inquiry, such as the inquiry into the deaths of civilians on Bloody Sunday in Derry in 1972, chaired by Lord Saville of Newdigate.

It is true that in Britain the judges have no power to strike down primary legislation (as in other countries). But, as we shall see, they have important powers to ensure that political decisions are made in accordance with the law which partly they determine, while their role has been greatly enhanced by membership of the European Community, and their powers greatly enhanced by the programme of constitutional reform introduced since 1997. Yet although questions arise about the composition and accountability of the bench, the different functions of the courts place a heavy premium on the independence of the judiciary as a core constitutional principle. The law should be applied by the courts without fear or favour of the government of the day, and government should be conducted in accordance with the law as it is, and not as the government of the day would like it to be. If governments are unhappy with the law, they have the opportunity to change it. It is in this sense that the courts play an important part in protecting the individual from the abuse of state power by ensuring that public officials have clear legal authority for their actions. In this way the independence of the judiciary is closely related to the principle of legality, another core constitutional principle on which democratic government stands.

Summary

- Judges perform an important role in ensuring that government is conducted in accordance with the law. Judges thus have the responsibility of policing the democratic process.
- The judicial role in the political process is expanding as a result of membership of the European Community and as a result of the programme of constitutional reform introduced since 1997.
- The enhanced role of the judiciary in the political process raises questions about the extent to which they can be said to be representative and accountable, in a manner which does not compromise their independence.

Who Are The Judges?

Most people are likely to go though life without setting foot in a court or speaking to a judge. Yet it does not follow from this that what the courts and judges do have no impact on our daily lives. The way in which we conduct our affairs is determined to some extent by law, whether consciously or not. In Britain, the law is made in one of two ways: by legislation passed by Parliament and interpreted by the judges, or by the common law made and developed by the judges. The role of the judges is therefore quite profound: much of the legal system continues to be governed by the common law – when we make a contract to buy a train ticket, a new car or a new house; when we are injured in an accident on the road or at work; when we suffer from the neglect of a doctor or make a will. In this sense it might be said that what the courts and judges do is essentially political. Although some lawyers may find the suggestion heretical, judges are engaged in an inherently legislative process: when they decide cases between private parties, they create precedents of general application, until overruled by a higher court. Who are these people?

How representative and accountable are the judges?

The appointment of judges is governed by legislation, which generally determines who may make the appointment and the conditions of eligibility for appointment. All appointments are made by the executive, either the Lord Chancellor in the case of the more junior appointments, the Crown on the advice of the Lord Chancellor (in the case of High Court judges), or the Crown on the advice of the Prime Minister (in the case of members of the Court of Appeal and the House of Lords). The Lord Chancellor is appointed by the Prime Minister and does not enjoy the security of tenure of other judges. High Court judges must be barristers or solicitors of at least ten years' standing, though in practice appointments are made from senior members of the profession with much longer experience. And although solicitors have been eligible for appointment since the Courts and Legal Services Act 1990, very few have been appointed. Court of Appeal judges must also be similarly qualified, though in practice no one is appointed directly from the legal profession, and all tend to be appointed directly from the High Court. Appointments to the House of Lords are made under the Appellate Jurisdiction Act 1876: those appointed are generally members of the Court of Appeal in England and Wales or the Court of Session in Scotland.

A common criticism of the British judiciary is that they are a very unrepresentative and homogeneous elite. This is certainly true of the highest levels. If we concentrate on the House of Lords we find that not one of the twelve Law Lords is a woman. Indeed, there never has been a female member of Britain's superior court, unlike in the superior courts of many other countries in the world (including notably – as countries which share British legal traditions – the USA, Canada and Australia). We also find that not one of the twelve Law Lords is black or Asian, and indeed that there never has been a black or Asian member of the court, despite the fact that blacks and Asians now account for a relatively significant proportion of the British population. It remains a curiously distinguishing feature of the British judiciary not only that it is overwhelmingly white men, but that they have very similar social origins, particularly in terms of education and training: private school, Oxbridge and the bar still dominate (see Table 24.1). All this matters, not necessarily to make crude points about the politics of the judiciary; it matters because judges exercise political power and authority; they develop the common law, they interpret legislation, and under the Human Rights Act 1998 they have the power to declare legislation incompatible with the European Convention on Human Rights. Those who exercise such formidable powers should arguably be representative of and accountable to the community they govern, yet there are no formal proposals to address these issues at official level.

Table 24.1 The Law Lords: how representative?

	DOB	Education
Lord Browne-Wilkinson	1930	Oxford
Lord Slynn of Hadley	1930	Cambridge
Lord Nicholls of Birkenhead	1933	Cambridge
Lord Steyn	1932	Oxford
Lord Hoffmann	1934	Oxford
Lord Hope of Craighead	1938	Cambridge
Lord Clyde	1932	Oxford
Lord Hutton	1931	Oxford
Lord Saville of Newdigate	1936	Oxford
Lord Hobhouse of Woodborough	1932	Oxford
Lord Millett	1932	Cambridge
Lord Phillips of Worth Maltravers	1938	Cambridge

Source: *Who's Who*

Concerns are also expressed about the lack of accountability of the judges, though this is not to underestimate the extent to which judges are in fact accountable. The courts must generally sit in public, and it is only exceptionally that the press may be excluded or required not to report evidence which may have been admitted in court. The judges give reasons (sometimes very lengthy) for their decisions, to explain why they have preferred the submissions and arguments of one side rather than the other. And judges (up to the House of Lords) are the subject of an appeal to a higher court if either party is unhappy about the way in which a judge has performed his or her duties. Even the House of Lords may now rehear a case if the circumstances warrant, though this has only ever happened once. Judges also regularly give public lectures and contribute articles to academic journals, expressing views on legal questions, some of which are contentious and controversial. But it remains the case that unlike other public officials, judges are not popularly accountable to the people or their parliamentary representatives. Appointed for life, they cannot easily be removed from office and they are not summoned to appear before parliamentary select committees. Some would argue that this lack of accountability is the price of judicial independence. Others might say that the price is too high.

The independence of the judiciary

Judicial independence is a highly valued prize in liberal democratic societies. It is a principle which has several dimensions. The judge should be independent of the parties to a dispute, and should not have a personal interest (financial or otherwise) in the outcome. The courts go to some length to ensure that this principle is followed in practice and that steps are taken to remove any appearance of bias or lack of impartiality on the part of a judge. This was the issue which led the House of Lords to decide to rehear a case involving a former Chilean dictator in 1998. The original decision was 3:2 against Pinochet, who was contesting his extradition to Spain, when it was revealed that one of the majority had connections with Amnesty International which had intervened in the case. But apart from independence of the parties in a dispute, the principle of judicial independence also means that the judges should be independent of the government of the day – to ensure that justice is administered according to the law, not the wishes of those in power. There are a number of ways in which this dimension could be compromised, and a number of safeguards are required to ensure that it is not.

There is little evidence in modern times of judges being appointed because of their political views, and certainly none of judges being appointed because of allegiance to the government of the day (which is not the same as saying that judges are not supporters of a particular administration). To some extent, British practice varies from that in the United States, where judicial appointments to courts with very significant powers are very heavily politicised. This is not to say that the British system of judicial appointments is beyond reproach, but the concerns relate mainly to the method of appointment by the Lord Chancellor's Department, secrecy and the lack of transparency in the procedures (based partly on soundings of other judges and senior members of the profession) rather than the political nature of the appointments. Nevertheless it could hardly be said that the senior bench covers a wide political spectrum (though in fairness the same could no doubt be said of the senior members of the parliamentary parties). Neither is there much evidence of political pressure being brought to bear on judges in the performance of their duties. There is in fact a convention that ministers do not criticise the judges, a convention which is not often breached. By the same token, the Standing Orders of the House of Commons prevent any criticism of a judge in the course of parliamentary proceedings except on a substantive motion, a rule which is rigorously enforced by the Speaker.

Perhaps the greatest safeguard of judicial independence lies in the protection against removal from office. Judges are appointed for life (or at least until retirement) and cannot easily be removed, and certainly not because the government finds their work inconvenient. High Court judges and judges of the Court of Appeal can only be removed from office for misconduct, and then only after an address presented to both Houses of Parliament. The same is true of members of the House of Lords. Quite what would constitute misconduct for this purpose is uncertain: there is no example in modern times of a senior judge being removed from office in this way. Resignation is likely to be the favoured option should questions arise about a judge's ability to continue in office. The security of lower judges is more precarious, in the sense that they may be removed from office by the Lord Chancellor for incapacity or misbehaviour. There is no need for parliamentary approval of any such proposal to dismiss, and in the exercise of this power the Lord Chancellor as a member of the House of Lords is evidently not responsible to the House of Commons.

Summary

- Judges are appointed by the Executive (the Lord Chancellor or the Prime Minister) and hold office until retirement: there is no parliamentary scrutiny of judicial appointments.
- British judges tend to be distinguished by their homogeneity in terms of gender, race and social class. There has never been a female member of the Appellate Committee of the House of Lords, which is the highest court.
- The independence of the judiciary is secured in a number of ways: judges must be independent of the parties appearing before them and of the government of the day. Judges may not engage in party politics.

What Do The Judges Do?

An important part of what the judges do is ensuring that government is conducted in accordance with the law. It is sometimes argued that the Rule of Law is a fundamental principle of liberal democracy, but as a principle the Rule of Law has been devalued by over-use and by the ideological purpose which it has served. Yet at its core is a sense that government should have legal authority for all that it does, and that government should be restrained where it lacks legal authority. But rather than talk about the Rule of Law and all the political baggage which it carries, it may be more appropriate now to refer simply to the principle of legality, as conveying the essence of the principle more accurately and more clearly. It is trite but important to observe that there can be no democracy without legality. Yet this is not to say that the role of the courts is uncontroversial, whether in terms of the principles of legality which they have developed to review and restrain governmental action, or in terms of the way in which these principles are applied and deployed in any particular case (see Box 24.4).

Box 24.4 The principle of legality

In *Malone v Metropolitan Police Commissioner* (1985), Mr Malone was charged with handling stolen goods. During the course of his trial, it emerged that his telephone had been tapped, though at the time there was no legal authority for the tapping of phones, whether by the police or the security service. The practice was nevertheless governed by warrants issued by the Home Secretary. Mr Malone challenged the tapping of his phone in the High Court, but failed. The government had not violated his property rights (the interception had been placed at the exchange), there was no breach of his rights to confidentiality (there is no confidence in an 'iniquity'), and there had been no breach of his right to privacy (there is no right to privacy in English law). So although the government had no express legal authority, it had done nothing unlawful. As a sequel, however, Mr Malone took his case to Strasbourg, alleging a breach of the European Convention on Human Rights, article 8 (see Box 24.10). He was successful and legislation was introduced in 1985 to regulate the practice of phone-tapping.

Judicial review of administrative action

The principle of legality means that the government must have legal authority for its actions (or as that principle applies weakly in Britain, that what the government does is not unlawful: there is an important distinction between these two positions). If the government acts without authority, it is for the courts to intervene to restrain the offending conduct. But it is important to note that the power of the courts historically has been confined to the review of administrative action. Unlike in other countries, there is no judicial review of legislative action. This is because of the doctrine of parliamentary sovereignty whereby Acts of Parliament cannot be called into question (see Box 24.5). So the courts may review the way in which statutory powers are exercised, but they may not review the legislation conferring the power. There are three issues which arise here:

- What is the source of the government's legal authority? Where does its legal authority come from?
- What are the grounds on which the courts may intervene to restrain governmental action?
- What remedies are available to the courts?

Box 24.5 Judicial review of Administrative Action

The Agricultural Marketing Act 1958 empowered the Minister of Agriculture, Fisheries and Food to set up a committee to investigate complaints from farmers about the price which they were paid for their milk, which at the time they were required to sell to the Milk Marketing Board. Following a complaint from producers in the south-east, the minister refused to refer the matter to a committee of investigation. In his letter to the complainants, he said that their complaint raised 'wide issues', and that if the complaint were upheld by the committee of investigation he would be expected to make a statutory order to give effect to its recommendations. In *Padfield v Minister of Agriculture, Fisheries and Food* (1968) the House of Lords held that these were not acceptable reasons for refusing to exercise the discretion which the Act conferred on the minister. The House of Lords also made it clear that if a minister should use a statutory power in a manner which runs contrary to the policy of an Act of Parliament (which it is for the courts to determine), the courts will intervene.

The legal authority for government action derives from two sources. One is the Royal Prerogative, and the other is Parliament in the form of legislation. The Royal Prerogative is the residue of power vested in the Crown which has not been displaced by legislation, and which the courts continue to recognise. The powers are exercised on behalf of the Crown by ministers, in most cases the Prime Minister. So when the country declares war, when troops are moved around the world, or when international treaties are signed, there is a need for legal authority for these steps to be taken. That authority is provided by the Royal Prerogative, which is no more than the common law powers of the Crown which continue in force (see Box 24.6). A more usual source of legal authority for government action in modern times is legislation passed by Parliament. In a parliamentary democracy this is what would be expected, and it is perhaps surprising that the legal system continues to authorise decisions to be taken under powers which have not been approved by Parliament. Legislation nevertheless presents difficulties, particularly in view of the fact that the legislative process is dominated by the executive. Often the executive will take very wide legislative powers: the courts have a role in regulating the way in which these powers are exercised.

The principles of review have evolved over a number of years, being a purely judicial creation (see Boxes 24.5, 24.6, 24.7 and 24.8). It is perhaps strange that the principles by which the government can be challenged in the courts continue to be determined by the courts rather than by Parliament. Nevertheless the principles were reformulated in a leading case in 1985 where three principles were identified:

- Illegality: meaning that the courts may intervene if a public authority acts unlawfully, for example because it purports to exercise a prerogative power which does not exist; or because it uses legislation for a purpose for which it was not intended.
- Irrationality: meaning that the decision taken with apparent legal authority (usually a wide discretionary power conferred by Parliament) was so unreasonable in defiance of logic that no reasonable person could possibly have made such a decision.

Box 24.6 Judicial review of the Royal Prerogative

In 1984 the government announced that trade unions would be banned from its spy station at GCHQ. The decision was taken under the authority of the Royal Prerogative to regulate the affairs of the civil service, and it was taken without consulting the unions concerned. In *Council of Civil Service Unions v Minister for the Civil Service* (1984) the unions sought a judicial review of the government decision, and in an historic judgment the House of Lords held that the fact that the decision was taken under the Royal Prerogative did not protect it from judicial review, as had previously been thought, provided the power in question was justiciable, that is to say giving rise to a dispute which a court was capable of resolving. In this case there was a procedural impropriety in the sense that the union should have been consulted before being removed from the sites. It had a legitimate expectation that its rights at GCHQ would continue. But the action failed, because the government claimed that its decision had been taken in the interests of national security which the House of Lords accepted was a full defence in judicial review proceedings which it could not challenge.

Box 24.7 Remedies in judicial review

The following remedies may be granted in judicial review proceedings:

- A mandatory order, which is an order compelling a public authority to comply with its legal duties. It is not often granted.
- A prohibitory order, which is an order prohibiting a public authority from doing something which would be a breach of its legal duties.
- A quashing order, which is an order quashing a decision of a public authority, where the decision is unlawful.
- An injunction, which may be mandatory (compelling a course of action) or, more usually, restraining (stopping a course of action).
- A declaration, which is an order declaring the rights of the parties, but which has no coercive effect, in the sense that there is no sanction for non-compliance.
- Damages, which are monetary compensation for losses suffered by the unlawful acts of another, though they may also have an exemplary or punitive element.

- Procedural impropriety: meaning that the decision has been taken without giving a hearing to a party whose rights or interests are affected by the decision, or who has a legitimate expectation that a hearing would be given. The right to be heard is a right to be heard before someone who has not prejudged the outcome of the case.

So far as remedies and procedures are concerned, a major reform was introduced in 1979 designed to simplify the procedures for challenging public bodies in the courts. Proceedings are governed by the Civil Procedure Rules, which provide that applications must be brought within three months of the decision complained of, and by someone who has a sufficient interest in the decision to be able to challenge it. It is also necessary to get the permission of the court to proceed with the application. The court is empowered to grant one or more of a number of remedies, some of which are peculiar to litigation against public bodies. Like the substantive law, the law relating to remedies also has its origins in the mists of time. The main change pioneered in the 1979 reforms was to give greater flexibility to the courts in the selection of remedies: previously different procedures had to be initiated for different remedies. Now there is a common procedure, designed to make life easier for applicants, by removing unnecessary procedural obstacles (see Box 24.7).

The judges and the European Community

The role of the courts has expanded, partly as a result of Britain's membership of the European Community. Now the courts are charged with the responsibility of ensuring that government is conducted not only in accordance with domestic law, but also in accordance with European law. The legal basis for Britain's membership of what was then the EEC is the European Communities Act 1972. This states in section 2:

> All such rights, powers, liabilities, obligations and restrictions from time to time created or arising by or under the Treaties, and all such remedies and procedures from time to time provided for by or under the Treaties, as in accordance with the Treaties are without further enactment to be given legal effect or used in the United Kingdom, shall be recognised and available in law, and be enforced, allowed and followed accordingly.

The upshot of this was to give European Community Law direct effect in British law. This means not only that the terms of the Treaty can be enforced (where appropriate) in the domestic courts, but perhaps more importantly that Community legislation (in the form of regulations and directives) can also be enforced in the domestic courts. This is fairly straightforward. But what happens if directly effective community law is inconsistent with an Act of Parliament? What would take priority? Where does final sovereignty lie? This is a matter which only the courts can decide, and which they have been called upon to decide.

The courts have been drawn into the heart of one the great contemporary political and constitutional issues, the question of political and legal sovereignty within the European Community. This is an issue which has caused difficulties for a number of countries as their constitutional traditions come into conflict with the claims of the Community. In order fully to understand the nature of the difficulty, it is necessary to begin with the claims of the European Court of Justice (ECJ), which sits in Luxembourg and is the final authority on the meaning of Community law. Cases may be referred to the ECJ in a number of ways: one European institution may bring an action against another, complaining of a breach of Community law; one member state may bring proceedings against another; or the European Commission may bring proceedings against a member state in default of Community obligations. Otherwise a matter may be referred to the ECJ by a domestic court under article 234 of the Treaty (previously article 177) for guidance on the meaning of a point of EC law which is unclear: although the

Box 24.8 The politics of the judiciary

There are a number of cases which fuel the concerns that in performing their duties the judges have not always been above politics. It is true that some of the cases are very old, but it is also true that the principles which they established live on long after the decisions in question to be applied to new circumstances. One such area relates to the activities of local authorities which have been subject to very close scrutiny by the courts. The starting point is a case called *Roberts v Hopwood* (1925) where the Poplar Borough Council introduced what it believed to be good employment practices which included equal pay for women, and an arrangement where they would not cut wages to reflect adjustments in the cost of living. In ruling this to be unlawful (and in doing so overruling the Court of Appeal), the House of Lords introduced a principle that local authorities owe a fiduciary duty to their ratepayers (local taxpayers, both individual and business). Notwithstanding any electoral mandate, the local authority was to conduct itself in accordance with good business principles, rather than in this case 'eccentric principles of socialist philanthropy', and a 'feminist ambition to secure equality of the sexes in the world of work'.

Judges are nowadays more restrained: but the principle of *Roberts v Hopwood* lives on in casebooks. Two examples highlight this in the context of local government:

> In *Prescott v Birmingham Corporation* (1955) the Court of Appeal held that a local authority could not introduce concessionary bus fares for pensioners. According to one of the members of the court, 'local authorities running an omnibus undertaking at the risk of their ratepayers, in the sense that any deficiencies must be met by an addition to the rates, are not, in our view, entitled . . . to charge different fares to different passengers, to make a gift to a particular class of persons of rights of free travel on their vehicles, simply because the local authority concerned are of the opinion that the favoured class of persons ought, on benevolent or philanthropic grounds, to be accorded that benefit'. Concessionary bus fares were subsequently made possible by legislation.

> *Bromley v Greater London Council* (1982) concerned the GLC and its famous 'fare's fair' policy whereby it reduced public transport fares by 25%, the costs being met by the ratepayers in the different London boroughs, leading to a cut in the rate support grant from central government. This was opposed by some of the boroughs. In a highly-controversial decision, the House of Lords held the arrangements to be unlawful, again influenced to some extent by the obligation of local authorities to conduct their activities on the basis of business-like principles, and the fiduciary duty owed to the ratepayers. The fact that the GLC had an electoral mandate for this policy was found not to be of great significance, and was certainly not accepted as a justification.

But it is not only in respect of local authorities that the courts are drawn into the political fray, sometimes exposed by the obligation to operate principles which at best cannot be said to be value-neutral. Central government departments are also prominent targets. There were, for example, a number of high-profile cases in the 1970s restraining the activities of the Home Secretary (in relation to television licences), the Secretary of State for Education (in relation to comprehensive schools), and the Secretary of State for Trade and Industry (in relation to airline competition), as well as cases involving powerful new public agencies created in the 1970s, such as ACAS (dealing with trade union rights) and the Commission for Racial Equality. But it would be a mistake to believe that judicial review has been an exclusive problem of Labour governments or Labour local authorities. The governments of Mrs Thatcher and Mr Major were also to feel the full blast of judicial review proceedings.

Box 24.8 (*continued*)

In *M v Home Office* (1994) a High Court judge issued a temporary order restraining the Home Secretary (Kenneth Baker) from deporting M to Zaire, until his application for asylum had been heard. The deportation nevertheless went ahead, and it proved impossible to return M to London after he had left. Legal proceedings were brought alleging that the Home Secretary had acted in contempt of court. The House of Lords – in another historic decision – held that the courts could properly issue injunctions against ministers, and that ministers and civil servants were subject to liability for contempt of court where these injunctions were ignored.

The Fire Brigades Union case (1995) was concerned with the Criminal Justice Act 1988 which had included a new statutory scheme for criminal injuries compensation, to replace the old scheme which had been introduced as an exercise of the Royal Prerogative. The Act said that the new scheme would come into force on a day to be appointed by the Secretary of State. The Home Secretary (Michael Howard) announced that the government had changed its mind and that the scheme would not now be introduced, and the power would not be used. The House of Lords held that the Home Secretary had acted unlawfully: where he had discretion under an Act of Parliament, he could not decide never to use the power which the Act conferred.

domestic courts are required to apply and enforce EC law, it is the ECJ which must determine what EC law means.

From the earliest days the ECJ has taken the view that Community law is supreme and takes priority over the domestic law of member states, expressing the view in one famous case that:

> By contrast with ordinary international treaties, the EEC Treaty has created its own legal system which, on the entry into force of the Treaty, became an integral part of the legal systems of the Member States and which their courts are bound to apply. By creating a Community of unlimited duration, having its own institutions, its own personality, its own legal capacity and capacity of representation on the international plane and, more particularly, real powers stemming from a limitation of sovereignty or a transfer of powers from the States to the Community, the Member States have limited their sovereign rights, albeit within limited fields, and have thus created a body of law which binds both their nationals and themselves.

In more recent cases the Court has expressed the view in a case from what was then West Germany that EC law must take priority over even the constitutional law of member states, stating that 'the validity of a Community measure or its effect within a Member State cannot be affected by allegations that it runs counter to either fundamental rights as formulated by the constitution of that State or the principles of a national constitutional structure'. But the problem which this presents is that, under British constitutional law, Parliament is supreme, and the duty of the courts is to give effect to an Act of Parliament: there is no higher law. Together with the principle of legality, the principle of parliamentary sovereignty is one of the two fundamental legal principles of the British Constitution. There is thus a great deal at stake here.

So what should the courts do if confronted with an Act of Parliament which is contrary to the provisions of the Treaty? The issue was confronted in the *Spanish Fishermen's* case in which a Spanish company challenged the Merchant Shipping Act 1988, arguing that some of its provisions were contrary to the Treaty. The Act provided that only British-owned vessels could be registered and thereby be eligible to fish in British waters. This requirement therefore excluded the Spanish owners from British waters, and they sought to assert their rights under EC law in the British courts. In lengthy proceedings, the European Court of Justice held that Community law must take priority over British constitutional law. This was accepted and applied by the House of Lords which held that in the event of conflict between domestic legislation and EC law, the latter must prevail. In the words of one member of the court:

> Thus, whatever limitation of its sovereignty Parliament accepted when it enacted the European Communities Act 1972 was entirely voluntary. Under the terms of the Act of 1972 it has always been clear that it was the duty of a United Kingdom court, when delivering final judgment, to override any rule of national law found to be in conflict with any directly enforceable rule of Community law. Similarly, when decisions of the European Court of Justice have exposed areas of United Kingdom statute law which failed to implement Council directives, Parliament has always loyally accepted the obligation to make appropriate and prompt amendments. Thus there is nothing in any way novel in according supremacy to rules of Community law in those areas to which they apply and to insist that, in the protection of rights under Community law, national courts must not be inhibited by rules of national law from granting interim relief in appropriate cases is no more than a logical recognition of that supremacy.

It has been argued that the effect of this decision has been to create a legal revolution, in the sense that it reflects a transfer of legal sovereignty from Westminster to Brussels, and that the European Communities Act has thus done what no Act of Parliament has done before or since, namely bind successor Parliaments. But this may exaggerate the position (see Box 24.9).

Summary

- It is an important part of the judicial function to ensure that government is conducted in accordance with the law. Legal authority for government action may be found in either the Royal Prerogative or legislation.
- The courts have developed a number of principles to ensure that prerogative and statutory powers are lawfully exercised. Power must not be used unlawfully, irrationally or in a manner which is procedurally improper.

Box 24.9 Sovereignty and the EC

It has been said that the effect of the European Communities Act 1972, section 2 and the *Spanish Fishermen's* case has been to effect a 'constitutional revolution', in the sense that there has been a transfer of legal sovereignty from Parliament to the courts. It is argued also that the 1972 Act has done what no other Act of Parliament has ever done, which is to bind future Parliaments, in the sense that all future Parliaments are required by section 2 of the 1972 Act to comply with EC law. But the position is not yet so clear. It is still open to Parliament to put into law a statute passed after 1972 a provision to the effect that the Act in question is to apply notwithstanding any EC obligation to the contrary. Although the European Court of Justice may claim the supremacy of community law in such a case, British constitutional law would still require the courts to give effect to the statute. It is true that this might create a diplomatic row, but that would be a matter for Brussels and the British government. It is not the concern, or indeed the business, of the courts. So although talk of constitutional revolution is heady stuff, it may be more accurate to talk at this stage of a constitutional accommodation.

- Membership of the European Community expanded the power of the courts which must now ensure that government is conducted in accordance with EC law. EC law will normally take priority over inconsistent domestic law.

Update and Debate

It would be true to say that the role of the courts has gradually extended and expanded over the course of the twentieth century, so that they are now important players on the political battlefield, not just policing the rules of engagement, but required from time to time to enter the fray. The traditional role of the courts was to review the way in which ministers, government departments and other public authorities exercised their powers – to ensure that they kept within the law. In recent years the courts have been willing to enlarge the circumstances in which they are prepared to intervene, and indeed the process of intervention was greatly encouraged by procedural reforms initiated by government in the late 1970s. But, the judicial role has expanded as a result of the programme of constitutional reform since 1997, including most notably the incorporation into domestic law of the European Convention on Human Rights, an international treaty – not of the European Community, but of the Council of Europe. Devolution also has an important part to play in enhancing the judicial role.

The Human Rights Act 1998

The power of the courts has been greatly increased by the Human Rights Act 1998 which came into force on 2 October 2000. The Act incorporates the European Convention on Human Rights (ECHR) into British law, which means that it can be enforced in the British courts (Box 24.10). The Convention was made by the Council of Europe in 1950 and came into force in 1953. It is not a treaty of the

Box 24.10 The European Convention on Human Rights

The main provisions of the ECHR are as follows:

article 2: the right to life
article 3: the right not to suffer torture, or inhuman or degrading treatment or punishment
article 4: the right not to suffer slavery or forced labour
article 5: the right to liberty and not to be arbitrarily detained
article 6: the right to a fair trial
article 7: the right to protection from retrospective criminal laws
article 8: the right to respect for private and family life, home and correspondence
article 9: the right to freedom of conscience and religion
article 10: the right to freedom of expression
article 11: the right to freedom of association and assembly
article 12: the right to marry and found a family

The main provisions of the First Protocol are as follows:

article 1: the right to 'peaceful enjoyment' of property and possessions
article 2: the right to education
article 3: the right to free elections

European Community, and the EC is not a party to it, though the European Court of Justice does have regard to the ECHR which is referred to in the European Union Treaty. However, at the time of writing the EC does not have the legal competence to accede to the ECHR. Made in the aftermath of the Second World War, the ECHR seeks to protect a wide range of civil and political rights, which are not to be compromised by ratifying states. The main text is supplemented by a number of Protocols, of which the most important substantively are Protocols 1 and 6 (the latter dealing with the abolition of the death penalty) and procedurally Protocol 11 (which streamlines the procedures for hearing complaints). With the expansion of the Council of Europe following the end of the Cold War the number of countries ratifying the ECHR has expanded to forty-one.

Since 1966 it has been possible for complaints alleging a breach of the Convention to be made to the European Court of Human Rights based in Strasbourg. There have been a number of such cases from Britain, with the court having challenged British law and practice in a number of areas: these include the killing of terrorist suspects by the security services in Gibraltar, 'inhuman' treatment of detainees in Northern Ireland, extradition of murder suspects to spend time on Death Row in the USA, detention of terrorist suspects for up to seven days without judicial authorisation, lack of protection against self-incrimination in criminal proceedings, security service surveillance and telephone-tapping, restrictions on gays and lesbians serving in the armed forces, banning books such as *Spycatcher* by retired MI5 officer Peter Wright, and the requirement that British Rail employees should be trade union members. Although it was thus possible for individuals to make applications of this kind, it was felt by many (including senior judges in Britain) that it should be possible to enforce the Convention in the domestic courts. The right to go to Strasbourg is all very well, it was claimed, but this causes unnecessary expense and delay when these rights could be enforced more cheaply and more speedily in the domestic courts (see Box 24.11).

The Human Rights Act 1998 permits legal proceedings in the domestic courts to enforce 'Convention rights' against public authorities. Unlike in a number of other countries, however, the courts may not challenge an Act of Parliament. They are required where possible to interpret Acts of Parliament always to comply with Convention rights, and where this is not possible they are empowered to issue a declaration that an Act of Parliament is incompatible with these rights. But the Act of Parliament will remain in force unless Parliament decides to repeal it. And there is no obligation on the part of Parliament to repeal any such legislation. This is a wise precaution against unpredictable judicial decision-making, with ultimate legal authority resting with a sovereign legislature. But unless a breach of the Convention is required by an Act of Parliament, it is now possible for a 'victim' of the breach to enforce his or her Convention rights in the domestic courts against a public authority. This means that ministers, civil servants, local authorities and others may now be restrained in the domestic courts if they fail to comply with the requirements of the Convention. It will, however, be possible only for a 'victim' of a breach to sue.

It is difficult to assess the likely long-term implications of the Human Rights Act. But two things are clear. The first is that it enables decisions of ministers to be challenged on a wider range of grounds than was previously the case, and these challenges may be made by companies, NGOs and individuals, provided that they are victims. Companies also have human rights. The second is that it will draw the courts even closer to the heart of the political battlefield, and will require the judges to make very political decisions on what will be very political questions. Many of the articles of the Convention are very highly qualified by provisions

---

Box 24.11 Britain in the dock at Strasbourg

Under the Representation of the People Act 1983, limits are imposed on the level of permitted expenditure incurred by parliamentary candidates. Partly in order to prevent these limits from being undermined, there are limits on how much may be spent by others. By virtue of section 75, it was an offence for anyone other than a candidate or his or her agent to incur election expenses of more than £10 without the consent of the candidate or the agent. If the consent was given, the expense incurred would count as part of the permitted expenditure of the candidate who consented or on behalf of whom consent was given. In *Bowman v UK* (1998), Mrs Bowman (a prominent member of the Society for the Protection of the Unborn Child) distributed literature in the constituency of Halifax during the general election in 1992 outlining the views of candidates on abortion and related issues. She did not have the consent of candidates or agents and was thought to have spent more than £10. Although her prosecution failed, she nevertheless applied to Strasbourg alleging that the prosecution itself violated her right to freedom of expression in article 10 of the ECHR. The application succeeded, the Court taking the view that the limit of £10 was too low, though appearing to accept that some limit on so-called third-party expenditure would be permitted, provided it was reasonable. The 1983 Act was amended by the Political Parties, Elections and Referendums Act 2000 which increased the £10 to £500.

which allow restrictions on the rights in question where these can be justified by the government as being 'prescribed by law' and 'necessary in a democratic society' (see Box 24.12). It will thus be necessary for the courts to construct a theory of a democratic society by which to judge the actions of elected and accountable officials. Apart from anything else, this is a task for which judges are wholly untrained and have no greater skills than the next 'armchair philosopher'. Given the record of the judges in the past, this is not a prospect which everyone will view without concern (see Box 24.8).

Box 24.12 ECHR, article 10

Freedom of expression

1. Everyone has the right to freedom of expression. The right shall include the right to hold opinions and to receive and impart information and ideas without interference by public authority and regardless of frontiers. This article shall not prevent states from requiring the licensing of broadcasting, television or cinema enterprises.
2. The exercise of these freedoms, since it carries with it duties and responsibilities, may be subject to such formalities, conditions, restrictions or penalties as are prescribed by law and are necessary in a democratic society, in the interests of national security, territorial integrity or public safety, for the prevention of disorder or crime, for the protection of health or morals, for the protection of the reputation or rights of others, for preventing the disclosure of information received in confidence, or for maintaining the authority and impartiality of the judiciary.

Devolution

The other area where the courts will be drawn more directly into the political fray is in relation to devolution. Since 1997, a number of new parliamentary bodies have been established in the United Kingdom: the Scottish Parliament, the National Assembly for Wales, and the Northern Ireland Assembly. These are in addition to the Greater London Assembly. A distinguishing feature of the programme of devolution is its lack of symmetry, with different powers having been devolved to each of the new parliamentary bodies. This arises most obviously when the powers of the Scottish Parliament to make primary legislation are compared with the powers of the Welsh Assembly to make secondary legislation only. But a common feature of the devolution programme is that each of the new parliamentary bodies is created by the Westminster Parliament, with powers defined and limited by the Westminster Parliament. This provides two opportunities for the courts: the first is that they have the responsibility to ensure that the devolved bodies act in accordance with the legislation which established them; and second, they have the responsibility to restrain these bodies should they legislate on a matter which is outside the scope of their statutory authority.

The Scottish Parliament has the competence to legislate on all matters except those which are 'reserved' (unlike the proposals in 1978 which specified the devolved matters). However, many subjects are expressly reserved, including the Crown, foreign affairs, the civil service, the defence of the realm, financial and economic matters (such as fiscal, economic and monetary policy, the currency and financial services), aspects of home affairs (such as the misuse of drugs and immigration and nationality), trade and industry (such as import and export policy and consumer protection), and social security. Legislation which falls within the categories of 'reserved items' is 'outside the legislative competence' of the Scottish Parliament and is 'not law' (Scotland Act, section 29). A measure is also outside the competence of the Scottish Parliament if it purports to legislate for a country or territory other than Scotland, or if it is incompatible with the European Convention on Human Rights or with European Community law (see Box 24.13).

The limited powers of the Scottish Parliament give rise to the possibility that it may exceed these powers. Part I of the Act seeks to minimise this risk. A minister introducing a bill must make a written statement that in his or her view the measure falls within the competence of the Scottish Parliament, while the Presiding Officer of the Parliament must also decide whether in his or her view the provisions of a bill would be within the legislative competence of the Parliament. But it is unavoidable that the courts will be drawn into policing the boundaries of the powers of the new Parliament. Indeed, a reference may be made to the Judicial Committee of the Privy Council within four weeks of the passing of a bill by the Lord Advocate, the Attorney General or the newly created Advocate General where there is concern that the bill may exceed the competence of the Parliament. A bill is not to be presented for the Royal Assent while such a reference is possible, and the effect of a reference is likely to be that the Royal Assent would be refused. Procedures also exist in Part V of the Act where the competence of an Act of the Scottish Parliament is challenged in legal proceedings: in these cases, too, the Privy Council is generally the court of last resort.

So the scene is set for a great constitutional drama. The Scottish Parliament may at some time in the future (in perhaps different political circumstances than those

Box 24.13 The ECHR in Scotland

The Human Rights Act 1998 was brought into operation in Scotland before the commencement date for the rest of the country, in the sense that both the Scottish Parliament and the Scottish Executive (creations of the Scotland Act 1998) could not act contrary to Convention rights. The restrictions on the Scottish Executive in particular has generated a number of cases by accused persons in criminal prosecutions alleging that their human rights had been violated at some stage in the proceedings. One such case is *Starrs v Ruxton* (2000) where the accused argued that their rights under article 6 (see Box 24.10) were infringed because they were tried before a temporary judge (temporary sheriff). The application was upheld on the ground that the reasonable observer might well conclude that a temporary judge (appointed for only a year at a time) would be influenced in deciding cases by a desire to please the appointing authorities (in this case the Secretary of State for Scotland, though since devolution the First Minister) in order to ensure further appointment or advancement. The entire system of judicial appointments in Scotland had to be reviewed as a result.

prevailing at the time of writing) legislate on an issue on the boundaries of its powers. There is also the possibility at some indeterminate future date of the Westminster Parliament trespassing on the powers of the Holyrood Parliament which may then wish to assert its authority to legislate a different solution to the same question. In these circumstances the courts will have a leading role to play, and they have already made it clear that they will not be shy in performing such a role. In one case the Court of Session in Scotland had no hesitation in pointing out that the Scottish Parliament is a body which 'has been created by statute and derives its powers from statute'. Moreover, it is not 'a parliament which is sovereign: on the contrary, it is subject to the laws and hence to the courts'. In the same case the court (which was concerned in the case in question with members' interests) rejected a submission that it should exercise 'a self-denying ordinance in relation to interfering with the proceedings' of the Scottish Parliament. There is no question of the Scottish Parliament being accorded the same judicial deference as its parent. The same applies to the Welsh and Northern Ireland Assemblies.

Summary

- The role of the courts has been enhanced by the Human Rights Act 1998 (by means of which rights in the European Convention on Human Rights may be enforced in the British courts) and by devolution.
- As a result of the Human Rights Act 1998, Convention rights may be enforced directly against public authorities in the British courts. The courts may not strike down but may declare Acts of Parliament incompatible with Convention rights.
- The devolved Parliament and Assemblies must exercise their powers in accordance with the legislation which created them. Otherwise, both their internal proceedings and their legislation may be challenged by the courts.

Conclusion

The judicial role in politics has always been present, but in recent years it has been increasing. Indeed, such has been the effect of the explosion of judicial review since 1979 that the government issued a booklet to civil servants entitled *The Judge over Your Shoulder*, as a safeguard against judicial review. Both Labour and Conservative ministers have suffered full judicial lashings. That trend will be reinforced by the Human Rights Act 1998. The nature of this activity (as well as the other law-making functions of the courts) raises important questions not only about the way in which judges are appointed, but also about the extent to which the judges are representative of, and accountable to, the community they serve. There is a great deal of effort invested in trying to make the magistrates as representative as possible. But the same effort does not appear to be devoted to the senior judiciary, yet they are the ones where the real authority lies. As the power of the courts continues to expand, so the case will become more compelling for a judiciary which is not only independent, but also representative of, and accountable to, the community over whom it is part of the governing process.

Chronology

1950 European Convention on Human Rights is made in Rome (see Box 24.10).

1951 United Kingdom ratifies the European Convention on Human Rights.

1966 United Kingdom permits individuals directly to take complaints against the UK government to the European Court of Human Rights in Strasbourg (see Box 24.11).

1968 *Padfield v Minister of Agriculture, Fisheries and Food*, beginning a new period of judicial activism in the field of judicial review of administrative action (see Box 24.5).

1972 European Communities Act 1972, enabling Community law to be enforced in British courts (see Box 24.9).

1979 Important procedural reforms facilitating applications for judicial review of administrative action. Beginning of significant increase in the number of applications (see Box 24.7).

1982 The 'fare's fair' case in which the House of Lords holds unlawful the GLC plan for cheaper fares on the London Underground (see Box 24.8).

1985 *Council of Civil Service Unions v Minister for the Civil Service*, holding that prerogative powers of the Crown may be subject to judicial review (see Box 24.6).

1991 *Spanish Fishermen's* case in which the House of Lords applied EC law in preference to an Act of Parliament. First time since 1688 that the courts refuse to apply an Act of Parliament and recognise a law-making body superior to Parliament (see Box 24.9).

1994 *M v Home Office* in which House of Lords hold that a Cabinet minister may be liable for contempt of court by ignoring or failing to comply with a judge's order (see Box 24.8).

1998 The Human Rights Act incorporates the European Convention on Human Rights into domestic law, enabling Convention rights to be enforced directly against public authorities in the British courts.

1998 Scotland Act, Government of Wales Act and Northern Ireland Act creating new legislative assemblies with limited powers.

2000 Human Rights Act brought into force on 2 October.

Discussion Questions

1. What part do the courts and judges play in British politics? How far can it be said that the courts and judges police the political process?

2. How are judges appointed? Should the present system of appointment be reformed? If so, why? And if so, how? If not, why not?

3. What are the main features of the Human Rights Act 1998? Should the courts have the power to strike down legislation incompatible with Convention rights?

Note

1. With the exception of the Stormont Parliament in Northern Ireland from 1921 to 1973.

Further reading

Bradley, A.W. and Ewing, K.D. (2002) *Constitutional and Administrative* Law (thirteenth edition), Harlow: Longman.

Brazier, R. (1999) *Constitutional Reform* (third edition), Oxford: Oxford University Press.

Brazier, R. (1999) 'The judiciary', in R. Blackburn and R. Plant (eds) *Constitutional Reform: The Labour Government's Constitutional Reform Agenda*, London: Addison-Wesley Longman, chapter 16.

Ewing, K.D. (1994) 'The Bill of Rights debate: democracy or juristocracy in Britain?', in K.D. Ewing, C.A. Greaty and B.A. Hepple (eds) *Human Rights and Labour Law: Essays for Paul O'Higgins*, London: Mansell.

Ewing, K.D. (2000) 'A theory of democratic adjudication: towards a representative, accountable and independent judiciary', *Alberta Law Review*, Vol. 38, No. 3, p. 135.

Griffith, J.A.G. (1997) *The Politics of the Judiciary* (fifth edition), London: Fontana.

Stevens, R. (1997) 'Judges, politics, politicians and the confusing role of the judiciary', in K. Hawkins (ed.) *The Human Face of the Law: Essays in Honour of Donald Harris*, Oxford: Oxford University Press.

Waldron, J. (1990) *The Law*, London: Routledge.

Index